Enterprise JavaBeans 3.1

SIXTH EDITION

Enterprise JavaBeans 3.1

Andrew Lee Rubinger and Bill Burke

O'REILLY®

Beijing · Cambridge · Farnham · Köln · Sebastopol · Tokyo

Enterprise JavaBeans 3.1, Sixth Edition

by Andrew Lee Rubinger and Bill Burke

Published by O'Reilly Media, Inc., 1005 Gravenstein Highway North, Sebastopol, CA 95472.

O'Reilly books may be purchased for educational, business, or sales promotional use. Online editions are also available for most titles (*http://my.safaribooksonline.com*). For more information, contact our corporate/institutional sales department: (800) 998-9938 or *corporate@oreilly.com*.

Editor: Mike Loukides
Production Editor: Teresa Elsey
Copyeditor: Genevieve d'Entremont
Proofreader: Teresa Elsey

Indexer: John Bickelhaupt
Cover Designer: Karen Montgomery
Interior Designer: David Futato
Illustrator: Robert Romano

Printing History:

June 1999:	First Edition.
March 2000:	Second Edition.
September 2001:	Third Edition.
June 2004:	Fourth Edition.
May 2006:	Fifth Edition.
September 2010:	Sixth Edition.

ISBN: 978-0-596-15802-6

[M]

1283528090

Table of Contents

Preface xv

Part I.   Why Enterprise JavaBeans?

1. **Introduction** **3**
   The Problem Domain   3
      Breaking Up Responsibilities   3
      Code Smart, Not Hard   6
      The Enterprise JavaBeans™ 3.1 Specification   8
      Review   10

2. **Component Types** **11**
   Server-Side Component Types   12
      Session Beans   12
      Message-Driven Beans (MDBs)   15
   Entity Beans   16
      The Java Persistence Model   17
   The Model Isn't Everything   17

3. **Container Services** **19**
   Dependency Injection (DI)   20
   Concurrency   21
   Instance Pooling/Caching   21
   Transactions   23
   Security   23
   Timers   24
   Naming and Object Stores   24
   Interoperability   25
   Lifecycle Callbacks   25
   Interceptors   26

Platform Integration   27
Bringing It Together   27

4. Developing Your First EJBs 29
Step 1: Preparation   29
   Definitions   29
   Naming Conventions   32
   Conventions for the Examples   32
Step 2: Coding the EJB   33
   The Contract   33
   The Bean Implementation Class   34
   Out-of-Container Testing   35
   Integration Testing   36
Summary   39

Part II.   Server-Side Component Models

5. The Stateless Session Bean 43
The XML Deployment Descriptor   45
SessionContext   46
   EJBContext   47
The Lifecycle of a Stateless Session Bean   49
   The Does Not Exist State   50
   The Method-Ready Pool   50
Example: The EncryptionEJB   52
   The Contract: Business Interfaces   53
   Application Exceptions   54
   Bean Implementation Class   55
   Accessing Environment Properties (Injection and Lookup)   57
Asynchronous Methods   60

6. The Stateful Session Bean 63
The Lifecycle of a Stateful Session Bean   64
   The Does Not Exist State   65
   The Method-Ready State   65
   The Passivated State   66
Example: The FileTransferEJB   68
   The Contract: Business Interfaces   69
   Exceptions   70
   Bean Implementation Class   70
   POJO Testing Outside the Container   74
   Integration Testing   77

7. The Singleton Session Bean **81**

   Concurrency   82
      Shared Mutable Access   84
      Container-Managed Concurrency   86
      Bean-Managed Concurrency   87
   Lifecycle   87
      Explicit Startup   87
   Example: The RSSCacheEJB   88
      Value Objects   89
      The Contract: Business Interfaces   92
      Bean Implementation Class   92

8. Message-Driven Beans **97**

   JMS and Message-Driven Beans   98
      JMS as a Resource   98
      JMS Is Asynchronous   99
      JMS Messaging Models   100
      Learning More About JMS   103
   JMS-Based Message-Driven Beans   103
      @MessageDriven   103
   The Lifecycle of a Message-Driven Bean   108
      The Does Not Exist State   109
      The Method-Ready Pool   109
   Connector-Based Message-Driven Beans   111
   Message Linking   114
      Session Beans Should Not Receive Messages   114
      The JMS APIs   115
      Example: The StatusUpdateEJBs   118

Part III. EJB and Persistence

9. Persistence: EntityManager **127**

   Entities Are POJOs   128
   Managed Versus Unmanaged Entities   130
      Persistence Context   130
   Packaging a Persistence Unit   133
      The Persistence Unit Class Set   135
   Obtaining an EntityManager   136
      EntityManagerFactory   137
      Obtaining a Persistence Context   138
   Interacting with an EntityManager   140
   Example: A Persistent Employee Registry   141

A Transactional Abstraction 141
Persisting Entities 142
Finding and Updating Entities 144
Removing Entities 147
refresh() 148
contains() and clear() 148
flush() and FlushModeType 148
Locking 149
unwrap() and getDelegate() 149

10. Mapping Persistent Objects **151**
The Programming Model 152
The Employee Entity 152
The Bean Class 152
XML Mapping File 154
Basic Relational Mapping 155
Elementary Schema Mappings 155
Primary Keys 157
@Id 157
Table Generators 158
Sequence Generators 159
Primary-Key Classes and Composite Keys 160
Property Mappings 164
@Transient 164
@Basic and FetchType 164
@Lob 166
@Temporal 166
@Enumerated 167
@Embedded Objects 167

11. Entity Relationships **171**
The Seven Relationship Types 171
One-to-One Unidirectional Relationship 173
One-to-One Bidirectional Relationship 176
One-to-Many Unidirectional Relationship 178
Many-to-One Unidirectional Relationship 181
One-to-Many Bidirectional Relationship 182
Many-to-Many Bidirectional Relationship 184
Many-to-Many Unidirectional Relationship 187
Mapping Collection-Based Relationships 188
Ordered List-Based Relationship 188
Map-Based Relationship 189
Detached Entities and FetchType 190

Cascading   191
    PERSIST   192
    MERGE   192
    REMOVE   193
    REFRESH   193
    ALL   193
    When to Use Cascading   194

12. Entity Inheritance **195**
Single Table per Class Hierarchy   196
    Advantages   198
    Disadvantages   198
Table per Concrete Class   199
    Advantages   200
    Disadvantages   200
Table per Subclass   200
    Advantages   203
    Disadvantages   203
Mixing Strategies   203
Nonentity Base Classes   203

13. Queries, the Criteria API, and JPA QL **205**
Query API   206
    Parameters   208
    Date Parameters   209
    Paging Results   209
    Hints   210
    FlushMode   210
JPA QL   211
    Abstract Schema Names   211
    Simple Queries   212
    Selecting Entity and Relationship Properties 213
    Constructor Expressions   215
    The IN Operator and INNER JOIN   215
    LEFT JOIN   216
    Fetch Joins   217
    Using DISTINCT   217
    The WHERE Clause and Literals   218
    The WHERE Clause and Operator Precedence 218
    The WHERE Clause and Arithmetic Operators 219
    The WHERE Clause and Logical Operators   219
    The WHERE Clause and Comparison Symbols   219
    The WHERE Clause and Equality Semantics   220

The WHERE Clause and BETWEEN   221
The WHERE Clause and IN   221
The WHERE Clause and IS NULL   222
The WHERE Clause and IS EMPTY   223
The WHERE Clause and MEMBER OF   223
The WHERE Clause and LIKE   224
Functional Expressions   224
The ORDER BY Clause   228
Bulk UPDATE and DELETE   229
Native Queries   230
Scalar Native Queries   230
Simple Entity Native Queries   230
Complex Native Queries   231
Named Queries   232
Named Native Queries   233

14. **Entity Callbacks and Listeners** **235**
Callback Events   235
Callbacks on Entity Classes   236
Entity Listeners   237
Default Entity Listeners   238
Inheritance and Listeners   238

Part IV. Container Services

15. **Security** **243**
Authentication and Identity   244
Authorization   245
Example: A Secured School   246
The Business Interface   246
Assigning Method Permissions   247
Programmatic Security   249
The RunAs Security Identity   251

16. **JNDI, the ENC, and Injection** **255**
Global JNDI   255
The JNDI ENC   256
What Can Be Registered in the JNDI ENC? 257
How Is the JNDI ENC Populated?   257
How Are Things Referenced from the ENC? 258
Reference and Injection Types   264
EJB References   264

EntityManagerFactory References   266
EntityManager References   269
Resource References   271
Resource Environment and Administered Objects   275
Environment Entries   275
Message Destination References   277

17. Transactions **279**
ACID Transactions   279
     Example: The BlackjackEJB   281
     Helper EJBs for Testing Transactions   283
     Is the BlackjackEJB Atomic?   284
     Is the BlackjackEJB Consistent?   285
     Is the BlackjackEJB Isolated?   285
     Is the BlackjackEJB Durable?   285
Declarative Transaction Management   286
     Transaction Scope   286
     Transaction Attributes   287
     Transaction Propagation   293
Isolation and Database Locking   298
     Dirty, Repeatable, and Phantom Reads   298
     Database Locks   299
     Transaction Isolation Levels   300
     Balancing Performance Against Consistency   301
     Optimistic Locking   302
     Programmatic Locking   303
Nontransactional EJBs   303
Explicit Transaction Management   304
     Transaction Propagation in Bean-Managed Transactions   307
     Heuristic Decisions   308
     UserTransaction   309
     Status   310
     EJBContext Rollback Methods   312
Exceptions and Transactions   313
     Application Exceptions Versus System Exceptions   313
Transactional Stateful Session Beans   318
     The Transactional Method-Ready State   320
Conversational Persistence Contexts   321

18. Interceptors **323**
Intercepting Methods   323
     Interceptor Class   325
     Applying Interceptors   327

Interceptors and Injection 331
Intercepting Lifecycle Events 333
   Custom Injection Annotations 333
Exception Handling 335
   Aborting a Method Invocation 336
   Catch and Rethrow Exceptions 336
Interceptor Lifecycle 338
Bean Class @AroundInvoke Methods 338

19. Timer Service **341**
Example: A Batch Credit Card Processing System 342
   The Business Interface 343
   javax.ejb.ScheduleExpression and @javax.ejb.Schedule 344
   The Bean Implementation Class 345
   The TimerService 347
   The Timer 348
Transactions 350
Stateless Session Bean Timers 351
Message-Driven Bean Timers 352

20. EJB 3.1: Web Services Standards **355**
Web Services Overview 355
XML Schema and XML Namespaces 356
   XML Schema 356
   XML Namespaces 361
SOAP 1.1 368
   Web Services Styles 369
   Exchanging SOAP Messages with HTTP 370
   Now You See It, Now You Don't 370
WSDL 1.1 371
   The <definitions> Element 372
   The <portType> and <message> Elements 374
   The <types> Element 375
   The <binding> and <service> Elements 377
UDDI 2.0 379
From Standards to Implementation 380

21. EJB 3.1 and Web Services **381**
Accessing Web Services with JAX-RPC 381
   Generating JAX-RPC Artifacts from WSDL 382
   Calling a Service from an EJB 387
   The <service-ref> Deployment Element 388
   The JAX-RPC Mapping File 389

Defining a Web Service with JAX-RPC 391
   The WSDL Document 392
   The Service Endpoint Interface 393
   The Stateless Bean Class 393
   The Deployment Files 394
Using JAX-WS 396
   The @WebService Annotation 396
   The @WebMethod Annotation 397
   The @SOAPBinding Annotation 398
   The @WebParam Annotation 399
   The @WebResult Annotation 400
   The @OneWay Annotation 401
   Separating the Web Services Contract 401
   The Service Class 402
   The Service Endpoint Interface 403
   The @WebServiceRef Annotation 403
Other Annotations and APIs 405
JAXB 405
   Taking JAXB Further 407
Conclusion 407

Part V. Examples

  A. **FirstEJB Example** 415

  B. **Stateless Session EJB: Encryption Example** 429

  C. **Stateful Session EJB: FTP Client Example** 453

  D. **Singleton Session EJB: RSS Cache Example** 505

  E. **Message-Driven EJB: Status Update Listeners Example** 527

  F. **Java Persistence APIs: Employee Registry Example** 557

  G. **Security: Secured School Example** 643

  H. **Transactions: Blackjack Game Example** 663

  I. **Interceptors: TV Channel Service Example** 691

J.   Timer Service: Credit Card Processor Example 719

Index 727

Preface

Author's Note

Reluctantly succumbing to my father's urging in the spring of 2000, I enrolled in my first software development course at the University of Massachusetts. Following years of frustration getting my computer to "just do what I want," I quickly found our roles inverted; I was in charge of the machine.

Academia proved a bit abstract to my sophomoric eyes, and after those first few months of study, I yearned to make programs that delivered real user value. Endless trial-and-error led me to the conclusion that it's best not to write every little thing on your own—it was more efficient to build upon the work of others.

By then the JBoss open source community was picking up steam with this thing called an "Application Server," a neat program that ran other programs. To a junior developer it meant no more networking code. No more manual database connections. No more object pools or caches. It meant no more speaking like a computer. It meant writing the programs I wanted to build, not the mechanics underneath.

My experience with this enterprise software miraculously made me marketable enough to snag a post-college job in the middle of the dot-com fallout, and during my tenure there we enrolled in a weeklong training session from the source—JBoss, Inc.

The reputation of our instructor preceded his arrival, his name sprinkled about the JBoss codebase, popular forums, and the upcoming EJB 3.0 specification. Bill Burke came to deliver course material, but in my eyes he planted the seed that it's possible to become part of a greater community where people talk about software problems, critique one another's ideas in public, and generally get paid to contribute to the global computing effort.

Over the next few years I stayed active on the user forums and submitted patches, looking to improve upon the new JBoss EJB3 container. One day my mail client blinked with an incoming message from the team lead, Carlo de Wolf:

> There is an opening for an EJB 3 developer in my team. Are you interested?

Why, yes.

The ethos of my development from inside JBoss and Red Hat have been the same as they were from the start: keep application programmers writing application code.

One fall night at a team dinner, Bill extended to me the reins of his hugely successful EJB book from O'Reilly, the same text that initially showed me the ropes. This edition is the product of that discussion.

Who Should Read This Book

This book explains and demonstrates the fundamentals of the EJB 3.1 and Java Persistence programming models. Although EJB makes application development much simpler, it is still a complex technology that requires a great deal of time and study to master. This book provides a straightforward, no-nonsense explanation of the underlying technology, Java™ classes and interfaces, the component model, and the runtime behavior of EJB. It does not include material on previous versions of the specification, however.

Although this book focuses on the fundamentals, it's not a "dummies" book. EJB is an extremely complex and ambitious enterprise technology. While using EJB may be fairly simple, the amount of work required to understand and master EJB is significant. Before reading this book, you should be fluent in the Java language and have some practical experience developing business solutions. Experience with distributed object systems is not a must, but you will need some experience with JDBC (or at least an understanding of the basics) to follow the examples in this book. If you are unfamiliar with the Java language, I recommend *Learning Java*; this book was formerly *Exploring Java* (both from O'Reilly). If you are unfamiliar with JDBC, I recommend *Database Programming with JDBC and Java* (O'Reilly). If you need a stronger background in distributed computing, I recommend *Java Distributed Computing* (O'Reilly).

How This Book Is Organized

This book is organized in five parts: Parts I through IV make up the technical manuscript, while Part V comprises the examples. The technical manuscript explains what EJB is, how it works, and when to use it. Part V provides step-by-step instructions for installing, configuring, and running the examples.

The technical manuscript was adapted from Bill Burke and Richard Monson-Haefel's fifth edition of this book by yours truly, Andrew Lee Rubinger. The code contained herein is not vendor-specific in any way, and it will often value concision over verbose code samples. The intent of this section is to focus on conceptual understanding.

Part I, Why Enterprise JavaBeans?

Multiuser distributed system are inherently complex. To ignore the issues they present is to ask for trouble down the line. Luckily, you don't have to do all the work yourself; Chapters 1 through 4 outline the benefits of taking advantage of EJB—a component model for simplified development of enterprise applications.

Part II, Server-Side Component Models

In Chapters 5 through 8 we dive into the mechanics of EJB with relation to business logic. We'll explore the various models available and discuss when each may be appropriate.

Part III, EJB and Persistence

While the server-side component models typically speak to actions, the EJB Entity model addresses the need to interact with persistent state. Java Persistence exposes relational data as objects, and EJB comes with integration built-in. Chapters 9 through 14 cover these topics.

Part IV, Container Services

EJB is armed with a powerful feature set ensuring secure and consistent execution of your application. Chapters 15 through 21 will uncover the utility and configuration of these helpful services. Jason T. Greene adapted Chapters 20 and 21.

Part V, Examples

The examples workbook shows how to execute examples from those chapters in the book that include at least one significant example. You'll want to read the introduction to the workbook to set up your build environment and configure it to run the examples. After that, just go to the workbook chapter that matches the chapter you're reading. The examples themselves will have a release cycle that outlives this book, so you may want to check back to get bug fixes, enhancements, and other updates as time goes on.

Software and Versions

This book covers EJB 3.1 and Java Persistence 2.0. It uses Java language features from the Java SE 6 platform. Because the focus of this book is on developing vendor-independent EJB components and solutions, we have stayed away from proprietary extensions and vendor-dependent idioms wherever possible. You can use any EJB-compliant server with this book, but you should be familiar with your server's specific installation, deployment, and runtime-management procedures to work with the examples.

Conventions Used in This Book

The following typographical conventions are used in this book:

Italic
> Indicates new terms, URLs, email addresses, filenames, and file extensions.

`Constant width`
> Used for program listings, as well as within paragraphs to refer to program elements such as variable or function names, databases, data types, environment variables, statements, and keywords.

`Constant width bold`
> Shows commands or other text that should be typed literally by the user.

`Constant width italic`
> Shows text that should be replaced with user-supplied values or by values determined by context.

 This icon signifies a tip, suggestion, or general note.

 This icon signifies a warning or caution.

Using Code Examples

This book is here to help you get your job done. In general, you may use the code in this book in your programs and documentation. You do not need to contact us for permission; in fact, all example code has open source licensing. Selling or distributing a CD-ROM of text from O'Reilly books does require permission, however. Answering a question by citing this book and quoting example code does not require permission.

We appreciate, but do not require, attribution. An attribution usually includes the title, author, publisher, copyright holder, and ISBN. For example: "*Enterprise JavaBeans 3.1*, Sixth Edition, by Andrew Lee Rubinger and Bill Burke (O'Reilly). Copyright 2010 Andrew Lee Rubinger and William J. Burke, Jr., 9780596158026."

If you feel your use of code examples falls outside fair use or the permission given here, feel free to contact us at *permissions@oreilly.com*.

Safari® Books Online

Safari Books Online is an on-demand digital library that lets you easily search over 7,500 technology and creative reference books and videos to find the answers you need quickly.

With a subscription, you can read any page and watch any video from our library online. Read books on your cell phone and mobile devices. Access new titles before they are available for print, and get exclusive access to manuscripts in development and post feedback for the authors. Copy and paste code samples, organize your favorites, download chapters, bookmark key sections, create notes, print out pages, and benefit from tons of other time-saving features.

O'Reilly Media has uploaded this book to the Safari Books Online service. To have full digital access to this book and others on similar topics from O'Reilly and other publishers, sign up for free at *http://my.safaribooksonline.com*.

Comments and Questions

Please address comments and questions concerning this book to the publisher:

O'Reilly Media, Inc.
1005 Gravenstein Highway North
Sebastopol, CA 95472
800-998-9938 (in the United States or Canada)
707-829-0515 (international or local)
707-829-0104 (fax)

There is a web page for this book, which lists errata, examples, and any additional information. You can access this page at:

http://oreilly.com/catalog/9780596158026

To comment on or ask technical questions about this book, send email to:

bookquestions@oreilly.com

For more information about books, conferences, software, Resource Centers, and the O'Reilly Network, see the O'Reilly website at:

http://www.oreilly.com

Acknowledgments

Many individuals share the credit for this book's development and delivery. Michael Loukides, the editor, and his team were pivotal to the success of every edition of this book. Without their experience, craft, and guidance, this book would not have been possible. I want to thank Jason T. Greene for taking over the web services chapters. I had no desire to learn JAX-WS beyond the `@WebService` annotation. Without the earlier work of Richard Monson-Haefel and Bill Burke, this book would not have been possible. It amazes me how the structure of this book could last six editions, and it is a testament to Bill and Richard's ability to succinctly structure complex topics into a cohesive text.

I particularly want to thank Bill for passing the baton to me on this series. A champion of my career from early on, you've encouraged me to get involved in coding, blogging, and accepting new challenges. You've been a force in our industry since I was learning a "for" loop, and your continued relevance now in the REST world is incredibly inspiring.

My coworkers, both within JBoss and around the community, have played no small part in the success of my software and this book.

Carlo de Wolf, whether he likes it or not, has been the technical mentor every developer should have. He's invested continually in my growth for years, and it's difficult to understate my appreciation for both his guidance and friendship.

Jaikiran Pai rounds out our EJB3 team at JBoss. Like me, he came from the community, and his dedication to our users and others in our group is noticeable every day, without fail, on our forums and mailing lists. You are certainly a jack of all trades.

The Application Server team and members of the #jboss-dev Freenode IRC Channel comprise a support system without which my code would surely be deficient. David Lloyd, Jason Greene, Brian Stansberry, Ales Justin, and Bob McWhirter: you boys are brilliant and selfless.

Our newly minted JBoss Testing team brings dedication to usability to a new level. Aslak Knutsen, Dan Allen, and Pete Muir: your work has made the examples portion of this book possible, and I've no doubt that we're on the cusp of a revolution that will bring simplicity back to functional testing of Enterprise Java. Let's keep plugging.

The JBoss Boston User's Group gave me a stage and place to geek out with friends. Until the next meeting, Jesper Pedersen, Shelly McGowan, Scott Marlow, and John Doyle.

Tim Roberts: You employed me as a college kid and let me learn open source on your dime. It was trial by fire, and I thank you for not breaking out the extinguisher before I developed my chops.

Marc Elliott and Matt Warren: You gave me my first job out of school, and your patience in cultivating a useful employee out of me will always be remembered.

Brian Weisenthal and Morgan Lang of 9mmedia in New York City: Together we built some of the slickest-looking applications I've seen to this day. You're deeply successful in rich media, and it was a pleasure building the backend for such impressive software. Thank you for graciously allowing me to pursue a career at JBoss.

Many expert technical reviewers helped ensure that the material was technically accurate and true to the spirit of EJB and Java Persistence. Of special note are Trenton D. Adams and Juraci Paixao Krohling, who've sent great comments throughout the process.

I'd also like to thank my personal entourage, though their influence was mostly detrimental to the completion of this book. Prelack, Fleischer, Halbert, Rudman, Clark: You locked me in a moving car and kidnapped me to a casino the weekend before my first draft was due. Jonathan Adam: You're smart and fair, and long ago eclipsed me in any number of ways. No brother could ever be more proud than I am of you.

Grandma Natalie and Grandpa Jerry Glass, you've invested in my education and have encouraged my intellectual curiosity. And you make the best bagels-n-lox breakfast known to man.

Mom and Dad, you supported me when you disagreed with me. You whipped me into shape when I was lazy. You're excellent at your jobs, and you're even finer human beings. Thank you for being such an excellent example.

## PART I

Why Enterprise JavaBeans?

If your path to Enterprise Java is anything like mine, you've arrived here hoping to be more productive in application development. Perhaps you've heard some good or bad things about this thing called "EJB," and you'd like to explore some more. Perhaps some EJB technology is already in place at work, and you're looking to understand it a bit deeper.

The fact is that Enterprise JavaBeans is much more than a set of APIs. It is a simplified programming model that, when understood at a conceptual level, has the power to easily adapt lightweight Java classes into powerful business components. In short, EJB lets you focus on the work you do best—writing your application logic.

In this section we'll start with a bird's-eye view of the issues facing every software developer, examining how EJB removes common problems from your concern.

## CHAPTER 1

Introduction

The Problem Domain

Application development can be a deceivingly complex undertaking.

Not only must our programs do their jobs, they must do them well. There's a laundry list of characteristics that Good Software implies:

- Secure
- Sound/maintains integrity
- Scalable
- Interoperable
- Robust/resilient
- Correct/functions as specified

And while these are all prerequisites to a finished product, not a single one is specific to any business. Across the world, programmers slave over their terminals, spinning up custom solutions to the same fundamental issues facing everyone else.

Bluntly put, this is a waste.

Breaking Up Responsibilities

For the sake of simplicity, we may categorize all code in a system into one of three flavors:

- Core concerns
- Cross-cutting concerns
- Plumbing

Core concerns

The primary purpose of an application is to satisfy *business logic*, the set of rules that dictate its expected behavior. More simply, this is *what* a program does. For instance, an email client must be able to let its users read, compose, send, and organize email. All functions related to the fulfillment of business logic fall into the category of *core concerns*.

Object-oriented principles lend themselves well toward modeling business logic. Typically done via *separation of concerns*,* a related set of functionality may be compartmentalized in a module, with well-defined interfaces for how each component will interact outside of its internals (see Figure 1-1). In the case of our email client example, this might lead to separate modules for interacting with remote servers, rendering HTML, composing new mail, etc.

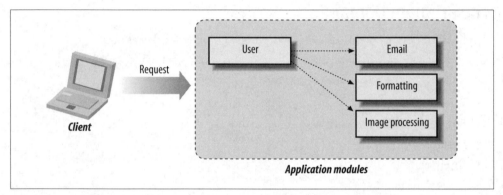

Figure 1-1. Modules, each addressing one business use-case, interacting with one another

The core is typically going to contain rules unique to your application, and no one can build it aside from you and your team. Our job as software engineers is to realize ideas, so the more time we can dedicate to business logic, the more efficient we become. And the best way to limit our scope to core concerns is to reduce or eliminate the energy we spend everywhere else.

Cross-cutting concerns

While the core of an application defines its primary function, there is a host of secondary operations necessary to keep things running correctly and efficiently. Security assertions, transactional boundaries, concurrency policies—all are helpful in ensuring the integrity of the system is in check. We define these as *aspects*.

The problem with aspects is that they're intrinsically tangential to core concerns. In other words, cross-cutting concerns are intended to stretch across modules (Figure 1-2).

---

* Edsger Dijkstra, "On the role of scientific thought" (1982). *http://www.cs.utexas.edu/users/EWD/ transcriptions/EWD04xx/EWD447.html*

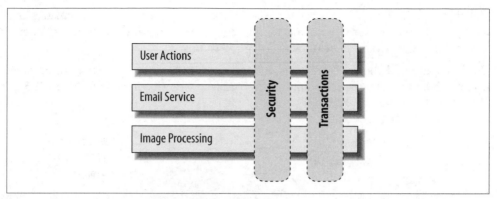

Figure 1-2. Aspects working uniformly across modules

This layout paints a picture of perpendicular, or *orthogonal*, aims. For this reason, it takes great care to integrate aspects with the core in complementary fashion, as opposed to weighing it down.

While it may seem that aspects violate good practice to separate concerns, in fact they're quite complementary in design. This is because they allow us to reuse shared code across modules, often transparently.

Banking software must allow users to withdraw money from their accounts, but it would make for an interesting solution if we could withdraw from any account we wanted; we need a security assertion at some point to ensure the requesting user has permission. If we hardcode this logic into the "withdraw" function, we've intermixed security with a core concern, and we'll likely end up copying/pasting similar checks all over the place. A much better approach is to apply security as an common aspect to be shared by many modules and configure where it's enforced separately.

This configuration ultimately regulates the direction of the invocation chain, but we don't want to give it too much of our attention.

Plumbing

Once modules have been built to address the core, there's still the matter of getting data and invocations from point A to point B. Plumbing provides this routing, and may take several forms:

- Forwarding control from an HTTP request to some action handler
- Obtaining a JDBC connection or JavaMail session
- Mapping a nonnative request (JSON, ActionScript, RDBMS SQL) into a Java object

A sufficiently decoupled system defines interfaces for each module. This ensures that components may be developed in isolation, limits the need for explicit dependencies, and encourages parallel development. All good things.

And like all good things, there's a cost: integration. Plumbing code is nothing more than an adapter between endpoints and provides few merits of its own (Figure 1-3).

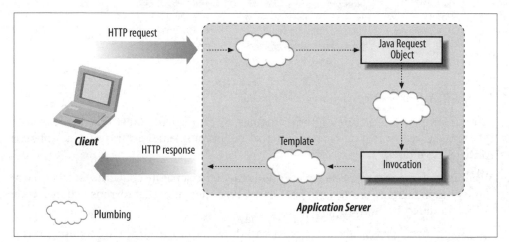

Figure 1-3. Plumbing as a connector between core concerns

Perhaps the worst characteristic of the integration layer is that it is notoriously difficult to test. Although Unit Tests, pieces of code that perform assertions on isolated functions, are quite easy to write given a properly designed module, Integration Tests are much more expansive; they typically require a more involved setup of the test environment, and they may take orders of magnitude longer to invoke. This makes for both a process prone to developer laziness (tests may not be written!) and increased time in the build/test cycle.

Plumbing is a means to an end, and therefore of little value in and of itself. It will benefit us to take an approach that minimizes the time we spend getting data from one endpoint to another. As we'll soon see, we may rely upon standards that remove this responsibility from our shoulders.

Code Smart, Not Hard

That's a lot to consider before even a single line of code is written. Ironically, the solutions we concoct to address these issues are prone to becoming problems in themselves, and we're at risk for introducing a tangled mess.

To state the obvious, the more that can be done for us, the less we have to do ourselves.

Do less

While it's a likely requirement that business logic be unique to your application, the machinery that moves things along is not held to the same supposition. On the contrary, if aspects and plumbing are provided in a generic fashion, the developer is freed to limit both scope and focus to more tangible requirements.

Let's say we want to register a new user with the system. Building everything in-house using traditional object-oriented methodology, we'd:

1. Check that we have permission to register someone new (*Security*)
2. Start a boundary so everything is ensured to complete together, without affecting anything else (*Transactions*)
3. Get a business worker delegate from some pool or cache, so we have control over concurrency (*Performance and Transactional Isolation*)
4. Make a hook into the database (*Resource Management*)
5. Store the user (*Business Logic*)
6. Get a hook to an SMTP (mail) server (*Resource Management*)
7. Email a confirmation (*Business Logic*)
8. Return our worker so another call may use it (*Performance and Transactional Isolation*)
9. Close our boundary (*Transactions*)

Even a simplified example shows that we're "speaking like a computer." All this talk about pools and boundaries and databases is undermining the utility of a programming language to help us express our ideas like humans. I'd much rather write:

```
pseudofunction registerUser(user)
{
  database.storeUser(user);
  mailService.emailUser(user);
}
```

If we could make the computational elements transparent, we'd be in position to pay greater attention to the business logic.

The Container

Now that we've identified candidates to be culled from our source tree, we may introduce an abstraction that provides the necessary features in a decoupled fashion. A commonly employed technique is to take advantage of a construct called a *Container*. Loosely defined:

> A Container is a host that provides services to guest applications.

The intent here is to provide generic services upon which applications may rely. The service support desired is usually defined by some combination of user code and metadata that together follow a *contract* for interaction between the application and container. In the case of Enterprise JavaBeans (EJB) 3.1, this contract is provided by a document jointly developed by experts under the authority of the Java Community Process (*http://jcp.org*). Its job is to do all the work you shouldn't be doing.

The Enterprise JavaBeans™ 3.1 Specification

Just as interfaces in code abstract the "what" from the "how," the EJB Specification dictates the capabilities required of a compliant EJB Container. This 626-page document is the result of lessons learned in the field, requests by the community, and subsequent debate by the JSR-318 Expert Group (*http://jcp.org/en/jsr/detail?id=318*).

It is the purpose of this book to introduce concepts provided by the spec in a concise manner, alongside examples where appropriate.

EJB defined

Let's dig in. The Specification defines itself (EJB 3.1 Specification, page 29):

> The Enterprise JavaBeans architecture is a [sic] architecture for the development and deployment of component-based business applications. Applications written using the Enterprise JavaBeans architecture are scalable, transactional, and multi-user secure. These applications may be written once, and then deployed on any server platform that supports the Enterprise JavaBeans specification.

More simply rewritten:

> Enterprise JavaBeans is a standard server-side component model for distributed business applications.

This means that EJB defines a model for piecing together a full system by integrating modules. Each component may represent a collection of business processes, and these will run centralized on the server (Figure 1-4).

Additionally, the "distributed" nature will provide a mechanism to spread modules across different processes, physical machines, or even entire networks (Figure 1-5).

As we'll soon discover, EJB is also an aggregate technology; it wires up other facets of the Java Enterprise Edition (*http://java.sun.com/javaee/*), such as messaging, transactions, resource management, persistence, and web services. It's this integration that will reduce the evil plumbing we'd identified earlier.

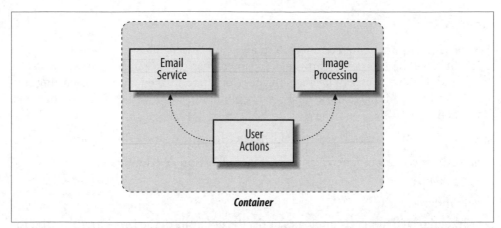

Figure 1-4. Modules operating inside a runtime container

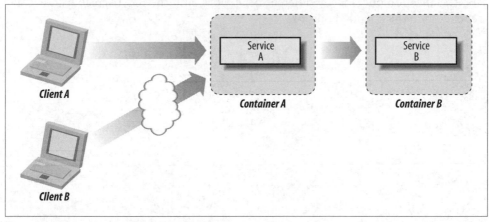

Figure 1-5. Using runtime containers to abstract the physical location of code

Embracing the standard of EJB has other, nontechnical benefits. Applications that take advantage of EJB architecture are portable across any compliant Container implementation. In practice, there may be some retrofitting required in order to resolve vendor-specific features, but applications written to spec alone should stay true to the Sun Microsystems "write once, run anywhere" philosophy of the Java language.

Finally, the familiarity of EJB means that developers already oriented to the technology may spend less time learning the control flow of a particular application, making hiring and training a much more simplified exercise.

Review

We've seen requirements common to many applications and how these can be met without recoding the same stuff the company across the street did last week. We've discussed the importance of keeping business logic uncluttered with cross-cutting concerns. And we've cringed at the unnecessary plumbing employed by the roll-your-own approach.

Most importantly, we've revealed the EJB Specification as a viable solution to:

- Address common/generic issues within application development
- Code less
- Standardize
- Integrate with other technologies under the umbrella of the Java Enterprise Edition

The specification offers a few different bean types, and the most sensible choice will depend upon the intended purpose.

## CHAPTER 2

Component Types

Modeling real-life objects and concepts is one of the first skills a programmer must develop. As such, we've become fairly adept at implementing object-oriented axioms such as reusability and extensibility on a daily basis. When we focus these principles on business logic, we end up with a set of *business objects* that encapsulate the rules of the road.

Starting with the 3.0 version of the Specification, EJB imposes no API coupling or restrictions upon the classes that will define our business objects. Commonly known as POJO (Plain Old Java Object)* development, this means that an application developer is under no obligation to extend, implement, or have any references tying the application to EJB. Now we can create class hierarchies however we see fit, and reuse our objects in some non-EJB environment (perhaps for quick testing outside of the Container).

Because a POJO class is just like any other class, it does not become an EJB until it's:

1. Assembled/packaged
2. Deployed
3. Accessed via the Container

This is an important distinction. EJBs become such only in the context of the EJB Container.

The Container, in turn, is responsible for equipping POJOs with EJB Services (covered in Chapter 3) as well as exposing their behavior via one of three personalities. We call these personalities *component types*, and while implementing their semantics is beyond scope for an application developer, it's important to know how, by contract, they'll behave.

We'll use the example of a fictitious casino to showcase where each component type might be applied.

---

* Fowler et al. *http://www.martinfowler.com/bliki/POJO.html*

Server-Side Component Types

Server-side component types reside exclusively on the server, and the client must interact with them via some indirection. There are two major server-side component types: session beans, which expose a view for the client to invoke upon, and message-driven beans, which act as event listeners.

Session Beans

If EJB is a grammar, session beans are the verbs. They take action, and they frequently contain business methods. Because of EJB's distributed nature, underlying bean instances that carry out the invocation live on the server and are accessed by way of a simple view the client may request of the EJB Container. This means that the client does not access the EJB directly, which allows the Container to perform all sorts of magic before a request finally hits the target method. It's this separation that allows for the client to be completely unaware of the location of the server, concurrency policies, or queuing of requests to manage resources. As far as the client is concerned, it's operating directly upon an EJB. In truth, the client is invoking upon a *proxy reference* that will delegate the request along to the Container and return the appropriate response (see Figure 2-1).

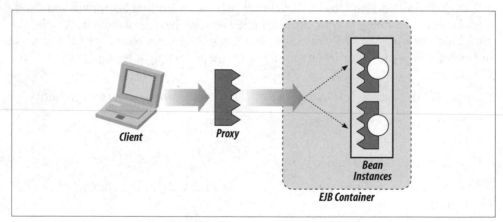

Figure 2-1. Client invoking upon a proxy object, responsible for delegating the call along to the EJB Container

Ultimately, it's the *bean instances* created and managed by the Container that the service client requests.

Stateless session beans (SLSBs)

Stateless session beans are useful for functions in which state does not need to be carried from invocation to invocation. A client cannot assume that subsequent requests will target any particular bean instance. In fact, the Container will often create and destroy instances however it feels will be most efficient (see Figure 2-2). How a Container chooses the target instance is left to the vendor's discretion.

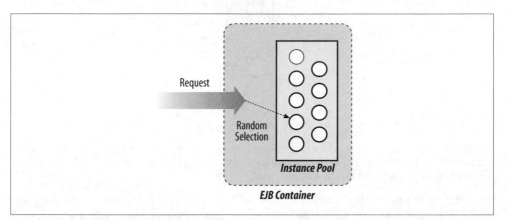

Figure 2-2. An SLSB Instance Selector picking an instance at random

Because there's no rule linking an invocation to a particular target bean instance, these instances may be used interchangeably and shared by many clients. This allows the Container to hold a much smaller number of objects in service, hence keeping memory footprint down.

One caveat to beware: though a SLSB has stateless semantics, it's backed by an instance of a class created by the application developer. Particular care must be employed to assure that any shared members (instance variables, for instance) are not leaked between invocations; this may lead to unpredictable behavior. We'll explain this gotcha when we cover SLSBs in greater detail in Chapter 5.

If we were to give our casino a game of roulette, SLSB would be a natural implementation choice. Roulette is a game with no memory—each spin operates independently from the last—so a function `getSpinResult` should return a random spot on the wheel.

Stateful session beans (SFSBs)

Stateful session beans differ from SLSBs in that every request upon a given proxy reference is guaranteed to ultimately invoke upon the same bean instance. This is to say, SFSB invocations share *conversational state*. Each SFSB proxy object has an isolated session context, so calls to one session will not affect another.

Stateful sessions, and their corresponding bean instances, are created sometime before the first invocation upon a proxy is made to its target instance (Figure 2-3). They live until the client invokes a method that the bean provider has marked as a *remove* event, or until the Container decides to evict the session (usually due to some timeout, though the spec leaves this out-of-scope and up to the vendor).

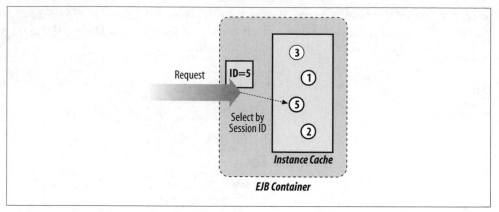

Figure 2-3. Stateful session bean creating and using the correct client instance, which lives inside the EJB Container, to carry out the invocation

In order to minimize the number of stateful sessions carried around in memory, the Container may *passivate* a SFSB bean instance. During passivation, the session's state is flushed to some persistent storage such that it may be removed from RAM. If the session is needed again before it's removed for good, the Container will *activate* it and bring the bean instance back into memory.

No casino is complete without a good game of poker, and we could build ours using SFSBs. Each game is played using a single deck, and we need to keep track of which cards have already been dealt—otherwise we risk giving the player next to us the impossible hand of five aces! If each table is scoped to its own stateful session, we could ensure that the integrity of the deck is intact.

We'll dive into SFSBs in Chapter 6.

Singleton beans

Sometimes we don't need any more than one backing instance for our business objects. EJB 3.1 therefore introduces a new session component type, the singleton bean. Because all requests upon a singleton are destined for the same bean instance, the Container doesn't have much work to do in choosing the target (Figure 2-4).

The singleton session bean may be marked to eagerly load when an application is deployed; therefore, it may be leveraged to fire application lifecycle events. This draws a relationship where deploying a singleton bean implicitly leads to the invocation of its lifecycle callbacks. We'll put this to good use when we discuss singleton beans in Chapter 7.

Dealers in a casino aren't granted complete autonomy; they've got to clear a set of privileged tasks such as changing money, cashout, and large betting with the pit boss. The pit boss, in turn, is the sole authority over what's permitted on his floor. If we model the boss as a singleton, all requests are passed along to the same source—one

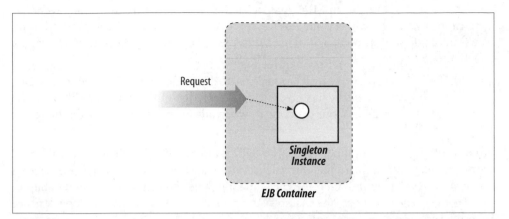

Figure 2-4. Conceptual diagram of a singleton session bean with only one backing bean instance

able to make informed, consistent decisions. In addition, at the start of the pit boss's shift, he can make the rounds and do whatever startup tasks he deems necessary.

Message-Driven Beans (MDBs)

Asynchronous messaging is a paradigm in which two or more applications communicate via a message describing a business event. EJB 3.1 interacts with messaging systems via the Java Connector Architecture (JCA) 1.6 (*http://jcp.org/en/jsr/detail?id=322*), which acts as an abstraction layer that enables any system to be adapted as a valid sender. The message-driven bean, in turn, is a *listener* that consumes messages and may either handle them directly or delegate further processing to other EJB components. The asynchronous characteristic of this exchange means that a message sender is not waiting for a response, so no return to the caller is provided (Figure 2-5).

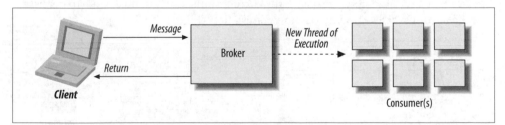

Figure 2-5. Asynchronous invocation of a message-driven bean, which acts as a listener for incoming events

One common provider of asynchronous messaging is the Java Message Service (JMS), and the EJB specification dictates that JMS is supported implicitly.[†] If a message is sent

---

† EJB 3.1 Specification 5.4.17.1

to a JMS Topic or Queue, an MDB may be created to take action upon that event. By extension, any service with a valid JCA Resource Adapter may use MDB as an endpoint. We'll untangle the various technologies that piece together asynchronous messaging in Chapter 8.

Like SLSBs, MDBs have no conversational state. Any instance may be used in servicing a message. In fact, the client has no view or knowledge of the MDB at all! Once the client sends a message, it's out of scope to worry about what may be listening to the event fired.

After a full night of gambling, visitors to our casino are likely to need their cars back from the valet. We may provide our valet service via MDBs; once a ticket (message) is received, the valet should fetch the car while its owner continues on to grab a cup of coffee or visit the gift shop. The casino visitor will have to frequently check back to see whether his car has arrived.

Message-driven beans are explored in Chapter 8.

Entity Beans

While session beans are our verbs, entity beans are the nouns. Their aim is to express an object view of resources stored within a Relational Database Management System (RDBMS)—a process commonly known as object-relational mapping.

Like session beans, the entity type is modeled as a POJO, and becomes a *managed object* only when associated with a construct called the `javax.persistence.EntityManager`, a container-supplied service that tracks state changes and synchronizes with the database as necessary. A client who alters the state of an entity bean may expect any altered fields to be propagated to persistent storage. Frequently the `EntityManager` will cache both reads and writes to transparently streamline performance, and may enlist with the current transaction to flush state to persistent storage automatically upon invocation completion (Figure 2-6).

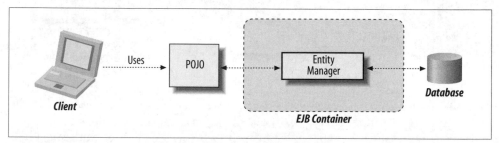

Figure 2-6. Using an EntityManager to map between POJO object state and a persistent relational database

Unlike session beans and MDBs, entity beans are not themselves a server-side component type. Instead, they are a view that may be detached from management and used just like any stateful object. When detached (disassociated from the `EntityManager`), there is no database association, but the object may later be re-enlisted with the `EntityManager` such that its state may again be synchronized. Just as session beans are EJBs only within the context of the Container, entity beans are managed only when registered with the `EntityManager`. In all other cases entity beans act as POJOs, making them extremely versatile.

Users familiar with EJB 2.x forms may be used to the former notion of Container Managed Persistence (CMP), which required dependence upon a verbose API. Although entity bean classes were once required to implement specific interfaces and their callback methods explicitly, these restrictions have been removed as of the 3.0 revision of the EJB Specification.

Our casino exists primarily to move money. Taking bets, paying winners, making change—all are transactions that need to be recorded for bookkeeping purposes. By modeling currency as an entity bean, all functions that interact with cash and chips may share the same object view that ultimately will be preserved in the database for future auditing.

Entity beans are introduced in Part III.

The Java Persistence Model

The sister to the EJB 3.1 Specification is the Java Persistence API (JPA) 2.0, developed in JSR-317 (*http://jcp.org/en/jsr/detail?id=317*). EJBs may become equipped with the facilities defined by JPA, such that modifying the properties of a managed object will be reflected automatically in the backing database. In addition to support within EJB, JPA may be used in standalone Java Standard Edition (SE) environments.

Persistence is simply a higher-level abstraction above Java Database Connectivity (JDBC). By exposing the database as objects to the developer, backing rows may be queried, loaded, updated, or removed without explicitly having to go through a contracted API or language such as SQL. In older versions of EJB, persistence was part of the specification, but starting with EJB 3.0, it has been spun off on its own. The entity bean is EJB's integration with JPA, and it is defined by enhancing a plain class definition with some additional persistence metadata.

The Model Isn't Everything

The various EJB Component types allow stateful, stateless, asynchronous, and persistent logic to be easily modeled. Now it's time to see how they'll shine under the bright lights of Container services.

## CHAPTER 3

Container Services

We see examples of efficient processes every day, even in our most mundane daily routines. A trip to the supermarket may involve ordering sliced meats from the deli counter, selecting grocery items from pre-stacked shelves, listening to advice from the butcher, and paying the cashier. If we were to model this errand as a business system, we'd notice that the whole is composed of many smaller pieces, and each task is serviced by a specialized worker. It is this same "do one thing and do it well"* approach that was introduced in French firearms production, powered the assembly lines pioneered by Henry Ford, and became omnipresent during the American industrial revolution as the preferred mechanism to maximize throughput.

The benefits of allowing each concern to be fulfilled by a specialist through *division of labor* are fairly obvious: a secretary should answer phones while a mail room attendant handles shipping. Similarly, application developers should write the rules of their business and leave the mechanics of reliable, distributed systems to middleware providers.

In the case of EJB, the Component Model defines our interchangeable parts, and the Container Services are specialists that perform work upon them. The Specification provides:

- Dependency injection
- Concurrency
- Instance pooling/caching
- Transactions
- Security
- Timers
- Naming and object stores
- Interoperability
- Lifecycle callbacks

* Doug McIlroy, *Basics of the Unix Philosophy*, *http://www.faqs.org/docs/artu/ch01s06.html*

- Interceptors
- Java Enterprise Platform integration

We'll introduce each at a high level here, and get into further detail later (Part III).

Dependency Injection (DI)

A component-based approach to software design brings with it the complication of inter-module communication. Tightly coupling discrete units together violates module independence and separation of concerns, while using common lookup code leads to the maintenance of more plumbing. Martin Fowler details this problem in his paper "Inversion of Control Containers and the Dependency Injection Pattern," which has spurred the development and success of many popular standalone DI containers.[†]

As EJB is a component-centric architecture, it provides a means to reference dependent modules in decoupled fashion. The end result is that you'll adhere to a contract and let the container provide the implementation at deployment time.

In pseudocode, this looks like:

```
prototype UserModule
{
  // Instance Member
  @DependentModule
  MailModule mail;

  // A function
  function mailUser()
  {
    mail.sendMail("me@ejb.somedomain");
  }
}
```

The fictitious `@DependentModule` annotation serves two purposes:

- Defines a dependency upon some service of type `MailModule`. `UserModule` may not deploy until this dependency is satisfied.
- Marks the instance member `mail` as a candidate for injection. The container will populate this field during deployment.

Dependency injection encourages coding to interfaces, and not to any particular implementation; we'll see it in action in Chapter 16.

† *http://martinfowler.com/articles/injection.html*

Concurrency

Assuming each Service is represented by one instance, dependency injection alone is a fine solution for a single-threaded application; only one client may be accessing a resource at a given time. However, this quickly becomes a problem in situations where a centralized server is fit to serve many simultaneous requests. Deadlocks, livelocks, and race conditions are some of the possible nightmares arising out of an environment in which threads may compete for shared resources. These are hard to anticipate, harder to debug, and are prone to first exposing themselves in production! Proper solutions lie outside the scope of this book,[‡] and for good reason: EJB allows the application developer to sidestep the problem entirely thanks to a series of concurrency policies.

That said, there are a series of effects upon performance to consider, so the specification allows for configuration in some cases. Otherwise, it's important to be aware how each component type views concurrency concerns; this is covered alongside the session bean in Chapters 5, 6, and 7.

Instance Pooling/Caching

Because of the strict concurrency rules enforced by the Container, an intentional bottleneck is often introduced where a service instance may not be available for processing until some other request has completed. If the service was restricted to a singular instance, all subsequent requests would have to queue up until their turn was reached (see Figure 3-1).

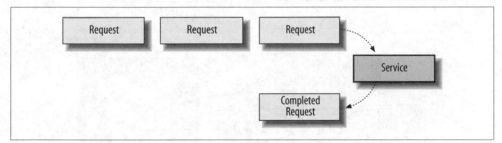

Figure 3-1. Client requests queuing for service

---

‡ Recommended reading is *Java Concurrency in Practice*, Goetz et al., *http://www.javaconcurrencyinpractice .com/*

Conversely, if the service was permitted to use any number of underlying instances, there would be no guard to say how many requests could be processed in tandem, and access across the physical machine could crawl to a halt as its resources were spread too thin (Figure 3-2).

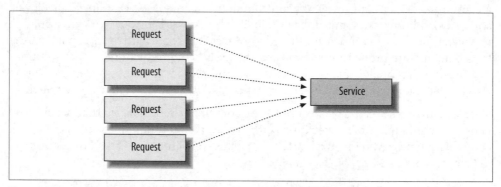

Figure 3-2. Many invocations executing concurrently with no queuing policy

EJB addresses this problem through a technique called *instance pooling*, in which each module is allocated some number of instances with which to serve incoming requests (Figure 3-3). Many vendors provide configuration options that allow the deployer to allocate pool sizes appropriate to the work being performed, providing the compromise needed to achieve optimal throughput.

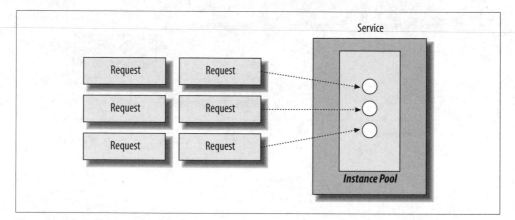

Figure 3-3. A hybrid approach using a pool

Instance pooling addresses performance, and it is explained alongside session beans in Chapters 5, 6, and 7.

Transactions

As a routine chugs along, it may perform half of its duties before encountering some exceptional circumstance that prevents successful completion. At this point, the system may be left in an unreliable or incorrect state. Take the popular "account transfer example":

1. User requests that $100 be transferred between her checking and savings accounts.
2. System deducts $100 from checking.
3. An unexpected error is thrown up the call chain.

The money has disappeared from record, and the customer is out $100. Although this may be a desirable scenario if you're a particularly scheming bank manager, in most cases we'd like our programs to reliably leave things in consistent state. EJB ensures this via its integration with the Java Transaction Service (JTS; *http://java.sun.com/jav aee/technologies/jts/*) and exposes an API that gives the *bean provider* (application developer) control over the properties specifying how a transaction-aware application behaves. Again, the nuts and bolts of *how* this is achieved is not a problem for the EJB developer; all that's required is some understanding of the ACID[§] fundamentals:

Atomicity
> Every instruction in a call completes or none do. If there's a failure halfway through, state is restored to the point before the request was made.

Consistency
> The system will be consistent with its governing rules both before and after the request.

Isolation
> Transactions in progress are not seen outside the scope of their request until successful completion. Shared resources may not be mutated by two transactions at once.

Durability
> Once a transaction successfully returns, it must commit to its changes. The system must process the result once a client has received word of normal completion.

There are a variety of options available to configure transactional behavior, and these are explored in Chapter 17.

Security

Multiuser applications are likely to expose a wide variety of operations, and not all callers are created equal. An unsecured banking system won't discriminate between a

---

[§] An acronym coined by Andreas Reuter and Theo Haerder in 1983, "Principles of Transaction-Oriented Database Recovery"

teller and a branch manager when confronted with a request to approve a loan, and manually baking this logic into the business method mixes two concerns. EJB therefore provides a role-based security mechanism that bolsters existing application code with a set of security policies governed by the Container (Figure 3-4).

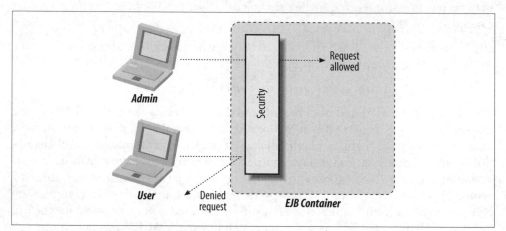

Figure 3-4. EJB Security permitting access based upon the caller's role

This allows the application developer to explicitly allow or deny access at a fine-grained level based upon the caller's identity.

We'll delve into the security model in Chapter 15.

Timers

So far, we've dealt exclusively with client-initiated requests. While this may handle the bulk of an application's requirements, it doesn't account for scheduled jobs:

- A ticket purchasing system must release unclaimed tickets after some timeout of inactivity.
- An auction house must end auctions on time.
- A cellular provider should close and mail statements each month.

The EJB Timer Service may be leveraged to trigger these events and has been enhanced in the 3.1 specification with a natural-language expression syntax.

We play with timers in Chapter 19.

Naming and Object Stores

All naming services essentially do the same thing: they provide clients with a mechanism for locating distributed objects or resources. To accomplish this, a naming service must fulfill two requirements: object binding and a lookup API. Object binding is the association of a distributed object with a natural language name or identifier. A lookup API provides the client with an interface to the naming system; it simply allows us to connect with a distributed service and request a remote reference to a specific object.

Enterprise JavaBeans mandates the use of Java Naming and Directory Interface (JNDI; *http://java.sun.com/products/jndi/*) as a lookup API on Java clients. JNDI supports just about any kind of naming and directory service. Although it can become extraordinarily complex, the way JNDI is used in Java Enterprise Edition (EE) applications is usually fairly simple. Java client applications can use JNDI to initiate a connection to an EJB server and locate a specific EJB.

There are many different kinds of directory and naming services, and EJB vendors can choose the one that best meets their needs, but all vendors must support the CORBA naming service in addition to any other directory services they choose to support.

Naming is a subset of the resource management features offered by EJB, and it is discussed in Chapter 16.

Interoperability

Although it's nice that the dependency injection facilities allow components within EJB to play nicely, we don't live in a bubble. Our application may want to consume data from or provide services to other programs, perhaps written in different implementation languages. There are a variety of open standards that address this inter-process communication, and EJB leverages these.

Interoperability is a vital part of EJB. The specification includes the required support for Java RMI-IIOP for remote method invocation and provides for transaction, naming, and security interoperability. EJB also requires support for JAX-WS, JAX-RPC, Web Services for Java EE, and Web Services Metadata for the Java Platform specifications (EJB 3.1 Specification, 2.6).

Lifecycle Callbacks

Some services require some initialization or cleanup to be used properly. For example, a file transfer module may want to open a connection to a remote server before processing requests to transfer files and should safely release all resources before being brought out of service.

For component types that have a lifecycle, EJB allows for callback notifications, which act as a hook for the bean provider to receive these events. In the case of our file transfer bean, this may look like:

```
prototype FileTransferService
{
```

```
    @StartLifecycleCallback
    function openConnection(){ ... }

    @StopLifecycleCallback
    function closeConnection() { ... }
}
```

Here we've annotated functions to open and close connections as callbacks; they'll be invoked by the container as their corresponding lifecycle states are reached.

Interceptors

While it's really nice that EJB provides aspectized handling of many of the container services, the specification cannot possibly identify all cross-cutting concerns facing your project. For this reason, EJB makes it possible to define custom *interceptors* upon business methods and lifecycle callbacks. This makes it easy to contain some common code in a centralized location and have it applied to the invocation chain without impacting your core logic.

Say we want to measure the execution time of all invocations to a particular method. We'd write an interceptor:

```
prototype MetricsInterceptor
{

    function intercept(Invocation invocation)
    {
      // Get the start time
      Time startTime = getTime();

      // Carry out the invocation
      invocation.continue();

      // Get the end time
      Time endTime = getTime();

      // Log out the elapsed time
      log("Took " + (endTime - startTime));
    }
}
```

Then we could apply this to methods as we'd like:

```
@ApplyInterceptor(MetricsInterceptor.class)
function myLoginMethod{ ... }

@ApplyInterceptor(MetricsInterceptor.class)
function myLogoutMethod{ ... }
```

Interceptors are explained in Chapter 18.

Platform Integration

As a key technology within the Java Enterprise Edition (JEE) 6 (*http://jcp.org/en/jsr/detail?id=313*), EJB aggregates many of the other platform frameworks and APIs:

- Java Transaction Service
- Java Persistence API
- Java Naming and Directory Interface (JNDI)
- Security Services
- Web Services

In most cases, the EJB metadata used to define this integration is a simplified view of the underlying services. This gives bean providers a set of powerful constructs right out of the box, without need for additional configuration.

EJB is also one of the target models recognized by the new Java Contexts and Dependency Injection specification (*http://jcp.org/en/jsr/detail?id=299*). This new kid on the block adds a unified binding to both Java Enterprise and Standard editions across many different component types.

Bringing It Together

Enough theory; up to this point, we've introduced topics only conceptually. In the next chapter we'll take off the gloves and ditch pseudocode for the real deal.

## CHAPTER 4

Developing Your First EJBs

Now that we've covered the concepts behind the various component models and container services provided by the specification, it's time to start putting these lessons into practice. In this chapter we'll introduce the terminology and syntax necessary to code, package, deploy, and test some functional EJBs.

Step 1: Preparation

Let's briefly lay out some definitions and conventions, and then we'll get to hacking away.

Definitions

EJBs are composed from the following.

Bean implementation class (session and message-driven beans)

This class, written by the bean provider, contains the business logic for a session or message-driven bean. It is annotated with the appropriate bean type: `@javax.ejb.Stateless`, `@javax.ejb.Stateful`, or `@javax.ejb.MessageDriven`. For instance:

```
@javax.ejb.Stateless
public class MyFirstBean{...}
```

is all that's needed to declare an SLSB.

Bean instance (session and message-driven beans)

The EJB Container internally contains one or more instances of the bean implementation class to service session or message-driven invocations. These are not exposed to the client, but are instead abstracted out by way of the *client view*. Entity bean instances are POJOs that may be created directly by the client using the new operator.

Client view (session and message-driven beans)

Because clients do not invoke upon bean instances directly, this is the contract with which a client will interact with the EJB. In the case of a session bean, the client view will take the form of a business, component, or endpoint interface—all to be implemented by the EJB Proxy. Message-driven beans have no client view, as they're received as messaging events, and entity beans also have no explicit view because clients will interact with a managed object directly. At least one view must be defined (either explicitly or implicitly) for an EJB.

EJB Proxy (session beans)

Session bean clients invoke upon the EJB Proxy, which adheres to the contract defined by the client view. Upon EJB deployment, the Container binds all appropriate Proxy objects into a predefined destination in Global JNDI (EJB 3.1 Specification Section 4.4), where a client may look up the reference. From the client's perspective, the proxy *is* the EJB, though in actuality the invocation mechanism is a bit more involved (Figure 4-1).

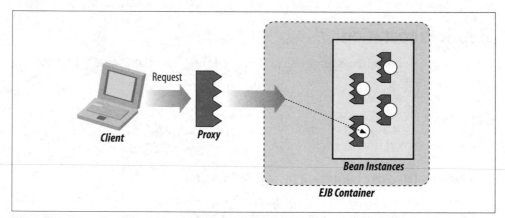

Figure 4-1. The role of the client, container, and bean instance in an EJB invocation

It's because of the Proxy indirection that the container is able to perform its extensive services outside of the client's concern.

Local versus remote (session beans)

The terms local and remote, when referring to business, home, or component interfaces, designate the relationship between the process running the client and the JVM running the EJB Container. This is often confused with distribution across physical boundaries. When the client is in-VM, invocations to the local interface are much more efficient than their remote counterpart; they may avoid the networking stack and pass object references instead of serializing values. For instance, EJBs within an application will often communicate with each other by means of a local business interface. The

EJB 3.1 Specification details key differences between local, remote, and endpoint views in Section 3.2.

Business interface (session beans)

This is the simplified view, introduced in EJB 3.0, defining business methods that are to be supported by session beans. The business interface is marked as such via an `@javax.ejb.Local` or `@javax.ejb.Remote` annotation, depending upon how it's to be used. However, any one interface may not be both local and remote. The EJB 3.1 Specification defines business interfaces in Section 4.9.7.

Component interface (session beans)

This is the legacy view defined by the EJB 2.x Specification. It has been left in place for backward compatibility with older clients, and it is detailed in EJB 3.1 Section 3.6. The Component interface (also known as the "local" or "remote" interface, contrasted with business interfaces, which are called "business local" or "business remote") must implement `javax.ejb.EJBObject` or `javax.ejb.EJBLocalObject` and will additionally define business methods available to the client. It is obtained via the `create<METHOD>` methods of the *home interface*.

Home interface (session beans)

The home interface is used to create, find, and remove session bean references according to the EJB 2.x client contract. Home interfaces extend `javax.ejb.EJBHome` or `javax.ejb.EJBLocalHome` and may define methods named with a prefix of "create" to return component interface references. Just like component interfaces, these are legacy and in place to support backward compatibility.

Endpoint interface (session beans)

The endpoint interface defines business methods that can be accessed from applications outside the EJB container via SOAP. The endpoint interface is based on Java API for XML-RPC (JAX-RPC) and is designed to adhere to the SOAP and WSDL standards. The endpoint interface is a plain Java interface that is annotated with the `@javax.jws.WebService` annotation.

Message interface (MDBs)

Message-driven beans implement the message interface, which defines the methods by which messaging systems, such as the JMS, can deliver messages to the bean. An MDB that listens to JMS events would therefore be defined like this:

```
@javax.ejb.MessageDriven(activationConfig={...})
public class MyMessageDrivenBean implements javax.jms.MessageListener{...}
```

Naming Conventions

Before going on, let's establish some conventions to be used throughout this book. These will be used for clarity; they are not prescriptive or even recommended for use in production. You may use any naming strategy you wish, but it's suggested that you stick to some predefined standard. There is no law dictating that each of the constructs listed next must be used for your EJBs; in fact, in most cases you'll use just one or two. The impositions of the EJB 2.x specifications are long gone.

Common business name

To describe an EJB's function, we'll assign it a common base from which we may derive other names. This should be descriptive of the business function; therefore, an EJB that handles ticket processing may contain the term `TicketProcessor`. All other classes that comprise an EJB may then be named according to the following table:

Construct	Suffix	Example
EJB (the sum of its parts)	EJB	TicketProcessorEJB
Bean Implementation Class	Bean	TicketProcessorBean
Remote Business Interface	RemoteBusiness	TicketProcessorRemoteBusiness
Local Business Interface	LocalBusiness	TicketProcessorLocalBusiness
Remote Home Interface	RemoteHome	TicketProcessorRemoteHome
Local Home Interface	LocalHome	TicketProcessorLocalHome
Remote Component Interface	Remote	TicketProcessorRemote
Local Component Interface	Local	TicketProcessorLocal
Endpoint Interface	WS (for WebService)	TicketProcessorWS

Conventions for the Examples

To maintain consistency, this text will adhere to the following conventions unless explicitly specified.

Vendor-agnostic
> All examples covered in Parts I through IV of this book will address syntax and concepts dictated by the EJB Specification only. As the EJB deployment mechanism is not covered by spec, these examples will not run unless bolstered by some additional instructions or metadata. To this end, each example will have a deployable counterpart in Part V, which is written to work specifically with the open source JBoss Application Server. The focus of the code fragments in this text may be intentionally incomplete to promote brevity, and they are in place primarily to illustrate concepts. Part V will serve as the real practice grounds for getting your hands dirty. You may want to flip back and forth between the lessons and their corresponding examples as you progress.

No XML

Generally speaking, EJB metadata may be supplied either by a standard XML descriptor (*ejb-jar.xml*), Java annotations, or some combination of the two. In cases where there's overlap, XML wins as an override. In order to cut down on the verbosity of our examples, we'll opt for annotations wherever possible. The corresponding XML syntax is available for reference by consulting the appropriate Document Type Definition (DTD) or schema.

Annotations on the bean implementation class

Many class-level annotations may be applied in a variety of locations. For instance, a remote business interface may be marked on the interface itself:

```
@javax.ejb.Remote
public interface SomeBusinessRemote{...}
```

Instead, we'll be declaring annotations upon the bean implementation class:

```
@javax.ejb.Stateless
@javax.ejb.Remote(SomeBusinessRemote.class)
public class SomeBean implements SomeBusinessRemote{...}
```

This means that a quick glance will reveal all metadata for the bean in question, and we'll minimize poking through various files to get the full picture.

Step 2: Coding the EJB

For this exercise we'll make a simple SLSB, a Calculator Service, to illustrate how the various pieces all fit together. In fact, we'll spin up two EJBs—one to show the path of least resistance, and another to expose all business, home, and component views. The full source and deployment instructions for this example are available in Appendix A.

The Contract

This is a great starting point, regardless of whether you're building EJBs. The contract, implemented as interfaces in Java, defines *what* our service will do, and leaves it up to the implementation classes to decide *how* it's done. Remember that the same interface cannot be used for both @Local and @Remote, so we'll make some common base that may be extended.

```
public interface CalculatorCommonBusiness
{
   /**
    * Adds all arguments
    *
    * @return The sum of all arguments
    */
   int add(int... arguments);
}

public interface CalculatorRemoteBusiness extends CalculatorCommonBusiness{}
```

As you can see, we've created `CalculatorRemoteBusiness` by extending the contract of `CalculatorCommonBusiness`. This will come in handy later when we want to add more views exposing the same method (so we don't have to rewrite its definition). Our remote business interface meets the requirement that our session bean will have at least one view, so we may now write the bean implementation class.

The Bean Implementation Class

Again we'll make a common base to contain the logic, and extend it to add our metadata that will define the SLSB.

```
public class CalculatorBeanBase implements CalculatorCommonBusiness
{
   /**
    * {@link CalculatorCommonBusiness#add(int...)}
    */
   @Override
   public int add(final int... arguments)
   {
      // Initialize
      int result = 0;

      // Add all arguments
      for (final int arg : arguments)
      {
         result += arg;
      }

      // Return
      return result;
   }
}
```

This contains the required implementation of `CalculatorCommonBusiness.add(int...)`. The bean implementation class therefore has very little work to do.

```
import javax.ejb.LocalBean;
import javax.ejb.Stateless;

@Stateless
@LocalBean
public class SimpleCalculatorBean extends CalculatorBeanBase

{
   /*
    * Implementation supplied by common base class
    */
}
```

The function of our bean implementation class here is to bring everything together and define the EJB metadata. Compilation will embed two important bits into the resultant *.class* file. First, we have an SLSB, as noted by the `@Stateless` annotation. And second, we're exposing a no-interface view, new to EJB 3.1, courtesy of the `@Local`

Bean annotation. Alternatively, we could have used an XML descriptor to hold this information, making an EJB out of `CalculatorBeanBase`. The EJB Container, upon deployment, will pick up on this information and take the necessary actions.

Before we use our new classes as an EJB, let's leverage the pure POJO programming model to make some quick tests.

Out-of-Container Testing

Unit testing, as contrasted with integration testing, aims to isolate small bits of functionality and assert that they're working as expected. The addition implementation of our `CalculatorEJB` is an excellent candidate for this kind of approach. By treating our EJB Implementation class as a POJO, we can keep test setup and execution time light and quick.

Testing in this book will be implemented using the popular open source framework JUnit (*http://www.junit.org/*):

```
import junit.framework.TestCase;

import org.junit.Test;

public class CalculatorUnitTestCase
{
    /**
     * Ensures that the CalculatorEJB adds as expected
     */
    @Test
    public void testAddition()
    {
        // Initialize
        final CalculatorCommonBusiness calc = new SimpleCalculatorBean();
        final int expectedSum = 2+3+5;

        // Add
        final int actualSum = calc.add(2, 3, 5);

        // Test
        TestCase.assertEquals("Addition did not return the expected result",
            expectedSum, actualSum);
    }
}
```

Here we make a new instance of `SimpleCalculatorBean` and use it to add a few integers. Again, this is *not* an EJB. The example showcases how the EJB Programming Model does not tie you to EJB at all; the test has no knowledge of the specification APIs.

Integration testing is where we'll ensure that the individual pieces play nicely together.

Integration Testing

There are three steps involved in performing integration testing upon an EJB. First, we must package the sources and any descriptors into a standard Java Archive (JAR; *http://java.sun.com/javase/6/docs/technotes/guides/jar/jar.html*) or Enterprise Archive (EAR; *http://java.sun.com/javaee/5/docs/tutorial/doc/bnaby.html#indexterm-47*). Next, the resultant deployable must be placed into the container according to a vendor-specific mechanism. Finally, we need a standalone client to obtain the proxy references from the Container and invoke upon them.

Packaging

The Sun Microsystems JDK, for example, ships with a standard `jar` tool that can be used to assemble classes, resources, and other metadata into a unified JAR file, which will both compress and encapsulate its contents. Typically your project's build will handle this step, often by way of an Apache Ant (*http://ant.apache.org/*) task or Maven (*http://maven.apache.org/*) goal. Whichever route you choose in packaging, the result might look a little bit like this if we were to print out the contents:

```
shell$> $JAVA_HOME/bin/jar -tvf firstejb.jar
     0 Wed Mar 25 01:59:22 GMT-08:00 2009 META-INF/
   129 Wed Mar 25 01:59:20 GMT-08:00 2009 META-INF/ejb-jar.xml // < OPTIONAL
     0 Wed Mar 25 01:59:20 GMT-08:00 2009 com/
     0 Wed Mar 25 01:59:20 GMT-08:00 2009 com/mycompany/
     0 Wed Mar 25 01:59:20 GMT-08:00 2009 com/mycompany/
     0 Wed Mar 25 01:59:20 GMT-08:00 2009 com/mycompany/
     0 Wed Mar 25 01:59:20 GMT-08:00 2009 com/mycompany/
     0 Wed Mar 25 01:59:20 GMT-08:00 2009 com/mycompany/firstejb/
   318 Wed Mar 25 01:59:20 GMT-08:00 2009 com/mycompany/firstejb/CalculatorLocal
Home.class
   248 Wed Mar 25 01:59:20 GMT-08:00 2009 com/mycompany/firstejb/CalculatorRemote
.class
   348 Wed Mar 25 01:59:20 GMT-08:00 2009 com/mycompany/firstejb/CalculatorRemote
Home.class
  1473 Wed Mar 25 01:59:20 GMT-08:00 2009 com/mycompany/firstejb/CalculatorBean
Base.class
   237 Wed Mar 25 01:59:20 GMT-08:00 2009 com/mycompany/firstejb/CalculatorRemote
Business.class
   939 Wed Mar 25 01:59:20 GMT-08:00 2009 com/mycompany/firstejb/ManyView
CalculatorBean.class
   251 Wed Mar 25 01:59:20 GMT-08:00 2009 com/mycompany/firstejb/CalculatorLocal
.class
   235 Wed Mar 25 01:59:20 GMT-08:00 2009 com/mycompany/firstejb/CalculatorLocal
Business.class
   189 Wed Mar 25 01:59:20 GMT-08:00 2009 com/mycompany/firstejb/CalculatorCommon
Business.class
   643 Wed Mar 25 01:59:20 GMT-08:00 2009 com/mycompany/firstejb/SimpleCalculator
Bean.class
```

The `ejb-jar.xml` line represents our optional XML descriptor, which is excluded from this example.

Deployment into the Container

The EJB Specification intentionally leaves the issue of deployment up to the vendor's discretion. Therefore, our examples will keep this out of scope until Part V, which will fully detail instructions for running examples.

The client

Again we'll implement our client as a JUnit test. This time, instead of creating POJOs via the new operator, we'll look up true EJB references via JNDI. For our purposes, JNDI is a simple store from which we may request objects keyed to some known address. The form of the address is supplied by the EJB 3.1 Portable Global JNDI Name Syntax, discussed in Chapter 16.

Let's walk through this step-by-step. The process looks a bit like the following:

1. Perform initialization of the test, and set up the JNDI Environment.
2. Look up the proxy reference to the EJB via JNDI.
3. Invoke upon the reference.
4. Test the result.

First, we declare some imports to show where some nonobvious types are coming from. Assume that the client is in the same package namespace as the `CalculatorEJB` classes:

```
import javax.naming.Context;
import javax.naming.InitialContext;
import org.junit.BeforeClass;
import org.junit.Test;
```

The `javax.naming` classes are used in obtaining the proxy references from JNDI, and the others are part of the test framework. Now to define the class and make for some `static` members used in testing:

```
public class CalculatorIntegrationTestCase
{
    /**
     * The JNDI Naming Context
     */
    private static Context namingContext;

    /**
     * The EJB 3.1 no-interface view view of the CalculatorEJB
     */
    private static SimpleCalculatorBean calc;


    /**
     * JNDI Name of the no-interface view
     */
    private static final String JNDI_NAME_CALC =
    "java:global/myJarName/SimpleCalculatorBean";
```

Here we've declared a JNDI naming `Context` for the lookups, and the names of the target JNDI Addresses under which we'll find the appropriate proxy reference. Our tests will check that the EJB 3.1 Business View works as expected, but before the test runs, a lifecycle method will obtain the reference and set the proxy reference accordingly:

```
@BeforeClass // Invoked by the test framework before any tests run
    public static void obtainProxyReferences() throws Throwable
    {
        // Create the naming context, using jndi.properties on the CP
        namingContext = new InitialContext();

        // Obtain EJB 3.1 Business Reference
        calc = (SimpleCalculatorBean)
          namingContext.lookup(JNDI_NAME_CALC);
    }
```

First we create the naming `Context`, using a standard *jndi.properties* file that we assume to be present on the classpath. The JNDI properties to be used are vendor-specific, so by pulling these out into a separate file, our test remains portable across EJB implementations.

From there, we obtain the business proxy by performing a simple JNDI lookup upon the portable Global JNDI name.

Let's define a central point to perform assertions within our tests:

```
private void assertAdditionSucceeds(CalculatorCommonBusiness calc)
    {
        // Initialize
        final int[] arguments = new int[]
        {2, 3, 5};
        final int expectedSum = 10;

        // Add
        final int actualSum = calc.add(arguments); // Real EJB Invocation!

        // Test
        TestCase.assertEquals("Addition did not return the expected result",
          expectedSum, actualSum);
    }
```

This time, the `calc` reference passed in will not be a POJO, but instead a true EJB Proxy.

```
@Test
    public void testAdditionUsingBusinessReference() throws Throwable
    {
        this.assertAdditionSucceeds(calc);
    }
}
```

Our two tests will merely pass the appropriate EJB Proxy to the assertion function. Assuming everything goes well, we'll get the all clear and may rest assured that the system is working as we expect.

The interesting thing to note about this setup is that nowhere have we declared the notion of remoting, transactions, or the like. Regardless, this test is a fully functional remote client to a distributed architecture. Client code has no idea that it's crossing process and network boundaries. This is a powerful argument in favor of the EJB Architecture.

Summary

This chapter has covered a lot of ground in terms of introducing some of the EJB APIs and grammars. In some cases, we've glossed over the more intimate details underpinning the creation, packaging, deployment, and testing of a stateless session bean to instead clearly focus upon the conceptual aspects involved. The next chapter contains an in-depth discussion of session beans and associated services.

## PART II

Server-Side Component Models

We've now seen how EJB's component types allow us to write less, allowing the container to equip us with services and other runtime support. In this section we'll more fully address the available server-side models: session beans and message-driven beans.

EJB's basic building block for implementing business logic—*taskflow*—is the session bean. Taskflow refers to all the steps required to service a request such as making a doctor's appointment or renting a video. Session beans frequently manage the interactions within persistent data—entity beans—describing how they work together to accomplish a specific goal.

Session beans are divided into three basic types: stateless, stateful, and singleton.

A *stateless* session bean (Chapter 5) is a collection of related services, each represented by a business method; the bean maintains no conversational state from one method invocation to the next. When you make a request upon a stateless session bean, the container executes the target method and returns the result without knowing or caring what other requests have gone before or might follow. Think of a stateless session bean as a set of procedures or batch programs that execute based on some parameters and return a result.

A *stateful* session bean (Chapter 6) is an extension of the client application. It performs tasks on behalf of the client and maintains state related to that client. This is called *conversational state* because it represents a continuing set of exchanges between the stateful session bean (SFSB) and the client. Methods invoked on a stateful session bean can write and read data to and from this conversational state, which is shared among all methods in the bean.

A *singleton* session bean (Chapter 7) is backed by only one target: an instance of the bean implementation class. All business requests are serviced by the same backing object, so state is shared throughout the application. This is especially useful for performing system-wide initialization or governing a process from a sole authority.

Message-driven beans (Chapter 8) act as listeners for incoming events. They are not invoked directly by the client, and they do not provide any return value. As we'll see, these may make a powerful utility for wiring together various pieces of an application.

## CHAPTER 5

The Stateless Session Bean

The stateless session bean is designed for efficiency and simplicity. Central to its design is the absence of conversational state, which is a topic worth exploring a bit further before delving into SLSB mechanics.

When we say *conversational state*, we refer to information exchanged and remembered within the context of a series of requests between the Client (caller) and EJB (service). We can illustrate this simply:

```
Mike: Hi, my name is Mike.
Service: Hello, Mike.
Mike: Do you know my name?
Service: Yes, your name is Mike.
```

Here, the state variable holding the name of the client is stored for the duration of the conversation. Stateless session beans are incapable of handling this exchange correctly; each invocation upon a SLSB proxy operates independently from those both before and after (see Figure 5-1). In fact, its underlying bean instances may be swapped interchangeably between requests.

Stateless session beans are EJB's answer to traditional transaction-processing applications, which are executed using a procedure call. The procedure runs from beginning to end, finally returning the result. Once the invocation completes, nothing about the data that was manipulated or the details of the request is available. When finished servicing a method invocation, an SLSB instance may be reused as the target for a new request. In short, stateless session beans are engineered to be lightweight and fast at the expense of conversational state. A much better usage of a SLSB looks like:

```
Mike: How much money is in savings account B?
SLSB: $100.
Mike: Please transfer $200 from checking account A to savings account B.
SLSB: OK, done.
Mike: How much money is in savings account B?
SLSB: $300.
```

Here Mike has supplied the SLSB with all the information it needs to process a request within the request itself.

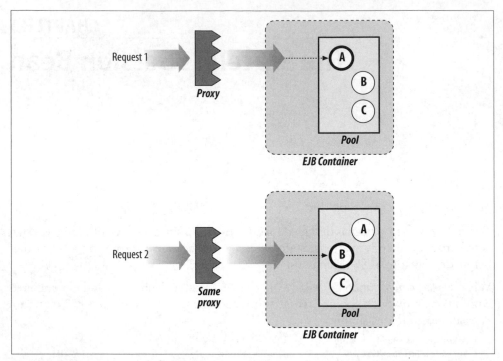

Figure 5-1. Two invocations upon the same proxy, where each invocation uses a different underlying bean instance as picked from the pool

Bypassing conversational state doesn't mean that a stateless session bean can't have instance variables or maintain any kind of *internal* state. Nothing prevents you from keeping a variable that tracks the number of times a bean instance has been called or a variable that saves data for debugging. However, it is important to remember that this state may never be visible to a client. The caller of an SLSB can't assume that the same bean instance will service all of its requests. Instance variables may have different values in different bean instances, so their state is likely to appear to change randomly as stateless session beans are swapped from one client to another. Therefore, anything you reference in instance variables should be generic and not leaked out through the API.

For example, an SLSB might reasonably record debugging messages—that might be the only way to figure out what is happening on a large server with many bean instances. The client doesn't know or care where debugging output is going. However, it would clearly be inappropriate for a stateless bean to remember that it was in the process of making a reservation for Madame X; the next time it is called, it may be servicing another client entirely. An SLSB used improperly might act a little like this:

```
Mike: Hi, my name is Mike.
SLSB: Hello, Mike.
Mike: Do you know my name?
SLSB: Yes, your name is Jason.
```

```
Mike: What?  That's wrong!  I'm going!
SLSB: OK, later, Dave.
```

This kind of behavior stems from an incorrect application of the SLSB type. Either the bean provider has leaked out internal state variables or a stateful session bean (Chapter 6) should have been used instead. As a result, bean instances that have previously serviced Jason and Dave are now being used for Mike's requests, and the system is in some inconsistent state.

Stateless session beans may be used for report generation, batch processing, or some stateless services such as validating credit cards. Another good application might be a StockQuoteEJB that returns a stock's current price. Any activity that can be accomplished in one method call is a good candidate for the high-performance stateless session bean.

Let's examine the semantics and grammars used to define session beans, and in particular, the SLSB.

The XML Deployment Descriptor

EJB has an optional XML deployment descriptor defined in the *META-INF/ejb-jar.xml* file of the EJB's JAR file. You can use this descriptor as an alternative to annotations, to augment metadata that is not declared as an annotation, or to override an annotation. The choice is up to you. While annotations are a quick, simple way to prototype or define default metadata, they do make for tight coupling as information becomes embedded into the bytecode.

What's interesting about an XML-only deployment is that your Java code may contain no references to any EJB-specific APIs. If you looked at the Java code, you wouldn't even know that it was an EJB.

The <enterprise-beans> element contained in <ejb-jar> defines the set of EJBs you are deploying. The <session> element denotes that you are deploying a session bean. <ejb-name> gives the session bean an identity that you can reference. The <remote> and <local> elements identify the business interfaces of the bean, and <ejb-class> declares the bean class. The <session-type> element identifies the session bean as a stateless session bean. <env-entry> initializes the values externalized from the bean class (details are provided in Chapter 16).

The XML deployment descriptor schema also supports partial XML definitions. This may be used to augment or override metadata provided via annotations, as we'll soon see.

SessionContext

The `javax.ejb.SessionContext` interface provides a view into the EJB container's environment. The `SessionContext` object can be used as the bean instance's interface to the EJB container to obtain information about the context of the method invocation call and to provide quick access to various EJB services. A session bean can obtain a reference to its `SessionContext` by using the `@Resource` annotation:

```
/**
 * SessionContext of this EJB; this will be injected by the EJB
 * Container because it's marked w/ @Resource
 */
@Resource
private SessionContext context;
```

`SessionContext` allows you to obtain information such as the current user that is invoking on the EJB, or to look up entries within the EJB's Enterprise Naming Context (ENC). Let's look at the `javax.ejb.SessionContext` interface:

```
public interface javax.ejb.SessionContext extends javax.ejb.EJBContext {
    EJBLocalObject getEJBLocalObject( ) throws IllegalStateException
    EJBObject getEJBObject( ) throws IllegalStateException;
    MessageContext getMessageContext( ) throws IllegalStateException;

    <T> getBusinessObject(Class<T> businessInterface)

throws IllegalStateException;
    Class getInvokedBusinessInterface( );
}
```

The `getEJBObject()` and `getEJBLocalObject()` methods are obsolete and will throw an exception if invoked upon. They are objects that are specific to the EJB 2.1 style of defining EJBs.

The `SessionContext.getBusinessObject()` method returns a reference to the current EJB that can be invoked by other clients. This reference is the EJB equivalent to Java's `this` pointer, but it returns a proper EJB proxy. The `businessInterface` parameter must be one of the EJB's `BusinessRemote` or `BusinessLocal` interfaces so that the container knows whether to create a remote or local reference to the current EJB. The `getBusinessObject()` method allows the bean instance to get its own EJB object reference, which it can then pass to other beans. Here is an example:

```
@Stateless
public class A_Bean implements A_BusinessRemote {
    @Resource private SessionContext context;
    public void someMethod( ) {
        B_BeanBusinessRemote  b = ... // Get a remote reference to B_Bean.
        A_BeanBusinessRemote mySelf =  getBusinessObject(A_BeanRemote.class);
        b.aMethod( mySelf );
    }
    ...
}
```

It is illegal for a bean instance to pass a this reference to another bean; instead, it passes its remote or local EJB object reference, which the bean instance gets from its Session Context.

The SessionContext.getInvokedBusinessInterface() method allows you to determine whether your EJB was invoked on through its remote, local, or web service interface. It returns the invoked business interface as a class.

EJBContext

SessionContext extends the javax.ejb.EJBContext class. EJBContext defines several methods that provide useful information to a bean at runtime.

Here is the definition of the EJBContext interface:

```
package javax.ejb;
public interface EJBContext {

    public Object lookup(String name);

    // EJB 2.1 only: TimerService
    public TimerService getTimerService( )
        throws java.lang.IllegalStateException;

    // security methods
    public java.security.Principal getCallerPrincipal( );
    public boolean isCallerInRole(java.lang.String roleName);

    // transaction methods
    public javax.transaction.UserTransaction getUserTransaction( )
        throws java.lang.IllegalStateException;
    public boolean getRollbackOnly( )
        throws java.lang.IllegalStateException;
    public void setRollbackOnly( )
        throws java.lang.IllegalStateException;

    // deprecated and obsolete methods
    public java.security.Identity getCallerIdentity( );
    public boolean isCallerInRole(java.security.Identity role);
    public java.util.Properties getEnvironment( );

    public EJBHome getEJBHome( )
        java.lang.IllegalStateException;
    public EJBLocalHome getEJBLocalHome( )
        java.lang.IllegalStateException;

}
```

EJBContext.lookup() is a convenience method that allows you to look up entries in the EJB's ENC. We've used it in the example just shown to obtain the cipher's passphrase.

The EJBContext.getTimerService() method returns a reference to the container's Timer Service, which allows the stateless bean to set up notifications of timed events for itself.

In other words, a session bean can set alarms so that the container will call it when a specific date arrives or some interval of time has passed. The Timer Service can also be injected using the @Resource annotation. The Timer Service is covered in detail in Chapter 19.

The EJBContext.getCallerPrincipal() method is used to obtain the java.security. Principal object representing the client that is currently accessing the bean. The Prin cipal object can, for example, be used by an EJB to track the identities of clients making updates:

```
@Stateless
public class BankBean implements Bank {
    @Resource SessionContext context;
    ...
    public void withdraw(int acctid, double amount) throws AccessDeniedException {
        String modifiedBy = principal.getName( );
        ...
    }
    ...
}
```

The EJBContext.isCallerInRole() method tells you whether the client accessing the bean is a member of a specific role, identified by a role name. This method is useful when more access control is needed than simple method-based access control can provide. In a banking system, for example, you might allow the Teller role to make most withdrawals but only the Manager role to make withdrawals of more than $10,000. This kind of fine-grained access control cannot be addressed through EJB's security attributes, because it involves a business logic problem. Therefore, we can use the isCaller InRole() method to augment the automatic access control provided by EJB. First, let's assume that all managers are also tellers. The business logic in the withdraw() method uses isCallerInRole() to make sure that only the Manager role can withdraw sums of more than $10,000:

```
@Stateless
public class BankBean implements Bank {
    @Resource SessionContext context;

    public void withdraw(int acctid, double amount) throws AccessDeniedException {

        if (amount > 10000) {
            boolean isManager = context.isCallerInRole("Manager");
            if (!isManager) {
                // Only Managers can withdraw more than 10k.
                throw new AccessDeniedException( );
            }
        }

    }
    ...
}
```

The transactional methods—`getUserTransaction()`, `setRollbackOnly()`, and `getRoll backOnly()`—are described in detail in Chapter 17.

`EJBContext` contains some methods that were used in older EJB specifications but have been abandoned in EJB 3.0. The security methods that interact with `Identity` classes, as well as the `getEnvironment()`, `EJBContext.getEJBHome()`, and `EJBContext.getEJBLocalHome()` methods, are now obsolete. A `RuntimeException` is thrown if these methods are executed.

The material on `EJBContext` covered in this section applies equally well to message-driven beans. There are some exceptions, however, and these differences are covered in Chapter 12.

The Lifecycle of a Stateless Session Bean

The lifecycle of a stateless session bean is very simple. It has only two states: *Does Not Exist* and *Method-Ready Pool*. The Method-Ready Pool is an instance pool of stateless session bean objects that are not in use. Because of all the injection and such that can happen, it can be more efficient to save stateless bean instances when they are not in use. This is an important difference between stateless and stateful session beans; stateless beans define instance pooling in their lifecycles and stateful beans do not.[*] Figure 5-2 illustrates the states and transitions an SLSB instance goes through.

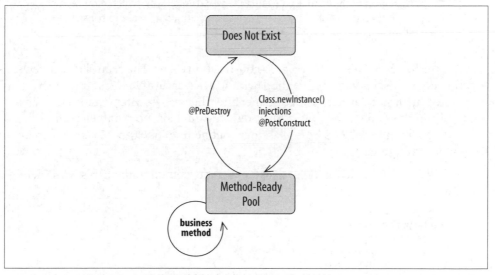

Figure 5-2. Stateless session bean lifecycle

---

[*] Some vendors may *not* pool stateless instances but may instead create and destroy instances with each method invocation. This is an implementation-specific decision that shouldn't affect the specified lifecycle of the stateless bean instance.

The Does Not Exist State

When a bean is in the Does Not Exist state, it is not an instance in the memory of the system. In other words, it has not been instantiated yet.

The Method-Ready Pool

Stateless bean instances enter the Method-Ready Pool as the container needs them. When the EJB server is first started, it may create a number of stateless bean instances and enter them into the Method-Ready Pool. (The actual behavior of the server depends on the implementation.) When the number of stateless instances servicing client requests is insufficient, more can be created and added to the pool.

Transitioning to the Method-Ready Pool

When an instance transitions from the Does Not Exist state to the Method-Ready Pool, three operations are performed on it. First, the bean instance is instantiated by invoking the `Class.newInstance()` method on the stateless bean class. Second, the container injects any resources that the bean's metadata has requested via an injection annotation or XML deployment descriptor.

 You must always provide a no-argument constructor. This is a constructor that accepts no parameters. The container instantiates instances of the bean class using `Class.newInstance()`, which requires a no-arg constructor. If no constructors are defined, the no-arg constructor is implicit.

Finally, the EJB container will fire a post-construction event. The bean class can register for this event by annotating a method with `@javax.annotation.PostConstruct`. This annotated method is called by the container after the bean is instantiated. The callback method can be of any name, but it must return `void`, have no parameters, and throw no checked exceptions. The bean class may define only one `@PostConstruct` method (but it is not required to do so).

Alternatively, you can declare your `@PostConstruct` method in the EJB's XML deployment descriptor:

```
<ejb-jar>
   <enterprise-beans>
      <session>
         <ejb-name>MyEJBName</ejb-name>
         <post-construct>
            <lifecycle-callback-method>initialize</lifecycle-callback-method>
         </post-construct>
      </session>
   </enterprise-beans>
</ejb-jar>
```

Stateless session beans are not subject to activation, so they can maintain open connections to resources for their entire lifecycles.[†] The @PreDestroy method should close any open resources before the stateless session bean is evicted from memory at the end of its lifecycle. You'll read more about @PreDestroy later in this section.

Life in the Method-Ready Pool

Once an instance is in the Method-Ready Pool, it is ready to service client requests. When a client invokes a business method on an EJB object, the method call is delegated to any available instance in the Method-Ready Pool. While the instance is executing the request, it is unavailable for use by other EJB objects. Once the instance has finished, it is immediately available to any EJB object that needs it. Stateless session instances are dedicated to an EJB object only for the duration of a single method call.

When an instance is swapped in, its SessionContext changes to reflect the context of the EJB object and the client invoking the method. The bean instance may be included in the transactional scope of the client's request and it may access SessionContext information specific to the client request: for example, the security and transactional methods. Once the instance has finished servicing the client, it is disassociated from the EJB object and returned to the Method-Ready Pool.

Clients that need a remote or local reference to a stateless session bean begin by having the reference injected (servlets support injection, for example) or by looking up the stateless bean in JNDI. The reference returned does not cause a session bean instance to be created or pulled from the pool until a method is invoked on it.

PostConstruct is invoked only once in the lifecycle of an instance: when it is transitioning from the Does Not Exist state to the Method-Ready Pool. It is not reinvoked every time a client requests a remote reference to the bean.

Transitioning out of the Method-Ready Pool: The death of a stateless bean instance

Bean instances leave the Method-Ready Pool for the Does Not Exist state when the server no longer needs them—that is, when the server decides to reduce the total size of the Method-Ready Pool by evicting one or more instances from memory. The process begins when a PreDestroy event on the bean is triggered. The bean class can register for this event by annotating a method with @javax.annotation.PreDestroy. The container calls this annotated method when the PreDestroy event is fired. This callback method can be of any name, but it must return void, have no parameters, and throw no checked exceptions. The bean class may define only one @PreDestroy method (but it is not required to do so). An @PreDestroy callback method can perform any cleanup operations, such as closing open resources.

[†] The duration of a stateless bean instance's life is assumed to be very long. However, some EJB servers may actually destroy and create instances with every method invocation, making this strategy less attractive. Consult your vendor's documentation for details on how your EJB server handles stateless instances.

```
@Stateless
public class MyBean implements MyLocalBusiness {

    @PreDestroy
    public void cleanup( ) {
        ...
    }
}
```

Alternatively, you can declare your @PreDestroy method in the EJB's XML deployment descriptor:

```
<ejb-jar>
    <enterprise-beans>
        <session>
            <ejb-name>MyEJBName</ejb-name>
            <pre-destroy>
                <lifecycle-callback-method>cleanup</lifecycle-callback-method>
            </pre-destroy>
        </session>
    </enterprise-beans>
</ejb-jar>
```

As with @PostConstruct, @PreDestroy is invoked only once: when the bean is about to transition to the Does Not Exist state. During this callback method, the SessionContext and access to the JNDI ENC are still available to the bean instance. Following the execution of the @PreDestroy method, the bean is dereferenced and eventually garbage-collected.

Example: The EncryptionEJB

Often we write applications that require users to choose a password or enter a credit card number. Storing this sensitive data in its raw form (called cleartext) represents a security risk: if someone were to gain unauthorized access to our database, he or she could query for this information and we'd be liable for any damage done. A nice alternative to persisting these fields in human-legible format is to encrypt them using our application. Because this is a simple request-response model requiring no conversational state, the stateless session bean is ideally suited to handle these requirements efficiently. Other EJBs or standalone clients may later leverage the generic encryption service we provide in this component.

The EncryptionEJB example is discussed in full detail in Appendix B.

There are two techniques we'll consider:

- Cryptographic hashing
- Cipher-based symmetrical encryption

Cryptographic hashing is the process in which some input is transformed into a reproducible, fixed-size result. The algorithm is unidirectional, meaning that it's not mathematically possible to un-hash the output back to its original form. By storing the hash of passwords only, we may compare hashes of login attempts against the stored value (see Figure 5-3).

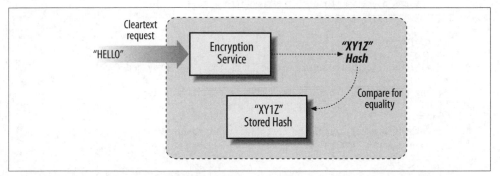

Figure 5-3. Comparing input with a hash of the expected result

Sometimes we need to be able to get the cleartext back out of an encrypted result. For example, perhaps our application offers storage of a previously used credit card number for future purchases. For this, we may employ symmetrical encryption, which dictates that some key (backed by a passphrase) may both encrypt and decrypt the data. Without the correct passphrase, attempts to decode become very tricky for potential attackers.

The Contract: Business Interfaces

Using the requirements described in the previous section, we can flesh out the contract for our EncryptionEJB:

```
public interface EncryptionCommonBusiness
{
   /**
    * Encrypts the specified String, returning the result
    *
    * @param input
    * @return
    * @throws IllegalArgumentException If no input was provided (null)
    */
   String encrypt(String input) throws IllegalArgumentException;

   /**
    * Decrypts the specified String, returning the result.  The general
    * contract is that the result of decrypting a String encrypted with
    * {@link EncryptionCommonBusiness#encrypt(String)} will be equal
    * by value to the original input (round trip).
    *
    * @param input
    * @return
    * @throws IllegalArgumentException If no input was provided (null)
    */
   String decrypt(String input) throws IllegalArgumentException;
```

Here we account for our symmetrical encryption functions:

```
/**
 * Returns a one-way hash of the specified argument.  Useful
 * for safely storing passwords.
 *
 * @param input
 * @return
 * @throws IllegalArgumentException If no input was provided (null)
 */
String hash(String input) throws IllegalArgumentException;

/**
 * Returns whether or not the specified input matches the specified
 * hash.  Useful for validating passwords against a
 * securely stored hash.
 *
 * @param hash
 * @param input
 * @return
 * @throws IllegalArgumentException If either the hash or input is not provided
(null)
 */
boolean compare(String hash, String input) throws IllegalArgumentException;
}
```

And these methods will handle our one-way cryptographic hashing. The `Encryption CommonBusiness` interface again becomes the base for both our local business and remote business views:

```
public interface EncryptionLocalBusiness extends EncryptionCommonBusiness {}
public interface EncryptionRemoteBusiness extends EncryptionCommonBusiness {}
```

A business interface can be a remote or local interface but not both. Remote business interfaces are able to receive method invocations from networked clients. When a client invokes a method on a session bean's remote interface, the parameter values and return value are *copied*. This is true regardless of whether the client is running in the same VM or on another machine in the network. This is known as *call-by-value* semantics.

Local interfaces are available only within the same JVM as the session bean. Invoking on a local interface does not copy the parameters or return value. Because of this, local interfaces are said to follow what is termed *call-by-reference* semantics.

Application Exceptions

Any business interface can throw application exceptions. These should describe a business logic problem—in this case, a problem in encryption/decryption. Application exceptions should be meaningful to the client, providing a brief and relevant identification of the error.

Our new `EncryptionException` will describe a specific business problem that is possibly recoverable; this makes it an application exception. The EJB container treats any exception that does not extend `RuntimeException` as an application exception. Here is the definition of `EncryptionException`:

```
@ApplicationException
// Explicit annotation, though this is inferred as default because we extend Exception
public class EncryptionException extends Exception{...}
```

An application exception is propagated to the calling client as is. Any instance variables you include in these exceptions should be serializable. Nonapplication exceptions are always wrapped, by the Container, in an `EJBException`. This means that any exception you throw that is or extends `RuntimeException` will be caught by the EJB container and wrapped in an `EJBException`. This is especially important for session beans that interact with entity beans. All exceptions thrown by Java Persistence interfaces are `RuntimeExceptions`. Your client code must be aware of this if it needs to take action on specific persistence exceptions. Exception behavior, preventing the wrapping in `EJBEx` `ception`, can be declared explicitly using the `@javax.ejb.ApplicationException` and the `<application-exception>` XML deployment descriptor metadata. These constructs are discussed in detail in Chapter 17, as they have a huge impact on transactional behavior.

Bean Implementation Class

The EncryptionEJB models a specific business process, so it is an excellent candidate for a stateless session bean. This bean really represents a set of independent operations—another indication that it is a good candidate for a stateless session bean.

First we'll reveal any nonobvious types to be imported (all will be discussed in turn):

```
import javax.annotation.PostConstruct;
import javax.annotation.Resource;
import javax.ejb.Local;
import javax.ejb.Remote;
import javax.ejb.SessionContext;
import javax.ejb.Stateless;
```

Annotations upon the bean implementation class provide the metadata declaring our SLSB and business interfaces:

```
@Stateless(name = "EncryptionEJB")
@Local(EncryptionLocalBusiness.class)
@Remote(EncryptionRemoteBusiness.class)
public class EncryptionBean implements EncryptionLocalBusiness,
    EncryptionRemoteBusiness
{ ...
```

The bean class is annotated with the `@javax.ejb.Stateless` annotation to identify that it is a stateless session bean. The `name()` attribute identifies the EJB name of the session bean. The EJB name defaults to the unqualified (simple) name of the bean class if you initialize this attribute; in this case, the EJB name would default to `EncryptionBean`. In most cases, you don't have to be aware of the concept of an EJB name, but it's useful when you want to override or augment metadata with an XML deployment descriptor. This will allow us to externalize properties and provide configuration for the service without requiring recompilation of the Java sources.

When used on the bean class, the `@Local` and `@Remote` annotations take an array of interface classes. It is not recommended that you use this approach unless you have to, as implementing your business interfaces directly enforces the contract between the bean class and these interfaces. These examples opt for the bean implementation class approach simply to centralize annotation metadata for readability, and the contract is honored by ensuring the bean implementation class explicitly implements all business interfaces.

The EncryptionEJB identifies its remote and local interfaces via the class-level annotations upon the bean implementation class. As we've mentioned before, `@Remote` and `@Local` could also go directly upon the `EncryptionBusinessRemote` and `EncryptionBusinessLocal` interfaces:

```
@Local
public interface EncryptionLocalBusiness extends EncryptionCommonBusiness {}
@Remote
public interface EncryptionRemoteBusiness extends EncryptionCommonBusiness {}
```

When an EJB is deployed, the container looks at the interfaces of the bean class to see whether they are annotated as business interfaces. This introspection may determine the business remote and business local interfaces of the bean class.

The art of creating a truly secure encryption service is beyond scope of this exercise, so we'll leave the implementation of the business methods for you to explore in runnable examples detailed in the appendix. Worthy of note, however, is that our bean implementation class must perform some initialization before it's able to do any real work. For this purpose, we introduce:

```
/**
 * Initializes this service before it may handle requests
 *
 * @throws Exception If some unexpected error occurred
 */
@PostConstruct
public void initialize() throws Exception
{
    // Log that we're here
    log.info("Initializing, part of " + PostConstruct.class.getName() + " life
cycle");

    // Get the passphrase for symmetric encryption
    final String passphrase = this.getCiphersPassphrase();

    // Do initialization tasks here
    ...
}
```

The @PostConstruct annotation defines a callback method to be executed at the proper point within the SLSB lifecycle. In this case, initialize() will be invoked by the Container after it has created the bean instance and performed any injection operations.

We've also defined the internal method getCiphersPassphrase(), which we'll use to obtain an externalized parameter as the passphrase (secret key) for use in symmetric encryption.

Accessing Environment Properties (Injection and Lookup)

Our bean implementation class declares a few instance members as part of its internal state:

```
/**
 * Passphrase to use  for the key in cipher operations; lazily initialized
 * and loaded via SessionContext.lookup
 */
private String ciphersPassphrase;

/**
 * Algorithm to use in message digest (hash) operations, injected
 * via @Resource annotation
 */
@Resource
private String messageDigestAlgorithm;
```

Remember that the internal state for each instance is permissible, so long as these don't leak out to the client. Stateless session beans may contain no conversational state!

Two of these properties, ciphersPassphrase and messageDigestAlgorithm, represent configurable attributes that we'll provide via externalized variables called *environment entries*. An environment entry is a value placed into JNDI under a private namespace called the *Enterprise Naming Context* (ENC), which is visible only to our EJB. There are a variety of ways to get at the values within the ENC, and this example will illustrate both manual lookup and injection.

The messageDigestAlgorithm is annotated with @Resource; this tells the EJB container that when an instance of the bean class is created, this field must be initialized with values in the container's ENC.

When the EJB container is deployed, the ENC is populated both with metadata embedded in annotations such as @Resource and with information stored in the optional EJB XML deployment descriptor. For example, the annotation alone suggests a named value within the ENC should be used to initialize the field externally. This named value can be configured by defining environment entries within the EJB's XML deployment descriptor:

```
<ejb-jar xmlns="http://java.sun.com/xml/ns/javaee"
   xmlns:xsi="http://www.w3.org/2001/XMLSchema-instance"
   xsi:schemaLocation="http://java.sun.com/xml/ns/javaee
                http://java.sun.com/xml/ns/javaee/ejb-jar_3_1.xsd"
```

```
        version="3.1">

        <enterprise-beans>

          <!--
            In this section we'll bolster our EncryptionEJB with some
            additional metadata to complement the info defined via
            annotations.
          -->
          <session>

            <!--
              This will match the value of @Stateless.name upon our bean
              implementation class
            -->
            <ejb-name>EncryptionEJB</ejb-name>

            <!-- Override the ciphers default passphrase -->
            <env-entry>
              <env-entry-name>ciphersPassphrase</env-entry-name>
              <env-entry-type>java.lang.String</env-entry-type>
              <env-entry-value>OverriddenPassword</env-entry-value>
            </env-entry>

            <!-- Override the default unidirectional hash MessageDigest algorithm -->
            <env-entry>
              <env-entry-name>messageDigestAlgorithm</env-entry-name>
              <env-entry-type>java.lang.String</env-entry-type>
              <env-entry-value>SHA</env-entry-value>
            </env-entry>

          </session>

        </enterprise-beans>

      </ejb-jar>
```

When this file, *META-INF/ejb-jar.xml*, is included in the packaging of the EJB, the Container will place the designated values within the ENC of our EncryptionEJB upon deployment. The messageDigestAlgorithm field may then be injected by the Container. But we've defined no annotation upon the field ciphersPassphrase, so we'll look it up manually.

The @Resource annotation is very versatile, and when placed upon a known type such as SessionContext, the Container knows how to handle this injection request. Through the lookup() method upon a SessionContext, we can poke into the ENC to obtain the value we're looking for:

```
    private String getEnvironmentEntryAsString(final String envEntryName) throws
  IllegalStateException
    {
        // Get the SessionContext from the injected instance member
        final SessionContext context = this.context;
```

```
        // Lookup in the Private JNDI ENC via the injected SessionContext
        Object lookupValue = null;
        try
        {
            lookupValue = context.lookup(envEntryName);
            log.debug("Obtained environment entry \"" + envEntryName + "\": " + look
    upValue);
        }
        catch (final IllegalArgumentException iae)
        {
            // Not found defined within this EJB's Component Environment,
            // so return null and let the caller handle it
            log.warn("Could not find environment entry with name: " + envEntryName);
            return null;
        }

        // Cast
        String returnValue = null;
        try
        {
            returnValue = String.class.cast(lookupValue);
        }
        catch (final ClassCastException cce)
        {
            throw new IllegalStateException("The specified environment entry, " +
            lookupValue + ", was not able to be represented as a "
            + String.class.getName(), cce);
        }

        // Return
        return returnValue;
    }
```

We may use something similar to the previous code to extract out the cipher passphrase from the ENC in a manual fashion. Because of this extra burden upon the developer, it's easy to see why injection is the preferred mechanism to obtain information from the Container.

Externalization of values is incredibly important. In this case, the application assembler or deployer of the EJB may choose a secret passphrase for the encryption scheme in production environments, and developers of the application never have to be exposed to this privileged information. We've also used environment entries to make our service configurable.

 It's worth noting: never, ever design to store passwords in a file to be placed on the filesystem. By definition, this is insecure. This example is in place to illustrate the absence of conversational state while maintaining internal state and should not be used as a real-world encryption system.

The exact semantics of the <env-entry> and @Resource annotation are discussed in detail in Chapter 16.

Asynchronous Methods

New in the EJB 3.1 Specification is the feature of fire-and-forget invocations upon session beans. Often we'll have requirements where a request may take some time to be fully processed, and the client may not need to wait for the result or confirmation of completion. In these cases, we can take advantage of the new @javax.ejb.Asynchro nous annotation to return control to the client before EJB is invoked. When the client does need access to the return value, it can do so via the facilities provided by java.util.concurrent.Future.

In the case of our EncryptionEJB, perhaps we have a very intensive hashing function that takes some time to complete:

```
/**
 * Returns a one-way hash of the specified argument, calculated
asynchronously.
 * Useful for safely storing passwords.
 *
 * @param input
 * @return
 * @throws IllegalArgumentException
 * @throws EncryptionException
 */
Future<String> hashAsync(String input) throws
IllegalArgumentException, EncryptionException;
```

During implementation, the bean provider may mark this method (either on the business interface or the bean class) as @Asynchronous, wrapping the real return value in a convenience implementation of java.util.concurrent.Future called javax.ejb.AsyncResult:

```
@Asynchronous
@Override
public Future<String> hashAsync(final String input) throws
IllegalArgumentException, EncryptionException
{
    // Get the real hash
    final String hash = this.hash(input);

    // Wrap and return
    return new AsyncResult<String>(hash);
}
```

Client usage therefore may look something like this:

```
// Declare the input
final String input = "Async Hashing Input";

// Hash
final Future<String> hashFuture =
myEjbProxyReference.hashAsync(input);

// Now we're free to do any work we want here while the
// EJB invocation runs concurrently
```

```
// ...[work]

// At this point we need the hash, so get the result,
// and block for up to 10 seconds to get it
final String hash = hashFuture.get(10,TimeUnit.SECONDS);
log.info("Hash of \"" + input + "\": " + hash);
```

Here control is returned to the client immediately after invoking upon hashAsync, and other work may be performed while the potentially expensive hashing function chugs along elsewhere concurrently. When we need the asynchronous result, we can use Future.get() or its derivatives to block until the result is available.

Methods with no return value (i.e., void) may also be marked as @Asynchronous. Any session bean business method (in Stateless, Stateful, or Singleton) is eligible to be made asynchronous, and @Asynchronous may be applied upon a business interface or bean class to denote that all methods should be handled async.

## CHAPTER 6

The Stateful Session Bean

While the strengths of the stateless session bean lie in its speed and efficiency, stateful session beans are built as a server-side extension of the client. Each SFSB is dedicated to one client for the life of the bean instance; it acts on behalf of that client as its agent (see Figure 6-1). Stateful session beans are not swapped among EJB objects, nor are they kept in an instance pool like their stateless session counterparts. Once a stateful session bean is instantiated and assigned to an EJB object, it is dedicated to that EJB object for its entire lifecycle.[*]

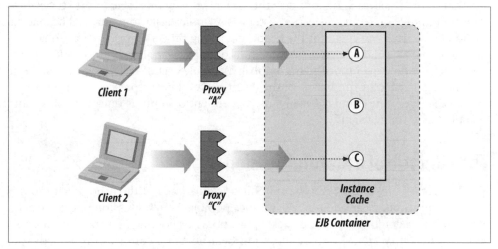

Figure 6-1. Client relationship with the EJB Container and backing bean instances

Stateful session beans maintain conversational state, which means that the instance variables of the bean class can maintain data specific to the client between method

---

[*] This is a conceptual model. Some EJB containers may actually use instance swapping with stateful session beans but make it appear as if the same instance is servicing all requests. Conceptually, however, the same stateful session bean instance services all requests.

invocations. This makes it possible for methods to be interdependent such that changes made to the bean's state in one method call can affect the results of subsequent method invocations. Therefore, every method call from a client must be serviced by the same instance (at least conceptually), so the bean instance's state can be predicted from one method invocation to the next. In contrast, stateless session beans don't maintain client-specific data from one method call to the next, so any instance can be used to service any method call from any client.

Although stateful session beans maintain conversational state, they are not themselves persistent; the state of a SFSB is lost when the session is removed, the session times out, or the server restarts. Persistent state in EJB is modeled by the entity bean, which we cover starting in Chapter 9.

Because SFSBs are often considered extensions of the client, we may think of a client as being composed from a combination of operations and state. Each task may rely on some information gathered or changed by a previous operation. A GUI client is a perfect example: when you fill in the fields on a GUI client, you are creating conversational state. Pressing a button executes an operation that might fill in more fields, based on the information you entered previously. The information in the fields is conversational state.

Stateful session beans allow you to encapsulate some of the business logic and conversational state of a client and move it to the server. Moving this logic to the server thins the client application and makes the system as a whole easier to manage. The stateful session bean acts as an agent for the client, managing processes or taskflow to accomplish a set of tasks; it manages the interactions of other beans in addition to direct data access over several operations to accomplish a complex set of tasks. By encapsulating and managing taskflow on behalf of the client, stateful beans present a simplified interface that hides the details of many interdependent operations on the database and other beans from the client.

The Lifecycle of a Stateful Session Bean

The biggest difference between the stateful session bean and the other bean types is that stateful session beans do not use instance pooling. Stateful session beans are dedicated to one client for their entire lives, so swapping or pooling of instances isn't possible.† When they are idle, stateful session bean instances are simply evicted from memory. The EJB object remains connected to the client, but the bean instance is dereferenced and garbage-collected during inactive periods. This means that each stateful bean must be passivated before it is evicted in order to preserve the conversational state of the instance, and it must be activated to restore its state when the EJB object becomes active again.

---

† Some vendors use pooling with stateful session beans, but that is a proprietary implementation and should not affect the specified lifecycle of the stateful session bean.

The bean's perception of its lifecycle depends on whether it implements a special interface called `javax.ejb.SessionSynchronization`. This interface defines an additional set of callback methods that notify the bean of its participation in transactions. A bean that implements `SessionSynchronization` can cache database data across several method calls before making an update. We have not discussed transactions in detail yet; we will consider this part of the bean's lifecycle in Chapter 17. This section describes the lifecycle of stateful session beans that do not implement the `SessionSynchronization` interface.

The lifecycle of a stateful session bean has three states: Does Not Exist, Method-Ready, and Passivated. This sounds a lot like a stateless session bean, but the Method-Ready state is significantly different from the Method-Ready Pool of stateless beans. Figure 6-2 shows the state diagram for stateful session beans.

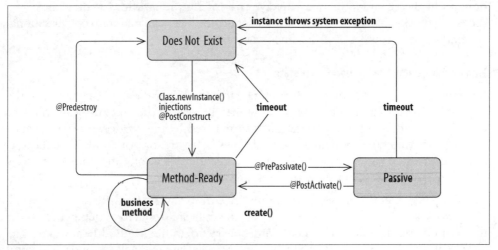

Figure 6-2. Stateful session bean lifecycle

The Does Not Exist State

A stateful bean instance in the Does Not Exist state has not been instantiated yet. It doesn't exist in the system's memory.

The Method-Ready State

The Method-Ready state is the state in which the bean instance can service requests from its clients. This section explores the instance's transition into and out of the Method-Ready state.

Transitioning into the Method-Ready state

When a client invokes the first method on the stateful session bean reference, the bean's lifecycle begins. The container invokes `newInstance()` on the bean class, creating a new instance of the bean. Next, the container injects any dependencies into the bean instance. At this point, the bean instance is assigned to the client referencing it. Finally, just like stateless session beans, the container invokes any `@PostConstruct` callbacks if there is a method in the bean class that has this annotation applied. Once `@PostConstruct` has completed, the container continues with the actual method call.

Life in the Method-Ready state

While in the Method-Ready state, the bean instance is free to receive method invocations from the client, which may involve controlling the taskflow of other beans or accessing the database directly. During this time, the bean can maintain conversational state and open resources in its instance variables.

Transitioning out of the Method-Ready state

Bean instances leave the Method-Ready state to enter either the Passivated state or the Does Not Exist state. Depending on how the client uses the stateful bean, the EJB container's load, and the passivation algorithm used by the vendor, a bean instance may be passivated (and activated) several times in its life, or not at all. If the bean is removed, it enters the Does Not Exist state. A client application can remove a bean by invoking a business interface method annotated as `@Remove`.

The container can also move the bean instance from the Method-Ready state to the Does Not Exist state if the bean times out. Timeouts are declared at deployment time in a vendor-specific manner. When a timeout occurs in the Method-Ready state, the container may, but is not required to, call any `@PreDestroy` callback methods. A stateful bean cannot time out while a transaction is in progress.

The Passivated State

During the lifetime of a stateful session bean, there may be periods of inactivity when the bean instance is not servicing methods from the client. To conserve resources, the container can passivate the bean instance by preserving its conversational state and evicting the bean instance from memory. A bean's conversational state may consist of primitive values, objects that are serializable, and the following special types:

- `javax.ejb.SessionContext`
- `javax.jta.UserTransaction` (bean transaction interface)
- `javax.naming.Context` (only when it references the JNDI ENC)
- `javax.persistence.EntityManager`

- `javax.persistence.EntityManagerFactory`
- References to managed resource factories (e.g., `javax.sql.DataSource`)
- References to other EJBs

The types in this list (and their subtypes) are handled specially by the passivation mechanism. They do not need to be serializable; they will be maintained through passivation and restored automatically when the bean instance is activated.

When a bean is about to be passivated, a method on the bean class may be annotated with `@PrePassivate` to receive a callback for this event. This can be used to alert the bean instance that it is about to enter the Passivated state. At this time, the bean instance should close any open resources and set all nontransient, nonserializable fields to `null`. This prevents problems from occurring when the bean is serialized. Transient fields are simply ignored.

How does the container store the bean's conversational state? It's largely up to the container. Containers can use standard Java serialization to preserve the bean instance, or some other mechanism that achieves the same result. Some vendors, for example, simply read the values of the fields and store them in a cache. The container is required to preserve remote references to other beans with the conversational state. When the bean is activated, the container must restore any bean references automatically. The container must also restore any references to the special types listed earlier.

When the client makes a request on an EJB object whose bean is passivated, the container activates the instance. This involves deserializing the bean instance and reconstructing the `SessionContext` reference, bean references, and managed resource factories held by the instance before it was passivated. When a bean's conversational state has been successfully restored, an `@PostActivate` callback method is invoked on the bean instance if one is declared on the bean class. The bean instance should open any resources that cannot be passivated and initialize the values of any transient fields within the `@PostActivate` method. Once `@PostActivate` is complete, the bean is back in the Method-Ready state and is available to service client requests delegated by the EJB object.

The activation of a bean instance follows the rules of Java serialization, regardless of how the bean's state was actually stored. The exception to this is transient fields. In Java serialization, transient fields are set to their default values when an object is deserialized; primitive numbers become zero, Boolean fields `false`, and object references `null`. In EJB, transient fields can contain arbitrary values when the bean is activated. The values held by transient fields following activation are unpredictable across vendor implementations, so do not depend on them to be initialized. Instead, use an `@PostActivate` callback method to reset their values.

The container can also move the bean instance from the Passivated state to the Does Not Exist state if the bean times out. When a timeout occurs in the Passivated state, any `@PreDestroy` callback methods are not invoked.

System exceptions

Whenever a system exception is thrown by a bean method, the container invalidates the EJB object and destroys the bean instance. The bean instance moves directly to the Does Not Exist state, and any `@PreDestroy` call methods are *not* invoked.[‡]

A system exception is any unchecked exception not annotated as an `@Application Exception`, including `EJBException`. Application and system exceptions are explained in more detail in Chapter 17.

Example: The FileTransferEJB

The File Transfer Protocol (FTP) defines a common language for exchanging data over network boundaries. Defined in RFC-959 (*http://www.ietf.org/rfc/rfc959.txt*), the specification mandates conversational state as part of the communication scheme; not all information required to service a request is present in the request itself. Because a session's invocation history plays a role in how an FTP client will operate, the SLSB is not a valid implementation choice. These requirements lie right in the wheelhouse of the stateful session bean.

This example's FTP client is covered in Appendix C. Most of the business logic contained in the bean implementation class has been stripped from the text in order to keep the focus upon SFSB semantics. All code is available in the appendix and from the companion website.

The simple operations we'll implement are:

- Print current directory (`pwd`)
- Make directory (`mkdir`)
- Change to directory (`cd`)

This will be enough to connect to an FTP server and interact with it a bit to show how conversational state is central to the design of the SFSB. Readers interested in extending the example to send files over the wire are encouraged to do so.

It's important to consider the additional lifecycle phases of the stateful session bean, as compared with the simpler SLSB. Not all of a bean's internal state is Serializable, and in the case of our FTP client, we need to explicitly handle the connection to the server. We won't attempt to serialize this out during passivation; we need to safely close all related resources and then reinitialize the value upon activation. The passivation and activation process must be completely transparent to the client such that from the caller's perspective, the SFSB must act as if these had never occurred.

[‡] Yes, this is a hole in the specification.

When it's completed all tasks, the client must signal when it's done with the session. This allows the container to perform cleanup operations and reduce the overhead inherent with hanging onto bean instances that are no longer needed.

The Contract: Business Interfaces

The operations explained in the previous section imply a contract:

```java
public interface FileTransferCommonBusiness
{
   // -------------------------------------------------------------------------||
   // Contracts --------------------------------------------------------------||
   // -------------------------------------------------------------------------||

   /**
    * Makes a directory of the specified name
    *
    * @throws IllegalStateException If the client connection has not been
initialized
    */
   void mkdir(String directory) throws IllegalStateException;

   /**
    * Changes into the named directory
    *
    * @param directory
    * @throws IllegalStateException If the client connection has not been
initialized
    */
   void cd(String directory) throws IllegalStateException;

   /**
    * Obtains the name of the current working directory
    *
    * @return
    * @throws IllegalStateException If the client connection has not been
initialized
    */
   String pwd() throws IllegalStateException;

   /**
    * Denotes that the client is done using this service; flushes
    * any pending operations and does all appropriate cleanup.  If
    * already disconnected, this is a no-op.
    */
   void disconnect();

   /**
    * Opens the underlying connections to the target FTP Server,
    * performs any other tasks required before commands may be sent
    * (ie. login, etc)
    *
    * @throws IllegalStateException If already initialized/connected
    */
```

```
    void connect() throws IllegalStateException;

}
```

There are five functions total to connect to, disconnect from, and play with directory structure of the FTP server. We build upon this base to create a remote business view:

```
public interface FileTransferRemoteBusiness extends FileTransferCommonBusiness
{
    /**
     * Ends the current session; will result in a SFSB @Remove call
     * as the bean implementation class will annotate this with
     * {@link javax.ejb.Remove}
     */
    void endSession();
}
```

The endSession() method here is specific to an EJB client, so we've excluded it from the POJO-friendly FileTransferCommonBusiness and instead placed it directly into the remote business interface. As noted in the JavaDoc, invocation of this method will tell the container that the client is done with the session and may discard its associated target instance after firing any @PreDestroy callbacks.

Exceptions

We'll include one general-purpose unchecked exception to denote a problem in executing the requested FTP command. Because this is a system-level problem from which a client typically cannot recover, it's not marked as @ApplicationException:

```
public class FileTransferException extends RuntimeException{...}
```

Bean Implementation Class

The bean implementation class will contain all of the business logic for our FTP client. The following imports are used:

```
import javax.annotation.PostConstruct;
import javax.annotation.PreDestroy;
import javax.annotation.Resource;
import javax.ejb.PostActivate;
import javax.ejb.PrePassivate;
import javax.ejb.Remote;
import javax.ejb.Remove;
import javax.ejb.Stateful;

import org.apache.commons.net.ftp.FTPClient;
import org.apache.commons.net.ftp.FTPFile;
import org.apache.commons.net.ftp.FTPReply;
```

The @PostConstruct and @PreDestroy annotations apply lifecycle callbacks when bean instances are created and destroyed, respectively. @PrePassivate and @PostActivate denote methods to be invoked during the stateful session passivation/activation phases.

@Remove is not a callback, but rather marks that when the client invokes its method, the session should be retired. Finally, we'll use the Apache Commons FTP Client (*http:// commons.apache.org/net/*) to handle the finer points of the FTP protocol for us. First comes the bean declaration:

```
@Stateful(name = FileTransferBean.EJB_NAME)
@Remote(FileTransferRemoteBusiness.class)
public class FileTransferBean implements FileTransferRemoteBusiness, Serializable
{
    /**
     * Name of the EJB, used in Global JNDI addresses
     */
    public static final String EJB_NAME = "FileTransferEJB";
```

Here we simply mark this class as a stateful session bean via the **@Stateful** annotation and assign it an explicit name such that we can construct the portable Global JNDI name in testing later. Also, we'll hardcode the host and port to be used in connecting to the FTP server. Typically this would be externalized, but for brevity's sake we'll keep things simple in this example:

```
    /**
     * The name of the host to which we'll connect.
     * In production systems would typically be externalized
     * via configurable environment entry
     */
    private static String CONNECT_HOST = "localhost";

    /**
     * The port to which we'll connect.
     * In production systems would typically be externalized
     * via configurable environment entry.  IANA standard
     * for FTP ports is 21, though this requires root access
     * on *nix for testing, so we'll use the nonstandard 12345.
     */
    private static int CONNECT_PORT = 12345;
```

Next, we'll account for the instance members that will comprise our SFSB's internal state:

```
    /**
     * The underlying FTP Client.  We don't want its state
     * getting Serialized during passivation.  We'll
     * reinitialize this client and its connections
     * upon activation.
     */
    private FTPClient client;

    /**
     * Name of the present working directory.  In cases where
     * we're passivated, if this is specified
     * we'll change into this directory upon activation.
     */
    private String presentWorkingDirectory;
```

The `client` will be our delegate for all FTP operations. Because we cannot serialize it during passivation, we'll have to null this out during passivation and automatically reconnect upon activation. Although it may be possible to achieve the same goal implicitly using the Java `transient` keyword, the EJB specification advises against this because not all containers will rely upon Java Serialization for the passivation process.

We'll also manually track the present working directory, our location within the FTP server, because once we go through the passivation/activation cycle we'll need to reconnect and move back to the same location.

Our lifecycle callbacks will account for the operations that must take place during instance construction, passivation, activation, and session removal:

```
/**
 * Called by the container when the instance has been created or re-activated
 * (brought out of passivated state).  Will construct the underlying FTP Client
 * and open all appropriate connections.
 *
 * @see FileTransferCommonBusiness#connect()
 */
@PostConstruct
@PostActivate
@Override
public void connect() throws IllegalStateException, FileTransferException
{
   /*
    * Precondition checks
    */
   final FTPClient clientBefore = this.getClient();
   if (clientBefore != null && clientBefore.isConnected())
   {
      throw new IllegalStateException("FTP Client is already initialized");
   }

   // Get the connection properties
   final String connectHost = this.getConnectHost();
   final int connectPort = this.getConnectPort();

   // Create the client
   final FTPClient client = new FTPClient();

   // Connect Logic Here

   // Login Logic Here

   // Change into the Present Working Directory Logic Here

}
```

The `@PostConstruct` and `@PostActivate` annotations denote to the server that it should call `connect()` after instance creation and activation (wakeup from passivation). Here we create a new client delegate, connect and log into the remote server, and finally switch into the present working directory (if we had one before passivation). After this callback has been made, our SFSB instance and session has been initialized and is ready for service:

```
/**
 * Called by the container when the instance is about to be passivated or
brought
 * out of service entirely.
 *
 * @see FileTransferCommonBusiness#disconnect()
 */
@PrePassivate
@PreDestroy
@Override
public void disconnect()
{
    // Obtain FTP Client
    final FTPClient client = this.getClient();

    // If exists
    if (client != null)
    {
        // If connected
        if (client.isConnected())
        {
            // Logout Logic Here

            // Disconnect Logic Here
        }

        // Null out so we don't serialize this field
        this.client = null;
    }
}
```

Due to the @PrePassivate and @PreDestroy annotations, the callback disconnect() is invoked by the container before passivation or the instance is removed from service. This is where we clean up any underlying resources by logging out and disconnecting from the FTP server.

We have the expected accessor and mutator methods:

```
public String getConnectHost() {// Logic here}
public void setConnectHost(final String connectHost) {// Logic here}
public int getConnectPort() {// Logic here}
public void setConnectPort(final int connectPort) {// Logic here}
```

Now all that's left is to do is implement the business interface methods that power the logic of the client. For brevity's sake, we'll omit the true code here; again, all of this is covered in the appendix:

```
/* (non-Javadoc)
 * @see FileTransferCommonBusiness#cd(java.lang.String)
 */
@Override
public void cd(final String directory)
```

```
{
    // Implementation Logic Here
}

/* (non-Javadoc)
 * @see FileTransferCommonBusiness#mkdir(java.lang.String)
 */
@Override
public void mkdir(final String directory)
{
    // Implementation Logic Here
}

/* (non-Javadoc)
 * @see FileTransferCommonBusiness#pwd()
 */
@Override
public String pwd()
{
    // Implementation Logic Here
}
}
```

POJO Testing Outside the Container

By directly creating an instance of our bean implementation class, we can use the
FileTransferEJB as a POJO. Of course, we won't be relying upon services such as injection and lifecycle callbacks, but we can mock the container's responsibilities by invoking these manually. Consider the following setup in a JUnit test class:

```
/**
 * Creates and initializes the FTP Client used in testing.
 * Fired before each test is run.
 */
@Before
public void createFtpClient() throws Exception
{

    // Create client
    final FileTransferBean ftpClient = new FileTransferBean();

    // Connect
    ftpClient.connect();

    // Set
    this.ftpClient = ftpClient;
    log.info("Set FTP Client: " + ftpClient);
}
```

Before each test case is run, we'll create a new POJO instance and manually connect. This essentially takes the place of the instance creation and @PostConstruct lifecycle callback performed by the EJB Container:

```
/**
 * Disconnects and resets the FTP Client.  Fired after each
 * test has completed.
 *
 * @throws Exception
 */
@After
public void cleanup() throws Exception
{
    // Get client
    final FileTransferBean ftpClient = this.ftpClient;

    // If set
    if (ftpClient != null)
    {
        // Disconnect and reset
        ftpClient.disconnect();
        this.ftpClient = null;
    }
}
```

After each test completes, we can mock the @PreDestroy callback to disconnect from the FTP server.

That covers our test setup; now let's ensure that our passivation logic is intact. Again, we can do this by explicitly invoking lifecycle callback methods as if our test client were the EJB Container:

```
/**
 * Mocks the passivation/activation process by manually invoking
 * upon the {@link PrePassivate} and {@link PostActivate} lifecycle
 * callbacks.  The client should function properly after these calls are made,
 * reconnecting as expected, and resuming into the correct present working
 * directory
 *
 * @throws Exception
 */
@Test
public void testPassivationAndActivation() throws Exception
{
    // Log
    log.info("testPassivationAndActivation");

    // Get the client
    final FileTransferCommonBusiness client = this.getClient();

    // Switch to home
    final String home = getFtpHome().getAbsolutePath();
    client.cd(home);
```

```
        // Test the pwd
        final String pwdBefore = client.pwd();
        TestCase.assertEquals("Present working directory should be set to home",
    home, pwdBefore);

        // Mock @PrePassivate
        log.info("Mock @" + PrePassivate.class.getName());
        client.disconnect();

        // Mock passivation
        log.info("Mock passivation");
        final ByteArrayOutputStream outStream = new ByteArrayOutputStream();
        final ObjectOutput objectOut = new ObjectOutputStream(outStream);
        objectOut.writeObject(client);
        objectOut.close();

        // Mock activation
        log.info("Mock activation");
        final InputStream inStream = new ByteArrayInputStream(outStream.toByteArray
    ());
        final ObjectInput objectIn = new ObjectInputStream(inStream);

        // Get a new client from passivation/activation roundtrip
        final FileTransferCommonBusiness serializedClient = (FileTransferCommon
    Business) objectIn.readObject();
        objectIn.close();

        // Mock @PostActivate
        log.info("Mock @" + PostActivate.class.getName());
        serializedClient.connect();

        // Test the pwd
        final String pwdAfter = serializedClient.pwd();
        TestCase.assertEquals("Present working directory should be the same as before
    passivation/activation", home,
                pwdAfter);
    }
```

This test is actually very simple. It:

1. Obtains the initialized FTP client from the test setup

2. Changes the working directory

3. Manually invokes the pre-passivation callback

4. Copies the instance via serialization (as the container may do during passivation and activation)

5. Manually invokes the post-activation callback

6. Ensures that the FTP client is connected and in the same working directory as before the passivation process

Testing passivation and activation manually is a wise habit, as it's difficult to get this fine-grained control in integration tests to true EJBs run within the context of the container. The specification does not define a mechanism to request that the container start passivation or activation upon a session.

Integration Testing

It's also important to consider context during testing, so we wouldn't be doing our job if we omitted integration tests to assert that our SFSB is working as a true EJB. This will also give us the opportunity to prove that the session isolation and removal contracts are holding true. Let's assume we have a method available in our test case:

```
/**
 * Obtains the SFSB Proxy from Global JNDI, creating a new user session
 */
private FileTransferRemoteBusiness createNewSession() throws Exception
{
   // Logic
}
```

This will use the test's JNDI Context to obtain a new Proxy, hence creating a new user session. We'll use createNewSession() in our tests.

It's important for a client to release its session once complete with work, allowing the server to reclaim the resources used in maintaining its state. We can write a test to validate that signaling we're done triggers the session removal:

```
/**
 * Tests that a call to {@link FileTransferRemoteBusiness#endSession()}
 * results in the SFSB's backing instance removal, and that subsequent
 * operations result in a {@link NoSuchEJBException}
 *
 * @throws Exception
 */
@Test
public void testSfsbRemoval() throws Exception
{
    // Get a new session
    final FileTransferRemoteBusiness sfsb = this.createNewSession();

    // cd into the home directory
    final String ftpHome = "myHome";
    sfsb.cd(ftpHome);

    // Get and test the pwd
    final String pwdBefore = sfsb.pwd();
    TestCase.assertEquals("Session should be in the FTP Home directory",
        ftpHome, pwdBefore);

    // End the session, resulting in an underlying instance
    // removal due to the annotation with @Remove upon
    // the bean implementation class
    sfsb.endSession();
```

```
            // Now try some other operation, and ensure that we get a NoSuchEJBException
            boolean gotExpectedException = false;
            try
            {
                // This should not succeed, because we've called a method marked as
@Remove
                sfsb.pwd();
            }
            catch (final NoSuchEJBException nsee)
            {
                gotExpectedException = true;
            }
            TestCase.assertTrue("Call to end the session did not result in underlying
removal
                of the SFSB bean instance",
                    gotExpectedException);
        }
```

As this test illustrates, invoking upon an SFSB's business method after session removal will result in a `javax.ejb.NoSuchEJBException`. This confirms that a call to `endSession()` correctly starts the removal of the current session and backing bean instance.

We may also show how the Container maintains conversational state for each session in an isolated context. Operations in discrete sessions may not leak out:

```
        /**
         * Tests that two separate sessions will act in isolation from each other
         *
         * @throws Exception
         */
        @Test
        public void testSessionIsolation() throws Exception
        {
            // Make two new sessions
            final FileTransferRemoteBusiness session1 = this.createNewSession();
            final FileTransferRemoteBusiness session2 = this.createNewSession();

            // cd into a home directory for each
            final String ftpHome = "myHome";
            session1.cd(ftpHome);
            session2.cd(ftpHome);

            // Now make a new directory for each session, and go into it
            final String newDirSession1 = "newDirSession1";
            final String newDirSession2 = "newDirSession2";
            session1.mkdir(newDirSession1);
            session1.cd(newDirSession1);
            session2.mkdir(newDirSession2);
            session2.cd(newDirSession2);

            // Get the current working directory for each session
            final String pwdSession1 = session1.pwd();
            final String pwdSession2 = session2.pwd();
```

```
        // Ensure each session is in the proper working directory
        TestCase.assertEquals("Session 1 is in unexpected pwd", ftpHome + File.
separator + newDirSession1, pwdSession1);
        TestCase.assertEquals("Session 2 is in unexpected pwd", ftpHome + File.
separator + newDirSession2, pwdSession2);

        // End the session manually for each session
        session1.endSession();
        session2.endSession();
    }
```

The stateless session bean is not capable of handling this test reliably. It's expected that
subsequent calls to `pwd()` will remember the current location, changed previously via
calls to `cd()`. Our SFSB is built primarily to handle conversational cases like the one
`testSessionIsolation()` illustrates.

## CHAPTER 7

The Singleton Session Bean

So far, we've enjoyed the isolated invocation context provided by stateless and stateful session beans. These bean types service requests independently of one another in separate bean instances, relieving the EJB developer of the burden introduced by explicit concurrent programming. Sometimes, however, it's useful to employ a scheme in which a single shared instance is used for all clients, and new to the EJB 3.1 Specification is the singleton session bean to fit this requirement.

Contrary to most late-generation feature additions, the singleton is actually a much simpler conceptual model than we've seen in SLSB and SFSB, as shown in Figure 7-1.

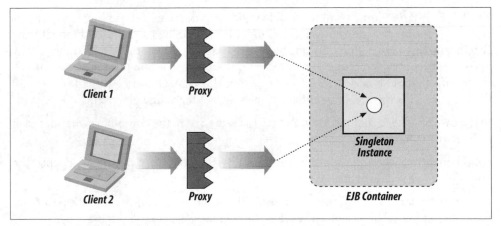

Figure 7-1. All invocations upon a singleton session bean using the same backing instance

Here all client requests are directed through the container to a sole target instance. This paradigm closely resembles that of a pure POJO service approach, and there are quite a few repercussions to consider:

- The instance's state is shared by all requests.
- There may be any number of requests pouring through the instance's methods at any one time.
- Due to concurrent invocations, the EJB must be designed as thread-safe.
- Locking or synchronization done to ensure thread safety may result in blocking (waiting) for new requests. This may not show itself in single-user testing, but will decimate performance in a production environment if we don't design very carefully.
- Memory footprint is the leanest of all session bean types. With only one backing instance in play, we don't take up much RAM.

In short, the singleton bean is poised to be an incredibly efficient choice if applied correctly. Used in the wrong circumstance, or with improper locking strategies, we have a recipe for disaster. Sitting at the very center of the difference between the two is the issue of concurrency.

Concurrency

Until now, EJB developers have been able to sidestep the issue of handling many clients at once by hiding behind the container. In both the stateless and stateful models, the specification mandates that only one request may access a backing bean instance at any one time. Because each request is represented by an invocation within a single thread, this means that SLSB and SFSB implementation classes need not be thread-safe. From the instance's perspective, one thread at most will enter at any given time.

In the case of many concurrent requests to the same SLSB, the container will route each to a unique instance (Figure 7-2).

SFSB concurrent requests must be serialized by the container but blocked until the underlying instance is available (Figure 7-3).

A bean provider may also optionally prohibit parallel invocations upon a particular stateful session via the use of `@javax.ejb.ConcurrencyManagement` (Figure 7-4).

A full discussion on concurrent programming is outside the scope of this book, but we'll introduce the main points of concern as they relate to EJB. Intentionally left out of this text are formal explanations of thread visibility, deadlock, livelock, and race conditions. If these are foreign concepts, a very good primer (and much more) is *Java Concurrency in Practice* by Brian Goetz, et al. (Addison-Wesley; *http://jcip.net/*).

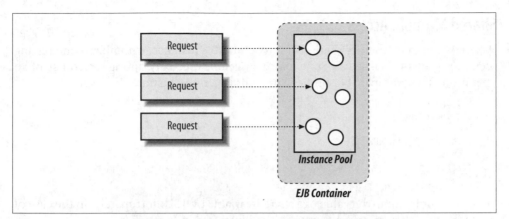

Figure 7-2. Stateless session bean invocations pulling from a pool of backing instances for service

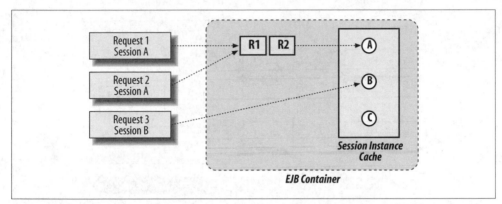

Figure 7-3. Stateful session bean invocations pulling from a cache of backing instances for service

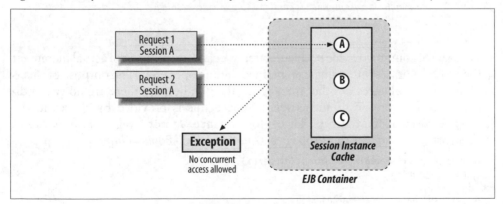

Figure 7-4. Concurrent requests upon the same session blocking until the session is available for use

Shared Mutable Access

When two or more threads share access to a mutable instance, a number of interesting scenarios present themselves. State may change unexpectedly during the course of an operation. The example of a simple increment function illustrates this well:

```
int shared = 1;
int increment()
{
  int new = shared + 1;
  shared = new;
  return shared;
}
```

Here we simply bump the value of a shared variable by 1. Unfortunately, in the case of many threads, this operation is not safe, as illustrated in Figure 7-5.

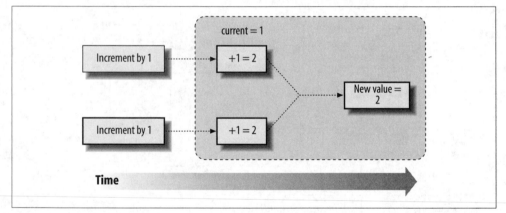

Figure 7-5. Poor synchronization policies can lead to incorrect results

There are two solutions to this problem. First, we can encapsulate the actual increment of the shared variable into a single, contained atomic operation. The purpose of this is to eliminate the chances of other threads sneaking in because there are no two individual read/writes to nestle in between. In Java this is provided by classes in the `java.util.concurrent.atomic` package—for instance, `AtomicInteger` (*http://java.sun .com/javase/6/docs/api/java/util/concurrent/atomic/AtomicBoolean.html*):

```
AtomicInteger shared = new AtomicInteger(1);
int increment()
{
  return shared.incrementAndGet();
}
```

In a multithreaded environment, the execution flow of this example is efficient and may look something like Figure 7-6.

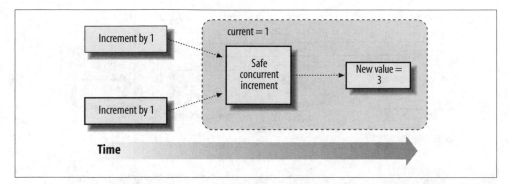

Figure 7-6. Proper synchronization policies allow many concurrent requests to execute in parallel and maintain reliable state

Behind the scenes, the backing increment is done all at once. Thus there can be no danger of inconsistent behavior introduced by multithreaded access.

Often, however, our requirements are more involved than simple increments upon a variable, and we cannot perform all of the work in one atomic unit. In this case, we need to make other threads wait until our mutable operations have completed. This is called "blocking" and is accomplished via the synchronized keyword in Java:

```
int shared = 1;
synchronized int increment()
{
  int new = shared + 1;
  shared = new;
  return shared;
}
```

The synchronized keyword here denotes that any executing thread must first gain rights to the method. This is done by acquiring what's called a *mutually exclusive lock*, a guard that may be held by only one thread at a time. The thread that owns the lock is permitted entry into the synchronized block, while others must block until the lock becomes available. In Java, every object has a corresponding lock, and when applied to a method, the synchronized keyword implicitly is using the this reference. So the previous example is analogous to:

```
int shared = 1;
int increment()
{
  synchronized(this)
  {
    int new = shared + 1;
    shared = new;
    return shared;
  }
}
```

The execution flow when using a locking strategy looks like Figure 7-7.

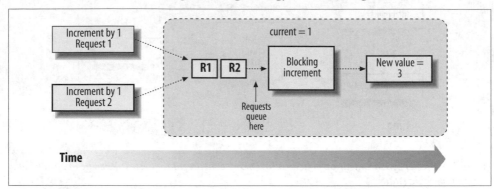

Figure 7-7. Blocking synchronization policy making new requests wait until it's safe to proceed

Although this code is safe, it does introduce a performance bottleneck, as only one thread may gain access to the mutable operation at any one time. Therefore we must be very selective about what and for how long we synchronize.

Container-Managed Concurrency

EJB 3.1 provides a simplistic locking abstraction to the bean provider in the form of *container-managed concurrency* (CMC). By introducing a few annotations (and corresponding XML metadata) into the API, the developer is freed from the responsibility of correctly implementing thread-safe code. The container will, in turn, transparently apply the appropriate locking strategy. Note that when using your bean implementation class as a POJO, however, the code is not safe for use in concurrent environments when using CMC.

By default, singleton beans employ a concurrency management type of CONTAINER, which takes the explicit form upon the bean implementation class:

```
@javax.ejb.ConcurrencyManagement(javax.ejb.ConcurrencyManagementType.CONTAINER)
public class MyBean{...}
```

Other types include BEAN and CONCURRENCY_NOT_SUPPORTED. Because only one instance of a singleton bean will exist (per VM) in an application, it makes sense to support concurrency in some fashion.

Each method in CMC will be assigned a lock type, which designates how the container should enforce access. By default, we use a *write lock*, which may be held by only one thread at a time. All other methods requesting the lock must wait their turn until the lock becomes available. The *read lock* may be explicitly specified, which will allow full concurrent access to all requests, provided that no write lock is currently being held. Locks are defined easily:

```
@javax.ejb.Lock(javax.ejb.LockType.READ)
public String concurrentReadOnlyMethod(){...}
```

```
@javax.ejb.Lock(javax.ejb.LockType.WRITE)
public void allowOnlyOneWriteAtATimeMethod(String stringToSet){...}
```

We may define the lock upon the method in the bean implementation class, on the class itself, or some combination of the two (with method-level overriding the class definition).

Requests upon a singleton bean employing CMC are not designed to block indefinitely until a lock becomes available. We may also specify sensible timeouts:

```
@javax.ejb.Lock(javax.ejb.LockType.READ)
@javax.ejb.AccessTimeout(timeout=15,unit=java.util.concurrent.TimeUnit.SECONDS)
public String concurrentReadOnlyMethod(){...}
```

In this example we denote that the read operation should wait on an available write lock a maximum of 15 seconds before giving up and returning a `javax.ejb.ConcurrentAccessTimeoutException`.

Bean-Managed Concurrency

Although convenient and resistant to developer error, container-managed concurrency does not cover the full breadth of concerns that multithreaded code must address. In these cases the specification makes available the full power of the Java language's concurrent tools by offering a bean-managed concurrency mode. This scenario opens the gates to full multithreaded access to the singleton bean, and it is the onus of the bean provider to manually apply the `synchronized` and `volatile` keywords to safeguard the bean instance in support of parallel invocations.

Lifecycle

The life of a singleton bean is very similar to that of the stateless session bean; it is either not yet instantiated or ready to service requests. In general, it is up to the Container to determine when to create the underlying bean instance, though this must be available before the first invocation is executed. Once made, the singleton bean instance lives in memory for the life of the application and is shared among all requests.

Explicit Startup

New in the EJB 3.1 Specification is the option to explicitly create the singleton bean instance when the application is deployed. This eager initialization is triggered simply:

```
@javax.ejb.Singleton
@javax.ejb.Startup
public class MySingletonBean implements MySingletonLocalBusiness{..}
```

The `@javax.ejb.Startup` annotation marks that the container must allocate and assign the bean instance alongside application startup. This becomes especially useful as an application-wide lifecycle listener. By additionally denoting a `@javax.ejb.Post Construct` method, this callback will be made at application start:

```
@javax.ejb.PostConstruct
public void applicationStartLifecycleMethod() throws Exception{...}
```

The method here will be invoked when the EJB is deployed. This application-wide callback was unavailable in previous versions of the specification.

Example: The RSSCacheEJB

Because the singleton bean represents one instance to be used by all incoming requests, we may take advantage of the extremely small impact this session type will have upon our overall memory consumption. The factors to beware are state consistency (thread-safety) and the potential blocking that this might impose. Therefore, it's best to apply this construct in high-read environments.

One such usage may be in implementing a simple high-performance cache. By letting parallel reads tear through the instance unblocked, we don't have the overhead of a full pool that might be supplied by an SLSB. The internal state of a cache is intended to be shared by many distinct sessions, so we don't need the semantics of an SFSB. Additionally, we may eagerly populate the cache when the application deploys, before any requests hit the system.

For this example, we'll define an RSS Caching service to read in a Really Simple Syndication (RSS; *http://en.wikipedia.org/wiki/RSS*) feed and store its contents for quick access. Relatively infrequent updates to the cache will temporarily block incoming read requests, and then concurrent operation will resume as normal, as illustrated in Figure 7-8.

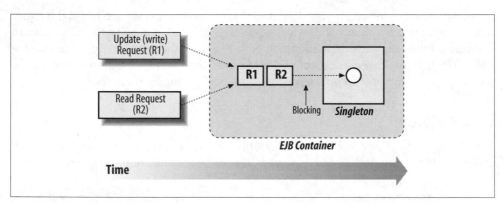

Figure 7-8. A concurrent singleton session bean servicing many requests in parallel

This example is covered in greater detail in Appendix D.

Value Objects

As we'll be representing the RSS entries in some generic form, first we should define what information we'll expose to the client:

```
public interface RssEntry
{
    /**
     * Obtains the author of the entry
     *
     * @return
     */
    String getAuthor();

    /**
     * Obtains the title of the entry
     *
     * @return
     */
    String getTitle();

    /**
     * Obtains the URL linking to the entry
     *
     * @return
     */
    URL getUrl();

    /**
     * Obtains the short description of the entry
     *
     * @return
     */
    String getDescription();
}
```

This is a very simple definition of properties. One thing that's important to note is that the type `java.net.URL` is itself mutable. We must take care to protect the internal state from being exported in a read request. Otherwise, a local client, which uses pass-by-reference, may change the contents of the URL returned from `getURL()`. To this end, we'll introduce a simple utility to copy the reference such that if a client writes back to it, only his view will be affected:

```
class ProtectExportUtil
{
    /**
     * Internal constructor; protects against instantiation
     */
    private ProtectExportUtil()
    {
    }

    /**
     * Returns a copy of the specified URL; used to ensure that mutable
```

```
 * internal state is not leaked out to clients
 * @param url
 * @return
 */
static URL copyUrl(final URL url)
{
    // If null, return
    if (url == null)
    {
        return url;
    }

    try
    {
        // Copy
        return new URL(url.toExternalForm());
    }
    catch (final MalformedURLException e)
    {
        throw new RuntimeException("Error in copying URL", e);
    }
}
}
```

Project ROME (*https://rome.dev.java.net/*) is an open source framework for dealing with RSS feeds, and we'll use it to back our implementation of `RssEntry`. In returning URLs, it will leverage the `ProtectExportUtil`:

```
public class RomeRssEntry implements RssEntry
{

    private String author;
    private String description;
    private String title;
    private URL url;

    /**
     * Constructor
     *
     * @param entry The Rome API's RSS Entry representation
     * @throws IllegalArgumentException If the entry is not specified
     */
    RomeRssEntry(final SyndEntry entry) throws IllegalArgumentException
    {
        // Set properties
        this.author = entry.getAuthor();
        final SyndContent content = entry.getDescription();
        this.description = content.getValue();
        this.title = entry.getTitle();
        final String urlString = entry.getLink();
        URL url = null;
        try
        {
            url = new URL(urlString);
        }
```

```
        catch (final MalformedURLException murle)
        {
            throw new RuntimeException("Obtained invalid URL from Rome RSS entry: "
+ entry, murle);
        }
        this.url = url;
    }

    @Override
    public String getAuthor()
    {
        return this.author;
    }

    @Override
    public String getDescription()
    {
        return this.description;
    }

    @Override
    public String getTitle()
    {
        return this.title;
    }

    @Override
    public URL getUrl()
    {
        return ProtectExportUtil.copyUrl(this.url);
    }

    /* (non-Javadoc)
     * @see java.lang.Object#toString()
     */
    @Override
    public String toString()
    {
        final StringBuilder sb = new StringBuilder();
        sb.append(this.getTitle());
        sb.append(" - ");
        sb.append(this.url.toExternalForm());
        return sb.toString();
    }
}
```

That should cover the case of the value object our EJB will need in order to return some results to the client. Note that the ROME implementation is completely separated from the contracted interface. Should we choose to use another library in the future, our clients won't require any recompilation.

The Contract: Business Interfaces

Now we need to define methods to read the cache's contents, obtain the URL that hosts the RSS feed, and refresh the cache from the URL:

```
public interface RssCacheCommonBusiness
{
   /**
    * Returns all entries in the RSS Feed represented by
    * {@link RssCacheCommonBusiness#getUrl()}.
    * This list will not support mutation and is read-only.
    */
   List<RssEntry> getEntries();

   /**
    * Returns the URL of the RSS Feed
    *
    * @return
    */
   URL getUrl();

   /**
    * Flushes the cache and refreshes the entries from the feed
    */
   void refresh();
}
```

Again, we must take care to protect the internal cache state from being exported in a read request. The point in question here is the List returned from getEntries(). Therefore we note in the documentation that the reference return will be read-only.

The refresh() operation will obtain the contents from the URL returned by getURL(), and parse these into the cache.

The cache itself is a List of the RssEntry type.

Bean Implementation Class

Once again, the bean implementation class contains the meat and potatoes of the business logic, as well as the annotations that round out the EJB's metadata:

```
@Singleton
@Startup
@Remote(RssCacheCommonBusiness.class)
// Explicitly declare Container Managed Concurrency, which is unnecessary; it's
the default
@ConcurrencyManagement(ConcurrencyManagementType.CONTAINER)
public class RssCacheBean implements RssCacheCommonBusiness {
```

The declaration marks our class as a Singleton Session type that should be initialized eagerly upon application deployment. We'll use container-managed concurrency (which is defined explicitly here for illustration, even though this is the default strategy).

Some internal members are next:

```
/**
 * Logger
 */
private static final Logger log = Logger.getLogger(RssCacheBean.class);

/**
 * URL pointing to the RSS Feed
 */
private URL url;

/**
 * Cached RSS Entries for the feed
 */
private List<RssEntry> entries;
```

The URL here will be used to point to the RSS feed we're caching. The List is our cache. Now to implement our business methods:

```
/* (non-Javadoc)
 * @see org.jboss.ejb3.examples.ch07.rsscache.spi.RssCacheCommonBusiness
#getUrl()
 */
@Lock(LockType.READ)
@Override
public URL getUrl()
{
    // Return a copy so we don't export mutable state to the client
    return ProtectExportUtil.copyUrl(this.url);
}
```

Again, we protect the internal URL from being changed from the outside. The lock type is READ and so concurrent access is permitted, given no WRITE locks are currently held:

```
/**
 * @see org.jboss.ejb3.examples.ch07.rsscache.spi.RssCacheCommonBusiness
#refresh()
 * @throws IllegalStateException If the URL has not been set
 */
@PostConstruct
@Override
// Block all readers and writers until we're done here;
// Optional metadata, WRITE is the default
@Lock(LockType.WRITE)
public void refresh() throws IllegalStateException
{

    // Obtain the URL
    final URL url = this.url;
    if (url == null)
    {
        throw new IllegalStateException("The Feed URL has not been set");
    }
    log.info("Requested: " + url);
```

```
    // Obtain the feed
    final FeedFetcher feedFetcher = new HttpClientFeedFetcher();
    SyndFeed feed = null;
    try
    {
        feed = feedFetcher.retrieveFeed(url);
    }
    catch (final FeedException fe)
    {
        throw new RuntimeException(fe);
    }
    catch (final FetcherException fe)
    {
        throw new RuntimeException(fe);
    }
    catch (final IOException ioe)
    {
        throw new RuntimeException(ioe);
    }

    // Make a new list for the entries
    final List<RssEntry> rssEntries = new ArrayList<RssEntry>();

    // For each entry
    @SuppressWarnings("unchecked")
    // The Rome API doesn't provide for generics, so suppress the warning
    final List<SyndEntry> list = (List<SyndEntry>) feed.getEntries();
    for (final SyndEntry entry : list)
    {
        // Make a new entry
        final RssEntry rssEntry = new RomeRssEntry(entry);

        // Place in the list
        rssEntries.add(rssEntry);
        log.debug("Found new RSS Entry: " + rssEntry);
    }

    // Protect the entries from mutation from exporting the client view
    final List<RssEntry> protectedEntries = Collections.unmodifiableList
(rssEntries);

    // Set the entries in the cache
    this.entries = protectedEntries;
}
```

There's a lot going on here. @PostConstruct upon the refresh() method means that this will be invoked automatically by the container when the instance is created. The instance is created at application deployment due to the @Startup annotation. So, transitively, this method will be invoked before the container is ready to service any requests.

The WRITE lock upon this method means that during its invocation, all incoming requests must wait until the pending request completes. The cache may not be read via getEntries() during refresh().

Also very important is that our cache is made immutable before being set. Accomplished via `Collections.unmodifiableList()`, this enforces the read-only contract of `getEntries()`.

The remainder of the method body simply involves reading in the RSS feed from the URL and parsing it into our value objects.

## CHAPTER 8

Message-Driven Beans

The message-driven bean (MDB) is an asynchronous listener. Its callers are systems that say, "Check out this message; do whatever you want with it" and don't have the decency to wait around for a response. In fact, clients of an MDB have no idea that the messages they send may be processed by an EJB at all. Messages are sent directly to some messaging system (it doesn't matter which), where they are routed via a standard inflow mechanism to the EJB subsystem and, eventually, a backing MDB instance (Figure 8-1).

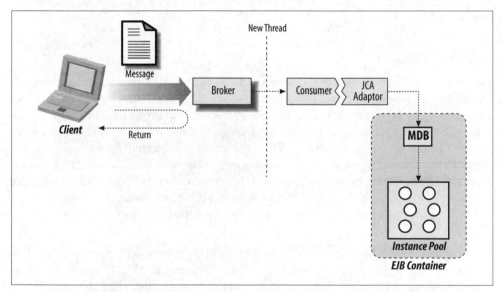

Figure 8-1. Message-driven bean listening on events via a messaging subsystem

The key to the generic plumbing shown in the figure is the Java Connector Architecture (JCA; *http://jcp.org/en/jsr/detail?id=322*), which provides an abstraction for the delivery of any message type. This means that EJB message-driven beans may act as a listener for events sent from any system for which there is a valid JCA inflow adaptor.

The message-driven bean was introduced in EJB 2.0 to support the processing of asynchronous messages from a Java Message Service (JMS; *http://java.sun.com/products/jms/*) provider. EJB 2.1 expanded the definition of the message-driven bean so that it can support any messaging system, not just JMS, via the facilities provided by JCA. EJB 3.x does not really expand on the feature set of earlier specification versions, but it does simplify configuration with the use of annotations. This chapter examines both JMS-based message-driven beans as well as the expanded message-driven bean model available to EJB 3.0 developers.

JMS and Message-Driven Beans

All EJB 3.x vendors must support a JMS provider. Most vendors supply a built-in provider, though it's possible to integrate a third-party implementation instead. Regardless, a JMS provider is an absolute necessity for supporting message-driven beans. By forcing the adoption of JMS, the EJB expert group has guaranteed that EJB developers can expect to have a working JMS provider to which messages can be both sent and received.

JMS as a Resource

JMS is a vendor-neutral API that can be used to access enterprise messaging systems. Enterprise messaging systems (aka message-oriented middleware) facilitate the exchange of messages between software applications, usually over a network. The role of JMS isn't unlike the role of JDBC; just as JDBC provides a common API for accessing many different relational databases, JMS provides vendor-independent access to enterprise messaging systems. Although messaging products aren't as familiar as database products, there's no shortage of messaging systems that support JMS, including OpenJMS, HornetQ, ActiveMQ, Qpid, and SonicMQ. Software applications that use the JMS API for sending or receiving messages are portable from one JMS vendor to another.

Applications that use JMS are called *JMS clients*, and the messaging system that handles routing and delivery of messages is called the *JMS provider*. A *JMS application* is a business system composed of many JMS clients and, generally, one JMS provider. A JMS client that sends a message is called a *producer*, and a client that receives a message is called a *consumer*. A single JMS client can be both a producer and a consumer.

In EJB, enterprise beans of all types can use JMS to send messages. These are later consumed by other applications or by message-driven beans. JMS facilitates sending messages from enterprise beans using a *messaging service*, sometimes called a *message broker* or *router*. Message brokers have been around for a couple of decades—the oldest and most established is IBM's MQSeries—but JMS is relatively new, and it is specifically designed to deliver a variety of message types from one Java application to another.

JMS Is Asynchronous

One of the principal advantages of JMS messaging is that it's *asynchronous*. In other words, a JMS client can send a message without having to wait for a reply. Contrast this flexibility with the synchronous messaging of Java RMI or JAX-RPC, in which each client invocation blocks the current thread until the method completes execution. This lockstep processing makes the client dependent on the availability of the EJB server, resulting in a tight coupling between the client and the enterprise bean.

JMS clients send messages asynchronously to a destination (Topic or Queue) from which other JMS clients can also receive messages. When a JMS client sends a message, it doesn't wait for a reply; it sends the message to a router, which is responsible for forwarding the message to other clients. There's no effect on the client if one or more recipients are unavailable; once delivered, the sender will continue with its work. It's the router's responsibility to make sure that the message eventually reaches its destination. Clients sending messages are decoupled from the clients receiving them; senders are not dependent on the availability of receivers.

The limitations of RMI make JMS an attractive alternative for communicating with other applications. Using the standard JNDI naming context, an enterprise bean can obtain a JMS connection to a JMS provider and use it to deliver asynchronous messages to other Java applications.

For example, a fictional `UserRegistrationEJB` may want to notify arbitrary systems of a new user, but it doesn't want to be coupled. By sending a JMS message to a system that is listening for incoming registration events, the `UserRegistrationEJB` can dispatch the request and continue along its way (Figure 8-2).

In this example, the applications receiving JMS messages initiated from the `UserRegistrationEJB` may be message-driven beans, other Java applications in the enterprise, or applications in other organizations that benefit from being notified that a new registration has been processed. Examples might include sending an email confirmation or an internal marketing application that adds customers to a catalog mailing list, and these may be plugged in or turned off at runtime without affecting the registration process itself.

Because messaging is inherently decoupled and asynchronous, the transactions and security contexts of the sender are not propagated to the receiver. For example, when the `UserRegistrationEJB` sends the message, the JMS provider may authenticate it, but the message's security context won't be propagated to the JMS client that received the message. When a JMS client receives the message, it has no idea about the security

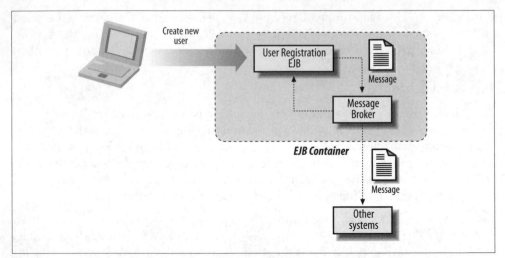

Figure 8-2. UserRegistrationEJB firing an event denoting that a new user has been created

context under which the message was sent. This is how it should be, because the sender and receiver often operate in environments with different security domains.

Similarly, transactions are never propagated from the sender to the receiver. For one thing, the sender has no idea who the receivers of the message will be. There could be one receiver or thousands; managing a distributed transaction under such ambiguous circumstances is not tenable. In addition, the clients receiving the message may not get it for a long time after it is sent. There may be a network problem, the client may be down, or there may be some other delay. Transactions are designed to be executed quickly because they lock up resources, and applications can't tolerate the possibility of a long transaction with an unpredictable end.

A JMS client can, however, have a distributed transaction with the JMS provider so that it manages the send or receive operation in the context of a transaction. For example, if the `UserRegistrationEJB`'s transaction fails for any reason, the JMS provider discards the message. Transactions and JMS are covered in more detail in Chapter 17.

JMS Messaging Models

JMS provides two types of messaging models: *publish-and-subscribe* and *point-to-point*. The JMS specification refers to these as *messaging domains*. In JMS terminology, publish-and-subscribe and point-to-point are frequently shortened to *pub/sub* and *p2p* (or *PTP*), respectively. This chapter uses both the long and short forms throughout.

In the simplest sense, publish-and-subscribe is intended for a one-to-many broadcast of messages, as illustrated in Figure 8-3.

Point-to-point, on the other hand, is intended for a message that is to be processed once (Figure 8-4).

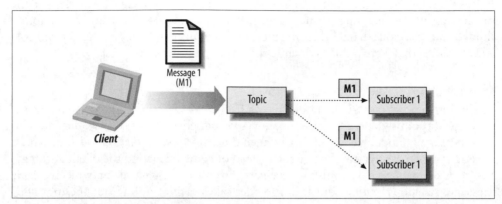

Figure 8-3. Publish-and-subscribe model of messaging

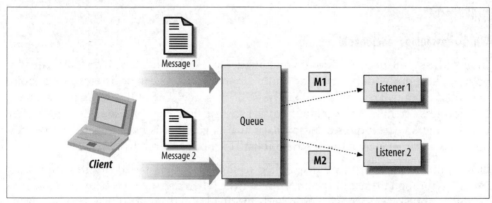

Figure 8-4. Point-to-point model of messaging

Each messaging domain (i.e., pub/sub and p2p) has its own set of interfaces and classes for sending and receiving messages. This results in two different APIs, which share some common types. JMS 1.1 introduced a Unified API that allows developers to use a single set of interfaces and classes for both messaging domains. Only the Unified API is used in this chapter.

Publish-and-subscribe

In publish-and-subscribe messaging, one producer can send a message to many consumers through a virtual channel called a *topic*. Consumers can choose to subscribe to a topic. Any messages addressed to a topic are delivered to all the topic's consumers. The pub/sub messaging model is largely a *push-based model*, in which messages are automatically broadcast to consumers without the consumers having to request or poll the topic for new messages.

In this pub/sub messaging model, the producer sending the message is not dependent on the consumers receiving the message. JMS clients that use pub/sub can establish durable subscriptions that allow consumers to disconnect and later reconnect and collect messages that were published while they were disconnected.

Point-to-point

The point-to-point messaging model allows JMS clients to send and receive messages both synchronously and asynchronously via virtual channels known as *queues*. The p2p messaging model has traditionally been a *pull-* or *polling-based model*, in which messages are requested from the queue instead of being pushed to the client automatically.[*] A queue may have multiple receivers, but only one receiver may receive each message. As shown earlier, the JMS provider takes care of doling out the messages among JMS clients, ensuring that each message is processed by only one consumer. The JMS specification does not dictate the rules for distributing messages among multiple receivers.

Which messaging model should you use?

In most cases, the decision about which model to use depends on how it'll be used by your application. With pub/sub, any number of subscribers can be listening on a topic, and all of them will receive copies of the same message. The publisher may not care if everybody is listening, or even if nobody is listening. For example, consider a publisher that broadcasts stock quotes. If any particular subscriber is not currently connected and misses out on a great quote, the publisher is not concerned.

Using pub/sub, messages are dispatched to the consumers based on filtering that is provided through the use of specific topics. Even when messaging is being leveraged to establish a one-on-one conversation with another known application, it can be advantageous to use pub/sub with multiple topics to segregate different kinds of messages. Each kind of message can be dealt with separately through its own unique consumer and onMessage() listener.

In contrast, a point-to-point session is likely to be intended for a one-on-one conversation with a specific application at the other end. In this scenario, every message really matters. The range and variety of the data the messages represent can be a factor as well.

Point-to-point is more convenient when you want to process a given message exactly once. This is perhaps the most critical difference between the two models: p2p guarantees that only one consumer processes each message. This ability is extremely important when messages need to be processed separately but in tandem.

---

[*] The JMS specification does not specifically state how the p2p and pub/sub models must be implemented. Either model can use push or pull—but conceptually, pub/sub is push and p2p is pull.

Learning More About JMS

JMS (and enterprise messaging in general) represents a powerful paradigm in distributed computing. While this chapter has provided a brief overview of JMS, it has presented only enough material to prepare you for the discussion of message-driven beans in the next section. To understand JMS and how it is used, you will need to study it independently.† Taking the time to learn JMS is well worth the effort.

JMS-Based Message-Driven Beans

Message-driven beans (MDBs) are stateless, server-side, transaction-aware components for processing asynchronous messages delivered via JMS. While a message-driven bean is responsible for consuming messages, its container manages the component's environment: transactions, security, resources, concurrency, and message acknowledgment. It's particularly important to note that the container manages concurrency. The thread safety provided by the container gives MDBs a significant advantage over traditional JMS clients, which must be custom built to manage resources, transactions, and security in a multithreaded environment. An MDB can process hundreds of JMS messages concurrently because many underlying bean instances of the MDB can execute concurrently in the container.

A message-driven bean is a complete enterprise bean, just like a session or entity bean, but there are some important differences. While a message-driven bean has a bean class, it does not have a business or component interface. These are absent because the message-driven bean responds only to asynchronous messages and not to direct client invocations.

@MessageDriven

MDBs are identified using the `@javax.ejb.MessageDriven` annotation or, alternatively, are described in an EJB deployment descriptor. An MDB can be deployed alone, but it's more frequently deployed with the other enterprise beans that it references.

@ActivationConfigProperty

We'll see later that because MDBs can receive messages from arbitrary messaging formats, the configuration must be very flexible to be able to describe the proprietary properties that different providers will have. JCA-based MDBs don't necessarily use JMS as the message service, so this requirement is very important. To facilitate this, the `@MessageDriven.activationConfig()` attribute takes an array of `@ActivationConfigProperty` annotations. These annotations are simply a set of generic name/value pairs that describe the configuration of your MDB.

---

† For a detailed treatment of JMS, see *Java Message Service* (O'Reilly).

```
@MessageDriven(activationConfig={
            @ActivationConfigProperty(
                propertyName="destinationType",

                propertyValue="javax.jms.Queue"),
            @ActivationConfigProperty(
                propertyName="messageSelector",

                propertyValue="MessageFormat = 'Version 3.4'"),
            @ActivationConfigProperty(
                propertyName="acknowledgeMode",

                propertyValue="Auto-acknowledge")})
public class ReservationProcessorBean implements javax.jms.MessageListener {
    ...
}
```

The property names and values used in the `activationConfig()` attribute to describe the messaging service vary depending on the type of message service used, but EJB 3.x defines a set of fixed properties for JMS-based message-driven beans. These properties are `acknowledgeMode`, `messageSelector`, `destinationType`, and `subscriptionDurability`.

Message selector

An MDB can declare a *message selector*, which allows an MDB to be more discerning about the messages it receives from a particular topic or queue. Message selectors use `Message` properties as criteria in conditional expressions.[‡] These conditional expressions use Boolean logic to declare which messages should be delivered. A message selector is declared using the standard property name, `messageSelector`, in an activation configuration element:

```
@ActivationConfigProperty(
            propertyName="messageSelector",
            propertyValue="MessageFormat = 'Version 3.4'"),
```

Message selectors are based on message properties, which are additional headers that can be assigned to a message; they allow vendors and developers to attach information to a message that isn't part of the message's body. The `Message` interface provides several methods for reading and writing properties. Properties can have a `String` value or one of several primitive values (`boolean`, `byte`, `short`, `int`, `long`, `float`, `double`). The naming of properties, together with their values and conversion rules, is strictly defined by JMS.

Here's how a JMS producer would go about setting a `MessageFormat` property on a `Message`:

```
Message message = session.createMapMessage();
message.setStringProperty("MessageFormat","Version 3.4");

// set the reservation named values
```

---

‡ Message selectors are also based on message headers, which are outside the scope of this chapter.

```
sender.send(message);
```

The message selectors are based on a subset of the SQL-92 conditional expression syntax that is used in the WHERE clauses of SQL statements. They can become fairly complex, including the use of literal values, Boolean expressions, unary operators, and so on.

Acknowledge mode

A JMS *acknowledgment* means that the JMS client notifies the JMS provider (message router) when a message is received. In EJB, it's the MDB container's responsibility to send an acknowledgment when it receives a message. Acknowledging a message tells the JMS provider that an MDB container has received and processed the message. Without an acknowledgment, the JMS provider does not know whether the MDB container has received the message, and unwanted redeliveries can cause problems.

The acknowledgment mode is set using the standard acknowledgeMode activation configuration property, as shown in the following code snippet:

```
@ActivationConfigProperty(
        propertyName="acknowledgeMode",
        propertyValue="Auto-acknowledge ")
```

Two values can be specified for acknowledgment mode: Auto-acknowledge and Dups-ok-acknowledge. Auto-acknowledge tells the container that it should send an acknowledgment to the JMS provider immediately after the message is given to an MDB instance to process. Dups-ok-acknowledge tells the container that it doesn't have to send the acknowledgment immediately; anytime after the message is given to the MDB instance will be fine. With Dups-ok-acknowledge, it's possible for the MDB container to delay acknowledgment for so long that the JMS provider assumes the message was not received and sends a "duplicate" message. Obviously, with Dups-ok-acknowledge, your MDBs must be able to handle duplicate messages correctly.

Auto-acknowledge avoids duplicate messages because the acknowledgment is sent immediately. Therefore, the JMS provider won't send a duplicate. Most MDBs use Auto-acknowledge to avoid processing the same message twice. Dups-ok-acknowledge exists because it can allow a JMS provider to optimize its use of the network. In practice, though, the overhead of an acknowledgment is so small, and the frequency of communication between the MDB container and the JMS provider is so high, that Dups-ok-acknowledge doesn't have a big impact on performance.

Having said all of this, the acknowledgment mode is ignored most of the time—in fact, it is ignored unless the MDB executes with bean-managed transactions or with the container-managed transaction attribute NotSupported (see Chapter 17). In all other cases, transactions are managed by the container, and acknowledgment takes place within the context of the transaction. If the transaction succeeds, the message is acknowledged. If the transaction fails, the message is not acknowledged. When using container-managed transactions with a `Required` transaction attribute, the acknowledgment mode is usually not specified; however, it is included in the deployment descriptor for the sake of discussion.

Subscription durability

When a JMS-based MDB uses a `javax.jms.Topic`, the deployment descriptor must declare whether the subscription is `Durable` or `NonDurable`. A `Durable` subscription outlasts an MDB container's connection to the JMS provider, so if the EJB server suffers a partial failure, shuts down, or otherwise disconnects from the JMS provider, the messages that it would have received are not lost. The provider stores any messages that are delivered while the container is disconnected; the messages are delivered to the container (and from there to the MDB) when the container reconnects. This behavior is commonly referred to as *store-and-forward messaging*. `Durable` MDBs are tolerant of disconnections, whether intentional or the result of a partial failure.

If the subscription is `NonDurable`, any messages the bean would have received while it was disconnected are lost. Developers use `NonDurable` subscriptions when it is not critical for all messages to be processed. Using a `NonDurable` subscription improves the performance of the JMS provider but significantly reduces the reliability of the MDBs.

```
@ActivateConfigProperty(
        propertyName="subscriptionDurability",
        propertyValue="Durable")
```

When the destination type is `javax.jms.Queue`, durability is not a factor, because of the nature of queue-based messaging systems. With a queue, messages may be consumed only once, and they remain in the queue until they are distributed to one of the queue's listeners.

MessageDrivenContext

Message-driven beans also have a context object that is similar in functionality to that of the `javax.ejb.SessionContext` described in Chapter 5. This object may be injected using the `@javax.annotation.Resource` annotation:

```
@Resource MessageDrivenContext context;
```

The `MessageDrivenContext` simply extends the `EJBContext`; it does not add any new methods. Only the transactional methods that `MessageDrivenContext` inherits from `EJBContext` are available to message-driven beans. The home methods—`getEJBHome()` and `getEJBLocalHome()`—throw a `RuntimeException` if invoked, because MDBs do not have home interfaces or EJB home objects. The security methods—`getCallerPrincipal()` and `isCallerInRole()`—also throw a `RuntimeException` if invoked on a `MessageDrivenContext`. When an MDB services a JMS message, there is no "caller," so there is no security context to be obtained from the caller. Remember that JMS is asynchronous and doesn't propagate the sender's security context to the receiver—that wouldn't make sense, since senders and receivers tend to operate in different environments.

MDBs usually execute in a container-initiated or bean-initiated transaction, so the transaction methods allow the MDB to manage its context. The transaction context is not propagated from the JMS sender; it is either initiated by the container or initiated by the bean explicitly using `javax.jta.UserTransaction`. The transaction methods in `EJBContext` are explained in more detail in Chapter 17.

Message-driven beans also have access to their own JNDI ENCs, which provide the MDB instances access to environment entries, other enterprise beans, and resources. For example, we may take advantage of the ENC to obtain references to an `EntityManager`, another EJB, or a JMS `ConnectionFactory` and `Queue`.

MessageListener interface

MDBs usually implement the `javax.jms.MessageListener` interface, which defines the `onMessage()` method. This method processes the JMS messages received by a bean.

```
package javax.jms;
public interface MessageListener {
    public void onMessage(Message message);
}
```

Although MDBs usually implement this interface, we will see later in this chapter that MDBs can integrate with other messaging systems besides JMS, which define a different interface contract.

Taskflow and integration for B2B: onMessage()

The `onMessage()` method is where all the business logic goes. As messages arrive, the container passes them to the MDB via the `onMessage()` method. When the method returns, the MDB instance is ready to process a new message.

```
public void onMessage(Message message) {
    try {
        // Extract out information from the message
        MapMessage mapMessage = (MapMessage)message;
        int userId = mapMessage.getInt("userId");
        String email = mapMessage.getInt("email");

        // Now perform business logic
    }
```

JMS is frequently used as an integration point for business-to-business (B2B) applications, so it's easy to imagine a message coming from an external business partner (perhaps a third-party processor or auditing system).

Like a session bean, the MDB can access any other session bean and use that bean to complete a task. An MDB can manage a process and interact with other beans as well as resources. For example, it is commonplace for an MDB to use the Java Persistence API (JPA) to access a database based on the contents of the message it is processing.

Sending messages from a message-driven bean

An MDB can also send messages using JMS. This hypothetical `deliverTicket()` method sends the ticket information to a destination defined by the sending JMS client:

```
public void deliverTicket(MapMessage reservationMsg, TicketDO ticket)
    throws JMSException{

    Queue queue = (Queue)reservationMsg.getJMSReplyTo();
    Connection connect = connectionFactory.createConnection();
    Session session = connect.createSession(true,0);
    MessageProducer sender = session.createProducer(queue);
    ObjectMessage message = session.createObjectMessage( );
    message.setObject(ticket);
    sender.send(message);
    connect.close( );
}
```

Every message type has two parts: a message header and a message body (aka the *payload*). The message header contains routing information and may also have properties for message filtering and other attributes. One of these attributes may be `JMSReplyTo`. The message's sender may set the `JMSReplyTo` attribute to any destination accessible to its JMS provider. In the case of the reservation message, the sender set the `JMSReplyTo` attribute to the queue to which the resulting ticket should be sent. Another application can access this queue to read tickets and distribute them to customers or store the information in the sender's database.

You can also use the `JMSReplyTo` address to report business errors. For example, if the cabin is already reserved, the preceding EJB might send an error message to the `JMSReplyTo` queue explaining that the reservation could not be processed. Including this type of error handling is left as an exercise for the reader.

The Lifecycle of a Message-Driven Bean

Just as session beans have well-defined lifecycles, so does the message-driven bean. The MDB instance's lifecycle has two states: *Does Not Exist* and *Method-Ready Pool*. The Method-Ready Pool is similar to the instance pool used for stateless session beans.[§] Figure 8-5 illustrates the states and transitions that an MDB instance goes through in its lifetime.

[§] Some vendors may *not* pool MDB instances but may instead create and destroy instances with each new message. This is an implementation-specific decision that should not affect the specified lifecycle of the stateless bean instance.

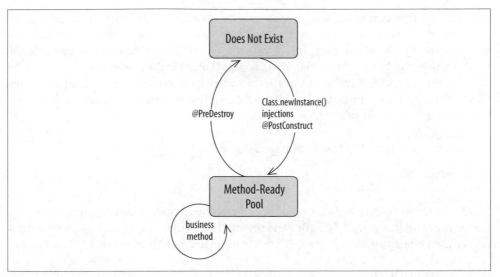

Figure 8-5. MDB lifecycle

The Does Not Exist State

When an MDB instance is in the Does Not Exist state, it is not an instance in the memory of the system. In other words, it has not been instantiated yet.

The Method-Ready Pool

MDB instances enter the Method-Ready Pool as the container needs them. When the EJB server is first started, it may create a number of MDB instances and enter them into the Method-Ready Pool (the actual behavior of the server depends on the implementation). When the number of MDB instances handling incoming messages is insufficient, more can be created and added to the pool.

Transitioning to the Method-Ready Pool

When an instance transitions from the Does Not Exist state to the Method-Ready Pool, three operations are performed on it. First, the bean instance is instantiated by invoking the `Class.newInstance()` method on the bean implementation class. Second, the container injects any resources that the bean's metadata has requested via an injection annotation or XML deployment descriptor.

 You must always provide a default constructor. A default constructor is a constructor with no parameters. The container instantiates instances of the bean class using `Class.newInstance()`, which requires a no-arg constructor. If no constructors are defined, the no-arg constructor is implicit.

Finally, the EJB container will invoke the `PostConstruct` callback if there is one. The bean class may or may not have a method that is annotated with `@javax.ejb.PostConstruct`. If it is present, the container will call this annotated method after the bean is instantiated. This `@PostConstruct` annotated method can be of any name and visibility, but it must return `void`, have no parameters, and throw no checked exceptions. The bean class may define only one `@PostConstruct` method (but it is not required to do so).

```
@MessageDriven
public class MyBean implements MessageListener {

    @PostConstruct
    public void myInit() {}
```

MDBs are not subject to activation, so they can maintain open connections to resources for their entire lifecycles.[||] The `@PreDestroy` method should close any open resources before the stateless session bean is evicted from memory at the end of its lifecycle.

Life in the Method-Ready Pool

When a message is delivered to an MDB, it is delegated to any available instance in the Method-Ready Pool. While the instance is executing the request, it is unavailable to process other messages. The MDB can handle many messages simultaneously, delegating the responsibility of handling each message to a different MDB instance. When a message is delegated to an instance by the container, the MDB instance's `MessageDrivenContext` changes to reflect the new transaction context. Once the instance has finished, it is immediately available to handle a new message.

Transitioning out of the Method-Ready Pool: The death of an MDB instance

Bean instances leave the Method-Ready Pool for the Does Not Exist state when the server no longer needs them—that is, when the server decides to reduce the total size of the Method-Ready Pool by evicting one or more instances from memory. The process begins by invoking an `@PreDestroy` callback method on the bean instance. Again, as with `@PostConstruct`, this callback method is optional to implement and its signature must return a `void` type, have zero parameters, and throw no checked exceptions. A `@PreDestroy` callback method can perform any cleanup operation, such as closing open resources.

```
@MessageDriven
public class MyBean implements MessageListener {

    @PreDestroy
    public void cleanup( ) {
```

[||] The duration of a stateless bean instance's life is assumed to be very long. However, some EJB servers may actually destroy and create instances with every method invocation, making this strategy less attractive. Consult your vendor's documentation for details on how your EJB server handles stateless instances.

```
        ...
    }
```

As with @PostConstruct, @PreDestroy is invoked only once: when the bean is about to transition to the Does Not Exist state. During this callback method, the MessageDriven Context and access to the JNDI ENC are still available to the bean instance. Following the execution of the @PreDestroy method, the bean is dereferenced and eventually garbage-collected.

Connector-Based Message-Driven Beans

Although the JMS-based MDB has proven very useful, it has limitations. Perhaps the most glaring limitation is that EJB vendors are able to support only a small number of JMS providers (usually only one). In pre-EJB 2.1 days, most vendors supported only their own JMS provider and no others. Obviously, this limits your choices: if your company or a partner company uses a JMS provider that is not supported by your EJB vendor, you will not be able to process messages from that JMS provider.[#]

The root of the problem is complex and requires a fairly deep understanding of transaction management. In a nutshell, the delivery of the message by the JMS provider to the MDB, and all the work performed by the MDB (e.g., using JDBC, invoking methods on other beans, etc.), must be part of the same transaction, which is initiated by the EJB container. This requires that the EJB container have prior knowledge that message delivery is imminent so that it can initiate a transaction before the message is actually delivered. Unfortunately, the JMS API doesn't support this kind of functionality. So in the early days of EJB, JMS providers had to perform custom integration with each and every EJB vendor. Custom integration was expensive (business-wise), so old EJB 2.0 vendors generally choose to integrate with very few JMS providers.

Another limitation with JMS-based MDBs is that you are tied to the JMS programming model; no other messaging systems are supported. Although JMS is very useful, it's not the only messaging system available. SOAP, email, CORBA messaging, proprietary messaging systems used in ERP systems (SAP, PeopleSoft, etc.), and legacy messaging systems are examples of other non-JMS messaging systems.

EJB 3.x (and 2.1) supports an expanded, more open definition of message-driven beans that allows them to service any kind of messaging system from any vendor. The only requirement is that new types of message-driven beans adhere to the message-driven bean lifecycle. EJB vendors can build custom code to support a new messaging system (something other than JMS), but they must also support any message-driven bean type that's based on JCA 1.6.

[#] A workaround is to use a JMS gateway, which routes messages from one JMS provider to another, but this is a custom solution outside the EJB specification.

The JCA provides a standard Service Provider Interface (SPI) that allows any EIS to plug into any Java EE container system. Version 1.0 of the connector architecture applies only to request/reply resources in which the Java EE component (EJB or servlet/JSP) initiates the request. The current version of the connector architecture (1.6), which is required by JEE6 and higher, is much more general and can work with any asynchronous messaging systems. In such systems, the Java EE component waits for messages to arrive instead of initiating an interaction with an EIS; the EIS initiates the interaction by delivering a message.

JCA defines a messaging contract specifically tailored to message-driven beans. It defines the contracts between an EJB container and an asynchronous Connector so that message-driven beans automatically process incoming messages from the EIS. MDBs based on an asynchronous Connector can implement a specific messaging interface defined by the Connector itself. Instead of implementing the `javax.jms.MessageListener` interface, the MDB implements some other type of interface that is specific to the EIS.

For example, consider a hypothetical Email Connector that allows MDBs to process email—similar to how JMS-based MDBs process JMS messages. The Email Connector is purchased from Vendor X and is delivered in a JAR file called a Resource ARchive (RAR). The RAR contains all the Connector code and deployment descriptors necessary to plug into the EJB container system. It also defines a messaging interface that the developer uses to create an email MDB. Here is a possible email messaging interface that must be implemented by an email MDB:

```
package com.vendorx.email;

public interface EmailListener
 {
     public void onMessage(javax.mail.Message message);
}
```

The bean class that implements this interface is responsible for processing email messages delivered by the Email Connector. The following code shows an MDB that implements the `EmailListener` interface and processes email:

```
package com.mycompany;

@MessageDriven(activationConfig={
                @ActivationConfigProperty(
                    propertyName="mailServer",
                    propertyValue="mail.ispx.com"),
                @ActivationConfigProperty(
                    propertyName="serverType",
                    propertyValue="POP3 "),
                @ActivationConfigProperty(
                    propertyName="messageFilter",
                    propertyValue="to='name@address.com'")})
public class EmailBean implements com.vendorx.email.EmailListener {

    public void onMessage(javax.mail.Message message){
```

```
        //  continue processing Email message
    }
}
```

In this example, the container calls onMessage() to deliver a JavaMail Message object, which represents an incoming email message. However, the messaging interfaces used by a Connector-based MDB don't have to use onMessage(). The method name and method signature can be whatever is appropriate to the EIS; it can even have a return type. For example, a Connector might be developed to handle request/reply-style messaging for SOAP. This connector might use the ReqRespListener defined by the Java API for XML Messaging (JAXM), which is a SOAP messaging API defined by Sun Microsystems that is not part of the Java EE platform:

```
package javax.xml.messaging;
import javax.xml.soap.SOAPMessage;


public interface ReqRespListener {
    public SOAPMessage onMessage(SOAPMessage message);
}
```

In this interface, onMessage() has a return type of SOAPMessage. This means the EJB container and Connector are responsible for coordinating the reply message back to the sender (or to some destination defined in the deployment descriptor). In addition to supporting different method signatures, the messaging interface may have several methods for processing different kinds of messages using the same MDB.

There's no limit to the new kinds of message-driven beans that EJB container systems can support. The real beauty of all of this is that Connector-based MDBs are completely portable across EJB vendors—because all vendors must support them. If you use a Connector-based MDB with EJB Vendor A and later change to EJB Vendor B, you can continue to use the same Connector-based MDB with no portability problems.

The activation configuration properties used with non-JMS-based MDBs depend on the type of Connector and its requirements. Let's see an example of this:

```
@MessageDriven(activationConfig={
            @ActivationConfigProperty(
                propertyName="mailServer",
                propertyValue="mail.ispx.com"),
            @ActivationConfigProperty(
                propertyName="serverType",
                propertyValue="POP3"),
            @ActivationConfigProperty(
                propertyName="messageFilter",
                propertyValue="to='name@address.com'")})
```

We talked about @ActivationConfigProperty annotations before. As you can see from the preceding example, any name/value pair is supported within this annotation, so it can easily support the email-specific configuration for this Connector type.

Message Linking

Message linking is a feature that allows the messages being sent by any enterprise bean to be routed to a specific message-driven bean in the same deployment. By using message linking, you can orchestrate a flow of messages between components in the same application. This is achieved by assigning logical names to destinations instead of using a real JCA endpoint; we may think of message destination references as virtual endpoints (see Figure 8-6).

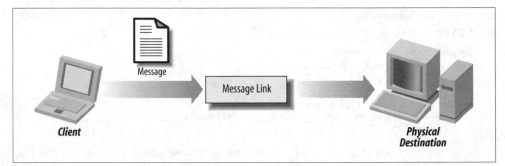

Figure 8-6. Sending events to the message-link abstraction, which delegates to a real destination

When we discussed this method earlier in the chapter, we never really mentioned where a user registration message was being sent; it could go to an emailing system or some other vendor listening in. However, message linking makes sure that the message goes directly to an explicit message-driven bean that we deploy.

For example, consider the following stateless session bean:

```
@Stateless(name = "MessageSendingEJB")
@Local(MessageSendingBusiness.class)
public class MessageSendingBean implements MessageSendingBusiness
{
   /**
    * Queue we'll send messages to; logical name as wired from
    * the message-destination-link
    */
   @Resource(name = "jms/MessageDestinationLinkQueue")
   // Name to match message-destination-ref-name
   private Queue queue;

   ...
}
```

Session Beans Should Not Receive Messages

Session beans respond to calls from EJB clients, and they cannot be programmed to respond to JMS messages; this is instead the motivation behind the message-driven bean component type. It's impossible to write a session or entity bean that is driven by incoming messages, though it is possible to develop a session bean that can consume a JMS message from a business method; in this case, an EJB client must call the method first. For example, when the business method on a `HypotheticalEJB` is called, it sets up a JMS session and then attempts to read a message from a queue:

```
@Stateless
public class HypotheticalBean implements HypotheticalRemoteBusiness {
    @Resource(mappedName="ConnectionFactory");
    private ConnectionFactory factory;

    @Resource(mappedName="MyQueue")
    private Queue queue;

    public String businessMethod( ) {
        try{
            Connection connect = factory.createConnection( );
            Session session = connect.createSession(true,0);
            MessageConsumer receiver = session.createConsumer(queue);
            TextMessage textMsg = (TextMessage)receiver.receive( );
            connect.close( );
            return textMsg.getText( );
        } catch(Exception e) {
            throws new EJBException(e);
        }
    }
}
```

The message consumer is used to proactively fetch a message from the queue. Although this operation has been programmed correctly, it is dangerous because a call to the `MessageConsumer.receive()` method blocks the thread until a message becomes available. If a message is never delivered, the thread is blocked indefinitely! If no one ever sends a message to the queue, the `MessageConsumer` just sits there waiting, forever.

To be fair, there are other `receive()` methods that are less dangerous. For example, `receive(long timeout)` allows you to specify a time after which the `MessageConsumer` should stop blocking the thread and give up waiting for a message. There is also `receiveNoWait()`, which checks for a message and returns `null` if none is waiting, thus avoiding a prolonged thread block. However, this operation is still dangerous. There is no guarantee that the less risky `receive()` methods will perform as expected, and the risk of programmer error (e.g., using the wrong `receive()` method) is too great.

The moral of the story is simple: don't write convoluted code trying to force session beans to receive messages. If you need to receive messages, use a message-driven bean. MDBs are specially designed to consume JMS messages.

The JMS APIs

We've alluded to some examples of JMS code earlier. Now let's get a better understanding of the underlying mechanics.

TopicConnectionFactory and Topic

In order to send a JMS message, we need a connection to the JMS provider and a destination address for the message. A JMS connection factory makes the connection to the provider possible, and the destination address is identified by a `Topic` object. Both the connection factory and the `Topic` object may be obtained either by using `@javax.annotation.Resource` to inject these objects directly (into a JEE managed object such as an EJB or Servlet) or by using a manual JNDI lookup.

```
@Resource(name="ResourceReferencename")
private TopicConnectionFactory connectionFactory;

@Resource(mappedName="jndiName")  // Non-portable, though some vendors may support
private TopicConnectionFactory connectionFactory;

public TopicConnectionFactory getConnectionFactory()
{
    return javax.naming.Context.lookup("jndiName");
}
```

The `ConnectionFactory` is similar to a `DataSource` in JDBC. Just as the `DataSource` provides a JDBC connection to a database, the `ConnectionFactory` provides a JMS connection to a message router.[*]

The `Topic` object itself represents a network-independent destination to which the message will be addressed. In JMS, messages aren't sent directly to applications; they're sent to topics or queues. A *topic* is analogous to an email list or newsgroup. Any application with the proper credentials can receive messages from and send messages to a topic. When a JMS client receives messages from a topic, the client is said to *subscribe* to that topic. JMS decouples applications by allowing them to send messages to each other through a destination, which serves as a virtual channel. A *queue* is another type of destination that we'll discuss in detail later.

Connection and Session

The `ConnectionFactory` is used to create a `Connection`, which is an actual connection to the JMS provider:

```
Connection connect = connectionFactory.createConnection();
Session session = connect.createSession(true,0);
```

Once you have a `Connection`, you can use it to create a `Session`. A `Session` allows you to group the actions of sending and receiving messages. In this case, you need only a single `Session`. Using multiple `Session`s is helpful if you wish to produce and consume messages in different threads. `Session` objects use a single-threaded model, which prohibits concurrent access to a single `Session` from multiple threads. The thread that creates a `Session` is usually the thread that uses that `Session`'s producers and consumers

---

[*] This analogy is not perfect. One might also say that the `Session` is analogous to the `DataSource`, since both represent transaction-resource connections.

(i.e., `MessageProducer` and `MessageConsumer` objects). If you wish to produce and consume messages using multithreading, you must create a different `Session` object for each thread.

The `createSession()` method has two parameters:

```
createSession(boolean transacted, int acknowledgeMode)
```

The EJB 3.1 specification's Section 13.3.5 stipulates that these arguments are ignored at runtime because the EJB container manages the transaction and acknowledgment mode of any JMS resource obtained from the JNDI ENC. The specification recommends that developers use the arguments `true` for `transacted` and `0` for `acknowledge Mode`, but since they are supposed to be ignored, it should not matter what you use.

It's good programming practice to close a `Connection` after it has been used:

```
Connection connect = factory.createConnection();
... // Do work
connect.close();
```

MessageProducer

The `Session` is used to create a `MessageProducer`, which sends messages from the caller to the destination specified by the `Topic` object. Any JMS clients that subscribe to that topic will receive a copy of the message:

```
MessageProducer producer = session.createProducer(topic);

TextMessage
 textMsg = session.createTextMessage();
textMsg.setText(ticketDescription);
producer.send(textMsg);
```

Message types

In JMS, a message is a Java object with two parts: a *header* and a *message body*. The header is composed of delivery information and metadata, and the message body carries the application data, which can take several forms: text, `Serializable` objects, byte streams, etc. The JMS API defines several message types (`TextMessage`, `MapMessage`, `ObjectMessage`, and others) and provides methods for delivering messages to and receiving from other applications.

For example, we can send a new user registration using a `MapMessage`:

```
User user = getUser(); // Assume we have this from somewhere
...
MessageProducer producer = session.createProducer(topic);
MapMessage mapMsg = session.createMapMessage();
mapMsg.setInt("userId", user.getUserId());
mapMsg.setString("firstname", user.getFirstname());
mapMsg.setString("email", user.getEmail());
producer.send(mapMsg);
```

The attributes of `MapMessage` (`userId`, `firstname`, and `email`) can be accessed by name from those JMS clients that receive it. As an alternative, we could use the `ObjectMessage` type, which would allow us to send the entire `User` object as the message using Java serialization:

```
User user = getUser(); // Assume we have this from somewhere

...
MessageProducer producer = session.createProducer(topic);
ObjectMessage objectMsg = session.createObjectMessage();
ObjectMsg.setObject(user);
producer.send(mapMsg);
```

In addition to `TextMessage`, `MapMessage`, and `ObjectMessage`, JMS provides two other message types: `StreamMessage` and `BytesMessage`. `StreamMessage` can take the contents of an I/O stream as its payload. `BytesMessage` can take any array of bytes, which it treats as opaque data.

Example: The StatusUpdateEJBs

To get a better idea of how JMS is used, we can create a Java application whose sole purpose is to broadcast out a generic status; listeners on the target topic can then take whatever action they'd like. Perhaps one consumer would like to log the status update, while another might act as an adapter to a third-party service such as Facebook or Twitter. The post-conditions are not the concern of the message producer, whose responsibility is fulfilled once the status is published to the target JMS endpoint.

To act as listeners for these updates, we may easily plug in some MDBs as subscribers to the topic.

This example is fully runnable, and it is covered in Appendix E.

JMS application client: Message producer

The application client for unit testing can take the form of any Java class. We use a JUnit test environment.

First, we have a simple value object to encapsulate the status update:

```
public class StatusUpdate
{

   /**
    * Internal status
    */
   private final String status;

   /**
    * Creates a new status update with the specified new status
    *
    * @throws IllegalArgumentException If either the status or username is not
specified
```

```
    */
    public StatusUpdate(final String status) throws IllegalArgumentException
    {
        // Precondition checks
        if (status == null || status.length() == 0)
        {
            throw new IllegalArgumentException("Status must be specified");
        }

        // Set
        this.status = status;
    }

    /**
     * Returns the new status
     * @return the status
     */
    public String getText()
    {
        return status;
    }
}
```

Our client will make use of the JMS and Naming APIs:

```
import javax.jms.Message;
import javax.jms.ObjectMessage;
import javax.jms.Topic;
import javax.jms.TopicConnection;
import javax.jms.TopicConnectionFactory;
import javax.jms.TopicPublisher;
import javax.jms.TopicSession;
import javax.naming.Context;
import javax.naming.InitialContext;
```

And using one method, we can publish to our topic:

```
void publishStatusUpdateToTopic(final StatusUpdate status) throws Exception,
IllegalArgumentException
{
    // Precondition check
    if (status == null)
    {
        throw new IllegalArgumentException("status must be provided");
    }

    // Make a JNDI Naming Context
    final Context namingContext = new InitialContext();  // Vendor-specific
properties required

    // Get the queue from JNDI
    final Topic topic = (Topic) namingContext.lookup("jndiNameOfTargetTopic");

    // Get the ConnectionFactory from JNDI
    final TopicConnectionFactory factory = (TopicConnectionFactory) namingContext
        .lookup("jndiNameOfConnectionFactory");
```

```
    // Make a Connection
    final TopicConnection connection = factory.createTopicConnection();
    final TopicSession sendSession = connection.createTopicSession(false,
TopicSession.AUTO_ACKNOWLEDGE);
    final TopicPublisher publisher = sendSession.createPublisher(topic);

    // Make the message
    final Message message = sendSession.createObjectMessage(status);

    // Publish the message
    publisher.publish(message);
    log.info("Published message " + message + " with contents: " + status);

    // Clean up
    sendSession.close();
    connection.close();
}
```

Here we obtain the TopicConnectionFactory and Topic from the JNDI Context, which is created with vendor-specific properties.

Once the client has the TopicConnectionFactory and Topic, it creates a TopicConnection and a TopicSession; from there we may further create a publisher through which we'll push messages.

It's worth noting that putting all of this logic in one location is guaranteed not to scale. In a real-world scenario, we should set up the session or publisher once and reuse it within the same thread.

Now that we've broadcasted our current status, we should make some listeners to take action.

Create a base listener

Because we'll make a couple of MDBs to listen for status updates, we should centralize some of the logic to extract the contents from the incoming JMS message. For this we declare a class that implements MessageListener:

```
public abstract class StatusUpdateBeanBase implements MessageListener
```

This will contain a contract to be fulfilled by subclasses:

```
/**
 * Updates status to the specified value.
 *
 * @throws IllegalArgumentException If the new status is not specified
 * @throws Exception If an error occured in processing
 */
public abstract void updateStatus(StatusUpdate newStatus) throws IllegalArgument
Exception, Exception;
```

The real meat of this class is done in onMessage, where we unwrap the status and delegate along to updateStatus:

```java
/**
 * {@inheritDoc}
 * @see javax.jms.MessageListener#onMessage(javax.jms.Message)
 */
@Override
public void onMessage(final Message message)
{
    /*
     * Precondition checks
     *
     */
    // Ensure the message is specified
    if (message == null)
    {
        throw new IllegalArgumentException("Message must be specified");
    }

    // Ensure the message is in expected form
    final ObjectMessage objMessage;
    if (message instanceof ObjectMessage)
    {
        objMessage = (ObjectMessage) message;
    }
    else
    {
        throw new IllegalArgumentException("Specified message must be of type " +
ObjectMessage.class.getName());
    }

    // Extract out the embedded status update
    final Serializable obj;
    try
    {
        obj = objMessage.getObject();
    }
    catch (final JMSException jmse)
    {
        throw new IllegalArgumentException(
          "Could not obtain contents of message " + objMessage);
    }

    // Ensure expected type
    final StatusUpdate status;
    if (obj instanceof StatusUpdate)
    {
        status = (StatusUpdate) obj;
    }
    else
    {
        throw new IllegalArgumentException("Contents of message should be of type " +
StatusUpdate.class.getName()
            + "; was instead " + obj);
    }

    // Process the update
```

```
    try
    {
        this.updateStatus(status);
    }
    catch (final Exception e)
    {
        throw new RuntimeException("Encountered problem with processing status upda
te " +
            status, e);
    }
}
```

Now we can make some MDBs to take advantage of the preceding logic, taking more specialized action:

```
@MessageDriven(activationConfig =
{
    @ActivationConfigProperty(propertyName = "destinationType", propertyValue = "java
x.jms.Topic"),
    @ActivationConfigProperty(propertyName = "destination", propertyValue = "nameOfThe
TopicInJndi")})
public class LoggingStatusUpdateMdb extends StatusUpdateBeanBase implements
    MessageListener
{

    /**
     * Logger
     */
    private static final Logger log =
        Logger.getLogger(LoggingStatusUpdateMdb.class.getName());

    /**
     * Logs status out at INFO-level
     */
    @Override
    public void updateStatus(final StatusUpdate newStatus) throws
        IllegalArgumentException, Exception
    {
        // Precondition checks
        if (newStatus == null)
        {
            throw new IllegalArgumentException("status must be specified");
        }

        // Get info
        final String status = newStatus.getText();

        // Log
        log.info("New status received: \"" + status + "\"");
    }
}
```

This simple MDB does nothing more than log out the new status update it has received. The activation configuration properties denote that this listener is for a JMS `Topic` and that the topic can be found in JNDI at the "destination" property value.

Surely we can do something more interesting. Remember that producers don't know or care who is listening to messages sent to a Topic, so we can create another listener and attach it. This one will propagate our status update to another service entirely. Twitter provides an external HTTP-based API, and we'll leverage the Twitter4J library (*http://yusuke.homeip.net/twitter4j/en/index.html*) to access it:

```
@MessageDriven(activationConfig =
{
        @ActivationConfigProperty(propertyName = "destinationType", propertyValue =
"javax.jms.Topic"),
        @ActivationConfigProperty(propertyName = "destination", propertyValue =
"nameOfTheTopicInJndi")})
```

Note that the activation configuration properties are the same as in the logging MDB. We're listening to the same Topic and receiving the same messages:

```
public class TwitterUpdateMdb extends StatusUpdateBeanBase implements Message
Listener
{
    /**
     * Logger
     */
    private static final Logger log = Logger.getLogger(TwitterUpdateMdb.class.get
Name());

    //-------------------------------------------------------------------------||
    // Instance Members -------------------------------------------------------||
    //-------------------------------------------------------------------------||

    /**
     * Underlying client used in updating Twitter by calling upon its API
     */
    private Twitter client;

    //-------------------------------------------------------------------------||
    // Lifecycle --------------------------------------------------------------||
    //-------------------------------------------------------------------------||

    /**
     * Lifecycle start to create the Twitter client from supplied environment
     * properties, if the environment has been configured to do so
     */
    @PostConstruct
    void createTwitterClient()
    {
        // Create the client
        client = new Twitter("username", "password");
        log.info("Created Twitter client " + client);
    }
```

MDBs, like any EJB component type, receive lifecycle events. In this one, we'll initialize the Twitter client:

```
    @Override
    public void updateStatus(final StatusUpdate newStatus)
```

```
         throws IllegalArgumentException, Exception
    {
        if (client == null)
        {
            throw new IllegalStateException("Twitter client has not been initialized
");
        }

        // Extract status
        final String status = newStatus.getText();

        // Update status
        client.updateStatus(status);

    }
}
```

This leaves us with the simple task of using the Twitter client to update the status as detailed in the incoming message.

Further testing

The appendix will explain further some techniques for reliably testing MDBs in both unit and integration environments. The asynchronicity inherent in the message-driven model makes for some interesting challenges in ensuring that our tests work as expected.

## PART III

EJB and Persistence

By now we've explored the various actions we can take within server-side component models. Of course, actions are nothing unless performed by some *thing*, and in EJB we address the nouns of our application via *entity beans*.

An entity is EJB's integration point with Java Persistence, a simple POJO that maps to an underlying relational database. By this mechanism, we're free to deal with objects as we're most comfortable—in Java—and we leave it to the container to translate simple method invocations to the appropriate SQL queries.

Additionally, we can form complex relationships between entity types, allowing us to form an object graph view of a database schema. The focus of entities is again on the ease-of-use provided to us as application developers, and under the hood the container may perform optimizations to keep things running efficiently.

These next chapters detail Java Persistence as it pertains to Enterprise Java Beans.

## CHAPTER 9

Persistence: EntityManager

Persistence is a key piece of the Java EE platform. In older versions of J2EE, the EJB 2.x specification was responsible for defining this layer. In Java EE 5, persistence was spun off into its own specification. Now, in EE6, we have a new revision called the Java Persistence API, Version 2.0, or more simply, JPA.

Persistence provides an ease-of-use abstraction on top of JDBC so that your code may be isolated from the database and vendor-specific peculiarities and optimizations. It can also be described as an object-to-relational mapping engine (ORM), which means that the Java Persistence API can automatically map your Java objects to and from a relational database. In addition to object mappings, this service also provides a query language that is very SQL-like but is tailored to work with Java objects rather than a relational schema.

In short, JPA handles the plumbing between Java and SQL. EJB provides convenient integration with JPA via the *entity bean*.

Entity beans, unlike session and message-driven types, are not server-side components. Instead, they are simple objects whose state can be synchronized with an underlying persistent storage provider. They are created just like any normal instance, typically using the new operator, and have no special APIs that must be implemented by the Entity class.

Much like EJB's server-side types, however, entity beans gain powerful services when used within the context of the container. In the case of persistence, Entity instances may become managed objects under the control of a service called the `javax.persistence.EntityManager`.

In the Java Persistence specification, the `EntityManager` is the central authority for all persistence actions. Because entities are plain Java objects, they do not become persistent until your code explicitly interacts with the `EntityManager` to make them persistent. The `EntityManager` manages the object-relational (O/R) mapping between a fixed set of entity classes and an underlying data source. It provides APIs for creating queries, finding objects, synchronizing, and inserting objects into the database. It also can provide caching and manage the interaction between an entity and transactional services in a Java EE environment such as the Java Transaction API (JTA). The `EntityManager` is well integrated with Java EE and EJB but is not limited to this environment; it also can be used in plain Java programs.

 You can use Java Persistence outside of an application server and in plain Java SE programs.

This chapter focuses on the details of the persistence service and how it can be accessed within Java EE.

Entities Are POJOs

Entities, in the Java Persistence specification, are plain old Java objects (POJOs). You allocate them with the `new()` operator just as you would any other plain Java object. Their state is not synchronized with persistent storage unless associated with an `EntityManager`. For instance, let's look at a simple example of an `Employee` entity:

```java
import javax.persistence.Entity;
import javax.persistence.Id;

/**
 * Represents an Employee in the system.  Modeled as a simple
 * value object with some additional EJB and JPA annotations.
 *
 * @author <a href="mailto:andrew.rubinger@jboss.org">ALR</a>
 * @version $Revision: $
 */
@Entity
// Mark that we're an Entity Bean, EJB's integration point
// with Java Persistence
public class Employee
{

   /**
    * Primary key of this entity
    */
   @Id
   // Mark that this field is the primary key
   private Long id;

   /**
    * Name of the employee
    */
   private String name;
```

```java
/**
 * Default constructor, required by JPA
 */
public Employee()
{

}

/**
 * Convenience constructor
 */
public Employee(final long id, final String name)
{
    // Set
    this.id = id;
    this.name = name;
}

/**
 * @return the id
 */
public Long getId()
{
    return id;
}

/**
 * @param id the id to set
 */
public void setId(final Long id)
{
    this.id = id;
}

/**
 * @return the name
 */
public String getName()
{
    return name;
}

/**
 * @param name the name to set
 */
public void setName(final String name)
{
    this.name = name;
}
```

```
/**
 * {@inheritDoc}
 * @see java.lang.Object#toString()
 */
@Override
public String toString()
{
    return "Employee [id=" + id + ", name=" + name + "]";
}
}
```

If we allocate instances of this Employee class, no magic happens when new() is invoked. Calling the new operator does not magically interact with some underlying service to create the Employee in the database:

```
// This is just an object
Employee hero = new Employee(1L,"Trey Anastasio");
```

Allocated instances of the Customer class remain POJOs until you ask the EntityManager to create the entity in the database.

Managed Versus Unmanaged Entities

Before we can go any deeper into the entity manager service, we need to delve more deeply into the lifecycle of entity object instances. An entity bean instance is either managed (aka attached) by an entity manager or unmanaged (aka detached). When an entity is attached to an EntityManager, the manager tracks state changes to the entity and synchronizes those changes to the database whenever the entity manager decides to flush its state. When an entity is detached, it is unmanaged. Any state changes to an entity that is detached are not tracked by the entity manager.

Persistence Context

A *persistence context* is a set of managed entity object instances. Persistence contexts are managed by an entity manager. The entity manager tracks all entity objects within a persistence context for changes and updates made, and flushes these changes to the database using the flush mode rules discussed later in this chapter. Once a persistence context is closed, all managed entity object instances become detached and are no longer managed. Once an object is detached from a persistence context, it can no longer be managed by an entity manager, and any state changes to this object instance will not be synchronized with the database.

When a persistence context is closed, all managed entity objects become detached and are unmanaged.

There are two types of persistence contexts: transaction-scoped and extended persistence contexts.

Transaction-scoped persistence context

Though we'll discuss transactions in much greater detail in Chapter 17, it's important to be aware of a transaction in simple terms to discuss Entities. For the purposes of this discussion, we may think of a transaction as a set of beginning and end boundaries. Everything executed in between must either fully succeed or fully fail, and state changes made within a transaction are visible elsewhere in the system only when the end boundary completes successfully.

Persistence contexts may live as long as a transaction and be closed when a transaction completes. This is called a *transaction-scoped persistence context*. When the transaction completes, the transaction-scoped persistence context will be destroyed and all managed entity object instances will become detached. Only persistence contexts managed by an application server may be transaction-scoped. In other words, only `EntityManager` instances injected with the `@PersistenceContext` annotation or its XML equivalent may be transaction-scoped.

```
@PersistenceContext(unitName="nameOfThePc")
EntityManager entityManager;

// Assume this method invocation takes place within
// the context of a running Transaction
public Employee getTheWorldsBestGuitarist()
{
    // Trey has key 1 in the DB
    Employee trey = entityManager.find(Employee.class, 1);
    trey.setName("Ernest Joseph Anastasio, III");
    return cust;
}
```

When `getTheWorldsBestGuitarist()` is executed, the EJB container invokes it within the context of a JTA transaction. An `Employee` reference is pulled from the `EntityManager`, and the `setName()` method is used to change the name of the employee. The `Employee` instance that the `EntityManager` returns will remain managed for the duration of the JTA transaction. This means that the change made by calling the `setName()` method will be synchronized with the database when the JTA transaction completes and commits.

The `Employee` instance is also returned by `getTheWorldsBestGuitarist()`. After the JTA transaction completes, the transaction-scoped persistence context is destroyed, and this `Employee` instance is no longer managed. This means that if `setName()` is called after it becomes detached, no changes will be made to any database.

Extended persistence context

Persistence contexts may also be configured to live longer than a transaction. This is called an *extended persistence context*. Entity object instances that are attached to an extended context remain managed even after a transaction is complete. This feature is extremely useful in situations where you want to have a conversation with your database but not keep a long-running transaction, as transactions hold valuable resources such as JDBC connections and database locks. Here's some small pseudocode to illustrate this concept:

```
Employee pageMcConnell = null;

transaction.begin(); // Start Tx 1
// Page has key 2 in the DB
pageMcConnell = extendedEntityManager.find(Employee.class, 2L);
transaction.commit(); // Tx 1 Ends

transaction.begin(); // Start Tx 2
pageMcConnell.setName("Leo!"); // Change Page's name to his nickname
extendedEntityManager.flush(); // Flush changes to the DB manually
// pageMcConnell instance is to remain managed, and changes are flushed
transaction.commit(); // End Tx 2
```

In this example, a local variable, `pageMcConnell`, is initialized by calling the `EntityManager.find()` method in transaction 1. Unlike a transaction-scoped persistence context, the `Employee` instance pointed to by this local variable remains managed. This is because extended persistence context stays alive past the completion of transaction 1. In transaction 2, the employee is updated and the changes are flushed to the database.

Extended persistence contexts may be created and managed by application code, and we'll see examples of this later in this chapter. They can also be created and managed by stateful session beans.

Detached entities

Entity instances become unmanaged and detached when a transaction scope or extended persistence context ends. An interesting side effect is that detached entities can be serialized and sent across the network to a remote client. The client can make changes remotely to these serialized object instances and send them back to the server to be merged back and synchronized with the database.

This behavior is very different from the EJB 2.1 entity model, where entities are always managed by the container. In EJB 2.1, applications using entity beans always had a proxy to the entity bean; in EJB 3.x, we work with concrete instances of plain Java classes. For EJB 2.1 developers, this behavior will seem strange at first, since you are used to the container managing every aspect of the entity. You'll find that after you get used to the new EJB 3.x model, your application code actually shrinks and is easier to manage.

The reason we can eliminate code is very simple to illustrate. EJB 2.1 code often used the Value Object Pattern (often called Data Transfer Objects). The idea of this pattern was that the entity bean exposed a method that copied its entire state into an object that could be serialized to remote clients (like a Swing application) that needed access to the entity's state:

```
// EJB 2.1 Entity bean class
public class CustomerBean implements javax.ejb.EntityBean {

    CustomerValueObject getCustomerVO() {
        return new CustomerValueObject(getFirstName(), getLastName(),
                                getStreet(), getCity(), getState, getZip());
    }
}
```

This is exactly the kind of plumbing we earlier deemed evil when discussing the benefits of using a Container and Application Server. Application code, armed with the right tools, should be free of this kind of error-prone and excessive noise.

Also, it is very expensive to make a remote method call to an entity bean from a client. If the client had to call `getFirstName()`, `getLastName()`, etc., to get information about a customer it was displaying, performance would suffer. This is where the Value Object Pattern came in. EJB 3.x eliminates the need for this pattern because persistent objects become value objects automatically when they are detached from a persistent context. One side effect we encounter in dealing with detached entities revolves around entity relationships, which we'll discuss later.

Packaging a Persistence Unit

An `EntityManager` maps a fixed set of classes to a particular database. This set of classes is called a *persistence unit*. Before you can even think about creating or querying entities with an entity manager, you must learn how to package a persistence unit for use within a Java SE (regular Java application) or Java EE (application server) environment. A persistence unit is defined in a *persistence.xml* file, which is described by the JPA2 specification in section 8.2.1. This file is a required deployment descriptor for the Java Persistence specification. A *persistence.xml* file can define one or more persistence units. The JAR file or directory that contains a *META-INF/persistence.xml* file is called the "root" of the persistence unit, and this may be:

- An EJB JAR file
- The *WEB-INF/classes* directory of a WAR file
- A JAR file in the *WEB-INF/lib* directory of a WAR file
- A JAR file in an EAR library directory
- An application client JAR file

The structure of one of these JAR files may look like the following:

```
/META-INF/
/META-INF/persistence.xml
/org/
/org/example/
/org/example/entity/
/org/example/entity/Employee.class
```

The *persistence.xml* deployment descriptor defines the identities and configuration properties of each persistence unit described within it. Each persistence unit must have an identity, although the empty string is a valid name.

The set of classes that belong to the persistence unit can be specified, or you can opt for the persistence provider to scan the JAR file automatically for the set of classes to deploy as entities. When scanning is used, the persistence provider will look at every class file within the JAR to determine whether it is annotated with the `@javax.persistence.Entity` annotation, and if it is, it will add it to the set of entities that must be mapped.

Each persistence unit is tied to one and only one data source. In Java SE environments, vendor-specific configuration must be used to define and configure these data sources. In Java EE environments, specific XML elements define this association.

The root of the *persistence.xml* XML schema is the `<persistence>` element, which contains one or more `<persistence-unit>` elements. Each `<persistence-unit>` has two attributes: `name` (required) and `transaction-type` (optional). The subelements of `<persistence-unit>` are `<description>` (optional), `<provider>` (optional), `<jta-data-source>` (optional), `<non-jta-data-source>` (optional), `<mapping-file>` (optional), `<jar-file>` (optional), `<class>` (optional), `<properties>` (optional), and `<exclude-unlisted-classes>` (optional).

Here's an example of a *persistence.xml* file:

```
<?xml version="1.0" encoding="UTF-8"?>
<persistence xmlns="http://java.sun.com/xml/ns/persistence"
  xmlns:xsi="http://www.w3.org/2001/XMLSchema-instance"
  xsi:schemaLocation="http://java.sun.com/xml/ns/persistence
    http://java.sun.com/xml/ns/persistence/persistence_2_0.xsd"
  version="2.0">
  <persistence-unit name="nameOfMyPu">
    <jta-data-source>java:/DataSourceNameInJndi</jta-data-source>
    <properties>
      <!-- Standard and Provider-specific config may go here -->
      <property name="myprovider.property.name" value="someValue"/>
    </properties>
  </persistence-unit>
</persistence>
```

The `name` attribute defines the name by which the unit will be referenced. This name is used by injection annotations and XML deployment descriptor elements to reference this unit. This attribute is required.

The `transaction-type` attribute defines whether you want your persistence unit to be managed by and integrated with Java EE transactions (JTA) or you want to use the resource local (`RESOURCE_LOCAL`) `javax.persistence.EntityTransaction` API to manage the integrity of your `EntityManager` instances. This attribute defaults to JTA in Java EE environments and to `RESOURCE_LOCAL` in SE environments.

The `<description>` element is really just a comment describing the given persistence unit and is not required.

The `<provider>` element is the fully qualified name of a class that implements the `javax.persistence.PersistenceProvider` interface. In Java EE and SE environments, the persistence implementation is pluggable: your vendor provides an appropriate implementation. Usually, you do not have to define this element and can rely on the default value.

If you are using JTA or `RESOURCE_LOCAL` persistence units, you will probably define a `<jta-data-source>` or `<non-jta-data-source>` element, respectively. These elements specify a vendor-specific identity of a particular data source. Usually, this string is the global JNDI name for referencing the data source. If neither is defined, then a vendor-provided default will be used.

The `<properties>` element defines the set of vendor-specific attributes passed to the persistence provider. They specify configuration that is specific to a vendor implementation. Since there is no registry or JNDI service within Java SE, this is usually how vendors configure data sources, instead of using the `<jta-data-source>` and `<non-jta-data-source>` elements.

The Persistence Unit Class Set

A persistence unit maps a fixed set of classes to a relational database. By default, if you specify no other metadata within your *persistence.xml* file, the JAR file that contains *persistence.xml* will be scanned from its root for any classes annotated with the `@javax.persistence.Entity` annotation. These classes are added to the set of classes the persistence unit will manage. You can specify additional JARs that you want to be scanned using the `<jar-file>` element. The value of this element is a path relative to the JAR file that contains *persistence.xml*:

```
<persistence>
   <persistence-unit name="nameOfMyPu">
      ...
      <jar-file>../lib/employee.jar</jar-file>
      ...
   </persistence-unit>
</persistence>
```

Scanning JAR files is guaranteed to work in Java EE environments but is not portable in Java SE applications. In theory, it may not be possible to determine the set of JAR files that must be scanned. In practice, however, this is not the case. Whether you do or do not rely on a JAR scan, classes can be listed explicitly with the `<class>` element:

```
<persistence>
    <persistence-unit name="nameOfMyPu">
        ...
        <class>org.example.entity.Employee</class>
        <class>org.example.entity.AnotherEntity</class>
        ...
    </persistence-unit>
</persistence>
```

The `Employee` and `AnotherEntity` classes listed within the `<class>` elements are added to the persistence unit set along with any other classes scanned in the persistence unit's archive. If you do not want the *persistence.xml*'s JAR file to be scanned, then you can use the `<exclude-unlisted-classes>` element.

```
<persistence>
    <persistence-unit name="nameOfMyPu">
        ...
        <exclude-unlisted-classes/>
        ...
    </persistence-unit>
</persistence>
```

The final set of classes is determined by a union of all of the following metadata:

- Classes annotated with `@Entity` in the *persistence.xml* file's JAR file (unless `<exclude-unlisted-classes>` is specified)
- Classes annotated with `@Entity` that are contained within any JARs listed with any `<jar-file>` elements
- Classes mapped in the *META-INF/orm.xml* file if it exists
- Classes mapped in any XML files referenced with the `<mapping-file>` element
- Classes listed with any `<class>` elements

Usually, you will find that you do not need to use the `<class>`, `<jar-file>`, or `<mapping-file>` element. One case where you might need one of these elements is when the same class is being used and mapped within two or more persistence units.

Obtaining an EntityManager

Now that you have packaged and deployed your persistence units, you need to obtain access to an `EntityManager` so that you can persist, update, remove, and query your entity beans within your databases. In Java SE, entity managers are created using a `javax.persistence.EntityManagerFactory`. Although you can use the factory interface in Java EE, the platform provides some additional features that make it easier and less verbose to manage entity manager instances.

EntityManagerFactory

EntityManagers may be created or obtained from an EntityManagerFactory. In a Java SE application, you must use an EntityManagerFactory to create instances of an EntityManager. Using the factory isn't a requirement in Java EE, and we recommend that you don't use it directly from application code.

```
package javax.persistence;

import java.util.Map;
import javax.persistence.metamodel.Metamodel;
import javax.persistence.criteria.CriteriaBuilder;

public interface EntityManagerFactory
{
    public EntityManager createEntityManager();
    public EntityManager createEntityManager(Map map);
    public CriteriaBuilder getCriteriaBuilder();
    public Metamodel getMetamodel();
    public boolean isOpen();
    public void close();
    public Map<String, Object> getProperties();
    public Cache getCache();
    public PersistenceUnitUtil getPersistenceUnitUtil();
}
```

The createEntityManager() methods return EntityManager instances that manage a distinct extended persistence context. You can pass in a java.util.Map parameter to override or extend any provider-specific properties you did not declare in your *persistence.xml* file. When you are finished using the EntityManagerFactory, you should close() it (unless it is injected; we'll discuss this later). The isOpen() method allows you to check whether the EntityManagerFactory reference is still valid.

Getting an EntityManagerFactory in Java EE

In Java EE, it is easy to get an EntityManagerFactory. It can be injected directly into a field or *setter* method of your EJBs using the @javax.persistence.PersistenceUnit annotation:

```
package javax.persistence;

@Target({ TYPE, METHOD, FIELD })
@Retention(RUNTIME)
public @interface PersistenceUnit
{
    String name() default "";

    String unitName() default "";
}
```

The `unitName()` is the identity of the `PersistenceUnit`. When the `PersistenceUnit` is used, it not only injects the `EntityManagerFactory`, it also registers a reference to it within the JNDI ENC of the EJB. (The JNDI ENC is discussed more in Chapter 16.) The EJB container is responsible for noticing the `@PersistenceUnit` annotation and injecting the correct factory:

```java
import javax.persistence.*;
import javax.ejb.*;

@Stateless
public MyBean implements MyBusinessInterface
{
    @PersistenceUnit(unitName="nameOfMyPu")
    private EntityManagerFactory factory1;
    private EntityManagerFactory factory2;

    @PersistenceUnit(unitName="nameOfAnotherPu")
    public void setFactory2(EntityManagerFactory f)
    {
        this.factory2 = f;
    }
}
```

When an instance of the stateless session bean is created, the EJB container sets the factory field to the persistence unit identified by `"nameOfMyPu"`. It also calls the `setFactory2()` method with the `"nameOfAnotherPu"` persistence unit.

In EJB, an injected `EntityManagerFactory` is automatically closed by the EJB container when the instance is discarded. In fact, if you call `close()` on an injected `EntityManagerFactory`, an `IllegalStateException` is thrown.

Obtaining a Persistence Context

A persistence context can be created by calling the `EntityManagerFactory.create` `EntityManager()` method. The returned `EntityManager` instance represents an extended persistence context. If the `EntityManagerFactory` is JTA-enabled, then you have to explicitly enlist the `EntityManager` instance within a transaction by calling the `EntityMan` `ager.joinTransaction()` method. If you do not enlist the `EntityManager` within the JTA transaction, the changes you make to your entities are not synchronized with the database.

 `EntityManager.joinTransaction()` is required to be invoked only when an `EntityManager` is created explicitly using an `EntityManagerFactory`. If you are using EJB container-managed persistence contexts, you do not need to perform this extra step.

Using the `EntityManagerFactory` API is a bit verbose and can be awkward when you are making nested EJB calls, for instance. Fortunately, EJB and the Java Persistence specification are nicely integrated. An `EntityManager` can be injected directly into an EJB using the `@javax.persistence.PersistenceContext` annotation.

```
package javax.persistence;

public enum PersistenceContextType
{
   TRANSACTION,
   EXTENDED
}

public @interface PersistenceProperty
{
   String name();
   String value();
}

@Target({TYPE, METHOD, FIELD})
@Retention(RUNTIME)
public @interface PersistenceContext
{
    String name() default "";
    String unitName() default "";
    PersistenceContextType type() default PersistenceContextType.TRANSACTION;
    PersistenceProperty[] properties() default {};
}
```

The `@PersistenceContext` annotation works in much the same way as `@PersistenceUnit`, except that an entity manager instance is injected instead of an `EntityManagerFactory`:

```
@Stateless
public class MyBean implements MyBusinessInterface
{
   @PersistenceContext(unitName="nameOfMyPu")
   private EntityManager entityManager;
}
```

The `unitName()` attribute identifies the persistence. By default, a transaction-scoped persistence context is injected when using this annotation. You can override this default with the `type()` attribute. When you access this transaction-scoped `EntityManager`, a persistence context becomes associated with the transaction until it finishes. This means that if you interact with any entity managers within the context of a transaction, even if they are different instances that are injected into different beans, the same persistence context will be used.

You must never call `close()` on an injected entity manager. Cleanup is handled by the application server. If you close an entity manager, an `IllegalStateException` is thrown.

An `EXTENDED` entity manager can only be injected into a stateful session bean; stateless session and message-driven beans are pooled, and there would be no way to close the persistence context and release any managed entity instances. In order to obtain an

extended context, a stateful session bean uses the @javax.persistence.Persistence
Context annotation with a type of EXTENDED:

```
@Stateful
public class MyBean implements MyBusinessInterface
{
    @PersistenceContext (unitName="nameOfMyPu", type=PersistenceContextType.EXTENDED)
    private EntityManager manager;
}
```

When this MyBean backing instance is created, a persistence context is also created for
the injected manager field. The persistence context has the same lifespan as the bean.
When the stateful session bean is removed, the persistence context is closed. This
means that any entity object instances remain attached and managed as long as the
stateful session bean is active.

 It is strongly suggested that you use the @PersistenceContext annotation
or the XML equivalent when using Java Persistence with EJBs. These
features were defined to make it easier for developers to interact with
entity beans. Entity managers created using EntityManagerFactory are
more error-prone because the application developer has to worry about
more things. For instance, the developer could forget to close() an entity manager and subsequently leak resources. Take advantage of the
ease-of-use facilities of your EJB container!

Interacting with an EntityManager

Now that you have learned how to deploy and obtain a reference to an entity manager,
you are ready to learn the semantics of interacting with it. The EntityManager API has
methods to insert and remove entities from a database as well as merge updates from
detached entity instances. There is also a rich query API that you can access by creating
query objects from certain EntityManager methods:

```
package javax.persistence;

import java.util.Map;
import javax.persistence.metamodel.Metamodel;
import javax.persistence.criteria.CriteriaBuilder;
import javax.persistence.criteria.CriteriaQuery;

public interface EntityManager
{
    public void persist(Object entity);
    public <T> T merge(T entity);
    public void remove(Object entity);
    public <T> T find(Class<T> entityClass, Object primaryKey);
    public <T> T find(Class<T> entityClass, Object primaryKey,
                      Map<String, Object> properties);
    public <T> T find(Class<T> entityClass, Object primaryKey,
                      LockModeType lockMode);
    public <T> T find(Class<T> entityClass, Object primaryKey,
```

```
                    LockModeType lockMode,
                        Map<String, Object> properties);
    public <T> T getReference(Class<T> entityClass,
                                    Object primaryKey);
    public void flush();
    public void setFlushMode(FlushModeType flushMode);
    public FlushModeType getFlushMode();
    public void lock(Object entity, LockModeType lockMode);
    public void lock(Object entity, LockModeType lockMode,
                    Map<String, Object> properties);
    public void refresh(Object entity);
    public void refresh(Object entity,
                            Map<String, Object> properties);
    public void refresh(Object entity, LockModeType lockMode);
    public void refresh(Object entity, LockModeType lockMode,
                    Map<String, Object> properties);
    public void clear();
    public void detach(Object entity);
    public boolean contains(Object entity);
    public LockModeType getLockMode(Object entity);
    public void setProperty(String propertyName, Object value);
    public Map<String, Object> getProperties();
    public Query createQuery(String qlString);
    public <T> TypedQuery<T> createQuery(CriteriaQuery<T> criteriaQuery);
    public <T> TypedQuery<T> createQuery(String qlString, Class<T> resultClass);
    public Query createNamedQuery(String name);
    public <T> TypedQuery<T> createNamedQuery(String name, Class<T> resultClass);
    public Query createNativeQuery(String sqlString);
    public Query createNativeQuery(String sqlString, Class resultClass);
    public Query createNativeQuery(String sqlString, String resultSetMapping);
    public void joinTransaction();
    public <T> T unwrap(Class<T> cls);
    public Object getDelegate();
    public void close();
    public boolean isOpen();
    public EntityTransaction getTransaction();
    public EntityManagerFactory getEntityManagerFactory();
    public CriteriaBuilder getCriteriaBuilder();
    public Metamodel getMetamodel();
}
```

Example: A Persistent Employee Registry

From our simple Employee entity defined earlier, we can use the EntityManager facilities to perform CRUD (Create, Read, Update, Delete) operations and build a simple persistent registry of employees. The full example is available in greater detail in Appendix F.

A Transactional Abstraction

Before we can take advantage of the EntityManager to flush and synchronize our changes with the database, we must set up a transactional context within which our code can run. Because we're not going to delve into the full features of transactions until later, let's define a simple abstraction that marks the beginning and end of the transactional context.

```
public interface TxWrappingLocalBusiness
{
   **
   * Wraps the specified tasks in a new Transaction
   *
   * @param task
   * @throws IllegalArgumentException If no tasks are specified
   * @throws TaskExecutionException If an error occurred in invoking
   * {@link Callable#call()}
   */
   void wrapInTx(Callable<?>... tasks) throws IllegalArgumentException,
      TaskExecutionException;
}
```

From here we can construct simple java.util.concurrent.Callable implementations that encapsulate our JPA operations, and these will all run within a transaction that starts and ends with the invocation to wrapInTx. Let's assume we have an instance called txWrapper that implements TxWrappingLocalBusiness for us.

Persisting Entities

Persisting an entity is the act of inserting it within a database. We persist entities that have not yet been created in the database. To create an entity, we first allocate an instance of it, set its properties, and wire up any relationships it might have with other objects. In other words, we initialize an entity bean just as we would any other Java object. Once we've done this, we can then interact with the entity manager service by calling the EntityManager.persist() method:

```
// Execute the addition of the employees, and conditional checks,
// in the context of a Transaction
txWrapper.wrapInTx(new Callable<Void>()
{
   @Override
   public Void call() throws Exception
   {
      // Create a few plain instances
      final Employee dave = new Employee(ID_DAVE, NAME_DAVE);
      final Employee josh = new Employee(ID_JOSH, NAME_JOSH);
      final Employee rick = new Employee(ID_RICK, NAME_RICK);

      // Get the EntityManager from our test hook
      final EntityManager em = emHook.getEntityManager();

      // Now first check if any employees are found in the underlying persistent
      // storage (shouldn't be)
      Assert
        .assertNull("Employees should not have been added to the EM yet",
           em.find(Employee.class, ID_DAVE));
```

```
        // Check if the object is managed (shouldn't be)
        Assert.assertFalse("Employee should not be managed yet", em.contains(josh));

        // Now persist the employees
        em.persist(dave);
        em.persist(josh);
        em.persist(rick);
        log.info("Added: " + rick + dave + josh);

        // The employees should be managed now
        Assert.assertTrue(
          "Employee should be managed now, after call to persist",
          em.contains(josh));

        // Return
        return null;
    }
});
```

When this method is called, the entity manager queues the `Employee` instances for insertion into the database, and the objects become managed. When the actual insertion happens depends on a few variables. If `persist()` is called within a transaction, the insert may happen immediately, or it may be queued until the end of the transaction, depending on the flush mode (described later in this chapter). You can always force the insertion manually within a transaction by calling the `EntityManager.flush()` method. You may call `persist()` outside of a transaction only if the entity manager is an `EXTENDED` persistence context. When you call `persist()` outside of a transaction with an `EXTENDED` persistence context, the insert is queued until the persistence context is associated with a transaction. An injected extended persistence context is automatically associated with a JTA transaction by the EJB container. For other extended contexts created manually with the `EntityManagerFactory` API, you must call `EntityManager.joinTransaction()` to perform the transaction association.

If the entity has any relationships with other entities, these entities may also be created within the database if you have the appropriate cascade policies set up. Cascading and relationships are discussed in detail in Chapter 11. Java Persistence can also be configured to automatically generate a primary key when the `persist()` method is invoked through the use of the `@GeneratedValue` annotation atop the primary key field or setter. So, in the previous example, if we had auto key generation enabled, we could view the generated key after the `persist()` method completed.

The `persist()` method throws an `IllegalArgumentException` if its parameter is not an entity type. `TransactionRequiredException` is thrown if this method is invoked on a transaction-scoped persistence context. However, if the entity manager is an extended persistence context, it is legal to call `persist()` outside of a transaction scope; the insert is queued until the persistence context interacts with a transaction.

Finding and Updating Entities

The entity manager provides two mechanisms for locating objects in your database. One way is with simple entity manager methods that locate an entity by its primary key. The other is by creating and executing queries.

find() and getReference()

The `EntityManager` has two different methods that allow you to find an entity by its primary key:

```
public interface EntityManager
{
    <T> T find(Class<T> entityClass, Object primaryKey);
    <T> T getReference(Class<T> entityClass, Object primaryKey);
}
```

Both methods take the entity's class as a parameter, as well as an instance of the entity's primary key. They use Java generics so that you don't have to do any casting. How do these methods differ? The `find()` method returns `null` if the entity is not found in the database. It also initializes the state based on the lazy-loading policies of each property (lazy loading is discussed in Chapter 10).

Once you have located an entity bean by calling `find()`, calling `getReference()`, or creating and executing a query, the entity bean instance remains managed by the persistence context until the context is closed. During this period, you can change the state of the entity bean instance as you would any other object, and the updates will be synchronized automatically (depending on the flush mode) or when you call the `flush()` method directly.

merge()

The Java Persistence specification allows you to merge state changes made to a detached entity back into persistence storage using the entity manager's `merge()` method.

If the entity manager isn't already managing an `Employee` instance with the same ID, a full copy of the parameter is made and returned from the `merge()` method. This copy is managed by the entity manager, and any additional *setter* methods called on this copy will be synchronized with the database when the `EntityManager` decides to flush. The original parameter remains detached and unmanaged.

The `merge()` method will throw an `IllegalArgumentException` if its parameter is not an entity type. The `TransactionRequiredException` is thrown if this method is invoked on a transaction-scoped persistence context. However, if the entity manager is an extended persistence context, it is legal to invoke this method outside of a transaction scope, and the update will be queued until the persistence context interacts with a transaction.

Now we can create a new `Employee` instance with new properties and synchronize this state with persistent storage:

```
// Now change Employee Dave's name in a Tx; we'll verify the changes were flushed
// to the DB later
txWrapper.wrapInTx(new Callable<Void>()
{
    @Override
    public Void call() throws Exception
    {
        // Get an EM
        final EntityManager em = emHook.getEntityManager();

        // Make a new "Dave" as a detached object with same primary key,
        // but a different name
        final Employee dave = new Employee(ID_DAVE, NAME_DAVE_NEW);

        // Merge these changes on the detached instance with the DB
        Employee managedDave = em.merge(dave);

        // Change Dave's name
        dave.setName(NAME_DAVE_NEW);
        log.info("Changing Dave's name: " + dave);

        // That's it - the new name should be flushed to the DB when the Tx completes
        return null;
    }
});
```

In this example, we are creating an `Employee` instance with a primary key ID of `ID_DAVE`. After we've performed this merge with the `EntityManager`, the `dave` instance's state is synced to the DB, and the object returned from the `merge` call is a managed object. Changing his name via a traditional call to the setter method for his name will change the state of this object, and the `EntityManager` will propagate these changes to the database when the transaction completes.

Alternatively, we could have used `EntityManager.find()` to look up `dave` from the DB, and then directly changed the name upon that reference.

`getReference()` differs from `find()` in that if the entity is not found in the database, this method throws a `javax.persistence.EntityNotFoundException` and there is no guarantee that the entity's state will be initialized.

Both `find()` and `getReference()` throw an `IllegalArgumentException` if their parameters are not an entity type. You are allowed to invoke them outside the scope of a transaction. In this case, any object returned is detached if the `EntityManager` is transaction-scoped but remains managed if it is an extended persistence context.

To prove that `dave`'s new name has been persisted, let's look him up again from a new transaction.

```
// Since we've changed Dave's name in the last transaction, ensure that we see the
// changes have been flushed and we can see them from a new Tx.
```

```
txWrapper.wrapInTx(new Callable<Void>()
{
    @Override
    public Void call() throws Exception
    {
        // Get an EM
        final EntityManager em = emHook.getEntityManager();

        // Look up "Dave" again
        final Employee dave = em.find(Employee.class, ID_DAVE);

        // Ensure we see the name change
        Assert.assertEquals("Employee Dave's name should have been changed",
         NAME_DAVE_NEW, dave.getName());

        // Now we'll detach Dave from the EM, this makes the object no longer managed
        em.detach(dave);

        // Change Dave's name again to some dummy value.  Because the object is
        // detached and no longer managed, we should not see this new value
        // synchronized with the DB
        dave.setName("A name we shouldn't see flushed to persistence");
        log.info("Changing Dave's name after detached: " + dave);

        // Return
        return null;
    }
});
```

To illustrate the difference between managed and unmanaged objects, here we manually detach dave from the EntityManager. We can still change his name just as we did before, but now these changes will not be synchronized with the database.

Queries

Persistent objects can also be located by using the JPA Query Language. Unlike EJB 2.1, there are no *finder* methods, and you must create a Query object by calling the EntityManager's createQuery(), createNamedQuery(), or createNativeQuery() methods:

```
public interface EntityManager
{
    public Query createQuery(String qlString);
    public <T> TypedQuery<T> createQuery(CriteriaQuery<T> criteriaQuery);
    public <T> TypedQuery<T> createQuery(String qlString, Class<T> resultClass);
    public Query createNamedQuery(String name);
    public <T> TypedQuery<T> createNamedQuery(String name, Class<T> resultClass);
    public Query createNativeQuery(String sqlString);
    public Query createNativeQuery(String sqlString, Class resultClass);
    public Query createNativeQuery(String sqlString, String resultSetMapping);
}
```

Creating and executing a JPA QL query is analogous to creating and executing a JDBC PreparedStatement:

```
Query query = entityManager.createQuery("from Employee c where id=2");
Employee employee = (Employee)query.getSingleResult();
```

New to JPA2 is the addition of the Criteria API, a fluent expression to programmatically build queries. In many ways this can be more flexible than the string-based JPA QL.

Queries and JPA QL are discussed in Chapter 13.

All object instances returned by find(), getResource(), or a query remain managed as long as the persistence context in which you accessed them remains active. This means that further calls to find() (or whatever) will return the same entity object instance.

Removing Entities

An entity can be removed from the database by calling the EntityManager.remove() method. The remove() operation does not immediately delete the employee from the database. When the entity manager decides to flush, based on the flush rules described later in this chapter, an SQL DELETE is executed:

```
// Uh oh, Rick has decided to leave the company. Let's delete his record.
txWrapper.wrapInTx(new Callable<Void>()
{
    @Override
    public Void call() throws Exception
    {
        // Get an EM
        final EntityManager em = emHook.getEntityManager();

        // Look up Rick
        final Employee rick = em.find(Employee.class, ID_RICK);

        // Remove
        em.remove(rick);
        log.info("Deleted: " + rick);

        // Return
        return null;
    }
});
```

After remove() is invoked, the rick instance will no longer be managed and will become detached. Also, if the entity has any relationships to other entity objects, those can be removed as well, depending on the cascading rules discussed in Chapter 11. The remove() operation can be undone only by recreating the entity instance using the persist() method.

The remove() method throws an IllegalArgumentException if its parameter is not an entity type. The TransactionRequiredException is thrown if this method is invoked on a transaction-scoped persistence context. However, if the EntityManager is an extended persistence context, it is legal to invoke this method outside of a transaction scope, and the remove will be queued until the persistence context interacts with a transaction.

refresh()

If you are concerned that a current managed entity is not up-to-date with the database, then you can use the EntityManager.refresh() method. The refresh() method refreshes the state of the entity from the database, overwriting any changes made to that entity. This effectively reverts any local changes.

If the entity bean has any related entities, those entities may also be refreshed, depending on the cascade policy set up in the metadata of the entity mapping.

The refresh() method throws an IllegalArgumentException if its parameter is not managed by the current entity manager instance. The TransactionRequiredException is thrown if this method is invoked on a transaction-scoped persistence context. However, if the entity manager is an extended persistence context, it is legal to invoke this method outside of a transaction scope. If the object is no longer in the database because another thread or process removed it, then this method will throw an EntityNotFoundException.

contains() and clear()

The contains() method takes an entity instance as a parameter. If this particular object instance is currently being managed by the persistence context, it returns true. It throws an IllegalArgumentException if the parameter is not an entity.

If you need to detach all managed entity instances from a persistence context, you can invoke the clear() method of the EntityManager. Be aware that when you call clear(), any changes you have made to managed entities are lost. It is wise to call flush() before clear() is invoked so you don't lose your changes.

flush() and FlushModeType

When you call persist(), merge(), or remove(), these changes are not synchronized with the database until the entity manager decides to flush. You can force synchronization at any time by calling flush(). By default, flushing automatically happens before a correlated query is executed (inefficient implementations may even flush before *any* query) and at transaction commit time. The exception to this default rule is find(). A flush does not need to happen when find() or getReference() is called, because finding by a primary key is not something that would be affected by any updates.

You can control and change this default behavior by using the `javax.persistence.Flush ModeType` enumeration:

```
public enum FlushModeType
{
    AUTO,
    COMMIT
}
```

`AUTO` is the default behavior described in the preceding code snippet. `COMMIT` means that changes are flushed only when the transaction commits, not before any query. You can set the `FlushModeType` by calling the `setFlushMode()` method on the `EntityManager`.

Why would you ever want to change the `FlushModeType`? The default flush behavior makes a lot of sense. If you are doing a query on your database, you want to make sure that any updates you've made within your transaction are flushed so that your query will pick up these changes. If the entity manager didn't flush, then these changes might not be reflected in the query. Obviously, you want to flush changes when a transaction commits.

`FlushModeType.COMMIT` makes sense for performance reasons. The best way to tune a database application is to remove unnecessary calls to the database. Some vendor implementations will do all required updates with a batch JDBC call. Using `COMMIT` allows the entity manager to execute all updates in one huge batch. Also, an `UPDATE` usually ends up in the row being write-locked. Using `COMMIT` limits the amount of time the transaction holds on to this database lock by holding it only for the duration of the JTA commit.

Locking

The `EntityManager` API supports both read and write locks. Because locking behavior is closely related to the concept of transactions, using the `lock()` method is discussed in detail in Chapter 17.

unwrap() and getDelegate()

The `unwrap()` method allows you to obtain a reference to the underlying persistence provider object that implements the `EntityManager` interface. Most vendors will have API extensions to the `EntityManager` interface that can be executed by obtaining and typecasting this delegate object to a provider's proprietary interface. In theory, you should be able to write vendor-independent code, but in practice, most vendors provide a lot of extensions to Java Persistence that you may want to take advantage of in your applications. The `getDelegate()` method was provided in JPA1; for now, it's recommended that users call `unwrap()`.

## CHAPTER 10

Mapping Persistent Objects

In this chapter, we take a thorough look at the process of developing entity beans—specifically, mapping them to a relational database. A good rule of thumb is that entity beans model business concepts that can be expressed as nouns. Although this is a guideline rather than a requirement, it helps determine when a business concept is a candidate for implementation as an entity bean. In grammar school, you learned that nouns are words that describe a person, place, or thing. The concepts of "person" and "place" are fairly obvious: a person entity might represent a customer or passenger, and a place entity might represent a city or port of call. Similarly, entity beans often represent "things": real-world objects, such as ships and credit cards, and abstractions, such as reservations. Entity beans describe both the state and behavior of real-world objects and allow developers to encapsulate the data and business rules associated with specific concepts; an `Employee` entity encapsulates the data and business rules associated with an employee, for example. This makes it possible for data associated with a concept to be manipulated consistently and safely.

Entities represent data in the database, so changes to an entity bean result in changes to the database. That's ultimately the purpose of an entity bean: to provide programmers with a simpler mechanism for accessing and changing data. It is much easier to change a customer's name by calling `Employee.setName()` than by executing an SQL command against the database. In addition, using entity beans provides opportunities for software reuse. Once an entity bean has been defined, its definition can be used throughout your application in a consistent manner. The concept of an employee, for example, is used in many areas of business, including booking, task assignment, and accounts payable. An `Employee` entity is also a unified model to information and thus ensures that access to its data is consistent and simple. Representing data as entity beans can make development easier and more cost-effective.

When a new entity is created and persisted into the entity manager service, a new record must be inserted into the database and a bean instance must be associated with that data. As the entity is used and its state changes, these changes must be synchronized with the data in the database: entries must be inserted, updated, and removed. The process of coordinating the data represented by a bean instance with the database is called *persistence*.

The Java Persistence specification gave a complete overhaul to entity beans. CMP 2.1 had a huge weakness in that applications written to that specification were completely nonportable between vendors because there was no object-to-relational (O/R) mapping. O/R mapping was completely left to the vendor's discretion. These next chapters focus solely on Java Persistence's object mappings to a relational database. This chapter focuses on basic entity bean mappings to a relational database. Chapter 11 will discuss how entities can have complex relationships to one another and how Java Persistence can map these to your database. Chapter 13 will cover how we interact with entity beans through the Java Persistence Query Language (JPA QL) and Criteria APIs.

The Programming Model

Entities are plain Java classes in Java Persistence. You declare and allocate these bean classes just as you would any other plain Java object. You interact with the entity manager service to persist, update, remove, locate, and query for entity beans. The entity manager service is responsible for automatically managing the entity beans' state. This service takes care of enrolling the entity bean in transactions and persisting its state to the database. We've seen this power in the previous chapter.

The Employee Entity

The `Employee` class is a simple entity bean that models the concept of an employee within a company. Java Persistence is all about relational databases. This section introduces the `Employee` entity's design and implementation. This entity will be refactored in many different ways throughout this chapter so that we can show you the multiple ways in which you can map the entity to a relational database.

The Bean Class

The `Employee` bean class is a plain Java object that you map to your relational database. It has fields that hold state and, optionally, it has *getter* and *setter* methods to access this state. It must have, at minimum, a no-argument constructor (which may be the default, implicit constructor):

```
import javax.persistence.Entity;
import javax.persistence.Id;
/**
 * Represents an Employee in the system.  Modeled as a simple
 * value object with some additional EJB and JPA annotations.
 *
```

```
   * @author <a href="mailto:andrew.rubinger@jboss.org">ALR</a>
   * @version $Revision: $
   */
@Entity
// Mark that we're an Entity Bean, EJB's integration point
// with Java Persistence
public class Employee
{

    /**
     * Primary key of this entity
     */
    @Id
    // Mark that this field is the primary key
    private Long id;

    /**
     * Name of the employee
     */
    private String name;

    /**
     * Default constructor, required by JPA
     */
    public Employee() { }

    /**
     * Convenience constructor
     */
    public Employee(final long id, final String name)
    {
        // Set
        this.id = id;
        this.name = name;
    }

    public Long getId() { return id; }
    public void setId(final Long id) { this.id = id; }
    public String getName() { return name; }
    public void setName(final String name) { this.name = name; }

    @Override
    public String toString()
    {
        return Employee.class.getSimpleName() + " [id=" + id + ", name=" + name + "
]";
    }
}
```

Java Persistence requires only two pieces of metadata when you are creating a persistent class: the `@javax.persistence.Entity` annotation denotes that the class should be mapped to your database, and the `@javax.persistence.Id` annotation marks which property in your class will be used as the primary key. The persistence provider will assume that all other properties in your class will map to a column of the same name and of the same type. The table name will default to the unqualified name of the bean class. Here is the table definition the persistence provider is assuming you are mapping to:

```
create table Employee(
    id long primary key not null,
    name VARCHAR(255)
);
```

The `@javax.persistence.Entity` annotation tells the persistence provider that your class can be persisted:

```
package javax.persistence;

@Target(TYPE) @Retention(RUNTIME)
public @interface Entity
{
    String name() default "";
}
```

The `@Entity` annotation has one `name()` attribute. This name is used to reference the entity within a JPA QL expression. If you do not provide a value for this attribute, the name defaults to the unqualified name of the bean class.

How you apply the `@javax.persistence.Id` annotation determines whether you will use the Java bean style for declaring your persistent properties or whether you will use Java fields. If you place the `@Id` annotation on a *getter* method, then you must apply any other mapping annotations on *getter* and *setter* methods in the class. The provider will also assume that any other *getter* and *setter* methods in your class represent persistent properties and will automatically map them based on their base name and type.

Earlier we placed the `@Id` annotation on a member field of the class. The persistence provider will also assume that any other member fields of the class are also persistent properties and will automatically map them based on their base name and type. Any mapping annotations must be placed on member fields in this example, not on *getter* or *setter* methods. Here, we are really defining the *access type*—that is, whether our relational mappings are defined on the fields or the methods of a class.

XML Mapping File

If you do not want to use annotations to identify and map your entity beans, you can alternatively use an XML mapping file to declare this metadata. By default, the persistence provider will look in the *META-INF* directory for a file named *orm.xml*, or you can declare the mapping file in the `<mapping-file>` element in the *persistence.xml* deployment descriptor.

The mapping file has a top element of `<entity-mappings>`. The `<entity>` element defines the entity class and access type: `PROPERTY` or `FIELD`. The `<id>` element is a subelement of the `<attributes>` element and defines what attribute your primary key is. Like annotated classes, the persistence provider will assume that any other property in your class is a persistent property, and you do not have to explicitly define them.

For brevity, we'll continue to use the annotation-based approach in our examples.

Basic Relational Mapping

A developer can take two directions when implementing entity beans. Some applications start from a Java object model and derive a database schema from this model. Other applications have an existing database schema from which they have to derive a Java object model.

The Java Persistence specification provides enough flexibility to start from either direction. If you are creating a database schema from a Java object model, most persistence vendors have tools that can autogenerate database schemas based on the annotations or XML metadata you provide in your code. In this scenario, prototyping your application is fast and easy, as you do not have to define much metadata in order for the persistence engine to generate a schema for you. When you want to fine-tune your mappings, the Java Persistence specification has the necessary annotations and XML mappings to do this.

If you have an existing database schema, many vendors have tools that can generate Java entity code directly from it. Sometimes, though, this generated code is not very object-oriented and doesn't map to your database very well. Luckily, the Java Persistence specification provides the necessary mapping capabilities to facilitate a solution to this problem.

You will find that your use of annotations and mapping XML will depend on the direction you are coming from. If you are autogenerating your schema from your entity classes, you probably will not need annotations such as @Table and @Column (covered in this chapter), as you will rely on well-defined specification defaults. If you have an existing schema or need to fine-tune the mapping, you may find that more metadata will need to be specified.

Elementary Schema Mappings

Let's assume we don't like the default table and column mappings of our original Employee entity class. Either we have an existing table we want to map to, or our DBA is forcing some naming conventions on us. Let's actually define the relational table we want to map our Employee entity to and use the @javax.persistence.Table and @javax.persistence.Column annotations to apply the mapping.

We want to change the table name and the column names of the id and name properties. We also want name to have a not-null constraint and want to set the VARCHAR length to 20. Let's modify our original Employee entity class and add the mapping annotations:

```
@Entity
@Table(name = "table_employees")
// Explicitly denote the name of the table in the DB
public class EmployeeWithCustomTableAndColumnMetadata
```

```
{
    @Id
    @Column(name="pk_employee_id")
    private Long id;

    @Column(name="employee_name",nullable=false, columnDefinition="integer")
    private String name;
    ...
}
```

@Table

The `@javax.persistence.Table` annotation tells the `EntityManager` service which relational table your bean class maps to. You do not have to specify this annotation if you do not want to, because, again, the table name defaults to the unqualified class name of the bean. Let's look at the full definition of this annotation:

```
package javax.persistence;

@Target({TYPE}) @Retention(RUNTIME)
public @interface Table
{
    String name() default "";
    String catalog() default "";
    String schema() default "";
    UniqueConstraint[] uniqueConstraints() default {};
}
```

The `catalog()` and `schema()` attributes are self-explanatory, as they identify the relational catalog and schema to which the table belongs.

```
public @interface UniqueConstraint
{
    /** Optional; chosen by provider if not specified **/
    String name default "";
    String[] columnNames();
}
```

The `@Table.uniqueConstraints()` attribute allows you to specify unique column constraints that should be included in a generated Data Definition Language (DDL). Some vendors have tools that can create DDLs from a set of entity classes or even provide automatic table generation when a bean is deployed. The `UniqueConstraint` annotation is useful for defining additional constraints when using these specific vendor features. If you are not using the schema generation tools provided by your vendor, then you will not need to define this piece of metadata.

@Column

Using the `@Column` annotation, we set the `name` property's column name to be `employee_name` and not nullable, and we set its database type to be an integer. We also set the `VARCHAR` length to 20. This is often important to save RAM in the database and keep things moving efficiently; if you don't need the extra space, it's a good idea to restrict your field types to take up the least amount of data as possible.

The `@javax.persistence.Column` annotation describes how a particular field or property is mapped to a specific column in a table:

```
public @interface Column
{
    String name() default "";
    boolean unique() default false;
    boolean nullable() default true;
    boolean insertable() default true;
    boolean updatable() default true;
    String columnDefinition() default "";
    String table() default "";
    int length() default 255;
    int precision() default 0;
    int scale() default 0;
}
```

The `name()` attribute obviously specifies the column name. If it is unspecified, the column name defaults to the property or field name. The `table()` attribute is used for multitable mappings, which we cover later in this chapter. The rest of the attributes are used when you are autogenerating the schema from vendor-provided tools. If you are mapping to an existing schema, you do not need to define any of these attributes. The `unique()` and `nullable()` attributes define constraints you want placed on the column. You can specify whether you want this column to be included in `SQL INSERT` or `UPDATE` by using `insertable()` and `updatable()`, respectively. The `columnDefinition()` attribute allows you to define the exact DDL used to define the column type. The `length()` attribute determines the length of a `VARCHAR` when you have a `String` property. For numeric properties, you can define the `scale()` and `precision()` attributes.

Primary Keys

A *primary key* is the identity of a given entity bean. Every entity bean must have a primary key, and it must be unique. Primary keys can map to one or more properties and must map to one of the following types: any Java primitive type (including wrappers), `java.lang.String`, or a primary-key class composed of primitives and/or strings. Let's first focus on simple one-property primary keys.

@Id

The `@javax.persistence.Id` annotation identifies one or more properties that make up the primary key for your table:

```
package javax.persistence;

@Target({METHOD, FIELD}) @Retention(RUNTIME)
public @interface Id
```

```
{
}
```

You can generate the primary key for your entity beans manually or have the persistence provider do it for you. When you want provider-generated keys, you have to use the `@javax.persistence.GeneratedValue` annotation:

```
package javax.persistence;

@Target({METHOD, FIELD}) @Retention(RUNTIME)
public @interface GeneratedValue
{
    GenerationType strategy() default AUTO;
    String generator() default "";
}

public enum GenerationType
{
    TABLE, SEQUENCE, IDENTITY, AUTO
}
```

Persistence providers are required to provide key generation for primitive primary keys. You can define the type of primary generator you would like to have using the **strategy()** attribute. The `GeneratorType.AUTO` strategy is the most commonly used configuration, and it is the default:

```
/**
 * Primary key
 */
@Id
@GeneratedValue
private Long id;
```

Table Generators

The `TABLE` strategy designates a user-defined relational table from which the numeric keys will be generated. A relational table with the following logical structure is used:

```
create table GENERATOR_TABLE
(
    PRIMARY_KEY_COLUMN
    VARCHAR not null,
    VALUE_COLUMN long not null
);
```

The `PRIMARY_KEY_COLUMN` holds a value that is used to match the primary key you are generating for. The `VALUE_COLUMN` holds the value of the counter.

To use this strategy, you must have already defined a table generator using the `@javax.persistence.TableGenerator` annotation. This annotation can be applied to a class or to the method or field of the primary key:

```
@Target({ TYPE, METHOD, FIELD })
@Retention(RUNTIME)
```

```
public @interface TableGenerator {
    String name();
    String table() default "";
    String catalog() default "";
    String schema() default "";
    String pkColumnName() default "";
    String valueColumnName() default "";
    String pkColumnValue() default "";
    int initialValue() default 0;
    int allocationSize() default 50;
    UniqueConstraint[] uniqueConstraints() default { };
}
```

The name() attribute defines the name of the @TableGenerator and is the name referenced in the @Id.generator() attribute. The table(), catalog(), and schema() attributes describe the table definition of the generator table. The pkColumnName() attribute is the name of the column that identifies the specific entity primary key you are generating for. The valueColumnName() attribute specifies the name of the column that will hold the counter for the generated primary key. pkColumnValue() is the value used to match up with the primary key you are generating for. The allocationSize() attribute is how much the counter will be incremented when the persistence provider queries the table for a new value. This allows the provider to cache blocks so that it doesn't have to go to the database every time it needs a new ID. If you are autogenerating this table, then you can also define some constraints using the uniqueConstraints() attribute.

Let's look at how you would actually use this generator on the Employee entity:

```
@Entity
public class Employee implements java.io.Serializable {
    @TableGenerator(name="MY_GENERATOR"
                    table="GENERATOR_TABLE"
                    pkColumnName="PRIMARY_KEY_COLUMN"
                    valueColumnName="VALUE_COLUMN"
                    pkColumnValue="EMPLOYEE_ID"
                    allocationSize=10)
    @Id
  @GeneratedValue (strategy=GenerationType.TABLE, generator="MY_GENERATOR")
    private long id;
    ...
}
```

Now if you allocate and persist() an Employee entity, the id property will be autogenerated when the persist() operation is called.

Sequence Generators

Some RDBMs, specifically Oracle, have an efficient built-in structure to generate IDs sequentially. This is the SEQUENCE generator strategy. This generator type is declared via the @javax.persistence.SequenceGenerator:

```
package javax.persistence;
```

```
@Target({METHOD, TYPE, FIELD}) @Retention(RUNTIME)
public @interface SequenceGenerator {

    String name();
    String sequenceName() default "";
    String catalog() default "";
    String schema() default "";
    int initialValue() default 1;
    int allocationSize() default 50;
}
```

The name() attribute specifies how this @SequenceGenerator is referenced in @Id annotations. Use the sequenceName() attribute to define what sequence table will be used from the database. initialValue() is the first value that will be used for a primary key, and allocationSize() is how much it will be incremented when it is accessed. schema() and catalog(), like their counterparts in @Table, refer to the schema and catalog of the sequence generator, respectively. Let's again look at applying the SEQUENCE strategy on our Employee entity bean:

```
@Entity
@SequenceGenerator(name="EMPLOYEE_SEQUENCE",
    sequenceName="EMPLOYEE_SEQ")
public class Employee implements java.io.Serializable {
  @Id
  @GeneratedValue(strategy=GenerationType.SEQUENCE, generator="EMPLOYEE_SEQUENCE")
  private Long id;
}
```

This example is a little different from our TABLE strategy example in that the generator is declared on the bean's class instead of directly on the property. TABLE and SEQUENCE generators can be defined in either place. As with the TABLE generation type, the primary key is autogenerated when the EntityManager.persist() operation is performed.

Primary-Key Classes and Composite Keys

Sometimes relational mappings require a primary key to be composed of multiple persistent properties. For instance, let's say that our relational model specified that our Employee entity should be identified by both its last name and its Social Security number instead of an autogenerated numeric key. These are called *composite keys*. The Java Persistence specification provides multiple ways to map this type of model. One is through the @javax.persistence.IdClass annotation; the other is through the @javax.persistence.EmbeddedId annotation.

@IdClass

The first way to define a primary-key class (and, for that matter, composite keys) is to use the @IdClass annotation. Your bean class does not use this primary-key class internally, but it does use it to interact with the entity manager when finding a persisted

---

object through its primary key. @IdClass is a class-level annotation and specifies what primary-key class you should use when interacting with the entity manager.

```
@Target(TYPE)
@Retention(RUNTIME)
public @interface IdClass
{
    Class value();
}
```

In your bean class, you designate one or more properties that make up your primary key, using the @Id annotation. These properties must map exactly to properties in the @IdClass. Let's look at changing our Employee bean class to have a composite key made up of last name and Social Security number. First, let's define our primary-key class:

```
import java.io.Serializable;

public class ExternalEmployeePK implements Serializable
{
    private static final long serialVersionUID = 1L;
    private String lastName;
    private Long ssn;

    public String getLastName() { return lastName; }
    public void setLastName(String lastName) { this.lastName = lastName; }
    public Long getSsn() { return ssn; }
    public void setSsn(Long ssn) { this.ssn = ssn; }

    @Override public int hashCode(){ // Assume implemented }
    @Override public boolean equals(Object obj) { // Assume implemented  }

}
```

The primary-key class must meet these requirements:

- It must be Serializable.
- It must have a public no-arg constructor.
- It must implement the equals() and hashCode() methods.

Our Employee bean must have the same exact properties as the ExternalEmployeePK class, and these properties are annotated with multiple @Id annotations:

```
import javax.persistence.Entity;
import javax.persistence.Id;
import javax.persistence.IdClass;

@Entity
@IdClass(ExternalEmployeePK.class)
// Use a composite primary key using a custom PK class
public class Employee
{
    @Id
    private String lastName;
```

```
@Id
private Long ssn;

...
}
```

 Primary-key autogeneration is not supported for composite keys and primary-key classes. You will have to manually create the key values in code.

The primary-key class is used whenever you are querying for the Employee:

```
ExternalEmployeePK pk = new ExternalEmployeePK();
pk.setLastName("Rubinger");
pk.setSsn(100L);
Employee employee = em.find(Employee.class, pk);
```

Whenever you call an EntityManager method such as find() or getReference(), you must use the primary-key class to identify the entity.

@EmbeddedId

A different way to define primary-key classes and composite keys is to embed the primary-key class directly in your bean class. The @javax.persistence.EmbeddedId annotation is used for this purpose in conjunction with the @javax.persistence.Embeddable annotation:

```
package javax.persistence;

public @interface EmbeddedId
{
}
```

```
public @interface Embeddable
{
}
```

When we use an @Embeddable class as the type for our primary key, we mark the property as @EmbeddedId. Let's first see an example of our embeddable primary key type:

```
import java.io.Serializable;

import javax.persistence.Column;
import javax.persistence.Embeddable;
import javax.persistence.EmbeddedId;

@Embeddable
// Flag to JPA that we're intended to be embedded into an Entity
// class as a PK
public class EmbeddedEmployeePK implements Serializable
{
    private static final long serialVersionUID = 1L;
```

```
@Column
private String lastName;

@Column
private Long ssn;

public String getLastName() { return lastName; }
public void setLastName(String lastName) { this.lastName = lastName; }
public Long getSsn() { return ssn; }
public void setSsn(Long ssn) { this.ssn = ssn; }

@Override
public int hashCode() { // Assume this is implemented }
@Override
public boolean equals(Object obj) { // Assume this is implemented }

}
```

We then change our `Employee` bean class to use the `EmbeddedEmployeePK` directly, using the `@EmbeddedId` annotation:

```
@Entity
public class Employee
{
    @EmbeddedId
    private EmbeddedEmployeePK id;
    ...
}
```

The `EmbeddedEmployeePK` primary-key class is used whenever you are fetching the `Employee` using `EntityManager` APIs:

```
// Create the Embedded Primary Key, and use this for lookup
EmbeddedEmployeePK pk = new EmbeddedEmployeePK();
pk.setLastName("Rubinger");
pk.setSsn(100L);

// Now look up using our custom composite PK value class
Employee employee = em.find(Employee.class, pk);
```

Whenever you call an `EntityManager` method such as `find()` or `getReference()`, you must use the primary-key class to identify the entity.

If you do not want to have the `@Column` mappings with the primary-key class, or you just want to override them, you can use `@AttributeOverrides` to declare them directly in your bean class:

```
@Entity
public class Employee implements java.io.Serializable
{
    @EmbeddedId
    @AttributeOverrides({
        @AttributeOverride(name="lastName", column=@Column(name="LAST_NAME")),
        @AttributeOverride(name="ssn", column=@Column(name="SSN"))
    })
    private EmbeddedEmployeePK pk;
```

```
    ...
}
```

The `@AttributeOverrides` annotation is an array list of `@AttributeOverride` annotations. The `name()` attribute specifies the property name in the embedded class you are mapping to. The `column()` attribute allows you to describe the column the property maps to.

Property Mappings

So far, we have only shown how to specify column mappings for simple primitive types. There are still a few bits of metadata that you can use to fine-tune your mappings. In this section, you'll learn more annotations for more complex property mappings. Java Persistence has mappings for JDBC `Blob`s and `Clob`s, serializable objects, and embeddable objects, as well as optimistic concurrency with version properties. We discuss all of these.

@Transient

In our first example of our `Employee` bean class, we showed that the persistence manager would assume that every nontransient property (*getter/setter* or field, depending on your access type) in your bean class is persistent, even if the property does not have any mapping metadata associated with it. This is great for fast prototyping of your persistent objects, especially when your persistence vendor supports autotable generation. However, you may have properties that you don't want to be persistent, and therefore this default behavior is inappropriate. For instance, let's assume we want to express what an employee is currently doing without tying this information to persistent storage. We may very simply declare:

```
/**
 * Description of what the Employee's currently
 * working on.  We don't need to store this in the DB.
 */
@Transient
// Don't persist this
private String currentAssignment;
```

When you annotate a property with `@javax.persistence.Transient`, the persistence manager ignores it and doesn't treat it as persistent.

@Basic and FetchType

The `@Basic` annotation is the simplest form of mapping for a persistent property. This is the default mapping type for properties that are primitives, primitive wrapper types, `java.lang.String`, `byte[]`, `Byte[]`, `char[]`, `Character[]`, `java.math.BigInteger`, `java.math.BigDecimal`, `java.util.Date`, `java.util.Calendar`, `java.sql.Date`, `java.sql.Time`, and `java.sql.Timestamp`. You do not need to tell your persistence manager explicitly that you're mapping a basic property, because it can usually figure out how to map it to JDBC using the property's type:

```
public @interface Basic
{
    FetchType fetch() default EAGER;
    boolean optional() default true;
}

public enum FetchType
{
    LAZY, EAGER
}
```

Usually, you would never annotate your properties with this annotation. However, at times you may need to specify the `fetch()` attribute, which allows you to specify whether a particular property is loaded lazily or eagerly when the persistent object is first fetched from the database. This attribute allows your persistence provider to optimize your access to the database by minimizing the amount of data you load with a query. So, if the `fetch()` attribute is LAZY, that particular property will not be initialized until you actually access this field. All other mapping annotations have this same attribute. The weird thing about the specification, though, is that the `fetch()` attribute is just a hint. Even if you mark the property as LAZY for a @Basic type, the persistence provider is still allowed to load the property eagerly. This is due to the fact that this feature requires class-level instrumentation. It should also be noted that lazy loading is neither really useful nor a significant performance optimization for standard, small objects, as loading these later requires the overhead of more SQL queries. It is best practice to eagerly load basic properties, and lazily load ones that may be large and infrequently accessed.

The `optional()` attribute is useful for when the persistence provider is generating the database schema for you. When this attribute is set to `true`, the property is treated as nullable.

Assuming employees may have a picture associated with their record, we probably don't need this picture all the time. We may lazily load it and allow the property to be nullable:

```
/**
 * Picture of the employee used in ID cards.
 */
@Lob
// Note that this is a binary large object
@Basic(fetch = FetchType.LAZY, optional = true)
// Don't load this by default; it's an expensive operation.
// Only load when requested.
private byte[] image;
```

Because we have a direct byte value here, we must also provide a mapping via the @Lob annotation.

@Lob

Sometimes your persistent properties require a lot of memory. One of your fields may represent an image or the text of a very large document. JDBC has special types for these very large objects. The `java.sql.Blob` type represents binary data, and `java.sql.Clob` represents character data. The `@javax.persistence.Lob` annotation is used to map these large object types. Java Persistence allows you to map some basic types to an `@Lob` and have the persistence manager handle them internally as either a `Blob` or a `Clob`, depending on the type of the property:

```
package javax.persistence;

public @interface Lob
{
}
```

Properties annotated with `@Lob` are persisted in a:

- `Blob` if the Java type is `byte[]`, `Byte[]`, or `java.io.Serializable`
- `Clob` if the Java type is `char[]`, `Character[]`, or `java.lang.String`

@Temporal

The `@Temporal` annotation provides additional information to the persistence provider about the mapping of a `java.util.Date` or `java.util.Calendar` property. This annotation allows you to map these object types to a date, a time, or a timestamp field in the database. By default, the persistence provider assumes that the temporal type is a timestamp:

```
package javax.persistence;

public enum TemporalType
{
   DATE,
   TIME,
   TIMESTAMP
}

public @interface Temporal
{
   TemporalType value() default TIMESTAMP;
}
```

For example, say we want to add the date of hire for an employee. We could add this support like so:

```
/**
 * Date the employee joined the company
 */
@Temporal(TemporalType.DATE)
// Note that we should map this as an SQL Date field;
```

```
        // could also be SQL Time or Timestamp
        private Date since;
```

The `since` property is stored in the database as a `DATE` SQL type.

@Enumerated

The `@Enumerated` annotation maps Java `enum` types to the database.

```
        package javax.persistence;

        public enum EnumType
        {
            ORDINAL,
            STRING
        }

        public @interface Enumerated
        {
            EnumTypes value() default ORDINAL;
        }
```

A Java `enum` property can be mapped either to the string representation or to the numeric ordinal number of the enum value. For example, let's say we want an `Employee` entity property that designates the kind of employee: manager or peon. This could be represented in a Java `enum` like so:

```
        public enum EmployeeType {
            MANAGER, PEON;
        }

        @Entity
        public class Employee
        {
            /**
             * Type of employee
             */
            @Enumerated(EnumType.STRING)
            // Show that this is an enumerated value, and the value to
            // be put in the DB is the value of the enumeration toString().
            private EmployeeType type;
        }
```

You are not required to use the `@Enumerated` annotation to map a property. If you omit this annotation, the `ORDINAL` EnumType value is assumed.

@Embedded Objects

The Java Persistence specification allows you to embed nonentity Java objects within your entity beans and map the properties of this embedded value object to columns within the entity's table. These objects do not have any identity, and they are owned exclusively by their containing entity bean class. The rules are very similar to the

`@EmbeddedId` primary-key example given earlier in this chapter. We first start out by defining our embedded object:

```
@Embeddable
public class Address implements java.io.Serializable
{
    private String street;
    private String city;
    private String state;

    public String getStreet() { return street; }
    public void setStreet(String street) { this.street = street; }
    public String getCity() { return city; }
    public void setCity(String city) { this.city = city; }
    public String getState() { return state; }
    public void setState(String state) { this.state = state; }
}
```

The embedded `Address` class has the `@Column` mappings defined directly within it. Next, let's use the `@javax.persistence.Embedded` annotation within our `Employee` bean class to embed an instance of this `Address` class:

```
package javax.persistence;

public @interface Embedded {}
```

As with `@EmbeddedId`, the `@Embedded` annotation can be used in conjunction with the `@AttributeOverrides` annotation if you want to override the column mappings specified in the embedded class. The following example shows how this overriding is done. If you don't want to override, leave out the `@AttributeOverrides`:

```
@Entity
@Table(name="table_employees"
public class Customer implements java.io.Serializable
{
    ...
    private Address address;
    ...
    @Embedded
 @AttributeOverrides({
  @AttributeOverride (name="street", column=@Column(name="employee_street")),
  @AttributeOverride(name="city", column=@Column(name="employee_city")),
  @AttributeOverride(name="state", column=@Column(name="employee_state"))
})
    public Address getAddress() {
        return address;
    }
...
}
```

In this example, we map the `Address` class properties to columns in `table_employees`. If you do not specify the `@Embedded` annotation and the `Address` class is serializable, then the persistence provider would assume that this was a `@Lob` type and serialize it as a byte stream to the column.

That's about it for basic property mappings. In the next chapter, we discuss how to map complex relationships between entity beans.

## CHAPTER 11

Entity Relationships

Chapter 10 covered basic persistence mappings, including various ways to define primary keys as well as simple and complex property-type mappings. This chapter retools our employee registry a bit further by discussing the relationships between entities.

In order to model real-world business concepts, entity beans must be capable of forming relationships. For instance, an employee may have an address; we'd like to form an association between the two in our database model. The address could be queried and cached like any other entity, yet a close relationship would be forged with the `Employee` entity. Entity beans can also have one-to-many, many-to-one, and many-to-many relationships. For example, the `Employee` entity may have many phone numbers, but each phone number belongs to only one employee (a one-to-many relationship). Similarly, an employee may belong to many teams within his or her organization, and teams may have any number of employees (a many-to-many relationship).

The Seven Relationship Types

Seven types of relationships can exist between entity beans. There are four types of cardinality: *one-to-one*, *one-to-many*, *many-to-one*, and *many-to-many*. In addition, each relationship can be either *unidirectional* or *bidirectional*. These options seem to yield eight possibilities, but if you think about it, you'll realize that one-to-many and many-to-one bidirectional relationships are actually the same thing. Thus, there are only seven distinct relationship types. To understand relationships, it helps to think about some simple examples:

One-to-one unidirectional
    The relationship between an employee and an address. You clearly want to be able to look up an employee's address, but you probably don't care about looking up an address's employee.

One-to-one bidirectional
    The relationship between an employee and a computer. Given an employee, we'll need to be able to look up the computer ID for tracing purposes. Assuming the

computer is in the tech department for servicing, it's also helpful to locate the employee when all work is completed.

One-to-many unidirectional

The relationship between an employee and a phone number. An employee can have many phone numbers (business, home, cell, etc.). You might need to look up an employee's phone number, but you probably wouldn't use one of those numbers to look up the employee.

One-to-many bidirectional

The relationship between an employee (manager) and direct reports. Given a manager, we'd like to know who's working under him or her. Similarly, we'd like to be able to find the manager for a given employee. (Note that a many-to-one bidirectional relationship is just another perspective on the same concept.)

Many-to-one unidirectional

The relationship between a customer and his or her primary employee contact. Given a customer, we'd like to know who's in charge of handling the account. It might be less useful to look up all the accounts a specific employee is fronting, although if you want this capability you can implement a many-to-one bidirectional relationship.

Many-to-many unidirectional

The relationship between employees and tasks to be completed. Each task may be assigned to a number of employees, and employees may be responsible for many tasks. For now we'll assume that given a task we need to find its related employees, but not the other way around. (If you think you need to do so, implement it as a bidirectional relationship.)

Many-to-many bidirectional

The relationship between an employee and the teams to which he or she belongs. Teams may also have many employees, and we'd like to do lookups in both directions.

Note that these relations represent the navigability of your domain model. Using JPA QL or the Criteria API (covered in Chapter 13), you'll be able to return even an unmapped association (for example, return the tasks for a given employee even if the association has been mapped as many-to-one unidirectional). Once again, the associations defined in the metadata represent the domain object navigation only.

In this chapter, we discuss how to specify relationships by applying annotations to your related entity beans. We also discuss several different common database schemas, and you will learn how to map them to your annotated relationships.

One-to-One Unidirectional Relationship

An example of a one-to-one unidirectional relationship is one between our Employee entity and an Address. In this instance, each employee has exactly one address, and each address has exactly one employee. Which bean references which determines the direction of navigation. While the Employee has a reference to the Address, the Address doesn't reference the Employee. The relationship is therefore unidirectional; you can only go from the employee to the address, not the other way around through object navigation. In other words, an Address entity has no idea who owns it. Figure 11-1 shows this relationship.

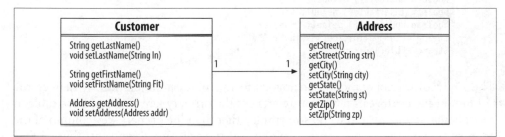

Figure 11-1. One-to-one unidirectional relationship

Relational database schema

One-to-one unidirectional relationships normally use a fairly typical relational database schema in which one table contains a foreign key (pointer) to another table. In this case, the Employee table contains a foreign key to the Address table, but the Address table doesn't contain a foreign key to the Employee table. This allows records in the Address table to be shared by other tables, a scenario explored in "Many-to-Many Unidirectional Relationship" on page 187.

Programming model

In unidirectional relationships (navigated only one way), one of the entity beans defines a property that lets it get or set the other bean in the relationship. Thus, inside the Employee class, you can call the getAddress()/setAddress() methods to access the Address entity, but there are no methods inside the Address class to access the Employee. Let's look at how we would mark up the Employee bean class to implement this one-to-one relationship to Address:

```
/**
 * The employee's address
 */
@OneToOne
@JoinColumn(name="ADDRESS_ID")
// Unidirectional relationship
private Address address;
```

A one-to-one relationship is specified using the @javax.persistence.OneToOne annotation and is mapped with the @javax.persistence.JoinColumn annotation. Let's first look at the @JoinColumn annotation:

```
package javax.persistence;

@Target({METHOD, FIELD})
@Retention(RUNTIME)
public @interface JoinColumn
{
    String name() default "";
    String referencedColumnName() default "";
    boolean unique() default false;
    boolean nullable() default true;
    boolean insertable() default true;
    boolean updatable() default true;
    String columnDefinition() default "";
    String table() default "";
}
```

The @JoinColumn annotation is analogous to the @Column annotation. It defines the column in the Employee's table that references the primary key of the Address table in the schema. If you are joining on something other than the primary-key column of the Address table, then you must use the referencedColumnName() attribute. This referencedColumnName() must be unique, since this is a one-to-one relationship.

If you need to map a one-to-one relationship in which the related entity has a composite primary key, use the @JoinColumns annotation to define multiple foreign-key columns:

```
public @interface @JoinColumns
{
    JoinColumn[] value();
}
```

Now let's learn about the @OneToOne annotation:

```
package javax.persistence;

@Target({METHOD, FIELD})
@Retention(RUNTIME)
public @interface OneToOne
{
    Class targetEntity() default void.class;
    CascadeType[] cascade() default {};
    FetchType fetch() default EAGER;
    boolean optional() default true;
    String mappedBy() default "";
    boolean orphanRemoval() default false;
}
```

The targetEntity() attribute represents the entity class you have a relationship to. Usually, you do not have to initialize this attribute, as the persistence provider can figure out the relationship you are setting up from the property's type.

The fetch() attribute works the same as we described in Chapter 10. It allows you to specify whether you want the association to be lazily or eagerly loaded. In Chapter 13, we'll show you how you can eagerly fetch a relationship with JPA QL or the Criteria API, even when you have marked the FetchType as LAZY.

The optional() attribute specifies whether this relationship can be null. If this is set to false, then a non-null relationship must exist between the two entities.

The cascade() attribute is a bit complicated. We'll discuss it later in this chapter, as all relationship types have this attribute.

The mappedBy() attribute is for bidirectional relationships and is discussed in the next section.

The orphanRemoval() attribute is new to JPA 2.0, and defines whether removing the relationship should also result in a removal of the referred entity.

Primary-key join columns

Sometimes the primary keys of the two related entities are used instead of a specific join column. In this case, the primary keys of the related entities are identical, and there is no need for a specific join column.

In this mapping scenario, you are required to use an alternative annotation to describe the mapping—@javax.persistence.PrimaryKeyJoinColumn:

```
public @interface PrimaryKeyJoinColumn
{
    String name() default "";
    String referencedColumnName() default "";
    String columnDefinition() default "";
}
```

The name() attribute refers to the primary-key column name of the entity the annotation is applied to. Unless your entity has a composite primary key, you can leave this blank and the persistence provider will figure it out.

The referencedColumnName() is the column to join to on the related entity. If this is left blank, it is assumed that the related entity's primary key will be used.

The columnDefinition() is used when the persistence provider is generating schema, and its value will specify the SQL type of the referencedColumnName().

If the primary-key join in question is of a composite nature, then the @javax.persistence.PrimaryKeyJoinColumns annotation is available to you:

```
public @interface PrimaryKeyJoinColumns
{
    PrimaryKeyJoinColumn[] value();
}
```

So, we could use this annotation to map the `Employee`/`Address` entities' one-to-one relationship:

```
@OneToOne(cascade={CascadeType.ALL})
@PrimaryKeyJoinColumn
private Address address;
```

Since we're joining on the primary keys of the `Employee` and `Address` entities and they are not composite keys, we can simply annotate the address property of `Employee` with the defaulted `@PrimaryKeyJoinColumn` annotation.

Default relationship mapping

If your persistence provider supports auto schema generation, you do not need to specify metadata such as `@JoinColumn` or `@PrimaryKeyJoinColumn`. Auto schema generation is great when you are doing fast prototypes:

```
@OneToOne
private Address address;
```

When you do not specify any database mapping for a unidirectional one-to-one relationship, the persistence provider will generate the necessary foreign-key mappings for you. In our employee/address relationship example, the following tables would be generated:

```
CREATE TABLE "PUBLIC"."EMPLOYEE"
(
    ID bigint PRIMARY KEY NOT NULL,
    ADDRESS_ID bigint
)
;

ALTER TABLE "PUBLIC"."EMPLOYEE"
ADD CONSTRAINT FK4AFD4ACEE5310533
FOREIGN KEY (ADDRESS_ID)
REFERENCES "PUBLIC"."ADDRESS"(ADDRESS_ID)
;
```

For unidirectional one-to-one relationships, the default mapping creates a foreign-key column named from a combination of the property you are mapping followed by an _ (underscore) character concatenated with the primary-key column name of the referenced table.

One-to-One Bidirectional Relationship

We can expand our `Employee` entity to include a reference to a `Computer` entity, which models the associate's company-provided computer. The employee will maintain a reference to his or her computer, and the computer will maintain a reference back to the employee. This makes good sense, since we may need to know the owner of a computer.

Relational database schema

The `Computer` has a corresponding `COMPUTER` table, which will contain a pointer to its `Employee` owner:

```
CREATE TABLE "PUBLIC"."COMPUTER"
(
    ID bigint PRIMARY KEY NOT NULL,
    MAKE varchar,
    MODEL varchar,
    OWNER_ID bigint
)
;
ALTER TABLE "PUBLIC"."COMPUTER"
ADD CONSTRAINT FKE023E33B5EAFBFC
FOREIGN KEY (OWNER_ID)
REFERENCES "PUBLIC"."EMPLOYEE"(OWNER_ID)
;
```

One-to-one bidirectional relationships may model relational database schemas in the same way as our one-to-one unidirectional relationship, in which one of the tables holds a foreign key that references the other. Remember that in a relational database model, there is no such notion of directionality, so the same database schema will be used for both unidirectional and bidirectional object relationships.

To model the relationship between the `Employee` and `Computer` entities, we need to declare a relationship property named `owner` in the `Computer` bean class:

```
@Entity
public class Computer
{
  ...
    @OneToOne
    // Bidirectional relationship, mappedBy
    // is declared on the non-owning side
    private Employee owner;
  ...
}
```

Similarly, the `Employee` class will have a reference to the `Computer`:

```
/**
 * The employee's computer
 */
@OneToOne(mappedBy = "owner")
// Bidirectional relationship
private Computer computer;
```

The `mappedBy()` attribute is new here. This attribute sets up the bidirectional relationship and tells the persistence manager that the information for mapping this relationship to our tables is specified in the `Computer` bean class, specifically to the `owner` property of `Computer`.

Here is an example for setting up a bidirectional relationship:

```
// Create a new Computer
final Computer computer = new Computer();
computer.setMake("Computicorp");
computer.setModel("ZoomFast 100");

// Create a new Employee
final Employee carloDeWolf = new Employee("Carlo de Wolf");

// Persist; now we have managed objects
EntityManager em = null;  // Assume we have this
em.persist(carloDeWolf);
em.persist(computer);

// Associate *both* sides of a bidirectional relationship
carloDeWolf.setComputer(computer);
computer.setOwner(carloDeWolf);
```

We have the `cascade()` attribute set to empty, so we must perform the association after each object is persisted and therefore managed. When we discuss cascading operations, you will see that there are ways to persist unmanaged objects as part of an association automatically.

There are some peculiarities with bidirectional relationships. With all bidirectional relationship types, including one-to-one, there is always the concept of an *owning* side of the relationship. Although a `setOwner()` method is available in the `Computer` bean class, it will not cause a change in the persistent relationship if we set it. When we marked the `@OneToOne` relationship in the `Employee` bean class with the `mappedBy()` attribute, this designated the `Employee` entity as the *inverse* side of the relationship. This means that the `Computer` entity is the *owning* side of the relationship.

 Always wire both sides of a bidirectional relationship when modifying relationships. Entities are like any other Java object that has an association to another object. You have to set the values of both sides of the relationship in memory for the relationship to be updated.

If the employee broke his computer, you would have to set the relationship to null on both sides and then remove the `Computer` entity from the database.

One-to-Many Unidirectional Relationship

Entity beans can also maintain relationships with multiplicity. This means one entity bean can aggregate or contain many other entity beans. For example, an employee may have relationships with many phones, each of which represents a phone number. This is very different from simple one-to-one relationships—or, for that matter, from multiple one-to-one relationships with the same type of bean. One-to-many and many-to-many relationships require the developer to work with a collection of references instead of a single reference when accessing the relationship field.

Relational database schema

To illustrate a one-to-many unidirectional relationship, we will use a new entity bean, the Phone, for which we must define a table, the PHONE table:

```
CREATE TABLE "PUBLIC"."PHONE"
(
    ID bigint PRIMARY KEY NOT NULL,
    NUMBER varchar,
    TYPE varchar
)
;
```

This is modeled as a simple Phone class:

```
@Entity
public class Phone
{
    ...
    /**
     * Phone number
     */
    private String number;
    ...
}
```

One-to-many unidirectional relationships between the EMPLOYEE and PHONE tables could be implemented in a variety of ways. For this example, we have chosen to introduce a new table, a join table, to map phones to employees:

```
CREATE TABLE "PUBLIC"."EMPLOYEE_PHONE"
(
    EMPLOYEE_ID bigint NOT NULL,
    PHONES_ID bigint NOT NULL
)
;
ALTER TABLE "PUBLIC"."EMPLOYEE_PHONE"
ADD CONSTRAINT FK1E56289D581FE7C
FOREIGN KEY (PHONES_ID)
REFERENCES "PUBLIC"."PHONE"(PHONES_ID)
;
ALTER TABLE "PUBLIC"."EMPLOYEE_PHONE"
ADD CONSTRAINT FK1E56289DD9454221
FOREIGN KEY (EMPLOYEE_ID)
REFERENCES "PUBLIC"."EMPLOYEE"(EMPLOYEE_ID)
;
```

Likewise, we can introduce a link from Employee to obtain a collection of Phones:

```
/**
 * All {@link Phone}s for this {@link Employee}
 */
@OneToMany
// Unidirectional relationship
private Collection<Phone> phones;
```

Our database schema illustrates that the structure and relationships of the actual database can differ from the relationships as defined in the programming model. In this case, the relationship in the object model is inferred from the reference Employee has to a Collection of Phones, but the database contains a join table. When you are dealing with legacy databases (i.e., databases that were established before the EJB application), it's important to have the mapping options JPA affords so that the object model is not dictated by the schema.

Programming model

You declare one-to-many relationships using the @javax.persistence.OneToMany annotation:

```
package javax.persistence;

@Target({METHOD, FIELD})
@Retention(RUNTIME)
public @interface OneToMany
{
    Class targetEntity() default void.class;
    CascadeType[] cascade() default {};
    FetchType fetch() default LAZY;
    String mappedBy() default "";
    boolean orphanRemoval() default false;
}
```

The attribute definitions are pretty much the same as those for the @OneToOne annotation.

In the programming model, we represent multiplicity by defining a relationship property that can point to many entity beans and annotating it with @OneToMany. To hold this type of data, we'll employ some data structures from the java.util package: Collection, List, Map, and Set. The Collection maintains a homogeneous group of entity object references, which means that it contains many references to one kind of entity bean. The Collection type may contain duplicate references to the same entity bean, and the Set type may not.

To illustrate how an entity bean uses a collection-based relationship, let's look at some code that interacts with the EntityManager:

```
// Create an Employee
final Employee jaikiranPai = new Employee("Jaikiran Pai");

// Create a couple Phones
final Phone phone1 = new Phone("800-USE-EJB3");
final Phone phone2 = new Phone("8675309");

// Persist
final EntityManager em = null; // Assume we have this
em.persist(jaikiranPai);
em.persist(phone1);
em.persist(phone2);
```

```
// Associate
jaikiranPai.getPhones().add(phone1);
jaikiranPai.getPhones().add(phone2);
```

If you need to remove a Phone from the relationship, you need to remove the Phone from both the collection and the database:

```
jaikiranPai.getPhones().remove(phone1);
em.remove(phone1);
```

Removing the Phone from the Employee's collection does not remove the Phone from the database. You have to delete the Phone explicitly; otherwise, it will be orphaned. The orphanRemoval attribute of @OneToMany may remove the orphaned phone automatically if set to true.

Many-to-One Unidirectional Relationship

Many-to-one unidirectional relationships result when many entity beans reference a single entity bean, but the referenced entity bean is unaware of the relationship. In our example company, we have a series of Customers who are each assigned to an Employee who is the primary contact for the customer account. An Employee may be the point person for many Customers, but the relationship will be one-way; customers will know who their primary contact is, but Employees will not refer to all of their Customers.

Relational database schema

Here we introduce a CUSTOMER table to model our customers:

```
CREATE TABLE "PUBLIC"."CUSTOMER"
(
    ID bigint PRIMARY KEY NOT NULL,
    NAME varchar,
    PRIMARYCONTACT_ID bigint
)
;
ALTER TABLE "PUBLIC"."CUSTOMER"
ADD CONSTRAINT FK27FBE3FE9BACAAF1
FOREIGN KEY (PRIMARYCONTACT_ID)
REFERENCES "PUBLIC"."EMPLOYEE"(PRIMARYCONTACT_ID)
;
```

Programming model

Many-to-one relationships are described with the @javax.persistence.ManyToOne annotation:

```
public @interface ManyToOne
{
    Class targetEntity() default void.class;
    CascadeType[] cascade() default {};
    FetchType fetch() default EAGER;
```

```
    boolean optional() default true;
}
```

The attribute definitions are pretty much the same as those for the @OneToOne annotation.

The programming model is quite simple for our relationship. We add a primaryContact property to our Customer entity bean class and annotate it with the @ManyToOne annotation:

```
@Entity
public class Customer
{
    ...
    /**
     * The primary {@link Employee} contact for this {@link Customer}
     */
    @ManyToOne
    // Unidirectional
    private Employee primaryContact;
    ...
}
```

The relationship between the Employee and Customer entities is unidirectional, so the Employee bean class doesn't define any relationship back to the Customer.

All of this should be mundane to you now. The impact of exchanging Employee references between Customer entities works just as we've seen with the previous relationship types.

One-to-Many Bidirectional Relationship

One-to-many and many-to-one bidirectional relationships sound like they're different, but they're not. A one-to-many bidirectional relationship occurs when one entity bean maintains a collection-based relationship property with another entity bean, and each entity bean referenced in the collection maintains a single reference back to its aggregating bean. For example, in our company an employee has a manager, and likewise a manager has many direct reports. The relationship is a one-to-many bidirectional relationship from the perspective of the manager (an Employee) and a many-to-one bidirectional relationship from the perspective of the report (also an Employee). For fun's sake, let's label "reports" in this sense as "peons." This becomes an interesting exercise as well, because it shows that relationships may exist within a single entity type.

Relational database schema

First, we need to equip our EMPLOYEE table with the support necessary to model the manager/peon relationship:

```
CREATE TABLE "PUBLIC"."EMPLOYEE"
(
    ID bigint PRIMARY KEY NOT NULL,
```

```
    NAME varchar,
    MANAGER_ID bigint
)
;
ALTER TABLE "PUBLIC"."EMPLOYEE"
ADD CONSTRAINT FK4AFD4ACE378204C2
FOREIGN KEY (MANAGER_ID)
REFERENCES "PUBLIC"."EMPLOYEE"(MANAGER_ID)
;
```

Now each `Employee` has a reference to his or her manager.

Programming model

Because this is a bidirectional relationship, the manager knows his or her reports, and also his or her own manager. The `Employee` class may therefore contain:

```
/**
 * Manager of the {@link Employee}
 */
@ManyToOne
private Employee manager;

/**
 * {@link Employee}s reporting to this {@link Employee}
 */
@OneToMany(mappedBy = "manager")
private Collection<Employee> peons;
```

The entire relationship here is contained within the `Employee` class. As with all bidirectional relationships, the inverse side specifies `mappedBy` to indicate the property to act as the owning side.

Java Persistence currently requires that the many-to-one side always be the owner. This may seem very confusing, but if you obey the cardinal rule of always wiring both sides of a relationship, then you will have no problems.

 Always wire both sides of a bidirectional relationship in your Java code.

Usage

Client usage is as we've seen before:

```
// Create a few Employees
final Employee alrubinger = new Employee("Andrew Lee Rubinger");
final Employee carloDeWolf = new Employee("Carlo de Wolf - SuperLead!");
final Employee jaikiranPai = new Employee("Jaikiran Pai");
final Employee bigD = new Employee("Big D");

// Persist
em.persist(jaikiranPai);
```

```
em.persist(alrubinger);
em.persist(carloDeWolf);
em.persist(bigD);

// Associate *both* sides of the bidirectional relationship
final Collection<Employee> peonsOfD = bigD.getPeons();
peonsOfD.add(alrubinger);
peonsOfD.add(carloDeWolf);
peonsOfD.add(jaikiranPai);
alrubinger.setManager(bigD);
carloDeWolf.setManager(bigD);
jaikiranPai.setManager(bigD);
```

Many-to-Many Bidirectional Relationship

Many-to-many bidirectional relationships occur when many beans maintain a collection-based relationship property with another bean, and each bean referenced in the collection maintains a collection-based relationship property back to the aggregating beans. For example, in our example company every Employee may belong to many Teams, and each Team may be composed of many Employees.

Relational database schema

The EMPLOYEE and TEAM tables may be fairly simple, and neither will have a direct reference to the other:

```
CREATE TABLE "PUBLIC"."TEAM"
(
    ID bigint PRIMARY KEY NOT NULL,
    NAME varchar
)
;
CREATE TABLE "PUBLIC"."EMPLOYEE"
(
    ID bigint PRIMARY KEY NOT NULL,
    NAME varchar
)
;
```

Again, we use a join table to establish a many-to-many bidirectional relationship, and we'll call this the TEAM_EMPLOYEE table. Here we maintain two foreign key columns—one for the EMPLOYEE table and another for the TEAM table:

```
CREATE TABLE "PUBLIC"."TEAM_EMPLOYEE"
(
    TEAMS_ID bigint NOT NULL,
    MEMBERS_ID bigint NOT NULL
)
;
ALTER TABLE "PUBLIC"."TEAM_EMPLOYEE"
ADD CONSTRAINT FKA63C2502B25E948
FOREIGN KEY (TEAMS_ID)
REFERENCES "PUBLIC"."TEAM"(TEAMS_ID)
```

```
;
ALTER TABLE "PUBLIC"."TEAM_EMPLOYEE"
ADD CONSTRAINT FKA63C25052E6C3D6
FOREIGN KEY (MEMBERS_ID)
REFERENCES "PUBLIC"."EMPLOYEE"(MEMBERS_ID)
```

Programming model

Many-to-many relationships are logically defined using the `@javax.persistence.Many`
`ToMany` annotation:

```
public @interface ManyToMany
{
    Class targetEntity( ) default void.class;
    CascadeType[] cascade( ) default {};
    FetchType fetch( ) default LAZY;
    String mappedBy( ) default "";
}
```

To model the many-to-many bidirectional relationship between the `Employee` and
`Team` entities, we need to include collection-based relationship properties in both bean
classes:

```
@Entity
public class Employee
{
    ...
    /**
     * The {@link Team}s to which this {@link Employee} belongs
     */
    @ManyToMany(mappedBy = "members")
    private Collection<Team> teams;
    ...
}

@Entity
public class Team
{
    ...
    /**
     * {@link Employee}s on this {@link Task}.
     */
    @ManyToMany
    private Collection<Employee> members;
    ...
}
```

The relationship is declared as a `java.util.Collection`. We could also use a `Set` type,
which would contain only unique `Teams` and no duplicates. The effectiveness of the
`Set` collection type depends largely on referential-integrity constraints established in
the underlying database.

As with all bidirectional relationships, there has to be an owning side. In this case, it is
the `Team` entity. Since the `Team` owns the relationship, its bean class may have the

`@JoinTable` mapping, though in our example we can accept the defaults. The `joinColumns()` attribute could identify the foreign-key column in the `TEAM_EMPLOYEE` table that references the `TEAM` table, whereas the `inverseJoinColumns()` attribute could identify the foreign key that references the `EMPLOYEE` table.

Like with `@OneToMany` relationships, if you are using your persistence provider's auto schema generation facilities, you do not need to specify a `@JoinTable` mapping. The Java Persistence specification has a default mapping for `@ManyToMany` relationships and will create the join table for you.

As with one-to-many bidirectional relationships, the `mappedBy()` attribute identifies the property on the `Team` bean class that defines the relationship. This also identifies the `Employee` entity as the inverse side of the relationship.

As far as modifying and interacting with the relationship properties, the same owner-ship rules apply as we saw in the one-to-many bidirectional example:

```
// Create a few employees
final Employee pmuir = new Employee("Pete Muir");
final Employee dallen = new Employee("Dan Allen");
final Employee aslak = new Employee("Aslak Knutsen");

// Create some teams
final Team seam = new Team("Seam");
final Team arquillian = new Team("Arquillian");

// Get EM
final EntityManager em = null; // Assume we have this

// Persist
em.persist(pmuir);
em.persist(dallen);
em.persist(aslak);
em.persist(seam);
em.persist(arquillian);

// Associate *both* directions
seam.getMembers().add(dallen);
seam.getMembers().add(pmuir);
seam.getMembers().add(aslak);
arquillian.getMembers().add(dallen);
arquillian.getMembers().add(pmuir);
arquillian.getMembers().add(aslak);
aslak.getTeams().add(seam);
aslak.getTeams().add(arquillian);
dallen.getTeams().add(seam);
dallen.getTeams().add(arquillian);
pmuir.getTeams().add(seam);
pmuir.getTeams().add(arquillian);
```

Many-to-Many Unidirectional Relationship

Many-to-many unidirectional relationships occur when many beans maintain a collection-based relationship with another bean, but the bean referenced in the `Collection` does not maintain a collection-based relationship back to the aggregating beans. In our example, we may assign any number of `Task`s to any number of `Employee`s, and `Employee`s may be assigned to any number of `Task`s. We'll maintain a reference from `Task` to `Employee`, but not the other way around.

Relational database schema

Our first order of business is to declare a `TASK` table:

```
CREATE TABLE "PUBLIC"."TASK"
(
    ID bigint PRIMARY KEY NOT NULL,
    DESCRIPTION varchar
)
;
```

Again, we'll make a join table to map `Task`s to `Employee`s:

```
CREATE TABLE "PUBLIC"."TASK_EMPLOYEE"
(
    TASK_ID bigint NOT NULL,
    OWNERS_ID bigint NOT NULL
)
;
ALTER TABLE "PUBLIC"."TASK_EMPLOYEE"
ADD CONSTRAINT FK7B1EDC2832EBEA41
FOREIGN KEY (TASK_ID)
REFERENCES "PUBLIC"."TASK"(TASK_ID)
;
ALTER TABLE "PUBLIC"."TASK_EMPLOYEE"
ADD CONSTRAINT FK7B1EDC28A3E4776F
FOREIGN KEY (OWNERS_ID)
REFERENCES "PUBLIC"."EMPLOYEE"(OWNERS_ID)
;
```

This many-to-many unidirectional relationship looks a lot like the join table mapping for the many-to-many bidirectional relationship discussed earlier. The big difference is that the object model will maintain a reference only in one direction.

Programming model

To model this relationship, we need to add a collection-based relationship field for `Employee` beans to the `Task`:

```
@Entity
public class Task
{
    ...
    /**
     * {@link Employee} in charge of this {@link Task}
```

```
   */
@ManyToMany
private Collection<Employee> owners;
   ...
}
```

Because the relationship is unidirectional, there are no owning or inverse sides, and we may omit the mappedBy attribute of @ManyToMany.

Usage is similar to what we've already seen:

```
// Create a couple of employees
final Employee smarlow = new Employee("Scott Marlow");
final Employee jpederse = new Employee("Jesper Pedersen");

// Create a couple of tasks
final Task task1 = new Task("Go to the Java User's Group in Boston");
final Task task2 = new Task("Help Shelly McGowan with testsuite setup");

// Persist
final EntityManager em = null; // Assume we have this
em.persist(smarlow);
em.persist(jpederse);
em.persist(task1);
em.persist(task2);

// Associate
task1.getOwners().add(smarlow);
task1.getOwners().add(jpederse);
task2.getOwners().add(smarlow);
task2.getOwners().add(jpederse);
```

Mapping Collection-Based Relationships

The one-to-many and many-to-many examples we've seen so far have used the java.util.Collection and java.util.Set types. The Java Persistence specification also allows you to represent a relationship with a java.util.List or a java.util.Map.

Ordered List-Based Relationship

The java.util.List interface can express collection-based relationships. You do not need any special metadata if you want to use a List rather than a Set or Collection type. (In this case, the List actually gives you a bag semantic, an unordered collection that allows duplicates). A List type can give you the additional ability to order the returned relationship based on a specific set of criteria. This requires the additional metadata provided by the @javax.persistence.OrderBy annotation:

```
package javax.persistence;

@Target({METHOD, FIELD}) @Retention(RUNTIME)
public @interface OrderBy
{
```

```
    String value( ) default "";
}
```

The `value()` attribute allows you to declare partial JPA QL that specifies how you want the relationship to be ordered when it is fetched from the database. If the `value()` attribute is left empty, the `List` is sorted in ascending order based on the value of the primary key.

Let's take the `Employee/Team` relationship, which is a many-to-many bidirectional relationship, and have the `teams` attribute of `Employee` return a `List` that is sorted alphabetically by the `Team` entity's name:

```
@Entity
public class Employee
{
    ...
    @ManyToMany
    @OrderBy("name ASC")
    private List<Team> teams;
    ...
}
```

`"name ASC"` tells the persistence provider to sort the `Team`'s `name` in ascending order. You can use `ASC` for ascending order and `DESC` for descending order. You can also specify additional restrictions, such as `@OrderBy('name asc, otherattribute asc")`. In this case, the list will be ordered by `lastname`, and for duplicate names, it will be ordered by the `otherattribute`.

Map-Based Relationship

The `java.util.Map` interface can be used to express collection-based relationships. In this case, the persistence provider creates a map, with the key being a specific property of the related entity and the value being the entity itself. If you use a `java.util.Map`, you must use the `@javax.persistence.MapKey` annotation:

```
package javax.persistence;

@Target({METHOD, FIELD}) @Retention(RUNTIME)
public @interface MapKey
{
    String name( ) default "";
}
```

The `name()` attribute is the name of the persistent property that you want to represent the key field of the map object. If you leave this blank, it is assumed you are using the primary key of the related entity as the key of the map.

For an example, let's use a map to represent the one-to-many unidirectional `Employee/Phone` relationship discussed earlier in this chapter:

```
@Entity
public class Employee
```

```
{
    ...
    @OneToMany
    @MapKey(name="number")
    private Map<String,Phone> phones;
    ...
}
```

In this example, the `phones` property of `Employee` will return a `java.util.Map` where the key is the `number` property of the `Phone` entity and the value is, of course, the `Phone` entity itself. There is no extra column to keep the map key, since the map key is borrowed from the `Phone` entity.

Detached Entities and FetchType

In Chapter 9, we discussed how managed entity instances become detached from a persistence context when the persistence context ends. Since these entity instances are no longer managed by any persistence context, they may have uninitialized properties or relationships. If you are returning these detached entities to your clients and basically using them as data transfer objects between the client and server, you need to fully understand the effects of accessing any uninitialized relationships.

When an entity instance becomes detached, its state might not be fully initialized, because some of its persistent properties or relationships may be marked as lazily loaded in the mapping metadata. Each relationship annotation has a `fetch()` attribute that specifies whether the relationship property is loaded when the entity is queried. If the `fetch()` attribute is set to `FetchType.LAZY`, then the relationship is not initialized until it is traversed in your code:

```
Employee employee = entityManager.find(Employee.class, id);
employee.getPhones().size();
```

Invoking the `size()` method of the `phones` collection causes the relationship to be loaded from the database. It is important to note that this lazy initialization does not happen unless the entity bean is being managed by a persistence context. If the entity bean is detached, the specification is not clear on what actions the persistence provider should perform when accessing an unloaded relationship of a detached entity. Most persistence providers throw some kind of lazy instantiation exception when you call the accessor of the relationship or when you try to invoke an operation on the relationship of a detached entity:

```
Employee employee = entityManager.find(Employee.class, id);
entityManager.detach(employee);
try
{
    int numPhones = employee.getPhones().size();
}
catch (SomeVendorLazyInitializationException ex)
{
}
```

In this code, the application has received an instance of a detached `Employee` entity and attempts to access the `phones` relationship. If the `fetch()` attribute of this relationship is `LAZY`, most vendor implementations will throw a vendor-specific exception. This lazy initialization problem can be overcome in two ways. The obvious way is just to navigate the needed relationships while the entity instance is still managed by a persistence context. The second way is to perform the fetch eagerly when you query the entity. In Chapter 13, you will see that the JPA QL query language has a `FETCH JOIN` operation that allows you to preinitialize selected relationships when you invoke a query.

How is the persistence provider able to throw an exception when accessing the relationship when the `Employee` class is a plain Java class? Although not defined in the specification, the vendor has a few ways to implement this. One is through bytecode manipulation of the `Employee` class. In Java EE, the application server is required to provide hooks for bytecode manipulation for persistence providers. In Java SE, the persistence provider may require an additional post-compilation step on your code base. Another way for vendors to implement this is to create a proxy class that inherits from `Employee` and that reimplements all the accessor methods to add lazy initialization checking. For collection-based relationships, the persistence provider can just provide its own implementation of the collection and do the lazy check there. Whatever the implementation, make a note to discover what your persistence provider will do in the detached lazy initialization scenario so that your code can take appropriate measures to handle this exception.

Cascading

There is one annotation attribute that we have ignored so far: the `cascade()` attribute of the `@OneToOne`, `@OneToMany`, `@ManyToOne`, and `@ManyToMany` relationship annotations. This section discusses in detail the behavior that is applied when using the `cascade()` attribute.

When you perform an entity manager operation on an entity bean instance, you can automatically have the same operation performed on any relationship properties the entity may have. This is called *cascading*. For example, if you are persisting a new `Employee` entity with a new address and phone number, all you have to do is wire the object, and the entity manager can automatically create the employee and its related entities, all in one `persist()` method call:

```
Employee employee = new Employee();
customer.setAddress(new Address());
customer.getPhoneNumbers().add(new Phone());

// create them all in one entity manager invocation
entityManager.persist(employee);
```

With the Java Persistence specification, cascading can be applied to a variety of entity manager operations, including `persist()`, `merge()`, `remove()`, and `refresh()`. This feature is enabled by setting the `javax.persistence.CascadeType` of the relationship annotation's `cascade()` attribute. The `CascadeType` is defined as a Java enumeration:

```
public enum CascadeType
{
    ALL, PERSIST,
    MERGE, REMOVE,
    REFRESH
}
```

The `ALL` value represents all of the cascade operations. The remaining values represent individual cascade operations. The `cascade()` attribute is an array of the cascade operations you want applied to your related entities.

PERSIST

`PERSIST` has to deal with the creation of entities within the database. If we had a `CascadeType` of `PERSIST` on the `Employee` side of our one-to-one relationship, you would not have to persist your created `Address` as well. It would be created for you. The persistence provider also will execute the appropriate SQL `INSERT` statements in the appropriate order for you.

If you did not have a cascade policy of `PERSIST`, then you would have to call `EntityManager.persist()` on the address object as well (as we do in the example).

MERGE

`MERGE` deals with entity synchronization, meaning inserts and, more importantly, updates. These aren't updates in the traditional sense. If you remember from previous chapters, we mentioned that objects could be detached from persistent management and serialized to a remote client, updates could be performed locally on that remote client, the object instance would be sent back to the server, and the changes would be merged back into the database. Merging is about synchronizing the state of a detached object instance back to persistent storage.

So, back to what `MERGE` means! `MERGE` is similar to `PERSIST`. If you have a cascade policy of `MERGE`, then you do not have to call `EntityManager.merge()` for the contained related entity:

```
employee.setName("William");
employee.getAddress().setCity("Boston");
entityManager.merge(employee);
```

In this example, when the `employee` variable is merged by the entity manager, the entity manager will cascade the merge to the contained `address` property and the `city` also will be updated in the database.

Another interesting thing about MERGE is that if you have added any new entities to a relationship that have not been created in the database, they will be persisted and created when the merge() happens:

```
Phone phone = new Phone();
phone.setNumber("617-666-6666");

employee.getPhoneNumbers().add(phone);
entityManager.merge(employee);
```

In this example, we allocate a Phone and add it to an Employee's list of phone numbers. We then call merge() with the employee, and since we have the MERGE CascadeType set on this relationship, the persistence provider will see that it is a new Phone entity and will create it within the database.

Remember that only the graph returned by the merge operation is in managed state, not the one passed as a parameter.

REMOVE

REMOVE is straightforward. In our Employee example, if you delete an Employee entity, its address will be deleted as well:

```
Employee employee = entityManager.find(Employee.class, id);
entityManager.remove(employee); // Also removes the address
```

REFRESH

REFRESH is similar to MERGE. Unlike merge, though, this CascadeType only pertains to when EntityManager.refresh() is called. Refreshing doesn't update the database with changes in the object instance. Instead, it refreshes the object instance's state from the database. Again, the contained related entities would also be refreshed:

```
Employee employee = entityManager.find(Employee.class, id);
entityManager.refresh(employee); // address would be refreshed too
```

So, if changes to the Employee's address were committed by a different transaction, the address property of the employee variable would be updated with these changes. This is useful in practice when an entity bean has some properties that are generated by the database (by triggers, for example). You can refresh the entity to read those generated properties. In this case, be sure to make those generated properties read-only from a persistence provider perspective, i.e., using the @Column (insertable=false, updatable=false).

ALL

ALL is a combination of all of the previous policies and is used for the purposes of simplicity.

When to Use Cascading

You don't always want to use cascading for every relationship you have. For instance, you would not want to remove the related `Computer` or `Tasks` when removing an `Employee` entity from the database, because these entities have a life span that is usually longer than the employee. You might not want to cascade merges because you may have fetched stale data from the database or simply not filled the relationship in one particular business operation. For performance reasons, you may also not want to refresh all the relationships an entity has because this would cause more round trips to the database. Be aware how your entities will be used before deciding on the cascade type. If you are unsure of their use, then you should turn off cascading entirely and enable it on a per-case basis. Remember, cascading is simply a convenient tool for reducing the `EntityManager` API calls. It's very easy to trigger expensive database calls, which may result in unnecessary multitable joins.

## CHAPTER 12

Entity Inheritance

In order to be complete, an object-to-relational mapping engine must support inheritance hierarchies. The Java Persistence specification supports entity inheritance, polymorphic relationships/associations, and polymorphic queries. These features were completely missing in the older EJB CMP 2.1 specification.

In this chapter, we'll modify the `Employee` entity that we defined in earlier chapters to make it fit into an inheritance hierarchy. We'll have it extend a base class called `Person` and redefine the `Employee` class to extend a `Customer` class. Figure 12-1 shows this class hierarchy.

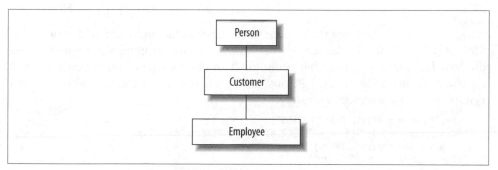

Figure 12-1. Customer class hierarchy

The Java Persistence specification provides three different ways to map an inheritance hierarchy to a relational database:

A single table per class hierarchy
> One table will have all properties of every class in the hierarchy.

A table per concrete class
> Each class will have a table dedicated to it, with all of its properties and the properties of its superclass mapped to this table.

A table per subclass

Each class will have its own table. Each table will have only the properties that are defined in that particular class. These tables will not have properties of any super-class or subclass.

In this chapter, we use these three strategies to map the Employee class hierarchy defined in Figure 12-1.

Single Table per Class Hierarchy

In the single table per class hierarchy mapping strategy, one database table represents every class of a given hierarchy. In our example, the Person, Customer, and Employee entities are represented in the same table, as shown in the following code:

```
CREATE TABLE "PUBLIC"."SINGLECLASS_PERSON"
(
    DISCRIMINATOR varchar NOT NULL,
    ID bigint PRIMARY KEY NOT NULL,
    FIRSTNAME varchar,
    LASTNAME varchar,
    CITY varchar,
    STATE varchar,
    STREET varchar,
    ZIP varchar,
    EMPLOYEEID integer
)
;
```

As you can see, all the properties for the Customer class hierarchy are held in one table, SINGLECLASS_PERSON. The single table per class hierarchy mapping also requires an additional *discriminator column*. This column identifies the type of entity being stored in a particular row of SINGLECLASS_PERSON. Let's look at how the classes will use annotations to map this inheritance strategy:

```
@Entity(name = "SINGLECLASS_PERSON")
@DiscriminatorColumn(name = "DISCRIMINATOR", discriminatorType =
    DiscriminatorType.STRING)
@DiscriminatorValue("PERSON")
@Inheritance(strategy = InheritanceType.SINGLE_TABLE)
public class Person
{
    @Id
    @GeneratedValue
    private Long id;

    private String firstName;
    private String lastName;

    ...
}
```

This is our base class for both Customers and Employees. It defines the discriminator column we've just seen as "DISCRIMINATOR", where Person rows will have a value of "PERSON".

Since one table is representing the entire class hierarchy, the persistence provider needs some way to identify which class the row in the database maps to. It determines this by reading the value from the discriminator column. The @javax.persistence.DiscriminatorColumn annotation identifies which column in our table will store the discriminator's value. The name() attribute identifies the name of the column, and the discriminatorType() attribute specifies what type the discriminator column will be. It can be a STRING, CHAR, or INTEGER. For our Employee class hierarchy mapping, you do not have to specify the discriminatorType(), as it defaults to being a STRING. If you're OK with the default column name, you can remove the @Discrimina torColumn entirely:

```
package javax.persistence;

@Target(TYPE) @Retention(RUNTIME)
public @interface DiscriminatorColumn
{
    String name( ) default "DTYPE";
    DiscriminatorType discriminatorType( ) default STRING;
    String columnDefinition( ) default "";
    int length( ) default 10;
}
```

The @javax.persistence.DiscriminatorValue annotation defines what value the discriminator column will take for rows that store an instance of a Person class. You can leave this attribute undefined if you want to. In that case, the persistence manager would generate a value for you automatically. This value will be vendor-specific if the DiscriminatorType is CHAR or INTEGER. The entity name is used by default when a type of STRING is specified. It is good practice to specify the value for CHAR and INTEGER values:

```
package javax.persistence;

@Target(TYPE) @Retention(RUNTIME)
public @interface DiscriminatorValue
{
    String value( )
}
```

The @javax.persistence.Inheritance annotation is used to define the persistence strategy for the inheritance relationship:

```
package javax.persistence;

@Target(TYPE) @Retention(RUNTIME)
public @interface Inheritance
{
    InheritanceType strategy( ) default SINGLE_TABLE;
}
```

```
public enum InheritanceType
{
    SINGLE_TABLE, JOINED, TABLE_PER_CLASS
}
```

The strategy() attribute defines the inheritance mapping that we're using. Since we're using the single table per class hierarchy, the SINGLE_TABLE enum is applied.

We can now extend this base into a more specialized Customer:

```
@Entity(name = "SINGLECLASS_CUSTOMER")
@DiscriminatorValue("CUSTOMER")
public class Customer extends Person
{
    private String street;
    private String city;
    private String state;
    private String zip;
    ...
}
```

Customer rows in the table will use a value of "CUSTOMER" in the discriminator column.

Finally, we have Employee:

```
@Entity (name="SINGLECLASS_EMPLOYEE")
@DiscriminatorValue("EMPLOYEE")
public class Employee extends Customer
{
    private Integer employeeId;
    ...
}
```

Advantages

The SINGLE_TABLE mapping strategy is the simplest to implement and performs better than all the inheritance strategies. There is only one table to administer and deal with. The persistence engine does not have to do any complex joins, unions, or subselects when loading the entity or when traversing a polymorphic relationship, because all data is stored in one table.

Disadvantages

One huge disadvantage of this approach is that all columns of subclass properties must be nullable. So, if you need or want to have any NOT NULL constraints defined on these columns, you cannot do so. Also, because subclass property columns may be unused, the SINGLE_TABLE strategy is not normalized.

Table per Concrete Class

In the table per concrete class strategy, a database table is defined for each concrete class in the hierarchy. Each table has columns representing its properties and all properties of any superclasses:

```
CREATE TABLE "PUBLIC"."TABLEPERCLASS_PERSON"
(
    ID bigint PRIMARY KEY NOT NULL,
    FIRSTNAME varchar,
    LASTNAME varchar
)
;

CREATE TABLE "PUBLIC"."TABLEPERCLASS_CUSTOMER"
(
    ID bigint PRIMARY KEY NOT NULL,
    FIRSTNAME varchar,
    LASTNAME varchar,
    CITY varchar,
    STATE varchar,
    STREET varchar,
    ZIP varchar
)
;

CREATE TABLE "PUBLIC"."TABLEPERCLASS_EMPLOYEE"
(
    ID bigint PRIMARY KEY NOT NULL,
    FIRSTNAME varchar,
    LASTNAME varchar,
    CITY varchar,
    STATE varchar,
    STREET varchar,
    ZIP varchar,
    EMPLOYEEID integer
)
;
```

One major difference between this strategy and the SINGLE_TABLE strategy is that no discriminator column is needed in the database schema. Also notice that each table contains every persistent property in the hierarchy. Let's now look at how we map this strategy with annotations:

```
@Entity(name = "TABLEPERCLASS_PERSON")
@Inheritance(strategy = InheritanceType.TABLE_PER_CLASS)
public class Person
{
    @Id
    @GeneratedValue(strategy = GenerationType.TABLE)
    // Cannot accept default generation strategy for table-per-class
    private Long id;

    private String firstName;
```

```
    private String lastName;
    ...
}

@Entity(name = "TABLEPERCLASS_CUSTOMER")
public class Customer extends Person
{
    private String street;
    private String city;
    private String state;
    private String zip;
    ...
}

@Entity(name = "TABLEPERCLASS_EMPLOYEE")
public class Employee extends Customer
{
    private Integer employeeId;
    ...
}
```

Notice that the only inheritance metadata required is the `InheritanceType`, and this is needed on only the base `Person` class.

Advantages

The advantage to this approach over the `SINGLE_TABLE` strategy is that you can define constraints on subclass properties. Another plus is that it might be easier to map a preexisting legacy schema using this strategy.

Disadvantages

This strategy is not normalized, as it has redundant columns in each of its tables for each of the base class's properties. Also, to support this type of mapping, the persistence manager has to do some funky things. One way it could be implemented is for the container to use multiple queries when loading an entity or polymorphic relationship. This is a huge performance hit because the container has to do multiple round-trips to the database. Another way a container could implement this strategy is to use `SQL UNIONs`. This still would not be as fast as the `SINGLE_TABLE` strategy, but it would perform much better than a multiselect implementation. The downside to an `SQL UNION` is that not all relational databases support this SQL feature. It is probably not wise to pick this strategy when developing your entity beans, unless you have good reason (e.g., an existing legacy schema).

Table per Subclass

In the table per subclass mapping, each subclass has its own table, but this table contains only the properties that are defined on that particular class. In other words, it is similar to the TABLE_PER_CLASS strategy, except the schema is normalized. This is also called the JOINED strategy:

```
CREATE TABLE "PUBLIC"."JOINED_PERSON"
(
    ID bigint PRIMARY KEY NOT NULL,
    FIRSTNAME varchar,
    LASTNAME varchar
)
;

CREATE TABLE "PUBLIC"."JOINED_CUSTOMER"
(
    CITY varchar,
    STATE varchar,
    STREET varchar,
    ZIP varchar,
    ID bigint PRIMARY KEY NOT NULL
)
;
ALTER TABLE "PUBLIC"."JOINED_CUSTOMER"
ADD CONSTRAINT FK65AE08146E93989D
FOREIGN KEY (ID)
REFERENCES "PUBLIC"."JOINED_PERSON"(ID)
;

CREATE TABLE "PUBLIC"."JOINED_EMPLOYEE"
(
    EMPLOYEEID integer,
    EMP_PK bigint PRIMARY KEY NOT NULL
)
;
ALTER TABLE "PUBLIC"."JOINED_EMPLOYEE"
ADD CONSTRAINT FK88AF6EE4D423ED9D
FOREIGN KEY (EMP_PK)
REFERENCES "PUBLIC"."JOINED_CUSTOMER"(EMP_PK)
;
```

When the persistence manager loads an entity that is a subclass or traverses a polymorphic relationship, it does an SQL join on all the tables in the hierarchy. In this mapping, there must be a column in each table that can be used to join each table. In our example, the JOINED_EMPLOYEE, JOINED_CUSTOMER, and JOINED_PERSON tables share the same primary-key values. The annotation mapping is quite simple:

```
@Entity(name="JOINED_PERSON")
@Inheritance(strategy=InheritanceType.JOINED)
public class Person
{
    ...
}

@Entity(name="JOINED_CUSTOMER")
public class Customer extends Person
{
    ...
```

```
    }

    @Entity(name = "JOINED_EMPLOYEE")
    @PrimaryKeyJoinColumn  (name="EMP_PK")
    public class Employee extends Customer
    {
       ...
    }
```

The persistence manager needs to know which columns in each table will be used to perform a join when loading an entity with a `JOINED` inheritance strategy. The `@javax.persistence.PrimaryKeyJoinColumn` annotation can be used to describe this metadata:

```
    package javax.persistence;

    @Target({TYPE, METHOD, FIELD})
    public @interface PrimaryKeyJoinColumn
    {
        String name( ) default "";
        String referencedColumnName( ) default "";
        String columnDefinition( ) default "";
    }
```

The `name()` attribute refers to the column contained in the current table on which you will perform a join. It defaults to the primary-key column of the superclass's table. The `referencedColumnName()` is the column that will be used to perform the join from the superclass's table. It can be any column in the superclass's table, but it defaults to its primary key. If the primary-key column names are identical between the base and subclasses, then this annotation is not needed. For instance, the `Customer` entity does not need the `@PrimaryKeyJoinColumn` annotation. The `Employee` class has a different primary-key column name than the tables of its superclasses, so the `@PrimaryKeyJoinColumn` annotation is required. If class hierarchy uses a composite key, there is a `@javax.persistence.PrimaryKeyJoinColumns` annotation that can describe multiple join columns:

```
    package javax.persistence;

    @Target({TYPE, METHOD, FIELD})
    public @interface PrimaryKeyJoinColumns
    {
        @PrimaryKeyJoinColumns[] value( );
    }
```

 Some persistence providers require a discriminator column for this mapping type. Most do not. Make sure to check your persistence provider implementation to see whether it is required.

Advantages

It is better to compare this mapping to other strategies to describe its advantages. Although it is not as fast as the SINGLE_TABLE strategy, you are able to define NOT NULL constraints on any column of any table, and your model is normalized.

This mapping is better than the TABLE_PER_CLASS strategy for two reasons. One, the relational database model is completely normalized. Two, it performs better than the TABLE_PER_CLASS strategy if SQL UNIONs are not supported.

Disadvantages

It does not perform as well as the SINGLE_TABLE strategy.

Mixing Strategies

The persistence specification currently makes mixing inheritance strategies optional. The rules for mixing strategies in an inheritance hierarchy may be defined in future versions of the spec.

Nonentity Base Classes

The inheritance mappings we described so far in this chapter concerned a class hierarchy of entity beans. Sometimes, however, you need to inherit from a nonentity superclass. This superclass may be an existing class in your domain model that you do not want to make an entity. The @javax.persistence.MappedSuperclass annotation allows you to define this kind of mapping. Let's modify our example class hierarchy and change Person into a mapped superclass:

```
@MappedSuperclass
public class Person
{
    @Id @GeneratedValue
    public int getId( ) { return id; }
    public void setId(int id) { this.id = is; }
    ...
}

@Entity
@Table(name="CUSTOMER")
@Inheritance(strategy=InheritanceType.JOINED)
@AttributeOverride(name="lastname", column=@Column(name="SURNAME"))
public class Customer extends Person {
...
}

@Entity
@Table(name="EMPLOYEE")
```

```
@PrimaryKeyJoinColumn(name="EMP_PK")
public class Employee extends Customer {
...
}
```

Since it is not an entity, the mapped superclass does not have an associated table. Any subclass inherits the persistence properties of the base class. You can override any mapped property of the mapped class by using the @javax.persistence.AttributeOverride annotation.

You can have @MappedSuperclass annotated classes in between two @Entity annotated classes in a given hierarchy. Also, nonannotated classes (i.e., not annotated with @Entity or @MappedSuperclass) are completely ignored by the persistence provider.

## CHAPTER 13

Queries, the Criteria API, and JPA QL

Querying is a fundamental feature of all relational databases. It allows you to pull complex reports, calculations, and information about intricately related objects from persistence storage. Queries in Java Persistence are done using the JPA QL query language, native Structured Query Language (SQL), and the new Criteria API.

JPA QL is a declarative query language similar to the SQL used in relational databases, but it is tailored to work with Java objects rather than a relational schema. To execute queries, you reference the properties and relationships of your entity beans rather than the underlying tables and columns these objects are mapped to. When a JPA QL query is executed, the entity manager uses the information you provided through the mapping metadata, discussed in the previous two chapters, and automatically translates it to an appropriate native SQL query. This generated native SQL is then executed through a JDBC driver directly on your database. Since JPA QL is a query language that represents Java objects, it is portable across vendor database implementations because the entity manager handles the conversion to raw SQL for you.

The JPA QL language is easy for developers to learn, yet precise enough to be interpreted into native database code. This rich and flexible query language empowers developers while executing in fast native code at runtime. Plus, because JPA QL is object-oriented, queries are usually much more compact and readable than their SQL equivalent. EJB QL existed in the EJB 2.1 specification, and it is really the only feature that survived in the new release. Since Persistence is completely spun off in its own specification, it's now known as JPA QL. Although it was well-formed, EJB QL in EJB 2.1 was incomplete, forcing developers to escape to JDBC or write really inefficient code. JPA QL has been greatly improved and expanded to be more parallel to SQL and should now meet most of your needs. Things such as projection, GROUP BY, and HAVING have been added, as well as bulk updates and deletes.

Like all query languages, JPA QL is modeled as a string, and therefore cannot be checked for structural correctness by the Java compiler. New to Java Persistence 2.0 is the Criteria API, a fluid interface for building queries using an object model.

Sometimes, though, JPA QL and the Criteria API are not enough. Because these are portable query language extensions, they cannot always take advantage of specific proprietary features of your database vendor. JPA QL does not allow you to execute stored procedures, for instance. The EJB 3.x Expert Group foresaw the need for this and has provided an API to map native SQL calls to your entity beans.

JPA QL and native SQL queries are executed through the `javax.persistence.Query` interface. The `Query` interface is analogous to the `java.sql.PreparedStatement` interface. This `Query` API gives you methods for paging your result set, as well as passing Java parameters to your query. Queries can be predeclared through annotations or XML or created dynamically at runtime through `EntityManager` APIs.

Similarly, the Criteria API has the `javax.persistence.criteria.CriteriaQuery` interface, through which we can construct queries via the object model and submit these via the `EntityManager`.

Query API

A query in Java Persistence is a full-blown Java interface that you obtain at runtime from the entity manager:

```
package javax.persistence;

public interface Query
{
    List getResultList();
    Object getSingleResult();
    int executeUpdate();
    Query setMaxResults(int maxResult);
    int getMaxResults();
    Query setFirstResult(int startPosition);
    int getFirstResult();
    Query setHint(String hintName, Object value);
    Map<String, Object> getHints();
    <T> Query setParameter(Parameter<T> param, T value);
    Query setParameter(Parameter<Calendar> param, Calendar value,
                    TemporalType temporalType);
    Query setParameter(Parameter<Date> param, Date value,
                    TemporalType temporalType);
    Query setParameter(String name, Object value);
    Query setParameter(String name, Calendar value,
                    TemporalType temporalType);
    Query setParameter(String name, Date value,
                    TemporalType temporalType);
    Query setParameter(int position, Object value);
    Query setParameter(int position, Calendar value,
                    TemporalType temporalType);
    Query setParameter(int position, Date value,
                    TemporalType temporalType);
    Set<Parameter<?>> getParameters();
    Parameter<?> getParameter(String name);
```

```
        <T> Parameter<T> getParameter(String name, Class<T> type);
        Parameter<?> getParameter(int position);
        <T> Parameter<T> getParameter(int position, Class<T> type);
        boolean isBound(Parameter<?> param);
        <T> T getParameterValue(Parameter<T> param);
        Object getParameterValue(String name);
        Object getParameterValue(int position);
        Query setFlushMode(FlushModeType flushMode);
        FlushModeType getFlushMode();
        Query setLockMode(LockModeType lockMode);
        LockModeType getLockMode();
        <T> T unwrap(Class<T> cls);
    }
```

Queries are created using these EntityManager methods:

```
    package javax.persistence;

    public interface EntityManager
    {
        public Query createQuery(String qlString);
        public <T> TypedQuery<T> createQuery(CriteriaQuery<T> criteriaQuery);
        public <T> TypedQuery<T> createQuery(String qlString, Class<T> resultClass);
        public Query createNamedQuery(String name);
        public <T> TypedQuery<T> createNamedQuery(String name, Class<T> resultClass);
        public Query createNativeQuery(String sqlString);
        public Query createNativeQuery(String sqlString, Class resultClass);
        public Query createNativeQuery(String sqlString, String resultSetMapping);
    }
```

Let's first look at using EntityManager.createQuery() to create a query dynamically at runtime:

```
    try
    {
        // Define query String
        final String jpaQlQuery = "FROM " + Employee.class.getSimpleName() +
            " e WHERE e.name='Dave'";
        // Query and get result
        final Employee roundtrip = (Employee)em.createQuery(jpaQlQuery)
            .getSingleResult();
    }
    catch (EntityNotFoundException notFound) {}
    catch (NonUniqueResultException nonUnique) {}
```

The previous query looks for a single, unique Employee entity named Dave. The query is executed when the getSingleResult() method is called. This method expects that the call will return only one result. If no result is returned, the method throws a javax.persistence.EntityNotFoundException runtime exception. If more than one result is found, a javax.persistence.NonUniqueResultException runtime exception is thrown. Since both of these exceptions are RuntimeExceptions, the example code is not required to have a full *try/catch* block.

There is a good chance that the `NonUniqueResultException` would be thrown by this example. Believe it or not, there are a lot of Daves in the world. You can change the query to use the `getResultList()` method to obtain a collection of results:

```
Query query = entityManager.creatQuery(
                "from Employee e where e.name='Dave'");
    java.util.List<?> bills = query.getResultList( );
```

The `getResultList()` method does not throw an exception if there are no Daves; the returned list would just be empty.

Parameters

Much like a `java.sql.PreparedStatement` in JDBC, JPA QL allows you to specify parameters in query declarations so that you can reuse and execute the query multiple times on different sets of parameters. Two syntaxes are provided: named parameters and positional parameters. Let's modify our earlier `Employee` query to take both last name and first name as named parameters:

```
// Define query String
final String jpaQlQuery = "FROM " + Employee.class.getSimpleName() +
    " e WHERE e.name=:name";
// Set parameter
jpaQlQuery.setParameter("name", "Dave");
// Query and get result
final Employee roundtrip = (Employee)em.createQuery(jpaQlQuery).getSingleResult();
```

The : character followed by the parameter name is used in JPA QL statements to identify a named parameter. The `setParameter()` method in this example takes the name of the parameter first, and then the actual value. EJB QL also supports positional parameters. Let's modify the previous example to see this mode in action:

```
// Define query String
final String jpaQlQuery = "FROM " + Employee.class.getSimpleName() +
    " e WHERE e.name=?1";
// Set parameter
jpaQlQuery.setParameter(1, "Dave");
// Query and get result
final Employee roundtrip = (Employee)em.createQuery(jpaQlQuery).getSingleResult();
```

Instead of a string named `parameter`, `setParameter()` also takes a numeric parameter position. The ? character is used instead of the : character used with named parameters. Numeric parameters are indexed (start at) 1, not 0.

 Using named parameters over positional parameters is recommended, as the JPA QL code becomes self-documenting. This is especially useful when working with predeclared queries.

Date Parameters

If you need to pass `java.util.Date` or `java.util.Calendar` parameters into a query, you need to use special `setParameter` methods:

```
package javax.persistence;

public enum TemporalType
{
    DATE, //java.sql.Date
    TIME, //java.sql.Time
    TIMESTAMP //java.sql.Timestamp
}

public interface Query
{
    Query setParameter(String name, java.util.Date value, TemporalType temporalTyp
e);
    Query setParameter(String name, Calendar value, TemporalType temporalType);
    Query setParameter(int position, Date value, TemporalType temporalType);
    Query setParameter(int position, Calendar value, TemporalType temporalType);
}
```

A `Date` or `Calendar` object can represent a real date, a time of day, or a numeric timestamp. Because these object types can represent different things at the same time, you need to tell your `Query` object how it should use these parameters. The `javax.persistence.TemporalType` passed in as a parameter to the `setParameter()` method tells the `Query` interface what database type to use when converting the `java.util.Date` or `java.util.Calendar` parameter to a native SQL type.

Paging Results

Sometimes an executed query returns too many results. For instance, maybe we're displaying a list of customers on a web page. The web page can display only so many customers, and maybe there are thousands or even millions of customers in the database. The `Query` API has two built-in functions to solve this type of scenario—`setMax Results()` and `setFirstResult()`:

```
public List getEmployees(int max, int index) {
    Query query = entityManager.createQuery("from Employee e");
    return query.setMaxResults(max).
                setFirstResult(index).
                getResultList();
}
```

The `getEmployees()` method executes a query that obtains all employees from the database. We limit the number of employees it returns by using the `setMaxResults()` method, passing in the `max` method parameter. The method is also designed so that you can define an arbitrary set of results that you want returned by the execution of the query. The `setFirstResult()` method tells the query what position in the executed query's result set you want returned. So, if you had a max result of 3 and a first result of 5, employees 5, 6, and 7 would be returned. We set this value in the `getEmployees()` method with the `index` parameter. Let's take this method and write a code fragment that lists all customers in the database:

```
List results;
int first = 0;
int max = 10;

do
{
   results = getEmployees(max, first);
   Iterator it = results.iterator();
   while (it.hasNext())
   {
      Employee employee = (Employee)it.next();
      System.out.println("Employee name: " + employee.getName());
   }
   entityManager.clear();
   first = first + results.getSize();
}
while(results.size() > 0);
```

In this example, we loop through all employees in the database and output their names to the system output stream. If we had thousands or even millions of employees in the database, we could quickly run out of memory, as each execution of the `getEmployees()` method would return customers that were still managed by the entity manager. So, after we are finished outputting a block of customers, we call `EntityManager.clear()` to detach these customers and let them be garbage-collected by the Java VM. Use this pattern when you need to deal with a lot of entity objects within the same transaction.

Hints

Some Java Persistence vendors will provide additional add-on features that you can take advantage of when executing a query. For instance, the JBoss EJB 3.x implementation allows you to define a timeout for the query. These types of add-on features can be specified as hints using the `setHint()` method on the query. Here's an example of defining a JBoss query timeout using hints:

```
Query query = entityManager.createQuery("from Employee e");
query.setHint("org.hibernate.timeout", 1000);
```

The `setHint()` method takes a string name and an arbitrary object parameter.

FlushMode

In Chapter 9, we talked about flushing and flush modes. Sometimes you would like a different flush mode to be enforced for the duration of a query. For instance, maybe a query wants to make sure that the entity manager does not flush before the query is executed (since the default value implies that the entity manager can). The `Query` interface provides a `setFlushMode()` method for this particular purpose:

```
Query query = manager.createQuery("from Employee e");
query.setFlushMode(FlushModeType.COMMIT);
```

In this example, we're telling the persistence provider that we do not want the query to do any automatic flushing before this particular query is executed. Using this commit mode can be dangerous if some correlated dirty entities are in the persistence context. You might return wrong entities from your query. Therefore, it is recommended that you use the `FlushModeType.AUTO`.

JPA QL

Now that you have a basic understanding of how to work with `Query` objects, you can learn what features are available to you for creating your own JPA QL queries. JPA QL is expressed in terms of the abstract persistence schema of an entity: its abstract schema name, basic properties, and relationship properties. JPA QL uses the abstract schema names to identify beans, the basic properties to specify values, and the relationship properties to navigate across relationships.

To discuss JPA QL, we will use the relationships defined in Chapter 11.

Abstract Schema Names

The abstract schema name can be defined by metadata, or it can default to a specific value. It defaults to the unqualified name of the entity bean class if the `name()` attribute is not specified when declaring the `@Entity` annotation.

In the following example, the `@Entity.name()` attribute is not specified on the `Employee` bean class, so `Employee` is used to reference the entity within JPA QL calls:

```
@Entity
public class Employee {...}

entityManager.createQuery("SELECT e FROM Employee AS e");
```

In the following example, since the `@Entity.name()` attribute is defined, you would reference `Employee` entities in JPA QL as `Emp`:

```
@Entity(name="Emp")
public class Employee {...}

entityManager.createQuery("SELECT e FROM Emp AS e");
```

Simple Queries

The simplest JPA QL statement has no WHERE clause and only one abstract schema type. For example, you could define a query method to select all Employee beans:

```
SELECT OBJECT( e ) FROM Employee AS e
```

The FROM clause determines which entity bean types will be included in the SELECT statement (i.e., it provides the *scope* of the select). In this case, the FROM clause declares the type to be Employee, which is the abstract schema name of the Employee entity. The AS e part of the clause assigns e as the identifier of the Employee entity. This is similar to SQL, which allows an identifier to be associated with a table. Identifiers can be any length and follow the same rules that are applied to field names in the Java programming language. However, identifiers cannot be the same as existing abstract schema name values. In addition, identification variable names are *not* case-sensitive, so an identifier of employee would be in conflict with an abstract schema name of Employee. For example, the following statement is illegal because Employee is the abstract schema name of the Employee EJB:

```
SELECT OBJECT ( employee ) FROM Employee AS employee
```

The AS operator is optional, but it is used in this book to help make the JPA QL statements clearer. The following two statements are equivalent:

```
SELECT OBJECT(e) FROM Employee AS e
```

```
SELECT e FROM Employee e
```

The SELECT clause determines the type of any values that are returned. In this case, the statement returns the Employee entity bean, as indicated by the e identifier.

The OBJECT() operator is optional and is a relic requirement of the EJB 2.1 specification. It is there for backward compatibility.

Identifiers cannot be EJB QL reserved words. In Java Persistence, the following words are reserved:

SELECT	FROM	WHERE	UPDATE	DELETE
JOIN	OUTER	INNER	GROUP	BY
HAVING	FETCH	DISTINCT	OBJECT	NULL
TRUE	FALSE	NOT	AND	OR
BETWEEN	LIKE	IN	AS	UNKNOWN
EMPTY	MEMBER	OF	IS	AVG
MAX	MIN	SUM	COUNT	ORDER
ASC	DESC	MOD	UPPER	LOWER
TRIM	POSITION	CHARACTER_LENGTH	CHAR_LENGTH	BIT_LENGTH
CURRENT_TIME	CURRENT_DATE	CURRENT_TIMESTAMP	NEW	

It's a good practice to avoid all SQL reserved words, because you never know which ones will be used by future versions of EJB QL. You can find more information in the appendix of *SQL in a Nutshell* (O'Reilly).

Selecting Entity and Relationship Properties

JPA QL allows SELECT clauses to return any number of basic or relationship properties. For example, we can define a simple SELECT statement to return the name of all of employees in the registry:

```
final String jpaQlQuery = "SELECT e.name FROM Employee AS e"
@SuppressWarnings("unchecked")
final List<String> names = em.createQuery(jpaQlQuery).getResultList();
```

The SELECT clause uses a simple path to select the Employee entity's name property as the return type. The persistence property names are identified by the access type of your entity bean class, regardless of whether you've applied your mapping annotations on a get or set method or on the member fields of the class.

If you use get or set methods to specify your persistent properties, then the property name is extracted from the method name. The get part of the method name is removed, and the first character of the remaining string is lowercase.

When a query returns more than one item, you must use the Query.getResultList() method. The return value of the earlier query is dependent upon the type of the field being accessed. In our case, we obtain a List of Strings because the name property is a String. If the SELECT clause queries more than one column or entity, the results are aggregated in an object array (Object[]) in the java.util.List returned by getResult List(). The following code shows how to access the returned results from a multi-property select:

```
// Create and persist
final Employee josh = new Employee(ID_JOSH, NAME_JOSH);
em.persist(josh);

// Lookup
final String jpaQlQuery = "SELECT e.name, e.id FROM " +
    Employee.class.getSimpleName() + " AS e";
@SuppressWarnings("unchecked")
final List<Object[]> properties = em.createQuery(jpaQlQuery).getResultList();

// Test
Assert.assertEquals(1, properties.size());
Assert.assertEquals(NAME_JOSH, properties.get(0)[0]);
Assert.assertEquals(ID_JOSH, properties.get(0)[1]);
```

Paths can be as long as required. It's common to use paths that navigate over one or more relationship fields to end at either a basic or a relationship property. For example, the following JPA QL statement selects the name of the manager of the employees:

```
@Entity
public class Employee
{
    /**
     * Manager of the {@link Employee}
     */
    @ManyToOne
    private Employee manager;
    ...
}
```

```
SELECT e.manager.name FROM Employee AS e
```

Using these relationships, we can specify more complex paths. Paths cannot navigate beyond persistent properties. For example, imagine that `Address` uses a `ZipCode` class as its `zip` property and this property is stored as a byte stream in the database:

```
public class ZipCode implements java.io.Serializable
{
    public int mainCode;
    public int codeSuffix;
    ...
}

@Entity
public class Address
{
    private ZipCode zip;
}
```

You can't navigate to one of the `ZipCode` class's instance fields:

```
// This is illegal
SELECT a.zip.mainCode FROM Address AS a
```

Of course, you could make the `ZipCode` class `@Embeddable`. If you did this, then you could obtain properties of the `ZipCode` class:

```
@Entity
public class Address {
    @Embedded private ZipCode zip;
}
```

This JPA QL would now be legal:

```
// @Embedded makes this legal now
SELECT a.zip.mainCode FROM Address AS a
```

It's illegal to navigate across a collection-based relationship field. The following JPA QL statement is illegal, even though the path ends in a single-type relationship field:

```
// This is illegal
SELECT e.phones.number FROM Employee AS e
```

If you think about it, this limitation makes sense. You can't use a navigation operator
(.) in Java to access elements of a `java.util.Collection` object. For example, if get
Phones() returns a `java.util.Collection` type, this statement is illegal:

```
// this is illegal in the Java programming language
employee.getPhones().getNumber();
```

Referencing the elements of a collection-based relationship field is possible, but it requires the use of an IN or JOIN operator and an identification assignment in the FROM
clause.

Constructor Expressions

One of the most powerful features of JPA QL is the ability to specify a constructor
within the SELECT clause that can allocate plain Java objects (nonentities) and pass
columns you select into that constructor. For example, let's say we want to aggregate
IDs and names from our Employee entity into a plain Java object called Name:

```java
package org.mypackage;
public class Name
{
   private Long id;
   private String name;

   public Name(final Long id, final String name)
   {
      this.setId(id);
      this.setName(name);
   }

   public Long getId() { return id; }
   public void setId(Long id) { this.id = id; }
   public String getName() { return name; }
   public void setName(String name) { this.name = name; }
}
```

We can actually have our query return a list of Name classes instead of a plain list of
strings. We do this by calling the constructor of Name directly within our query:

```
SELECT new org.mypackage.Name(e.id,e.name) FROM Employee e
```

The Query object will automatically allocate an instance of Name for each row returned,
passing in the id and name columns as arguments to the Name's constructor. This feature
is incredibly useful for generating typed reports and can save you a lot of typing.

The IN Operator and INNER JOIN

Many relationships between entity beans are collection-based, and being able to access
and select beans from these relationships is important. We've seen that it is illegal to
select elements directly from a collection-based relationship. To overcome this

limitation, JPA QL introduces the `IN` operator, which allows an identifier to represent individual elements in a collection-based relationship field.

The following query uses the `IN` operator to select the elements from a collection-based relationship. It returns all the Phones for an Employee:

```
SELECT p FROM Employee AS e, IN( e.phones ) p
```

The `IN` operator assigns the individual elements in the phones property to the p identifier. Once we have an identifier to represent the individual elements of the collection, we can reference them directly and even select them in the JPA QL statement. We can also use the element identifier in path expressions. For example, the following statement selects all phone numbers (a property of Phone) for an Employee:

```
SELECT p.number FROM Employee AS e, IN( e.phones ) p
```

The identifiers assigned in the `FROM` clause are evaluated from left to right. Once you declare an identifier, you can use it in subsequent declarations in the `FROM` clause. The e identifier, which was declared first, was subsequently used in the `IN` operator to define the p identifier.

This query can also be expressed as an `INNER JOIN`:

```
SELECT p.number FROM Employee e INNER JOIN e.phones p
```

The `INNER JOIN` syntax parallels the SQL language much better and is more intuitive for developers coming from the relational world.

LEFT JOIN

The `LEFT JOIN` syntax enables retrieval of a set of entities where matching values in the join statement may not exist. For values that do not exist, a null value is placed in the result set.

For example, let's say we want to generate a report with an employee's name and all the employee's phone numbers. Some employees may not have specified a phone number, but we still want to list their names. We would use a `LEFT JOIN` to acquire all of this information, including employees with no phone numbers:

```
SELECT e.name, p.number From Employee e LEFT JOIN e.phones p
```

If there were three employees in our system, and Bill Burke did not provide any phone numbers, the return values might look like this:

```
David Ortiz 617-555-0900
David Ortiz 617-555-9999
Trot Nixon 781-555-2323
Bill Burke null
```

The previous query can also be expressed as a `LEFT OUTER JOIN`. This is just syntax sugar to parallel SQL-92:

```
SELECT e.name, p.number From Employee e LEFT OUTER JOIN e.phones p
```

Fetch Joins

The `JOIN FETCH` syntax allows you to preload a returned entity's relationships, even if the relationship property has a `FetchType` of `LAZY`. For example, let's say we have defined our employee's one-to-many relationship to `Phone` as follows:

```
/**
 * All {@link Phone}s for this {@link Employee}
 */
@OneToMany (fetch=FetchType.LAZY)
private Collection<Phone> phones;
```

If we want to print out all employee information, including their phone numbers, usually we would just query for all employees and then traverse the `getPhones()` method inside a `for` loop:

```
Query query = manager.createQuery("SELECT e FROM Employee e"); ❶
List results = query.getResultList( );
Iterator it = results.iterator( );
while (it.hasNext( )) {
  Employee e = (Employee)it.next( );
  System.out.print(e.getName( ));
  for (Phone p : e.getPhones( )) { ❷
  System.out.print(p.getNumber( ));
  }
    System.out.println("");
  }
```

❶ There are performance problems with the preceding code. Because the `Phone` relationship is annotated as being lazily loaded in the `Employee` bean class, the `Phone` collection will not be initialized when we do the initial query.

❷ When `getPhones()` is executed, the persistence engine has to do an additional query to get the `Phone` entities associated with the `Employee`. This is called the *N + 1 problem*, as we have to do *N* extra queries beyond our initial query. When tuning database applications, it is always important to reduce the number of round-trips made to the database as much as possible. This is where the `JOIN FETCH` syntax comes into play. Let's modify our query to preload the `Phone` association:

```
SELECT e FROM Employee e LEFT JOIN FETCH e.phones
```

Using `LEFT JOIN FETCH` will additionally preload the `Phone` association. This can have a dramatic effect on performance because instead of *N + 1* queries, only one query is made to the database.

Using DISTINCT

The `DISTINCT` keyword ensures that the query does not return duplicates. For example, the following query finds all employees on a team. This query will return duplicates:

```
SELECT emp FROM Team t INNER JOIN t.members emp
```

If an `Employee` belongs to more than one `Team`, there will be duplicate references to that employee in the result. Using the `DISTINCT` keyword ensures that each `Employee` is represented only once in the result:

```
SELECT DISTINCT emp FROM Team t INNER JOIN t.members emp
```

The WHERE Clause and Literals

You can use literal values to narrow the scope of the elements selected. This is accomplished through the `WHERE` clause, which behaves in much the same way as the `WHERE` clause in SQL.

For example, you can define a JPA QL statement that selects all the `Employee` entities that have a specific name. The literal in this case is a `String` literal. Literal strings are enclosed by single quotes. Literal values that include a single quote, such as the restaurant name *Wendy's*, use two single quotes to escape the quote: `Wendy''s`. The following statement returns employees who have the name "Natalie Glass":

```
SELECT e FROM Employee AS e WHERE e.name = 'Natalie Glass'
```

Path expressions in the `WHERE` clause may be used in the same way as in the `SELECT` clause. When making comparisons with a literal, the path expression must evaluate to a basic property; you can't compare a relationship field with a literal.

In addition to literal strings, literals can be exact numeric values (`long` types) and approximate numeric values (`double` types). Exact numeric literal values are expressed using the Java integer literal syntax (`321`, `-8932`, `+22`). Approximate numeric literal values are expressed using Java floating-point literal syntax in scientific (`5E3`, `-8.932E5`) or decimal (`5.234`, `38282.2`) notation. Boolean literal values use `TRUE` and `FALSE`.

The WHERE Clause and Operator Precedence

The `WHERE` clause is composed of conditional expressions that reduce the scope of the query and limit the number of items selected. Several conditional and logical operators can be used in expressions; they are listed here in order of precedence:

- Navigation operator (`.`)
- Arithmetic operators: `+`, `-` (unary); `*`, `/` (multiplication and division); `+`, `-` (addition and subtraction)
- Comparison operators: `=`, `>`, `>=`, `<`, `<=`, `<>` (not equal), `LIKE`, `BETWEEN`, `IN`, `IS NULL`, `IS EMPTY`, `MEMBER OF`
- Logical operators: `NOT`, `AND`, `OR`

The WHERE Clause and Arithmetic Operators

The arithmetic operators allow a query to perform arithmetic in the process of doing a comparison. Arithmetic operators can be used only in the `WHERE` clause, not in the `SELECT` clause.

The following JPA QL statement returns references to all the `Employee`s who have an ID less than 100:

```
SELECT e FROM Employee AS e WHERE e.id < (1 * 10)
```

The rules applied to arithmetic operations are the same as those used in the Java programming language, where numbers are *widened*, or *promoted*, in the process of performing a calculation. For example, multiplying a `double` and an `int` value requires that the `int` first be promoted to a `double` value. (The result will always be that of the widest type used in the calculation, so multiplying an `int` and a `double` results in a `double` value.)

`String`, `boolean`, and entity object types cannot be used in arithmetic operations. For example, using the addition operator with two `String` values is considered an illegal operation. There is a special function for concatenating `String` values, covered in "Functional expressions in the WHERE clause" on page 225.

The WHERE Clause and Logical Operators

Logical operators such as `AND`, `OR`, and `NOT` operate the same way in JPA QL as their corresponding logical operators in SQL.

Logical operators evaluate only Boolean expressions, so each operand (i.e., each side of the expression) must evaluate to `true`, `false`, or `NULL`. Logical operators have the lowest precedence so that all the expressions can be evaluated before they are applied.

The `AND` and `OR` operators don't behave like their Java language counterparts, `&&` and `||`. JPA QL does not specify whether the righthand operands are evaluated conditionally. For example, the `&&` operator in Java evaluates its righthand operand *only* if the lefthand operand is `true`. Similarly, the `||` logical operator evaluates the righthand operand *only* if the lefthand operand is `false`. We can't make the same assumption for the `AND` and `OR` operators in JPA QL. Whether these operators evaluate righthand operands depends on the native query language into which the statements are translated. It's best to assume that both operands are evaluated on all logical operators.

`NOT` simply reverses the Boolean result of its operand; expressions that evaluate to the Boolean value of `true` become `false`, and vice versa

The WHERE Clause and Comparison Symbols

Comparison operators, which use the symbols =, >, >=, <, <=, and <> should be familiar to you. Only the = and <> (equals and not equals) operators may be used on `boolean` and entity object identifiers. The greater-than and less-than symbols (>, >=, <, <=) can be used on numeric values as well as strings. However, the semantics of these operations are not defined by the Java Persistence specification. Is character case (upper or lower) important? Does leading and trailing whitespace matter? Issues like these affect the ordering of string values. In order for JPA QL to maintain its status as an abstraction of native query languages, it cannot dictate `String` ordering, because native query languages may have very different ordering rules. In fact, even different relational database vendors vary on the question of `String` ordering, which makes it all but impossible to standardize ordering, even for SQL "compliant" databases.

Of course, this is all academic if you plan on using the same database well into the future. In such a case, the best thing to do is to examine the documentation for the database you are using to find out how it orders strings in comparisons. This tells you exactly how your JPA QL comparisons will work.

The WHERE Clause and Equality Semantics

Although it is legal to compare an exact numeric value (`short`, `int`, `long`) to an approximate numeric value (`double`, `float`), all other equality comparisons must compare the same types. You cannot, for example, compare a `String` value of `123` to the `Integer` literal `123`. However, you can compare two `String` types for equality.

You can compare numeric values for which the rules of numeric promotion apply. For example, a `short` may be compared to an `int`, an `int` to a `long`, etc. Java Persistence also states that primitives may be compared to primitive wrapper types—the rules of numeric promotion apply.

In older versions of the spec, `String` type comparisons had to match exactly, character for character. EJB 2.1 dropped this requirement, making the evaluation of equality between `String` types more ambiguous. This continued in Java Persistence. Again, this ambiguity arises from the differences between kinds of databases (relational versus object-oriented versus file), as well as differences between vendors of relational databases. Consult your vendor's documentation to determine exactly how `String` equality comparisons are evaluated.

You can also compare entity objects for equality, but these too must be of the same type. To be more specific, they must both be entity object references to beans from the same deployment. Once it's determined that the bean is the correct type, the actual comparison is performed on the beans' primary keys. If they have the same primary key, they are considered equal.

You may use `java.util.Date` objects in equality comparisons. See "Date Parameters" on page 209.

The WHERE Clause and BETWEEN

The BETWEEN clause is an inclusive operator specifying a range of values. In this example, we use it to select all Employees with an ID between 100 and 200:

```
SELECT e FROM Employee AS e WHERE e.id BETWEEN 100 AND 200
```

The BETWEEN clause may be used only on numeric primitives (byte, short, int, long, double, float) and their corresponding java.lang.Number types (Byte, Short, Integer, etc.). It cannot be used on String, boolean, or entity object references.

Using the NOT logical operator in conjunction with BETWEEN excludes the range specified. For example, the following JPA QL statement selects all the Employees that have an ID less than 100 or greater than 200:

```
SELECT e FROM Employee AS e WHERE e.id NOT BETWEEN 100 AND 200
```

The net effect of this query is the same as if it had been executed with comparison symbols:

```
SELECT e FROM Employee AS e
WHERE e.id < 100 OR e.id > 200
```

The WHERE Clause and IN

The IN conditional operator used in the WHERE clause is not the same as the IN operator used in the FROM clause (that's why the JOIN keyword in the FROM clause should be preferred over the IN keyword for collection navigation). In the WHERE clause, IN tests for membership in a list of literal values. For example, the following JPA QL statement uses the IN operator to select all the customers who reside in a specific set of states:

```
SELECT e FROM Employee AS e WHERE e.address.state IN ('FL', 'TX', 'MI', 'WI', 'MN')
```

Applying the NOT operator to this expression reverses the selection, excluding all customers who reside in the list of states:

```
SELECT e FROM Employee AS e WHERE e.address.state NOT IN ('FL', 'TX', 'MI', 'WI',
  'MN')
```

If the field tested is null, the value of the expression is "unknown," which means it cannot be predicted.

The IN operator can be used with operands that evaluate to either string or numeric values. For example, the following JPA QL fragment uses the IN operator to select values 1, 3, 5, and 7:

```
WHERE e.property IN (1,3,5,7)
```

The IN operator can also be used with input parameters. For example, the following query selects all the parameters:

```
WHERE e.property IN (?1,?2,?3)
```

In this case, the input parameters (?1, ?2, and ?3) are combined with parameters sent to the query during runtime execution.

The WHERE Clause and IS NULL

The IS NULL comparison operator allows you to test whether a path expression is null. For example, the following EJB QL statement selects all the Employees who do not have a manager (those who are self-managing):

```
SELECT e FROM Employee AS e WHERE e.manager IS NULL
```

Using the NOT logical operator, we can reverse the results of this query, selecting all Employees who report to a manager:

```
SELECT e FROM Employee AS e WHERE e.manager IS NOT NULL
```

Path expressions are composed using "inner join" semantics. If an entity has a null relationship field, any query that uses that field as part of a path expression eliminates that entity from consideration. For example, if the Employee entity representing "John Smith" has a null value for its address relationship field, then the "John Smith" Employee entity won't be included in the result set for the following query:

```
SELECT e FROM Employee AS e
WHERE e.address.state = 'TX'
AND c.name = 'John Smith'
```

This seems obvious at first, but stating it explicitly helps eliminate much of the ambiguity associated with null relationship fields.

The NULL comparison operator can also be used to test input parameters. In this case, NULL is usually combined with the NOT operator to ensure that an input parameter is not a null value. For example, this query can be used to test for null input parameters. The JPA QL statement first checks that the city and state input parameters are not null and then uses them in comparison operations:

```
SELECT e FROM Employee AS e
WHERE :city IS NOT NULL AND :state IS NOT NULL
AND e.address.state = :state
AND e.address.city = :city
```

In this case, if either of the input parameters is a null value, the query returns an empty List, avoiding the possibility of UNKNOWN results from null input parameters. Your Java code should do these null checks (input assertions) up front to avoid an unnecessary database round-trip.

If the results of a query include a null relationship or a basic field, the results must include null values. For example, the following query selects the addresses of customers whose name is "John Smith":

```
SELECT e.address FROM Employee AS e WHERE e.name = 'John Smith'
```

If the Employee entity representing "John Smith" has a null value for its address relationship field, the previous query returns a List that includes a null value—the null represents the address relationship field of "John Smith"—in addition to a bunch of Address entity references. You can eliminate null values by including the NOT NULL operator in the query, as shown here:

```
SELECT e.address.city FROM Employee AS e
WHERE e.address.city NOT NULL AND e.address.state = 'FL'
```

The WHERE Clause and IS EMPTY

The IS EMPTY operator allows the query to test whether a collection-based relationship is empty. Remember from Chapter 11 that a collection-based relationship will never be null. If a collection-based relationship field has no elements, it returns an empty Collection or Set.

Testing whether a collection-based relationship is empty has the same purpose as testing whether a single relationship field or basic field is null: it can be used to limit the scope of the query and items selected. For example, the following query selects all the Employees who have no Phones:

```
SELECT e FROM Employee AS e
WHERE e.phones IS EMPTY
```

The NOT operator reverses the result of IS EMPTY. The following query selects all the Employees who have at least one Phone:

```
SELECT e FROM Employee AS e
WHERE e.phones IS NOT EMPTY
```

The WHERE Clause and MEMBER OF

The MEMBER OF operator is a powerful tool for determining whether an entity is a member of a specific collection-based relationship. The following query determines whether a particular Employee entity (specified by the input parameter) is a member of any of the Team/Employee relationships:

```
SELECT t
FROM Team AS t, IN (t.members) AS m, Employee AS e
WHERE
e = :myCustomer
   AND
e MEMBER OF m.members
```

Applying the NOT operator to MEMBER OF has the reverse effect, selecting all the customers on which the specified customer does not have a team:

```
SELECT t
FROM Team AS t, IN (t.members) AS m, Employee AS e
WHERE
e = :myCustomer
```

```
                  AND
        e NOT MEMBER OF m.members
```

Checking whether an entity is a member of an empty collection always returns `false`.

The WHERE Clause and LIKE

The `LIKE` comparison operator allows the query to select `String` type fields that match a specified pattern. For example, the following JPA QL statement selects all the customers with hyphenated names, like "Monson-Haefel" and "Berners-Lee":

```
SELECT OBJECT( e ) FROM Employee AS e WHERE e.name LIKE '%-%'
```

You can use two special characters when establishing a comparison pattern: % (percent) stands for any sequence of characters, and _ (underscore) stands for any single character. You can use these characters at any location within a string pattern. If a % or _ actually occurs in the string, you can escape it with the \ (backslash) character. The `NOT` logical operator reverses the evaluation so that matching patterns are excluded. The following examples show how the `LIKE` clause evaluates `String` type fields:

`phone.number LIKE '617%'`
> True for "617-322-4151"
>
> False for "415-222-3523"

`cabin.name LIKE 'Suite _100'`
> True for "Suite A100"
>
> False for "Suite A233"

`phone.number NOT LIKE '608%'`
> True for "415-222-3523"
>
> False for "608-233-8484"

`someField.underscored LIKE '\_%'`
> True for "_xyz"
>
> False for "abc"

`someField.percentage LIKE '\%%'`
> True for "% XYZ"
>
> False for "ABC"

The `LIKE` operator can also be used with input parameters:

```
SELECT e FROM Employee AS e WHERE e.name LIKE :param
```

Functional Expressions

JPA QL has numerous functions that you can use to process strings and numeric values.

Functional expressions in the WHERE clause

JPA QL has seven functional expressions that allow for simple `String` manipulation and three functional expressions for basic numeric operations. The `String` functions are:

`LOWER(String)`
> Converts a string to lowercase.

`UPPER(String)`
> Converts a string to uppercase.

`TRIM([[LEADING | TRAILING | BOTH] [trim_char] FROM] String)`
> Allows you to trim a specified character from the beginning (`LEADING`), end (`TRAILING`), or both (`BOTH`). If you do not specify a trim character, the space character will be assumed.

`CONCAT(String1, String2)`
> Returns the `String` that results from concatenating `String1` and `String2`.

`LENGTH(String)`
> Returns an `int` indicating the length of the string.

`LOCATE(String1, String2 [, start])`
> Returns an `int` indicating the position at which `String1` is found within `String2`. If it's present, `start` indicates the character position in `String2` at which the search should start. Support for the `start` parameter is optional; some containers will support it and others will not. Don't use it if you want to ensure that the query is portable.

`SUBSTRING(String1, start, length)`
> Returns the `String` consisting of `length` characters taken from `String1`, starting at the position given by `start`.

The `start` and `length` parameters indicate positions in a `String` as integer values. You can use these expressions in the `WHERE` clause to refine the scope of the items selected. Here's how the `LOCATE` and `LENGTH` functions might be used:

```
SELECT e
FROM Employee AS e
WHERE
LENGTH(e.name) > 6
  AND
LOCATE(e.name, 'Monson') > -1
```

This statement selects all the employees with `Monson` somewhere in their last names but specifies that the names must be longer than six characters. Therefore, "Monson-Haefel" and "Monson-Ares" would evaluate to `true`, but "Monson" would return `false` because it has only six characters.

The arithmetic functions in JPA QL may be applied to primitive as well as corresponding primitive wrapper types:

```
ABS(number)
```
Returns the absolute value of a number (`int`, `float`, or `double`)

```
SQRT(double)
```
Returns the square root of a `double`

```
MOD(int, int)
```
Returns the remainder for the first parameter divided by the second (e.g., `MOD(7, 5)` is equal to 2)

Functions returning dates and times

JPA QL has three functions that can return you the current date, time, and timestamp: `CURRENT_DATE`, `CURRENT_TIME`, and `CURRENT_TIMESTAMP`. Here's an example of searching for employees who joined the company on the current date:

```
SELECT e FROM Employee e WHERE e.startDate = CURRENT_DATE
```

Aggregate functions in the SELECT clause

Aggregate functions are used with queries that return a collection of values. They are fairly simple to understand and can be handy, especially the `COUNT()` function.

COUNT (identifier or path expression). This function returns the number of items in the query's final result set. The return type is a `java.lang.Long`, depending on whether it is the return type of the query method. For example, the following query provides a count of all the customers who live in Wisconsin:

```
SELECT COUNT( c )
FROM Customers AS c
WHERE c.address.state = 'WI'
```

The `COUNT()` function can be used with an identifier, in which case it always counts entities, or with path expressions, in which case it counts fields. For example, the following statement provides a count of all the zip codes that start with the numbers 554:

```
SELECT COUNT(c.address.zip)
FROM Customers AS c
WHERE c.address.zip LIKE '554%'
```

In some cases, queries that count a path expression have a corresponding query that can be used to count an identifier. For example, the result of the following query, which counts `Customers` instead of the `zip` field, is equivalent to the previous query:

```
SELECT COUNT( c )
FROM Customers AS c
WHERE c.address.zip LIKE '554%'
```

MAX(path expression), MIN(path expression). These functions can be used to find the largest or smallest value from a collection of any type of field. They cannot be used with identifiers or paths that terminate in a relationship field. The result type will be the type of field that is being evaluated. For example, the following query returns the highest price paid for an order:

```
SELECT MAX( o.totalAmount )
FROM ProductOrder AS o
```

The `MAX()` and `MIN()` functions can be applied to any valid value, including primitive types, strings, and even serializable objects. The result of applying the `MAX()` and `MIN()` functions to serializable objects is not specified, because there is no standard way to determine which serializable object is greater than or less than another one.

The result of applying the `MAX()` and `MIN()` functions to a `String` field depends on the underlying data store. This has to do with the inherent problems associated with `String` type comparisons.

AVG(numeric), SUM(numeric). The `AVG()` and `SUM()` functions can be applied only to path expressions that terminate in a numeric primitive field (`byte`, `long`, `float`, etc.) or in one of their corresponding numeric wrappers (`Byte`, `Long`, `Float`, etc.). The result of a query that uses the `SUM()` function has the same type as the numeric type it's evaluating. The result type of the `AVG()` function is a `java.lang.Double`, depending on whether it is used in the return type of the `SELECT` method.

For example, the following query uses the `SUM()` function to get the total amount for all orders:

```
SELECT SUM( o.totalAmount )
FROM ProductOrder o
```

DISTINCT, nulls, and empty arguments. The `DISTINCT` operator can be used with any of the aggregate functions to eliminate duplicate values. The following query uses the `DISTINCT` operator to count the number of *different* zip codes that match the pattern specified:

```
SELECT DISTINCT COUNT(c.address.zip)
FROM Customers AS c
WHERE c.address.zip LIKE '554%'
```

The `DISTINCT` operator first eliminates duplicate zip codes. If 100 customers live in the same area with the same zip code, their zip code is counted only once. After the duplicates have been eliminated, the `COUNT()` function counts the number of items left.

Any field with a `null` value is automatically eliminated from the result set operated on by the aggregate functions. The `COUNT()` function also ignores values with null values. The aggregate functions `AVG()`, `SUM()`, `MAX()`, and `MIN()` return `null` when evaluating an empty collection.

The `COUNT()` function returns 0 (zero) when the argument it evaluates is an empty collection. If the following query is evaluated on an order with no line items, the result is 0 (zero) because the argument is an empty collection:

```
SELECT COUNT( li )
FROM ProductOrder AS o, IN( o.lineItems ) AS li
WHERE o = ?1
```

The ORDER BY Clause

The ORDER BY clause allows you to specify the order of the entities in the collection returned by a query. The semantics of the ORDER BY clause are basically the same as in SQL. For example, we can construct a simple query that uses the ORDER BY clause to return an alphabetical list of all employees:

```
SELECT e
FROM Employee AS e
ORDER BY e.name
```

This will return a Collection of Employee entities in alphabetical order by name.

You can use the ORDER BY clause with or without the WHERE clause. For example, we can refine the previous query by listing only those U.S. employees who reside in Boston:

```
SELECT e
FROM Employee AS e
WHERE e.address.city = 'Boston' AND e.address.state = 'MA'
ORDER BY e.name
```

The default order of an item listed in the ORDER BY clause is always ascending, which means that the lesser values are listed first and the greater values last. You can explicitly specify the order as *ascending* or *descending* by using the keywords ASC and DESC. The default is ASC. Null elements will be placed either on top or at the bottom of the query result, depending on the underlying database. Here's a statement that lists customers in reverse (descending) order:

```
SELECT e
FROM Employee AS e
ORDER BY e.name DESC
```

You can specify multiple order-by items. For example, you can sort customers by lastName in ascending order and firstName in descending order:

```
SELECT c
FROM Customers AS c
ORDER BY c.lastName ASC, c.firstName DESC
```

If you have five Customer entities with the lastName equal to Brooks, this query sorts the results as follows:

```
Brooks, William
Brooks, Henry
Brooks, Hank
Brooks, Ben
Brooks, Andy
```

Although the fields used in the ORDER BY clause must be basic fields, the value selected can be an entity identifier, a relationship field, or a basic field. For example, the following query returns an ordered list of all zip codes:

```
SELECT addr.zip
FROM Address AS addr
ORDER BY addr.zip
```

The following query returns all the `Address` entities for customers named Smith, ordered by their zip code:

```
SELECT c.address
FOR Customer AS c
WHERE c.lastName = 'Smith'
ORDER BY c.address.zip
```

You must be careful which basic fields you use in the `ORDER BY` clause. If the query selects a collection of entities, then the `ORDER BY` clause can be used with only basic fields of the entity type that is selected. The following query is illegal, because the basic field used in the `ORDER BY` clause is not a field of the entity type selected:

```
// Illegal JPA QL
SELECT e
FROM Employee AS e
ORDER BY e.address.city
```

Because the `city` field is not a direct field of the `Employee` entity, you cannot use it in the `ORDER BY` clause.

A similar restriction applies to results. The field used in the `ORDER BY` clause must also be in the `SELECT` clause. The following query is illegal because the field identified in the `SELECT` clause is not the same as the one used in the `ORDER BY` clause:

```
// Illegal JPA QL
SELECT e.address.city
FROM Employee AS e
ORDER BY e.address.state
```

In the previous query, we wanted a list of all the cities ordered by their state. Unfortunately, this is illegal. You can't order by the `state` field if you are not selecting the `state` field.

Bulk UPDATE and DELETE

Java Persistence has the ability to perform bulk `UPDATE` and `DELETE` operations. This can save you a lot of typing. For example, let's say we want to give a $10 credit across the board to any customer named Bill Burke. We can do the following bulk `UPDATE`:

```
UPDATE ProductOrder o SET o.amountPaid = (o.amountPaid + 10)
WHERE EXISTS (
    SELECT c FROM o.customer c
    WHERE c.name = 'Bill Burke'
)
```

As an example of `DELETE`, say that we want to remove all orders placed by Bill Burke:

```
DELETE FROM ProductOrder o
WHERE EXISTS (
    SELECT c FROM o.customer c
    WHERE c.name = 'Bill Burke'
)
```

Be very careful how you use bulk UPDATE and DELETE. It is possible, depending on the vendor implementation, to create inconsistencies between the database and entities that are already being managed by the current persistence context. Vendor implementations are required only to execute the update or delete directly on the database. They do not have to modify the state of any currently managed entity. For this reason, it is recommended that you do these operations within their own transaction or at the beginning of a transaction (before any entities are accessed that might be affected by these bulk operations). Alternatively, executing EntityManager.flush() and EntityManager.clear() before executing a bulk operation will keep you safe.

Native Queries

JPA QL is a very rich syntax and should meet most of your querying needs. Sometimes, though, you want to take advantage of certain proprietary capabilities that are available only on a specific vendor's database.

The entity manager service provides a way to create native SQL queries and map them to your objects. Native queries can return entities, column values, or a combination of the two. The EntityManager interface has three methods for creating native queries: one for returning scalar values, one for returning one entity type, and one for defining a complex result set that can map to a mix of multiple entities and scalar values.

 You can always get the underlying JDBC connection through a javax.sql.DataSource injected by the @Resource and execute any SQL statement you need. Be aware that your changes will not be reflected in the current persistence context.

Scalar Native Queries

```
Query createNativeQuery(String sql)
```

This creates a native query that returns scalar results. It takes one parameter: your native SQL. It executes as is and returns the result set in the same form as JPA QL returns scalar values.

Simple Entity Native Queries

```
Query createNativeQuery(String sql, Class entityClass)
```

A simple entity native query takes an SQL statement and implicitly maps it to one entity based on the mapping metadata you declared for that entity. It expects that the columns returned in the result set of the native query will match perfectly with the entity's O/R mapping. The entity that the native SQL query maps to is determined by the entity Class parameter:

```
Query query = manager.createNativeQuery(
    "SELECT p.phone_PK, p.phone_number, p.type
```

```
        FROM PHONE AS p", Phone.class
    );
```

All the properties of the entities must be pulled.

Complex Native Queries

```
    Query createNativeQuery(String sql, String mappingName)
```

This entity manager method allows you to have complex mappings for your native SQL. You can return multiple entities and scalar column values at the same time. The map pingName parameter references a declared @javax.persistence.SqlResultSetMapping. This annotation is used to define how the native SQL results hook back into your O/R model. If your returned column names don't match the parallel annotated property mapping, you can provide a field-to-column mapping for them using @javax.persistence.FieldResult:

```
    package javax.persistence;

    public @interface SqlResultSetMapping {
        String name( );
        EntityResult[] entities( ) default {};
        ColumnResult[] columns( ) default {};
    }

    public @interface EntityResult {
        Class entityClass( );
        FieldResult[] fields( ) default {};
        String discriminatorColumn( ) default "";
    }

    public @interface FieldResult {
        String name( );
        String column( );
    }

    public @interface ColumnResult {
        String name( );
    }
```

Let's create an example to show how this would work.

Native queries with multiple entities

First, let's create a native query that returns multiple entity types—a Customer and its CreditCard:

```
    @Entity
    @SqlResultSetMapping(name="customerAndCreditCardMapping",
            entities={@EntityResult(entityClass=Customer.class),
                    @EntityResult(entityClass=CreditCard.class,
                            fields={@FieldResult(name="id",
                                            column="CC_ID"),
                                    @FieldResult(name="number",
```

```
                                        column="number")}
                        )})
    public class Customer {...}

    // execution code
    {
        Query query = manager.createNativeQuery(
            "SELECT c.id, c.firstName, cc.id As CC_ID,
     cc.number" +
                    "FROM CUST_TABLE c, CREDIT_CARD_TABLE cc" +
                    "WHERE c.credit_card_id = cc.id",
            "customerAndCreditCardMapping");
    }
```

Because the result set returns multiple entity types, we must define an `@SqlResultSet`
`Mapping`. This annotation can be placed on an entity class or method. The `entities()`
attribute is set to an array of `@EntityResult` annotations. Each `@EntityResult` annotation
specifies the entities that will be returned by the native SQL query.

The `@javax.persistence.FieldResult` annotation is used to explicitly map columns in
the query with properties of an entity. The `name()` attribute of `@FieldResult` identifies
the entity bean's property, and the `column()` attribute identifies the result set column
returned by the native query.

In this example, we do not need to specify any `@FieldResult`s for `Customer`, as the native
query pulls in each column for this entity. However, since we are querying only the ID
and number columns of the `CreditCard` entity, an `@FieldResult` annotation should be
specified. In the `@EntityResult` annotation for `CreditCard`, the `fields()` attribute defines what `CreditCard` properties each queried column maps to. Because the `Customer`
and `CreditCard` primary-key columns have the same name, the SQL query needs to
distinguish that they are different. The `cc.id As CC_ID` SQL fragment performs this
identification.

Named Queries

Java Persistence provides a mechanism so that you can predefine JPA QL or native SQL
queries and reference them by name when creating a query. You would want to pre-
declare queries for the same reason you create `String` constant variables in Java: to
reuse them in multiple situations. If you predefine your queries in one place, you have
an easy way to fine-tune or modify them as time goes on. The `@javax.persistence.Named`
`Query` annotation is used for predefining JPA QL queries:

```
package javax.persistence;

public @interface NamedQuery {
    String name( );
    String query( );
    QueryHint[] hints( ) default {};
}
```

```
public @interface QueryHint {
    String name( );
    String value( );
}

public @interface NamedQueries {
    NamedQuery[] value( );
}
```

You use the `@javax.persistence.NamedQueries` annotation when you are declaring more than one query on a class or package. The `@javax.persistence.QueryHint` annotation declares vendor-specific hints. These hints work in the same way as the `Query.setHint` () method described earlier in this chapter. Here's an example:

```
@NamedQueries({
    @NamedQuery
(name="getAverageProductOrderAmount",
            query=
                "SELECT AVG( o.amountPaid )
                FROM ProductOrder as o")
})
@Entity
public class ProductOrder {...}
```

This example declares a JPA QL query on the `ProductOrder` entity bean class. You can then reference these declarations in the `EntityManager.createNamedQuery()` method:

```
Query query = em.createNamedQuery("getAverageProductOrderAmount");
```

Named Native Queries

The `@javax.persistence.NamedNativeQuery` annotation is used for predefining native SQL queries:

```
package javax.persistence;

public @interface NamedNativeQuery {
    String name( );
    String query( );
    Class resultClass( ) default void.class;
    String resultSetMapping( ) default "";
}

public @interface NamedNativeQueries {
    NamedNativeQuery[] value( );
}
```

The `resultClass()` attribute is for when you have a native query that returns only one entity type (see "Native Queries" on page 230). The `resultSetMapping()` attribute must resolve to a predeclared `@SqlResultSetMapping`. Both attributes are optional, but you must declare at least one of them. Here is an example of predeclaring an `@NamedNative Query`:

```
@NamedNativeQuery(
    name="findCustAndCCNum",
    query="SELECT c.id, c.firstName, c.lastName, cc.number AS CC_NUM
              FROM CUST_TABLE c, CREDIT_CARD_TABLE cc
              WHERE c.credit_card_id = cc.id",
    resultSetMapping="customerAndCCNumMapping")
@SqlResultSetMapping(name="customerAndCCNumMapping",
      entities={@EntityResult(entityClass=Customer.class)},
      columns={@ColumnResult(name="CC_NUM")}
)
@Entity
public class Customer {...}
```

You can then reference this declaration in the `EntityManager.createNamedQuery()` method:

```
Query query = em.createNamedQuery("findCustAndCCNum");
```

## CHAPTER 14

Entity Callbacks and Listeners

When you execute `EntityManager` methods such as `persist()`, `merge()`, `remove()`, and `find()`, or when you execute JPA QL queries or use the `Criteria` API, a predefined set of lifecycle events are triggered. For instance, the `persist()` method triggers database inserts. Merging triggers updates to the database. The `remove()` method triggers database deletes. Querying entities triggers a load from the database. Sometimes it is very useful to have your entity bean class be notified as these events happen. For instance, maybe you want to create an audit log of every interaction done on each row in your database. The Java Persistence specification allows you to set up callback methods on your entity classes so that your entity instances are notified when these events occur. You can also register separate listener classes that can intercept these same events. These are called *entity listeners*. This chapter discusses how you register your entity bean classes for lifecycle callbacks as well as how to write entity listeners that can intercept lifecycle events on your entities.

Callback Events

An annotation may represent each phase of an entity's lifecycle:

```
@javax.persistence.PrePersist
@javax.persistence.PostPersist
@javax.persistence.PostLoad
@javax.persistence.PreUpdate
@javax.persistence.PostUpdate
@javax.persistence.PreRemove
@javax.persistence.PostRemove
```

The `@PrePersist` and `@PostPersist` events have to do with the insertion of an entity instance into the database. The `@PrePersist` event occurs immediately when the `EntityManager.persist()` call is invoked or whenever an entity instance is scheduled to be inserted into the database (as with a cascaded merge). The `@PostPersist` event is not triggered until the actual database insert.

The `@PreUpdate` event is triggered just before the state of the entity is synchronized with the database, and the `@PostUpdate` event happens after. This synchronization could occur at transaction commit time, when `EntityManager.flush()` is executed, or whenever the persistence context deems it necessary to update the database.

The `@PreRemove` and `@PostRemove` events have to do with the removal of an entity bean from the database. `@PreRemove` is triggered whenever `EntityManager.remove()` is invoked on the entity bean, directly or because of a cascade. The `@PostRemove` event happens immediately after the actual database delete occurs.

The `@PostLoad` event is triggered after an entity instance has been loaded by a `find()` or `getReference()` method call on the `EntityManager` interface, or when a JPA QL or `Criteria` query is executed. It is also called after the `refresh()` method is invoked.

Callbacks on Entity Classes

You can have an entity bean instance register for a callback on any of these lifecycle events by annotating a public, private, protected, or package-protected method on the bean class. This method must return **void**, throw no checked exceptions, and have no arguments:

```
import javax.persistence.Entity;
import javax.persistence.PostPersist;
import javax.persistence.PrePersist;

/**
 * Represents an Employee which is able to receive JPA
 * events.
 */
@Entity
public class EntityListenerEmployee
{

    private String name;

    public String getName() { return name; }
    public void setName(final String name) { this.name = name; }

    /*
     * Event Listeners; fired by JPA and track state in the EventTracker
     */

    @PrePersist
    @SuppressWarnings("unused")
    private void prePersist(){ ... }

    @PostPersist
    @SuppressWarnings("unused")
    private void postPersist(){ ... }
```

```
        ...
    }
```

When an event is triggered on a particular managed entity instance, the entity manager will invoke the appropriate annotated method on the entity bean class.

Entity Listeners

Entity listeners are classes that can generically intercept entity callback events. They are not entity classes themselves, but they can be attached to an entity class through a binding annotation or XML. You can assign methods on an entity listener class to intercept a particular lifecycle event. These methods return void and take one Object parameter that is the entity instance on which the event is being triggered. The method is annotated with the callback in which it is interested:

```
public class Auditor {

    @PostPersist void postInsert(final Object entity)
    {
        System.out.println("Inserted entity: " + entity.getClass().getName( ));
    }

    @PostLoad void postLoad(final Object entity)
    {
        System.out.println("Loaded entity: " + entity.getClass().getName( ));
    }

}
```

The entity listener class must have a public no-arg constructor. It can be applied to an entity class by using the @javax.persistence.EntityListeners annotation:

```
package javax.persistence;

@Target(TYPE) @Retention(RUNTIME)
public @interface EntityListeners
{
    Class[] value();
}
```

You may specify one or more entity listeners that intercept the callback events of an entity class:

```
@Entity
@EntityListeners  ({Auditor.class})
public class EntityListenerEmployee
{
    ...
}
```

By using the @EntityListeners annotation on the EntityListenerEmployee entity class, any callback methods within those entity listener classes will be invoked whenever EntityListenerEmployee entity instances interact with a persistence context.

Default Entity Listeners

You can specify a set of default entity listeners that are applied to every entity class in the persistence unit by using the `<entity-listeners>` element under the top-level `<entity-mappings>` element in the ORM mapping file. For instance, if you wanted to apply the `Auditor` listener to every entity class in a particular persistence unit, you would do the following:

```
<entity-mappings>
    <entity-listeners>
        <entity-listener class="org.package.Auditor">
            <post-persist name="postInsert"/>
            <post-load name="postLoad"/>
        </entity-listener>
    </entity-listeners>
</entity-mappings
```

If you want to turn off default entity listeners to a particular entity class, you can use the `@javax.persistence.ExcludeDefaultListeners` annotation:

```
@Entity
@ExcludeDefaultListeners
public class NoEntityListenersEmployee {
...
}
```

If either the `@ExcludeDefaultListeners` annotation or its XML equivalent is applied to the `EntityListenerEmployee` entity, the `Auditor` is turned off for that entity.

Inheritance and Listeners

If you have an inheritance entity hierarchy in which the base class has entity listeners applied to it, any subclass will inherit these entity listeners. If the subclass also has entity listeners applied to it, then both the base and the subclass's listeners will be attached:

```
@Entity
@EntityListeners(Auditor.class)
public class SingleEntityListenerEmployee
{
    ...
}

@Entity
@EntityListeners(AnotherListener.class)
public class DoubleEntityListenerEmployee extends SingleEntityListenerEmployee
{
    ...
}
```

In this example, the `Auditor` entity listener and `AnotherListener` will be attached to the `DoubleEntityListenerEmployee` entity. If all of these listeners have an `@PostPersist` callback, the order of callback execution will be as follows:

1. `Auditor`'s `@PostPersist` method
2. `AnotherListener`'s `@PostPersist` method

Entity listeners applied to a base class happen before any listeners attached to a subclass. Callback methods defined directly in an entity class happen last.

You can turn off inherited entity listeners by using `@javax.persistence.ExcludeSuper classListeners`:

```
@Entity
@EntityListeners(Auditor.class)
public class EntityListenerEmployee {

}

@Entity
@ExcludeSuperclassListeners

public class NoEntityListenersEmployee extends EntityListenerEmployee {
...
}
```

In this example, no listeners would be executed for `NoEntityListenerEmployee` entity instances. `@ExcludeSuperclassListeners` has an XML equivalent in the `<exclude-super class-listeners/>` element.

## PART IV

Container Services

While server-side component types handle business logic and entities address state, the EJB Container can continue to make our jobs easier by providing a wide range of generic and configurable services. Enterprise applications generally handle a large number of concurrent users, and each request might need to be handled carefully so it does not violate the security or integrity of the application. Additionally, we shouldn't waste our time wiring our modules together; the container can do this for us. Perhaps we have some other cross-cutting concern we'd like to model and apply on our own. For these requirements, EJB offers a range of container services.

Security (Chapter 15) addresses the need to authorize and authenticate users uniformly across the application. Not all requests should be given *carte blanche* access to the whole application, and this is EJB's mechanism to declaratively or programmatically restrict access.

Injection (Chapter 16) allows our modules to communicate with one another without the explicit need to perform service lookups. We can also use injection to define dependency relationships between resources.

Transactions (Chapter 17) ensure that our application's state maintains its integrity while under load from concurrent use. Although traditionally this is a very difficult paradigm to achieve manually, EJB provides us with a declarative syntax to guard our business logic methods and, by extension, associated resources such as the `EntityManager`.

Interceptors (Chapter 18) are a generic utility for defining your own application logic to be applied in a cross-cutting manner. This is a powerful way to promote code reuse, and it's built into the platform.

The Timer Service (Chapter 19) allows the EJB container to fire time-based events into business logic methods. Instead of servicing a client request, we may instead set triggers to, for instance, process a batch job every hour.

Web Services (Chapters 20 and 21) address the need for interoperability with other platforms outside Enterprise Java.

## CHAPTER 15

Security

Most enterprise applications are designed to serve a large number of clients, and users are not necessarily equal in terms of their access rights. An administrator might require hooks into the configuration of the system, whereas unknown guests may be allowed a read-only view of data.

It's bad practice, however, to hardcode users' access directly into your application's logic. We shouldn't have to rebuild an EJB each time a new employee comes into the company or an existing one is promoted to a new position with greater privileges.

If we group users into categories with defined *roles*, we can then allow or restrict access to the role itself, as illustrated in Figure 15-1.

This technique is called *role-based security*. As we've seen before, embedding such rules within business logic tangles up concerns, so we're best off enforcing these constraints at another level.

The Java EE and EJB specifications provide a core set of security services that application developers can integrate declaratively and programmatically. These include:

Authentication
> This is the process of validating the identity of a user who is trying to access a secured system. When authenticating, the application server verifies that the user actually exists in the system and has provided the correct credentials, such as a password.

Authorization
> Once a user is authenticated in a system, he will want to interact with the application. Authorization involves determining whether a user is allowed to execute a certain action. Authorization can police a user's access to subsystems, data, and business objects, or it can monitor more general behavior. Certain users, for example, may be allowed to update information, whereas others are allowed only to view the data. For web applications, maybe only certain users are permitted to access certain URLs. For EJB applications, the user can be authorized on a per-method basis.

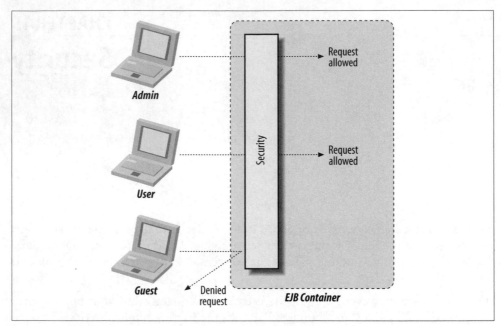

Figure 15-1. EJB security permitting access based upon the caller's role

Although a small programmatic API is available for interacting with Java EE security services, users rarely have to write any code to secure their applications, because setting up security is usually a static, declarative process. Only session beans can be secured in EJB. This chapter focuses on how to set up authentication and authorization for your session beans.

Authentication and Identity

In a secure EJB application, *authentication* involves verifying that a user is who she says she is. When a remote client logs on to the EJB system, it is associated with a security identity for the duration of that session. Once a remote client application has been associated with a security identity, it is ready to use beans to accomplish some task. When a client invokes a method on a bean, the EJB server implicitly passes the client's identity with the method invocation. When the EJB container receives the method invocation, it checks the identity to ensure that the client is valid and is allowed to invoke the target method.

Unfortunately (or fortunately, depending on your perspective), the EJB specification does not specify how authentication happens. Although it defines how security information is propagated from a client to the server, it does not specify how the client is supposed to obtain and associate identity and credentials with an EJB invocation. It also does not define how the application server stores and retrieves authentication information. The vendor must decide how to package and provide these services on the client and server.

When invoking on a remote EJB, many application servers accomplish authentication by using the JNDI API. For example, a client using JNDI can provide authenticating information using the JNDI API to access a server or resource in the server. This information is frequently passed when the client attempts to initiate a JNDI connection on the EJB server. The following code shows how a client's password and username can be added to the connection properties for obtaining a JNDI connection to the EJB server:

```
properties.put(Context.SECURITY_PRINCIPAL, "username");
properties.put(Context.SECURITY_CREDENTIALS, "password");

Context ctx = new InitialContext(properties);
Object ref = jndiContext.lookup("SecureBean/remote");
SecureRemoteBusiness remote = (SecureRemoteBusiness)ref;
```

In this example, the user is authenticated with the connection to the JNDI InitialContext. The username and password are associated with the client thread and propagated to the server internally when calls are made to remote EJBs.

Although JNDI is a common way for most application servers to perform authentication, sometimes users need a better abstraction for obtaining security information. For instance, what if the credentials were a thumbprint instead of a password? Many application servers provide a mechanism other than JNDI with which to authenticate. For instance, the JBoss application server uses the JAAS specification, which provides a rich API for performing authentication.

Authorization

Once a user is authenticated by a vendor-specific mechanism, he must be checked to see if he is allowed to invoke a particular EJB method. Authorization is performed in Java EE and EJB by associating one or more roles with a given user and then assigning method permissions based on that role. While an example of a user might be "Carlo" or "Jaikiran," roles are used to identify a group of users—for instance, "administrator," "manager," or "employee." In EJB, you assign access control at method granularity. You do not assign these permissions on a per-user basis, but rather on a per-role basis. This allows the authentication process to remain a separate configuration from authorization.

The roles used to describe authorization are considered logical roles because they do not directly reflect users, groups, or any other security identities in a specific operational environment. EJB security roles are mapped to real-world user groups and users when the bean is deployed. This mapping allows a bean to be portable; every time the bean is deployed in a new system, the roles can be mapped to the users and groups specific to that operational environment.

Unlike authentication, authorization is something that the EJB specification clearly defines. You begin by declaring the roles that are accessed programmatically in your code base. Then, you assign permissions for each method in your class. This is done declaratively through Java annotations or through the `ejb-jar.xml` deployment descriptor.

Example: A Secured School

To illustrate, let's secure access to a `SecureSchoolEJB`; anyone can see whether a school is open, but only enrolled students may enter the front door during operating hours. Additionally, only janitors may use the service door, and administrators have total access, including the ability to open and close the school each day. The full example is covered in Appendix G.

The Business Interface

As always, we'll start by fleshing out the API for our little school. It'll support both a front and service entrance, and access to each will be defined by the user looking to enter as well as whether the school is open or closed:

```
/**
 * Represents a school holding doors which may be
 * opened by various users.  Using the EJB Security model,
 * access to open a particular door may be blocked
 * to certain users.
 *
 * @author <a href="mailto:andrew.rubinger@jboss.org">ALR</a>
 * @version $Revision: $
 */
public interface SecureSchoolLocalBusiness
{

   /**
    * Closes the school for business.  At this point the
    * front door will be unlocked for all.
    * This method may only be called by users in role
    * {@link Roles#ADMIN}.
    */
   void open();

   /**
    * Closes the school for business.  At this point the
    * front door will be locked for all but users
    * in role {@link Roles#ADMIN}
    * This method may only be called by admins.
    */
   void close();

   /**
    * Opens the front door.  While school is open,
```

```
 * any authenticated user may open the door, else
 * only the {@link Roles#ADMIN} may open.
 *
 * @throws SchoolClosedException If the current user
 * is not in {@link Roles#ADMIN} and is attempting to open
 * the door while {@link SecureSchoolLocalBusiness#isOpen()}
 * is false.
 */
void openFrontDoor() throws SchoolClosedException;

/**
 * Opens the service door. Users in {@link Roles#STUDENT}
 * role may not open this door, but {@link Roles#ADMIN}
 * and {@link Roles#JANITOR} may.
 */
void openServiceDoor();

/**
 * Returns whether or not the school is open.  When closed, only
 * the {@link Roles#ADMIN} is allowed access to all doors.  Anyone,
 * even unauthenticated users, may check if school is open.
 * @return
 */
boolean isOpen();

}
```

Assigning Method Permissions

We must be very careful when determining to whom we grant access within the Secure
SchoolEJB.

As a first step, let's define the roles that are permitted:

```
/**
 * Holds the list of roles with which users of the school
 * may be affiliated.  EJB Security is role-based, so this
 * is how we'll determine access.
 *
 * @author <a href="mailto:andrew.rubinger@jboss.org">ALR</a>
 * @version $Revision: $
 */
public interface Roles
{
   /*
    * Roles of callers to the system
    */

   /**
    * Role denoting the user is a school administrator
    */
   String ADMIN = "Administrator";

   /**
    * Role denoting the user is a student
```

```
 */
String STUDENT = "Student";

/**
 * Role denoting the user is a janitor
 */
String JANITOR = "Janitor";

}
```

We need to make the EJB aware now of the roles it'll respect; this is done using the `@javax.annotation.security.DeclareRoles` annotation and placing the declaration atop the bean implementation class:

```
@DeclareRoles(
{Roles.ADMIN, Roles.STUDENT, Roles.JANITOR})
```

Alternatively, we can use the `security-role-ref` element within the bean deployment descriptor.

By default, it's good practice to restrict access to everyone at the highest level, and then enable access as necessary at a finer granularity. The `@javax.annotation.security.RolesAllowed` annotation is used to assign access rights at either the class or method level. This annotation defines one or more logical roles that are allowed to access the method. When placed on the bean class, the `@RolesAllowed` annotation specifies the default set of roles that are permitted to access bean methods. Each individual EJB method can override this behavior by using the same annotation. Let's block everyone at the class level first, which gives us a full bean implementation class definition that looks a little like the following:

```
/**
 * A secure school which may block requests to
 * open doors depending upon the EJB Security
 * model's configuration
 *
 * @author <a href="mailto:andrew.rubinger@jboss.org">ALR</a>
 * @version $Revision: $
 */
@Singleton
@Local(SecureSchoolLocalBusiness.class)
// Declare the roles in the system
@DeclareRoles(
{Roles.ADMIN, Roles.STUDENT, Roles.JANITOR})
// By default allow no one access, we'll enable access at a finer-grained level
@RolesAllowed(
{})
@Startup
public class SecureSchoolBean implements SecureSchoolLocalBusiness { ... }
```

Now that the whole EJB is secured to block outside callers, we can drill down to the method level and enable access to fit our requirements.

The `@javax.annotation.security.PermitAll` annotation specifies that any authenticated user is permitted to invoke the method. As with `@RolesAllowed`, you can use this annotation on the bean class to define the default for the entire bean class, or you can use it on a per-method basis. `@PermitAll` is also the default value if no default or explicit security metadata is provided for a method. This means that if you do not use any security annotations on your bean class, every user is implicitly granted unlimited access.

Because anyone can check to see whether the school is open, we apply `@PermitAll` to the `isOpen()` method:

```
@PermitAll
// Anyone can check if school is open
public boolean isOpen() { ... }
```

With `@PermitAll`, all callers—including unauthenticated anonymous users—may invoke `isOpen()`.

Now we need to allow the `Administrator` role to open and close the school for business. We can assign permissions to the relevant methods easily, again using `@RolesAllowed`:

```
@RolesAllowed(Roles.ADMIN)
// Only let admins open and close the school
public void close(){ ... }

@PostConstruct
// School is open when created
@RolesAllowed(Roles.ADMIN)
// Only let admins open and close the school
public void open(){ ... }
```

Upon invocation, the EJB container will check that the caller is in the configured role before allowing the target method to be invoked upon the bean instance. If the client does not have the appropriate permissions, a `javax.ejb.EJBAccessException` will be raised.

Janitors need to be able to access the service door, so we'll grant this role the right to do so:

```
@RolesAllowed(
{Roles.ADMIN, Roles.JANITOR})
// Students cannot open this door
public void openServiceDoor(){ ... }
```

Programmatic Security

At this point, we've locked down each method in a declarative fashion, and the EJB container is responsible for blocking and allowing invocations at the method level. However, it's likely that your application will have some contextual security requirements. In our case, students and janitors may open the front doors to the school only during its operating hours, so we'll need to code this logic programmatically.

Most of the security features in this chapter have focused solely on declarative security metadata, or metadata that is statically defined before an application even runs. To fit this need, EJB also has a small programmatic API for gathering information about a secured session. Specifically, the `javax.ejb.EJBContext` interface has a method for determining the concrete user who is invoking on the EJB. It also has a method that allows you to check whether the current user belongs to a certain role.

First, we'll let the authenticated roles access the method:

```
// Give everyone access to this method, we may restrict them later
@RolesAllowed(
{Roles.ADMIN, Roles.STUDENT, Roles.JANITOR})
public void openFrontDoor()
{
```

Now it's our responsibility as bean provider to do some manual checking on our own, and we do this via the `javax.ejb.EJBContext` interface (or its child, `SessionContext`). As we've seen before, this is the hook for bean instances to interact with the container, so we'll inject the following as an instance member:

```
/**
 * Hook to the container to get security information
 */
@Resource
private SessionContext context;
```

We use the `getCallerPrincipal()` method to return a standard Java SE `javax.security.Principal` security interface. A `Principal` object represents the individual user who is currently invoking on the EJB.

The `EJBContext.isCallerInRole()` method allows you to determine whether the current calling user belongs to a certain role. According to our business interface contract, we only let users in the `Administrator` role open the front doors after closing hours.

From `EJBContext` we can access the caller principal's name (i.e., the username) and also check that he is in the desired role. If so, we'll let the client open the door:

```
// If we've reached this point, EJB security has let us through.  However,
// we may want to apply some contextual rules.  Because EJB security is
// declarative at the method level, we use the API to enforce specific logic.

// Get the caller
final String callerName = context.getCallerPrincipal().getName();

// Ensure the school is open
if (!this.isOpen())
{
    // School's closed, so only let admins open the door
    if (!context.isCallerInRole(Roles.ADMIN))
    {
        // Kick 'em out
        throw SchoolClosedException
            .newInstance("Attempt to open the front door after hours " +
                "is prohibited to all but admins, denied to: "
```

```
                        + callerName);
        }
    }

    // Log
    log.info("Opening front door for: " + callerName);
```

The RunAs Security Identity

In addition to specifying the roles that have access to an enterprise bean's methods, the deployer can also specify the *run as* role for the entire enterprise bean. Whereas the `@RolesAllowed` annotation specifies which roles have access to the bean's methods, `@javax.annotation.security.RunAs` specifies the role under which the method will run. In other words, the "run as" role is used as the enterprise bean's identity when it tries to invoke methods on other beans—and this identity isn't necessarily the same as the identity that's currently accessing the bean.

Although they are not allowed to use method permissions, message-driven beans can use the `@RunAs` feature. Message-driven beans have only a `@RunAs` identity; they never execute under the caller identity, because there is no "caller." The messages that a message-driven bean processes are not considered calls, and the clients that send them are not associated with the messages. With no caller identity to propagate, message-driven beans must always specify a `@RunAs` security identity if they interact with other secured session beans.

In the case of our secured school example, we can imagine that a firehouse nearby is able to service requests for emergency response. As an extreme precautionary measure when this occurs, we'll close the school and send all kids home.

It would be irresponsible to let only administrators raise a fire alert; anyone passing by might notice danger. But because admin privileges are required to close the school, we can let the current user masquerade with the correct rights in this emergency situation.

First, to flesh out the fire department's limited capabilities:

```
/**
 * Represents a fire department capable of declaring
 * a state of emergency.  Anyone may invoke this support,
 * and when an alert is raised we'll close the local school.
 *
 * @author <a href="mailto:andrew.rubinger@jboss.org">ALR</a>
 * @version $Revision: $
 */
public interface FireDepartmentLocalBusiness
{

    /**
     * Declares a state of emergency, so we must close the local school
     */
```

```
            void declareEmergency();

    }
```

Our bean implementation class is very simple. It invokes upon the school's `close()` method but runs as an administrator, thanks to the `@RunAs` annotation atop the class:

```
@Singleton
@RunAs(Roles.ADMIN)
@PermitAll
// Implicit, but included here to show access policy
public class FireDepartmentBean implements FireDepartmentLocalBusiness
{

    /**
     * School to close in case of emergency
     */
    @EJB
    private SecureSchoolLocalBusiness school;

    /**
     * Ordinarily we can't close the school with no permissions,
     * but because of @RunAs, we have ADMIN rights.
     */
    @Override
    public void declareEmergency()
    {
        // We run as admin here, so go ahead and close the school
        school.close();
    }

}
```

As is usually the case, the client view ends up being the most illustrative to show the effect of `@RunAs`.

We can easily construct a test that takes the following steps:

- Obtains EJB proxies using an authenticated security context (anonymous user)
- Tries to close the school directly
- Ensures we can't close directly, as we're not admins
- Declares an emergency with the fire department
- Ensures that the school is closed as a postcondition

This might look a little like the following:

```
/**
 * Ensures that any unauthenticated user can declare an emergency,
 * hence closing the school
 */
@Test
public void anyoneCanDeclareEmergencyAndCloseSchool() throws NamingException
{
```

```
    // Assume we have a couple EJB proxies with unauthenticated caller
    final SecureSchoolLocalBusiness school = null; // From somewhere
    final FireDepartmentLocalBusiness fireDepartment = null; // From somewhere

    // First check that school's open
    Assert.assertTrue("School should be open to start the test", school.isOpen());

    // Ensure we can't close the school directly (we don't have access)
    boolean gotAccessException = false;
    try
    {
        school.close();
    }
    catch (final EJBAccessException e)
    {
        // Expected
        log.info("We can't close the school on our own, make an emergency");
        gotAccessException = true;
    }
    Assert.assertTrue("We shouldn't be able to close school directly",
            gotAccessException);

    // Now declare an emergency via the fire department
    fireDepartment.declareEmergency();

    // The school should now be closed, even though we
    // don't have rights to do that directly on our own.
    Assert.assertFalse("School should be closed after emergency was declared",
            school.isOpen());

}
```

## CHAPTER 16

JNDI, the ENC, and Injection

Every EJB container that is deployed in an application server has its own personal internal registry called the Enterprise Naming Context (ENC). This is implemented by JNDI and is an object store where the EJB container can hold specific references to its environment. Think of it as the EJB container's personal address book, where it writes down addresses to various Java EE services that it wants to look up and use within its business logic.

In previous chapters, we started to talk a little bit about the ENC, showing how you can use annotations such as `@javax.annotation.EJB` and `@javax.annotation.Resource` to inject references to Java EE services directly into the fields of your bean. This injection process is driven by the EJB container's ENC. In this chapter, we show you how you can populate the ENC and use it as your own JNDI registry, and we show you how you can use it to inject environment references into your bean fields.

Global JNDI

While previous versions of the EJB Specification left it up to the vendor to decide exactly how clients were to look up session bean proxies, the 3.1 revision in Chapter 4.4 introduces a portable syntax required of all container providers. No matter which vendor's implementation you choose, SLSBs and SFSBs views must be available in Global JNDI under this syntax:

```
java:global[/app-name]/module-name/bean-name [!FQN]
```

In this arrangement, *app-name* refers to the name of the application (or EAR; this is optional), *module-name* is the name of the module (the JAR or WAR), and *FQN* is the fully qualified interface name. Elements in brackets are optional. So, for instance, an EJB outside of an enterprise archive and exposing a no-interface view would leave out *app-name* and *FQN*.

Let's see an example:

```
@Stateless(name="MyEJB")
public class MyEJBBean implements MyEJBRemoteBusiness, MyEJBLocalBusiness
{
   ...
}
```

We'll assume that this EJB is packaged in a module, *myejb.jar*, which is located at the root of an encompassing application *myapp.ear*. Clients could then reliably expect to obtain a reference to the remote business interface by using the following code:

```
javax.naming.Context jndiContext = new InitialContext(); // Assume we have this

// Define the contracted value
final String jndiName = "java:global/myapp/myejb/MyEJB!" +
        MyEJBRemoteBusiness.class.getName();

MyEJBRemoteBusiness bean = (MyEJBRemoteBusiness)jndiContext.lookup(jndiName);
```

This gives us a portable contract where we may expect to find our EJBs in the same place, no matter our vendor.

Although this works wonderfully for clients operating in nonmanaged environments, there are a few places we can improve this setup. For starters, the lookup code depends upon obtaining a vendor-specific JNDI Context. More importantly, we require a cast, and the lookup is not typesafe. Finally, because we must construct the JNDI name on our own, there's a point for potential errors.

Luckily the EJB container provides a series of typesafe injection mechanisms, paving the way for a cleaner separation of logic from plumbing:

```
@EJB
MyEJBLocalBusiness bean;
```

In many cases, this is all we need to obtain a usable reference. These injection facilities will be the focus of this chapter.

The JNDI ENC

The ENC has been around in the EJB specification since the early 1.0 days. It began as a local JNDI namespace that was specific to an EJB container. Developers could define aliases to resources, EJBs, and environment entries in the JNDI ENC through EJB XML deployment descriptors. These aliases could then be looked up directly in JNDI within business logic. In EJB 3.x, this mechanism was enhanced so that JNDI ENC references can be injected directly into the fields of a bean class. Annotations are the primary mechanism for doing this, but XML deployment descriptor support is available for those who wish to use that abstraction.

What Can Be Registered in the JNDI ENC?

Many different items can be bound to the ENC: references to any EJB interface, a JMS queue or topic destination, JMS connection factories, data sources, any JCA resource, and even primitive values. Java EE services such as `javax.transaction.UserTransaction`, `javax.ejb.TimerService`, and `org.omg.CORBA.ORB` are also available in the ENC.

How Is the JNDI ENC Populated?

The ENC's JNDI namespace is populated in two separate ways: via XML or via annotations. Any reference that you declare in XML to a service or resource automatically populates the JNDI ENC with the reference's name. Any environment annotation that you use in your bean class also causes the ENC to be populated. Once an item is bound to the JNDI ENC of the EJB container, it can be referenced by a JNDI lookup.

XML population

To illustrate how XML population works, let's define a reference to the stateless session bean we wrote in Chapter 4. Here we define a local interface reference from one EJB to another:

```
<ejb-jar>
    <enterprise-beans>
        <session>
            <ejb-name>MyEJB</ejb-name>
            <ejb-local-ref>
                <ejb-ref-name>ejbs/referenceToMyEJB2</ejb-ref-name>
                <ejb-ref-type>Session</ejb-ref-type>
                <local>org.ejb3book.example.MyEJB2LocalBusiness</local>
                <ejb-link>MyEJB2</ejb-link>
            </ejb-local-ref>
    </enterprise-beans>
</ejb-jar>
```

The `<ejb-local-ref>` element tells the EJB container that the `MyEJB` wants a reference to the local business interface of `MyEJB2`. A reference to this bean is registered in the `MyEJB`'s JNDI ENC under the name `ejbs/referenceToMyEJB2`, as noted by the `<ejb-ref-name>` element. Other referenceable types such as resources and JMS destinations have elements similar to `<ejb-local-ref>` that specify how and where the reference will be bound into their JNDI ENCs. Each service type in Java EE has its own reference syntax. We'll see examples of all of them in this chapter.

Annotation population

Each referenceable type also has a corresponding annotation that can be used as an alternative to XML. If you specify these annotations on the bean class, they will cause the JNDI ENC to be populated with the information defined in the annotation:

```
@Stateful(name="MyEJB")
@EJB(name="ejbs/referenceToMyEJB2",
  beanInterface=MyEJB2LocalBusiness.class,
      beanName="MyEJB2")
public class MyEJBBean implements MyEJBLocalBusiness
{
  ...
}
```

In this example, we are registering a reference to the MyEJB2 under the ejb/reference
ToMyEJB2 name. Business logic running inside the MyEJBBean is able to do JNDI lookups
to find this reference. Each environment annotation, such as @javax.annotation.EJB,
has a name() attribute that specifies the JNDI ENC name to which you want the service
reference to be bound.

The second half of this chapter describes all the details of each of these different environment annotations.

How Are Things Referenced from the ENC?

Anything registered in the JNDI ENC can be looked up by name under the java:comp/
env context. The comp part of this name corresponds to *component*. The JNDI name
resolves to a different context depending on where you invoke the lookup. For example,
if you invoke jndi.lookup("java:comp/env") within the MyEJB, you will get that EJB
container's ENC. If you do the same within another EJB, you will get a different ENC
registry specific to that bean. The application server knows which ENC is active when
you perform the lookup:

```
@Stateful(name="MyEJB")
@EJB(name="ejbs/referenceToMyEJB2",
    beanInterface=MyEJB2LocalBusiness.class,
        beanName="MyEJB2")
public class MyEJBBean implements MyEJBLocalBusiness
{
    public void lookEjbFromEnc()
    {
        MyEJB2LocalBusiness otherBean = null;
        try
        {
            javax.naming.InitialContext ctx = new InitialContext();
            otherBean = (MyEJB2LocalBusiness)
                    ctx.lookup("java:comp/env/ejbs/referenceToMyEJB2");
        }
        catch (javax.naming.NamingException ne)
        {
            throw new EJBException(ne);
        }
        // ...
    }
}
```

In this example, the `lookupEjbFromEnc` method needs a reference to `MyEJB2`. This reference was created in `MyEJB`'s ENC by annotating the bean class with the `@EJB` annotation, and the preceding code does a JNDI lookup to find this reference.

Using EJBContext

In Chapters 5 and 8, we talked a little bit about the `javax.ejb.SessionContext` and `javax.ejb.MessageDrivenContext` interfaces. Both extend the `javax.ejb.EJBContext`, and they can be used to look up ENC entries. The `EJBContext` interface has a convenience ENC lookup method, and it's a bit simpler than a direct JNDI lookup because it does not throw a checked exception and it takes a relative name into the ENC instead of the full `java:comp/env` string we saw before. `SessionContext` or `MessageDrivenContext` can be injected into your session or message-driven beans by using the `@javax.annotation.Resource` annotation:

```
@Stateful(name="MyEJB")
@EJB(name="ejbs/referenceToMyEJB2",
    beanInterface=MyEJB2LocalBusiness.class,
        beanName="MyEJB2")
public class MyEJBBean implements MyEJBLocalBusiness
{
    @Resource private javax.ejb.SessionContext ejbContext;

    public void lookEjbFromContext()
    {
        MyEJB2LocalBusiness otherBean = ejbContext.lookup("ejbs/referenceToMyEJB2");
        // ...
    }
}
```

This example uses the `EJBContext.lookup()` method to look up the reference. This context object is injected into the `ejbContext` field using the `@Resource` annotation. Here we do not append the `java:comp/env` string to the name when performing the lookup but instead use the relative name defined in the annotation or XML reference.

Annotation injection

Instead of an ENC lookup, EJB references can be injected directly into a member variable. This injection can be done through environment annotations or an XML deployment descriptor fragment:

```
@Stateful(name="MyEJB")
public class MyEJBBean implements MyEJBLocalBusiness
{
    @EJB // Field-level injection
    private MyEJB2LocalBusiness otherBean;

}
```

By using the `@javax.ejb.EJB` annotation on the `otherBean` field of the `MyEJBBean` class, the EJB container will automatically inject a reference when the bean instance is created.

Alternatively, if you do not like this form of injection, the specification also supports injecting via a bean *setter* method:

```
@Stateful(name="MyEJB")
public class MyEJBBean implements MyEJBLocalBusiness
{
    private MyEJB2LocalBusiness otherBean;

    @EJB // Setter method injection
    public void setOtherBean(final MyEJB3LocalBusiness otherBean)
    {
        this.otherBean = otherBean;
    }

}
```

Unlike the previous example, when the bean instance is allocated, the EJB container will instead invoke the setOtherBean method, passing in the EJB reference as a parameter. This pattern works for all other injection annotations discussed in this chapter. Setter method injection is more verbose than direct field injection, but its advantage is that it can be mocked more easily in unit tests.

A number of different environment annotations like @EJB are described in detail in the second half of this chapter. All of them function similarly and follow the same usage patterns as @EJB.

Default ENC name

Annotating a field or a setter method of a bean class also creates an entry in the JNDI ENC for the injected element. This is true for all environment annotations, not just @EJB. If the name() attribute of the injection annotation is specified, then the reference is stored in the ENC under that name. If no name is specified, then the ENC name is extracted from the name of the annotated field or setter method. In this case, a default ENC name is derived from the fully qualified class name of the field or method, as well as the base name of the field or method. So, for the otherBean field or setOtherBean method of the previous example, the ENC name would be org.ejb3book.example.MyEJB Bean/otherBean. These injected EJB references can then be looked up in JNDI under java:comp/env/org.ejb3book.example.MyEJBBean/otherBean. The ENC name becomes very important when you want to override an injection annotation within XML.

XML injection

If you prefer not to use annotations to initialize the fields of your bean class, then the <injection-target> element is available to you in your ejb-jar.xml deployment descriptor:

```
<ejb-jar>
    <enterprise-beans>
        <session>
            <ejb-name>MyEJB</ejb-name>
```

```
        <ejb-local-ref>
            <ejb-ref-name>MyEJB2</ejb-ref-name>
            <ejb-ref-type>Session</ejb-ref-type>
            <local>org.ejb3book.examples.MyEJB2LocalBusiness</local>
            <ejb-link>MyEJB2Bean</ejb-link>
            <injection-target>
               <injection-target-class>
                   org.ejb3book.examples.MyEJBBean
               </injection-target-class>
               <injection-target-name>otherBean</injection-target-name>
            </injection-target>
        </ejb-ref>
    </enterprise-beans>
</ejb-jar>
```

Each XML environment element such as `<ejb-local-ref>` can use `<injection-target>` to populate a field or call a setter method with the referenced item. The `<injection-target-class>` element is the class where your field or method is declared. This may seem unnecessarily verbose, but this becomes important when there are inheritance hierarchies. The `<injection-target-name>` specifies the target field or method name into which you want the reference injected. In this case, we're injecting into the `otherBean` field or `setOtherBean` method.

You cannot inject into a field and method with the same base name. In our example, you cannot simultaneously define injections upon an `otherBean` field and `setOtherBean` method, as they will represent the same ENC name and will not be distinguishable by the EJB container. If your logic requires injection into both a field and a method, simply assign different base names.

XML overrides

Using injection annotations is sometimes considered hardcoding configuration into the code of your bean class, though one could also make the argument that this is a static wiring of the application, not a configurable element. Either way, the EJB specification allows you to override injection annotations via the XML deployment descriptor. Let's reexamine our use of the `@EJB` annotation:

```
@Stateful(name="MyEJB")
public class MyEJBBean implements MyEJBLocalBusiness
{
    @EJB // Field-level injection
    private MyEJB2LocalBusiness otherBean;

}
```

In the original deployment of the `MyEJB`, the EJB container could figure out what EJB reference to inject based on the type of the annotated `otherBean` field. `MyEJB2LocalBusiness` was unique across the application. What if in a new deployment, multiple implementations of this type were deployed into the same application? You might want to configure, per deployment of your application, which reference is injected. You can override this annotation within XML:

```
<ejb-jar>
   <enterprise-beans>
      <session>
         <ejb-name>MyEJB</ejb-name>
         <ejb-local-ref>
            <ejb-ref-name>
               org.ejb3book.examples.MyEJBBean/otherBean
            </ejb-ref-name>
            <ejb-ref-type>Session</ejb-ref-type>
            <local>org.ejb3book.examples.MyEJB2LocalBusiness</local>
            <ejb-link>MyEJB2</ejb-link>
         </ejb-local-ref>
      </session>
   </enterprise-beans>
</ejb-jar>
```

In this example, we are providing a more exact mapping for the @EJB annotation within XML. The <ejb-ref-name> must match the default ENC name of the injected field; this is how the EJB container knows you are overriding an annotated field. The <ejb-link> element provides a more explicit reference to the EJB with the name MyEJB2.

If the name() attribute were used with the @EJB annotation, then <ejb-ref-name> would have to match that value. For example, consider this declaration in Java:

```
@Stateful(name="MyEJB")
public class MyEJBBean implements MyEJBLocalBusiness
{
    @EJB(name="nonDefaultReference") // Defines the name in the ENC
    private MyEJB2LocalBusiness otherBean;

}
```

The @EJB annotation tells the EJB container that it wants to inject an EJB with the MyEJB2LocalBusiness interface into the otherBean field, and that it should be registered in the ENC under the nonDefaultReference entry. The XML must use this ENC name to override what is injected:

```
<ejb-jar>
   <enterprise-beans>
      <session>
         <ejb-name>MyEJB</ejb-name>
         <ejb-local-ref>
            <ejb-ref-name>nonDefaultReference</ejb-ref-name>
            <ejb-ref-type>Session</ejb-ref-type>
            <local>org.ejb3book.examples.MyEJB2LocalBusiness</local>
            <ejb-link>MyEJB2</ejb-link>
         </ejb-local-ref>
      </session>
   </enterprise-beans>
</ejb-jar>
```

The same nonDefaultReference name is referenced using the <ejb-ref-name> element.

XML always takes precedence over annotation metadata. XML provides the means to reconfigure hardcoded annotation configuration.

Injection and inheritance

It is possible for a bean class to be part of a class hierarchy. If any fields or methods have injection annotations on them, they will still be populated, but certain injection rules are followed:

```java
public class BaseClass
{
    private SomeBusinessInterface bean;

    @EJB(beanName="SomeEJB")
    public void someMethod(SomeBusinessInterface bean)
    {
        this.bean = bean;
        // ...
    }
}

@Stateless
public class MySessionBean extends BaseClass implements MySessionLocalBusiness
{
    // ...
}
```

In this example, we have a stateless session bean class that inherits from a base class. All instances of MySessionBean would have the appropriate resource injected into the base class's someMethod method. It is possible to change what is injected by reimplementing and overriding it in the subclass:

```java
@Stateless
public class MySessionBean extends BaseClass implements MySessionLocalBusiness
{
    private SomeBusinessInterface bean;

    @EJB(beanName="AnotherEJB")
    public void someMethod(SomeBusinessInterface bean)
    {
        // ...
    }
}
```

The SomeEJB would no longer be injected into the someMethod method; instead, the new overridden reference, AnotherEJB, would be injected. There is one exception to this rule: if someMethod in the BaseClass was a private method rather than a protected or public method, then the base class would still be injected with the old reference.

Reference and Injection Types

The first half of this chapter focused on the semantics of the JNDI ENC and how to reference things within it. You learned the base semantics of both annotation and XML injection. This section dives into the various services and configurations you can reference from your ENC. Other chapters within this book have touched briefly on most of these injectable and referenceable types, but this chapter groups all of it into one place and discusses the intricacies and dirty details.

EJB References

As you saw earlier in this chapter, your EJB bean classes can reference and aggregate other EJBs either through JNDI ENC lookups or by directly injecting these references into member fields.

@javax.ejb.EJB

The `@javax.ejb.EJB` annotation can be used on your bean class's setter methods, on member fields, or directly on the class itself:

```
package javax.ejb;

@Target({TYPE, METHOD, FIELD}) @Retention(RUNTIME)
public @interface EJB {
   String name( ) default "";
   String description( ) default "";
   Class beanInterface( ) default Object.class;
   String beanName( ) default "";
   String mappedName( ) default "";
   String lookup( ) default "";
}
```

The `name()` attribute refers to what the JNDI ENC name will be for the referenced EJB. This name is relative to the `java:comp/env` context.

The `beanInterface()` attribute is the interface you are interested in and usually is used by the container to distinguish whether you want a remote or local reference to the EJB. If your EJB needs to be integrated with EJB 2.1 beans, `beanInterface()` can also be a reference to a home interface.

The `beanName()` is the EJB name of the EJB referenced. It is equal to either the value you specify in the `@Stateless.name()` or `@Stateful.name()` annotation or the value you put in the `<ejb-name>` field in the XML deployment descriptor.

The `mappedName()` attribute is a placeholder for a vendor-specific identifier. This identifier may be a key into the vendor's global registry. Many vendors store references to EJBs within the global JNDI tree so that clients can reference them, and `mappedName()` may reference that global JNDI name.

The `lookup()` attribute, new to EJB 3.1, defines the JNDI name that should be used to find the target EJB reference. Although `mappedName()` for many vendors defines the same feature, this addition is spec-compliant.

As we've seen, when placed on the bean class, the `@EJB` annotation will register a reference into the JNDI ENC of the bean. In this scenario, the `name()` and `beanInterface()` attributes are required. Most of the time, only the bean's interface is needed to distinguish which EJB you are referring to. Sometimes, though, you may be reusing the same business interface for multiple deployed EJBs. In that case, the `bean Name()` or `lookup()` (or, if your vendor supports it, `mappedName()`) attribute must be used to provide a unique identifier for the EJB you want to reference.

The `@EJB` annotation can be used only once on your bean class. When you need to reference multiple EJBs, the `@javax.ejb.EJBs` annotation is available:

```
package javax.ejb;

@Target({TYPE}) @Retention(RUNTIME)
public @interface EJBs {
    EJB[] value( );
}
```

This kind of annotation is required because only one annotation of a given type can be applied to any given artifact in the Java language. This plural name pattern is duplicated for the other reference annotations described in this chapter:

```
@Stateless
@EJBs({
    @EJB(name="SomeEJB1",
            beanInterface=SomeEJBLocalBusiness1.class),
    @EJB(name="SomeEJB2",
            beanInterface=SomeEJBLocalBusiness2.class)
})
public class MyEJBBean implements MyEJBLocalBusiness
{
    // ...
}
```

In this example, we create an ENC reference to both the `SomeEJB1` and `SomeEJB2` beans through their local business views.

Ambiguous and overloaded EJB names

The `<ejb-name>` element and any `@Stateless.name()` or `@Stateful.name()` attributes must be unique within a given EJB-JAR deployment. Unfortunately, this is not the case for all EJB JARs deployed in an Enterprise ARchive (*.ear*) file. In an *.ear* file, EJB names can be duplicated in different EJB-JAR deployments. To differentiate references with duplicate EJB names, the EJB specification has an extended syntax for `<ejb-link>` and the `beanName()` attribute of the `@EJB` annotation. This extended syntax has a relative path to the JAR file in which the EJB is located, followed by the # character, followed by the EJB name of the referenced bean:

```
@EJB(beanName="myejbs.jar#SomeEJB")
private SomeEJBLocalBusiness bean;
```

In this example, the *myejbs.jar* file is in the root directory of the EAR file along with the JAR the referencing EJB is deployed in. The @EJB annotation references SomeEJB specifically.

Resolving EJB references

The simplest example of the @javax.ejb.EJB annotation is using it with no other annotation attributes:

```
@EJB
private SomeEJBLocalBusiness bean;
```

The specification isn't very detailed in terms of exactly how the EJB container should resolve this reference. To give you a feel for how this process works, let's see how the JBoss application server resolves this reference:

1. The only possible identifier for this EJB reference is the business interface type. The application server first looks for a unique EJB in the referencing EJB's EJB-JAR deployment that uses SomeEJBLocalBusiness as one of its business interfaces. If more than one EJB uses the same business interface, it throws a deployment exception.

2. If the EJB-JAR is deployed as part of an Enterprise ARchive (*.ear*), it looks in other EJB-JARs for a unique EJB that uses the SomeEJBLocalBusiness interface. Again, if more than one EJB uses the same business interface, it throws a deployment exception.

3. If the EJB reference is not found in the *.ear* file, it looks for it in other global EJB-JAR deployments.

If the beanName() attribute is specified, then JBoss uses the same search process, but it uses the beanName()'s value as an additional identifier.

If the mappedName() or lookup() attribute is specified, then no search process is performed. The application server expects that a specific EJB is bound into the global JNDI under the attribute's value.

EntityManagerFactory References

A javax.persistence.EntityManagerFactory can be registered in the JNDI ENC of an EJB and then injected. It is sometimes useful to obtain a reference to an EntityManager Factory directly so that you can have full control over the EntityManager instance and persistence context you want to work with. Although you can obtain an EntityManagerFactory through the javax.persistence.Persistence API, it is always better to use the facilities of Java EE so that the lifecycle of the EntityManagerFactory can be controlled by the application server. When you let the application server populate your ENC or inject your `EntityManagerFactory`, the Java EE runtime will handle the cleanup of this instance and you do not have to call `EntityManagerFactory.close()`. Like all other services and resources, an `EntityManagerFactory` can be bound to the JNDI ENC or injected into your bean class by using either annotations or XML.

@javax.persistence.PersistenceUnit

The `@javax.persistence.PersistenceUnit` annotation can be used on your bean class's setter methods or member fields, or directly on the class itself:

```
package javax.persistence;

@Target({TYPE, METHOD, FIELD}) @Retention(RUNTIME)
public @interface PersistenceUnit {
    String name( ) default "";
    String unitName( ) default "";
}
```

The `name()` attribute refers to what the JNDI ENC name will be for the referenced `EntityManagerFactory`. This name is relative to the `java:comp/env` context.

The `unitName()` attribute identifies which `EntityManagerFactory` you are interested in referencing and refers to the name given your persistence unit that you declared in a *persistence.xml* file. If left unspecified, a deployment error is raised, unless the EJB-JAR has only one persistence unit deployed within it. In that case, it defaults to this sole persistence unit.

When placed on the bean class, the `@PersistenceUnit` annotation will register a reference to the `EntityManagerFactory` in the JNDI ENC of the EJB bean class:

```
@Stateless(name="MyEJB")
@PersistenceUnit(name="persistence/MyDB",
     unitName="MyDB")
public class MyEJBBean implements MyEJBLocalBusiness
{
  ...
}
```

In this example, code within the `MyEJBBean` can look up an `EntityManagerFactory` that manages a `MyDB` persistence unit under the `java:comp/env/persistence/MyDB` JNDI ENC name. Here's how a client bean would use this context to look up the reference to this `EntityManagerFactory`:

```
InitialContext jndiContext = new InitialContext( );
EntityManagerFactory emf = (EntityManagerFactory)
     jndiContext.lookup("java:comp/env/persistence/MyDB");
```

When the `@PersistenceUnit` annotation is used on the bean class, the `name()` attribute is always required so that the EJB container knows where in the JNDI ENC to bind the `EntityManagerFactory`.

The `@PersistenceUnit` annotation can be used only once on your bean class. So when you need to reference multiple persistence units, the `@javax.persistence.PersistenceUnits` annotation is available:

```
package javax.persistence;

@Target({TYPE}) @Retention(RUNTIME)
public @interface PersistenceUnits {
    PersistenceUnit[] value();
}
```

This is used just as we've seen with `@EJBs`; it allows us to aggregate a series of `@PersistenceUnit` annotations together.

The `@PersistenceUnit` annotation can also be placed on a setter method or member field so that the `EntityManagerFactory` that is referenced is injected directly into the bean class instance. When used on a setter method or member field, no annotation attribute is required, because both the `name()` and the `unitName()` attributes have valid defaults, as described earlier in this chapter.

XML-based EntityManagerFactory references

The `<persistence-unit-ref>` element defines a reference to a given `EntityManagerFactory`. It contains the subelements `<description>` (optional), `<persistence-unit-ref-name>` (required), and `<persistence-unit-name>` (required), as well as the element `<injection-target>` (optional) described in the first section of this chapter. Here is an example of a reference that provides the same metadata as our annotation-based one shown earlier:

```
<ejb-jar>
    <enterprise-beans>
        <session>
            <ejb-name>MyEJB</ejb-name>
            <persistence-unit-ref>
                <persistence-unit-ref-name>persistence/MyDB</persistence-unit-ref-name>
                <persistence-unit-name>MyDB</persistence-unit-name>
            </persistence-unit-ref>
    </enterprise-beans>
</ejb-jar>
```

The `<persistence-unit-ref-name>` element is equivalent to the `name()` attribute of the `@PersistenceUnit` annotation, in that it represents the ENC name to which the reference will be bound. The `<persistence-unit-name>` element is equivalent to the `unitName()` attribute of the `@PersistenceUnit` annotation. It represents the same name you have declared in your *persistence.xml* deployment descriptor.

The `<injection-target>` element is used if you want to inject your `EntityManagerFactory` into your EJB's bean class. Here is an example of using `<injection-target>`:

```
<ejb-jar>
    <enterprise-beans>
```

```
<session>
    <ejb-name>TravelAgentBean</ejb-name>
    <persistence-unit-ref>
        <persistence-unit-ref-name>persistence/MyDB</persistence-unit-ref-name>
        <persistence-unit-name>MyDB</persistence-unit-name>
        <injection-target>
            <injection-target-class>org.ejb3book.examples.MyEJBBean
                </injection-target-class>
            <injection-target-name>pu</injection-target-name>
        </injection-target>
    </persistence-unit-ref>
</enterprise-beans>
</ejb-jar>
```

In this example, the `EntityManagerFactory` would be injected into field named `pu` or passed as a parameter to a setter method named `setPu()` in the `MyEJBBean` class.

Scoped and overloaded unit names

A persistence unit can be declared in many different places. It can be defined in an EJB-JAR, an EAR/lib JAR, or even a WAR file. Persistence units are scoped when defined in a WAR or EJB-JAR file, and they cannot be referenced by components deployed outside of that archive. Persistence units deployed in a JAR in the *.ear*'s *lib/* directory are available to all other components in that enterprise archive. Sometimes you may have the same persistence unit name defined in your EJB or WAR file as the name you declared in a persistence JAR in the *EAR/lib* directory. To differentiate references with duplicate persistence unit names, the specification has an extended syntax for `<persistence-unit-name>` and the `unitName()` attribute of the `@PersistenceUnit` annotation. This extended syntax has a relative path to a JAR file that contains the persistence unit, followed by the # character, followed by the persistence unit name:

```
@PersistenceUnit(unitName="myejbs.jar#MyDB")
EntityManagerFactory emf;
```

In this example, the *myejbs.jar* is in the same directory of the EAR file as the persistence unit's JAR file. The `@PersistenceUnit` annotation references the `MyDB` persistence unit within that deployment.

EntityManager References

An `EntityManager` can be registered in the JNDI ENC of an EJB. When you are registering an `EntityManager` into the JNDI ENC or injecting it into your EJB, the EJB container has full control over the lifecycle of the underlying persistence context of the `EntityManager`. The `EntityManager` object reference itself is really just a proxy around an actual persistence context that may not even exist yet, depending on the type of persistence context you are injecting. When you let the application server populate your ENC or inject your `EntityManager`, the EJB container handles the cleanup of this instance and you do not have to call `EntityManager.close()`. In fact, it is illegal to call `close()` on an injected `EntityManager` instance, and an exception will be thrown if you do. Like all other services and resources, an `EntityManager` can be bound to the JNDI ENC or injected into your bean class by using either annotations or XML.

@javax.persistence.PersistenceContext

The `@javax.persistence.PersistenceContext` annotation can be used on your bean class's setter methods or member fields or directly on the class itself:

```
package javax.persistence;

public enum PersistenceContextType
{
   TRANSACTION,
   EXTENDED
}

@Target({}) @Retention(RUNTIME)
public @interface PersistenceProperty {
   String name( );
   String value( );
}

@Target({TYPE, METHOD, FIELD}) @Retention(RUNTIME)
public @interface PersistenceContext {
   String name( ) default "";
   String unitName( ) default "";
   PersistenceContextType type( ) default TRANSACTION;
   PersistenceProperty[] properties( ) default {};
}
```

The `name()` attribute refers to the JNDI ENC name under which the `EntityManager` is referenced. This name is relative to the `java:comp/env` context.

The `unitName()` attribute identifies which persistence unit you are interested in referencing. This identifier is the same as what you have declared in your *persistence.xml* file. If left unspecified, a deployment error is raised unless the EJB-JAR has only one persistence unit deployed within it. In that case, it defaults to this sole persistence unit.

The `type()` attribute specifies the type of persistence context you want. `Persistence ContextType.TRANSACTION` specifies that you want a transaction-scoped persistence context. This is the default. `PersistenceContextType.EXTENDED` gives you an extended persistence context. The `EXTENDED` type can be used only on stateful session beans. You will receive a deployment error if you use it with any other bean type. Review Chapter 17 for more information on the differences between `EXTENDED`- and `TRANSACTION`-based persistence contexts.

The `properties()` attribute allows you to pass in additional vendor-specific properties for the created `EntityManager` instance. You set this attribute with an array of `@javax.persistence.PersistenceProperty` annotation declarations.

When placed on the bean class, the `@PersistenceContext` annotation will register a reference to the `EntityManager` into the JNDI ENC of the EJB bean class:

```
@Stateful
@PersistenceContext(name="persistence/MyDB",
    unitName="MyDB"
   type=PersistenceContextType.EXTENDED)
public class MyEJBBean implements MyEJBLocalBusiness
{
   // ...
}
```

In this example, code within the `MyEJB` can look up an `EntityManager` that manages a `MyDB` persistence unit under the `java:comp/env/persistence/MyDB` JNDI ENC name. Here's how a client bean would use this context to look up the reference to this `EntityManager`:

```
InitialContext jndiContext = new InitialContext( );
EntityManager em = (EntityManager)
        jndiContext.lookup("java:comp/env/persistence/MyDB");
```

When the `@PersistenceContext` annotation is used on the bean class, the `name()` attribute is required so that the EJB container knows where in the JNDI ENC to bind the `EntityManager`. The `type()` and `unitName()` attributes have valid defaults.

The `@PersistenceContext` annotation can be used only once on your bean class. So when you need to reference multiple persistence contexts, the `@javax.persistence.PersistenceContexts` annotation is available.

The `@PersistenceContext` annotation can also be placed on a setter method or member field so that the `EntityManager` referenced is injected directly into the bean class instance:

```
@Stateful
public class MyEJBBean implements MyEJBLocalBusiness
{
    @PersistenceContext(unitName="MyDB")
    private EntityManager em;
}
```

When used on a setter method or member field, no annotation attribute is required, as the `name()`, `unitName()`, and `type()` attributes have valid defaults.

XML-based injection for `EntityManager` types works similarly to the previous examples for `<persistence-unit-ref>`.

Resource References

EJBs need access to more than just other EJBs and persistence contexts, and they use the JNDI ENC to look up external resources that they need to access. The mechanism for doing this is similar to the mechanism used for referencing other EJB and environment entries: the external resources are mapped into a name within the JNDI ENC namespace and are optionally injected into member fields or setter methods of bean instances. This is accomplished using annotations or an XML deployment descriptor fragment.

Resource injection is detailed in the Java Enterprise Edition 6 Specification, Chapter EE.5.

External resources can be of the following types:

- `javax.sql.DataSource`
- `javax.jms.Queue`
- `javax.jms.Topic`
- `javax.jms.QueueConnectionFactory`
- `javax.jms.ConnectionFactory`
- `javax.jms.TopicConnectionFactory`
- `javax.mail.Session`
- `java.net.URL`
- `java.lang`: `String`, `Character`, `Byte`, `Short`, `Integer`, `Long`, `Boolean`, `Double`, `Float`, `Class`, and all `Enum` types.
- `javax.transaction.UserTransaction`
- `javax.transaction.TransactionSynchronizationRegistry`
- CORBA ORB references
- JPA `PersistenceUnit` and `PersistenceContext`

In this section, we focus on `javax.sql.DataSource` as an example.

@javax.annotation.Resource

The `@javax.annotation.Resource` annotation is used to reference an external resource. It can be applied to your bean class's setter methods or member fields, or directly on the class itself. This annotation is highly overloaded and overused in the Java EE specification; in addition to external resources, it is also used to reference JMS message destinations, environment entries, `EJBContexts`, and Java EE core services. For now, we'll focus solely on using this annotation to access external resources:

```
package javax.annotation;

@Target({TYPE, METHOD, FIELD}) @Retention(RUNTIME)
public @interface Resource
{

    public enum AuthenticationType {
        CONTAINER,
        APPLICATION
    }

    String name( ) default "";
    Class type( ) default Object.class;
    AuthenticationType authenticationType( ) default AuthenticationType.CONTAINER;
    boolean shareable( ) default true;
    String description( ) default "";
```

```
    String mappedName( ) default "";
    String lookup( ) default "";
}
```

The `name()` attribute refers to what the JNDI ENC name is for the referenced external resource. This name is relative to the `java:comp/env` context.

The `type()` attribute declares the fully qualified class name of the resource's Java type. When the `@Resource` annotation is applied to the bean class, this attribute may be important to the EJB container to truly identify the resource in which you are interested. Usually, this attribute is unneeded and the default value is good enough.

The `mappedName()` attribute is a vendor-specific identifier for the external resource. Since Java EE has no specified mechanism or global registry for finding global resources, many vendors require this attribute so that they can locate and bind the resource. Many times, this `mappedName()` attribute will be equivalent to a global JNDI name.

The `lookup()` attribute, new in JEE6, is the spec-defined mechanism pointing to a resource in global JNDI.

When placed on the bean class, the `@Resource` annotation registers a reference to the external resource into the JNDI ENC of the EJB bean class:

```
@Stateless
@Resource(name="jdbc/PostgresDB",
          type=javax.sql.DataSource,
          lookup="java:/DefaultDS")
public class MyEJBBean implements MyEJBLocalBusiness
{
  // ...
}
```

In this example, the `@Resource` annotation is binding a `javax.sql.DataSource` into the `jdbc/PostgresDB` ENC name. The `lookup()` attribute provides the global JNDI name so that the application server can locate the desired resource. Code within the `MyEJB` can now locate this data source under the `java:comp/env/jdbc/PostgresDB` JNDI ENC name.

When the `@Resource` annotation is used on the bean class, the `name()` and `type()` attributes are required. Here `lookup()` is used to truly identify the resource.

The `authenticationType()` attribute tells the server who is responsible for authentication when the resource is accessed. It can have one of two values: `CONTAINER` or `APPLICATION`. If `CONTAINER` is specified, the container will automatically perform authentication (sign on or log in) to use the resource, as specified at deployment time. If `APPLICATION` is specified, the bean itself must perform the authentication before using the resource. Here's how a bean might sign on to a connection factory when `APPLICATION` is specified:

```
@Stateful
@Resource(name="jdbc/PostgresDB",
          type=javax.sql.DataSource,
```

```
            authenicationType=AuthenticationType.APPLICATION,
            lookup="java:/DefaultDS")
public class MyEJBBean implements MyEJBLocalBusiness
{
    @Resource SessionContext ejbContext;

    private java.sql.Connection getConnection( )
    {
        DataSource source = (DataSource)
            ejbContext.lookup("jdbc/PostgresDB");
        String loginName = ejbContext.getCallerPrincipal().getName();
        String password = ...;  // get password from somewhere

        // use login name and password to obtain a database connection
        java.sql.Connection con = source.getConnection(loginName, password);
}
```

In this case, the connection will be authenticated programmatically. In the CONTAINER option, the caller principal could be extracted internally by the resource itself or configured statically by the application deployment.

The @Resource annotation can be used only once on your bean class. When you need to reference multiple persistence units, the @javax.annotation.Resources annotation is available.

The @Resource annotation can also be placed on a setter method or member field so that the resources referenced will be injected directly into the bean class instance. When used on a setter method or member field, only the lookup( ) attribute may be required to identify the resource, as the type and ENC name can be determined from the type and name of the method or field.

Shareable resources

When several enterprise beans in a transaction use the same resource, you will want to configure your EJB server to share that resource. Sharing a resource means that each EJB will use the same connection to access the resource (e.g., database or JMS provider), a strategy that is more efficient than using separate resource connections.

In terms of a database, EJBs that are referencing the same database will probably want to use the same database connection during a transaction so that all create, read, update, and delete (CRUD) operations return consistent results. EJB containers share resources by default, but resource sharing can be turned on or off explicitly with the shareable( ) attribute of the @Resource annotation.

Occasionally, advanced developers may run into situations where resource sharing is not desirable, and having the option to turn off resource sharing is beneficial. But unless you have a good reason for turning off resource sharing, we recommend that you accept the default shareable( ) setting of true.

Resource Environment and Administered Objects

Resource environment entries are objects that do not fall into the resource reference category. Some resources may have other, additional administered objects that need to be obtained from the JNDI ENC or injected into your bean class. An administered object is a resource that is configured at deployment time and is managed by the EJB container at runtime. They are usually defined and deployed by a JCA resource adapter.

Besides administered objects, resource environment entries are also used to reference services such as `javax.transaction.UserTransaction` and `javax.transaction.TransactionSynchronizationRegistry`.

To obtain a reference to one of these services, the `@Resource` annotation can be used. When using this annotation, the `authenticationType()` and `shareable()` attributes are meaningless and are illegal even to specify.

Environment Entries

In Chapter 5, the `EncryptionEJB` had a configurable property for the cipher's passphrase. These types of configurable properties are called *environment entries*. The bean can use environment entries to customize its behavior.

Although they can be defined using annotations, environment entries are almost always configured via XML, as they really are configuration values and not metadata. The `<env-entry>` element is used to define them. This element contains the subelements `<description>` (optional), `<env-entry-name>` (required), `<env-entry-type>` (required), and `<env-entry-value>` (optional), as well as the element `<injection-target>` (optional). Here is a typical `<env-entry>` declaration:

```
<ejb-jar>
  <enterprise-beans>
    <session>
      <ejb-name>EncryptionEJB</ejb-name>

      <!-- Override the ciphers' default  passphrase -->
      <env-entry>
        <env-entry-name>ciphersPassphrase</env-entry-name>
        <env-entry-type>java.lang.String</env-entry-type>
        <env-entry-value>OverriddenPassword</env-entry-value>
      </env-entry>

    </session>
  </enterprise-beans>
</ejb-jar>
```

The `<env-entry-name>` element is relative to the `java:comp/env` context. For example, the `ciphersPassphrase` entry can be accessed using the path `java:comp/env/ciphersPassphrase` in a JNDI ENC lookup:

```
InitialContext jndiContext = new InitialContext( );
String passphrase = (String) jndiContext.lookup("java:comp/env/ciphersPassphrase");
```

Alternatively, it can be looked up with the `EJBContext.lookup()` method using the `ciphersPassphrase` name.

`<env-entry-type>` can be of type `String` or one of the several primitive wrapper types, including `Integer`, `Long`, `Double`, `Float`, `Byte`, `Boolean`, `Short`, or any `Enum` type.

`<env-entry-value>` is optional. The value can be specified by the bean developer or deferred to the application assembler or deployer.

The `<injection-target>` element can be used to initialize a field or setter method with the environment entry's value:

```
<ejb-jar>
  <enterprise-beans>
    <session>
      <ejb-name>EncryptionEJB</ejb-name>

      <!-- Override the ciphers' default  passphrase -->
      <env-entry>
        <env-entry-name>ciphersPassphrase</env-entry-name>
        <env-entry-type>java.lang.String</env-entry-type>
        <env-entry-value>OverriddenPassword</env-entry-value>
          <injection-target>
            <injection-target-class>
              org.ejb3book.examples.MyEJBBean
            </injection-target-class>
            <injection-target-name>ciphersPassphrase</injection-target-name>
          </injection-target>
      </env-entry>

    </session>
  </enterprise-beans>
</ejb-jar>
```

The preceding XML will inject the value `OverriddenPassword` into the field named `ciphersPassphrase` or invoke a setter method named `setCiphersPassphrase` in the bean class.

The `@javax.annotation.Resource` annotation can be used to pull in the environment entry instead of the `<injection-target>` element:

```
@Resource(name="ciphersPassphrase") private String passphrase = "defaultPassphrase";
```

In this example, the value will be pulled from the environment entry described in XML and injected into the `passphrase` field. If no XML is used to configure this value, the default will be `"defaultPassphrase"`, but no entry is created in the ENC. A common pattern is to annotate your field with `@Resource` and provide a default value for the field that can optionally be overridden in XML. Using the `@Resource` annotation with a `String` or primitive value type identifies it as an environment entry to the EJB container. When `@Resource` designates an environment entry, only the `name()` attribute is allowed to be specified. Also, it doesn't make much sense to use `@Resource` for environment entries at the class level, as there is no way to initialize the value in the annotation.

Message Destination References

Message destination references populate the JNDI ENC with a pointer to a JMS topic or queue. You need these references if you are sending messages within your EJB. Chapter 8 gave a more complete description of this type of reference, so only an overview will be provided here, with additional instructions on how to inject using an annotation instead.

XML-based resource references

The `<message-destination-ref>` element defines a reference to a JMS message destination. It contains the subelements `<description>` (optional), `<message-destination-ref-name>` (required), `<message-destination-type>` (required), `<message-destination-usage>` (required), `<message-destination-link>` (optional), and `<mapped-name>` (optional), as well as the element `<injection-target>` (optional) described in the first section of this chapter. Here is an example of a reference to a topic:

```
<ejb-jar>
    <enterprise-beans>
        <session>
            <ejb-name>MyEJB</ejb-name>
            <message-destination-ref>
                <message-destination-ref-name>
                    jms/MyTopic
                </message-destination-ref-name>
                <message-destination-type>javax.jms.Topic</message-destination-type>
                <message-destination-usage>Produces</message-destination-usage>
                <message-destination-link>Distributor</message-destination-link>
                <mapped-name>topic/MyTopic</mapped-name>
                <injection-target>
                    <injection-target-class>org.ejb3book.examples.MyEJBBean
                    </ injection-target-class>
                    <injection-target-name>myTopic</injection-target-name>
                </injection-target>
            </message-destination-ref>
        </session>
    </enterprise-beans>
</ejb-jar>
```

The `<message-destination-ref-name>` element is the JNDI ENC name the topic will be bound to and is relative to the path `java:comp/env`.

The `<message-destination-type>` element is either a `javax.jms.Topic` or a `javax.jms.Queue` and is required.

The `<message-destination-usage>` element specifies whether the EJB produces or consumes messages to or from this destination.

The `<message-destination-link>` element creates a message flow, as described in Chapter 8.

Sometimes a vendor-specific identify is required, and `<mapped-name>` optionally fulfills this role.

As with all other resource reference types, the `<injection-target>` element can be used to inject the destination into a field or setter method.

Using @Resource

The `@javax.annotation.Resource` annotation is overloaded to support referencing JMS destinations. Unfortunately, the specification does not provide annotation metadata to set up a message destination link, so you'll have to rely on XML to do this sort of thing.

When placed on the bean class, the `@Resource` annotation registers a reference to the JMS queue or topic destination into the JNDI ENC of the EJB bean class:

```
@Stateless
@Resource(name="jms/MyTopic",
          type=javax.jms.Topic,
          lookup="topic/MyTopic")
public class MyEJBBean implements MyEJBLocalBusiness
{
    // ...
}
```

In this example, the `@Resource` annotation is binding a `javax.jms.Topic` into the `jms/MyTopic` ENC name. The `mappedName()` attribute provides a global, vendor-specific identifier so that the application server can locate the desired destination.

When the `@Resource` annotation is used on the bean class, the `name()` and `type()` attributes are required. As stated earlier, `lookup()` may be required by the vendor to truly identify the resource from global JNDI. Only these three attributes can be set by application code. All others are illegal, and they will create a deployment error.

The `@Resource` annotation can also be placed on a setter method or member field so that the destination referenced will be injected directly into the bean class instance:

```
@Stateless
public class MyEJBBean implements MyEJBLocalBusiness
{
    @Resource(mappedName="topic/MyTopic")
    private javax.jms.Topic myTopic;
}
```

When used on a setter method or member field, only the `lookup()` attribute may be required to identify the resource, as the type and ENC name can be determined from the field type and name.

## CHAPTER 17

Transactions

ACID Transactions

Unfortunately, good business-object design is not enough to make EJBs useful in an industrial-strength application. The problem is not with the definition of the EJBs or the taskflow; the problem is that a good design does not, in and of itself, guarantee that a business method represents a good *transaction*. To understand why, we will take a closer look at what a transaction is and what criteria a transaction must meet to be considered reliable.

In business, a transaction usually involves an exchange between two parties. When you purchase an ice cream cone, you exchange money for food; when you work for a company, you exchange skill and time for money (which you use to buy more ice cream). When you are involved in these exchanges, you monitor the outcome to ensure that you aren't "ripped off." If you give the ice cream vendor a $20 bill, you don't want him to drive off without giving you your change; likewise, you want to make sure that your paycheck reflects all the hours that you worked. By monitoring these commercial exchanges, you are attempting to ensure the reliability of the transactions; you are making sure that each transaction meets everyone's expectations.

In business software, a transaction embodies the concept of a commercial exchange. A business system transaction (transaction for short) is the execution of a unit-of-work that accesses one or more shared resources, usually databases. A *unit-of-work* is a set of activities that relate to each other and must be completed together. The reservation process is a unit-of-work made up of several activities: recording a reservation, debiting a credit card, and generating a ticket.

The object of a transaction is to execute a unit-of-work that results in a reliable exchange. Here are some types of business systems that employ transactions:

ATM

   The ATM (automatic teller machine) you use to deposit, withdraw, and transfer funds executes these units-of-work as transactions. In an ATM withdrawal, for example, the ATM checks to make sure you don't overdraw, and then it debits your account and spits out some money.

Online book order

You've probably purchased many of your Java books—maybe even this book—from an online bookseller. This type of purchase is also a unit-of-work that takes place as a transaction. In an online book purchase, you submit your credit card number, it is validated, and a charge is made for the price of the book. Finally, an order to ship the book is sent to the bookseller's warehouse.

Medical system

In a medical system, important data—some of it critical—is recorded about patients every day, including information about clinical visits, medical procedures, prescriptions, and drug allergies. The doctor prescribes the drug, and then the system checks for allergies, contraindications, and appropriate dosages. If all tests pass, the drug can be administered. These tasks make up a unit-of-work. A unit-of-work in a medical system may not be financial, but it's just as important. Failure to identify a drug allergy in a patient could be fatal.

As you can see, transactions are often complex and usually involve the manipulation of a lot of data. Mistakes in data can cost money, or even lives. Transactions must therefore preserve data integrity, which means that the transaction must work perfectly every time or not be executed at all. This is a pretty tall order. As difficult as this requirement is, however, when it comes to commerce, there is no room for error. Units-of-work involving money or anything of value always require the utmost reliability because errors affect the revenues and the well-being of the parties involved.

To give you an idea of the accuracy required by transactions, think about what would happen if a transactional system suffered from even infrequent errors. ATMs provide customers with convenient access to their bank accounts and represent a significant percentage of the total transactions in personal banking. The transactions handled by ATMs are simple but numerous, providing us with a great example of why transactions must be error-proof. Let's say that a bank has 100 ATMs in a metropolitan area, and each ATM processes 300 transactions (deposits, withdrawals, and transfers) a day, for a total of 30,000 transactions per day. If each transaction involves the deposit, withdrawal, or transfer of an average of $100, then about $3 million will move through the ATM system per day. In the course of a year, that's a little more than $1 billion:

365 days × 100 ATMs × 300 transactions × $100 = $1,095,000,000

How well do the ATMs have to perform to be considered reliable? For the sake of argument, let's say that ATMs execute transactions correctly 99.99% of the time. This seems to be more than adequate; after all, only one out of every 10,000 transactions executes incorrectly. But if you do the math, that could result in more than $100,000 in errors over the course of a year!

$1,095,000,000 × .01% = $109,500

Obviously, this example is an oversimplification of the problem, but it illustrates that even a small percentage of errors is unacceptable in high-volume or mission-critical systems. For this reason, experts have identified four characteristics of a transaction that must be met for a system to be considered safe. Transactions must be *atomic*, *consistent*, *isolated*, and *durable* (ACID)—the four horsemen of transaction services:

Atomic
> An atomic transaction must execute completely or not at all. This means that every task within a unit-of-work must execute without error. If any of the tasks fail, the entire unit-of-work or transaction is aborted, meaning that any changes to the data are undone. If all the tasks execute successfully, the transaction is committed, which means that the changes to the data are made permanent or durable.

Consistent
> Consistency refers to the integrity of the underlying data store. It must be enforced by both the transactional system and the application developer. The transactional system fulfills this obligation by ensuring that a transaction is atomic, isolated, and durable. The application developer must ensure that the database has appropriate constraints (primary keys, referential integrity, and so forth) and that the unit-of-work—the business logic—doesn't result in inconsistent data (i.e., data that is not in harmony with the real world it represents). In an account transfer, for example, the debit to one account must equal the credit to another account.

Isolated
> Isolation means that a transaction must be allowed to execute without interference from other processes or transactions. In other words, the data that a transaction accesses cannot be affected by any other part of the system until the transaction or unit-of-work is completed.

Durable
> Durability means that all the data changes made during the course of a transaction must be written to some type of physical storage before the transaction is successfully completed. This ensures that the changes are not lost if the system crashes.

To get a better idea of what these principles mean, we will introduce a `BlackjackEJB` to model an online blackjack game in terms of the four ACID properties.

Example: The BlackjackEJB

In this example, we're not so much interested with handling the business rules of a real game of blackjack. However, the outputs of gameplay (whether money exchanges parties as expected) are centrally important to the function of the service. As such, we'll expose a single business method that allows users to play single trials, which compose a single unit of work.

The full example is covered in Appendix H.

```
/**
 * Contract of a service capable of simulating
 * a single game of blackjack.  The actual gameplay is not modeled,
 * only the inputs and outputs of a single trial.
 */
public interface BlackjackGameLocalBusiness
{
    /**
     * Places a single bet, returning if the bet won or lost.  If the result
     * is a win, the amount specified will be transferred from the Blackjack Service
     * account to {@link User#getAccount()}, else it will be deducted from the
     * user account and placed into the Blackjack Service account.
     *
     * @return Whether the bet won or lost
     * @param userId The ID of the user placing the bet
     * @param amount The amount of the bet
     * @throws IllegalArgumentException If either the user of the amount is not
     *         specified or the amount is a negative number.
     * @throws InsufficientBalanceException If the user does not have enough in
     *         his/her account to cover the bet
     */
    boolean bet(long userId, BigDecimal amount) throws IllegalArgumentException,
        InsufficientBalanceException;
}
```

Depending upon the result of the bet, the designated amount should either be added
to the user's account or transferred into the game service's account.

To facilitate the transfers of money, we'll also expose a simple bank:

```
/**
 * Defines the contract for a bank, supporting common
 * account activities
 */
public interface BankLocalBusiness
{
    /**
     * Withdraws the specified amount from the account with
     * the specified ID, returning the new balance.
     * @param amount
     * @throws IllegalArgumentException If the amount is not specified, the account
     * ID is not valid, or the amount to be withdrawn is less than 0
     * @throws InsufficientBalanceException If the amount to be withdrawn is greater
     * than the value of {@link Account#getBalance()}.
     */
    BigDecimal withdraw(long accountId, BigDecimal amount) throws
        IllegalArgumentException, InsufficientBalanceException;

    /**
     * Deposits the specified amount to the account with the
     * specified ID, returning the new balance.
     * @param amount
     * @throws IllegalArgumentException If the amount is not specified, the account
     * ID is not valid, or the amount to be deposited is less than 0
     */
    BigDecimal deposit(long accountId, BigDecimal amount) throws
```

```
    IllegalArgumentException;

/**
 * Obtains the current balance from the account with the specified ID
 * @param accountId
 * @return
 * @throws IllegalArgumentException If the account ID is not valid
 */
BigDecimal getBalance(long accountId) throws IllegalArgumentException;

/**
 * Transfers the specified amount from one account to another
 * @param accountIdFrom The ID of the account from which we'll withdraw
 * @param accountIdTo The ID of the account to which we'll deposit
 * @param amount The amount to be transferred
 * @throws IllegalArgumentException If the amount is not specified, the amount
is
 *    less than 0, or either account ID is invalid
 * @throws InsufficientBalanceException If the amount is greater than the
current
 *    balance of the "from" account
 */
void transfer(long accountIdFrom, long accountIdTo, BigDecimal amount)
    throws IllegalArgumentException, InsufficientBalanceException;

/**
 * Transfers the specified amount from one account to another
 * @param accountFrom The account from which we'll withdraw
 * @param accountTo The account to which we'll deposit
 * @param amount The amount to be transferred
 * @throws IllegalArgumentException If the amount is not specified, the amount
is
 *    less than 0, or either account ID is invalid
 * @throws InsufficientBalanceException If the amount is greater than the
current
 *    balance of the "from" account
 */
void transfer(Account accountFrom, Account accountTo, BigDecimal amount)
    throws IllegalArgumentException, InsufficientBalanceException;
}
```

Through the BankEJB, we'll expect to safely exchange funds.

Helper EJBs for Testing Transactions

During testing and development, it's often helpful to get a hook into the underlying
system to manually specify the boundaries that mark the beginning and end of a unit
of work. For this we'll provide another simple view:

```
public interface TxWrappingLocalBusiness
{
    /**
     * Wraps the specified task in a new Transaction, returning the value
     *
```

```
 * @param task
 * @throws IllegalArgumentException If no task is specified
 * @throws TaskExecutionException If an error occurred in
 *    invoking {@link Callable#call()}
 */
<T> T wrapInTx(Callable<T> task) throws IllegalArgumentException,
    TaskExecutionException;

/**
 * Wraps the specified tasks in a new Transaction
 *
 * @param task
 * @throws IllegalArgumentException If no tasks are specified
 * @throws TaskExecutionException If an error occurred in invoking
 *    {@link Callable#call()}
 */
void wrapInTx(Callable<?>... tasks) throws IllegalArgumentException,
    TaskExecutionException;
}
```

Although we would not ever let a real client arbitrarily submit `java.util.concurrent.Callable` types for execution, this is a nice way to allow tests to run business logic inside the scope of a transaction. As we saw in Chapter 9, this has the added benefit of providing access to managed JPA entities before they're detached from the `EntityManager` at transaction completion. We can also force rollbacks via this mechanism to test that our application's state is left consistent in the case of an exceptional condition.

Is the BlackjackEJB Atomic?

Our first measure of the `BlackjackEJB`'s reliability is its atomicity: does it ensure that the transaction executes completely or not at all? What we are really concerned with are the critical tasks that change or create information. When placing a bet, the gameplay must succeed without error, and funds must leave the user's account and be added to the winner's. All of these tasks must be successful for the entire transaction to be successful.

To understand the importance of the atomic characteristic, imagine what would happen if even one of the subtasks failed to execute. For example, if the withdrawal from the loser's account succeeded but the money failed to be placed in the winner's account, the money would be lost from the system and no longer accounted for (loss of consistency).

So the only way `bet()` can be completed is if all the critical tasks execute successfully. If something goes wrong, the entire process must be aborted. Aborting a transaction requires more than simply not finishing the tasks; in addition, all the tasks that did execute within the transaction must be undone. In our example failure case, this means that the money must be restored to the loser's account, and an exception must be thrown to signal that the game didn't complete successfully.

Is the BlackjackEJB Consistent?

In order for a transaction to be consistent, the business system must make sense after the transaction has completed. In other words, the *state* of the business system must be consistent with the reality of the business. This requires the transaction to enforce the atomic, isolated, and durable characteristics, and it also requires diligent enforcement of integrity constraints by the application developer. In our failure example, failing to deposit funds after withdrawing from another as part of a transfer constitutes a loss of consistency; the money has evaporated from the system.

In addition, the database must be set up to enforce integrity constraints. For example, it should not be possible for a bank account to be associated with a null user or have a foreign key reference to a user ID that does not exist.

Is the BlackjackEJB Isolated?

If you are familiar with the concept of thread synchronization in Java or row-locking schemes in relational databases, isolation will be a familiar concept. To be isolated, a transaction must protect the data it is accessing from other transactions. This is necessary to prevent other transactions from interacting with data that is in transition. During a transfer between accounts in our blackjack game's bank, the transaction is isolated to prevent other transactions from modifying the entities and tables that are being updated. Imagine the problems that would arise if separate transactions were allowed to change any entity bean at any time—transactions would walk all over one another. Several account transfers could take place at the same time and withdraw from the same account, possibly overdrawing it.

The isolation of data accessed by EJBs does not mean that the entire application shuts down during a transaction. Only those entity beans and data directly affected by the transaction are isolated. That is to say, during an account transfer, only the removal and destination accounts need isolation.

Is the BlackjackEJB Durable?

To be durable, a business method must write all changes and new data to a permanent data store before it can be considered successful. This may seem like a no-brainer, but often it does not happen in real life. In the name of efficiency, changes are often maintained in memory for long periods of time before being saved on a disk drive. The idea is to reduce disk accesses—which slow systems down—and only periodically write the cumulative effect of data changes. Although this approach is great for performance, it is also dangerous because data can be lost when the system goes down and memory is wiped out. Durability requires the system to save all updates made within a transaction as the transaction successfully completes, thus protecting the integrity of the data.

Only when data is made durable are those specific records accessible through their respective entities from other transactions. Hence, durability also plays a role in isolation. A transaction is not finished until the data is successfully recorded.

Ensuring that transactions adhere to the ACID principles requires careful design. The system has to monitor the progress of a transaction to ensure that it does all of its work, that the data is changed correctly, that transactions do not interfere with each other, and that the changes can survive a system crash. Engineering all of this functionality into a system is a lot of work, and not something you would want to reinvent for every business system on which you work. Fortunately, EJB is designed to support transactions automatically, making the development of transactional systems easier. The rest of this chapter examines how EJB supports transactions implicitly (through declarative transaction attributes) and explicitly (through the Java Transaction API, or JTA).

Declarative Transaction Management

One of the primary advantages of Enterprise JavaBeans is that it allows for *declarative transaction management*. Without this feature, transactions must be controlled using explicit transaction demarcation, which involves the use of explicit APIs such as the Java Transaction Service (JTS). At best, explicit demarcation is difficult if you use the aforementioned APIs, particularly if you are new to transactional systems. In addition, it requires that the transactional code be written within the business logic, which reduces the clarity of the code. We talk more about explicit transaction management and EJB later in this chapter.

With declarative transaction management, the transactional behavior of EJBs can be controlled using the `@javax.ejb.TransactionAttribute` annotation or the EJB *deployment descriptor*, both of which can set transaction attributes for individual enterprise bean methods. This means that the transactional behavior of an EJB can be changed without changing the EJB's business logic by simply annotating the method in a different way or modifying XML. Declarative transaction management reduces the complexity of transactions for EJB developers and application developers and makes it easier to create robust transactional applications. Where no explicit declarative transaction properties have been defined, EJB will provide a default (which we'll soon see).

Transaction Scope

Transaction scope is a crucial concept for understanding transactions. In this context, transaction scope refers to managed resources (such as EJBs and entities) that are participating in a particular transaction. In the `wrapInTx()` method of the test-only `TxWrappingEJB`, all of the business logic designated in the supplied `Callable` is executed within a single transaction. When the method invocation completes, the transaction is over and its scope is no longer in context.

As you know, a transaction is a unit-of-work made up of one or more tasks. In a transaction, all the tasks that make up the unit-of-work must succeed for the entire transaction to succeed; in other words, the transaction must be atomic. If any task fails, the updates made by all the other tasks in the transaction will be rolled back or undone. In EJB, tasks are generally expressed as enterprise bean methods, and a unit-of-work consists of every enterprise bean method invoked in a transaction. The scope of a transaction includes every EJB that participates in the unit-of-work.

It is easy to trace the scope of a transaction by following the thread of execution. If the invocation of the `wrapInTx()` method begins a transaction, then logically, the transaction ends when the method completes. The scope of the `wrapInTx()` transaction would include any transaction-aware service it contains—every EJB, entity, or other managed resources. A transaction is propagated to an EJB when that EJB's method is invoked and included in the scope of that transaction. The transaction is also propagated to the persistence context of an `EntityManager`. The persistence context keeps track of changes made to persistent managed objects and commits them if the transaction succeeds.

A transaction can end if an exception is thrown while the `wrapInTx()` method is executing. The exception can be thrown from any referenced code or the `wrapInTx()` method itself. An exception may or may not cause a rollback, depending on its type. We discuss exceptions and transactions in more detail later.

The thread of execution is not the only factor that determines whether an EJB is included in the scope of a transaction; the EJB's transaction attributes also play a role. Determining whether an EJB participates in the transaction scope of any unit-of-work is accomplished implicitly, using the EJB's transaction attributes, or explicitly, using the JTA.

Transaction Attributes

As an application developer, you normally don't need to control transactions explicitly when using an EJB server. EJB servers can manage transactions implicitly, based on the transaction attributes established at deployment time. When an EJB is deployed, you can set its runtime transaction attribute in the `@javax.ejb.TransactionAttribute` annotation or deployment descriptor to one of several values:

```
NotSupported
Supports
Required
RequiresNew
Mandatory
Never
```

You may set a transaction attribute for the entire EJB (in which case it applies to all methods) or at different transaction attributes for individual methods. The former method is much simpler and less error-prone, but setting attributes at the method level offers more flexibility. The code in the following sections shows how to set the default transaction attribute of an EJB via annotations.

Using the @TransactionAttribute annotation

The @javax.ejb.TransactionAttribute annotation can be used to apply transaction attributes to your EJB's bean class or business methods. The attribute is defined using the javax.ejb.TransactionAttributeType Java enum:

```
public enum TransactionAttributeType
{
    MANDATORY,
    REQUIRED,
    REQUIRES_NEW,
    SUPPORTS,
    NOT_SUPPORTED,
    NEVER
}

@Target({METHOD, TYPE})
public @interface TransactionAttribute
{
    TransactionAttributeType value( ) default TransactionAttributeType.REQUIRED;
}
```

The @TransactionAttribute can be applied per method, or you can use it on the bean class to define the default transaction attribute for the entire bean class. In the case of our test TxWrappingEJB, the bean implementation class achieves the proper transaction isolation by always starting a new transaction and by running the business method inside of its context. This is implemented by using TransactionAttribute Type.REQUIRES_NEW:

```
import javax.ejb.Local;
import javax.ejb.Stateless;
import javax.ejb.TransactionAttribute;
import javax.ejb.TransactionAttributeType;

/**
 * EJB which wraps a specified series of {@link Callable}
 * tasks within the context of a new Transaction
 */
@Stateless
@Local(TxWrappingLocalBusiness.class)
@TransactionAttribute(TransactionAttributeType.REQUIRES_NEW)
// We always require a new Tx here, so we ensure to wrap
public class TxWrappingBean implements TxWrappingLocalBusiness
{
    ...
}
```

In this example, the default transaction attribute will be REQUIRES_NEW for every method of the class because we have applied the @TransactionAttribute annotation to the bean class. This default can be overridden by applying @TransactionAttribute individually to the business methods.

If you do not specify any `@TransactionAttribute` and there is no XML deployment descriptor, the default transaction attribute will be `REQUIRED`. One of the ideas behind EJB 3.0 is to provide common defaults so that you do not have to be explicit about transaction demarcation. In the majority of cases, EJB methods will be transactional, especially if they are interacting with an entity manager.

Transaction attributes defined

Here are the definitions of the transaction attributes listed earlier. In a few of the definitions, the client transaction is described as *suspended*. This means the transaction is not propagated to the enterprise bean method being invoked; propagation of the transaction is temporarily halted until the enterprise bean method returns. To make things easier, we will talk about attribute types as if they were bean types. For example, we'll say "a `Required` EJB" as shorthand for "an enterprise bean with the `Required` transaction attribute." The attributes are:

NotSupported

Invoking a method on an EJB with this transaction attribute suspends the transaction until the method is completed. This means that the transaction scope is not propagated to the `NotSupported` EJB or to any of the EJBs it calls. Once the method on the `NotSupported` EJB is done, the original transaction resumes its execution.

Figure 17-1 shows that a `NotSupported` EJB does not propagate the client transaction when one of its methods is invoked.

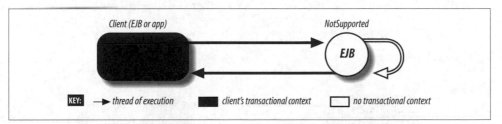

Figure 17-1. The NotSupported attribute

Supports

This attribute means that the enterprise bean method will be included in the transaction scope if it is invoked within a transaction. In other words, if the EJB or client that invokes the `Supports` EJB is part of a transaction scope, the `Supports` EJB and all EJBs accessed by it become part of the original transaction. However, the `Supports` EJB doesn't have to be part of a transaction and can interact with clients and other EJBs that are not included in a transaction scope.

Figure 17-2a shows the `Supports` EJB being invoked by a transactional client and propagating the transaction. Figure 17-2b shows the `Supports` EJB being invoked by a nontransactional client.

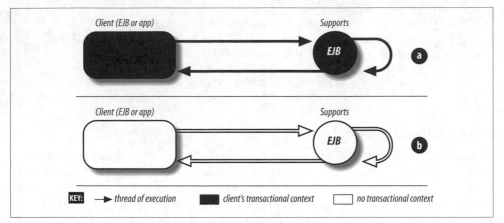

Figure 17-2. The Supports attribute

Required

This attribute means that the enterprise bean method must be invoked within the scope of a transaction. If the calling client or EJB is part of a transaction, the `Required` EJB is automatically included in its transaction scope. If, however, the calling client or EJB is not involved in a transaction, the `Required` EJB starts its own new transaction. The new transaction's scope covers only the `Required` EJB and all other EJBs accessed by it. Once the method invoked on the `Required` EJB is done, the new transaction's scope ends.

Figure 17-3a shows the `Required` EJB being invoked by a transactional client and propagating the transaction. Figure 17-3b shows the `Required` EJB being invoked by a nontransactional client, which causes it to start its own transaction.

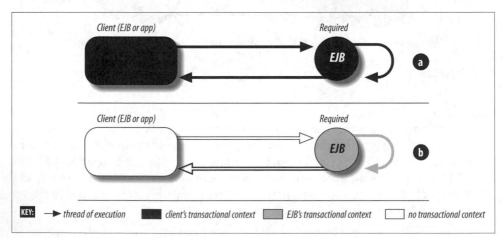

Figure 17-3. The Required attribute

RequiresNew

This attribute means that a new transaction is always started. Regardless of whether the calling client or EJB is part of a transaction, a method with the `RequiresNew` attribute begins a new transaction when invoked. If the calling client is already involved in a transaction, that transaction is suspended until the `RequiresNew` EJB's method call returns. The new transaction's scope covers only the `RequiresNew` EJB and all the EJBs accessed by it. Once the method invoked on the `RequiresNew` EJB is done, the new transaction's scope ends and the original transaction resumes.

Figure 17-4a shows the `RequiresNew` EJB being invoked by a transactional client. The client's transaction is suspended while the EJB executes under its own transaction. Figure 17-4b shows the `RequiresNew` EJB being invoked by a nontransactional client; the `RequiresNew` EJB executes under its own transaction.

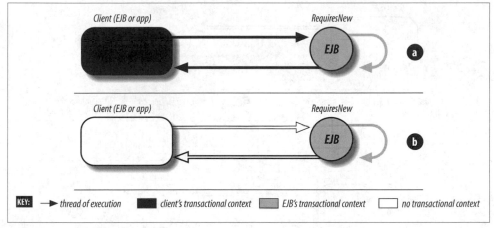

Figure 17-4. The RequiresNew attribute

Mandatory

This attribute means that the enterprise bean method must always be made part of the transaction scope of the calling client. The EJB may not start its own transaction; the transaction must be propagated from the client. If the calling client is not part of a transaction, the invocation will fail, throwing a `javax.ejb.EJBTransactionRequiredException`.

Figure 17-5a shows the `Mandatory` EJB invoked by a transactional client and propagating the transaction. Figure 17-5b shows the `Mandatory` EJB invoked by a nontransactional client; the method throws an `EJBTransactionRequiredException` because there is no transaction scope.

Never

This attribute means that the enterprise bean method must not be invoked within the scope of a transaction. If the calling client or EJB is part of a transaction, the `Never` EJB will throw an `EJBException`. However, if the calling client or EJB is not involved in a transaction, the `Never` EJB will execute normally without a transaction.

Figure 17-6a shows the `Never` EJB being invoked by a nontransactional client. Figure 17-6b shows the `Never` EJB being invoked by a transactional client; the method throws an `EJBException` to EJB clients because a client or EJB that is included in a transaction can never invoke the method.

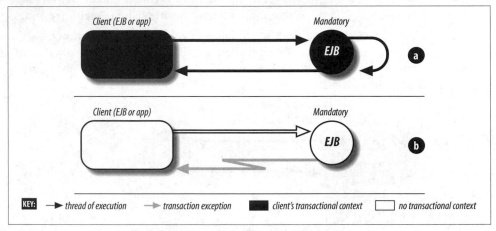

Figure 17-5. The Mandatory attribute

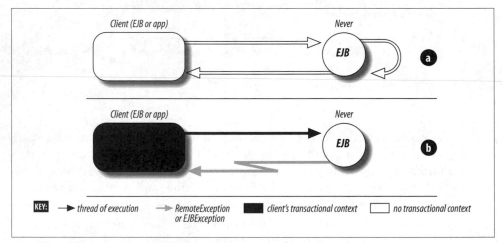

Figure 17-6. The Never attribute

EJB 3.0 persistence and transaction attributes

The EJB specification strongly advises that `EntityManager`s be accessed within the scope of a JTA transaction. So, if you are wrapping access to your persistent entities with EJBs, use only the `Required`, `RequiresNew`, and `Mandatory` transaction attributes. This restriction ensures that all database access occurs in the context of a transaction, which is important when the container is automatically managing persistence. There are valid exceptions to this rule when using extended persistence contexts with stateful session beans, but we'll talk about these exceptions later in the chapter.

Message-driven beans and transaction attributes

Message-driven beans may declare only the `NotSupported` or `Required` transaction attribute. The other transaction attributes don't make sense in message-driven beans, because they apply to client-initiated transactions. The `Supports`, `RequiresNew`, `Mandatory`, and `Never` attributes are all relative to the transaction context of the client. For example, the `Mandatory` attribute requires the client to have a transaction in progress before calling the enterprise bean. This is meaningless for a message-driven bean, which is decoupled from the client.

The `NotSupported` transaction attribute indicates that the message will be processed without a transaction. The `Required` transaction attribute indicates that the message will be processed with a container-initiated transaction.

EJB endpoints and transaction attributes

The `Mandatory` transaction attribute cannot be used with EJB endpoints, because an EJB endpoint does not propagate a client transaction. This may change when web service transactions become standardized, but for now, using `Mandatory` with an EJB endpoint method is prohibited.

Transaction Propagation

To illustrate the impact of transaction attributes, we'll test a bank account transfer as we saw earlier. Using the test `TxWrappingEJB` will ensure all operations must be initiated from the same client transaction. If any operation fails, the entire transaction fails. We'll take the following steps in the context of one transaction:

1. Transfer $100 from Account A to Account B.
2. Check that Account A has $100 less than before, and Account B has $100 more.
3. Force a rollback.

Because we'll encounter a mock error to make a rollback, checking the account balance of Account A after the transaction completes should yield the same balance as before we started, as if the transfer was never made.

First, let's see some of the transaction attributes for the `BankEJB`:

```
@Stateless
public class BankBean implements BankLocalBusiness
{
  ...
  @Override
```

```
@TransactionAttribute(TransactionAttributeType.SUPPORTS)
// Don't require a Tx is in play, but respect a currently operating
// one so we get the correct visibility from inside the Tx
public BigDecimal getBalance(long accountId) throws IllegalArgumentException
{
  ...
}

@Override
@TransactionAttribute(TransactionAttributeType.REQUIRED)
// Default Tx Attribute; create a new Tx if not present, else use the existing
public void transfer(long accountIdFrom, long accountIdTo, BigDecimal amount)
throws IllegalArgumentException,
      InsufficientBalanceException
{
  ...
}

  ...
}
```

The getBalance() method does not require a currently running transaction from the caller. Because this is a read-only operation, it does not honor atomicity, consistency, or durability. However, because of the "I" in ACID, for transaction isolation, when we have a currently running transaction, it needs to have the correct visibility to see any potential changes made within that transaction. Marking this method as SUPPORTS means we don't impose any transactional overhead for obtaining a current balance, but we'll respect the current balance inside of a running transaction.

The transfer() method, however, does involve write operations, and as such requires a transaction to be in play. This may be supplied as either a currently running transaction from the caller or a new one started by the EJB container if a transactional context is not present. This will guarantee that the transfer operation is treated as a single unit of work. Remember that REQUIRED does not need to be defined explicitly; this is the default value for EJBs if left out.

Now we can write our test:

```
/**
 * Ensures that Transfers between accounts obey the ACID properties of Transactions
 */
@Test
public void transferRetainsIntegrity() throws Throwable
{

  // Init
  final long alrubingerAccountId = ExampleUserData.ACCOUNT_ALRUBINGER_ID;
  final long blackjackAccountId = BlackjackServiceConstants.ACCOUNT_BLACKJACK
GAME_ID;

  // Ensure there's the expected amounts in both the ALR and Blackjack accounts
  final BigDecimal expectedinitialALR = ExampleUserData.INITIAL_ACCOUNT_BALANCE_
ALR;
```

```
final BigDecimal expectedinitialBlackjack =
  BlackjackServiceConstants.INITIAL_ACCOUNT_BALANCE_BLACKJACKGAME;
this.executeInTx(new CheckBalanceOfAccountTask(alrubingerAccountId, expected
initialALR),
        new CheckBalanceOfAccountTask(blackjackAccountId, expectedinitialBlackjack));
```

As a precondition check, we ensure that the balances of the two accounts in question are as expected. The executeInTx() method uses our TxWrappingEJB as we've described:

```
// Transfer $100 from ALR to Blackjack
final BigDecimal oneHundred = new BigDecimal(100);
bank.transfer(alrubingerAccountId, blackjackAccountId, oneHundred);
```

Here we make a transfer. Because we have no currently running transaction and the BankEJB's transfer() method has TransactionAttributeType.REQUIRED, a new transaction is created for us to handle the exchange:

```
// Ensure there's $100 less in the ALR account, and $100 more in the blackjack
account
this.executeInTx(new CheckBalanceOfAccountTask(alrubingerAccountId, expected
initialALR.subtract(oneHundred)),
        new CheckBalanceOfAccountTask(blackjackAccountId, expectedinitialBlack
jack.add(oneHundred)));
```

After checking the balances of the accounts to ensure the money was moved as expected, we throw a wrench into the system. In the next step, we'll force a transaction rollback by making another transfer but raising an exception before the transaction finishes:

```
// Now make a transfer, check it succeeded within the context of a Transaction,
// then intentionally throw an exception. The Tx should complete as rolled back,
// and the state should be consistent (as if the xfer request never took place).
boolean gotExpectedException = false;
final Callable<Void> transferTask = new Callable<Void>()
{
    @Override
    public Void call() throws Exception
    {
        bank.transfer(alrubingerAccountId, blackjackAccountId, oneHundred);
        return null;
    }
};
try
{
    this.executeInTx(transferTask, new CheckBalanceOfAccountTask(alrubinger
AccountId, expectedinitialALR.subtract(
            oneHundred).subtract(oneHundred)), new CheckBalanceOfAccountTask
(blackjackAccountId, expectedinitialBlackjack
            .add(oneHundred).add(oneHundred)), ForcedTestExceptionTask.INSTANCE);
}
// Expected
catch (final ForcedTestException fte)
{
    gotExpectedException = true;
}
```

```
    Assert.assertTrue("Did not receive expected exception as signaled from the
test; was not rolled back",
        gotExpectedException);

    // Now that we've checked the transfer succeeded from within the Tx, then
    // we threw an exception before committed, ensure the Tx rolled back and the
    // transfer was reverted from the
    // perspective of everyone outside the Tx.
    this.executeInTx(new CheckBalanceOfAccountTask(alrubingerAccountId, expected
initialALR.subtract(oneHundred)),
        new CheckBalanceOfAccountTask(blackjackAccountId, expectedinitialBlack
jack.add(oneHundred)));
}
```

Finally, we check that we've gotten the expected exception, and that the account transfer did not take place outside the context of the transaction. In other words, the state kept by the transaction before the error was encountered is ditched, and the system is left in consistent state.

As a transaction monitor, an EJB server watches each method call in the transaction. If any of the updates fail, all the updates to all the EJBs and entities will be reversed, or *rolled back*. A rollback is like an undo command. If you have worked with relational databases, the concept of a rollback should be familiar to you. Once an update is executed, you can either *commit* the update or roll it back. A commit makes the changes requested by the update permanent; a rollback aborts the update and leaves the database in its original state. Making EJBs transactional provides the same kind of rollback/commit control.

In cases in which the container implicitly manages the transaction, the commit and rollback decisions are handled automatically. When transactions are managed explicitly within an enterprise bean or by the client, the responsibility falls on the enterprise bean or application developer to commit or roll back a transaction. Programmatic demarcation of transactions is covered in detail later in this chapter.

The transaction manager coordinates transactions, propagating the transaction scope from one EJB to the next to ensure that all EJBs touched by a transaction are included in the transaction's unit-of-work. That way, the transaction manager can monitor the updates made by each enterprise bean and decide, based on the success of those updates, whether to commit all changes made by all enterprise beans to the database or roll them all back. If a *system exception* or a *rollback application exception* is thrown by a business method, the transaction is automatically rolled back. We talk more about exceptions later in this chapter.

When all the EJBs and persistence contexts are registered and their updates are made, the transaction manager checks to ensure that their updates will work. If all the updates will work, the transaction manager allows the changes to become permanent. If one of the EJBs or entity managers reports an error or fails, any changes made are rolled back by the transaction manager.

In addition to managing transactions in its own environment, an EJB server can coordinate with other transactional systems. If, for example, an EJB actually came from a different application server than the `BankEJB`, the two application servers would cooperate to manage the transaction as one unit-of-work. This is called a *distributed transaction*.[*] A distributed transaction requires what is called a *two-phase commit* (2-PC or TPC). A 2-PC allows transactions to be managed across different servers and resources (e.g., databases and JMS providers). The details of a 2-PC are beyond the scope of this book, but a system that supports it will not require any extra operations by an EJB or application developer. If distributed transactions are supported, the protocol for propagating transactions, as discussed earlier, will be supported. In other words, as an application or EJB developer, you should not notice a difference between local and distributed transactions.

A number of books on transaction processing and 2-PC are available. Perhaps the best books on the subject are *Principles of Transaction Processing* (Morgan Kaufmann) and *Transaction Processing: Concepts and Techniques* (Morgan Kaufmann). A much lighter resource is the series of "XA Exposed" articles (I, II, and III) by Mike Spille, which you can find at *http://jroller.com/page/pyrasun/?anchor=xa_exposed*.

Transactions and persistence context propagation

There are some transaction propagation rules to consider when invoking on multiple different EJBs within the same transaction that use entity managers. Here is a detailed list of persistence context-propagation rules:

- When a transaction-scoped entity manager is invoked outside the scope of a transaction, it creates a persistence context for the duration of that method call. After the method call completes, any managed objects produced by the call are immediately detached.

- If a transaction-scoped entity manager is invoked from within a transaction, a new persistence context is created (if there isn't one already) and associated with that transaction.

- If an entity manager is invoked upon and a persistence context is already associated with the transaction, use that persistence context. The persistence context is propagated between EJB invocations in the same transaction. This means that if an EJB interacts with an injected entity manager within a transaction and then invokes on another EJB within that same transaction, that EJB call will use the same enlisted persistence context.

- If an EJB with a transaction-scoped persistence context invokes on a stateful session bean that uses an extended persistence context, an error is thrown.

---

[*] Not all EJB servers support distributed transactions.

- If a stateful session bean with an extended persistence context calls another EJB that has injected a transaction-scoped persistence context, the extended persistence context is propagated.

- If an EJB calls another EJB with a different transaction scope, the persistence context, regardless of whether it is extended, is not propagated.

- If a stateful session bean with an extended persistence context calls another non-injected stateful session bean with an extended persistence context, an error is thrown. If you inject a stateful session bean into another stateful session bean, those beans share the same extended persistence context. However, if you manually create a stateful session, there is no sharing of persistence contexts.

Isolation and Database Locking

Transaction isolation (the "I" in ACID) is a critical part of any transactional system. This section explains isolation conditions, database locking, and transaction isolation levels. These concepts are important when deploying any transactional system.

Dirty, Repeatable, and Phantom Reads

Transaction isolation is defined in terms of isolation conditions called *dirty reads*, *repeatable reads*, and *phantom reads*. These conditions describe what can happen when two or more transactions operate on the same data.[†] When two users execute data access methods concurrently, different problems can surface or be avoided entirely, depending on the isolation level used by the database. Transaction isolation seeks to avoid these situations.

Dirty reads

A *dirty read* occurs when a transaction reads uncommitted changes made by a previous transaction. If the first transaction is rolled back, the data read by the second transaction becomes invalid because the rollback undoes the changes. The second transaction will not be aware that the data it has read has become invalid.

Repeatable reads

A *repeatable read* occurs when the data read is guaranteed to look the same if read again during the same transaction. Repeatable reads are guaranteed in one of two ways: either the data read is locked against changes, or it is a snapshot that doesn't reflect changes. If the data is locked, it cannot be changed by any other transaction until the current transaction ends. If the data is a snapshot, other transactions can change the data, but these changes will not be seen by this transaction if the read is repeated.

---

† Isolation conditions are covered in detail by the ANSI SQL-92 Specification, Document Number: ANSI X3. 135-1992 (R1998).

A *nonrepeatable read* occurs when the data retrieved in a subsequent read within the same transaction can return different results. In other words, the subsequent read can see the changes made by other transactions.

Phantom reads

A *phantom read* occurs when new records added to the database are detectable by transactions that started prior to the insert. Queries will include records added by other transactions after their transaction has started.

Database Locks

Databases, especially relational databases, normally use several different locking techniques. The most common are *read locks*, *write locks*, and *exclusive write locks*. (We've taken the liberty of adding *snapshots* to this list of techniques, although this isn't a formal term.) These locking mechanisms control how transactions access data concurrently. Locking mechanisms impact the read conditions described in the previous section. These types of locks are simple concepts that are addressed to a degree by the Java Persistence specification, but we'll discuss this later. Database vendors implement these locks differently, so you should understand how your database addresses these locking mechanisms to best predict how the isolation levels described in this section will work.

The four types of locks are:

Read locks
> Read locks prevent other transactions from changing data read during a transaction until the transaction ends, thus preventing nonrepeatable reads. Other transactions can read the data but not write to it. The current transaction is also prohibited from making changes. Whether a read lock locks only the records read, a block of records, or a whole table depends on the database being used.

Write locks
> Write locks are used for updates. A write lock prevents other transactions from changing the data until the current transaction is complete but allows dirty reads by other transactions and by the current transaction itself. In other words, the transaction can read its own uncommitted changes.

Exclusive write locks
> Exclusive write locks are used for updates. An exclusive write lock prevents other transactions from reading or changing the data until the current transaction is complete. It also prevents dirty reads by other transactions. Some databases do not allow transactions to read their own data while it is exclusively locked.

Snapshots
> A snapshot is a frozen view of the data that is taken when a transaction begins. Some databases get around locking by providing every transaction with its own

snapshot. Snapshots can prevent dirty reads, nonrepeatable reads, and phantom reads. They can be problematic because the data is not real-time data; it is old the instant the snapshot is taken.

Transaction Isolation Levels

Transaction isolation is defined in terms of the isolation conditions (dirty reads, repeatable reads, and phantom reads). Isolation levels are commonly used in database systems to describe how locking is applied to data within a transaction. The following terms are used to discuss isolation levels:

Read Uncommitted
> The transaction can read uncommitted data (i.e., data changed by a different transaction that is still in progress). Dirty reads, nonrepeatable reads, and phantom reads can occur. Bean methods with this isolation level can read uncommitted changes.

Read Committed
> The transaction cannot read uncommitted data; data that is being changed by a different transaction cannot be read. Dirty reads are prevented; nonrepeatable reads and phantom reads can occur. Bean methods with this isolation level cannot read uncommitted data.

Repeatable Read
> The transaction cannot change data that is being read by a different transaction. Dirty reads and nonrepeatable reads are prevented; phantom reads can occur. Bean methods with this isolation level have the same restrictions as those in the Read Committed level and can execute only repeatable reads.

Serializable
> The transaction has exclusive read and update privileges; different transactions can neither read nor write to the same data. Dirty reads, nonrepeatable reads, and phantom reads are prevented. This isolation level is the most restrictive.

These isolation levels are the same as those defined for JDBC. Specifically, they map to the static final variables in the `java.sql.Connection` class. The behavior modeled by the isolation levels in the connection class is the same as the behavior described here.

The exact behavior of these isolation levels depends largely on the locking mechanism used by the underlying database or resource. How the isolation levels work depends in large part on how your database supports them.

In EJB, the deployer sets transaction isolation levels in a vendor-specific way if the container manages the transaction. The EJB developer sets the transaction isolation level if the enterprise bean manages its own transactions. Up to this point, we have discussed only container-managed transactions; we discuss bean-managed transactions later in this chapter.

Balancing Performance Against Consistency

Generally speaking, as the isolation levels become more restrictive, the performance of the system decreases because transactions are prevented from accessing the same data. If isolation levels are very restrictive—in other words, if they are at the Serializable level—then all transactions, even simple reads, must wait in line to execute. This can result in a system that is very slow. EJB systems that process a large number of concurrent transactions and need to be very fast will therefore avoid the Serializable isolation level where it is not necessary.

Isolation levels, however, also enforce consistency of data. More restrictive isolation levels help to ensure that invalid data is not used for performing updates. The old adage, "garbage in, garbage out," applies. The Serializable isolation level ensures that data is never accessed concurrently by transactions, thus ensuring that the data is always consistent.

Choosing the correct isolation level requires some research about the database you are using and how it handles locking. You must also carefully analyze how each piece of data in your application is being used. For instance, most systems have some entities which will rarely, if ever, change. Even if these types of data do change, they would rarely affect the integrity of the system. Therefore, a low isolation level can be specified when a piece of business logic is viewing only this type of data. Other data, such as the current balance in an `Account`, on the other hand, can greatly affect the integrity of our `BankEJB`; this may require isolation to be more restrictive.

Controlling isolation levels

Different EJB servers allow different levels of granularity for isolation levels, and some servers defer this responsibility to the database. Most EJB servers and `EntityManager` implementations control the isolation level through the resource access API (e.g., JDBC and JMS) and may allow different resources to have different isolation levels. However, they will generally require a consistent isolation level for access to the same resource within a single transaction. Consult your vendor's documentation to find out the level of control your server offers.

Bean-managed transactions in session beans and message-driven beans, however, allow you to specify the transaction isolation level using the database's API. The JDBC API, for instance, provides a mechanism for specifying the isolation level of the database connection. For example:

```
DataSource source = (javax.sql.DataSource)
    jndiCntxt.lookup("java:comp/env/jdbc/titanDB");
Connection con = source.getConnection( );
con.setTransactionIsolation(Connection.TRANSACTION_SERIALIZABLE);
```

You can have different isolation levels for different resources within the same transaction, but all enterprise beans using the same resource in a transaction should use the same isolation level.

Optimistic Locking

Using an isolation level that's too restrictive results in the locking of resources. When many clients contend for the same resource, they must block until it's their turn. This leads to a natural bottleneck and scalability problem that results in both high latency and reduced overall throughput.

So, how can we solve this concurrency problem? One solution is to use the *optimistic locking* design pattern. Optimistic locking isn't locking in the traditional sense. Instead, we assume that no other client is trying to access the same data at the same time. Then, at transaction commit time, we let the database resolve whether the data has been altered by another transaction. If it has, we throw an exception and roll back our transaction. In other words, we are being optimistic that the data hasn't been touched until we need to commit. How does this work? How does this avoid table-level locks? Well, to use optimistic locking, we have to use a special feature of Java Persistence.

The first thing we need to do is model our `Account` for use in the `BankEJB`:

```
@Entity
public class Account
{
    ...

    /**
     * Current balance of the account
     */
    private BigDecimal balance = new BigDecimal(0, new MathContext(2));

    /**
     * Version used for optimistic locking
     */
    @Version
    private Long version;
    ...
}
```

The new and interesting property is the `version` property, which is annotated with `@javax.persistence.Version`. An `@Version` property is a column in the `Account` table that will hold a version ID of a particular row. Whenever the `Account` entity class is updated, the version column is incremented automatically by JPA. When a transaction beginning the commit process and business logic has updated the `Account`, the entity manager first checks to see whether the `version` property of the in-memory `Account` instance matches the version column currently stored in the database. If the versions match, then the `version` property is incremented. If they don't match, then the entity manager throws an exception and the whole transaction rolls back. When the entity manager detects that the `Account` has been updated by another transaction and a concurrency error has occurred, it throws the `javax.persistence.OptimisticLock-Exception` and rolls back the transaction. Otherwise, the transaction completes successfully, and the queried `Account` is updated as requested and its `version` property is incremented. This optimistic locking solution creates a quick *write-lock* on one row in our database instead of the vastly unscalable table lock in the `Serializable` solution that was presented earlier in this chapter.

It should be noted that the optimistic locking design pattern does not work all the time. If you have a row in your database that has a high concurrent write contention, then it is probably less efficient to use the optimistic locking pattern because it will create a lot of rollbacks, which create a lot of overhead in your system. In that scenario, the `Serializable` solution is possibly more scalable. A redesign of your data model is probably more appropriate in this situation, however. If you have high concurrent access to one particular row in your database, then your system probably won't scale much anyway.

Programmatic Locking

The `EntityManager` interface has a specific `lock()` method for performing entity locks. To use it, you pass in the entity object you want to lock and indicate whether you want a read or write lock:

```
package javax.persistence;

public enum LockModeType
{
   READ,
   WRITE
}

public interface EntityManager {
   void lock(Object entity, LockModeType type);
}
```

`LockModeType.READ` ensures that no dirty and nonrepeatable reads can occur on the locked entity. `LockModeType.WRITE` has the same semantics as `READ`, but it also forces an increment of the entity's `@Version` property. To implement these semantics, a database row lock is usually performed (i.e., `SELECT ... FOR UPDATE`).

 Vendor implementations are not required to support locking on entities that do not have an `@Version` property.

Programmatic locking becomes important when you want to ensure nonrepeatable reads on entity beans that may be read within the transaction but not updated.

Nontransactional EJBs

Beans outside of a transaction's scope normally provide some kind of stateless service that does not manipulate data in a data store. While these types of enterprise beans may be necessary as utilities during a transaction, they do not need to meet the ACID requirements. Consider a nontransactional stateless session bean, the `QuoteEJB`, which provides live stock quotes. This EJB may respond to a request from an EJB involved in a stock purchase transaction. The success or failure of the stock purchase as a transaction will not impact the state or operations of the `QuoteEJB`, so it does not need to be part of the transaction. Beans that are involved in transactions are subjected to the isolated ACID property, which means that their services *cannot* be shared during the life of the transaction. Making an enterprise bean transactional can be expensive at runtime. Declaring an EJB to be nontransactional (i.e., `NotSupported`) leaves it out of the transaction scope, which may improve the performance and availability of that service.

Explicit Transaction Management

 Although this section covers JTA, it is strongly recommended that you not attempt to manage transactions explicitly. Through transaction attributes, Enterprise JavaBeans provides a comprehensive and simple mechanism for delimiting transactions at the method level and propagating transactions automatically. Only developers with a thorough understanding of transactional systems should attempt to use JTA with EJB.

EJB provides implicit transaction management on the method level: we can define transactions that are delimited by the scope of the method being executed. This is one of the primary advantages of EJB over cruder distributed object implementations because it reduces complexity, and therefore, programmer error. In addition, declarative transaction demarcation, as used in EJB, separates the transactional behavior from the business logic, meaning that a change to transactional behavior does not require changes to the business logic. In rare situations, however, it may be necessary to take control of transactions explicitly.

Explicit management of transactions is normally accomplished using the Object Management Group's (OMG) Object Transaction Service (OTS) or the Java implementation of OTS, the Java Transaction Service (JTS). OTS and JTS provide APIs that allow developers to work with transaction managers and resources (e.g., databases and JMS providers) directly. While the JTS implementation of OTS is robust and complete, it is not the easiest API to work with; it requires clean and intentional control over the bounds of enrollment in transactions.

Enterprise JavaBeans supports a much simpler API, the Java Transaction API (JTA), for working with transactions. This API is implemented by the `javax.transaction` package. JTA actually consists of two components: a high-level transactional client interface and a low-level X/Open XA interface. We are concerned with the high-level client interface, since it is accessible to enterprise beans and is recommended for client applications. The low-level XA interface is used by the EJB server and container to coordinate transactions with resources such as databases.

Your use of explicit transaction management will probably focus on one simple interface: javax.transaction.UserTransaction. UserTransaction allows you to manage the scope of a transaction explicitly. Here's how explicit demarcation might be used in an EJB:

```
@Singleton
@Startup
@TransactionManagement(TransactionManagementType.BEAN)
public class InitializerBean
{

    /**
     * Because @PostConstruct runs in an unspecified
     * Tx context (as invoked by the container), we'll
     * make one via this manager.  For EJBs that use
     * TransactionManagementType.BEAN, this is the hook
     * we use to programmatically demarcate transactional
     * boundaries.
     */
    @Resource(mappedName = "java:/TransactionManager")
    // mappedName is vendor-specific, and in this case points to an
    // address in JNDI
    private TransactionManager txManager;

    /**
     * Called by the container on startup.
     * Because EJB lifecycle operations are invoked outside of a
     * transactional context, we manually demarcate the Tx boundaries
     * via the injected {@link TransactionManager}.
     */
    @PostConstruct
    public void initialize() throws Exception
    {
        // Get the current Tx (if we have one, we may have been invoked via
        // a business method which has provided a Tx
        final Transaction tx = txManager.getTransaction();
        final boolean startOurOwnTx = tx == null;
        // If we need to start our own Tx (ie. this was called by the container as @Post
Construct)
        if (startOurOwnTx)
        {
            // Start a Tx via the injected TransactionManager
            txManager.begin();
        }

        try
        {
            // Do some work inside of a transaction, for instance
            // via en EntityManager or calls to another EJB
        }
        // Any errors should result in a rollback
        catch(final Throwable t)
```

```
    {
        if(startOurOwnTx)
        {
            txManager.setRollbackOnly();
        }
    }
    finally
    {
        // Mark the end of the Tx if we started it; will trigger an
        // EntityManager to flush outgoing changes
        if (startOurOwnTx)
        {

            txManager.commit();
        }
    }
    }
}
```

Here's an interesting case. In the previous example, `initialize()` is both a business method and a lifecycle callback through `@PostConstruct`. Because `@PostConstruct` methods are executed by the container inside of an unspecified transactional context, if we need to interact with managed resources such as an `EntityManager`, we must initiate our own transaction. For this we use the injected `TransactionManager` APIs to demarcate the beginning and end of the transaction. Note that it's very important to attempt the `commit()` in a `finally` block, such that any exceptional conditions are accounted for. We catch any exceptions and mark the transaction to roll back later if encountered.

Obviously, this example is contrived, but the point it makes is clear. Transactions can be controlled directly instead of depending on method scope to delimit them. The advantage of using explicit transaction demarcation is that it gives the client control over the bounds of a transaction. The client, in this example, could be a client application or another enterprise bean.[‡] In either case, the same `javax.transaction.User Transaction` is used, but it is obtained from different sources, depending on whether it is needed on the client or in an enterprise bean.

Java Enterprise Edition (Java EE) specifies how a client application can obtain a `User Transaction` object using JNDI. Here's how a client obtains a `UserTransaction` object if the EJB container is part of a Java EE system:

```
Context jndiCntx = new InitialContext( );
UserTransaction tran = (UserTransaction)
    jndiCntx.lookup("java:comp/UserTransaction");
utx.begin( );
...
utx.commit( );
```

Enterprise beans can also manage transactions explicitly. Only session beans and message-driven beans that define a `javax.ejb.TransactionManagementType` of `Bean` using

[‡] Only beans declared as managing their own transactions (bean-managed transaction beans) can use the `UserTransaction` interface.

the `@javax.ejb.TransactionManager` annotation can manage their own transactions. Enterprise beans that manage their own transactions are frequently referred to as bean-managed transaction (BMT) beans. Entity beans can never be BMT beans.

Transaction Propagation in Bean-Managed Transactions

With stateless session beans, transactions that are managed using `UserTransaction` must be started and completed within the same method. In other words, `UserTransaction` transactions cannot be started in one method and ended in another. This makes sense because stateless session bean instances are shared across many clients; while one stateless instance may service a client's first request, a completely different instance may service a subsequent request by the same client. With stateful session beans, however, a transaction can begin in one method and be committed in another because a stateful session bean is used by only one client. Therefore, a stateful session bean can associate itself with a transaction across several different client-invoked methods.

When a client that is already involved in a transaction invokes a bean-managed transaction method, the client's transaction is suspended until the method returns. This suspension occurs regardless of whether the BMT bean explicitly started its own transaction within the method or the transaction was started in a previous method invocation. The client transaction is always suspended until the BMT method returns.

 Transaction control across methods is strongly discouraged because it can result in improperly managed transactions and long-lived transactions that lock up or even leak resources. It's best practice to let the method defining the transaction start also dictate where the transaction ends.

Message-driven beans and bean-managed transactions

Message-driven beans also have the option of managing their own transactions. In the case of MDBs, the scope of the transaction must begin and end within the `onMessage()` method. It is not possible for a bean-managed transaction to span `onMessage()` calls.

It is important to understand that in a BMT, the message consumed by the MDB is not part of the transaction. When an MDB uses container-managed transactions, the message it handles is a part of the transaction, so if the transaction is rolled back, the consumption of the message is also rolled back, forcing the JMS provider to redeliver the message. But with bean-managed transactions, the message is not part of the transaction, so if the BMT is rolled back, the JMS provider will not be aware of the transaction's failure. However, all is not lost, because the JMS provider can still rely on message acknowledgment to determine whether the message was delivered successfully.

The EJB container will acknowledge the message if the onMessage() method returns successfully. If, however, a RuntimeException is thrown by the onMessage() method, the container will not acknowledge the message, and the JMS provider will suspect a problem and probably attempt to redeliver the message. If redelivery of a message is important when a transaction fails, your best course of action is to ensure that the onMessage() method throws an EJBException so that the container will *not* acknowledge the message received from the JMS provider.

 Vendors use proprietary (declarative) mechanisms to specify the number of attempts to redeliver messages to BMT/NotSupported MDBs that "fail" to acknowledge receipt. The JMS-MDB provider may provide a "dead message" area into which such messages will be placed if they cannot be processed successfully according to the retry count. Administrators can monitor the dead message area so that delivered messages can be detected and handled manually.

Other than the message, everything between the UserTransaction.begin() and UserTransaction.commit() methods is part of the same transaction. If a transaction failure occurs, these operations will be rolled back and the message will not be sent.

Heuristic Decisions

Transactions are normally controlled by a *transaction manager* (often the EJB server), which manages the ACID characteristics across several enterprise beans, databases, and servers. The transaction manager uses a two-phase commit (2-PC) to manage transactions. 2-PC is a protocol for managing transactions that commits updates in two stages. 2-PC is complex, but basically it requires that servers and databases cooperate through an intermediary—the transaction manager—in order to ensure that all of the data is made durable together. Some EJB servers support 2-PC and others do not, and the value of this transaction mechanism is a source of some debate. The important point to remember is that a transaction manager controls the transaction; based on the results of a poll against the resources (databases, JMS providers, and other resources), it decides whether all the updates should be committed or rolled back. A *heuristic decision* takes place when one of the resources makes a unilateral decision to commit or roll back without permission from the transaction manager. When a heuristic decision has been made, the atomicity of the transaction is lost and data-integrity errors can occur.

UserTransaction throws a few different exceptions related to heuristic decisions, discussed in the following section.

UserTransaction

EJB servers are required to support UserTransaction but are not required to support the rest of JTA, nor are they required to use JTS for their transaction service. UserTransaction is defined as follows:

```
public interface javax.transaction.UserTransaction
{

    public abstract void begin( ) throws IllegalStateException, SystemException;
    public abstract void commit( ) throws IllegalStateException, SystemException,
        TransactionRolledbackException, HeuristicRollbackException,
        HeuristicMixedException;
    public abstract int getStatus( );
    public abstract void rollback( ) throws IllegalStateException, SecurityException,
        SystemException;
    public abstract void setRollbackOnly( ) throws IllegalStateException,
        SystemException;
    public abstract void setTransactionTimeout(int seconds)
        throws SystemException;

}
```

Here's what the methods defined in this interface do:

begin()

Invoking the begin() method creates a new transaction. The thread that executes the begin() method is immediately associated with the new transaction, which is then propagated to any EJB that supports existing transactions. The begin() method can throw one of two checked exceptions. An IllegalStateException is thrown when begin() is called by a thread that is already associated with a transaction. You must complete any transactions associated with that thread before beginning a new transaction. A SystemException is thrown if the transaction manager (i.e., the EJB server) encounters an unexpected error condition.

commit()

The commit() method completes the transaction that is associated with the current thread. When commit() is executed, the current thread is no longer associated with a transaction. This method can throw several checked exceptions. An IllegalStateException is thrown if the current thread is not associated with a transaction. A SystemException is thrown if the transaction manager (the EJB server) encounters an unexpected error condition. A TransactionRolled-backEx ception is thrown when the entire transaction is rolled back rather than committed; this can happen if one of the resources was unable to perform an update or if the UserTransaction.rollBackOnly() method was called. A HeuristicRollback Exception indicates that one or more resources made a heuristic decision to roll back the transaction. A HeuristicMixedException indicates resources made heuristic decisions to both roll back and commit the transaction; that is, some resources decided to roll back and others decided to commit.

rollback()

The rollback() method is invoked to roll back the transaction and undo updates. The rollback() method can throw one of three different checked exceptions. A SecurityException is thrown if the thread using the UserTransaction object is not allowed to roll back the transaction. An IllegalStateException is thrown if the current thread is not associated with a transaction. A SystemException is thrown if the transaction manager (the EJB server) encounters an unexpected error condition.

setRollbackOnly()

The setRollbackOnly() method is invoked to mark the transaction for rollback. This means that, regardless of whether the updates executed within the transaction succeed, the transaction must be rolled back when completed. This method can be invoked by any BMT EJB participating in the transaction or by the client application. The setRollBackOnly() method can throw one of two checked exceptions: an IllegalStateException is thrown if the current thread is not associated with a transaction, and a SystemException is thrown if the transaction manager (the EJB server) encounters an unexpected error condition.

setTransactionTimeout(int seconds)

The setTransactionTimeout(int seconds) method sets the lifespan of a transaction (i.e., how long it will live before timing out). The transaction must complete before the transaction timeout is reached. If this method is not called, the transaction manager (EJB server) automatically sets the timeout. If this method is invoked with a value of 0 seconds, the default timeout of the transaction manager will be used. This method must be invoked after the begin() method. A SystemException is thrown if the transaction manager (EJB server) encounters an unexpected error condition.

getStatus()

The getStatus() method returns an integer that can be compared to constants defined in the javax.transaction.Status interface. A sophisticated programmer can use this method to determine the status of a transaction associated with a UserTransaction object. A SystemException is thrown if the transaction manager (EJB server) encounters an unexpected error condition.

Status

Status is a simple interface that contains constants but no methods. Its sole purpose is to provide a set of constants that describe the status of a transactional object—in this case, UserTransaction:

```
interface javax.transaction.Status
{
    public final static int STATUS_ACTIVE;
```

```
    public final static int STATUS_COMMITTED;
    public final static int STATUS_COMMITTING;
    public final static int STATUS_MARKED_ROLLBACK;
    public final static int STATUS_NO_TRANSACTION;
    public final static int STATUS_PREPARED;
    public final static int STATUS_PREPARING;
    public final static int STATUS_ROLLEDBACK;
    public final static int STATUS_ROLLING_BACK;
    public final static int STATUS_UNKNOWN;
}
```

The value returned by getStatus() tells the client using the UserTransaction the status of a transaction. Here's what the constants mean:

STATUS_ACTIVE

An active transaction is associated with the UserTransaction object. This status is returned after a transaction has been started and prior to a transaction manager beginning a two-phase commit. (Transactions that have been suspended are still considered active.)

STATUS_COMMITTED

A transaction is associated with the UserTransaction object, and the transaction has been committed. It is likely that heuristic decisions have been made; otherwise, the transaction would have been destroyed and the STATUS_NO_TRANSACTION constant would have been returned instead.

STATUS_COMMITTING

A transaction is associated with the UserTransaction object, and the transaction is in the process of committing. The UserTransaction object returns this status if the transaction manager has decided to commit but has not yet completed the process.

STATUS_MARKED_ROLLBACK

A transaction is associated with the UserTransaction object, and the transaction has been marked for rollback, perhaps as a result of a UserTransaction.setRoll backOnly() operation invoked somewhere else in the application.

STATUS_NO_TRANSACTION

No transaction is currently associated with the UserTransaction object. This occurs after a transaction has completed or if no transaction has been created. This value is returned instead of throwing an IllegalStateException.

STATUS_PREPARED

A transaction is associated with the UserTransaction object. The transaction has been prepared, which means that the first phase of the two-phase commit process has completed.

STATUS_PREPARING

A transaction is associated with the UserTransaction object, and the transaction is in the process of preparing, which means that the transaction manager is in the middle of executing the first phase of the two-phase commit.

STATUS_ROLLEDBACK

A transaction is associated with the `UserTransaction` object, and the outcome of the transaction has been identified as a rollback. It is likely that heuristic decisions have been made; otherwise, the transaction would have been destroyed and the `STATUS_NO_TRANSACTION` constant would have been returned.

STATUS_ROLLING_BACK

A transaction is associated with the `UserTransaction` object, and the transaction is in the process of rolling back.

STATUS_UNKNOWN

A transaction is associated with the `UserTransaction` object, and its current status cannot be determined. This is a transient condition and subsequent invocations will ultimately return a different status.

EJBContext Rollback Methods

Only BMT beans can access `UserTransaction` from `EJBContext` and the JNDI ENC. Container-managed transaction (CMT) beans cannot use `UserTransaction`. Instead, CMT beans use the `setRollbackOnly()` and `getRollbackOnly()` methods of `EJBContext` to interact with the current transaction. Later in this chapter, we'll see that exceptions can be used to roll back the transaction.

The `setRollbackOnly()` method gives an enterprise bean the power to veto a transaction, which can be used if the enterprise bean detects a condition that would cause inconsistent data to be committed when the transaction completes. Once an enterprise bean invokes the `setRollbackOnly()` method, the current transaction is marked for rollback and cannot be committed by any other participant in the transaction, including the container.

The `getRollbackOnly()` method returns `true` if the current transaction has been marked for rollback. This information can be used to avoid executing work that would not be committed anyway. For example, if an exception is thrown and captured within an enterprise bean method, `getRollbackOnly()` can be used to determine whether the exception caused the current transaction to be rolled back. If it did, there is no sense in continuing the processing. If it did not, the EJB has an opportunity to correct the problem and retry the task that failed. Only expert EJB developers should attempt to retry tasks within a transaction. Alternatively, if the exception did not cause a rollback (i.e., `getRollbackOnly()` returns `false`), a rollback can be forced using the `setRollbackOnly()` method.

BMT beans must *not* use the `setRollbackOnly()` and `getRollbackOnly()` methods of the `EJBContext`. BMT beans should use the `getStatus()` and `rollback()` methods on the `UserTransaction` object to check for rollback and force a rollback, respectively.

Exceptions and Transactions

Exceptions have a large impact on the outcome of transactions.

Application Exceptions Versus System Exceptions

System exceptions represent unknown internal errors. The EJB container throws system exceptions when it encounters an internal application server failure. Business logic can throw system exceptions when it wants to abort the business process. Application exceptions are exceptions that are part of your business logic. They denote a strongly typed definition of a specific business problem or failure but do not necessarily abort or roll back the business process.

System exceptions

System exceptions include `java.lang.RuntimeException` and its subclasses. `EJBException` is a subclass of `RuntimeException`, so it is considered a system exception. System exceptions also include `java.rmi.RemoteException` and its subclasses. The `RuntimeException` and `RemoteException` subclasses differ in that they can be turned into application exceptions using the `@javax.ejb.ApplicationException` annotation. This annotation is discussed later in this chapter.

System exceptions always cause a transaction to roll back when they are thrown from an enterprise bean method. Any `RuntimeException` not annotated with `@ApplicationException` that is thrown within a business method (for instance, `EJBException`, `NullPointerException`, `IndexOutOfBoundsException`, and so on) is handled by the container automatically and results in a transaction rollback. In Java, `RuntimeException` types do not need to be declared in the throws clause of the method signature or handled using try/catch blocks; they are automatically thrown from the method.

The container handles system exceptions automatically and it will always do the following:

1. Roll back the transaction.
2. Log the exception to alert the system administrator.
3. Discard the EJB instance.

When a system exception is thrown from any callback method (`@PostConstruct`, `@PostActivate`, and so on), it is treated the same way as exceptions thrown from any business method.

Although EJB requires system exceptions to be logged, it does not specify how they should be logged or the format of the logfile. The exact mechanism for recording exceptions and reporting them to the system administrator is left to the vendor.

When a system exception occurs, the EJB instance is discarded, which means that it is dereferenced and garbage-collected. The container assumes that the EJB instance may have corrupt variables or otherwise be unstable and is therefore unsafe to use.

The impact of discarding an EJB instance depends on the enterprise bean's type. In the case of stateless session beans, the client does not notice that the instance has been discarded. These instance types are not dedicated to a particular client; they are swapped in and out of an instance pool, and so any instance can service a new request. With stateful session beans, however, the impact on the client is severe. Stateful session beans are dedicated to a single client and maintain conversational state. Discarding a stateful bean instance destroys the instance's conversational state and invalidates the client's reference to the EJB. When stateful session instances are discarded, subsequent invocations of the EJB's methods by the client result in a `NoSuchEJBException`, which is a subclass of `RuntimeException`.§

With message-driven beans, a system exception thrown by the `onMessage()` method or one of the callback methods (`@PostConstruct` or `@PreDestroy`) will cause the bean instance to be discarded. If the MDB was a BMT bean, the message it was handling may or may not be redelivered, depending on when the EJB container acknowledges delivery. In the case of container-managed transactions, the container will roll back the transaction, so the message will not be acknowledged and may be redelivered.

In session beans, when a system exception occurs and the instance is discarded, a `RuntimeException` is always thrown, regardless of whether the client is a remote or a local invocation. If the client started the transaction, which was then propagated to the EJB, a system exception (thrown by the enterprise bean method) will be caught by the container and rethrown as a `javax.ejb.EJBTransactionRolledbackException`. `EJBTransactionRolledbackException` is a subtype of `RuntimeException` and gives a more explicit indication to the client that a rollback occurred. If the client did not propagate a transaction to the EJB, the system exception will be caught and rethrown as an `EJBException`.

An `EJBException` generally should be thrown when a nonbusiness subsystem throws an exception, such as JDBC throwing an `SQLException` or JMS throwing a `JMSException`. In some cases, however, the bean developer may attempt to handle the exception and retry an operation instead of throwing an `EJBException`. This should be done only when the exceptions thrown by the subsystem and their repercussions on the transaction are well understood. As a rule of thumb, rethrow nonbusiness subsystem exceptions as `EJBException`s (or `@ApplicationException`s that cause a rollback) and allow the EJB container to roll back the transaction and discard the bean instance automatically.

---

§ Although the instance is always discarded with a `RuntimeException`, the impact on the remote reference may vary depending on the vendor.

Application exceptions

An *application exception* is normally thrown in response to a business-logic error, as opposed to a system error. Application exceptions are always delivered directly to the client without being repackaged as an EJBException type. By default, they do not cause a transaction to roll back. In this case, the client has an opportunity to recover after an application exception is thrown. Application errors are frequently used to report validation errors in this manner. In this case, the exception is thrown before tasks are started and is clearly not the result of a subsystem failure (e.g., JDBC, JMS, Java RMI, and JNDI).

The @javax.ejb.ApplicationException annotation may be used to force an application exception to roll back the transaction automatically:

```
package javax.ejb;

@Target(TYPE) @Retention(RUNTIME)
public @interface ApplicationException
{
    boolean rollback( ) default false;
}
```

For instance, our BankEJB makes use of an application exception to denote that a withdrawal or transfer operation cannot complete due to an insufficient balance:

```
/**
 * Exception thrown when attempting to invoke an operation that requires
 * more funds than are currently available
 */
@ApplicationException(rollback = true)
public class InsufficientBalanceException extends Exception
{
    ...
}
```

We want the transaction to be rolled back automatically, but business logic may be able to catch InsufficientBalanceException and retry the transaction automatically (by depositing more funds first, for example).

The @ApplicationException annotation can also be used on subclasses of java.lang.RuntimeException and java.rmi.RemoteException. This is useful because you may not want a thrown RuntimeException to be wrapped in an EJBException, or you may not want a particular subclass of RemoteException to roll back the exception.

Table 17-1 summarizes the interactions among different types of exceptions and transactions in session and entity beans.

Table 17-1. Exception summary for session and entity beans

Transaction scope	Transaction type attributes	Exception thrown	Container's action	Client's view
Client-initiated transaction. The transaction is started by the client (application or EJB) and propagated to the enterprise bean method.	transaction-type = Container transaction-attribute = Required | Mandatory |Supports	Application exception	If the EJB invoked `setRoll backOnly()` or the application exception is annotated with `@ApplicationException (rollback=true)`, mark the client's transaction for rollback. Rethrow the application exception.	Receives the application exception. The client's transaction may or may not have been marked for rollback.
		System exception	Mark the client's transaction for rollback. Log the error. Discard the instance. Rethrow the `javax.ejb.EJBTransac tionRolledback Exception`.	Clients receive the JTA `javax.ejb.EJB TransactionRol ledbackExcep tion`. The client's transaction has been rolled back.
Container-managed transaction. The transaction started when the EJB's method was invoked and will end when the method completes.	transaction-type = Container transaction-attribute = Required | RequiresNew	Application exception	If the EJB invoked `setRoll backOnly()` or the application exception is annotated with `@ApplicationException (rollback=true)`, roll back the transaction and rethrow the application exception. If the EJB did not explicitly roll back the transaction, attempt to commit the transaction and rethrow the application exception.	Receives the application exception. The EJB's transaction may or may not have been rolled back. The client's transaction is not affected.
		System exception	Roll back the transaction. Log the error. Discard the instance. Rethrow the `RemoteExcep tion` or `EJBException`.	Remote clients receive the `RemoteExcep tion` or `EJBExcep tion`. The EJB's transaction was rolled back. The client's transaction may be marked for rollback, depending on the vendor.
The bean is not part of a transaction. The EJB was invoked but doesn't propagate the client's transaction and doesn't start its own transaction.	transaction-type = Container transaction-attribute = Never | NotSupported | Supports |	Application exception	Rethrow the application exception.	Receives the application exception. The client's transaction is not affected.

Transaction scope	Transaction type attributes	Exception thrown	Container's action	Client's view
		System exception	Log the error. Discard the instance. Rethrow the `RemoteException` or `EJBException`.	Remote clients receive the `RemoteException` or `EJBException`. The client's transaction may or may not be marked for rollback, depending on the vendor.
Bean-managed transaction. The stateful or stateless session EJB uses the `EJBContext` to explicitly manage its own transaction.	transaction-type = Bean transaction-attribute = Bean-managed transaction EJBs do not use transaction attributes.	Application exception	Rethrow the application exception.	Receives the application exception. The client's transaction is not affected.
		System exception	Roll back the transaction. Log the error. Discard the instance. Rethrow the `RemoteException` or `EJBException`.	Remote clients receive the `RemoteException` or `EJBException`. The client's transaction is not affected.

Table 17-2 summarizes the interactions among different types of exceptions and transactions in message-driven beans.

Table 17-2. Exception summary for message-driven beans

Transaction scope	Transaction type attributes	Exception thrown	Container's action
Container-initiated transaction. The transaction started before the `onMessage()` method was invoked and will end when the method completes.	transaction-type =Container transaction-attribute = Required	System exception	Roll back the transaction. Log the error. Discard the instance.
		Application exception	If the instance called `setRollbackOnly()` or the exception is annotated with `@ApplicationException (rollback=true)`, roll back the transaction and rethrow to the resource adapter.

Transaction scope	Transaction type attributes	Exception thrown	Container's action
Container-initiated transaction. No transaction was started.	transaction-type =Container transaction-attribute = Not-Supported	System exception	Log the error. Discard the instance.
		Application exception	Rethrow the exception to the resource adapter.
Bean-managed transaction. The message-driven bean uses EJBContext to manage its own transaction explicitly.	transaction-type = Bean transaction-attribute = Bean-managed transaction attributes.	System exception	Roll back the transaction. Log the error. Discard the instance.
All Tx Scopes		Application exception	Rethrow the exception to the resource adapter.

Transactional Stateful Session Beans

Session beans can interact directly with the database as easily as they can manage the taskflow of other enterprise beans. Stateless session beans have no conversational state, so each method invocation must make changes to the database immediately. With stateful session beans, however, we may not want to make changes to the database until the transaction is complete. Remember, a stateful session bean can be one of many participants in a transaction, so it might be advisable to postpone database updates until the entire transaction is committed or to avoid updates if it is rolled back.

There are several different scenarios in which a stateful session bean might cache changes before applying them to the database. For example, think of a shopping cart implemented by a stateful session bean that accumulates several items for purchase. If the stateful bean implements SessionSynchronization, it can cache the items and write them to the database only when the transaction is complete.

The javax.ejb.SessionSynchronization interface allows a session bean to receive additional notification of the session's involvement in transactions. The addition of these transaction callback methods by the SessionSynchronization interface expands the EJB's awareness of its lifecycle to include a new state, the *Transactional Method-Ready state*. This is always a part of the lifecycle of a transactional stateful session bean. Implementing the SessionSynchronization interface simply makes it visible to the application provider. Figure 17-7 shows the stateful session bean with the additional state.

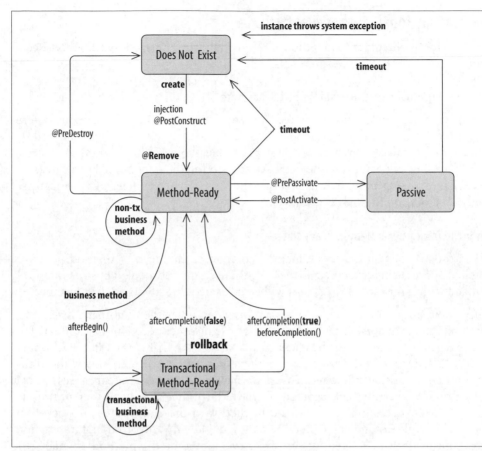

Figure 17-7. Lifecycle of a stateful session bean

The SessionSynchronization interface is defined as follows:

```
package javax.ejb;

public interface javax.ejb.SessionSynchronization
{
    public abstract void afterBegin( ) throws RemoteException;
    public abstract void beforeCompletion( ) throws RemoteException;
    public abstract void afterCompletion(boolean committed)
        throws RemoteException;
}
```

When a method of the SessionSynchronization bean is invoked outside of a transaction scope, the method executes in the Method-Ready state. However, when a method is invoked within a transaction scope (or creates a new transaction), the EJB moves into the Transactional Method-Ready state.

The Transactional Method-Ready State

The `SessionSynchronization` methods are called in the Transactional Method-Ready state.

Transitioning into the Transactional Method-Ready state

When a transactional method is invoked on a `SessionSynchronization` bean, the stateful bean becomes part of the transaction, causing the `afterBegin()` callback method defined in the `SessionSynchronization` interface to be invoked. This method should take care of reading any data from the database and storing the data in the bean's instance fields. The `afterBegin()` method is called before the EJB object delegates the business-method invocation to the EJB instance.

Life in the Transactional Method-Ready state

When the `afterBegin()` callback method completes, the business method originally invoked by the client is executed on the EJB instance. Any subsequent business methods invoked within the same transaction will be delegated directly to the EJB instance.

Once a stateful session bean is a part of a transaction—whether it implements `Session Synchronization` or not—it cannot be accessed by any other transactional context. This is true regardless of whether the client tries to access the EJB with a different context or the EJB's own method creates a new context. If, for example, a method with a transaction attribute of `RequiresNew` is invoked, the new transactional context causes an error to be thrown. Since the `NotSupported` and `Never` attributes specify a different transactional context (no context), invoking a method with these attributes also causes an error. A stateful session bean cannot be removed while it is involved in a transaction. This means that invoking an `@Remove` annotated method while the `SessionSynchronization` bean is in the middle of a transaction will cause an error to be thrown.

At some point, the transaction in which the `SessionSynchronization` bean has been enrolled will come to an end. If the transaction is committed, the `SessionSynchronization` bean will be notified through its `beforeCompletion()` method. At this time, the EJB should write its cached data to the database. If the transaction is rolled back, the `beforeCompletion()` method will not be invoked, avoiding the pointless effort of writing changes that won't be committed to the database.

The `afterCompletion()` method is always invoked, whether the transaction ended successfully with a commit or unsuccessfully with a rollback. If the transaction was a success—which means that `beforeCompletion()` was invoked—the `committed` parameter of the `afterCompletion()` method will be `true`. If the transaction was unsuccessful, then the `committed` parameter will be `false`.

It may be desirable to reset the stateful session bean's instance variables to some initial state if the `afterCompletion()` method indicates that the transaction was rolled back.

Conversational Persistence Contexts

Entity managers participate in transactions just like any other resource. We've seen examples of this throughout this book. Extended persistence contexts have some interesting transactional behavior that you can exploit. You are allowed to invoke `EntityManager` operations such as `persist()`, `merge()`, and `remove()` outside of a transaction when you interact with an extended persistence context. These inserts, updates, and deletes are queued until the extended persistence context is enlisted in an active transaction and is committed. In other words, the database is not touched until the persistence context becomes involved with a transaction. Also, any executed queries do not hold their database connection after they complete. Let's look at an example of this:

```
1   EntityManager manager = entityManagerFactory.createEntityManager(EXTENDED);
2   manager.persist(entityA);
3   manager.merge(entityB);
4   manager.remove(entityC);
5   userTransaction.begin();
6   manager.flush();
7   userTransaction.commit();
```

Line 1 creates an extended persistence context. Lines 2–4 create, update, and delete some entity beans. These actions are queued until the persistence context becomes enlisted in a transaction in Line 5. The act of calling an `EntityManager` method enlists the persistence context in the transaction. The batched actions are then committed in Line 7.

You can really exploit this behavior by using it with stateful session beans.

The combination of stateful session beans, extended persistence contexts, and specific transaction demarcation gives you a lot of power to optimize and control your conversational state. Without these integrated features, you would have the painstaking task of managing all of these state changes within the stateful session bean itself. Now you can let the entity manager do most of the work for you.

## CHAPTER 18

Interceptors

From the very start, we've been focusing on finding a proper home for all code in an application. Business logic is accessible from session or message-driven beans, domain nouns are in entities, and services such as security and transactions are handled as configurable aspects by the container. However, there might be cross-cutting concerns demanded by your unique requirements that are too specific to be handled by an open specification. For these cases, EJB 3.1 provides a generic interception framework in the form of the Interceptors 1.1 Specification.

Interceptors are objects that can interpose themselves on method calls or the lifecycle events of session and message-driven beans. They allow you to encapsulate common behavior that cuts across large parts of your application. This behavior is usually common code that you don't want polluting your business logic. Where most of the changes to the EJB 3.x specifications were designed to make EJB easier to use for application developers, interceptors are an advanced feature that provide you another way to modularize your application or even extend your EJB container. This chapter teaches you how to write an interceptor and shows you various real-world examples of where interceptors can be used.

Intercepting Methods

To understand when to use interceptors, we'll first take a look at an example of poor code reuse.

We'll be building an online television station, and part of the backing application is a `TunerEJB`. Incoming requests to get a channel will return an `InputStream` pointer to read in the content:

```
public interface TunerLocalBusiness
{
    /**
     * Obtains the stream containing viewable content
     * for the specified television channel.  Supported channels are 1 and 2.
     *
```

```
 * @param channel
 * @return
 * @throws IllegalArgumentException If the channel is not valid
 */
InputStream getChannel(int channel) throws IllegalArgumentException;

}
```

Management may have the requirement that we keep track of all incoming requests to the system so that we can analyze its real-world use during the product launch. So, as obedient developers, we might code something into the implementation as follows:

```
/**
 * {@inheritDoc}
 * @see org.jboss.ejb3.examples.chxx.echo.TunerLocalBusiness#getChannel(int)
 */
@Override
public InputStream getChannel(final int channel) throws IllegalArgumentException
{
    // Obtain a cache to store invocation context information
    final InvocationCache cache = InvocationCache.get(); // Assume this type
exists

    // Get some context about this invocation
    final Method method;
    try{
        method = TunerLocalBusiness.class.getMethod("getChannel", int.class);
    }
    catch(final NoSuchMethodException nmse)
    {
        throw new RuntimeException(
          "Developer error, could not get target method invoked");
    }
    final Object[] params = new Object[]{channel};

    // Put this context into the cache
    cache.put(new MyInvocationDO(method,params));

    ... // Rest of method business logic follows

}
```

Already we have a few lines of code embedded into our business method that have nothing to do with obtaining channel content. We might encourage code reuse by extracting out into some common utilities, but even then every function that needs this behavior will have to explicitly call the shared logic.

Additionally, company management may decide to restrict access to some methods, from some callers, at some times. As you can see, we very quickly get to a situation in which we're layering unrelated business logic across the system.

In fact, there are a lot of design flaws:

- The `getChannel()` method is polluted with code that has nothing to do with the business logic of the method. Not only has the developer added seven lines of code to the method, but he has also made the code a bit harder to read.

- It is difficult to turn auditing off and on since you have to comment out the code and recompile the bean class.

- This auditing logic is obviously a template that could be reused across many methods of your application. If this code is littered throughout your EJB methods, you would need to potentially modify a lot of different classes to expand the functionality.

Interceptors define a much cleaner separation for business logic that may run across many modules in your system. They provide a mechanism to encapsulate this business logic and an easy way to apply it to your methods without making the code harder to read. Interceptors provide a structure for this type of behavior so that it can easily be extended and expanded in one class. Finally, they provide a simple, configurable mechanism for applying their behavior wherever you like.

Interceptor Class

Encapsulating this auditing logic into an interceptor is as simple as creating a plain Java class that has a method with the `@javax.interceptor.AroundInvoke` annotation and the following signature:

```
@AroundInvoke

Object <any-method-name>(javax.interceptor.InvocationContext
   invocation)
      throws Exception;
```

The `@AroundInvoke` method in an interceptor class does just what it implies. It wraps around the call to your business method and is actually invoked in the same Java call stack and in the same transaction and security context as the bean method it is intercepting. The `javax.interceptor.InvocationContext` parameter is a generic representation of the business method the client is invoking. You can obtain information such as the target bean instance on which you are invoking, access to its parameters expressed as an array of objects, and a reference to a `java.lang.reflect.Method` object that is the generic representation of the actual invoked method. `InvocationContext` is also used to drive the invocation. Let's convert our auditing logic into an `@AroundInvoke` method:

```
/**
 * Aspect which records all incoming invocations
 * such that we may perform auditing later
 *
 * @author <a href="mailto:andrew.rubinger@jboss.org">ALR</a>
 * @version $Revision: $
 */
```

```
public class RecordingAuditor
{
    /**
     * Logger
     */
    private static final Logger log =
        Logger.getLogger(RecordingAuditor.class.getName());

    /**
     * Writable store for incoming invocations; imagine this is available to us
     * and that it'll either log or otherwise store persistently in a DB
     */
    private final Recorder<InvocationContext> invocations ; // We made up "Recorder"

    /**
     * Persistently records the intercepted {@link InvocationContext} such that
     * we may examine it later
     */
    @AroundInvoke
    public Object audit(final InvocationContext context) throws Exception
    {
        // Precondition checks
        assert context != null : "Context was not specified";

        // Record the invocation
        invocations.add(context);

        // Carry out the invocation, noting where we've intercepted
        // before and after the call (around it)
        try
        {
            // Log
            log.info("Intercepted: " + context);

            // Return
            return context.proceed();
        }
        finally
        {
            // Log
            log.info("Done with: " + context);
        }
    }
}
```

The @AroundInvoke method of our interceptor class is the audit() method. It looks pretty much the same as the code in our getChannel() method, except that the business logic is gone and all that is left is our generic auditing logic. Additionally, we can take advantage of the descriptor given to us (InvocationContext) for the current request rather than construct our own representation. After we've recorded the invocation, the InvocationContext.proceed() method is called. If another interceptor must be invoked as part of the method call, then proceed() calls the @AroundInvoke method of that other interceptor. If no other interceptors need executing, then the EJB container calls the bean method on which the client is invoking. Because the `getChannel()` method is invoked in the same Java call stack as the business method on which you are invoking, `proceed()` must be called by the interceptor code, or the actual EJB method is not called at all.

The only responsibility of our auditor is to record the incoming request for future analysis. The `InvocationContext.getMethod()` operation gives us access to the `java.lang.reflect.Method` object that represents the actual bean method being invoked. Besides `getMethod()`, the `InvocationContext` interface has some other interesting methods:

```
package javax.interceptor;

public interface InvocationContext {
    public Object getTarget( );
    public Method getMethod( );
    public Object[] getParameters( );
    public void setParameters(Object[] newArgs);
    public java.util.Map<String, Object> getContextData( );
    public Object proceed( ) throws Exception;
    public Object getTimer();
}
```

The `getTarget()` method returns a reference to the target bean instance. We could change our `audit()` method to also print out the parameters of the invoked bean method by using the `getParameters()` method. The `setParameters()` method allows you to actually modify the parameters of the method that is being invoked. Use this with care. The `getContextData()` method returns a `Map` object that is active for the entire method invocation. Interceptors can use this map to pass contextual data between themselves within the same method invocation.

Applying Interceptors

Now that the interceptor class has been written, it is time to apply it to an EJB. One or more interceptors can be applied to all EJBs within a deployment (default interceptors), to all methods of one EJB, or to a single method of an EJB. Interceptors can be applied via an annotation or by using an XML deployment descriptor. We discuss all options in this section.

Annotated methods and classes

The `@javax.interceptor.Interceptors` annotation can be used to apply interceptors to individual methods or to every method in the EJB's bean class:

```
package javax.interceptor;

import java.lang.annotation.*;

@Retention(RetentionType.RUNTIME)
@Target({ElementType.CLASS, ElementType.METHOD})
```

```
public @interface Interceptors {
    Class[] value( );
}
```

When the `@Interceptors` annotation is applied to an individual method, that interceptor is executed only when that particular method is invoked. If you use the `@Interceptors` annotation on the bean class, all interceptor classes listed will interpose on every method invocation of every business method of the EJB.

Therefore, auditing all the methods of our `TunerEJB` is as easy as applying the `@Interceptors` annotation at the class level:

```
@Stateless
// Class-level interceptors will be run upon requests to every method of this EJB
@Interceptors(RecordingAuditor.class)
@Local(TunerLocalBusiness.class)
public class TunerBean implements TunerLocalBusiness{
  ...
}
```

We may also have another aspect in charge of blocking access to a particular channel when management would like to restrict access. This can be declared to run only on specific methods, like so:

```
/**
 * {@inheritDoc}
 * @see org.ejb3book.examples.chxx.echo.TunerLocalBusiness#getChannel(int)
 */
// Here we declare method-level interceptors, which will only take place on this
method
@Interceptors(Channel2Restrictor.class)
@Override
public InputStream getChannel(final int channel) throws IllegalArgumentException
{
  ...
}
```

Whether you want to apply the `@Interceptors` annotation on the class or the method is really determined by your requirements.

Applying interceptors through XML

Although the `@Interceptors` annotation allows you to apply the auditing interceptor easily, it does force you to modify and recompile your class every time you want to remove profiling from or add it to a particular method or EJB. Unless an interceptor is a required part of your business logic, it may not be the best idea to annotate your code; using XML bindings instead might be a better approach. Because the EJB 3.x specification supports partial XML deployment descriptors, it is quite painless and easy to apply an interceptor through XML:

```
<ejb-jar
      xmlns="http://java.sun.com/xml/ns/javaee"
      xmlns:xsi="http://www.w3.org/2001/XMLSchema-instance"
```

```
            xsi:schemaLocation="http://java.sun.com/xml/ns/javaee
                                http://java.sun.com/xml/ns/javaee/ejb-jar_3_1.xsd"
            version="3.1">
    <assembly-descriptor>
        <interceptor-binding>
            <ejb-name>TunerBean</ejb-name>
            <interceptor-class>org.ejb3book.RecordingAuditor</interceptor-class>
            <method-name>getChannel</method-name>
            <method-params>
                <method-param>int</method-param>
            </method-params>
        </interceptor-binding>
    </assembly-descriptor>
</ejb-jar>
```

The preceding XML is a complete deployment descriptor. The <interceptor-binding> element specifies that we want the RecordingAuditor interceptor to be executed whenever the getChannel() method of the TunerEJB is invoked. Because the getChannel() method is not overloaded in the bean class, the <method-params> element isn't explicitly required.

If you want to apply an interceptor to every business method of a particular EJB, then leave out the <method-name> and <method-params> elements:

```
<ejb-jar
        xmlns="http://java.sun.com/xml/ns/javaee"
        xmlns:xsi="http://www.w3.org/2001/XMLSchema-instance"
        xsi:schemaLocation="http://java.sun.com/xml/ns/javaee
                            http://java.sun.com/xml/ns/javaee/ejb-jar_3_1.xsd"
        version="3.1">
    <assembly-descriptor>
        <interceptor-binding>
            <ejb-name>TunerBean</ejb-name>
            <interceptor-class>org.ejb3book.RecordingAuditor</interceptor-class>
        </interceptor-binding>
    </assembly-descriptor>
</ejb-jar>
```

As you can see, you can use an XML deployment descriptor only when you need it and leave the rest of the EJB metadata expressed as annotations. In this particular interceptor use case, it makes more sense to use XML than an annotation because auditing is probably something you'd want to do for a limited time.

Default interceptors

XML has some other advantages as well. For instance, the <ejb-name> element in an <interceptor-binding> can take a wildcard. In this case, you are applying one or more interceptors that you declare in the interceptor-binding to every EJB in that particular JAR file deployment:

```
<ejb-jar
        xmlns="http://java.sun.com/xml/ns/javaee"
        xmlns:xsi="http://www.w3.org/2001/XMLSchema-instance"
```

```
            xsi:schemaLocation="http://java.sun.com/xml/ns/javaee
                             http://java.sun.com/xml/ns/javaee/ejb-jar_3_1.xsd"
            version="3.1">
    <assembly-descriptor>
      <interceptor-binding>
        <ejb-name>*</ejb-name>
        <interceptor-class>org.ejb3book.RecordingAuditor</interceptor-class>
      </interceptor-binding>
    </assembly-descriptor>
</ejb-jar>
```

Disabling interceptors

If you are using default interceptors or class-level interceptors, there may be times when you want to disable them for a particular EJB or for a particular method of an EJB. You can do this via an annotation or through XML. Let's look at disabling default interceptors first.

In the preceding XML, we have enabled the RecordingAuditor interceptor for every EJB deployed in the particular JAR file in which the XML is placed. Let's say we do not want the auditor to be executed for our TunerEJB. We can turn off all default interceptors by using the @javax.interceptor.ExcludeDefaultInterceptors annotation:

```
@Stateless
@ExcludeDefaultInterceptors
@Interceptors
(org.ejb3book.SomeOtherInterceptor.class)
@Local(TunerLocalBusiness.class)
public class TunerBean implements TunerLocalBusiness {
...
}
```

In the preceding example, the RecordingAuditor will not be executed. Just because the @ExcludeDefaultInterceptors annotation has been used, it does not mean we cannot specify an @Interceptors annotation that triggers other interceptor classes. This exclusion can be done within XML as well:

```
<ejb-jar
      xmlns="http://java.sun.com/xml/ns/javaee"
      xmlns:xsi="http://www.w3.org/2001/XMLSchema-instance"
      xsi:schemaLocation="http://java.sun.com/xml/ns/javaee
                            http://java.sun.com/xml/ns/javaee/ejb-jar_3_1.xsd"
      version="3.1">
  >
      <interceptor-binding>
        <ejb-name>*</ejb-name>
        <interceptor-class>org.ejb3book.RecordingAuditor</interceptor-class>
      </interceptor-binding>
      <interceptor-binding>
        <ejb-name>TunerBean</ejb-name>
        <exclude-default-interceptors/>
        <interceptor-class>org.ejb3book.SomeOtherInterceptor</interceptor-class>
      </interceptor-binding>
```

```
        </assembly-descriptor>
    </ejb-jar>
```

What we're really doing in the preceding examples is giving the TunerEJB a brand-new interceptor stack that overrides and supersedes any default interceptors.

The same overriding and disabling of interceptors can be done at the method level as well. You can turn off interceptors entirely for a particular method by using the @javax.interceptor.ExcludeDefaultInterceptors and @javax.interceptor.Exclude ClassInterceptors annotations:

```
@Stateless
@Interceptors
(org.ejb3book.SomeOtherInterceptor.class)
@Local(TunerLocalBusiness.class)
public class TunerBean implements TunerLocalBusiness
{
...
    @ExcludeClassInterceptors
    @ExcludeDefaultInterceptors
    public InputStream getChannel(final int channel) throws IllegalArgumentException
    {
        ...
    }
...
}
```

The @ExcludeClassInterceptors annotation turns off any applied class-level interceptors, and the @ExcludeDefaultInterceptors annotation turns off any default interceptors defined in XML. You could also specify an @Interceptors annotation on the getChannel() method to define a different interceptor stack compared to the rest of the methods in the bean class. This is also available in XML format.

Usually, you will not be concerned with disabling interceptors, but it is good to know you have the tools to do so if you need to.

Interceptors and Injection

Interceptors belong to the same ENC as the EJBs they intercept. Like the EJBs they intercept, interceptor classes have full support for all the injection annotations, as well as injection through XML. So, you can use annotations such as @Resource, @EJB, and @PersistenceContext within your interceptor class if you so desire. Let's illustrate this in a revised view of our auditing interceptor:

```
public class RecordingAuditor
{

    ...

    /**
     * The current EJB Context; to be injected by the Container
     */
```

```
@Resource
EJBContext beanContext;

/**
 * Persistently records the intercepted {@link InvocationContext} such that
 * we may examine it later
 */
@AroundInvoke
public Object audit(final InvocationContext invocationContext) throws Exception
{
   // Precondition checks
   assert invocationContext != null : "Context was not specified";

   // Obtain the caller
   final Principal caller = beanContext.getCallerPrincipal();

   // Create a new view
   final AuditedInvocation audit =
      new AuditedInvocation(invocationContext, caller);

   // Record the invocation
   invocations.add(audit);

   ... // The rest omitted for brevity

}

}
```

The purpose of this interceptor is to log in a persistent view every method invocation done on a particular bean so that an audit trail is created. From this audit trail, system administrators can research security breaches or replay the actions of a particular user. The interceptor obtains the calling user by invoking getCallerPrincipal() on the javax.ejb.EJBContext injected into the beanContext member variable. It allocates an AuditedInvocation object and sets properties such as the method being invoked and the calling principal. We could even fashion AuditedInvocation as an entity bean, and persist to the database by an injected EntityManager. Any members the container may inject into a session or message-driven bean is also available to interceptors.

As with bean classes, interceptor injection annotations create additional entries in the ENC of the EJB to which the interceptor class is bound. This means that the persistence context referenced by the beanContext field is also available in JNDI with the string java:comp/env/org.ejb3book.AuditInterceptor/beanContext.

As always, if you do not want to use annotations to inject dependencies into your interceptor classes, the XML alternative is to define an <interceptor> element within your *ejb-jar.xml* deployment descriptor.

Intercepting Lifecycle Events

Not only can you intercept EJB method invocations, but you can also intercept EJB lifecycle events. These callbacks can be used to initialize the state of your EJB bean classes, as well as the interceptor class itself. Lifecycle interception looks very similar to the @AroundInvoke style:

```
@callback-annotation> voidmethod-name(InvocationContext
    ctx);
```

To intercept an EJB callback, define a method within your interceptor class that is annotated with the callback in which you are interested. The return value of the method must be **void** because EJB callbacks have no return value. The method name can be anything and must not throw any checked exceptions (no **throws** clause). **Invocation Context** is the only parameter to this method. As with **@AroundInvoke** methods, callback interception is invoked in one big Java call stack. This means you must call **Invocation Context.proceed()** to complete the lifecycle event. When calling **proceed()**, the next interceptor class that has the same callback is invoked. If there are no other interceptors, then the callback method of the EJB's bean class is invoked, if one exists. If the EJB has no callback method, then **proceed()** is a no-op. Because there may be no callback method, **InvocationContext.getMethod()** always returns **null**.

Custom Injection Annotations

Why would you want to intercept an EJB callback? One concrete example is when you want to create and define your own injection annotations. The EJB specification has a bunch of annotations for injecting Java EE resources, services, and EJB references into your bean classes. Some application servers or applications like to use JNDI as a global registry for configuration or for non-Java EE services. Unfortunately, the specification defines no way to inject something directly from global JNDI into your beans. What we can do is define our own annotation for providing this functionality and implement it as an interceptor.

The first thing we must do is to define the annotation we will use to inject from JNDI:

```
package org.ejb3book.annotations;

import java.lang.annotation.*;

@Target({ElementType.METHOD, ElementType.FIELD})
@Retention(RetentionPolicy.RUNTIME)
public @interface JndiInjected {
    String value();
}
```

The `value()` attribute of the `@org.ejb3book.annotations.JndiInjected` annotation is the global JNDI name of the object we want injected into our field or *setter* method. Here is an example of how we might use this custom annotation:

```
@Stateless
public class MySessionBean implements MySession {
    @JndiInject("java:/TransactionManager")
    private javax.transaction.TransactionManager tm;

...

}
```

Some applications might be interested in obtaining a reference to the Java EE JTA Transaction Manager service. Many application servers store a reference to this service in global JNDI. In this instance, we use the `@JndiInjected` annotation to pull a reference to the Transaction Manager directly into the field of our session bean. Now that we have defined our custom injection annotation and we've defined how it might be used, we need to code the interceptor class that implements this behavior:

```
package org.ejb3.interceptors;

import java.lang.reflect.*;
import com.titan.annotations.JndiInjected;
import javax.ejb.*;
import javax.naming.*;
import javax.interceptor.*;
import javax.annotation.*;

public class JndiInjector
{

    @PostConstruct
    public void jndiInject(InvocationContext invocation) {
        Object target = invocation.getTarget( );
        Field[] fields = target.getClass().getDeclaredFields( );
        Method[] methods = target.getClass().getDeclaredMethods( );

        // find all @JndiInjected
    fields/methods and set them
        try {
            InitialContext ctx = new InitialContext( );
            for (Method method : methods) {
                JndiInjected inject = method.getAnnotation(JndiInjected.class);
                if (inject != null) {
                    Object obj = ctx.lookup(inject.value( ));
                    method.setAccessible(true);
                    method.invoke(target, obj);
                }
            }
            for (Field field : fields) {
                JndiInjected inject = field.getAnnotation(JndiInjected.class);
                if (inject != null) {
                    Object obj = ctx.lookup(inject.value( ));
                    field.setAccessible(true);
```

```
                    field.set(target, obj);
                }
            }
            invocation.proceed( );
        } catch (Exception ex) {
            throw new EJBException

("Failed to execute @JndiInjected", ex);
        }
    }
}
```

The `jndiInject()` method is annotated with `@javax.annotation.PostConstruct` to tell the EJB container that the `JndiInjector` interceptor is interested in intercepting that particular EJB callback. The method begins by obtaining a reference to the bean instance it is intercepting. It then reflects on the object to find all methods and fields that are annotated with `@JndiInjected`, looks up the referenced JNDI name, and initializes the field or method of the target bean instance. Notice that this is done in a *try/catch* block. When intercepting a callback method, you can never throw a checked exception; therefore, all checked exceptions must be caught and wrapped in an `EJBException`.

Now that the interceptor class has been implemented, we can apply this interceptor to our EJBs just as we've done before.

One particularly interesting thing about this example is that it shows that you can use EJB interceptors as a framework for writing custom annotations that add your own customer behavior to your EJBs. Default interceptors, through XML, give you a clean, simple way of applying the interceptors that implement the behavior of your annotations. Finally, this custom behavior is portable and can be used in any vendor implementation. Not only is EJB 3.x easy to use, but it is easy to extend as well.

Exception Handling

Exception handling with interceptors is simple yet powerful. Since interceptors sit directly in the Java call stack of the bean method or callback that is being invoked, you can put a *try/catch/finally* block around the `InvocationContext.proceed()` method. You can abort an invocation before it reaches the actual bean method by throwing an exception within the `@AroundInvoke` or callback method. You are also allowed to catch a bean-method-thrown exception and throw a different exception or suppress the exception. With `@AroundInvoke` interception, you are even allowed to retry the bean method call after catching an exception from the bean method. Let's look at some examples.

Aborting a Method Invocation

It's conceivable that the management of our online television station would like to restrict access to a premium channel at their discretion. In this case, we might short-circuit an incoming request to instead return a descriptive `Exception`:

```java
public class Channel2Restrictor
{
...
    /**
     * Examines the specified request to determine if the caller is attempting
     * to obtain content for Channel 2.  If so, and Channel 2 is currently closed,
     * will block the request, instead throwing {@link Channel2ClosedException}
     */
    @AroundInvoke
    public Object checkAccessibility(final InvocationContext context) throws Exception
    {
        // Precondition checks
        assert context != null : "Context was not specified";

        // See if we're requesting Channel 2
        if (isRequestForChannel2(context))
        {
            // See if Channel 2 is open
            if (!Channel2AccessPolicy.isChannel2Permitted())
            {
                // Block access
                throw Channel2ClosedException.INSTANCE;
            }
        }

        // Otherwise carry on
        return context.proceed();
    }
}
```

Here we've encapsulated the logic determining whether we should allow the request to continue along for processing, ultimately to return content for Channel 2. In this example we're, in effect, implementing our own custom security framework. EJB security is pretty basic and sometimes you have more specific contextual requirements. For instance, you may want to integrate your EJB with a rules engine that analyzes the user as well as the method and parameters to determine whether the user is allowed to invoke the method. This can also be done from within an interceptor.

Catch and Rethrow Exceptions

Besides aborting a given method invocation, you can also catch exceptions thrown by the bean method within the interceptor's `@AroundInvoke` method. For example, you can use interceptor classes as an abstraction mechanism to create exception-handling frameworks. Consider JDBC and the `java.sql.SQLException`. When an `SQLException` is thrown, your code, programmatically, does not know the cause of the exception without looking at the error number or the message of the exception. Unfortunately, error codes and messages differ per database vendor and thus, if you wanted to handle certain exceptions in certain ways, your code would be nonportable between database vendors.

Let's take two common SQLExceptions: deadlocking and cursor not available. First, we will create concrete exceptions that extend SQLException:

```
@ApplicationException(rollback=true)
public class DatabaseDeadlockException extends java.sql.SQLException {
    public DatabaseDeadlockException(Exception cause) {
        Super(cause);
    }
}
@ApplicationException(rollback=true)
public class DatabaseCursorNotAvailable extends java.sql.SQLException {
    public DatabaseCursorNotAvailable(Exception cause) {
        super(cause);
    }
}
```

With these exceptions, we have abstracted away the dependency on the error number to determine the actual database error that occurred. Our client code can use these exceptions in a portable way and not be concerned with the underlying database vendor. But before we can use these exceptions, we need to write the interceptor class that does the exception handling:

```
public class MySQLExceptionHandler {
    @AroundInvoke
    public Object handleException(InvocationContext ctx) Exception {
        try {
            return ctx.proceed( );
        } catch (SQLException sql) {
            int ernum = sql.getErrorCode( );
            switch(ernum) {
            case 32343:
                throw new DatabaseDeadlockException(sql);
            case 22211:
                throw new DatabaseCursorNotAvailable(sql);
            ...
            default:
                throw new RollbackAlwaysOnException(sql);
            }
        }
    }
}
```

The @AroundInvoke method simply catches any SQLException thrown by the bean method and converts it to an appropriate exception type that you can catch in your client code. Of course, there would be one exception-handler interceptor class per database vendor. Here's how your application code could then take advantage of this interceptor behavior:

```
// application client code
{
```

```
    try {
        ejbref.invokeSomeDatabaseOperation( );
    } catch (DatabaseDeadlockException deadlock) {
        // handle this specific error case in a special way
    }
}
```

So, combining the exception handler interceptor with EJB invocations allows you to have specific code that handles specific database errors such as deadlock, without having to worry that your code is not portable between vendors.

Interceptor Lifecycle

Interceptor classes have the same lifecycles as the EJBs they intercept. Consider an interceptor class as an extension of the EJB's bean instance. They are created along with bean instances. They are destroyed, passivated, and activated along with their bean instances as well. Also, it is important to note that interceptor classes have the same restrictions as the beans to which they are attached. For instance, you cannot inject an extended persistence context into an interceptor class if that interceptor does not intercept a stateful session bean.

Because interceptors have lifecycles and hook into lifecycle events, they can also hold internal state. This might be extremely useful when you want the interceptor class to obtain an open connection to a remote system and then close that connection at destroy time. You may also be interested in maintaining state that is particular to the bean instance on which the interceptor class is intercepted. Maybe you have a custom injection annotation that you have built and it needs special cleanup after the bean instance is destroyed. You can hold internal state within the interceptor class and do the cleanup when the interceptor and bean instance are destroyed.

Bean Class @AroundInvoke Methods

This chapter has mostly discussed interceptor classes. @AroundInvoke methods can also exist inside EJB bean classes. When used inside a bean class, the @AroundInvoke method will be the last "interceptor" to be invoked before the actual bean method:

```
@Stateless
public class MySessionBean implements MySessionRemote {

    public void businessMethod( ) {
        ...
    }

    @AroundInvoke
    public Object beanClassInterceptor(InvocationContext ctx) {
        try {
            System.out.println("entering: " + ctx.getMethod( ));
            return ctx.proceed( );
```

```
      } finally {
        System.out.println("leaving: " + ctx.getMethod( ));
      }
    }
  }
```

This is a simple example of a bean class `@AroundInvoke` method. For what sorts of things would you want to use it? You may want to have a dynamic implementation of your bean class, or you may have an interceptor whose logic is specific to the bean.

## CHAPTER 19

Timer Service

Business systems frequently use scheduling systems to run programs at specified times. Scheduling systems typically run applications that generate reports, reformat data, or do audit work at night. In other cases, scheduling systems provide callback APIs that can alert subsystems of events such as due dates, deadlines, etc. Scheduling systems often run *batch jobs* (aka *scheduled jobs*), which perform routine work automatically at a prescribed time. Users in the Unix world frequently run scheduled jobs using *cron*, a simple but useful scheduling system that runs programs listed in a configuration file.

Regardless of the software, scheduling systems are used in many different scenarios:

- In a credit card processing system, credit card charges are processed in batches so that all the charges made for a block of time are settled together rather than separately. This work may be scheduled to be done in the evening to reduce the impact of processing on the system.

- In a hospital or clinical system, Electronic Data Interface (EDI) software is used to send medical claims to various HMOs. Each HMO has its own processing requirements, but all of them are routine, so jobs are scheduled to gather claim data, put it in the proper format, and transfer it to the HMO.

- In just about any company, managers need specific reports run on a regular basis. A scheduling system can be configured to run those reports automatically and deliver them via email to managers.

Scheduling systems are also common in *workflow applications*, which are systems that manage document processing that typically spans days or months and involves many systems and lots of human intervention. In workflow applications, scheduling is employed for auditing tasks that periodically take inventory of the state of an application, invoice, sales order, etc., in order to ensure everything is proceeding as scheduled. The scheduling system maintains timers and delivers events to alert applications and components when a specified date and time are reached, or when some period has expired.

Here are some examples of workflow scheduling:

- In a mortgage system, a lot of tasks have to be completed (e.g., appraisal, rate lock-in, closing appointment, etc.) before the mortgage can be closed. Timers can be set on mortgage applications to perform periodic audits that ensure everything is proceeding on schedule.

- In a healthcare claims-processing system, claims must be processed within 90 days according to terms negotiated by in-network physicians and clinics. Each claim could have a timer set to go off seven days before the deadline.

- In a stockbroker system, buy-at-limit orders can be created for a specific number of shares, but only at a specified price or lower. These buy-at-limit orders typically have a time limit. If the stock price falls below the specified price before the time limit, the buy-at-limit order is carried out. If the stock price does not fall below the specified price before the time limit, the timer expires and the buy-at-limit order is canceled.

The EJB 2.1 specification introduced a standard Java EE scheduling system called the *EJB Timer Service*. The 3.1 revision of the spec has overhauled the mechanism in which users define scheduling events, bringing forth a new natural-language syntax that is much friendlier than previous versions and the *cron* format.

 The Java Standard Edition includes the `java.util.Timer` class, which allows threads to schedule tasks for future execution in a background thread. This facility is useful for a variety of applications, but it's too limited to be used in enterprise computing. Note, however, that the scheduling semantics of `java.util.Timer` are similar to those of the EJB Timer Service.

The Timer Service is a facility of the EJB container system that provides a timed-event API, which can be used to schedule timers for specified dates, periods, and intervals. A timer is associated with the enterprise bean that set it, and it calls that bean's `ejbTimeout()` method or a method annotated with `@javax.ejb.Timeout` when it goes off. The rest of this chapter describes the EJB Timer Service API and its use with stateless session and message-driven beans.

Example: A Batch Credit Card Processing System

Imagine we have a popular retail store with a series of 20 registers. Every minute, sales transactions take place that eventually must be processed with a third-party credit provider. Considering that we're only one store out of potentially millions using the provider, this adds up to a lot of traffic. If our business rules allow, we might be better served caching transactions in a pending state, and then processing a batch altogether in a single request. With the EJB Timer Service, we can schedule this job to fire within our EJBs. This full example is covered in detail in Appendix J.

The Business Interface

For the credit-card-processing subsystem, we only need to support a few features. First, we must be able to accept new transactions, which will be added to the pending queue. Next, we'll supply callers with a mechanism to schedule a batch-processing job. As a convenience, we'll also expose support to obtain the current pending transactions and a way to immediately process them. When a scheduled processing event is fired, it'll be able to simply call upon the business method to process.

```java
/**
 * Contract of a service capable of storing a series
 * of {@link CreditCardTransaction}s to be processed,
 * scheduling processing, and processing payment of
 * all pending transactions.
 *
 * @author <a href="mailto:andrew.rubinger@jboss.org">ALR</a>
 * @version $Revision: $
 */
public interface CreditCardTransactionProcessingLocalBusiness
{
   //-------------------------------------------------------------------------
-||
   // Contracts --------------------------------------------------------------
-||
   //-------------------------------------------------------------------------
-||

   /**
    * Returns an immutable view of all transactions
    * pending processing
    * @return
    */
   List<CreditCardTransaction> getPendingTransactions();

   /**
    * Proceses all pending {@link CreditCardTransaction}s,
    * clearing them from the pending list when complete
    */
   void process();

   /**
    * Adds the specified {@link CreditCardTransaction} to be processed
    * @param transaction
    * @throws IllegalArgumentException If the transaction is null
    */
   void add(CreditCardTransaction transaction) throws IllegalArgumentException;

   /**
    * Schedules a new {@link Timer} to process pending payments
    * according to the supplied {@link ScheduleExpression}.  Returns
```

```
    * the {@link Date} representing when the next job is to fire.
    * @param expression
    * @return
    * @throws IllegalArgumentException If the expression is null
    */
   Date scheduleProcessing(ScheduleExpression expression)
       throws IllegalArgumentException;
}
```

javax.ejb.ScheduleExpression and @javax.ejb.Schedule

The scheduleProcessing method just shown accepts a type we haven't yet seen. New to EJB 3.1, javax.ejb.ScheduleExpression encapsulates an intuitive, flexible syntax for defining when timer events should fire. It's here that we can programmatically indicate scheduling by year, month, day of the month, day of the week, hour, minute, and second. Additionally, we can specify a wildcard character (*) to denote "every", a list such as 0,2,6, or ranges such as 0-10. Section 18.2.1 of the EJB 3.1 Specification defines the format in full, but some examples are shown in Table 19-1.

Table 19-1. Attributes of @javax.ejb.Schedule

Attribute	Allowed values
second	[0,59]
minute	[0,59]
hour	[0,23]
dayOfMonth	[1,31], or [-x], where x is the number of days from the end of the month, or "Last"
month	[1,12] or {"Jan", "Feb", "Mar"..."Dec"}
dayOfWeek	[0,7] or {"Sun","Mon","Tue"..."Sat"} (0 and 7 are both equal to "Sun")
year	Four-digit calendar year

The ScheduleExpression is used to programatically create a new javax.ejb.Timer via the javax.ejb.TimerService (we'll see both in a bit). Alternatively, it's possible to create new Timers in a declarative fashion via the @javax.ejb.Schedule annotation:

```
package javax.ejb;
@Target(value=METHOD)
@Retention(value=RUNTIME)
public @interface Schedule {
   String dayOfMonth() default "*";

   String dayOfWeek() default "*";

   String hour() default "0";

   String info() default "";

   String minute() default "0";
```

```
    String month() default "*";

    boolean persistent() default true;

    String second() default "0";

    String timezone() default "";

    String year() default "*";
}
```

The Timer Service enables an enterprise bean to be notified when a specific date has arrived, when some period of time has elapsed, or at recurring intervals. To use the Timer Service, an enterprise bean must implement the `javax.ejb.TimedObject` interface, which defines a single callback method, `ejbTimeout()`:

```
package javax.ejb;

public interface TimedObject
{
    public void ejbTimeout(Timer timer) ;
}
```

In EJB 3.x, the `@javax.ejb.Timeout` annotation can be applied to a method whose signature returns **void** and has either no parameters or one `javax.ejb.Timer` parameter. It's a matter of developer preference which technique is chosen to mark a method as a timeout; here we'll use the annotation.

When the scheduled time is reached or the specified interval has elapsed, the container system invokes the enterprise bean's timeout callback method. The enterprise bean can then perform any processing it needs to respond to the timeout, such as run reports, audit records, modify the states of other beans, etc. In our case, we'd like to delegate along to the logic that processes pending transactions.

The Bean Implementation Class

First, we'll make a simple singleton bean, though we could also use a stateless session bean or message-driven bean. Stateful session beans are not valid targets for the Timer Service:

```
@Singleton
@Local(CreditCardTransactionProcessingLocalBusiness.class)
@ConcurrencyManagement(ConcurrencyManagementType.CONTAINER)
public class CreditCardTransactionProcessingBean implements
        CreditCardTransactionProcessingLocalBusiness
{
```

An enterprise bean schedules itself for a timed notification using a reference to the `TimerService`, which can be obtained from the `EJBContext` or injected directly into your bean using the `@javax.annotation.Resource` annotation. The `TimerService` allows a

bean to register itself for notification on a specific date, after some period of time, or
at recurring intervals:

```
/**
 * {@link SessionContext} hook to the EJB Container;
 * from here we may obtain a {@link TimerService} via
 * {@link SessionContext#getTimerService()}.
 */
@Resource
private SessionContext context;

/**
 * We can directly inject the {@link TimerService} as well.
 */
@Resource
private TimerService timerService;
```

Now that we have a hook into the TimerService, we can implement the
scheduleProcessing business method easily:

```
@Override
public Date scheduleProcessing(final ScheduleExpression expression) throws
IllegalArgumentException
{
    // Precondition checks
    if (expression == null)
    {
        throw new IllegalArgumentException("Timer expression must be specified");
    }

    // Programmatically create a new Timer from the given expression
    // via the TimerService from the SessionContext
    final TimerService timerService = context.getTimerService();
    final Timer timer = timerService.createCalendarTimer(expression);
    final Date next = timer.getNextTimeout();
    log.info("Created " + timer + " to process transactions; next fire is at: " +
        timer.getNextTimeout());
    return next;
}
```

Here we accept the ScheduleExpression from the client and use it to create a new
Timer from the TimerService. As the API implies, this will result in a new scheduled
event to fire upon our timeout method.

The specification also makes room for automatic timer creation via @Schedule, as we
saw earlier. To use this facility, simply create a timeout method and annotate it as
desired:

```
@Timeout
// Mark this method as the EJB timeout method for timers created
programmatically.
// If we're just creating a timer via @Schedule, @Timer is not required.
@Schedule(dayOfMonth = EVERY, month = EVERY, year = EVERY, second = ZERO,
    minute = ZERO, hour = EVERY)
// This timeout will be created on deployment and fire every hour on the hour;
```

```
// declarative creation
public void processViaTimeout(final Timer timer)
{
    // Just delegate to the business method
    this.process();
}
```

Here we've defined a timer that will be created by the container to fire every hour on the hour.

The TimerService

The TimerService interface provides an enterprise bean with access to the EJB container's Timer Service so that new timers can be created and existing timers can be listed. The TimerService interface is part of the *javax.ejb* package in EJB 3.x and has the following definition:

```
package javax.ejb;
public interface javax.ejb.TimerService
{
    public Timer createTimer(long duration,
            java.io.Serializable info);

    public Timer createTimer(java.util.Date expiration,
        java.io.Serializable info);

    public Timer createSingleActionTimer(long duration,
                                    TimerConfig timerConfig);

    public Timer createSingleActionTimer(java.util.Date expiration,
                                    TimerConfig timerConfig);

    public Timer createTimer(long initialDuration,
        long intervalDuration, java.io.Serializable info);

    public Timer createTimer(java.util.Date initialExpiration,
        long intervalDuration, java.io.Serializable info);

    public Timer createIntervalTimer(long initialDuration,
        long intervalDuration, TimerConfig timerConfig);

    public Timer createIntervalTimer(java.util.Date initialExpiration,
        long intervalDuration, TimerConfig timerConfig);

    public Timer createCalendarTimer(ScheduleExpression schedule);

    public Timer createCalendarTimer(ScheduleExpression schedule,
                                TimerConfig timerConfig);

    public Collection<Timer> getTimers();
}
```

Each of the TimerService.create*Timer() methods establishes a timer with a different type of configuration. There are essentially two types of timers: *single-action* and *interval*. A single-action timer expires once, and an interval timer expires many times, at specified intervals. When a timer expires, the Timer Service calls the bean's `ejbTime out()` method or a callback method with `@javax.ejb.Timeout`.

At this point, we are discussing only the `expiration` and `duration` parameters and their uses. The `Serializable info` parameter is discussed later in this chapter.

When a timer is created, the Timer Service makes it persistent in some type of secondary storage, so it will survive system failures. If the server goes down, the timers are still active when the server comes back up. Although the specification isn't clear, it's assumed that any timers that expire while the system is down will go off when it comes back up again. If an interval timer expires many times while the server is down, it may go off multiple times when the system comes up again. Consult your vendor's documentation to learn how they handle expired timers following a system failure.

The `TimerService.getTimers()` method returns all the timers that have been set for a particular enterprise bean. The `getTimers()` method returns a `java.util.Collection`, an unordered collection of zero or more `javax.ejb.Timer` objects. Each `Timer` object represents a different timed event that has been scheduled for the bean using the Timer Service.

The `getTimers()` method is often used to manage existing timers. A bean can look through the `Collection` of `Timer` objects and cancel any timers that are no longer valid or need to be rescheduled.

The Timer

A `Timer` is an object that implements the `javax.ejb.Timer` interface. It represents a timed event that has been scheduled for an enterprise bean using the Timer Service. `Timer` objects are returned by the `TimerService.createTimer()` and `TimerService.getTimers()` methods, and a `Timer` is the (optional) only parameter of the `TimedObject.ejbTimeout()` method or annotated `@javax.ejb.Timeout` callback. The `Timer` interface is:

```
package javax.ejb;

public interface javax.ejb.Timer
{
    public void cancel();

    public long getTimeRemaining();

    public java.util.Date getNextTimeout();

    public javax.ejb.ScheduleExpression getSchedule();

    public javax.ejb.TimerHandle getHandle();

    public java.io.Serializable getInfo();
```

```
    public boolean isPersistent();

    public boolean isCalendarTimer();
}
```

A `Timer` instance represents exactly one timed event and can be used to cancel the timer, obtain a `Serializable` handle, obtain the application data associated with the timer, and find out when the timer's next scheduled expiration will occur.

Canceling timers

`Timer.cancel()` is used to cancel a specific timer from the Timer Service so that it never expires/fires. It is useful when a particular timer needs to be removed completely or simply rescheduled. To reschedule a timed event, cancel the timer and create a new one.

Identifying timers

Of course, comparing descriptions is a fairly unreliable way of identifying timers, since descriptions tend to vary over time. What is really needed is a far more robust information object that can contain both a description and a precise identifier.

All of the `TimeService.createTimer()` methods declare an `info` object as their last parameter. The `info` object is application data that is stored by the Timer Service and delivered to the enterprise bean when its timeout callback is invoked. The serializable object used as the `info` parameter can be anything, as long as it implements the `java.io.Serializable` interface and follows the rules of serialization.[*] The `info` object can be put to many uses, but one obvious use is to associate the timer with some sort of identifier.

To get the `info` object from a timer, you call the timer's `getInfo()` method. This method returns a serializable object, which you'll have to cast to an appropriate type. So far, we've been using strings as `info` objects, but there are much more elaborate (and reliable) possibilities.

Retrieving other information from timers

The `Timer.getNextTimeout()` method simply returns the date—represented by a `java.util.Date` instance—on which the timer will expire next. If the timer is a single-action timer, the `Date` returned is the time at which the timer will expire. If, however, the timer is an interval timer, the `Date` returned is the time remaining until the next expiration. Oddly, there is no way to determine subsequent expirations or the interval at which an interval timer is configured. The best way to handle this is to put that information into your `info` object.

---

[*] In the most basic cases, all an object needs to do to be serializable is implement the `java.io.Serializable` interface and make sure any nonserializable fields (e.g., JDBC connection handles) are marked as `transient`.

The `Timer.getTimeRemaining()` method returns the number of milliseconds before the timer will next expire. Like the `getNextTimeout()` method, this method only provides information about the next expiration.

The TimerHandle object

The `Timer.getHandle()` method returns a `TimerHandle` object. The `TimerHandle` object is similar to the `javax.ejb.Handle` and `javax.ejb.HomeHandle`. It's a reference that can be saved to a file or some other resource and then used later to regain access to the `Timer`. The `TimerHandle` interface is simple:

```
package javax.ejb;
public interface TimerHandle extends java.io.Serializable {
    public Timer getTimer( ) throws NoSuchObjectLocalException, EJBException;
}
```

The `TimerHandle` is valid only as long as the timer has not expired (if it's a single-action timer) or been canceled. If the timer no longer exists, calling the `TimerHandle.get Timer()` method throws a `javax.ejb.NoSuchObjectException`.

`TimerHandle` objects are local, which means they cannot be used outside the container system that generated them. Passing the `TimerHandle` as an argument to a remote or endpoint interface method is illegal. However, a `TimerHandle` can be passed between local enterprise beans using their local interface, because local enterprise beans must be co-located in the same container system.

Exceptions

All the methods defined in the `Timer` interface declare two exceptions:

`javax.ejb.NoSuchObjectLocalException`
> This exception is thrown if you invoke any method on an expired single-action timer or a canceled timer.

`javax.ejb.EJBException`
> This exception is thrown when some type of system-level exception occurs in the Timer Service.

Transactions

When a bean calls `createTimer()`, the operation is performed in the scope of the current transaction. If the transaction rolls back, the timer is undone and it's not created (or, more precisely, it's uncreated).

In most cases, the timeout callback method on beans should have a transaction attribute of `RequiresNew`. This ensures that the work performed by the callback method is in the scope of container-initiated transactions. Transactions are covered in more detail in Chapter 17.

Stateless Session Bean Timers

Stateless session bean timers can be used for *auditing* or *batch processing*. As an auditing agent, a stateless session timer can monitor the state of the system to ensure that tasks are being completed and that data is consistent. This type of work spans entities and possibly data sources. Such EJBs can also perform batch-processing work such as database cleanup, transfer of records, etc. Stateless session bean timers can also be deployed as agents that perform some type of intelligent work on behalf of the organization they serve. An agent can be thought of as an extension of an audit: it monitors the system, but it also fixes problems automatically.

Stateless session bean timers are associated with only a specific type of session bean. When a timer for a stateless session bean goes off, the container selects an instance of that stateless bean type from the instance pool and calls its timeout callback method. This makes sense because all stateless session beans in the instance pool are logically equivalent. Any instance can serve any client, including the container itself.

Stateless session timers are often used to manage taskflow; they're also used when the timed event applies to a collection of entities instead of just one. For example, stateless session timers might be used to audit all maintenance records to ensure that a cruise line's ships meet state and federal guidelines. At specific intervals, a timer notifies the bean to look up the maintenance records from all the ships and generate a report. A stateless session timer can also be used to do something like send notifications to all the passengers for a particular cruise.

The stateless session bean can access an injected `TimerService` from the `Session Context` in the `@PostConstruct`, `@PreDestroy`, or any business method, but it cannot access the Timer Service from any *setter* injection method. This means a client must call some method on a stateless session bean (either `create` or a business method) in order for a timer to be set. This is the only way to guarantee that the timer is set.

Setting a timer on the `@PostConstruct` method within a stateless session bean is problematic. First, there is no guarantee that an `@PostConstruct` callback will ever be called. We might instead use a singleton configured to eagerly load on application startup to ensure the timer is registered. An SLSB `@PostConstruct` callback method's stateless session bean is called sometime after the bean is instantiated, before it enters the Method-Ready Pool. However, a container might not create a pool of instances until the first client accesses that bean, so if a client (remote or otherwise) never attempts to access the bean, the `@PostConstruct` callback may never be called and the timer will never be set. Another problem with using SLSB `@PostConstruct` is that it's called on every instance before it enters the pool; you have to prevent subsequent instances (instances created after the first instance) from setting the timer, because the first instance created would have already done this. It's tempting to use a static variable to avoid recreating timers, as in the following code, but this can cause problems:

```
public class StatelessTimerBean javax.ejb.TimedObject {
```

```
static boolean isTimerSet = false;

@Resource TimerService timerService;
@Resource SessionContext ctx;

@PostConstruct
public void init( ){
    if( isTimerSet == false) {
        long expirationDate = (Long)ctx.lookup("expirationDate");
        timerService.createTimer(expirationDate, null );
        isTimerSet = true;
    }
}
```

Although this may seem like a good solution, it works only when your application is deployed within a single server with one VM and one classloader. If you are using a clustered system, a single server with multiple VMs, or multiple classloaders (which is very common), it won't work, because bean instances that are not instantiated in the same VM with the same classloader will not have access to the same static variable. In this scenario, it's easy to end up with multiple timers doing the same thing. An alternative is to have `@PostCreate` access and remove all preexisting timers to see whether the timer is already established, but this can affect performance because it's likely that new instances will be created and added to the pool many times, resulting in many calls to `@PostCreate` and, therefore, many calls to `TimerService.getTimers()`. Also, there is no requirement that the Timer Service work across a cluster, so timers set on one node in a cluster may not be visible to timers set on some other node in the cluster.

With stateless session beans, you should never use the `@PreDestroy` callback method to cancel or create timers. The `@PreDestroy` callback is called on individual instances before they are evicted from memory. It is not called in response to client calls to the remote or local remove method. Also, the `@PreDestroy` callback doesn't correspond to an undeployment of a bean; it's specific to only a single instance. As a result, you cannot determine anything meaningful about the EJB as a whole from a call to the `ejbRemove()` method, and you should not use it to create or cancel timers.

When a stateless session bean implements the `javax.ejb.TimedObject` interface, or contains an `@javax.ejb.Timeout` callback method, its lifecycle changes to include the servicing of timed events. The Timer Service pulls an instance of the bean from the instance pool when a timer expires; if there are no instances in the pool, the container creates one. Figure 19-1 shows the lifecycle of a stateless session bean that implements the `TimedOut` interface.

Message-Driven Bean Timers

Message-driven bean timers are similar to stateless session bean timers in several ways. Timers are associated only with the type of bean. When a timer expires, a message-driven bean instance is selected from a pool to execute the timeout callback method.

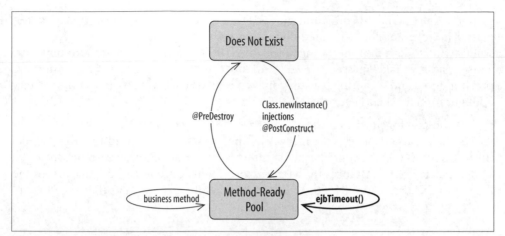

Figure 19-1. Stateless session bean lifecycle with TimedObject

In addition, message-driven beans can be used for performing audits or other types of batch jobs. The primary difference between a message-driven bean timer and a stateless session bean timer is the way in which they're initiated: timers are created in response to an incoming message or, if the container supports it, from a configuration file.

In order to initialize a message-driven bean timer from an incoming message, you simply put the call to the `TimerService.createTimer()` method in the message-handling method. For a JMS-based message-driven bean, the method call goes in the `onMessage()` method:

```
@MessageDriven
public class JmsTimerBean implements MessageListener {
    @Resource TimerService timerService

    public void onMessage(Message message){
        MapMessage mapMessage = (MapMessage)message;
        long expirationDate = mapMessage.getLong("expirationDate");

        timerService.createTimer(expirationDate, null );
}

    @Timeout

    public void timeout( ){
        // put timeout logic here
    }
```

The incoming JMS message should contain information about the timer: the beginning (start) date, duration, or even the `Serializable info` object. Combining JMS with the Timer Service can offer some powerful design options for implementing audits, batch processing, and agent-like solutions.

Although it's not standardized, it is possible that vendors will allow message-driven bean timers to be configured at deployment time. This would require a proprietary solution, since standard configuration options for message-driven bean timers do not exist. The advantage of configured timers is that they do not require a client to initiate some action to start the timer. When the bean is deployed, its timer is set automatically. This capability makes message-driven bean timers more like Unix *cron* jobs, which are preconfigured and then run. Consult your vendor to see whether it offers a proprietary configuration for message-driven bean timers.

As was the case for stateless session beans, the `TimedObject` interface or the presence of an `@Timeout` method changes the lifecycle of the message-driven bean slightly. When a timed event occurs, the container must pull a message-driven bean instance from the pool. If there are no instances in the pool, then an instance must be moved from the Does Not Exist state to the Method-Ready Pool before it can receive the timed event.

## CHAPTER 20

EJB 3.1: Web Services Standards

Web services have taken the enterprise computing industry by storm in the past couple of years, and for good reason. They present the opportunity for real interoperability across hardware, operating systems, programming languages, and applications. Based on the XML, SOAP, and WSDL standards, web services have enjoyed widespread adoption by nearly all of the major enterprise players, including Microsoft, IBM, BEA, JBoss, Oracle, Hewlett-Packard, and others. Sun Microsystems has integrated web services into the Java EE platform; specifically, Sun and the Java Community Process have introduced several web services APIs, including the Java API for XML Web Services (JAX-WS), the Java API for XML-based RPC (JAX-RPC), the SOAP with Attachments API for Java (SAAJ), and the Java API for XML Registries (JAXR). These web services APIs were integrated into J2EE 1.4 and have been expanded upon in subsequent releases, including Java EE 6 and EJB 3.1.

This chapter provides an overview of the technologies that are the foundation of web services: XML Schema and XML Namespaces, SOAP, and WSDL. Chapter 21 provides an overview of JAX-WS and JAX-RPC, the most important web services APIs.

Web Services Overview

The term *web services* means different things to different people, but thankfully, the definition is straightforward for EJB developers because the Java EE platform has adopted a rather narrow view of them. Specifically, a web service is a remote application described using the Web Service Description Language (WSDL) and accessed using the Simple Object Access Protocol (SOAP) according to the rules defined by the WS-I Basic Profile 1.1. The WS-I (Web Services Integration Organization) is a group of vendors (Microsoft, IBM, BEA, Sun Microsystems, Oracle, HP, and others) that have banded together to ensure web services are interoperable across all platforms. To do this, they have created a recommendation called the Basic Profile 1.1, which defines a set of rules for using XML, SOAP, and WSDL together to create interoperable web services.

In order to understand SOAP and WSDL, you must understand XML Schema and XML Namespaces. The rest of this chapter conducts a whirlwind tour of XML, SOAP, and WSDL. Although it's not the purpose of this book to cover these subjects in depth, you should be able to understand the basics.

XML Schema and XML Namespaces

We'll start with the basics of XML Schema and XML Namespaces. It's assumed that you already understand how to use basic XML elements and attributes. If you don't, you should probably read a primer on XML before proceeding. We recommend the book *Learning XML* (O'Reilly). If you already understand how XML Schema and XML Namespaces work, skip ahead to the section on SOAP.

XML Schema

An *XML Schema* is similar in purpose to a *Document Type Definition* (DTD), which validates the structure of an XML document. To illustrate some of the basic concepts of XML Schema, let's start with an XML document with address information:

```
<?xml version='1.0' encoding='UTF-8' standalone='yes'?>
<address>
  <street>800 Langdon Street</street>
  <city>Madison</city>
  <state>WI</state>
  <zip>53706</zip>
</address>
```

In order to ensure that the XML document contains the proper type of elements and data, the address information must be evaluated for *correctness*. You measure the correctness of an XML document by determining two criteria: whether the document is *well formed* and whether it is *valid*. To be well formed, an XML document must obey the syntactic rules of the XML markup language: it must use proper attribute declarations, the correct characters to denote the start and end of elements, and so on. Most XML parsers based on standards such as SAX and DOM automatically detect documents that aren't well formed.

In addition to being well formed, the document must use the right types of elements and attributes in the correct order and structure. A document that meets these criteria is called *valid*. However, the criteria for validity have nothing to do with XML itself; they have more to do with the application in which the document is used. For example, the Address document would not be valid if it didn't include the zip code or state elements. In order to validate an XML document, you need a way to represent these application-specific constraints.

The XML Schema for the Address XML document looks like this:

```
<?xml version='1.0' encoding='UTF-8' ?>
<schema xmlns="http://www.w3.org/2001/XMLSchema"
```

```
    xmlns:titan="http://www.titan.com/Reservation"
    targetNamespace="http://www.titan.com/Reservation">

  <element name="address" type="titan:AddressType"/>

  <complexType name="AddressType">
    <sequence>
      <element name="street" type="string"/>
      <element name="city" type="string"/>
      <element name="state" type="string"/>
      <element name="zip" type="string"/>
    </sequence>
  </complexType>

</schema>
```

The first thing to focus on in this XML Schema is the `<complexType>` element, which declares a type of element in much the same way that a Java class declares a type of object. The `<complexType>` element explicitly declares the names, types, and order of elements that an `AddressType` element may contain. In this case, it may contain four elements of type `string`, in the following order: `street`, `city`, `state`, and `zip`. Validation is pretty strict, so any XML document that claims conformity to this XML Schema must contain exactly the right elements with the right data types, in the correct order.

XML Schema automatically supports about two dozen simple data types, called *built-in types*. Built-in types are a part of the XML Schema language and are automatically supported by any XML Schema–compliant parser. Table 20-1 provides a short list of some of the built-in types. It also includes Java types that correspond to each built-in type. (Table 20-1 presents only a subset of all the XML Schema [XSD] built-in types, but it's more than enough for this book.)

Table 20-1. XML Schema built-in types and their corresponding Java types

XML Schema built-in type	Java type
byte	Byte, byte
boolean	Boolean, boolean
short	Short, short
int	Integer, int
long	Long, long
float	Float, float
double	Double, double
string	java.lang.String
dateTime	java.util.Calendar
integer	java.math.BigInteger
decimal	java.math.BigDecimal

By default, each element declared by a `<complexType>` must occur once in an XML document, but you can specify that an element is optional or that it must occur more than once by using the occurrence attributes. For example, we can say that the `street` element *must* occur once but *may* occur twice:

```
<complexType name="AddressType">
  <sequence>
    <element name="street" type="string" maxOccurs="2"
minOccurs="1"
/>
    <element name="city" type="string"/>
    <element name="state" type="string"/>
    <element name="zip" type="string"/>
  </sequence>
</complexType>
```

By default, the `maxOccurs` and `minOccurs` attributes are always `1`, indicating that the element must occur exactly once. Setting `maxOccurs` to `2` allows an XML document to have either two `street` elements or just one. You can also set `maxOccurs` to `unbounded`, which means the element may occur as many times as needed. Setting `minOccurs` to `0` means the element is optional and can be omitted.

The `<element>` declarations are nested under a `<sequence>` element, which indicates that the elements must occur in the order they are declared. You can also nest the elements under an `<all>` declaration, which allows the elements to appear in any order. The following shows the `AddressType` declared with an `<all>` element rather than a `<sequence>` element:

```
<complexType name="AddressType">
  <all>
    <element name="street" type="string" maxOccurs="2" minOccurs="1" />
    <element name="city" type="string"/>
    <element name="state" type="string"/>
    <element name="zip" type="string"/>
  </all>
</complexType>
```

In addition to declaring elements of XSD built-in types, you can declare elements based on complex types. This is similar to how Java class types declare fields that are other Java class types. For example, we can define a `CustomerType` that uses the `AddressType`:

```
<?xml version='1.0' encoding='UTF-8' ?>
<schema xmlns="http://www.w3.org/2001/XMLSchema"
    xmlns:titan="http://www.titan.com/Reservation"
    targetNamespace="http://www.titan.com/Reservation">
  <element name="customer" type="titan:CustomerType"/>


<complexType name="CustomerType">
  <sequence>
    <element name="last-name" type="string"/>
    <element name="first-name" type="string"/>
    <element name="address" type="titan:AddressType"/>
```

```
      </sequence>
    </complexType>
  <complexType name="AddressType">
      <sequence>
       <element name="street" type="string" />
       <element name="city" type="string"/>
       <element name="state" type="string"/>
       <element name="zip" type="string"/>
      </sequence>
    </complexType>

  </schema>
```

This XSD tells us that an element of `CustomerType` must contain a `<last-name>` and `<first-name>` element of the built-in type `string`, and an element of type `AddressType`. This is straightforward, except for the `titan:` prefix on `AddressType`. That prefix identifies the XML Namespace of the `AddressType`; we'll discuss namespaces later in the chapter. For now, just think of it as declaring that the `AddressType` is a custom type defined by Titan Cruises. It's not a standard XSD built-in type. An XML document that conforms to the Customer XSD would look like this:

```
<?xml version='1.0' encoding='UTF-8' ?>
<customer>
  <last-name>Jones</last-name>
  <first-name>Sara</first-name>
  <address>
    <street>3243 West 1st Ave.</street>
    <city>Madison</city>
    <state>WI</state>
    <zip>53591</zip>
  </address>
</customer>
```

Building on what you've learned so far, we can create a Reservation schema using the `CustomerType`, the `AddressType`, and a new `CreditCardType`:

```
<?xml version='1.0' encoding='UTF-8' ?>
<schema xmlns="http://www.w3.org/2001/XMLSchema"
    xmlns:titan="http://www.titan.com/Reservation"
    targetNamespace="http://www.titan.com/Reservation">

<element name="reservation" type="titan:ReservationType"/>

<complexType name="ReservationType">
    <sequence>
      <element name="customer" type="titan:CustomerType"/>
      <element name="cruise-id" type="int"/>
      <element name="cabin-id" type="int"/>
      <element name="price-paid" type="double"/>
    </sequence>
  </complexType>
  <complexType name="CustomerType">
    <sequence>
      <element name="last-name" type="string"/>
      <element name="first-name" type="string"/>
```

```
      <element name="address" type="titan:AddressType"/>
      <element name="credit-card" type="titan:CreditCardType"/>
    </sequence>
  </complexType>
  <complexType name="CreditCardType">
    <sequence>
      <element name="exp-date" type="dateTime"/>
      <element name="number" type="string"/>
      <element name="name" type="string"/>
      <element name="organization" type="string"/>
    </sequence>
  </complexType>
  <complexType name="AddressType">
    <sequence>
      <element name="street" type="string"/>
      <element name="city" type="string"/>
      <element name="state" type="string"/>
      <element name="zip" type="string"/>
    </sequence>
  </complexType>
</schema>
```

An XML document that conforms to the Reservation XSD would include information describing the customer (name and address), credit card information, and the identity of the cruise and cabin that are being reserved. This document might be sent to Titan Cruises from a travel agency that cannot access the TravelAgent EJB to make reservations. Here's an XML document that conforms to the Reservation XSD:

```
<?xml version='1.0' encoding='UTF-8' ?>
<reservation>
  <customer>
    <last-name>Jones</last-name>
    <first-name>Sara</first-name>
    <address>
      <street>3243 West 1st Ave.</street>
      <city>Madison</city>
      <state>WI</state>
      <zip>53591</zip>
    </address>
    <credit-card>
      <exp-date>09-2007</exp-date>
      <number>0394029302894028930</number>
      <name>Sara Jones</name>
      <organization>VISA</organization>
    </credit-card>
  </customer>
  <cruise-id>123</cruise-id>
  <cabin-id>333</cabin-id>
  <price-paid>6234.55</price-paid>
</reservation>
```

At runtime, the XML parser compares the document to its schema, ensuring that the document conforms to the schema's rules. If the document doesn't adhere to the schema, it is considered invalid, and the parser produces error messages. An XML

Schema checks that XML documents received by your system are properly structured, so you won't encounter errors while parsing the documents and extracting the data. For example, if someone sent your application a Reservation document that omitted the credit card element, the XML parser could reject the document as invalid before your code even sees it; you don't have to worry about errors in your code caused by missing information in the document.

This brief overview represents only the tip of the iceberg. XML Schema is a very rich XML typing system and can be given sufficient attention only in a text dedicated to the subject. For in-depth and insightful coverage of XML Schema, read *XML Schema: The W3C's Object-Oriented Descriptions for XML* (O'Reilly), or read the XML Schema specification, starting with the primer at the World Wide Web Consortium (W3C) website (*http://www.w3.org/TR/xmlschema-0*).

XML Namespaces

The Reservation schema defines an XML markup language that describes the structure of a specific kind of XML document. Just as a class is a type of Java object, an *XML markup language* is a type of XML document defined by an XML Schema. In some cases, it's convenient to combine two or more XML markup languages into a single document so that the elements from each markup language can be validated separately using different XML Schema. This is especially useful when you want to reuse a markup language in many different contexts. For example, the `AddressType` defined in the previous section is useful in a variety of contexts, not just the Reservation XSD, so it could be defined as a separate markup language in its own XML Schema:

```
<?xml version='1.0' encoding='UTF-8' ?>
<schema xmlns="http://www.w3.org/2001/XMLSchema"
    targetNamespace="http://www.titan.com/Address">

  <complexType name="AddressType">
    <sequence>
      <element name="street" type="string"/>
      <element name="city" type="string"/>
      <element name="state" type="string"/>
      <element name="zip" type="string"/>
    </sequence>
  </complexType>
</schema>
```

To use different markup languages in the same XML document, you must clearly identify the markup language to which each element belongs. The following example is an XML document for a reservation, but this time we are using XML Namespaces to separate the address information from the reservation information:

```
<?xml version='1.0' encoding='UTF-8' ?>
<res:reservation xmlns:res="http://www.titan.com/Reservation">
  <res:customer>
    <res:last-name>Jones</res:last-name>
    <res:first-name>Sara</res:first-name>
```

```
<addr:address xmlns:addr="http://www.titan.com/Address">
  <addr:street>3243 West 1st Ave.</addr:street>
  <addr:city>Madison</addr:city>
  <addr:state>WI</addr:state>
  <addr:zip>53591</addr:zip>
</addr:address>

<res:credit-card>
  <res:exp-date>09-2007</res:exp-date>
  <res:number>0394029302894028930</res:number>
  <res:name>Sara Jones</res:name>
  <res:organization>VISA</res:organization>
</res:credit-card>
</res:customer>
<res:cruise-id>123</res:cruise-id>
<res:cabin-id>333</res:cabin-id>
<res:price-paid>6234.55</res:price-paid>
</res:reservation>
```

All of the elements for the address information are prefixed with the characters `addr:`, and all the reservation elements are prefixed with `res:`. These prefixes allow parsers to identify and separate the elements that belong to the Address markup from those that belong to the Reservation markup. As a result, the address elements can be validated against the Address XSD, and the reservation elements can be validated against the Reservation XSD. The prefixes are assigned using XML Namespace declarations, which are shown in bold in the previous listing. An XML Namespace declaration follows this format:

```
xmlns:prefix="URI"
```

The prefix can be anything you like, as long as it does not include blank spaces or any special characters. We use prefixes that are abbreviations for the name of the markup language: `res` stands for Reservation XSD, and `addr` stands for Address XSD. Most XML documents follow this convention, but it's not a requirement; you could use a prefix like `foo` or `bar` or anything else you fancy.

While the prefix can be any arbitrary token, the Universal Resource Identifier (URI) must be very specific. A *URI* is an identifier that is a superset of the Universal Resource Locator (URL), which you use every day to look up web pages. In most cases, people use the stricter URL format for XML Namespaces because URLs are familiar and easy to understand. The URI used in the XML Namespace declaration identifies the exact markup language that is employed. It doesn't have to point at a web page or an XML document; it only needs to be unique to that markup language. For example, the XML Namespace used by the Address markup is different from the URL used for the Reservation markup:

```
xmlns:addr="http://www.titan.com/Address"
xmlns:res="http://www.titan.com/Reservation"
```

The URI in the XML Namespace declaration should match the target namespace declared by the XML Schema. The following example shows the Address XSD with the target namespace declaration in bold. The URL value of the `targetNamespace` attribute is identical to the URL assigned to the `add:` prefix in the Reservation document:

```xml
<?xml version='1.0' encoding='UTF-8' ?>
<schema xmlns="http://www.w3.org/2001/XMLSchema"
    targetNamespace="http://www.titan.com/Address">

  <complexType name="AddressType">
    <sequence>
      <element name="street" type="string"/>
      <element name="city" type="string"/>
      <element name="state" type="string"/>
      <element name="zip" type="string"/>
    </sequence>
  </complexType>
</schema>
```

The `targetNamespace` attribute identifies the unique URI of the markup language; it is the permanent identifier for that XML Schema. Whenever elements from the Address XSD are used in some other document, the document must use an XML Namespace declaration to identify those elements as belonging to the Address markup language.

Prefixing every element in an XML document with its namespace identifier is a bit tedious, so the XML Namespace allows you to declare a default namespace that applies to all nonprefixed elements. The default namespace is simply an XML Namespace declaration that has no prefix (`xmlns="URL"`). For example, we can use a default name in the Reservation document for all reservation elements:

```xml
<?xml version='1.0' encoding='UTF-8' ?>
<reservation xmlns="http://www.titan.com/Reservation">
  <customer>
    <last-name>Jones</last-name>
    <first-name>Sara</first-name>

    <addr:address xmlns:addr="http://www.titan.com/Address">
      <addr:street>3243 West 1st Ave.</addr:street>
      <addr:city>Madison</addr:city>
      <addr:state>WI</addr:state>
      <addr:zip>53591</addr:zip>
    </addr:address>
    <credit-card>
      <exp-date>09-2007</exp-date>
      <number>0394029302894028930</number>
      <name>Sara Jones</name>
      <organization>VISA</organization>
    </credit-card>
  </customer>
  <cruise-id>123</cruise-id>
  <cabin-id>333</cabin-id>
  <price-paid>6234.55</price-paid>
</reservation>
```

None of the reservation element names are prefixed. Any nonprefixed element belongs to the default namespace. The address elements do not belong to the *http://www.titan .com/Reservation* namespace, so they are prefixed to indicate to which namespace they belong. The default namespace declaration has *scope*; in other words, it applies to the element in which it is declared (if that element has no namespace prefix), and to all nonprefixed elements nested under that element. We can apply the scoping rules of namespace to simplify the Reservation document further by allowing the address elements to override the default namespace with their own default namespace:

```
<?xml version='1.0' encoding='UTF-8' ?>
<reservation xmlns="http://www.titan.com/Reservation">
  <customer>
    <last-name>Jones</last-name>
    <first-name>Sara</first-name>

    <address xmlns="http://www.titan.com/Address">
      <street>3243 West 1st Ave.</street>
      <city>Madison</city>
      <state>WI</state>
      <zip>53591</zip>
    </address>

    <credit-card>
      <exp-date>09-2007</exp-date>
      <number>0394029302894028930</number>
      <name>Sara Jones</name>
      <organization>VISA</organization>
    </credit-card>
  </customer>
  <cruise-id>123</cruise-id>
  <cabin-id>333</cabin-id>
  <price-paid>6234.55</price-paid>
</reservation>
```

The `Reservation` default namespace applies to the `<reservation>` element and all of its children, except for the address elements. The `<address>` element and its children have defined their own default namespace, which overrides the default namespace of the `<reservation>` element.

Default namespaces do not apply to attributes. As a result, any attributes used in an XML document should be prefixed with a namespace identifier. The only exceptions to this rule are attributes defined by the XML language itself, such as the `xmlns` attribute, which establishes an XML Namespace declaration. This attribute doesn't need to be prefixed, because it is part of the XML language.

XML Namespaces are URIs that uniquely identify a namespace but do not actually point at a resource. In other words, you don't normally use the URI of an XML Namespace to look something up. It's usually only an identifier. However, you might want to indicate the location of the XML Schema associated with an XML Namespace so that a parser can upload it and use it in validation. This is accomplished using the `schemaLocation` attribute:

```
<?xml version='1.0' encoding='UTF-8' ?>
<reservation xmlns="http://www.titan.com/Reservation"
             xmlns:xsi="http://www.w3.org/2001/XMLSchema-Instance"
             xsi:schemaLocation="http://www.titan.com/Reservation
                                 http://www.titan.com/schemas/reservation.xsd">
   <customer>
     <last-name>Jones</last-name>
     <first-name>Sara</first-name>

     <address xmlns="http://www.titan.com/Address"
                  xsi:schemaLocation="http://www.titan.com/Address
         http://www.titan.com/schemas/address.xsd">
       <street>3243 West 1st Ave.</street>
       <city>Madison</city>
       <state>WI</state>
       <zip>53591</zip>
     </address>

     <credit-card>
       <exp-date>09-2007</exp-date>
       <number>0394029302894028930</number>
       <name>Sara Jones</name>
       <organization>VISA</organization>
     </credit-card>
   </customer>
   <cruise-id>123</cruise-id>
   <cabin-id>333</cabin-id>
   <price-paid>6234.55</price-paid>
</reservation>
```

The schemaLocation attribute provides a list of values as Namespace-Location value pairs. The first value is the URI of the XML Namespace; the second is the physical location (URL) of the XML Schema. The following schemaLocation attribute states that all elements belonging to the Reservation namespace (*http://www.titan.com/ Reservation*) can be validated against an XML Schema located at the URL *http:// www.titan.com/schemas/reservation.xsd*:

```
xsi:schemaLocation="http://www.titan.com/Reservation
                    http://www.titan.com/schemas/reservation.xsd">
```

The schemaLocation attribute is not a part of the XML language, so we'll actually need to prefix it with the appropriate namespace in order to use it. The XML Schema specification defines a special namespace that can be used for schemaLocation (as well as other attributes). That namespace is *http://www.w3.org/2001/XMLSchema-Instance*. To declare the schemaLocation attribute properly, you must declare its XML Namespace and prefix it with the identifier for that namespace, as shown in the following snippet:

```
<?xml version='1.0' encoding='UTF-8' ?>
<reservation xmlns=http://www.titan.com/Reservation
                 xmlns:xsi="http://www.w3.org/2001/XMLSchema-Instance"
                 xsi:schemaLocation="http://www.titan.com/Reservation
                                     http://www.titan.com/schemas/reservation.xsd">
```

A namespace declaration needs to be defined only once; it applies to all elements nested under the element in which it's declared. The convention is to use the prefix xsi for the XML Schema Instance namespace (*http://www.w3.org/2001/XMLSchema-Instance*).

XML Schema also use XML Namespaces. Let's look at the XML Schema for the Address markup language with a new focus on the use of XML Namespaces:

```
<?xml version='1.0' encoding='UTF-8' ?>
<schema
    xmlns=http://www.w3.org/2001/XMLSchema
    targetNamespace="http://www.titan.com/Address"
    xmlns:addr="http://www.titan.com/Address">

  <element name="address" type="addr:AddressType"/>

  <complexType name="AddressType">
    <sequence>
      <element name="street" type="string"/>
      <element name="city" type="string"/>
      <element name="state" type="string"/>
      <element name="zip" type="string"/>
    </sequence>
  </complexType>
```

In this file, namespaces are used in three separate declarations. The first declaration states that the default namespace is *http://www.w3.org/2001/XMLSchema*, which is the namespace of the XML Schema specification. This declaration makes it easier to read the XSD because most of the elements do not need to be prefixed. The second declaration states that the target namespace of the XML Schema is the namespace of the Address markup. This tells us that all the types and elements defined in this XSD belong to that namespace. Finally, the third namespace declaration assigns the prefix addr to the target namespace so that types can be referenced exactly. For example, the top-level <element> definition uses the name addr:AddressType to state that the element is of type AddressType, belonging to the namespace *http://www.titan.com/Address*.

Why do you have to declare a prefix for the target namespace? The reason is clearer when you examine the Reservation XSD:

```
<?xml version='1.0' encoding='UTF-8' ?>
<schema
    xmlns=http://www.w3.org/2001/XMLSchema
    xmlns:xsi=http://www.w3.org/2001/XMLSchema-Instance
    xmlns:addr=http://www.titan.com/Address
    xmlns:res=http://www.titan.com/Reservation
    targetNamespace="http://www.titan.com/Reservation">

  <import namespace="http://www.titan.com/Address"
                xsi:schemaLocation="http://www.titan.com/Address.xsd" />

  <element name="reservation" type="res:ReservationType"/>

  <complexType name="ReservationType">
    <sequence>
```

```
            <element name="customer" type="res:CustomerType "/>
            <element name="cruise-id" type="int"/>
            <element name="cabin-id" type="int"/>
            <element name="price-paid" type="double"/>
         </sequence>
      </complexType>
      <complexType name="CustomerType">
         <sequence>
            <element name="last-name" type="string"/>
            <element name="first-name" type="string"/>
            <element name="address" type="addr:AddressType"/>
            <element name="credit-card" type="res:CreditCardType"/>
         </sequence>
      </complexType>
      <complexType name="CreditCardType">
         <sequence>
            <element name="exp-date" type="dateTime"/>
            <element name="number" type="string"/>
            <element name="name" type="string"/>
            <element name="organization" type="string"/>
         </sequence>
      </complexType>
   </schema>
```

The Reservation XSD imports the Address XSD so that the AddressType can be used to define the CustomerType. You can see the use of namespaces in the definition of CustomerType, which references types from both the Address and Reservation namespaces (prefixed by addr and res, respectively):

```
<?xml version='1.0' encoding='UTF-8' ?>
<schema
    xmlns="http://www.w3.org/2001/XMLSchema"
    xmlns:xsi=http://www.w3.org/2001/XMLSchema-Instance
    xmlns:addr=http://www.titan.com/Address
    xmlns:res=http://www.titan.com/Reservation
    targetNamespace="http://www.titan.com/Reservation">
...
  <complexType name="CustomerType">
     <sequence>
        <element name="last-name" type="string"/>
        <element name="first-name" type="string"/>
        <element name="address" type="addr:AddressType"/>
        <element name="credit-card" type="res:CreditCardType"/>
     </sequence>
  </complexType>
```

Assigning a prefix to the Reservation namespace allows us to distinguish between elements that are defined as Reservation types (e.g., credit-card) and elements that are defined as Address types (e.g., address). All the type attributes that reference the built-in string and int types also belong to the XML Schema namespace, so we don't need to prefix them. We could, though, for clarity. That is, we'd replace string and int with xsd:string and xsd:int. The prefix xsd references the XML Schema namespace; it allows us to identify built-in types defined as XML Schema more clearly. It's not a problem that the default namespace is the same as the namespace prefixed by xsd. By convention, the xsd prefix is the one used in most XML Schema.

SOAP 1.1

SOAP 1.1 is simply a distributed object protocol, similar to DCOM, CORBA's IIOP, and JRMP (the primary transport used by RMI). The most significant difference between SOAP 1.1 and other distributed object protocols is that SOAP 1.1 is based on XML.

SOAP is defined by its own XML Schema and relies heavily on the use of XML Namespaces. Every SOAP message that is sent across the wire is an XML document consisting of standard SOAP elements and application data. The use of namespaces differentiates the standard SOAP elements from the application data. Here's a SOAP request message that might be sent from a client to a server:

```
<?xml version='1.0' encoding='UTF-8' ?>
<env:Envelope xmlns:env="http://schemas.xmlsoap.org/soap/envelope/">
    <env:Header />
    <env:Body>
        <reservation xmlns="http://www.titan.com/Reservation">
            <customer>
                    <!-- customer info goes here -->
            </customer>
            <cruise-id>123</cruise-id>
            <cabin-id>333</cabin-id>
            <price-paid>6234.55</price-paid>
        </reservation>
    </env:Body>
</env:Envelope>
```

The standard SOAP elements are shown in bold, and the application data, or the Reservation XML document fragment, is shown in regular text. SOAP's primary purpose is to establish a standard XML framework for packaging application data that is exchanged between different software platforms, such as Java and Perl, or Java and .NET. To do this, SOAP defines a set of elements, each designed to carry different data. The <Envelope> element is the root of the SOAP message; all other elements are contained by it. Within the <Envelope> element are two direct children: the <Header> element and the <Body> element.

The <Header> element is generally used for carrying infrastructure data such as security tokens, transaction IDs, routing information, and so on. In the previous example, the <Header> element is empty, which is not unusual for basic web services. In many cases, we are only interested in exchanging information and not in more advanced issues, such as those relating to security and transactions. Although the <Body> element is required, the <Header> element is not. From this point forward, the <Header> element will be omitted from examples.

The <Body> element carries the application information that is being exchanged. In the previous example, the <Body> element contains a <reservation> element, which is the application data. It's an XML document fragment based on the Reservation XSD developed earlier in this chapter. It's called a "fragment" because it's embedded inside a SOAP message instead of standing alone.

Web Services Styles

The SOAP message in the previous example is a *Document/Literal message*, which means that the message body is a single XML Schema instance document, and thus the full message can be validated. For this reason, Document/Literal is becoming the preferred message style of the web services community.

The schemaLocation attribute could have been included, but it's omitted because we assume that the receiver is already familiar with the schema used for that type of SOAP message.

The other style allowed by the WS-I Basic Profile 1.1 and supported by EJB 3.1 is *RPC/Literal*. RPC/Literal represents SOAP messages as RPC calls with parameters and return values, each with its own schema type. The following Java interface defines a single method called makeReservation():

```
public interface TravelAgent {
    public void makeReservation(int cruiseID, int cabinID,
                                int customerId, double price);
}
```

The makeReservation() method can be modeled as a SOAP message using the RPC/Literal messaging style:

```
<env:Envelope
    xmlns:env="http://schemas.xmlsoap.org/soap/envelope/"
    xmlns:titan="http://www.titan.com/TravelAgent"/>
    <env:Body>
    <titan:makeReservation>
        <cruiseId>23</cruiseId>
        <cabinId>144</cabinId>
        <customerId>9393</customerId>
        <price>5677.88</price>
    </titan:makeReservation>
    </env:Body>
</env:Envelope>
```

The first element within the <Body> identifies the web services operation being invoked. In this case, it is the makeReservation operation. Directly beneath the <titan:makeReservation> element are the parameters of the RPC call, each represented by an element with a value.

EJB 3.1, but not the WS-I Basic Profile 1.1, supports the *RPC/Encoded* mode of SOAP messaging. Most SOAP applications used RPC/Encoded when web services were first created. However, the web services industry has moved toward Document/Literal and

RPC/Literal, primarily because interoperability between platforms using RPC/Encoded proved to be less than perfect and sometimes downright difficult. Whereas RPC/Encoded SOAP messages rely on SOAP-defined types for arrays, enumeration, unions, lists, and the like, RPC/Literal and Document/Literal depend only on XML Schema for their data types, which seems to provide a better system for interoperability across programming languages. Although EJB 3.1 supports RPC/Encoded messaging, it's not a very good option to use in web services. RPC/Encoded messaging is not addressed in this book.

Exchanging SOAP Messages with HTTP

SOAP messages are *network-protocol agnostic*, which means that a SOAP message is not aware of or dependent on the type of network or protocol used to carry it. With that said, SOAP is primarily exchanged using HTTP. The reason for using HTTP is simple. Most Internet products, including web servers, application servers, and wireless devices, are designed to handle the HTTP protocol. This widespread support provides an instant infrastructure for SOAP messaging. The fact that SOAP can leverage the ubiquity of HTTP is one of the reasons it has become so popular so quickly.

Another advantage of using HTTP is that SOAP messages can slip through firewalls without any hassles. If you have ever tried to support internal or external customers who are separated from you by a firewall (yours or theirs), you know the headaches it can create. Unless you have direct control over the firewall, your chances of communicating with arbitrary clients using anything but HTTP or SMTP (email) are slim to none. However, because SOAP can be transmitted with HTTP, it slips through the firewall unnoticed. This ability makes life a lot simpler for the application developer, but it's a point of contention with the security folks. Understandably, they're a bit irked by the idea of application developers circumventing their defenses. Using HTTP to carry an application protocol such as SOAP is commonly called *HTTP tunneling*. In the past, support for tunneling by vendors of other distributed object protocols (CORBA IIOP, DCOM, and so on) was sporadic and proprietary, making interoperability extremely difficult. However, tunneling over HTTP is built into the SOAP 1.1 specification, which means interoperability is no longer a problem. Because almost every application server vendor rapidly adopts SOAP, SOAP-HTTP tunneling is becoming ubiquitous.

You can use SOAP 1.2 with other protocols, such as SMTP, FTP, and even raw TCP/IP, but HTTP is the only protocol for which a binding is currently specified. As a result, EJB 3.1 and Java EE 6 require support for SOAP 1.1 over HTTP 1.1, but not other protocols.

Now You See It, Now You Don't

All this talk about SOAP is intended to give you a better idea of what is going on under the hood, but in practice, you are unlikely to interact with the protocol directly. As with most protocols, SOAP is designed to be produced and consumed by software and is usually encapsulated by a developer API. In EJB 3.1, the API you use to exchange SOAP messages is the Java API for XML-based Web Services (JAX-WS), which hides the details of SOAP messaging so that you can focus on developing and invoking web services. While using JAX-WS, you will rarely have to deal with the SOAP protocol, which is nice because it makes you a lot more productive. JAX-WS is covered in Chapter 21.

WSDL 1.1

The Web Service Description Language (WSDL) is an XML document used to describe a web service. WSDL is programming-language, platform, and protocol agnostic. The fact that WSDL is protocol agnostic means that it can describe web services that use protocols other than SOAP and HTTP. This ability makes WSDL very flexible, but it has the unfortunate side effect of also making WSDL abstract and difficult to understand. Fortunately, the WS-I Basic Profile 1.1 endorses only SOAP 1.1 or 1.2 over HTTP, so we'll discuss WSDL as if that's the only combination of protocols supported.

Imagine that you want to develop a web services component that implements the following interface:

```java
public interface TravelAgent {
    public String makeReservation(int cruiseID, int cabinID,
                                  int customerId, double price);
}
```

Any application should be able to invoke this method using SOAP, regardless of the language in which it was written or the platform on which it is running. Because other programming languages don't understand Java, we have to describe the web service in a language they do understand: XML. Using XML, and specifically the WSDL markup language, we can describe the type of SOAP messages that must be sent to invoke the makeReservation() method. A WSDL document that describes the makeReservation() method might look like this:

```xml
<?xml version="1.0"?>
<definitions name="TravelAgent"
  xmlns="http://schemas.xmlsoap.org/wsdl/"
  xmlns:soap="http://schemas.xmlsoap.org/wsdl/soap/"
  xmlns:xsd="http://www.w3.org/2001/XMLSchema"
  xmlns:titan="http://www.titan.com/TravelAgent"
  targetNamespace="http://www.titan.com/TravelAgent">

<!-- message elements describe the parameters and return values -->
<message name="RequestMessage">
  <part name="cruiseId"   type="xsd:int" />
  <part name="cabinId"    type="xsd:int" />
  <part name="customerId" type="xsd:int" />
  <part name="price"      type="xsd:double" />
</message>
<message name="ResponseMessage">
```

```
      <part name="reservationId" type="xsd:string" />
    </message>

    <!-- portType element describes the abstract interface of a web service -->
    <portType name="TravelAgent">
      <operation name="makeReservation">
        <input message="titan:RequestMessage"/>
        <output message="titan:ResponseMessage"/>
      </operation>
    </portType>

    <!-- binding element tells us which protocols and encoding styles are used -->
    <binding name="TravelAgentBinding" type="titan:TravelAgent">
      <soap:binding style="rpc"
                    transport="http://schemas.xmlsoap.org/soap/http"/>
      <operation name="makeReservation">
        <soap:operation soapAction="" />
        <input>
          <soap:body use="literal"
                namespace="http://www.titan.com/TravelAgent"/>
        </input>
        <output>
          <soap:body use="literal"
                namespace="http://www.titan.com/TravelAgent"/>
        </output>
      </operation>
    </binding>

    <!-- service element tells us the Internet address of a web service -->
    <service name="TravelAgentService">
      <port name="TravelAgentPort" binding="titan:TravelAgentBinding">
        <soap:address location="http://www.titan.com/webservices/TravelAgent" />
      </port>
    </service>

</definitions>
```

If you find the previous WSDL listing indecipherable, don't despair. Most people can't understand a WSDL document the first time they see one. Like many things that are complicated, the best approach to understanding WSDL is to study it in pieces. And fortunately, modern web services platforms, such as JBoss, provide tools to generate the WSDL for you. WSDL should be something you need to look at only when things break. At this point, things still break often, so it's helpful to be familiar with WSDL; it will show you what the server expects when a method is called. But don't think that you'll be called on to write a WSDL document by yourself.

The <definitions> Element

The root element of a WSDL document is the <definitions> element. Usually, a WSDL document declares all the XML Namespaces used in the root element. In the previous example, the <definitions> element makes four XML Namespace declarations:

```
<?xml version="1.0"?>
<definitions name="TravelAgent"
   xmlns="http://schemas.xmlsoap.org/wsdl/"
   xmlns:soap="http://schemas.xmlsoap.org/wsdl/soap/"
   xmlns:xsd="http://www.w3.org/2001/XMLSchema"
   xmlns:titan="http://www.titan.com/TravelAgent"
   targetNamespace="http://www.titan.com/TravelAgent">
```

The default namespace (xmlns="*http://schemas.xmlsoap.org/wsdl/*") is the WSDL namespace. The xsd prefix is assigned to the XMLSchema namespace. It is used primarily to identify simple data types such as xsd:string, xsd:int, and xsd:dateTime in <message> elements:

```
<message name="RequestMessage">
   <part name="cruiseId"   type="xsd:int" />
   <part name="cabinId"    type="xsd:int" />
   <part name="customerId" type="xsd:int" />
   <part name="price"      type="xsd:double" />
</message>
<message name="ResponseMessage">
   <part name="reservationId" type="xsd:string" />
</message>
```

The titan prefix is assigned to a Titan Cruises URL, which indicates that it's an XML Namespace belonging to Titan Cruises. This namespace is also the value of the target Namespace attribute. This attribute is similar to the one used in XML Schema. For example, the <portType> element references <message> elements and the <binding> element references a <portType> element using the target namespace:

```
<!-- message elements describe the parameters and return values -->
<message name="RequestMessage">
   <part name="cruiseId"   type="xsd:int" />
   <part name="cabinId"    type="xsd:int" />
   <part name="customerId" type="xsd:int" />
   <part name="price"      type="xsd:double" />
</message>
<message name="ResponseMessage">
   <part name="reservationId" type="xsd:string" />
</message>

<!-- portType element describes the abstract interface of a web service -->
<portType name="TravelAgent">
  <operation name="makeReservation">
     <input message="titan:RequestMessage"/>
     <output message="titan:ResponseMessage"/>
  </operation>
</portType>

<!-- binding element tells us which protocols and encoding styles are used  -->
<binding name="TravelAgentBinding" type="titan:TravelAgent">
   ...
</binding>
```

As you can see, the different WSDL types reference each other by name, and a named WSDL type automatically takes on the namespace declared by the `targetNamespace` attribute.

The <portType> and <message> Elements

The `<portType>` and `<message>` elements are the immediate children of the `<definitions>` element. Here's what they look like:

```
<!-- message elements describe the parameters and return values -->
<message name="RequestMessage">
   <part name="cruiseId"   type="xsd:int" />
   <part name="cabinId"    type="xsd:int" />
   <part name="customerId" type="xsd:int" />
   <part name="price"      type="xsd:double" />
</message>
<message name="ResponseMessage">
   <part name="reservationId" type="xsd:string" />
</message>

<!-- portType element describes the abstract interface of a web service -->
<portType name="TravelAgent">
  <operation name="makeReservation">
     <input message="titan:RequestMessage"/>
     <output message="titan:ResponseMessage"/>
  </operation>
</portType>
```

The `<portType>` element describes the web services operations (Java methods) that are available. An operation can have input, output, and fault messages. An *input message* describes the type of SOAP message a client should send to the web service. An *output message* describes the type of SOAP message a client should expect to get back. A *fault message* (not shown in the example) describes any SOAP error messages that the web service might send back to the client. A fault message is similar to a Java exception.

JAX-WS, and therefore EJB 3.1, supports two styles of web services messaging: *request-response* and *one-way*. You know you are dealing with request-response if the `<operation>` element contains a single `<input>` element, followed by a single `<output>` element and, optionally, zero or more `<fault>` elements. The `TravelAgent` `<portType>` is an example of the request-response messaging style:

```
<!-- portType element describes the abstract interface of a web service -->
<portType name="TravelAgent">
  <operation name="makeReservation">
     <input message="titan:RequestMessage"/>
     <output message="titan:ResponseMessage"/>
  </operation>
</portType>
```

The one-way message style, on the other hand, is implied by the presence of a single `<input>` element but no `<output>` or `<fault>` element. Here is a web service that supports one-way messaging:

```
<!-- portType element describes the abstract interface of a web service -->
<portType name="ReservationProcessor">
  <operation name="submitReservation">
    <input message="titan:ReservationMessage"/>
  </operation>
</portType>
```

The request-response style of messaging is the kind you expect in RPC programming;
you send a message and get a response. The one-way style tends to be used for
asynchronous messaging; you send a message but do not expect a response. In addition,
one-way messaging is frequently used to deliver XML documents, such as the
Reservation document, rather than parameters and return values. However, both
request-response and one-way messaging styles can be used with either RPC or
document-style messaging.

WSDL also supports two other messaging styles: *notification* (a single `<output>` and no
`<input>`) and *solicitation* (a single `<output>` followed by a single `<input>`). Although
WSDL makes these messaging styles available, they are not supported by WS-I Basic
Profile 1.1 or JAX-RPC.

The `<types>` Element

If your service needs any custom types, they are defined in the `<types>` element, which
is the first child of the `<definitions>` element. The complete WSDL document shown
earlier did not include a `<types>` element because it didn't define any new types (it used
XML Schema built-in types). The `<types>` element allows us to declare more complex
XML types. For example, instead of declaring each parameter of the makeReservation
operation as an individual part, you can combine them into a single structure that serves
as the parameter of the operation:

```
<?xml version="1.0"?>
<definitions name="TravelAgent"
    xmlns="http://schemas.xmlsoap.org/wsdl/"
    xmlns:soap="http://schemas.xmlsoap.org/wsdl/soap/"
    xmlns:xsd="http://www.w3.org/2001/XMLSchema"
    xmlns:titan="http://www.titan.com/TravelAgent"
    targetNamespace="http://www.titan.com/TravelAgent">

<!-- types element describes complex XML data types -->
<types>
  <xsd:schema
    targetNamespace="http://www.titan.com/TravelAgent">

    <xsd:complexType name="ReservationType">
      <xsd:sequence>
        <xsd:element name="cruiseId" type="xsd:int"/>
        <xsd:element name="cabinId" type="xsd:int"/>
        <xsd:element name="customerId" type="xsd:int"/>
        <xsd:element name="price-paid" type="xsd:double"/>
      </xsd:sequence>
    </xsd:complexType>
```

```
      </xsd:schema>
  </types>

  <!-- message elements describe the parameters and return values -->
  <message name="RequestMessage">
      <part name="reservation" type="titan:ReservationType" />
  </message>
  <message name="ResponseMessage">
      <part name="reservationId" type="xsd:string" />
  </message>
```

The <types> element is frequently used with document-oriented messaging. For example, the following WSDL binding defines an XML Schema for the Reservation markup so that Reservation documents can be submitted to Titan as one-way messages. The schema is embedded within the WSDL document as the content of the <types> element:

```
  <?xml version="1.0"?>
  <definitions name="Reservation"
    xmlns="http://schemas.xmlsoap.org/wsdl/"
    xmlns:soap="http://schemas.xmlsoap.org/wsdl/soap/"
    xmlns:xsd="http://www.w3.org/2001/XMLSchema"
    xmlns:titan="http://www.titan.com/Reservation"
    targetNamespace="http://www.titan.com/Reservation">

  <!-- types element describes complex XML data types -->
  <types>
    <xsd:schema
      targetNamespace="http://www.titan.com/Reservation">

    <xsd:element name="reservation" type="titan:ReservationType"/>

    <xsd:complexType name="ReservationType">
      <xsd:sequence>
        <xsd:element name="customer" type="titan:CustomerType"/>
        <xsd:element name="cruise-id" type="xsd:int"/>
        <xsd:element name="cabin-id" type="xsd:int"/>
        <xsd:element name="price-paid" type="xsd:double"/>
      </xsd:sequence>
    </xsd:complexType>
    <xsd:complexType name="CustomerType">
      <xsd:sequence>
        <xsd:element name="last-name" type="xsd:string"/>
        <xsd:element name="first-name" type="xsd:string"/>
        <xsd:element name="address" type="titan:AddressType"/>
        <xsd:element name="credit-card" type="titan:CreditCardType"/>
      </xsd:sequence>
    </xsd:complexType>
    <xsd:complexType name="CreditCardType">
      <xsd:sequence>
        <xsd:element name="exp-date" type="xsd:dateTime"/>
        <xsd:element name="number" type="xsd:string"/>
        <xsd:element name="name" type="xsd:string"/>
        <xsd:element name="organization" type="xsd:string"/>
      </xsd:sequence>
```

```
      </xsd:complexType>
      <xsd:complexType name="AddressType">
        <xsd:sequence>
          <xsd:element name="street" type="xsd:string"/>
          <xsd:element name="city" type="xsd:string"/>
          <xsd:element name="state" type="xsd:string"/>
          <xsd:element name="zip" type="xsd:string"/>
        </xsd:sequence>
      </xsd:complexType>
    </xsd:schema>
  </types>

  <!-- message elements describe the parameters and return values -->
  <message name="ReservationMessage">
    <part name="inmessage" element="titan:reservation"/>
  </message>
  <!-- portType element describes the abstract interface of a web service -->
  <portType name="ReservationProcessor">
    <operation name="submitReservation">
      <input message="titan:ReservationMessage"/>
    </operation>
  </portType>
  <!-- binding tells us which protocols and encoding styles are used  -->
  <binding name="ReservationProcessorBinding" type="titan:ReservationProcessor">
    <soap:binding style="document"
                  transport="http://schemas.xmlsoap.org/soap/http"/>
    <operation name="submitReservation">
      <soap:operation soapAction="" />
      <input>
        <soap:body use="literal"/>
      </input>
    </operation>
  </binding>
  <!-- service tells us the Internet address of a web service -->
  <service name="ReservationProcessorService">
    <port name="ReservationProcessorPort" binding="titan:ReservationProcessorBinding">
      <soap:address location="http://www.titan.com/webservices/Reservation" />
    </port>
  </service>

</definitions>
```

The <binding> and <service> Elements

In addition to the <portType> and <message> elements, a WSDL document also defines <binding> and <service> elements. JAX-WS specifies these elements to generate marshaling and network communication code that is used to send and receive messages.

The `<binding>` element describes the type of encoding used to send and receive messages as well as the protocol on which the SOAP messages are carried. The `<binding>` definition for the `TravelAgent` port type looks like this:

```
<!-- binding element tells us which protocols and encoding styles are used  -->
<binding name="TravelAgentBinding" type="titan:TravelAgent">
   <soap:binding style="rpc"
                 transport="http://schemas.xmlsoap.org/soap/http"/>
   <operation name="makeReservation">
     <soap:operation soapAction="" />
     <input>
       <soap:body use="literal"
             namespace="http://www.titan.com/TravelAgent"/>
     </input>
     <output>
       <soap:body use="literal"
             namespace="http://www.titan.com/TravelAgent"/>
     </output>
   </operation>
</binding>
```

A binding element is always interlaced with protocol-specific elements—usually, the elements describe the SOAP protocol binding. (In fact, this is the only binding that is allowed by the WS-I Basic Profile 1.1.) Because Java EE web services must support SOAP with attachments, the MIME binding is also supported when attachments (images, documents, and so on) are sent with SOAP messages. However, that subject is a bit involved and is outside the scope of this book.

Similar to the `<portType>` element, the `<binding>` element contains `<operation>`, `<input>`, `<output>`, and `<fault>` elements. In fact, a binding is specific to a particular `<portType>`: its `<operation>`, `<input>`, and `<output>` elements describe the implementation details of the corresponding `<portType>`. The previous example used the HTTP protocol with RPC/Literal-style messaging. The WSDL binding for Document/Literal-style messaging is different:

```
<!-- binding element tells us which protocols and encoding styles are used  -->
<binding name="TravelAgentBinding" type="titan:TravelAgent">
   <soap:binding style="document"
     transport="http://schemas.xmlsoap.org/soap/http"/>
   <operation name="submitReservation">
     <soap:operation soapAction=""/>
     <input>
       <soap:body use="literal"/>
     </input>
   </operation>
</binding>
```

The `<binding>` element describes a one-way web service that accepts an XML document fragment. The `<portType>` associated with this `<binding>` also defines a single input message (consistent with one-way messaging) within an operation called `submitReservation`:

```
<!-- portType element describes the abstract interface of a web service -->
<portType name="ReservationProcessor">
  <operation name="submitReservation">
    <input message="titan:ReservationMessage"/>
  </operation>
</portType>
```

UDDI 2.0

Universal Description, Discovery, and Integration (UDDI) is a specification that describes a standard for publishing and discovering web services on the Internet. It's essentially a repository with a rigid data structure describing companies and the web services they provide. UDDI is not as fundamental to web services as XML, SOAP, and WSDL, but it is considered a basic constituent of web services in Java EE.

The analogy normally used to describe UDDI is that it provides electronic White, Yellow, and Green pages for companies and their web services. You can look up companies by name or identifier (White pages) or by business or product category (Yellow pages). You can also discover information about web services hosted by a company by examining the technical entities of a UDDI registry (Green pages). In other words, UDDI is an electronic directory that allows organizations to advertise their business and web services and to locate other organizations and web services.

Not only does a UDDI registry provide information about web services and their hosts, a UDDI repository is itself a web service. You can search, access, add, update, and delete information in a UDDI registry using a set of standard SOAP messages. All UDDI registry products must support the standard UDDI data structures and SOAP messages, which means that you can access any UDDI-compliant registry using the same standard set of SOAP messages.

Although organizations can set up private UDDI registries, there is a free UDDI registry that anyone can use, called the Universal Business Registry (UBR). This registry is accessed at one of four sites hosted by Microsoft, IBM, SAP, and NTT. If you publish information about your company in any one of these sites, the data will be replicated to each of the other three. You can find out more about the UBR and the sites that host it at *http://uddi.xml.org/*.

From Standards to Implementation

Understanding the fundamental web services standards (XML, SOAP, and WSDL) is essential to becoming a competent web services developer. However, you'll also need to understand how to implement web services in software. Numerous web services platforms allow you to build production systems based on the web services standards, including .NET, Perl, and Java EE. The focus of this book is obviously the Java EE platform, and specifically, support for web services in EJB. The next chapter explains how JAX-WS and its precursor (JAX-RPC) are used to support web services in Enterprise JavaBeans.

## CHAPTER 21

EJB 3.1 and Web Services

Support for web services in EJB 3.1 is based on the Java API for XML-based Web Services (JAX-WS) 2.1 specification, as well its predecessor, the Java API for XML-based RPC (JAX-RPC) 1.1. The name was changed primarily to avoid the common misconception that web services are only about RPC. Other specifications included in EJB 3.1 are the SOAP with Attachments API for Java (SAAJ) and the Java API for XML Registries (JAXR). JAX-WS and JAX-RPC are similar to RMI and CORBA, except they use the SOAP protocol; SAAJ is an API for manipulating the structure of a SOAP message; and JAXR allows you to access web services registries, usually UDDI.

Although this chapter and Chapter 20 provide you with a launching pad for learning about web services in Java EE (specifically EJB), the subject is too huge to cover in a book about EJB. In order to cover Java EE web services comprehensively, we would need another 500 pages. Since you'll need to lift this book to read it, we wrote a lighter approach to the subject. This chapter provides you with an introduction to both JAX-WS and JAX-RPC, but you should not consider it a comprehensive guide to the APIs.

The main purpose of a web services API is to bridge Java components with the standard web services protocols. Unlike other distributed technologies, web services were designed to be very flexible and very extendable. Although this makes the technology more open and more adaptable, it also makes transparency harder to achieve. A good web services API will go to great lengths to achieve transparency. The process of invoking and defining a web service in Java should be as close as possible to invoking and defining a normal object in Java. Both JAX-RPC and JAX-WS attempt to achieve this goal, although we think you will see that JAX-WS does a much better job. We will start with the aging JAX-RPC specification and then move into the newer JAX-WS API.

Accessing Web Services with JAX-RPC

JAX-RPC provides a client-side programming model that allows you to access web services on other platforms from your EJBs. In other words, by using JAX-RPC, EJBs can access web services across the network hosted on both Java and non-Java platforms

(Perl, .NET, C++, and so on). There are three APIs for accessing web services: generated stubs, dynamic proxies, and the Dynamic Invocation Interface (DII). When JAX-RPC is accessed from a Java EE/EJB 3.1 environment, the decision to use a dynamic proxy or a stub is up to the specific container on which you are running. In this case, however, a dynamic proxy will most likely be used, because a stub is not portable between Java EE platforms.

A *dynamic proxy* is very much like the classic Java RMI or CORBA programming model, where the client accesses a remote service via a remote interface implemented by a network stub. The stub translates calls made on the remote interface into network messages that are sent to the remote service. It's similar to using an EJB remote reference; however, the protocol is SOAP over HTTP rather than CORBA IIOP. Figure 21-1 illustrates the remote execution loop executed with a JAX-RPC dynamic proxy.

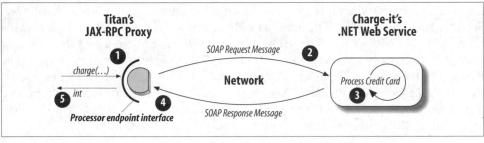

Figure 21-1. The JAX-RPC RMI loop

The execution loop in JAX-RPC is the same as any other RMI loop. In Step 1, the client invokes a method on the JAX-RPC proxy that implements the service endpoint interface. The method invocation is transformed into a SOAP message that is sent to the server in Step 2. In Step 3, the web service processes the request and sends the results back as a SOAP response message in Step 4. In Step 5, the SOAP response message is transformed into either a return value or an exception (if it was a SOAP fault) and is then returned to the client.

Generating JAX-RPC Artifacts from WSDL

The primary interface that describes a JAX-RPC web service is called a *service endpoint interface*. A JAX-RPC-compliant compiler generates the endpoint interface from a WSDL `<portType>` definition. This interface, when combined with WSDL `<binding>` and `<port>` definitions, is used to create the dynamic proxy at deploy time. The organization that hosts the web service provides the WSDL document.

Imagine that Titan Cruises subcontracts a company, Charge-It Inc., to process payments made by customers using credit cards. Charge-It runs a system based on .NET and exposes its credit card processing application to clients via a web service. A WSDL document describes the web service. The WSDL document for Charge-It's web service looks like this:

```
<?xml version="1.0" encoding="UTF-8"?>
<definitions xmlns="http://schemas.xmlsoap.org/wsdl/"
    xmlns:wsdl="http://schemas.xmlsoap.org/wsdl/"
    xmlns:xsd="http://www.w3.org/2001/XMLSchema"
    xmlns:soap="http://schemas.xmlsoap.org/wsdl/soap/"
    xmlns:tns="http://charge-it.com/Processor"
    targetNamespace="http://charge-it.com/Processor">

<message name="chargeRequest">
  <part name="name" type="xsd:string"/>
  <part name="number" type="xsd:string"/>
  <part name="exp-date" type="xsd:dateTime"/>
  <part name="card-type" type="xsd:string"/>
  <part name="amount" type="xsd:float"/>
</message>
<message name="chargeResponse">
  <part name="return" type="xsd:int"/>
</message>
<portType name="Processor">
  <operation name="charge">
    <input message="tns:chargeRequest"/>
    <output message="tns:chargeResponse"/>
  </operation>
</portType>
<binding name="ProcessorSoapBinding" type="tns:Processor">
  <soap:binding style="rpc"
      transport="http://schemas.xmlsoap.org/soap/http"/>
  <operation name="charge">
    <soap:operation soapAction="" style="rpc"/>
    <input>
      <soap:body use="literal"
          namespace="http://charge-it.com/Processor"/>
    </input>
    <output>
      <soap:body use="literal"
          namespace="http://charge-it.com/Processor"/>
    </output>
  </operation>
</binding>
<service name="ProcessorService">
  <port name="ProcessorPort" binding="tns:ProcessorSoapBinding">
    <soap:address
     location="http://www.charge-it.com/ProcessorService"/>
  </port>
</service>
</definitions>
```

The endpoint interface is based on the WSDL `<portType>` and its corresponding
`<message>` definitions. Based on these definitions, a JAX-RPC compiler would generate
the following interface:

```
package com.charge_it;

public interface Processor
 extends java.rmi.Remote
```

```
{
    public int charge(String name, String number, java.util.Calendar expDate,
                       String cardType, float amount)
        throws java.rmi.RemoteException;
}
```

An endpoint interface is a plain Java interface that extends the `java.rmi.Remote` interface. All methods on the service endpoint interface must throw `RemoteException`, although the bean implementation class is not required to. Application exceptions can be thrown from any business method. The interface name, method names, parameters, and exceptions are derived from the WSDL document. Figure 21-2 shows the mapping between the `<portType>` and `<message>` definitions and the endpoint interface.

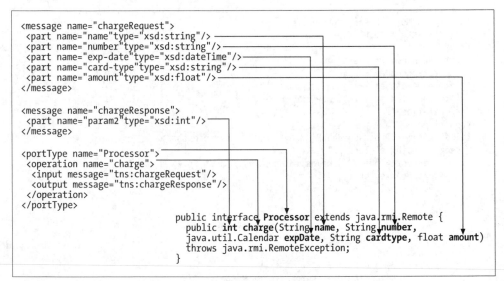

Figure 21-2. Mapping a WSDL <portType> to a JAX-RPC endpoint interface

The name of the endpoint interface comes from the name of the `<portType>`, which is Processor. The methods defined by the endpoint interface are derived from the `<operation>` elements declared by the WSDL `<portType>`. In this case, there is one `<operation>` element, which maps a single method: `charge()`. The parameters of the `charge()` method are derived from the `<operation>` element's input message. For each `<part>` element of the input message, there will be a corresponding parameter in the `charge()` method. The output message, in this case, declares a single `<part>` element, which maps to the return type of the `charge()` method.

The JAX-RPC specification defines an exact mapping between many of the XML Schema built-in types and Java. This is how the XML Schema types declared by the WSDL `<part>` elements are mapped to the parameters and the return type of an endpoint method. Table 21-1 shows the mapping between XML Schema built-in types and Java primitives and classes.

Table 21-1. XML Schema built-in types and their corresponding Java types

XML Schema built-in type	Java type
xsd:byte	Byte
xsd:Boolean	Boolean
xsd:short	Short
xsd:int	Int
xsd:long	Long
xsd:float	float
xsd:double	Double
xsd:string	java.lang.String
xsd:dateTime	java.util.Calendar
xsd:integer	java.math.BigInteger
xsd:decimal	java.math.BigDecimal
xsd:QName	java.xml.namespace.QName
xsd:base64Binary	byte []
xsd:hexBinary	byte []

JAX-RPC also maps *nillable* types (types that can be null), based on XML Schema built-in types, to Java primitive wrappers. For example, a nillable xsd:int type would map to a java.lang.Integer type, and a nillable xsd:double would map to a java.lang.Double type.

In addition, JAX-RPC defines a mapping between complex types defined in the WSDL <types> element and Java bean classes.

When a service is deployed, the proxy, which implements the endpoint interface, is generated from the <binding> and <port> definitions. The JAX-RPC proxy translates the messaging style specified by the <binding> definition into a marshaling algorithm for converting method calls made on the endpoint stub into SOAP request and reply messages. Charge-It's WSDL document defines the following <binding> element:

```
<binding name="ProcessorSoapBinding" type="tns:Processor">
  <soap:binding style="rpc"
      transport="http://schemas.xmlsoap.org/soap/http"/>
  <operation name="charge">
    <soap:operation soapAction="" style="rpc"/>
    <input>
      <soap:body use="literal"
          namespace="http://charge-it.com/Processor"/>
    </input>
    <output>
      <soap:body use="literal"
          namespace="http://charge-it.com/Processor"/>
    </output>
```

```
          </operation>
        </binding>
```

According to the <binding> element, the web service employs RPC/Literal SOAP 1.1 messages with a request-response-style operation. The proxy is responsible for converting method calls made on the endpoint interface into SOAP messages that are sent to the web service. It's also responsible for converting SOAP response messages sent back to the stub into a return value—or, if it's a SOAP fault message, into an exception thrown by the endpoint method.

The proxy also takes into consideration the <port> definition, which declares the Internet address where the web service is located. The Charge-It WSDL document defines the following <port> element:

```
<service name="ProcessorService">

    <port name="ProcessorPort" binding="tns:ProcessorSoapBinding">
        <soap:address
         location="http://www.charge-it.com/ProcessorService"/>
    </port>
</service>
```

The address attribute (*http://www.charge-it.com/ProcessorService*) specifies the URL with which the proxy will exchange SOAP messages. Figure 21-1, shown earlier, illustrates how the processor endpoint interface and stub are used to access the Charge-It credit card processing web service.

In addition to the service endpoint interface, the JAX-RPC compiler also creates a service interface, which is used to get an instance of the proxy at runtime. The service interface is based on the <service> element of the WSDL document. Here's the definition of the ProcessorService interface generated from Charge-It's WSDL document:

```
package com.charge_it;

public interface ProcessorService extends javax.xml.rpc.Service {
    public com.charge_it.Processor getProcessorPort( )
        throws javax.xml.rpc.ServiceException;
    public java.lang.String getProcessorPortAddress( );
    public com.charge_it.Processor getProcessorPort(java.net.URL portAddress)
        throws javax.xml.rpc.ServiceException;
}
```

The getProcessorPort() method returns a proxy that is ready to invoke methods on the web service. The getProcessPortAddress() method returns the URL that the proxy accesses by default. The getProcessorPort(URL) method allows you to create an endpoint stub that accesses a different URL than the default defined in the WSDL document.

Calling a Service from an EJB

As with other resources (JDBC, JMS, and so on), the generated JAX-RPC service can be injected directly into a field or *setter* method of the bean class. It can also be bound to a specific namespace in the JNDI ENC at deployment time. The service can then obtain the proxy, as described in the previous section.

To illustrate how EJBs use a service, we will modify the bookPassage() method of a fictitious TravelAgentBean. The TravelAgent EJB will use Charge-It's Processor web service. We could look up the service directly using JNDI, but injection will save us the extra step. The following code shows the changes to the TravelAgentBean class:

```
package com.titan.travelagent;
import com.charge_it.Processor;
import com.charge_it.ProcessorService;
...

@Stateful
public class TravelAgentBean implements TravelAgentRemote {
    @PersistenceContext(unitName="titanDB")
    private EntityManager em;

    @PersistenceContext EntityManager em;

    Customer customer;
    Cruise cruise;
    private Cabin cabin;

    private ProcessorService processorService;
    ...
    public TicketDO bookPassage(CreditCardDO card, double price)
        throws IncompleteConversationalState {

        if (customer == null || cruise == null || cabin == null)
        {
            throw new IncompleteConversationalState( );
        }
        try {
            Reservation reservation = new Reservation(
                customer, cruise, cabin, price, new Date( ));

            em.persist(reservation);

            String customerName = customer.getFirstName( )+" "+
                                  customer.getLastName( );
            java.util.Calendar expDate = new Calendar(card.date);
            Processor processor = processorService.getProcessorPort( );
            processor.charge(customerName, card.number,
                             expDate, card.type, price);
            TicketDO ticket = new TicketDO(customer, cruise, cabin, price);
            return ticket;
        } catch(Exception e) {
            throw new EJBException(e);
```

```
        }
    }
    ...
}
```

`ProcessorService` is injected directly into the `processorService` field on the bean class. From this field, we can obtain the proxy object that implements the service endpoint interface. You will see in the next section how to configure an XML deployment descriptor to populate the field.

Invoking this proxy within a transactional business process such as `bookPassage()` presents a few problems of which you should be aware. If the proxy encounters a networking problem or SOAP processing error, it throws a `RemoteException`, which is caught and rethrown as an `EJBException`, causing the entire transaction to roll back. However, if an error occurs after the web service has executed but before the EJB method successfully returns, a partial rollback occurs; the reservation is rolled back, but the charge made using the Charge-It web service is not. *Invocations on web services do not participate in the caller's transaction context!*

The <service-ref> Deployment Element

We still need to specify where and how this web service reference is defined. To do this we need a `<service-ref>` element in our EJB deployment descriptor. This XML element binds a JAX-RPC service to the JNDI ENC and injects it into the `processorService` field of our bean class. EJB XML is allowed to be a partial deployment descriptor. This means that we do not have to define every single piece of metadata in XML just because we want to inject a web service into our bean class. The partial XML deployment descriptor of the TravelAgent EJB declares a `<service-ref>` element that looks like this:

```xml
<?xml version='1.0' encoding='UTF-8' ?>
<ejb-jar
 xmlns="http://java.sun.com/xml/ns/j2ee"
 xmlns:xsi=http://www.w3.org/2001/XMLSchema-instance
 xmlns:chargeIt="http://charge-it.com/Processor"
 xsi:schemaLocation="http://java.sun.com/xml/ns/j2ee
                     http://java.sun.com/xml/ns/j2ee/ejb-jar_3_1.xsd"
 version="3.1">
  <enterprise-beans>
    <session>
      <ejb-name>TravelAgentEJB</ejb-name>
      <service-ref>
        <service-ref-name>service/ChargeItProcessorService</service-ref-name>
        <service-interface>com.charge_it.ProcessorService</service-interface>
        <wsdl-file>META-INF/wsdl/ChargeItProcessor.wsdl</wsdl-file>
        <jaxrpc-mapping-file>META-INF/mapping.xml</jaxrpc-mapping-file>
        <service-qname>chargeIt:ProcessorService</service-qname>
        <mapped-name>webservices/ProcessorService</mapped-name>
    <injection-target>
      <injection-target-class>
              com.titan.travelagent.TravelAgentBean</injection-target-class>
          <injection-target-name>processorService </ injection-target-name>
```

```
      </injection-target>
      </service-ref>
      </session>
    </enterprise-beans>
  </ejb-jar>
```

The `<service-ref-name>` element declares the name of the JAX-RPC service in the JNDI ENC—it's always relative to the `java:comp/env` context. The `<service-interface>` element identifies the JAX-RPC service interface, which is implemented by a JAX-RPC service object. The `<wsdl-file>` identifies the location of the WSDL document that describes the Charge-It web service. The WSDL document must be packaged in the same EJB-JAR file as the EJB that is making the web service call, whether you are using a `<service-ref>` element or an annotation to inject your web service. The path is always relative to the root of the EJB-JAR file. In this case, a copy of the Charge-It WSDL document, *ChargeItProcessor.wsdl*, is stored in the *META-INF* directory of the EJB-JAR file. The `<jaxrpc-mapping-file>` element identifies the location of the JAX-RPC mapping file relative to the root of the EJB-JAR file. In this case, it's also located in the *META-INF* directory. (The *JAX-RPC mapping file* is an additional deployment file that helps the EJB container to understand the mapping between the WSDL document and the service endpoint interfaces.) The `<service-qname>` element identifies the fully qualified XML name of the WSDL `<service>` definition to which this reference pertains. The qualified service name is relative to the WSDL document identified by the `<wsdl-file>` element. The `<mapped-named>` element is a vendor-specific identifier that can map to a global registry of the application server (usually the global JNDI). The `<injection-target>` element is used to tell the EJB container to inject an instance of `ProcessorService` into the `processorService` field of the `TravelAgentBean` class. You can find more information about using `<injection-target>` in Chapter 16.

The JAX-RPC Mapping File

A JAX-RPC service or client in a Java EE environment must have a JAX-RPC mapping file. The mapping file format is defined in the "Implementing Enterprise Web Services" (JSR-109) specification. There are many possible ways to map or bind Java to WSDL, and WSDL to Java. This can cause portability problems between different JAX-RPC implementations, since they may bind Java and WSDL in different ways. The JAX-RPC mapping file addresses this problem by configuring the specific details for how binding is supposed to occur. This allows for a service and a client to be portable across different Java EE implementations. The mapping file for the *ChargeItProcessor.wsdl* document follows:

```
    <?xml version='1.0' encoding='UTF-8' ?>
    <java-wsdl-mapping
      xmlns="http://java.sun.com/xml/ns/j2ee"
      xmlns:chargeIt="http://charge-it.com/Processor"
      xmlns:xsi="http://www.w3.org/2001/XMLSchema-instance"
      xmlns:xsd="http://www.w3.org/2001/XMLSchema"
```

```
xsi:schemaLocation="http://java.sun.com/xml/ns/j2ee
        http://www.ibm.com/webservices/xsd/j2ee_jaxrpc_mapping_1_1.xsd"
version="1.1">

<package-mapping>
 <package-type>com.charge_it</package-type>
 <namespaceURI>http://charge-it.com/Processor</namespaceURI>
</package-mapping>
<service-interface-mapping>
  <service-interface>com.charge_it.ProcessorService</service-interface>
  <wsdl-service-name>chargeIt:ProcessorService</wsdl-service-name>
  <port-mapping>
    <port-name>chargeIt:ProcessorPort</port-name>
    <java-port-name>ProcessorPort</java-port-name>
  </port-mapping>
</service-interface-mapping>
<service-endpoint-interface-mapping>
  <service-endpoint-interface>com.charge_it.Processor
  </service-endpoint-interface>
  <wsdl-port-type>chargeIt:Processor</wsdl-port-type>
  <wsdl-binding>chargeIt:ProcessorSoapBinding</wsdl-binding>
  <service-endpoint-method-mapping>
    <java-method-name>charge</java-method-name>
    <wsdl-operation>chargeIt:charge</wsdl-operation>
    <method-param-parts-mapping>
      <param-position>0</param-position>
      <param-type>java.lang.String</param-type>
      <wsdl-message-mapping>
        <wsdl-message>chargeIt:chargeRequest</wsdl-message>
        <wsdl-message-part-name>name</wsdl-message-part-name>
        <parameter-mode>IN</parameter-mode>
      </wsdl-message-mapping>
    </method-param-parts-mapping>
    <method-param-parts-mapping>
      <param-position>1</param-position>
      <param-type>java.lang.String</param-type>
      <wsdl-message-mapping>
        <wsdl-message>chargeIt:chargeRequest</wsdl-message>
        <wsdl-message-part-name>number</wsdl-message-part-name>
        <parameter-mode>IN</parameter-mode>
      </wsdl-message-mapping>
    </method-param-parts-mapping>
    <method-param-parts-mapping>
      <param-position>2</param-position>
      <param-type>java.util.Calendar</param-type>
      <wsdl-message-mapping>
        <wsdl-message>chargeIt:chargeRequest</wsdl-message>
        <wsdl-message-part-name>exp-date</wsdl-message-part-name>
        <parameter-mode>IN</parameter-mode>
      </wsdl-message-mapping>
    </method-param-parts-mapping>
    <method-param-parts-mapping>
      <param-position>3</param-position>
      <param-type>java.lang.String</param-type>
      <wsdl-message-mapping>
```

```
        <wsdl-message>chargeIt:chargeRequest</wsdl-message>
        <wsdl-message-part-name>card-type</wsdl-message-part-name>
        <parameter-mode>IN</parameter-mode>
      </wsdl-message-mapping>
    </method-param-parts-mapping>
    <method-param-parts-mapping>
      <param-position>4</param-position>
      <param-type>float</param-type>
      <wsdl-message-mapping>
        <wsdl-message>chargeIt:chargeRequest</wsdl-message>
        <wsdl-message-part-name>amount</wsdl-message-part-name>
        <parameter-mode>IN</parameter-mode>
      </wsdl-message-mapping>
    </method-param-parts-mapping>
    <wsdl-return-value-mapping>
      <method-return-value>int</method-return-value>
      <wsdl-message>chargeIt:chargeResponse</wsdl-message>
      <wsdl-message-part-name>return</wsdl-message-part-name>
    </wsdl-return-value-mapping>
    </service-endpoint-method-mapping>
  </service-endpoint-interface-mapping>
</java-wsdl-mapping>
```

As you can see, the service interface is mapped to a WSDL `<service>` element, the endpoint interface is mapped to a WSDL `<portType>`, each method is mapped to a WSDL `<operation>`, and every parameter and return value is mapped to a specific WSDL `<part>` of a specific WSDL `<message>` definition.

The complete JAX-RPC mapping file is too complicated to discuss in detail. Don't worry, though; you normally don't write these by hand. A Java EE implementation will provide tools to generate these files for you. Also, the JAX-RPC mapping file is no longer used in JAX-WS. We will discuss how it handles binding in the section "Using JAX-WS" on page 396.

Defining a Web Service with JAX-RPC

Java EE provides two different programming models for defining a JAX-RPC web service: the web container model (or servlet model) and the EJB container model. Given that this book is about EJB 3.1, we assume you are more interested in the EJB model.

The core component in the EJB model is called an *EJB endpoint*. An EJB endpoint is a stateless session bean that is exposed as a web service. In addition to the remote and local component interfaces, there is another component interface, called the *service endpoint interface*. The service endpoint interface defines the abstract web services contract that the EJB endpoint provides to a web services client.

Because an EJB endpoint is simply a SOAP-accessible stateless session bean, it has the same advantages as other EJBs. An EJB endpoint runs in the same EJB container that automatically manages transactions and security, and provides access to other EJBs and resources via injection or the JNDI ENC.

The WSDL Document

Every EJB endpoint must have a WSDL document that describes the web service. You can create this document by hand, or you can use the tools provided by your Java EE vendor to generate it. The <portType> declared by the WSDL document must be aligned with the endpoint interface of the web service. In other words, the mapping between the WSDL <portType> and the endpoint interface must be correct according to the JAX-RPC specification. One way to ensure this is to create the WSDL document first, and then use it to generate the service endpoint interface:

```
<?xml version="1.0"?>
<definitions name="TravelAgent"
    xmlns="http://schemas.xmlsoap.org/wsdl/"
    xmlns:soap="http://schemas.xmlsoap.org/wsdl/soap/"
    xmlns:xsd="http://www.w3.org/2001/XMLSchema"
    xmlns:titan="http://www.titan.com/TravelAgent"
    targetNamespace="http://www.titan.com/TravelAgent">

<!-- message elements describe the parameters and return values -->
<message name="RequestMessage">
    <part name="cruiseId"   type="xsd:int" />
    <part name="cabinId"    type="xsd:int" />
    <part name="customerId" type="xsd:int" />
    <part name="price"      type="xsd:double" />
</message>
<message name="ResponseMessage">
    <part name="reservationId" type="xsd:string" />
</message>

<!-- portType element describes the abstract interface of a web service -->
<portType name="TravelAgentEndpoint">
  <operation name="makeReservation">
     <input message="titan:RequestMessage"/>
     <output message="titan:ResponseMessage"/>
  </operation>
</portType>

<!-- binding element tells us which protocols and encoding styles are used -->
<binding name="TravelAgentBinding" type="titan:TravelAgentEndpoint">
    <soap:binding style="rpc"
                  transport="http://schemas.xmlsoap.org/soap/http"/>
    <operation name="makeReservation">
      <soap:operation soapAction="" />
      <input>
        <soap:body use="literal"
               namespace="http://www.titan.com/TravelAgent"/>
      </input>
      <output>
        <soap:body use="literal"
               namespace="http://www.titan.com/TravelAgent"/>
      </output>
    </operation>
</binding>
```

```
<!-- service element tells us the Internet address of a web service -->
<service name="TravelAgentService">
  <port name="TravelAgentPort" binding="titan:TravelAgentBinding">
     <soap:address location="http://www.titan.com/webservices/TravelAgent" />
  </port>
</service>

</definitions>
```

The Service Endpoint Interface

The process for generating a service endpoint interface for an EJB endpoint is identical to the process we used to generate a JAX-RPC client. The JAX-RPC compiler generates it from the `<portType>` and `<message>` definitions (and `<types>`, if present). The resulting interface looks like the following:

```
package com.titan.webservice;

public interface TravelAgentEndpoint extends java.rmi.Remote {
    public java.lang.String makeReservation(int cruiseId, int cabinId,
                                    int customerId, double price)
                    throws java.rmi.RemoteException;
}
```

Alternatively, you can start from Java by writing the service endpoint interface by hand. You can then generate the WSDL and the JAX-RPC mapping file from this interface. Refer to Table 21-1, earlier in this chapter, to determine the schema types that will be mapped from the Java parameters in each method.

The Stateless Bean Class

The bean class defined for the TravelAgent endpoint must implement the methods defined by the endpoint interface. As with remote and local interfaces, a stateless bean class can implement the service endpoint interface directly. Here's the new definition for the TravelAgentBean class:

```
package com.titan.webservice;
import com.titan.domain.*;
import com.titan.cabin.*;
import com.titan.processpayment.*;
import javax.ejb.EJBException;
import java.util.Date;
import java.util.Calendar;
import javax.persistence.*;

@Stateless
public class TravelAgentBean implements TravelAgentEndpoint {
    @PersistenceContext EntityManager em;

    @EJB ProcessPaymentLocal process;

    public String makeReservation(int cruiseId, int cabinId,
```

```
                              int customerId, double price){
        try {
            Cruise cruise = em.find(Cruise.class, cruiseId);
            Cabin cabin = em.find(Cabin.class, cabinId);
            Customer customer = em.find(Customer.class, customerId);
            CreditCardDO card = this.getCreditCard(customer);

            Reservation reservation = new Reservation(
                        customer, cruise, cabin, price, new Date( ));
            process.byCredit(customer, card, price);

            return reservation.getId( );

        } catch(Exception e) {
            throw new EJBException(e);
        }
    }

    public CreditCardDO getCreditCard(Customer cust) throws Exception{
        CreditCard card = customer.getCreditCard( );
        return new CreditCardDO(card.getNumber(),card.getExpirationDate( ),
                            card.getCreditOrganization( ));
    }
}
```

The `TravelAgentBean` class is not that different from the TravelAgent EJB developed
earlier in this chapter (the version that uses the Charge-It credit card processing web
service). The primary differences are that it responds to web service calls rather than
remote or local calls, and it is a stateless session bean rather than a stateful session bean.

The Deployment Files

The TravelAgent endpoint requires three deployment files: a WSDL file, a JAX-RPC
mapping file, and a *webservices.xml* file. In this section, we will create these files manually, although you would typically use the tools provided by your Java EE implementation to assist in this process.

The WSDL file

The WSDL file used to represent the endpoint interface must be packaged with the EJB
endpoint. Normally, the WSDL document is placed in the *META-INF* directory of the
JAR file, but it can go anywhere as long as it's in the same JAR file as the EJB endpoint.

The JAX-RPC mapping file

EJB endpoints, like JAX-RPC service references, require you to define a JAX-RPC mapping file. The mapping file can have any name, but it should be descriptive, and the file
type should be XML. It's common to name this file *jaxrpc-mapping.xml* or *travel-
agent_mapping.xml*, or something along those lines. We covered the JAX-RPC mapping
file in "The JAX-RPC Mapping File" on page 389.

The webservices.xml file

The *webservices.xml* file is the baling wire that ties the separate deployment files together. It defines the relationships between the stateless session bean, the WSDL file, and the JAX-RPC mapping file:

```
<?xml version='1.0' encoding='UTF-8' ?>
<webservices
    xmlns="http://java.sun.com/xml/ns/j2ee"
    xmlns:xsi="http://www.w3.org/2001/XMLSchema-instance"
    xmlns:titan="http://www.titan.com/TravelAgent"
    xsi:schemaLocation="http://java.sun.com/xml/ns/j2ee
                http://www.ibm.com/webservices/xsd/j2ee_web_services_1_1.xsd"
    version="1.1">

    <webservice-description>
        <webservice-description-name>TravelAgentService
        </webservice-description-name>
        <wsdl-file>META-INF/travelagent.wsdl</wsdl-file>
        <jaxrpc-mapping-file>/META-INF/travelagent_mapping.xml
        </jaxrpc-mapping-file>
        <port-component>
            <port-component-name>TravelAgentEndpoint</port-component-name>
            <wsdl-port>titan:TravelAgentPort</wsdl-port>
            <service-endpoint-interface>
                com.titan.webservice.TravelAgentEndpoint
            </service-endpoint-interface>
            <service-impl-bean>
                <ejb-link>TravelAgentBean</ejb-link>
            </service-impl-bean>
        </port-component>
    </webservice-description>
</webservices>
```

The `<webservice-description>` element describes an EJB endpoint; there may be one or more of these elements in a single *webservices.xml* file.* `<webservice-description-name>` is a unique name assigned to the web services description. It can be anything you like. The `<wsdl-file>` element points to the WSDL document of the EJB endpoint. Each EJB endpoint has exactly one WSDL document, which is usually located in the *META-INF* directory of the EJB-JAR file. When the EJB endpoint is deployed, your deployment tool will probably provide you with the option of copying the WSDL document to some type of public URL or registry so that others can discover the web service. The `<jaxrpc-mapping-file>` element indicates the location of the JAX-RPC mapping file that is associated with the EJB endpoint and the WSDL document. It, too, is usually located in the *META-INF* directory of the EJB-JAR file.

The `<port-component>` element maps a stateless session bean declared in the *ejb-jar.xml* file to a specific `<port>` in the WSDL document. `<port-component-name>` is the

---

* The `<webservice-description>` element can also describe a JAX-RPC service endpoint, which is a servlet-based web service that is outside the scope of this book.

logical name you assign the EJB endpoint. It can be anything. The `<wsdl-port>` element maps the EJB endpoint deployment information to a specific WSDL `<port>` element in the WSDL document. `<service-endpoint-interface>` is the fully qualified name of the endpoint interface; it must be the same interface declared by the `<service-endpoint>` element for the EJB in the *ejb-jar.xml* file. `<service-impl-bean>` and its `<ejb-link>` element link the `<port-component>` to a specific EJB. The value of `<ejb-link>` must match the value of the EJB name, which is `TravelAgentBean` in this example.

Using JAX-WS

The WSDL, JAX-RPC mapping, and *webservices.xml* files sure are a lot of things to define just to expose your stateless EJB as a web service. It should be easier to publish an EJB as a web service—and it is. One of the goals of the JAX-WS specification was to make the JAX-RPC API and deployment model easier to use. To this end, the specification provides an extensive set of annotations, most of which are based on JSR-181 ("Web Services Metadata for the Java Platform"). These annotations make it much simpler to define a web service. Keeping with the spirit of EJB 3.1, all JAX-WS annotations have reasonable defaults. In the following example, it takes nothing more than adding two annotations to transform a stateless EJB into a web service:

```
package com.titan.webservice;

import javax.ejb.Stateless;
import javax.jws.WebService;
import javax.jws.WebMethod;

@Stateless
@WebService
public class TravelAgentBean
{
    @WebMethod
    public String makeReservation(int cruiseId, int cabinId,
                                  int customerId, double price) {
    ...
    }
}
```

The @WebService Annotation

The main annotation for defining a web service is `@javax.jws.WebService`. This annotation must be placed on the stateless session bean implementation class in order to expose it as a web service:

```
package javax.jws;

@Target({TYPE}) @Retention(value=RetentionPolicy.RUNTIME)
public @interface WebService {
```

```
    String name( ) default "";
    String targetNamespace( ) default "";
    String serviceName( ) default "";
    String wsdlLocation( ) default "";
    String portName( ) default "";
    String endpointInterface( ) default "";
}
```

The name() attribute is the name of the web service, and it is used as the name of the
portType when mapped to WSDL. This defaults to the short name of the Java class or
Java interface to which you are applying it. The targetNamespace() attribute specifies
the XML namespace used for the WSDL and XML elements that are generated from
this annotation. The default value is generated from the package name of the annotated
type. The wsdlLocation() attribute defines the URL of the WSDL document that represents this web service. You need this attribute only if you are mapping your service
to a preexisting WSDL document. The endpointInterface() attribute is used to externalize the contract of the web service by specifying that contract in the form of a Java
interface. We'll talk more about this option later. The portName() attribute specifies
which WSDL port you will use. In most cases, you can use the default values for each
of these attributes.

The @WebMethod Annotation

If a stateless session bean is annotated with @java.jws.WebService, and it contains no
methods that are annotated with @javax.jws.WebMethod, then all methods are made
available to the web service. Otherwise, only those methods that are annotated with
@javax.jws.WebMethod will be made available. This is an important feature because web
services tend to be coarser-grained than a standard EJB. Also, it is generally considered
good design practice to reduce dependencies between modules. The @javax.jws.Web
Method annotation also offers attributes for customizing the generated WSDL:

```
package javax.jws;

@Target({ElementType.METHOD}) @Retention(value = RetentionPolicy.RUNTIME)
public @interface WebMethod
{
    String operationName( ) default "";
    String action( ) default "";
}
```

The operationName() attribute is used to define the WSDL operation that the annotated
method implements. If it is not specified, the literal Java method name is used. The
action() attribute is used to set the SOAPAction hint that corresponds with this operation. This hint allows a service endpoint to determine the destination by simply looking
at the SOAPAction HTTP header instead of analyzing the contents of the SOAP message
body. This has the potential for a slight performance increase, although it depends on
the Java EE implementation you are using.

The following example demonstrates setting the operation name for a Java method:

```
package com.titan.webservice;

import javax.ejb.Stateless;
import javax.jws.WebService;
import javax.jws.WebMethod;

@Stateless
@WebService(name = "TravelAgent")
public class TravelAgentBean
{
    @WebMethod(operationName = "Reserve")
    public String makeReservation(int cruiseId, int cabinId,
                                  int customerId, double price) {

    ...
    }
}
```

This will result in the following WSDL portType definition:

```
<portType name="TravelAgent">
    <operation name="Reserve">
    ...
    </operation>
</portType>
```

The @SOAPBinding Annotation

In Chapter 20, we discussed the web services styles supported in EJB 3.1. You can customize the web services style that the EJB endpoint uses with the @javax.jws.soap.SOAPBinding annotation:

```
@Target(value = {ElementType.TYPE}) @Retention(value = RetentionPolicy.RUNTIME)
public @interface SOAPBinding {
    public enum Style {DOCUMENT, RPC};
    public enum Use {LITERAL,
 ENCODED};

    public enum ParameterStyle {BARE, WRAPPED}

    Style style( ) default Style.DOCUMENT;
    Use use( ) default Use.LITERAL;
    ParameterStyle parameterStyle( ) default ParameterStyle.WRAPPED;
}
```

Table 21-2 describes the supported attribute value combinations. It is important to note that the use() attribute must always be set to LITERAL. ENCODED refers to SOAP encoding, which has been disallowed by the WS-I Basic Profile 1.1. Furthermore, an EJB implementation is not required to support it. If this annotation is not specified, the default style is Document/Literal Wrapped.

Table 21-2. @SOAPBinding behavior

Style	Use	Parameter style	Description
RPC	LITERAL	N/A	Each parameter is mapped to a wsdl:part, which is mapped to a schema type definition.
DOCUMENT	LITERAL	BARE	Only one parameter is allowed, and that parameter is mapped to a root schema element that fully defines the content of the message.
DOCUMENT	LITERAL	WRAPPED	All parameters are wrapped in a root schema element with the same name as the operation to which they belong.

The @WebParam Annotation

The @javax.jws.WebParam annotation allows you to control the WSDL that is generated for a Java method annotated with @javax.jws.WebMethod:

```
package javax.jws;

@Target({PARAMETER})@Retention(value=RetentionPolicy.RUNTIME)
public @interface WebParam {
    public enum Mode {IN, OUT, INOUT};
    String name( ) default "";
    String targetNamespace( ) default "";
    Mode mode( ) default Mode.IN;
    boolean header( ) default false;
}
```

If the style is RPC/Literal, the name() attribute sets the wsdl:part name. Otherwise, it sets the XML local name of the element within the schema document that corresponds to the annotated parameter. If it is not specified, the default value is computed in the form of argN, where N is the 0-based position of the parameter in the method signature. The targetNamespace() attribute is used only if the style is Document/Literal or the parameter is a header. It sets the targetNamespace of the schema definition that contains the element. The header() attribute is used to indicate that the parameter should be put in a SOAP header rather than in the SOAP body. The mode() attribute is used to indicate whether the parameter is to be used for input, output, or both. Due to Java semantics, if a parameter is used for output, it must be wrapped using a special holder type. The following example shows the use of a JAX-WS holder on an RPC-style service:

```
@WebMethod(operationName = "CheckStatus")
public int checkStatus(
    @WebParam(name = "ReservationID")
    String reservationId,
    @WebParam(name = "CustomerID", mode = WebParam.Mode.OUT)
    javax.xml.ws.Holder<Integer> customerId
){
    ...
    // return customer id and status
    customerId.value = getCustomerId(reservationId);
```

```
        return status;
    }
```

This produces the following WSDL:

```
<message name="CheckStatus">
    <part name="ReservationID" type="xsd:string"/>
</message>
<message name="CheckStatusResponse">
    <part name="return" type="xsd:int"/>
    <part name="CustomerID" type="xsd:int"/>
</message>
<portType name="TravelAgent">
    <operation name="CheckStatus" parameterOrder="ReservationID CustomerID">
        <input message="tns:CheckStatus"/>
        <output message="tns:CheckStatusResponse"/>
    </operation>
</portType>
```

The @WebResult Annotation

This @javax.jws.WebResult annotation provides the same, although somewhat reduced, functionality for return values that @javax.jws.WebParam provides for method parameters:

```
@Target(value = {ElementType.METHOD}) @Retention(value = RetentionPolicy.RUNTIME)
public @interface WebResult
{
    String name( ) default "";
    String targetNamespace( ) default "";
}
```

The attributes behave the same as they do in @javax.jws.WebParam, with the exception of the default value for name(). If the name() attribute is not specified, and the style is Document/Literal bare, then its value will be the WSDL operation name concatenated with "Response". For all other styles, the default is "return". The following example demonstrates the use of this annotation:

```
package com.titan.webservice;

import javax.ejb.Stateless;
import javax.jws.WebService;
import javax.jws.WebMethod;
import javax.jws.WebResult;


@Stateless
@WebService(name = "TravelAgent")
public class TravelAgentBean
{
    @WebMethod(operationName = "Reserve")
    @WebResult(name = "ReservationID")
    public String makeReservation(int cruiseId, int cabinId,
                                  int customerId, double price) {
```

```
        ...
      }
    }
```

This produces the following relevant WSDL sections:

```xml
<xs:element name="ReserveResponse" type="ReserveResponse"/>
<xs:complexType name="ReserveResponse">
  <xs:sequence>
      <xs:element name="ReservationID" type="xs:string" nillable="true"/>
  </xs:sequence>
</xs:complexType>
...
<message name="ReserveResponse">
    <part name="parameters" element="tns:ReserveResponse"/>
</message>
...
<portType name="TravelAgent">
    <operation name="Reserve">
       <input message="tns:Reserve"/>
       <output message="tns:ReserveResponse"/>
    </operation>
</portType>
```

The @OneWay Annotation

The @javax.jws.OneWay annotation is used to declare that the corresponding web services operation will return an empty message. This allows the server and the client to optimize the operation by performing the method invocation asynchronously. Whether the method is actually executed asynchronously is determined by the Java EE implementation. The resulting WSDL for a one-way operation will not have an <output> tag.

Separating the Web Services Contract

Up to this point, we have been defining everything within the EJB implementation class. An alternative approach is to use the endpointInterface() attribute of the @javax.jws.WebService annotation. The web services contract can then be maintained in an external Java interface. With this methodology, the *only required annotation* on the endpoint interface is @javax.jws.WebService. All other annotations are optional. Unlike the previous approach of keeping everything within the EJB implementation, *all methods in the interface are exposed* in the web service. Technically, the EJB implementation does not have to implement this interface, although there is no reason not to. We can modify the TravelAgentBean example to utilize this approach by first extracting the desired web methods:

```java
package com.titan.webservice;

import javax.jws.WebService;

@WebService
public interface TravelAgentEndpoint{
```

```
    public java.lang.String makeReservation(int cruiseId, int cabinId,
                                            int customerId, double price);
}
```

The implementation bean then references the endpoint interface from the
@javax.jws.WebService annotation:

```
package com.titan.webservice;

import javax.jws.WebService;

@WebService(endpointInterface = "com.titan.webservice.TravelAgentEndpoint")
public class TravelAgentBean implements TravelAgentEndpoint {
...
}
```

The Service Class

Similar to the JAX-RPC client methodology we discussed earlier, JAX-WS contains a
service class that the JAX-WS client uses to communicate with a web service. The
service class must extend javax.xml.ws.Service and provide a method to retrieve the
service endpoint interface. It should also use the @javax.xml.ws.WebServiceClient
annotation to define the name, namespace, and WSDL location of the service. The
@javax.xml.ws.WebEndpoint annotation is necessary to resolve for which WSDL
<port> to return a proxy. The following is an example Service class that communicates
with the Charge-It web service:

```
package com.charge_it;

import javax.xml.ws.WebServiceClient;
import javax.xml.ws.WebEndpoint;

@WebServiceClient(name="ProcessorService",
                  targetNamespace="http://charge-it.com/Processor"
                  wsdlLocation="http://charge-it.com/Processor?wsdl")
public class ProcessorService extends javax.xml.ws.Service {
    public ProcessorService( ) {
        super(new URL("http://charge-it.com/Processor?wsdl"),
            new QName("http://charge-it.com/Processor", "ProcessorService"));
    }

    public ProcessorService(String wsdlLocation, QName serviceName) {
        super(wsdlLocation, serviceName);
    }

    @WebEndpoint(name = "ProcessorPort")
    public Processor getProcessorPort( ) {
        return (Processor)
            super.getPort(
                new QName("http://charge-it.com/Processor", "ProcessorPort"),
                Processor.class);
    }
}
```

The Service Endpoint Interface

We discussed a JAX-WS service endpoint interface in "Separating the Web Services Contract" on page 401. Our client can use the same interface. This means that the client uses all of the annotations we defined for the server side. However, remember that you are not limited to just talking to JAX-WS web services. A web service can be running on *any platform* in *any language*. So, in those scenarios, you will not reuse the service endpoint interface but will instead use a tool to generate one for you. However, we will go ahead and do this by hand:

```
package com.charge_it;

import javax.jws.WebService;
import javax.jws.soap.SOAPBinding;

@WebService
@SOAPBinding(style = SOAPBinding.Style.RPC)
public interface Processor{
    public int charge(String name, String number, java.util.Calendar expDate,
                      String cardType, float amount);
}
```

The @WebServiceRef Annotation

In addition to the <service-ref> XML tag in *ejb-jar.xml*, a JAX-WS client can use the @javax.xml.ws.WebServiceRef annotation to reference either a service interface or a service endpoint interface directly:

```
package javax.xml.ws;

@Target({TYPE, METHOD, FIELD}) @Retention(RUNTIME)
public @interface WebServiceRef {
    String name( ) default "";
    String wsdlLocation( ) default "";
    Class type default Object.class;
    Class value default Object.class;
    String mappedName( ) default "";
};
```

The name() attribute defines how the web service will be bound into the JNDI ENC. The wsdlLocation() attribute specifies the URL where the WSDL file lives in the EJB-JAR. HTTP URLs are allowed. If not specified, the value for this attribute will be pulled from the service class, provided it is annotated with the @javax.xml.ws.WebService Client annotation.

The mappedName() attribute is a vendor-specific global identifier for the web service. Consult your vendor documentation to determine whether you need this attribute.

The type() and value() attributes are used to determine whether to inject a service class or service endpoint interface into a field or property. In order to inject a service endpoint interface, value() must be set to the service interface. The type() attribute can then refer to the service endpoint interface that will be injected. This does not have to be specified if the container can infer that information from the field type:

```
// Injected SEI, inferred from type
@WebServiceRef(ProcessorService.class)
private Processor endpoint;
```

In order to inject a service interface, both the **value()** and **type()** attributes can be set to the service interface class; otherwise, it can be inferred from the type:

```
// Inject Service, inferred from type
@WebServiceRef
private ProcessorService service;
```

Let's modify our TravelAgent EJB bean class to use this annotation:

```
package com.titan.travelagent;
import com.charge_it.ProcessorService;
import com.charge_it.Processor;
...

@Stateful
public class TravelAgentBean implements TravelAgentRemote {
    @PersistenceContext(unitName="titanDB")
    private EntityManager em;

    @PersistenceContext EntityManager em;

    Customer customer;
    Cruise cruise;
    private Cabin cabin;

    @WebServiceRef(ProcessorService.class)
    Processor processor;
      ...
    public TicketDO bookPassage(CreditCardDO card, double price)
        throws IncompleteConversationalState {

        if (customer == null || cruise == null || cabin == null)
        {
            throw new IncompleteConversationalState( );
        }
        try {
            Reservation reservation = new Reservation(
                customer, cruise, cabin, price, new Date( ));

            em.persist(reservation);

            String customerName = customer.getFirstName( )+" "+
                                    customer.getLastName( );
            java.util.Calendar expDate = new Calendar(card.date);
            processor.charge(customerName, card.number,
                                expDate, card.type, price);
            TicketDO ticket = new TicketDO(customer, cruise, cabin, price);
            return ticket;
        } catch(Exception e) {
```

```
            throw new EJBException(e);
        }
    }
    ...
}
```

In this example, the annotation will cause a dynamic proxy that implements the Processor interface to be injected into the processor field. Because we are injecting a service endpoint interface directly into the field, the `value()` attribute must be employed to specify which JAX-WS service class will be used to create the endpoint.

You can also override attributes of this annotation with the `<service-ref>` tag we covered earlier.

Other Annotations and APIs

JAX-WS also provides a few more annotations for advanced customization, as well as some additional client APIs for invoking services dynamically and supporting some of the latest WS-* specifications. However, this book does not expand on those topics because they would detract from our focus—building Enterprise Java Beans. For more information on them, please see the relevant specifications.

JAXB

The Java Architecture for XML Binding, or JAXB for short, is a framework for mapping XML content to and from Java objects. Mapping is performed in accordance to annotations specified on the relevant Java class. These annotations are either written by hand or alternatively generated from a schema file. Since a custom marshaling engine is created from the annotations, schema parsing is not necessary. Also, the generated engine is reused across multiple requests, which makes it ideal for web services. For these reasons, JAX-WS uses JAXB for all complex type processing.

Following the schema first methodology, we can construct a simple address type:

```
<xs:schema version="1.0" xmlns:xs="http://www.w3.org/2001/XMLSchema" targetName
space="http://titan.com/custom">
  <xs:complexType name="address">
    <xs:sequence>
      <xs:element name="street" type="xs:string" minOccurs="0"/>
      <xs:element name="city" type="xs:string" minOccurs="0"/>
      <xs:element name="zip" type="xs:string" minOccurs="0"/>
    </xs:sequence>
  </xs:complexType>
</xs:schema>
```

This can then be passed to the JAXB *xjc* tool to generate a Java object that represents this custom type:

```
$xjc address.xsd
parsing a schema...
```

```
compiling a schema...
com/titan/custom/Address.java
com/titan/custom/ObjectFactory.java
com/titan/custom/package-info.java
```

The resulting **Address** type looks like a standard JavaBean:

```
@XmlAccessorType(XmlAccessType.FIELD)
@XmlType(name = "address", propOrder = {"street","city","zip"})
public class Address {
    protected String street;
    protected String city;
    protected String zip;

    public String getStreet() {
        return street;
    }
    public void setStreet(String value) {
        this.street = value;
    }
    public String getCity() {
        return city;
    }
    public void setCity(String value) {
        this.city = value;
    }
    public String getZip() {
        return zip;
    }
    public void setZip(String value) {
        this.zip = value;
    }
}
```

The resulting **Address** class can now be modified, or added to any JAX-WS service endpoint as described earlier. The resulting service will use a complex type according to the schema, and the WSDL generated from the service endpoint will include an equivalent schema to the one passed to *xjc*.

```
@WebService
public class TravelAgentEndpoint{
    public java.lang.String makeReservation(int cruiseId, int cabinId,
                                            int customerId, double price,
                                            Address shipTo) {...}
}
```

When passed to a JAX-WS tool, such as the JDK6-provided *wsgen*, the following custom type appears (as expected):

```
<xs:complexType name="address">
  <xs:sequence>
    <xs:element name="city" type="xs:string" minOccurs="0"/>
    <xs:element name="street" type="xs:string" minOccurs="0"/>
    <xs:element name="zip" type="xs:string" minOccurs="0"/>
  </xs:sequence>
</xs:complexType>
```

Taking JAXB Further

The previous examples just demonstrate the basic capabilities of JAXB. The framework has facilities for much more advanced cases, and supports almost all of XML Schema fairly well without customization. There are, however, some limitations. These are mostly caused by the fact that XML Schema supports concepts with no clear mapping to the Java language (e.g., unions, restrictions). In such cases, specialized annotations may need to be added. See the official JAXB specification and/or javadoc for more information on how it addresses these issues.

Conclusion

EJB 3.1 provides a rich number of APIs and tools to map your business logic to modern invocation and remoting technologies, and this includes web services. Web services have evolved during the history of Java EE, and EJB 3.1 has adapted accordingly. Notably, this includes the recent support for JAX-WS and JAXB that support the latest web service technologies, with a major usability improvement over JAX-RPC.

This section is dedicated to the examples of concepts covered in the explanatory chapters of this edition. While EJB Specification addresses concerns in a vendor-independent way, to get code running in a real EJB container requires the use of some vendor-specific hooks for operations like startup and deployment. From this point forward, code may be geared to a particular implementation.

The online companion to this text lives at:

http://community.jboss.org/groups/oreillyejb6th

From this site hosted by the JBoss Community, readers are encouraged to participate in forum discussion, the issue tracker, and article comments in order to further understand EJB concepts in practice.

All examples in this book are LGPL Open-Source software, and these examples serve as a guide to users looking to run the code on their own. The examples will have a lifecycle extending beyond the book's publishing date to account for explanations requested by users, new features, documentation updates and bug fixes.

Building from Source

Prerequisites

Product	Version	Required
JDK (Java Development Kit)	1.6.0+ (but less than 1.7.0)	Yes
Apache Maven	>= 2.0.9	Yes
Git Client		
Eclipse IDE		
m2eclipse	0.10.0	Recommended if using Eclipse
IntelliJ IDEA		

Obtain the Source Using Subversion SCM

Anonymous access

```
$> git clone
git://github.com/jbossejb3/oreilly-ejb-6thedition-book-examples.git
```

Committers

```
$> git clone
git@github.com:jbossejb3/oreilly-ejb-6thedition-book-examples.git
```

Switch into the checked-out location

```
$> cd oreilly-ejb-6thedition-book-examples
```

The above links will pull in the latest (unreleased) updates to the project. If you'd prefer to obtain the latest stable release, grab the most recent version under the **tags** location:

http://github.com/jbossejb3/oreilly-ejb-6thedition-book-examples

The version released for this book is "**1.0.0**", though subsequent releases may have more features, bug fixes, or be updated to use more recently released versions of backing EJB containers.

Build and Test

Build and run tests, installing into the local Maven repository:

```
myLocation $> mvn clean install
```

Notes

- The first build may take some time, as all required dependencies are downloaded from the JBoss Nexus Repository.
- Some projects may require environment-specific setup to fully run all examples; see each project's description page for more info if this is the case.

The Test Harness

To illustrate the pure POJO programming model of EJB, many of the chapters have examples using test which operate outside the scope of an EJB Container. In this setup, we test not real EJBs, but only the business logic contained in instances of regular objects. These are intended to execute quickly without any vendor reliance, and the test setup may manually mock services like injection.

All tests are written using the excellent JUnit Testing Framework (*http://www.junit .org/*), which allows us to code simple classes bolstered with additional annotations to specify things like lifecycle callbacks and test methods. JUnit has become a well-known standard for testing, and it is likely to improve your efficiency as contrasted with manual test setups.

It should be noted that none of the tests rely on JUnit-specific features (just the API), so if you desire to swap in an alternate framework (such as TestNG; *http://testng.org*), this should be possible with a little bit of refactoring. Either way, we recommend the use of some test framework to continue along the theme of writing less plumbing and taking advantage of declarative behaviour whenever possible.

In addition to the underlying test framework, these examples take advantage of two exciting, young projects within the JBoss.org Community, both focused on keeping the task of writing testable integration tests as simple and painfree as possible.

ShrinkWrap

http://jboss.org/shrinkwrap

Skip the Build!

Shrinkwrap provides a simple API to assemble archives like JARs, WARs, and EARs in Java.

Description

Packaging specifications such as Java Archives (JAR) and Enterprise Archives (EAR) are standard mechanisms for declaring a collection of Classes and resources into one unit. Often these are intended to be run directly or deployed into a web or application server. Archives carry with them implicit metadata regarding their structure, from which concerns like ClassLoading scope and manifest parameters may be inferred.

However useful, archives typically require the addition of a build step within the development lifecycle, either via a script or extra tool. The ShrinkWrap project provides a simple API to programmatically assemble archives in code, optionally allowing for export into ZIP or Exploded File formats. This makes it very fast to prototype "virtual" archives from resources scattered about the classpath, the filesystem, or remote URLs.

We primarily use ShrinkWrap in these examples to define the contents of our deployments. There's no need to run a full build to assemble the file-based JARs or EARs in testing; with a backing EJB Container that supports deployment of ShrinkWrap archives, we can take advantage of IDE incremental compilation and test immediately after making changes, with no step in between.

The adaptor that provides a hook in between ShrinkWrap and backing containers is a library that integrates with our test classes. Just as EJB brings a powerful backend to server-side business objects, the Arquillian framework arms POJO tests with services and an EJB Container abstraction.

Arquillian

http://jboss.org/arquillian

Test In-Container!

Arquillian provides a easy mechanism to test your application code inside a remote or embedded container or by interacting as a client of the container.

Mission Statement

Arquillian provides developers a simple test harness for a broad range of integration tests for their Java applications (most likely enterprise applications). A test case may be executed within the container, deployed alongside the code under test, or by coordinating with the container, acting as a client to the deployed code.

Arquillian defines two styles of container, remote and embedded. A remote container resides in a separate JVM from the test runner. Its lifecycle may be managed by Arquillian, or Arquillian may bind to a container that is already started. An embedded container resides in the same JVM and is mostly likely managed by Arquillian. Containers can be further classified by their capabilities. Examples include a fully compliant Java EE application server (e.g., GlassFish, JBoss AS, Embedded GlassFish), a Servlet container (e.g., Tomcat, Jetty) and a bean container (e.g., Weld SE). Arquillian ensures that the container used for testing is pluggable, so the developer is not locked into a proprietary testing environment.

Arquillian seeks to minimize the burden on the developer to carry out integration testing by handling all aspects of test execution, including:

1. Managing the lifecycle of the container (start/stop)
2. Bundling the test class with dependent classes and resources into a deployable archive

3. Enhancing the test class (e.g., resolving `@Inject`, `@EJB`, and `@Resource` injections)
4. Deploying the archive to test (deploy/undeploy)
5. Capturing results and failures

To avoid introducing unnecessary complexity into the developer's build environment, Arquillian integrates transparently with familiar testing frameworks (e.g., JUnit 4, TestNG 5), allowing tests to be launched using existing IDE, Ant, and Maven test plugins without any add-ons.

Arquillian makes integration testing a breeze.

FirstEJB Example

Description

In this exercise, we'll model an extremely simple business process: addition. The core logic is the same as one would write in a CS100-level undergraduate class, and we'll create real EJBs from these small classes using a few annotations. In addition, this example shows how we may expose our EJBs through a variety of "views": as business interfaces, as EJB 2.x legacy components, and as the new EJB 3.1 no-interface view.

The tests for this section come in both unit and integration flavors. The unit tests simply instantiate our classes as POJO objects and invoke their business methods directly, while the integration tests use a real backing container to make EJBs and invoke upon their proxy references. This shows the versatility of the EJB POJO programming model.

Online Companion Information

Wiki article: *http://community.jboss.org/docs/DOC-15566*

Source location: *http://github.com/jbossejb3/oreilly-ejb-6thedition-book-examples/tree/master/ch04-firstejb/*

Source Listing

Following is a full listing of all source code used in this runnable example.

Implementation Resources

CalculatorBeanBase.java

```java
package org.jboss.ejb3.examples.ch04.firstejb;

import org.jboss.logging.Logger;

/**
 * Base for bean implementation classes of the CalculatorEJB,
 * provides business logic for required contracts
 *
 * @author <a href="mailto:andrew.rubinger@jboss.org">ALR</a>
 */
public class CalculatorBeanBase implements CalculatorCommonBusiness
{
   // -------------------------------------------------------------------------||
   // Class Members -----------------------------------------------------------||
   // -------------------------------------------------------------------------||

   /**
    * Logger
    */
   private static final Logger log = Logger.getLogger(CalculatorBeanBase.class);

   // -------------------------------------------------------------------------||
   // Required Implementations ------------------------------------------------||
   // -------------------------------------------------------------------------||

   /**
    * {@inheritDoc}
    * @see org.jboss.ejb3.examples.ch04.firstejb.CalculatorCommonBusiness#add(int
[])
    */
   @Override
   public int add(final int... arguments)
   {
      // Initialize
      final StringBuffer sb = new StringBuffer();
      sb.append("Adding arguments: ");
      int result = 0;

      // Add all arguments
      for (final int arg : arguments)
      {
         result += arg;
         sb.append(arg);
         sb.append(" ");
      }

      // Return
      log.info(sb.toString());
      log.info("Result: " + result);
```

```
            return result;
        }

    }
```

CalculatorCommonBusiness.java

```java
package org.jboss.ejb3.examples.ch04.firstejb;

/**
 * Contains the contract for operations common to
 * all business interfaces of the CalculatorEJB
 *
 * @author <a href="mailto:andrew.rubinger@jboss.org">ALR</a>
 */
public interface CalculatorCommonBusiness
{

    // ---------------------------------------------------------------------||
    // Contracts -----------------------------------------------------------||
    // ---------------------------------------------------------------------||

    /**
     * Adds all arguments
     *
     * @return The sum of all arguments
     */
    int add(int... arguments);

}
```

CalculatorLocal.java

```java
package org.jboss.ejb3.examples.ch04.firstejb;

import javax.ejb.EJBLocalObject;

/**
 * EJB 2.x Local Component interface of the CalculatorEJB
 *
 * @author <a href="mailto:andrew.rubinger@jboss.org">ALR</a>
 */
public interface CalculatorLocal extends CalculatorCommonBusiness, EJBLocalObject
{

}
```

CalculatorLocalBusiness.java

```java
package org.jboss.ejb3.examples.ch04.firstejb;

/**
 * Local business interface for the CalculatorEJB
 *
 * @author <a href="mailto:andrew.rubinger@jboss.org">ALR</a>
```

```
 */
public interface CalculatorLocalBusiness extends CalculatorCommonBusiness
{

}
```

CalculatorLocalHome.java

```
package org.jboss.ejb3.examples.ch04.firstejb;

import javax.ejb.CreateException;
import javax.ejb.EJBLocalHome;

/**
 * EJB 2.x Local Home of the CalculatorEJB
 *
 * @author <a href="mailto:andrew.rubinger@jboss.org">ALR</a>
 */
public interface CalculatorLocalHome extends EJBLocalHome
{
   // --------------------------------------------------------------------------||
   // create<METHOD> Methods ---------------------------------------------------||
   // --------------------------------------------------------------------------||

   /**
    * Returns a reference to a local component view of the CalculatorEJB
    */
   CalculatorLocal create() throws CreateException;

}
```

CalculatorRemote.java

```
package org.jboss.ejb3.examples.ch04.firstejb;

import javax.ejb.EJBObject;

/**
 * EJB 2.x Remote Component interface of the CalculatorEJB
 *
 * @author <a href="mailto:andrew.rubinger@jboss.org">ALR</a>
 */
public interface CalculatorRemote extends CalculatorCommonBusiness, EJBObject
{

}
```

CalculatorRemoteBusiness.java

```
package org.jboss.ejb3.examples.ch04.firstejb;

/**
 * Remote business interface for the CalculatorEJB
 *
 * @author <a href="mailto:andrew.rubinger@jboss.org">ALR</a>
```

```
    */
    public interface CalculatorRemoteBusiness extends CalculatorCommonBusiness
    {

    }
```

CalculatorRemoteHome.java

```java
package org.jboss.ejb3.examples.ch04.firstejb;

import java.rmi.RemoteException;

import javax.ejb.CreateException;
import javax.ejb.EJBHome;

/**
 * EJB 2.x Remote Home of the CalculatorEJB
 *
 * @author <a href="mailto:andrew.rubinger@jboss.org">ALR</a>
 */
public interface CalculatorRemoteHome extends EJBHome
{
    // ----------------------------------------------------------------------||
    // create<METHOD> Methods -----------------------------------------------||
    // ----------------------------------------------------------------------||

    /**
     * Returns a reference to a remote component view of the CalculatorEJB
     */
    CalculatorRemote create() throws CreateException, RemoteException;

}
```

ManyViewCalculatorBean.java

```java
package org.jboss.ejb3.examples.ch04.firstejb;

import javax.ejb.Local;
import javax.ejb.LocalBean;
import javax.ejb.LocalHome;
import javax.ejb.Remote;
import javax.ejb.RemoteHome;
import javax.ejb.Stateless;

/**
 * Bean implementation class of the CalculatorEJB which
 * exposes local and remote business and component views,
 * as well as an EJB 3.1 no-interface view
 *
 * @author <a href="mailto:andrew.rubinger@jboss.org">ALR</a>
 */
@Stateless
@Local(CalculatorLocalBusiness.class)
@Remote(CalculatorRemoteBusiness.class)
@LocalHome(CalculatorLocalHome.class)
```

```
@RemoteHome(CalculatorRemoteHome.class)
@LocalBean // No-interface view
public class ManyViewCalculatorBean extends CalculatorBeanBase implements
CalculatorCommonBusiness
{
   /*
    * Implementation supplied by common base class
    */
}
```

NoInterfaceViewCalculatorBean.java

```
package org.jboss.ejb3.examples.ch04.firstejb;

import javax.ejb.LocalBean;
import javax.ejb.Stateless;

/**
 * Bean implementation class of the CalculatorEJB which
 * has a no-interface view
 *
 * @author <a href="mailto:andrew.rubinger@jboss.org">ALR</a>
 */
@Stateless
@LocalBean
public class NoInterfaceViewCalculatorBean extends CalculatorBeanBase
{
   // Implementation in base class
}
```

SimpleCalculatorBean.java

```
package org.jboss.ejb3.examples.ch04.firstejb;

import javax.ejb.Local;
import javax.ejb.Stateless;

/**
 * Bean implementation class of the CalculatorEJB which
 * exposes one local business view
 *
 * @author <a href="mailto:andrew.rubinger@jboss.org">ALR</a>
 */
@Stateless
@Local(CalculatorLocalBusiness.class)
public class SimpleCalculatorBean extends CalculatorBeanBase implements
CalculatorCommonBusiness
{
   /*
    * Implementation supplied by common base class
    */
}
```

Test Resources

CalculatorAssertionDelegate.java

```java
package org.jboss.ejb3.examples.ch04.firstejb;

import junit.framework.TestCase;

import org.jboss.logging.Logger;

/**
 * Contains functions to assert that implementations
 * of {@link CalculatorCommonBusiness} are working
 * as expected
 *
 * @author <a href="mailto:andrew.rubinger@jboss.org">ALR</a>
 */
class CalculatorAssertionDelegate
{
   // -------------------------------------------------------------------------||
   // Class Members -----------------------------------------------------------||
   // -------------------------------------------------------------------------||

   /**
    * Logger
    */
   private static final Logger log = Logger.getLogger(CalculatorAssertionDelegate
.class);

   // -------------------------------------------------------------------------||
   // Functional Methods ------------------------------------------------------||
   // -------------------------------------------------------------------------||

   /**
    * Uses the supplied Calculator instance to test the addition
    * algorithm
    */
   void assertAdditionSucceeds(final CalculatorCommonBusiness calc)
   {
      // Initialize
      final int[] arguments = new int[]
      {2, 3, 5};
      final int expectedSum = 10;

      // Add
      final int actualSum = calc.add(arguments);

      // Test
      TestCase.assertEquals("Addition did not return the expected result",
expectedSum, actualSum);

      // Log
      final StringBuffer sb = new StringBuffer();
      sb.append("Obtained expected result, ");
      sb.append(actualSum);
```

```
        sb.append(", from arguments: ");
        for (final int arg : arguments)
        {
            sb.append(arg);
            sb.append(" ");
        }
        log.info(sb.toString());
    }
}
```

CalculatorIntegrationTestCase.java

```
package org.jboss.ejb3.examples.ch04.firstejb;

import java.net.MalformedURLException;

import javax.ejb.EJB;

import org.jboss.arquillian.api.Deployment;
import org.jboss.arquillian.junit.Arquillian;
import org.jboss.logging.Logger;
import org.jboss.shrinkwrap.api.ShrinkWrap;
import org.jboss.shrinkwrap.api.spec.JavaArchive;
import org.junit.BeforeClass;
import org.junit.Test;
import org.junit.runner.RunWith;

/**
 * Integration tests for the CalculatorEJB exposing one
 * business view
 *
 * @author <a href="mailto:andrew.rubinger@jboss.org">ALR</a>
 */
@RunWith(Arquillian.class)
public class CalculatorIntegrationTestCase
{
    // -------------------------------------------------------------------------||
    // Class Members -----------------------------------------------------------||
    // -------------------------------------------------------------------------||

    /**
     * Logger
     */
    private static final Logger log = Logger.getLogger(CalculatorIntegrationTest
Case.class);

    /**
     * The EJB 3.x local business view of the CalculatorEJB
     */
    @EJB
    private static CalculatorLocalBusiness calcLocalBusiness;

    /**
     * Delegate for ensuring that the obtained Calculators are working as expected
     */
```

```
        private static CalculatorAssertionDelegate assertionDelegate;

        /**
         * Define the deployment
         */
        @Deployment
        public static JavaArchive createDeployment() throws MalformedURLException
        {
            final JavaArchive archive = ShrinkWrap.create("firstejb.jar", JavaArchive.
    class).addPackage(
                    CalculatorBeanBase.class.getPackage());
            log.info(archive.toString(true));
            return archive;
        }

        // --------------------------------------------------------------------------||
        // Lifecycle Methods --------------------------------------------------------||
        // --------------------------------------------------------------------------||

        /**
         * Run once before any tests
         */
        @BeforeClass
        public static void beforeClass() throws Throwable
        {
            // Create Assertion Delegate
            assertionDelegate = new CalculatorAssertionDelegate();
        }

        // --------------------------------------------------------------------------||
        // Tests --------------------------------------------------------------------||
        // --------------------------------------------------------------------------||

        /**
         * Ensures that the CalculatorEJB adds as expected,
         * using the EJB 3.x business view
         */
        @Test
        public void testAdditionUsingBusinessReference() throws Throwable
        {
            // Test
            log.info("Testing EJB via business reference...");
            assertionDelegate.assertAdditionSucceeds(calcLocalBusiness);
        }

    }
```

CalculatorUnitTestCase.java

```
    package org.jboss.ejb3.examples.ch04.firstejb;

    import junit.framework.TestCase;

    import org.jboss.logging.Logger;
    import org.junit.BeforeClass;
```

```java
import org.junit.Test;

/**
 * Tests to ensure that the business methods of the CalculatorEJB
 * are working as expected
 *
 * @author <a href="mailto:andrew.rubinger@jboss.org">ALR</a>
 */
public class CalculatorUnitTestCase
{
   // -------------------------------------------------------------------------||
   // Class Members -----------------------------------------------------------||
   // -------------------------------------------------------------------------||

   /**
    * Logger
    */
   private static final Logger log = Logger.getLogger(CalculatorUnitTestCase.
class);

   /**
    * The POJO instance to test
    */
   private static CalculatorCommonBusiness calc;

   // -------------------------------------------------------------------------||
   // Lifecycle Methods -------------------------------------------------------||
   // -------------------------------------------------------------------------||

   @BeforeClass
   public static void beforeClass()
   {
      // Make a POJO instance adhering to the
      // CalculatorCommonBusiness contract
      calc = new SimpleCalculatorBean();
   }

   // -------------------------------------------------------------------------||
   // Tests -------------------------------------------------------------------||
   // -------------------------------------------------------------------------||

   /**
    * Ensures that the business logic behind the
    * CalculatorEJB adds as expected when used
    * as a pure POJO
    */
   @Test
   public void testAddition()
   {
      // Initialize
      final int[] arguments = new int[]
      {3, 7, 2};
      final int expectedSum = 12;

      // Add
```

```
        final int actualSum = calc.add(arguments);

        // Test
        TestCase.assertEquals("Addition did not return the expected result",
expectedSum, actualSum);

        // Log
        final StringBuffer sb = new StringBuffer();
        sb.append("Obtained expected result, ");
        sb.append(actualSum);
        sb.append(", from arguments: ");
        for (final int arg : arguments)
        {
            sb.append(arg);
            sb.append(" ");
        }
        log.info(sb.toString());
    }
}
```

MultiViewCalculatorIntegrationTestCase.java

```
package org.jboss.ejb3.examples.ch04.firstejb;

import java.net.MalformedURLException;

import javax.naming.Context;
import javax.naming.InitialContext;

import org.jboss.arquillian.api.Deployment;
import org.jboss.arquillian.junit.Arquillian;
import org.jboss.logging.Logger;
import org.jboss.shrinkwrap.api.ShrinkWrap;
import org.jboss.shrinkwrap.api.spec.JavaArchive;
import org.junit.BeforeClass;
import org.junit.Test;
import org.junit.runner.RunWith;

/**
 * Integration tests for the CalculatorEJB, testing many views
 *
 * @author <a href="mailto:andrew.rubinger@jboss.org">ALR</a>
 */
@RunWith(Arquillian.class)
public class MultiViewCalculatorIntegrationTestCase
{
    // -------------------------------------------------------------------------||
    // Class Members -----------------------------------------------------------||
    // -------------------------------------------------------------------------||

    /**
     * Logger
     */
    private static final Logger log = Logger.getLogger(MultiViewCalculator
IntegrationTestCase.class);
```

```
    /**
     * The JNDI Naming Context
     */
    private static Context namingContext;

    /**
     * The EJB 3.x local business view of the CalculatorEJB
     */
    private static CalculatorLocalBusiness calcLocalBusiness;

    /**
     * The EJB 2.x local component view of the CalculatorEJB
     */
    private static CalculatorLocal calcLocal;

    /**
     * Delegate for ensuring that the obtained Calculators are working as expected
     */
    private static CalculatorAssertionDelegate assertionDelegate;

    /**
     * JNDI Name of the Local Business Reference
     */
    //TODO Use Global JNDI Syntax
    private static final String JNDI_NAME_CALC_LOCAL_BUSINESS = ManyViewCalculator
Bean.class.getSimpleName() + "Local";

    /**
     * JNDI Name of the Local Home Reference
     */
    //TODO Use Global JNDI Syntax
    private static final String JNDI_NAME_CALC_REMOTE_HOME = ManyViewCalculator
Bean.class.getSimpleName() + "LocalHome";

    /**
     * Define the deployment
     */
    @Deployment
    public static JavaArchive createDeployment() throws MalformedURLException
    {
        final JavaArchive archive = ShrinkWrap.create("firstejb.jar", JavaArchive.
class).addPackage(
                CalculatorBeanBase.class.getPackage());
        log.info(archive.toString(true));
        return archive;
    }

    // --------------------------------------------------------------------------||
    // Lifecycle Methods --------------------------------------------------------||
    // --------------------------------------------------------------------------||

    /**
     * Run once before any tests
     */
```

```
    @BeforeClass
    public static void beforeClass() throws Throwable
    {
        // Create the naming context, using jndi.properties on the CP
        namingContext = new InitialContext();

        // Obtain EJB 3.x Business Reference
        calcLocalBusiness = (CalculatorLocalBusiness) namingContext.lookup(JNDI_
NAME_CALC_LOCAL_BUSINESS);

        // Create Assertion Delegate
        assertionDelegate = new CalculatorAssertionDelegate();

        // Obtain EJB 2.x Component Reference via Home
        final Object calcLocalHomeReference = namingContext.lookup(JNDI_NAME_CALC_
REMOTE_HOME);
        final CalculatorLocalHome calcRemoteHome = (CalculatorLocalHome) calcLocal
HomeReference;
        calcLocal = calcRemoteHome.create();
    }

    // --------------------------------------------------------------------------||
    // Tests --------------------------------------------------------------------||
    // --------------------------------------------------------------------------||

    /**
     * Ensures that the CalculatorEJB adds as expected,
     * using the EJB 3.x business view
     */
    @Test
    public void testAdditionUsingBusinessReference() throws Throwable
    {
        // Test
        log.info("Testing remote business reference...");
        assertionDelegate.assertAdditionSucceeds(calcLocalBusiness);
    }

    /**
     * Ensures that the CalculatorEJB adds as expected,
     * using the EJB 2.x component view
     */
    @Test
    public void testAdditionUsingComponentReference() throws Throwable
    {
        // Test
        log.info("Testing remote component reference...");
        assertionDelegate.assertAdditionSucceeds(calcLocal);
    }

}
```

jndi.properties

```
# JNDI Properties for Local interaction with OpenEJB Naming Provider
java.naming.factory.initial=org.apache.openejb.client.LocalInitialContextFactory
```

Stateless Session EJB: Encryption Example

Description

The stateless session bean is a fantastic implementation choice for business processes which require no server-side state to be retained in between client invocations. If all information needed to process a request can be found in the request itself, the SLSB may be used as a highly efficient endpoint. In this example we build an encryption service capable of performing both one-way hashing and encryption/decryption operations.

Additionally, we show here that SLSBs may indeed have their own internal state, so long as that it's not leaked out to the client during requests. Finally, we introduce the use of XML via environment entries to externalize configurable elements of the service.

Online Companion Information

Wiki article: *http://community.jboss.org/docs/DOC-15567*

Source location: *http://github.com/jbossejb3/oreilly-ejb-6thedition-book-examples/tree/master/ch05-encryption/*

Source Listing

Following is a full listing of all source code used in this runnable example.

Implementation Resources

EncryptionBean.java

```java
package org.jboss.ejb3.examples.ch05.encryption;

import java.io.UnsupportedEncodingException;
import java.security.MessageDigest;
import java.security.NoSuchAlgorithmException;
import java.security.spec.AlgorithmParameterSpec;
import java.security.spec.KeySpec;

import javax.annotation.PostConstruct;
import javax.annotation.Resource;
import javax.crypto.Cipher;
import javax.crypto.SecretKey;
import javax.crypto.SecretKeyFactory;
import javax.crypto.spec.PBEKeySpec;
import javax.crypto.spec.PBEParameterSpec;
import javax.ejb.Local;
import javax.ejb.Remote;
import javax.ejb.SessionContext;
import javax.ejb.Stateless;

import org.apache.commons.codec.binary.Base64;
import org.jboss.logging.Logger;

/**
 * Bean implementation class of the EncryptionEJB.  Shows
 * how lifecycle callbacks are implemented (@PostConstruct),
 * and two ways of obtaining externalized environment
 * entries.
 *
 * @author <a href="mailto:alr@jboss.org">ALR</a>
 */
@Stateless(name = EncryptionBean.EJB_NAME)
@Local(EncryptionLocalBusiness.class)
@Remote(EncryptionRemoteBusiness.class)
public class EncryptionBean implements EncryptionLocalBusiness, EncryptionRemote
Business
{
    // ------------------------------------------------------------------------||
    // Class Members ----------------------------------------------------------||
    // ------------------------------------------------------------------------||

    /**
     * Logger
     */
    private static final Logger log = Logger.getLogger(EncryptionBean.class);

    /**
     * Name we'll assign to this EJB, will be referenced in the corresponding
     * META-INF/ejb-jar.xml file
     */
    static final String EJB_NAME = "EncryptionEJB";
```

```java
    /**
     * Name of the environment entry representing the ciphers' passphrase supplied
     * in ejb-jar.xml
     */
    private static final String ENV_ENTRY_NAME_CIPHERS_PASSPHRASE = "ciphersPass
phrase";

    /**
     * Name of the environment entry representing the message digest algorithm
supplied
     * in ejb-jar.xml
     */
    private static final String ENV_ENTRY_NAME_MESSAGE_DIGEST_ALGORITHM = "message
DigestAlgorithm";

    /**
     * Default Algorithm used by the Digest for one-way hashing
     */
    private static final String DEFAULT_ALGORITHM_MESSAGE_DIGEST = "MD5";

    /**
     * Charset used for encoding/decoding Strings to/from byte representation
     */
    private static final String CHARSET = "UTF-8";

    /**
     * Default Algorithm used by the Cipher Key for symmetric encryption
     */
    private static final String DEFAULT_ALGORITHM_CIPHER = "PBEWithMD5AndDES";

    /**
     * The default passphrase for symmetric encryption/decryption
     */
    private static final String DEFAULT_PASSPHRASE = "LocalTestingPassphrase";

    /**
     * The salt used in symmetric encryption/decryption
     */
    private static final byte[] DEFAULT_SALT_CIPHERS =
    {(byte) 0xB4, (byte) 0xA2, (byte) 0x43, (byte) 0x89, 0x3E, (byte) 0xC5, (byte)
0x78, (byte) 0x53};

    /**
     * Iteration count used for symmetric encryption/decryption
     */
    private static final int DEFAULT_ITERATION_COUNT_CIPHERS = 20;

    // -------------------------------------------------------------------------||
    // Instance Members --------------------------------------------------------||
    // -------------------------------------------------------------------------||

    /*
     * The following members represent the internal
     * state of the Service.  Note how these are *not* leaked out
```

```java
     * via the end-user API, and are hence part of "internal state"
     * and not "conversational state".
     */

    /**
     * SessionContext of this EJB; this will be injected by the EJB
     * Container because it's marked w/ @Resource
     */
    @Resource
    private SessionContext context;

    /**
     * Passphrase to use  for the key in cipher operations; lazily initialized
     * and loaded via SessionContext.lookup
     */
    private String ciphersPassphrase;

    /**
     * Algorithm to use in message digest (hash) operations, injected
     * via @Resource annotation with name property equal to env-entry name
     */
    @Resource(name = ENV_ENTRY_NAME_MESSAGE_DIGEST_ALGORITHM)
    private String messageDigestAlgorithm;

    /**
     * Digest used for one-way hashing
     */
    private MessageDigest messageDigest;

    /**
     * Cipher used for symmetric encryption
     */
    private Cipher encryptionCipher;

    /**
     * Cipher used for symmetric decryption
     */
    private Cipher decryptionCipher;

    // --------------------------------------------------------------------------||
    // Lifecycle ----------------------------------------------------------------||
    // --------------------------------------------------------------------------||

    /**
     * Initializes this service before it may handle requests
     *
     * @throws Exception If some unexpected error occurred
     */
    @PostConstruct
    public void initialize() throws Exception
    {
        // Log that we're here
        log.info("Initializing, part of " + PostConstruct.class.getName() +
" lifecycle");
```

```
    /*
     * Symmetric Encryption
     */

    // Obtain parameters used in initializing the ciphers
    final String cipherAlgorithm = DEFAULT_ALGORITHM_CIPHER;
    final byte[] ciphersSalt = DEFAULT_SALT_CIPHERS;
    final int ciphersIterationCount = DEFAULT_ITERATION_COUNT_CIPHERS;
    final String ciphersPassphrase = this.getCiphersPassphrase();

    // Obtain key and param spec for the ciphers
    final KeySpec ciphersKeySpec = new PBEKeySpec(ciphersPassphrase.toCharArray
(), ciphersSalt, ciphersIterationCount);
    final SecretKey ciphersKey = SecretKeyFactory.getInstance(cipherAlgorithm).
generateSecret(ciphersKeySpec);
    final AlgorithmParameterSpec paramSpec = new PBEParameterSpec(ciphersSalt,
ciphersIterationCount);

    // Create and init the ciphers
    this.encryptionCipher = Cipher.getInstance(ciphersKey.getAlgorithm());
    this.decryptionCipher = Cipher.getInstance(ciphersKey.getAlgorithm());
    encryptionCipher.init(Cipher.ENCRYPT_MODE, ciphersKey, paramSpec);
    decryptionCipher.init(Cipher.DECRYPT_MODE, ciphersKey, paramSpec);

    // Log
    log.info("Initialized encryption cipher: " + this.encryptionCipher);
    log.info("Initialized decryption cipher: " + this.decryptionCipher);

    /*
     * One-way Hashing
     */

    // Get the algorithm for the MessageDigest
    final String messageDigestAlgorithm = this.getMessageDigestAlgorithm();

    // Create the MessageDigest
    try
    {
        this.messageDigest = MessageDigest.getInstance(messageDigestAlgorithm);
    }
    catch (NoSuchAlgorithmException e)
    {
        throw new RuntimeException("Could not obtain the " + MessageDigest.class
.getSimpleName() + " for algorithm: "
                + messageDigestAlgorithm, e);
    }
    log.info("Initialized MessageDigest for one-way hashing: " + this.message
Digest);
    }

    // -------------------------------------------------------------------------||
    // Required Implementations ------------------------------------------------||
    // -------------------------------------------------------------------------||

    /**
```

```
 * {@inheritDoc}
 * @see org.jboss.ejb3.examples.ch05.encryption.EncryptionCommonBusiness#
compare(java.lang.String, java.lang.String)
 */
@Override
public boolean compare(final String hash, final String input) throws Illegal
ArgumentException, EncryptionException
{
    // Precondition checks
    if (hash == null)
    {
        throw new IllegalArgumentException("hash is required.");
    }
    if (input == null)
    {
        throw new IllegalArgumentException("Input is required.");
    }

    // Get the hash of the supplied input
    final String hashOfInput = this.hash(input);

    // Determine whether equal
    final boolean equal = hash.equals(hashOfInput);

    // Return
    return equal;
}

/**
 * {@inheritDoc}
 * @see org.jboss.ejb3.examples.ch05.encryption.EncryptionCommonBusiness
#decrypt(java.lang.String)
 */
@Override
public String decrypt(final String input) throws IllegalArgumentException,
IllegalStateException,
        EncryptionException
{
    // Get the cipher
    final Cipher cipher = this.decryptionCipher;
    if (cipher == null)
    {
        throw new IllegalStateException("Decryption cipher not available, has
this service been initialized?");
    }

    // Run the cipher
    byte[] resultBytes = null;;
    try
    {
        final byte[] inputBytes = this.stringToByteArray(input);
        resultBytes = cipher.doFinal(Base64.decodeBase64(inputBytes));
    }
    catch (final Throwable t)
    {
```

```
            throw new EncryptionException("Error in decryption", t);
        }
        final String result = this.byteArrayToString(resultBytes);

        // Log
        log.info("Decryption on \"" + input + "\": " + result);

        // Return
        return result;
    }

    /**
     * {@inheritDoc}
     * @see org.jboss.ejb3.examples.ch05.encryption.EncryptionCommonBusiness
#encrypt(java.lang.String)
     */
    @Override
    public String encrypt(final String input) throws IllegalArgumentException,
EncryptionException
    {
        // Get the cipher
        final Cipher cipher = this.encryptionCipher;
        if (cipher == null)
        {
            throw new IllegalStateException("Encryption cipher not available, has
this service been initialized?");
        }

        // Get bytes from the String
        byte[] inputBytes = this.stringToByteArray(input);

        // Run the cipher
        byte[] resultBytes = null;
        try
        {
            resultBytes = Base64.encodeBase64(cipher.doFinal(inputBytes));
        }
        catch (final Throwable t)
        {
            throw new EncryptionException("Error in encryption of: " + input, t);
        }

        // Log
        log.info("Encryption on \"" + input + "\": " + this.byteArrayToString
(resultBytes));

        // Return
        final String result = this.byteArrayToString(resultBytes);
        return result;
    }

    /**
     * Note:
     *
     * This is a weak implementation, but is enough to satisfy the example.
```

```
 * If considering real-world stresses, we would be, at a minimum:
 *
 * 1) Incorporating a random salt and storing it alongside the hashed result
 * 2) Additionally implementing an iteration count to re-hash N times
 */
/* (non-Javadoc)
 * @see org.jboss.ejb3.examples.ch05.encryption.EncryptionCommonBusiness#hash
(java.lang.String)
 */
@Override
public String hash(final String input) throws IllegalArgumentException,
EncryptionException
{
    // Precondition check
    if (input == null)
    {
        throw new IllegalArgumentException("Input is required.");
    }

    // Get bytes from the input
    byte[] inputBytes = this.stringToByteArray(input);

    // Obtain the MessageDigest
    final MessageDigest digest = this.messageDigest;

    // Update with our input, and obtain the hash, resetting the messageDigest
    digest.update(inputBytes, 0, inputBytes.length);
    final byte[] hashBytes = digest.digest();
    final byte[] encodedBytes = Base64.encodeBase64(hashBytes);

    // Get the input back in some readable format
    final String hash = this.byteArrayToString(encodedBytes);
    log.info("One-way hash of \"" + input + "\": " + hash);

    // Return
    return hash;
}

/**
 * Override the way we get the ciphers' passphrase so that we may
 * define it in a secure location on the server.  Now our production
 * systems will use a different key for encoding than our development
 * servers, and we may limit the likelihood of a security breach
 * while still allowing our programmer to use the default passphrase
 * transparently during development.
 *
 * If not provided as an env-entry, fall back upon the default.
 *
 * Note that a real system won't expose this method in the public API, ever.  We
 * do here for testing and to illustrate the example.
 *
 * @see org.jboss.ejb3.examples.ch05.encryption.EncryptionBeanBase#getCiphers
Passphrase()
 */
@Override
```

```java
   public String getCiphersPassphrase()
   {
      // Obtain current
      String passphrase = this.ciphersPassphrase;

      // If not set
      if (passphrase == null)
      {

         // Do a lookup via SessionContext
         passphrase = this.getEnvironmentEntryAsString(ENV_ENTRY_NAME_CIPHERS_
PASSPHRASE);

         // See if provided
         if (passphrase == null)
         {

            // Log a warning
            log.warn("No encryption passphrase has been supplied explicitly via "
                  + "an env-entry, falling back on the default...");

            // Set
            passphrase = DEFAULT_PASSPHRASE;
         }

         // Set the passphrase to be used so we don't have to do this lazy init
again
         this.ciphersPassphrase = passphrase;
      }

      // In a secure system, we don't log this. ;)
      log.info("Using encryption passphrase for ciphers keys: " + passphrase);

      // Return
      return passphrase;
   }

   /**
    * Obtains the message digest algorithm as injected from the env-entry element
    * defined in ejb-jar.xml.  If not specified, fall back onto the default,
logging a warn
    * message
    *
    * @see org.jboss.ejb3.examples.ch05.encryption.EncryptionRemoteBusiness#get
MessageDigestAlgorithm()
    */
   @Override
   public String getMessageDigestAlgorithm()
   {
      // First see if this has been injected/set
      if (this.messageDigestAlgorithm == null)
      {
         // Log a warning
         log.warn("No message digest algorithm has been supplied explicitly via "
               + "an env-entry, falling back on the default...");
```

```java
        // Set
        this.messageDigestAlgorithm = DEFAULT_ALGORITHM_MESSAGE_DIGEST;
    }

    // Log
    log.info("Configured MessageDigest one-way hash algorithm is: " + this.
messageDigestAlgorithm);

    // Return
    return this.messageDigestAlgorithm;
}

// --------------------------------------------------------------------------||
// Internal Helper Methods --------------------------------------------------||
// --------------------------------------------------------------------------||

/**
 * Obtains the environment entry with the specified name, casting to a String,
 * and returning the result.  If the entry is not assignable
 * to a String, an {@link IllegalStateException} will be raised.  In the event
that the
 * specified environment entry cannot be found, a warning message will be logged
 * and we'll return null.
 *
 * @param envEntryName
 * @return
 * @throws IllegalStateException
 */
private String getEnvironmentEntryAsString(final String envEntryName) throws
IllegalStateException
{
    // See if we have a SessionContext
    final SessionContext context = this.context;
    if (context == null)
    {
        log.warn("No SessionContext, bypassing request to obtain environment
entry: " + envEntryName);
        return null;
    }

    // Lookup in the Private JNDI ENC via the injected SessionContext
    Object lookupValue = null;
    try
    {
        lookupValue = context.lookup(envEntryName);
        log.debug("Obtained environment entry \"" + envEntryName + "\": " + look
upValue);
    }
    catch (final IllegalArgumentException iae)
    {
        // Not found defined within this EJB's Component Environment,
        // so return null and let the caller handle it
        log.warn("Could not find environment entry with name: " + envEntryName);
        return null;
```

```
            }

        // Cast
        String returnValue = null;
        try
        {
            returnValue = String.class.cast(lookupValue);
        }
        catch (final ClassCastException cce)
        {
            throw new IllegalStateException("The specified environment entry, " +
lookupValue
                    + ", was not able to be represented as a " + String.class.getName(),
cce);
        }

        // Return
        return returnValue;
    }

    /**
     * Returns a String representation of the specified byte array
     * using the charset from {@link EncryptionBeanBase#getCharset()}.  Wraps
     * any {@link UnsupportedEncodingException} as a result of using an invalid
     * charset in a {@link RuntimeException}.
     *
     * @param bytes
     * @return
     * @throws RuntimeException If the charset was invalid, or some other unknown
error occurred
     * @throws IllegalArgumentException If the byte array was not specified
     */
    private String byteArrayToString(final byte[] bytes) throws RuntimeException,
IllegalArgumentException
    {
        // Precondition check
        if (bytes == null)
        {
            throw new IllegalArgumentException("Byte array is required.");
        }

        // Represent as a String
        String result = null;
        final String charset = this.getCharset();
        try
        {
            result = new String(bytes, charset);
        }
        catch (final UnsupportedEncodingException e)
        {
            throw new RuntimeException("Specified charset is invalid: " + charset, e);
        }

        // Return
        return result;
```

```
    }

    /**
     * Returns a byte array representation of the specified String
     * using the charset from {@link EncryptionBeanBase#getCharset()}.  Wraps
     * any {@link UnsupportedEncodingException} as a result of using an invalid
     * charset in a {@link RuntimeException}.
     *
     * @param input
     * @return
     * @throws RuntimeException If the charset was invalid, or some other unknown
error occurred
     * @throws IllegalArgumentException If the input was not specified (null)
     */
    private byte[] stringToByteArray(final String input) throws RuntimeException,
IllegalArgumentException
    {
        // Precondition check
        if (input == null)
        {
            throw new IllegalArgumentException("Input is required.");
        }

        // Represent as a String
        byte[] result = null;
        final String charset = this.getCharset();
        try
        {
            result = input.getBytes(charset);
        }
        catch (final UnsupportedEncodingException e)
        {
            throw new RuntimeException("Specified charset is invalid: " + charset, e);
        }

        // Return
        return result;
    }

    /**
     * Obtains the charset used in encoding/decoding Strings
     * to/from byte representation
     *
     * @return The charset
     */
    private String getCharset()
    {
        return CHARSET;
    }

}
```

EncryptionCommonBusiness.java

```java
package org.jboss.ejb3.examples.ch05.encryption;

/**
 * Contains the contract for operations common to
 * all business interfaces of the EncryptionEJB
 *
 * @author <a href="mailto:alr@jboss.org">ALR</a>
 */
public interface EncryptionCommonBusiness
{
   // -----------------------------------------------------------------------||
   // Contracts -------------------------------------------------------------||
   // -----------------------------------------------------------------------||

   /**
    * Encrypts the specified String, returning the result
    *
    * @param input
    * @return
    * @throws IllegalArgumentException If no input was provided (null)
    * @throws EncryptionException If some problem occurred with encryption
    */
   String encrypt(String input) throws IllegalArgumentException, Encryption
Exception;

   /**
    * Decrypts the specified String, returning the result.  The general
    * contract is that the result of decrypting a String encrypted with
    * {@link EncryptionCommonBusiness#encrypt(String)} will be equal
    * by value to the original input (round trip).
    *
    * @param input
    * @return
    * @throws IllegalArgumentException If no input was provided (null)
    * @throws EncryptionException If some problem occurred with decryption
    */
   String decrypt(String input) throws IllegalArgumentException, Encryption
Exception;

   /**
    * Returns a one-way hash of the specified argument.  Useful
    * for safely storing passwords.
    *
    * @param input
    * @return
    * @throws IllegalArgumentException If no input was provided (null)
    * @throws EncryptionException If some problem occurred making the hash
    */
   String hash(String input) throws IllegalArgumentException, EncryptionException;

   /**
    * Returns whether or not the specified input matches the specified
    * hash.  Useful for validating passwords against a
    * securely stored hash.
```

```
 *
 * @param hash
 * @param input
 * @return
 * @throws IllegalArgumentException If either the hash or input is not
provided (null)
 * @throws EncryptionException If some problem occurred making the hash
 */
boolean compare(String hash, String input) throws IllegalArgumentException,
EncryptionException;

/*
 * This comment applies to all below this marker.
 *
 * In real life it's a security risk to expose these internals,
 * but they're in place here for testing and to show
 * functionality described by the examples.
 */

/**
 * Obtains the passphrase to be used in the key for
 * the symmetric encryption/decryption ciphers
 *
 * @return
 */
String getCiphersPassphrase();

/**
 * Obtains the algorithm to be used in performing
 * one-way hashing
 *
 * @return
 */
String getMessageDigestAlgorithm();

}
```

EncryptionException.java

```
package org.jboss.ejb3.examples.ch05.encryption;

import javax.ejb.ApplicationException;

/**
 * A checked Application Exception denoting
 * some unexpected problem with Encryption operations
 *
 * @author <a href="mailto:alr@jboss.org">ALR</a>
 */
@ApplicationException
// Explicit annotation, though this is inferred as default because we extend
Exception
public class EncryptionException extends Exception
{
```

```
// ------------------------------------------------------------------||
// Class Members ------------------------------------------------------||
// ------------------------------------------------------------------||

/**
 * To satisfy explicit serialization hints to the JVM
 */
private static final long serialVersionUID = 1L;

// ------------------------------------------------------------------||
// Constructors ------------------------------------------------------||
// ------------------------------------------------------------------||

/*
 * All constructors will delegate to the superclass implementation
 */

public EncryptionException()
{
    super();
}

public EncryptionException(String message, Throwable cause)
{
    super(message, cause);
}

public EncryptionException(String message)
{
    super(message);
}

public EncryptionException(Throwable cause)
{
    super(cause);
}

}
```

EncryptionLocalBusiness.java

```
package org.jboss.ejb3.examples.ch05.encryption;

/**
 * EJB 3.x Local Business View of the EncryptionEJB
 *
 * @author <a href="mailto:alr@jboss.org">ALR</a>
 */
public interface EncryptionLocalBusiness extends EncryptionCommonBusiness
{
    // Contracts in hierarchy
}
```

EncryptionRemoteBusiness.java

```java
package org.jboss.ejb3.examples.ch05.encryption;

/**
 * EJB 3.x Remote Business View of the EncryptionEJB
 *
 * @author <a href="mailto:alr@jboss.org">ALR</a>
 */
public interface EncryptionRemoteBusiness extends EncryptionCommonBusiness
{
    // Contracts in hierarchy
}
```

META-INF/ejb-jar.xml

```xml
<ejb-jar xmlns="http://java.sun.com/xml/ns/javaee" xmlns:xsi="http://www.w3.org/
2001/XMLSchema-instance"
   xsi:schemaLocation="http://java.sun.com/xml/ns/javaee
                 http://java.sun.com/xml/ns/javaee/ejb-jar_3_1.xsd"
   version="3.1">

  <enterprise-beans>

    <!--
      In this section we'll bolster our EncryptionEJB with some
      additional metadata to complement the info defined via
      annotations.
    -->
    <session>

      <!--
        This will match the value of @Stateless.name upon our bean
        implementation class
      -->
      <ejb-name>EncryptionEJB</ejb-name>

      <!-- Override the ciphers' default  passphrase -->
      <env-entry>
        <env-entry-name>ciphersPassphrase</env-entry-name>
        <env-entry-type>java.lang.String</env-entry-type>
        <env-entry-value>OverriddenPassword</env-entry-value>
      </env-entry>

      <!-- Override the default unidirectional hash MessageDigest algorithm -->
      <env-entry>
        <env-entry-name>messageDigestAlgorithm</env-entry-name>
        <env-entry-type>java.lang.String</env-entry-type>
        <env-entry-value>SHA</env-entry-value>

      </env-entry>

    </session>

  </enterprise-beans>
```

```
    </ejb-jar>
```

Test Resources

EncryptionIntegrationTestCase.java

```java
package org.jboss.ejb3.examples.ch05.encryption;

import java.net.MalformedURLException;
import java.net.URL;

import javax.ejb.EJB;

import junit.framework.TestCase;

import org.jboss.arquillian.api.Deployment;
import org.jboss.arquillian.junit.Arquillian;
import org.jboss.logging.Logger;
import org.jboss.shrinkwrap.api.ShrinkWrap;
import org.jboss.shrinkwrap.api.spec.JavaArchive;
import org.junit.Test;
import org.junit.runner.RunWith;

/**
 * Integration tests for the EncryptionEJB
 *
 * @author <a href="mailto:andrew.rubinger@jboss.org">ALR</a>
 */
@RunWith(Arquillian.class)
public class EncryptionIntegrationTestCase extends EncryptionTestCaseSupport
{
    // --------------------------------------------------------------------------||
    // Class Members -----------------------------------------------------------||
    // --------------------------------------------------------------------------||

    /**
     * Logger
     */
    private static final Logger log = Logger.getLogger(EncryptionIntegrationTest
Case.class);

    /**
     * The EJB 3.x local business view of the EncryptionEJB
     */
    @EJB
    private static EncryptionLocalBusiness encryptionLocalBusiness;

    /**
     * Correlates to the env-entry within ejb-jar.xml, to be used as an override
from the default
     */
    private static final String EXPECTED_CIPHERS_PASSPHRASE = "OverriddenPassword";
```

```
    /**
     * Correlates to the env-entry within ejb-jar.xml, to be used as an override
from the default
     */
    private static final String EXPECTED_ALGORITHM_MESSAGE_DIGEST = "SHA";

    /**
     * Define the deployment
     */
    @Deployment
    public static JavaArchive createDeployment() throws MalformedURLException
    {
        final JavaArchive archive = ShrinkWrap.create("slsb.jar", JavaArchive.class)
.addClasses(EncryptionBean.class,
                EncryptionCommonBusiness.class, EncryptionLocalBusiness.class,
EncryptionRemoteBusiness.class,
                EncryptionException.class).addManifestResource(
                new URL(EncryptionIntegrationTestCase.class.getProtectionDomain().get
CodeSource().getLocation(),
                    "../classes/META-INF/ejb-jar.xml"), "ejb-jar.xml");
        //TODO SHRINKWRAP-141 Make addition of the ejb-jar less verbose
        log.info(archive.toString(true));
        return archive;
    }

    // ------------------------------------------------------------------------||
    // Tests -----------------------------------------------------------------||
    // ------------------------------------------------------------------------||

    /*
     * These tests will use the EJB set up in test initialization
     */

    /**
     * @see {@link EncryptionTestCaseSupport#assertHashing(EncryptionCommon
Business)}
     */
    @Test
    public void testHashing() throws Throwable
    {
        // Log
        log.info("testHashing");

        // Test via superclass
        this.assertHashing(encryptionLocalBusiness);
    }

    /**
     * @see {@link EncryptionTestCaseSupport#assertEncryption(EncryptionCommon
Business)}
     */
    @Test
    public void testEncryption() throws Throwable
    {
        // Log
```

```
        log.info("testEncryption");

        // Test via superclass
        this.assertEncryption(encryptionLocalBusiness);
    }

    /**
     * Ensures that the hashing algorithm was overridden
     * from the environment entry declared in ejb-jar.xml
     *
     * @throws Throwable
     */
    @Test
    public void testMessageDigestAlgorithmOverride() throws Throwable
    {
        // Log
        log.info("testMessageDigestAlgorithmOverride");

        // Get the algorithm used
        final String algorithm = encryptionLocalBusiness.getMessageDigestAlgorithm();
        log.info("Using MessageDigest algorithm: " + algorithm);

        // Ensure expected
        TestCase.assertEquals("MessageDigest algorithm should have been overridden
from the environment entry",
                EXPECTED_ALGORITHM_MESSAGE_DIGEST, algorithm);
    }

    /**
     * Ensures that the cipher passphrase was overridden
     * from the environment entry declared in ejb-jar.xml
     *
     * @throws Throwable
     */
    @Test
    public void testCiphersPassphraseOverride() throws Throwable
    {
        // Log
        log.info("testCiphersPassphraseOverride");

        // Get the algorithm used
        final String passphrase = encryptionLocalBusiness.getCiphersPassphrase();
        log.info("Using Encryption passphrase: " + passphrase);

        // Ensure expected
        TestCase.assertEquals("Encryption passphrase should have been overridden
from the environment entry",
                EXPECTED_CIPHERS_PASSPHRASE, passphrase);
    }

}
```

EncryptionTestCaseSupport.java

```java
package org.jboss.ejb3.examples.ch05.encryption;

import junit.framework.TestCase;

import org.jboss.logging.Logger;

/**
 * Common base for centralizing test logic used
 * for the Encryption POJO and EncryptionEJB
 *
 * @author <a href="mailto:alr@jboss.org">ALR</a>
 */
public class EncryptionTestCaseSupport
{
   // -------------------------------------------------------------------------||
   // Class Members -----------------------------------------------------------||
   // -------------------------------------------------------------------------||

   /**
    * Logger
    */
   private static final Logger log = Logger.getLogger(EncryptionTestCaseSupport.
class);

   /**
    * A simple String used in testing
    */
   private static final String TEST_STRING = "EJB 3.1 Examples Test String";

   // -------------------------------------------------------------------------||
   // Test Support ------------------------------------------------------------||
   // -------------------------------------------------------------------------||

   /**
    * Ensures that the hashing functions are working as expected:
    *
    * 1) Passing through the hash returns a result inequal to the input
    * 2) Comparison upon the hash result and the original input matches
    *
    * @param service The service to use (either POJO or EJB)
    * @throws Throwable
    */
   protected void assertHashing(final EncryptionCommonBusiness service) throws
Throwable
   {
      // Log
      log.info("assertHashing");

      // Declare the input
      final String input = TEST_STRING;

      // Hash
      final String hash = service.hash(input);
      log.info("Hash of \"" + input + "\": " + hash);
```

```
        // Test that the hash function had some effect
        TestCase.assertNotSame("The hash function had no effect upon the supplied
input", input, hash);

        // Get the comparison result
        final boolean equal = service.compare(hash, input);

        // Test that the input matches the hash we'd gotten
        TestCase.assertTrue("The comparison of the input to its hashed result
failed", equal);
    }

    /**
     * Ensures that the encryption functions are working as expected:
     *
     * 1) Passing through the encryption returns a result inequal to the input
     * 2) Round-trip through decryption again returns a result equal to the
original input
     *
     * @param service The service to use (either POJO or EJB)
     * @throws Throwable
     */
    protected void assertEncryption(final EncryptionCommonBusiness service) throws
Throwable
    {
        // Log
        log.info("assertEncryption");

        // Declare the input
        final String input = TEST_STRING;

        // Hash
        final String encrypted = service.encrypt(input);
        log.info("Encrypted result of \"" + input + "\": " + encrypted);

        // Test that the hash function had some effect
        TestCase.assertNotSame("The encryption function had no effect upon the
supplied input", input, encrypted);

        // Get the round-trip result
        final String roundTrip = service.decrypt(encrypted);

        // Test that the result matches the original input
        TestCase.assertEquals("The comparison of the input to its encrypted result
failed", input, roundTrip);
    }
}
```

EncryptionUnitTestCase.java

```
package org.jboss.ejb3.examples.ch05.encryption;

import org.jboss.logging.Logger;
import org.junit.BeforeClass;
```

```java
import org.junit.Test;

/**
 * Tests to ensure that the business methods of the EncryptionEJB
 * are working as expected
 *
 * @author <a href="mailto:alr@jboss.org">ALR</a>
 */
public class EncryptionUnitTestCase extends EncryptionTestCaseSupport
{
   // -----------------------------------------------------------------------||
   // Class Members ---------------------------------------------------------||
   // -----------------------------------------------------------------------||

   /**
    * Logger
    */
   private static final Logger log = Logger.getLogger(EncryptionUnitTestCase.
class);

   /**
    * POJO Encryption Service
    */
   private static EncryptionBean encryptionService;

   // -----------------------------------------------------------------------||
   // Lifecycle -------------------------------------------------------------||
   // -----------------------------------------------------------------------||

   /**
    * Initializes the suite, invoked once before any tests are run
    */
   @BeforeClass
   public static void initialize() throws Throwable
   {
      // Create the encryption service as a POJO
      encryptionService = new EncryptionBean();
      encryptionService.initialize(); // We call init manually here
   }

   // -----------------------------------------------------------------------||
   // Tests -----------------------------------------------------------------||
   // -----------------------------------------------------------------------||

   /*
    * These tests will use the POJO set up in test initialization
    */

   /**
    * @see {@link EncryptionTestCaseSupport#assertHashing(EncryptionCommon
Business)}
    */
   @Test
   public void testHashing() throws Throwable
   {
```

```java
        // Log
        log.info("testHashing");

        // Test via superclass
        this.assertHashing(encryptionService);
    }

    /**
     * @see {@link EncryptionTestCaseSupport#assertEncryption(EncryptionCommon
Business)}
     */
    @Test
    public void testEncryption() throws Throwable
    {
        // Log
        log.info("testEncryption");

        // Test via superclass
        this.assertEncryption(encryptionService);
    }
}
```

Stateful Session EJB: FTP Client Example

Description

Often it's necessary for the server to remember information about a specific client in between requests; this is modeled by components that have "conversational state." For instance, the File Transfer Protocol is "stateful"—the server knows the current working directory used by each client, for example. In this example we'll model an FTP client using the stateful session bean.

In order to save resources (i.e., RAM), SFSBs may go through a processes called "passivation" whereby an instance/client session is removed from memory and persisted to disk after some timeout. If the client session is needed again, the state may be activated back into use. Here we must explicitly ensure that our state is properly accounted for in this serialization/deserialization process such that passivation is completely transparent to the client.

Online Companion Information

Wiki article: *http://community.jboss.org/docs/DOC-15568*

Source location: *http://github.com/jbossejb3/oreilly-ejb-6thedition-book-examples/tree/master/ch06-filetransfer/*

Source Listing

Following is a full listing of all source code used in this runnable example.

Implementation Resources

FileTransferBean.java

```java
package org.jboss.ejb3.examples.ch06.filetransfer;

import java.io.IOException;
import java.io.Serializable;

import javax.annotation.PostConstruct;
import javax.annotation.PreDestroy;
import javax.ejb.PostActivate;
import javax.ejb.PrePassivate;
import javax.ejb.Remote;
import javax.ejb.Remove;
import javax.ejb.Stateful;

import org.apache.commons.net.ftp.FTPClient;
import org.apache.commons.net.ftp.FTPFile;
import org.apache.commons.net.ftp.FTPReply;
import org.jboss.logging.Logger;

/**
 * Bean Implementation class of the FileTransferEJB, modeled
 * as a Stateful Session Bean
 *
 * @author <a href="mailto:andrew.rubinger@jboss.org">ALR</a>
 */
@Stateful(name = FileTransferBean.EJB_NAME)
@Remote(FileTransferRemoteBusiness.class)
public class FileTransferBean implements FileTransferRemoteBusiness, Serializable
{

    //-------------------------------------------------------------------------||
    // Class Members ----------------------------------------------------------||
    //-------------------------------------------------------------------------||

    /**
     * Serial Version UID
     */
    private static final long serialVersionUID = 1L;

    /**
     * Logger
     */
    private static final Logger log = Logger.getLogger(FileTransferBean.class);

    /**
     * Name of the EJB, used in Global JNDI addresses
     */
    public static final String EJB_NAME = "FileTransferEJB";

    /**
     * The name of the host to which we'll connect.
     * In production systems would typically be externalized
```

```
    * via configurable environment entry
    */
   private static String CONNECT_HOST = "localhost";

   /**
    * The port to which we'll connect.
    * In production systems would typically be externalized
    * via configurable environment entry.  IANA standard
    * for FTP ports is 21, though this requires root access
    * on *nix for testing, so we'll use the nonstandard 12345.
    */
   private static int CONNECT_PORT = 12345;

   //-------------------------------------------------------------------------||
   // Instance Members -------------------------------------------------------||
   //-------------------------------------------------------------------------||

   /**
    * The underlying FTP Client.  We don't want its state
    * getting Serialized during passivation.  We'll
    * reinitialize this client and its connections
    * upon activation.
    */
   private FTPClient client;

   /**
    * Name of the present working directory.  In cases where
    * we're passivated, if this is specified
    * we'll change into this directory upon activation.
    */
   private String presentWorkingDirectory;

   //-------------------------------------------------------------------------||
   // Lifecycle Callbacks ----------------------------------------------------||
   //-------------------------------------------------------------------------||

   /**
    * Called by the container when the instance is about to be passivated or
brought
    * out of service entirely.
    *
    * @see org.jboss.ejb3.examples.ch06.filetransfer.FileTransferCommonBusiness#
disconnect()
    */
   @PrePassivate
   @PreDestroy
   @Override
   public void disconnect()
   {
      // Obtain FTP Client
      final FTPClient client = this.getClient();

      // If exists
      if (client != null)
      {
```

```java
            // If connected
            if (client.isConnected())
            {
                // Logout
                try
                {
                    client.logout();
                    log.info("Logged out of: " + client);
                }
                catch (final IOException ioe)
                {
                    log.warn("Exception encountered in logging out of the FTP
    client", ioe);
                }

                // Disconnect
                try
                {
                    log.debug("Disconnecting: " + client);
                    client.disconnect();
                    log.info("Disconnected: " + client);
                }
                catch (final IOException ioe)
                {
                    log.warn("Exception encountered in disconnecting the FTP
    client", ioe);
                }

                // Null out the client so it's not serialized
                this.client = null;
            }
        }
    }

    /**
     * Called by the container when the instance has been created or re-activated
     * (brought out of passivated state).  Will construct the underlying FTP Client
     * and open all appropriate connections.
     *
     * @see org.jboss.ejb3.examples.ch06.filetransfer.FileTransferCommonBusiness
#connect()
     */
    @PostConstruct
    @PostActivate
    @Override
    public void connect() throws IllegalStateException, FileTransferException
    {
        /*
         * Precondition checks
         */
        final FTPClient clientBefore = this.getClient();
        if (clientBefore != null && clientBefore.isConnected())
        {
            throw new IllegalStateException("FTP Client is already initialized");
        }
```

```java
        // Get the connection properties
        final String connectHost = this.getConnectHost();
        final int connectPort = this.getConnectPort();

        // Create the client
        final FTPClient client = new FTPClient();
        final String canonicalServerName = connectHost + ":" + connectPort;
        log.debug("Connecting to FTP Server at " + canonicalServerName);
        try
        {
            client.connect(connectHost, connectPort);
        }
        catch (final IOException ioe)
        {
            throw new FileTransferException("Error in connecting to " + canonical
ServerName, ioe);
        }

        // Set
        log.info("Connected to FTP Server at: " + canonicalServerName);
        this.setClient(client);

        // Check that the last operation succeeded
        this.checkLastOperation();

        try
        {
            // Login
            client.login("user", "password");

            // Check that the last operation succeeded
            this.checkLastOperation();
        }
        catch (final Exception e)
        {
            throw new FileTransferException("Could not log in", e);
        }

        // If there's a pwd defined, cd into it.
        final String pwd = this.getPresentWorkingDirectory();
        if (pwd != null)
        {
            this.cd(pwd);
        }

    }

    //-------------------------------------------------------------------------||
    // Required Implementations -----------------------------------------------||
    //-------------------------------------------------------------------------||

    /* (non-Javadoc)
     * @see org.jboss.ejb3.examples.ch06.filetransfer.FileTransferCommonBusiness
#cd(java.lang.String)
```

```java
    */
    @Override
    public void cd(final String directory)
    {
        // Get the client
        final FTPClient client = this.getClient();

        // Exec cd
        try
        {
            // Exec cd
            client.changeWorkingDirectory(directory);

            // Check reply for success
            this.checkLastOperation();
        }
        catch (final Exception e)
        {
            throw new FileTransferException("Could not change working directory to \
"" + directory + "\"", e);
        }

        // Set the pwd (used upon activation)
        log.info("cd > " + directory);
        this.setPresentWorkingDirectory(directory);
    }

    /* (non-Javadoc)
     * @see org.jboss.ejb3.examples.ch06.filetransfer.FileTransferCommonBusiness
#mkdir(java.lang.String)
     */
    @Override
    public void mkdir(final String directory)
    {
        // Get the client
        final FTPClient client = this.getClient();

        // Exec cd
        try
        {
            // Exec mkdir
            client.makeDirectory(directory);

            // Check reply for success
            this.checkLastOperation();
        }
        catch (final Exception e)
        {
            throw new FileTransferException("Could not make directory \"" +
directory + "\"", e);
        }

    }
```

```
    /* (non-Javadoc)
     * @see org.jboss.ejb3.examples.ch06.filetransfer.FileTransferCommonBusiness
#pwd()
     */
    @Override
    public String pwd()
    {
        // Get the client
        final FTPClient client = this.getClient();

        // Exec pwd
        try
        {
            final FTPFile[] files = client.listFiles();
            for (final FTPFile file : files)
            {
                log.info(file);
            }

            // Exec pwd
            return client.printWorkingDirectory();

        }
        catch (final IOException ioe)
        {
            throw new FileTransferException("Could not print working directory", ioe);
        }
    }

    //--------------------------------------------------------------------------||
    // Internal Helper Methods --------------------------------------------------||
    //--------------------------------------------------------------------------||

    /**
     * Ensures that the last operation succeeded with a positive
     * reply code.  Otherwise a {@link FileTransferException}
     * is raised, noting the reply code denoting the error.
     *
     * @throws FileTransferException
     */
    protected void checkLastOperation() throws FileTransferException
    {
        // Get the client
        final FTPClient client = this.getClient();

        // Obtain and check the reply from the connection
        final int connectReply = client.getReplyCode();
        if (!FTPReply.isPositiveCompletion(connectReply))
        {
            // Indicate the problem
            throw new FileTransferException("Did not receive positive completion
code from server, instead code was: "
                    + connectReply);
        }
```

```
    }

    /* (non-Javadoc)
     * @see org.jboss.ejb3.examples.ch06.filetransfer.FileTransferRemoteBusiness
#endSession()
     */
    @Remove
    @Override
    public void endSession()
    {
        log.info("Session Ending...");
    }

    //-------------------------------------------------------------------------||
    // Accessors / Mutators ---------------------------------------------------||
    //-------------------------------------------------------------------------||

    /**
     * @return the connectHost
     */
    public String getConnectHost()
    {
        return CONNECT_HOST;
    }

    /**
     * @return the connectPort
     */
    public int getConnectPort()
    {
        return CONNECT_PORT;
    }

    /**
     * @return the client
     */
    protected final FTPClient getClient()
    {
        return client;
    }

    /**
     * @param client the client to set
     */
    private void setClient(final FTPClient client)
    {
        this.client = client;
    }

    /**
     * @return the presentWorkingDirectory
     */
    private String getPresentWorkingDirectory()
    {
        return presentWorkingDirectory;
```

```
    }

    /**
     * @param presentWorkingDirectory the presentWorkingDirectory to set
     */
    private void setPresentWorkingDirectory(String presentWorkingDirectory)
    {
        this.presentWorkingDirectory = presentWorkingDirectory;
    }

}
```

EncryptionBean.java

```java
package org.jboss.ejb3.examples.ch05.encryption;

import java.io.UnsupportedEncodingException;
import java.security.MessageDigest;
import java.security.NoSuchAlgorithmException;
import java.security.spec.AlgorithmParameterSpec;
import java.security.spec.KeySpec;

import javax.annotation.PostConstruct;
import javax.annotation.Resource;
import javax.crypto.Cipher;
import javax.crypto.SecretKey;
import javax.crypto.SecretKeyFactory;
import javax.crypto.spec.PBEKeySpec;
import javax.crypto.spec.PBEParameterSpec;
import javax.ejb.Local;
import javax.ejb.Remote;
import javax.ejb.SessionContext;
import javax.ejb.Stateless;

import org.apache.commons.codec.binary.Base64;
import org.jboss.logging.Logger;

/**
 * Bean implementation class of the EncryptionEJB.  Shows
 * how lifecycle callbacks are implemented (@PostConstruct),
 * and two ways of obtaining externalized environment
 * entries.
 *
 * @author <a href="mailto:alr@jboss.org">ALR</a>
 */
@Stateless(name = EncryptionBean.EJB_NAME)
@Local(EncryptionLocalBusiness.class)
@Remote(EncryptionRemoteBusiness.class)
public class EncryptionBean implements EncryptionLocalBusiness, EncryptionRemote
Business
{
    // -------------------------------------------------------------------------||
    // Class Members -----------------------------------------------------------||
    // -------------------------------------------------------------------------||
```

```java
/**
 * Logger
 */
private static final Logger log = Logger.getLogger(EncryptionBean.class);

/**
 * Name we'll assign to this EJB, will be referenced in the corresponding
 * META-INF/ejb-jar.xml file
 */
static final String EJB_NAME = "EncryptionEJB";

/**
 * Name of the environment entry representing the ciphers' passphrase supplied
 * in ejb-jar.xml
 */
private static final String ENV_ENTRY_NAME_CIPHERS_PASSPHRASE = "ciphersPass
phrase";

/**
 * Name of the environment entry representing the message digest algorithm
supplied
 * in ejb-jar.xml
 */
private static final String ENV_ENTRY_NAME_MESSAGE_DIGEST_ALGORITHM = "message
DigestAlgorithm";

/**
 * Default Algorithm used by the Digest for one-way hashing
 */
private static final String DEFAULT_ALGORITHM_MESSAGE_DIGEST = "MD5";

/**
 * Charset used for encoding/decoding Strings to/from byte representation
 */
private static final String CHARSET = "UTF-8";

/**
 * Default Algorithm used by the Cipher Key for symmetric encryption
 */
private static final String DEFAULT_ALGORITHM_CIPHER = "PBEWithMD5AndDES";

/**
 * The default passphrase for symmetric encryption/decryption
 */
private static final String DEFAULT_PASSPHRASE = "LocalTestingPassphrase";

/**
 * The salt used in symmetric encryption/decryption
 */
private static final byte[] DEFAULT_SALT_CIPHERS =
{(byte) 0xB4, (byte) 0xA2, (byte) 0x43, (byte) 0x89, 0x3E, (byte) 0xC5, (byte)
0x78, (byte) 0x53};

/**
 * Iteration count used for symmetric encryption/decryption
 */
```

```
    */
    private static final int DEFAULT_ITERATION_COUNT_CIPHERS = 20;

    // ---------------------------------------------------------------------||
    // Instance Members ----------------------------------------------------||
    // ---------------------------------------------------------------------||

    /*
     * The following members represent the internal
     * state of the Service.  Note how these are *not* leaked out
     * via the end-user API, and are hence part of "internal state"
     * and not "conversational state".
     */

    /**
     * SessionContext of this EJB; this will be injected by the EJB
     * Container because it's marked w/ @Resource
     */
    @Resource
    private SessionContext context;

    /**
     * Passphrase to use  for the key in cipher operations; lazily initialized
     * and loaded via SessionContext.lookup
     */
    private String ciphersPassphrase;

    /**
     * Algorithm to use in message digest (hash) operations, injected
     * via @Resource annotation with name property equal to env-entry name
     */
    @Resource(name = ENV_ENTRY_NAME_MESSAGE_DIGEST_ALGORITHM)
    private String messageDigestAlgorithm;

    /**
     * Digest used for one-way hashing
     */
    private MessageDigest messageDigest;

    /**
     * Cipher used for symmetric encryption
     */
    private Cipher encryptionCipher;

    /**
     * Cipher used for symmetric decryption
     */
    private Cipher decryptionCipher;

    // ---------------------------------------------------------------------||
    // Lifecycle -----------------------------------------------------------||
    // ---------------------------------------------------------------------||

    /**
     * Initializes this service before it may handle requests
```

```
 *
 * @throws Exception If some unexpected error occurred
 */
@PostConstruct
public void initialize() throws Exception
{
    // Log that we're here
    log.info("Initializing, part of " + PostConstruct.class.getName() + " life
cycle");

    /*
     * Symmetric Encryption
     */

    // Obtain parameters used in initializing the ciphers
    final String cipherAlgorithm = DEFAULT_ALGORITHM_CIPHER;
    final byte[] ciphersSalt = DEFAULT_SALT_CIPHERS;
    final int ciphersIterationCount = DEFAULT_ITERATION_COUNT_CIPHERS;
    final String ciphersPassphrase = this.getCiphersPassphrase();

    // Obtain key and param spec for the ciphers
    final KeySpec ciphersKeySpec = new PBEKeySpec(ciphersPassphrase.toCharArray
(), ciphersSalt, ciphersIterationCount);
    final SecretKey ciphersKey = SecretKeyFactory.getInstance(cipherAlgorithm).
generateSecret(ciphersKeySpec);
    final AlgorithmParameterSpec paramSpec = new PBEParameterSpec(ciphersSalt,
ciphersIterationCount);

    // Create and init the ciphers
    this.encryptionCipher = Cipher.getInstance(ciphersKey.getAlgorithm());
    this.decryptionCipher = Cipher.getInstance(ciphersKey.getAlgorithm());
    encryptionCipher.init(Cipher.ENCRYPT_MODE, ciphersKey, paramSpec);
    decryptionCipher.init(Cipher.DECRYPT_MODE, ciphersKey, paramSpec);

    // Log
    log.info("Initialized encryption cipher: " + this.encryptionCipher);
    log.info("Initialized decryption cipher: " + this.decryptionCipher);

    /*
     * One-way Hashing
     */

    // Get the algorithm for the MessageDigest
    final String messageDigestAlgorithm = this.getMessageDigestAlgorithm();

    // Create the MessageDigest
    try
    {
        this.messageDigest = MessageDigest.getInstance(messageDigestAlgorithm);
    }
    catch (NoSuchAlgorithmException e)
    {
        throw new RuntimeException("Could not obtain the " + MessageDigest.class
.getSimpleName() + " for algorithm: "
                + messageDigestAlgorithm, e);
```

```
      }
      log.info("Initialized MessageDigest for one-way hashing: " + this.message
Digest);
   }

   // -------------------------------------------------------------------------||
   // Required Implementations ------------------------------------------------||
   // -------------------------------------------------------------------------||

   /**
    * {@inheritDoc}
    * @see org.jboss.ejb3.examples.ch05.encryption.EncryptionCommonBusiness
#compare(java.lang.String, java.lang.String)
    */
   @Override
   public boolean compare(final String hash, final String input) throws Illegal
ArgumentException, EncryptionException
   {
      // Precondition checks
      if (hash == null)
      {
         throw new IllegalArgumentException("hash is required.");
      }
      if (input == null)
      {
         throw new IllegalArgumentException("Input is required.");
      }

      // Get the hash of the supplied input
      final String hashOfInput = this.hash(input);

      // Determine whether equal
      final boolean equal = hash.equals(hashOfInput);

      // Return
      return equal;
   }

   /**
    * {@inheritDoc}
    * @see org.jboss.ejb3.examples.ch05.encryption.EncryptionCommonBusiness
#decrypt(java.lang.String)
    */
   @Override
   public String decrypt(final String input) throws IllegalArgumentException,
IllegalStateException,
         EncryptionException
   {
      // Get the cipher
      final Cipher cipher = this.decryptionCipher;
      if (cipher == null)
      {
         throw new IllegalStateException("Decryption cipher not available, has
this service been initialized?");
      }
```

```java
        // Run the cipher
        byte[] resultBytes = null;;
        try
        {
            final byte[] inputBytes = this.stringToByteArray(input);
            resultBytes = cipher.doFinal(Base64.decodeBase64(inputBytes));
        }
        catch (final Throwable t)
        {
            throw new EncryptionException("Error in decryption", t);
        }
        final String result = this.byteArrayToString(resultBytes);

        // Log
        log.info("Decryption on \"" + input + "\": " + result);

        // Return
        return result;
    }

    /**
     * {@inheritDoc}
     * @see org.jboss.ejb3.examples.ch05.encryption.EncryptionCommonBusiness
#encrypt(java.lang.String)
     */
    @Override
    public String encrypt(final String input) throws IllegalArgumentException,
EncryptionException
    {
        // Get the cipher
        final Cipher cipher = this.encryptionCipher;
        if (cipher == null)
        {
            throw new IllegalStateException("Encryption cipher not available, has
this service been initialized?");
        }

        // Get bytes from the String
        byte[] inputBytes = this.stringToByteArray(input);

        // Run the cipher
        byte[] resultBytes = null;
        try
        {
            resultBytes = Base64.encodeBase64(cipher.doFinal(inputBytes));
        }
        catch (final Throwable t)
        {
            throw new EncryptionException("Error in encryption of: " + input, t);
        }

        // Log
        log.info("Encryption on \"" + input + "\": " + this.byteArrayToString
(resultBytes));
```

```java
        // Return
        final String result = this.byteArrayToString(resultBytes);
        return result;
    }

    /**
     * Note:
     *
     * This is a weak implementation, but is enough to satisfy the example.
     * If considering real-world stresses, we would be, at a minimum:
     *
     * 1) Incorporating a random salt and storing it alongside the hashed result
     * 2) Additionally implementing an iteration count to re-hash N times
     */
    /* (non-Javadoc)
     * @see org.jboss.ejb3.examples.ch05.encryption.EncryptionCommonBusiness#hash
(java.lang.String)
     */
    @Override
    public String hash(final String input) throws IllegalArgumentException,
EncryptionException
    {
        // Precondition check
        if (input == null)
        {
            throw new IllegalArgumentException("Input is required.");
        }

        // Get bytes from the input
        byte[] inputBytes = this.stringToByteArray(input);

        // Obtain the MessageDigest
        final MessageDigest digest = this.messageDigest;

        // Update with our input, and obtain the hash, resetting the messageDigest
        digest.update(inputBytes, 0, inputBytes.length);
        final byte[] hashBytes = digest.digest();
        final byte[] encodedBytes = Base64.encodeBase64(hashBytes);

        // Get the input back in some readable format
        final String hash = this.byteArrayToString(encodedBytes);
        log.info("One-way hash of \"" + input + "\": " + hash);

        // Return
        return hash;
    }

    /**
     * Override the way we get the ciphers' passphrase so that we may
     * define it in a secure location on the server.  Now our production
     * systems will use a different key for encoding than our development
     * servers, and we may limit the likelihood of a security breach
     * while still allowing our programmer to use the default passphrase
     * transparently during development.
```

```
     *
     * If not provided as an env-entry, fall back upon the default.
     *
     * Note that a real system won't expose this method in the public API, ever.  We
     * do here for testing and to illustrate the example.
     *
     * @see org.jboss.ejb3.examples.ch05.encryption.EncryptionBeanBase#getCiphers
 Passphrase()
     */
    @Override
    public String getCiphersPassphrase()
    {
        // Obtain current
        String passphrase = this.ciphersPassphrase;

        // If not set
        if (passphrase == null)
        {

            // Do a lookup via SessionContext
            passphrase = this.getEnvironmentEntryAsString(ENV_ENTRY_NAME_CIPHERS_
 PASSPHRASE);

            // See if provided
            if (passphrase == null)
            {

                // Log a warning
                log.warn("No encryption passphrase has been supplied explicitly via "
                    + "an env-entry, falling back on the default...");

                // Set
                passphrase = DEFAULT_PASSPHRASE;
            }

            // Set the passphrase to be used so we don't have to do this lazy init
 again
            this.ciphersPassphrase = passphrase;
        }

        // In a secure system, we don't log this. ;)
        log.info("Using encryption passphrase for ciphers keys: " + passphrase);

        // Return
        return passphrase;
    }

    /**
     * Obtains the message digest algorithm as injected from the env-entry element
     * defined in ejb-jar.xml.  If not specified, fall back onto the default,
 logging a warn
     * message
     *
     * @see org.jboss.ejb3.examples.ch05.encryption.EncryptionRemoteBusiness#get
 MessageDigestAlgorithm()
```

```
     */
    @Override
    public String getMessageDigestAlgorithm()
    {
        // First see if this has been injected/set
        if (this.messageDigestAlgorithm == null)
        {
            // Log a warning
            log.warn("No message digest algorithm has been supplied explicitly via "
                    + "an env-entry, falling back on the default...");

            // Set
            this.messageDigestAlgorithm = DEFAULT_ALGORITHM_MESSAGE_DIGEST;
        }

        // Log
        log.info("Configured MessageDigest one-way hash algorithm is: " + this.
messageDigestAlgorithm);

        // Return
        return this.messageDigestAlgorithm;
    }

    // -------------------------------------------------------------------------||
    // Internal Helper Methods -------------------------------------------------||
    // -------------------------------------------------------------------------||

    /**
     * Obtains the environment entry with the specified name, casting to a String,
     * and returning the result.  If the entry is not assignable
     * to a String, an {@link IllegalStateException} will be raised.  In the event
that the
     * specified environment entry cannot be found, a warning message will be logged
     * and we'll return null.
     *
     * @param envEntryName
     * @return
     * @throws IllegalStateException
     */
    private String getEnvironmentEntryAsString(final String envEntryName) throws
IllegalStateException
    {
        // See if we have a SessionContext
        final SessionContext context = this.context;
        if (context == null)
        {
            log.warn("No SessionContext, bypassing request to obtain environment
entry: " + envEntryName);
            return null;
        }

        // Lookup in the Private JNDI ENC via the injected SessionContext
        Object lookupValue = null;
        try
        {
```

```
            lookupValue = context.lookup(envEntryName);
            log.debug("Obtained environment entry \"" + envEntryName + "\": " +
    lookupValue);
        }
        catch (final IllegalArgumentException iae)
        {
            // Not found defined within this EJB's Component Environment,
            // so return null and let the caller handle it
            log.warn("Could not find environment entry with name: " + envEntryName);
            return null;
        }

        // Cast
        String returnValue = null;
        try
        {
            returnValue = String.class.cast(lookupValue);
        }
        catch (final ClassCastException cce)
        {
            throw new IllegalStateException("The specified environment entry, " +
    lookupValue
                    + ", was not able to be represented as a " + String.class.getName(),
    cce);
        }

        // Return
        return returnValue;
    }

    /**
     * Returns a String representation of the specified byte array
     * using the charset from {@link EncryptionBeanBase#getCharset()}.  Wraps
     * any {@link UnsupportedEncodingException} as a result of using an invalid
     * charset in a {@link RuntimeException}.
     *
     * @param bytes
     * @return
     * @throws RuntimeException If the charset was invalid, or some other unknown
    error occurred
     * @throws IllegalArgumentException If the byte array was not specified
     */
    private String byteArrayToString(final byte[] bytes) throws RuntimeException,
    IllegalArgumentException
    {
        // Precondition check
        if (bytes == null)
        {
            throw new IllegalArgumentException("Byte array is required.");
        }

        // Represent as a String
        String result = null;
        final String charset = this.getCharset();
        try
```

```
        {
            result = new String(bytes, charset);
        }
        catch (final UnsupportedEncodingException e)
        {
            throw new RuntimeException("Specified charset is invalid: " + charset, e);
        }

        // Return
        return result;
    }

    /**
     * Returns a byte array representation of the specified String
     * using the charset from {@link EncryptionBeanBase#getCharset()}.  Wraps
     * any {@link UnsupportedEncodingException} as a result of using an invalid
     * charset in a {@link RuntimeException}.
     *
     * @param input
     * @return
     * @throws RuntimeException If the charset was invalid, or some other unknown
error occurred
     * @throws IllegalArgumentException If the input was not specified (null)
     */
    private byte[] stringToByteArray(final String input) throws RuntimeException,
IllegalArgumentException
    {
        // Precondition check
        if (input == null)
        {
            throw new IllegalArgumentException("Input is required.");
        }

        // Represent as a String
        byte[] result = null;
        final String charset = this.getCharset();
        try
        {
            result = input.getBytes(charset);
        }
        catch (final UnsupportedEncodingException e)
        {
            throw new RuntimeException("Specified charset is invalid: " + charset, e);
        }

        // Return
        return result;
    }

    /**
     * Obtains the charset used in encoding/decoding Strings
     * to/from byte representation
     *
     * @return The charset
     */
```

```
    private String getCharset()
    {
        return CHARSET;
    }

}
```

EncryptionCommonBusiness.java

```java
package org.jboss.ejb3.examples.ch05.encryption;

/**
 * Contains the contract for operations common to
 * all business interfaces of the EncryptionEJB
 *
 * @author <a href="mailto:alr@jboss.org">ALR</a>
 */
public interface EncryptionCommonBusiness
{
    // -------------------------------------------------------------------------||
    // Contracts ---------------------------------------------------------------||
    // -------------------------------------------------------------------------||

    /**
     * Encrypts the specified String, returning the result
     *
     * @param input
     * @return
     * @throws IllegalArgumentException If no input was provided (null)
     * @throws EncryptionException If some problem occurred with encryption
     */
    String encrypt(String input) throws IllegalArgumentException, Encryption
Exception;

    /**
     * Decrypts the specified String, returning the result.  The general
     * contract is that the result of decrypting a String encrypted with
     * {@link EncryptionCommonBusiness#encrypt(String)} will be equal
     * by value to the original input (round trip).
     *
     * @param input
     * @return
     * @throws IllegalArgumentException If no input was provided (null)
     * @throws EncryptionException If some problem occurred with decryption
     */
    String decrypt(String input) throws IllegalArgumentException, Encryption
Exception;

    /**
     * Returns a one-way hash of the specified argument.  Useful
     * for safely storing passwords.
     *
     * @param input
     * @return
     * @throws IllegalArgumentException If no input was provided (null)
```

```
     * @throws EncryptionException If some problem occurred making the hash
     */
    String hash(String input) throws IllegalArgumentException, EncryptionException;

    /**
     * Returns whether or not the specified input matches the specified
     * hash.  Useful for validating passwords against a
     * securely stored hash.
     *
     * @param hash
     * @param input
     * @return
     * @throws IllegalArgumentException If either the hash or input is not
provided (null)
     * @throws EncryptionException If some problem occurred making the hash
     */
    boolean compare(String hash, String input) throws IllegalArgumentException,
EncryptionException;

    /*
     * This comment applies to all below this marker.
     *
     * In real life it's a security risk to expose these internals,
     * but they're in place here for testing and to show
     * functionality described by the examples.
     */

    /**
     * Obtains the passphrase to be used in the key for
     * the symmetric encryption/decryption ciphers
     *
     * @return
     */
    String getCiphersPassphrase();

    /**
     * Obtains the algorithm to be used in performing
     * one-way hashing
     *
     * @return
     */
    String getMessageDigestAlgorithm();

}
```

EncryptionException.java

```
package org.jboss.ejb3.examples.ch05.encryption;

import javax.ejb.ApplicationException;

/**
 * A checked Application Exception denoting
 * some unexpected problem with Encryption operations
 *
```

```
 * @author <a href="mailto:alr@jboss.org">ALR</a>
 */
@ApplicationException
// Explicit annotation, though this is inferred as default because we extend
Exception
public class EncryptionException extends Exception
{

   // --------------------------------------------------------------------------||
   // Class Members ------------------------------------------------------------||
   // --------------------------------------------------------------------------||

   /**
    * To satisfy explicit serialization hints to the JVM
    */
   private static final long serialVersionUID = 1L;

   // --------------------------------------------------------------------------||
   // Constructors -------------------------------------------------------------||
   // --------------------------------------------------------------------------||

   /*
    * All constructors will delegate to the superclass implementation
    */

   public EncryptionException()
   {
      super();
   }

   public EncryptionException(String message, Throwable cause)
   {
      super(message, cause);
   }

   public EncryptionException(String message)
   {
      super(message);
   }

   public EncryptionException(Throwable cause)
   {
      super(cause);
   }

}
```

EncryptionLocalBusiness.java

```
package org.jboss.ejb3.examples.ch05.encryption;

/**
 * EJB 3.x Local Business View of the EncryptionEJB
 *
 * @author <a href="mailto:alr@jboss.org">ALR</a>
```

```
 */
public interface EncryptionLocalBusiness extends EncryptionCommonBusiness
{
    // Contracts in hierarchy
}
```

EncryptionRemoteBusiness.java

```
package org.jboss.ejb3.examples.ch05.encryption;

/**
 * EJB 3.x Remote Business View of the EncryptionEJB
 *
 * @author <a href="mailto:alr@jboss.org">ALR</a>
 */
public interface EncryptionRemoteBusiness extends EncryptionCommonBusiness
{
    // Contracts in hierarchy
}
```

META-INF/ejb-jar.xml

```
<ejb-jar xmlns="http://java.sun.com/xml/ns/javaee" xmlns:xsi="http://www.w3.org/
2001/XMLSchema-instance"
  xsi:schemaLocation="http://java.sun.com/xml/ns/javaee
                http://java.sun.com/xml/ns/javaee/ejb-jar_3_1.xsd"
  version="3.1">

    <enterprise-beans>

      <!--
        In this section we'll bolster our EncryptionEJB with some
        additional metadata to complement the info defined via
        annotations.
      -->
      <session>

        <!--
          This will match the value of @Stateless.name upon our bean
          implementation class
        -->
        <ejb-name>EncryptionEJB</ejb-name>

        <!-- Override the ciphers' default  passphrase -->
        <env-entry>
          <env-entry-name>ciphersPassphrase</env-entry-name>
          <env-entry-type>java.lang.String</env-entry-type>
          <env-entry-value>OverriddenPassword</env-entry-value>
        </env-entry>

        <!-- Override the default unidirectional hash MessageDigest algorithm -->
        <env-entry>
          <env-entry-name>messageDigestAlgorithm</env-entry-name>
          <env-entry-type>java.lang.String</env-entry-type>
          <env-entry-value>SHA</env-entry-value>
```

```
        </env-entry>

    </session>

  </enterprise-beans>

</ejb-jar>
```

Test Resources

EncryptionIntegrationTestCase.java

```java
package org.jboss.ejb3.examples.ch05.encryption;

import java.net.MalformedURLException;
import java.net.URL;

import javax.ejb.EJB;

import junit.framework.TestCase;

import org.jboss.arquillian.api.Deployment;
import org.jboss.arquillian.junit.Arquillian;
import org.jboss.logging.Logger;
import org.jboss.shrinkwrap.api.ShrinkWrap;
import org.jboss.shrinkwrap.api.spec.JavaArchive;
import org.junit.Test;
import org.junit.runner.RunWith;

/**
 * Integration tests for the EncryptionEJB
 *
 * @author <a href="mailto:andrew.rubinger@jboss.org">ALR</a>
 */
@RunWith(Arquillian.class)
public class EncryptionIntegrationTestCase extends EncryptionTestCaseSupport
{
    // -------------------------------------------------------------------------||
    // Class Members -----------------------------------------------------------||
    // -------------------------------------------------------------------------||

    /**
     * Logger
     */
    private static final Logger log = Logger.getLogger(EncryptionIntegrationTest
Case.class);

    /**
     * The EJB 3.x local business view of the EncryptionEJB
     */
    @EJB
    private static EncryptionLocalBusiness encryptionLocalBusiness;
```

```java
    /**
     * Correlates to the env-entry within ejb-jar.xml, to be used as an override
from the default
     */
    private static final String EXPECTED_CIPHERS_PASSPHRASE = "OverriddenPassword";

    /**
     * Correlates to the env-entry within ejb-jar.xml, to be used as an override
from the default
     */
    private static final String EXPECTED_ALGORITHM_MESSAGE_DIGEST = "SHA";

    /**
     * Define the deployment
     */
    @Deployment
    public static JavaArchive createDeployment() throws MalformedURLException
    {
        final JavaArchive archive = ShrinkWrap.create("slsb.jar", JavaArchive.class
).addClasses(EncryptionBean.class,
                EncryptionCommonBusiness.class, EncryptionLocalBusiness.class,
EncryptionRemoteBusiness.class,
                EncryptionException.class).addManifestResource(
                new URL(EncryptionIntegrationTestCase.class.getProtectionDomain().get
CodeSource().getLocation(),
                        "../classes/META-INF/ejb-jar.xml"), "ejb-jar.xml");
        //TODO SHRINKWRAP-141 Make addition of the ejb-jar less verbose
        log.info(archive.toString(true));
        return archive;
    }

    // ---------------------------------------------------------------------------||
    // Tests ---------------------------------------------------------------------||
    // ---------------------------------------------------------------------------||

    /*
     * These tests will use the EJB set up in test initialization
     */

    /**
     * @see {@link EncryptionTestCaseSupport#assertHashing(EncryptionCommon
Business)}
     */
    @Test
    public void testHashing() throws Throwable
    {
        // Log
        log.info("testHashing");

        // Test via superclass
        this.assertHashing(encryptionLocalBusiness);
    }
```

```
/**
 * @see {@link EncryptionTestCaseSupport#assertEncryption(EncryptionCommon
Business)}
 */
@Test
public void testEncryption() throws Throwable
{
    // Log
    log.info("testEncryption");

    // Test via superclass
    this.assertEncryption(encryptionLocalBusiness);
}

/**
 * Ensures that the hashing algorithm was overridden
 * from the environment entry declared in ejb-jar.xml
 *
 * @throws Throwable
 */
@Test
public void testMessageDigestAlgorithmOverride() throws Throwable
{
    // Log
    log.info("testMessageDigestAlgorithmOverride");

    // Get the algorithm used
    final String algorithm = encryptionLocalBusiness.getMessageDigestAlgorithm();
    log.info("Using MessageDigest algorithm: " + algorithm);

    // Ensure expected
    TestCase.assertEquals("MessageDigest algorithm should have been overridden
from the environment entry",
            EXPECTED_ALGORITHM_MESSAGE_DIGEST, algorithm);
}

/**
 * Ensures that the cipher passphrase was overridden
 * from the environment entry declared in ejb-jar.xml
 *
 * @throws Throwable
 */
@Test
public void testCiphersPassphraseOverride() throws Throwable
{
    // Log
    log.info("testCiphersPassphraseOverride");

    // Get the algorithm used
    final String passphrase = encryptionLocalBusiness.getCiphersPassphrase();
    log.info("Using Encryption passphrase: " + passphrase);
```

```
        // Ensure expected
        TestCase.assertEquals("Encryption passphrase should have been overridden
from the environment entry",
            EXPECTED_CIPHERS_PASSPHRASE, passphrase);
    }

}
```

EncryptionTestCaseSupport.java

```java
package org.jboss.ejb3.examples.ch05.encryption;

import junit.framework.TestCase;

import org.jboss.logging.Logger;

/**
 * Common base for centralizing test logic used
 * for the Encryption POJO and EncryptionEJB
 *
 * @author <a href="mailto:alr@jboss.org">ALR</a>
 */
public class EncryptionTestCaseSupport
{
    // -------------------------------------------------------------------------||
    // Class Members -----------------------------------------------------------||
    // -------------------------------------------------------------------------||

    /**
     * Logger
     */
    private static final Logger log = Logger.getLogger(EncryptionTestCaseSupport.
class);

    /**
     * A simple String used in testing
     */
    private static final String TEST_STRING = "EJB 3.1 Examples Test String";

    // -------------------------------------------------------------------------||
    // Test Support ------------------------------------------------------------||
    // -------------------------------------------------------------------------||

    /**
     * Ensures that the hashing functions are working as expected:
     *
     * 1) Passing through the hash returns a result inequal to the input
     * 2) Comparison upon the hash result and the original input matches
     *
     * @param service The service to use (either POJO or EJB)
     * @throws Throwable
     */
    protected void assertHashing(final EncryptionCommonBusiness service) throws
Throwable
    {
```

```
        // Log
        log.info("assertHashing");

        // Declare the input
        final String input = TEST_STRING;

        // Hash
        final String hash = service.hash(input);
        log.info("Hash of \"" + input + "\": " + hash);

        // Test that the hash function had some effect
        TestCase.assertNotSame("The hash function had no effect upon the supplied
input", input, hash);

        // Get the comparison result
        final boolean equal = service.compare(hash, input);

        // Test that the input matches the hash we'd gotten
        TestCase.assertTrue("The comparison of the input to its hashed result failed",
equal);
    }

    /**
     * Ensures that the encryption functions are working as expected:
     *
     * 1) Passing through the encryption returns a result inequal to the input
     * 2) Round-trip through decryption again returns a result equal to the
original input
     *
     * @param service The service to use (either POJO or EJB)
     * @throws Throwable
     */
    protected void assertEncryption(final EncryptionCommonBusiness service) throws
 Throwable
    {
        // Log
        log.info("assertEncryption");

        // Declare the input
        final String input = TEST_STRING;

        // Hash
        final String encrypted = service.encrypt(input);
        log.info("Encrypted result of \"" + input + "\": " + encrypted);

        // Test that the hash function had some effect
        TestCase.assertNotSame("The encryption function had no effect upon the
supplied input", input, encrypted);

        // Get the round-trip result
        final String roundTrip = service.decrypt(encrypted);

        // Test that the result matches the original input
        TestCase.assertEquals("The comparison of the input to its encrypted result
failed", input, roundTrip);
```

```
      }
   }
```

EncryptionUnitTestCase.java

```java
package org.jboss.ejb3.examples.ch05.encryption;

import org.jboss.logging.Logger;
import org.junit.BeforeClass;
import org.junit.Test;

/**
 * Tests to ensure that the business methods of the EncryptionEJB
 * are working as expected
 *
 * @author <a href="mailto:alr@jboss.org">ALR</a>
 */
public class EncryptionUnitTestCase extends EncryptionTestCaseSupport
{
   // -------------------------------------------------------------------------||
   // Class Members -----------------------------------------------------------||
   // -------------------------------------------------------------------------||

   /**
    * Logger
    */
   private static final Logger log = Logger.getLogger(EncryptionUnitTestCase.
class);

   /**
    * POJO Encryption Service
    */
   private static EncryptionBean encryptionService;

   // -------------------------------------------------------------------------||
   // Lifecycle ---------------------------------------------------------------||
   // -------------------------------------------------------------------------||

   /**
    * Initializes the suite, invoked once before any tests are run
    */
   @BeforeClass
   public static void initialize() throws Throwable
   {
      // Create the encryption service as a POJO
      encryptionService = new EncryptionBean();
      encryptionService.initialize(); // We call init manually here
   }

   // -------------------------------------------------------------------------||
   // Tests -------------------------------------------------------------------||
   // -------------------------------------------------------------------------||

   /*
    * These tests will use the POJO set up in test initialization
```

```
    */

    /**
     * @see {@link EncryptionTestCaseSupport#assertHashing(EncryptionCommon
Business)}
     */
    @Test
    public void testHashing() throws Throwable
    {
        // Log
        log.info("testHashing");

        // Test via superclass
        this.assertHashing(encryptionService);
    }

    /**
     * @see {@link EncryptionTestCaseSupport#assertEncryption(EncryptionCommon
Business)}
     */
    @Test
    public void testEncryption() throws Throwable
    {
        // Log
        log.info("testEncryption");

        // Test via superclass
        this.assertEncryption(encryptionService);
    }
}
```

FileTransferCommonBusiness.java

```
    package org.jboss.ejb3.examples.ch06.filetransfer;

/**
 * Contains the contract for operations common to all
 * business interfaces of the FileTransferEJB.
 *
 * Includes support for switching present working directories,
 * printing the current working directory, and making directories.
 *
 * @author <a href="mailto:andrew.rubinger@jboss.org">ALR</a>
 */
public interface FileTransferCommonBusiness
{
    // ---------------------------------------------------------------------------||
    // Contracts -----------------------------------------------------------------||
    // ---------------------------------------------------------------------------||

    /**
     * Makes a directory of the specified name
     *
     * @throws IllegalStateException If the client connection has not been
initialized
```

```
      */
    void mkdir(String directory) throws IllegalStateException;

    /**
     * Changes into the named directory
     *
     * @param directory
     * @throws IllegalStateException If the client connection has not been
initialized
     */
    void cd(String directory) throws IllegalStateException;

    /**
     * Obtains the name of the current working directory
     *
     * @return
     * @throws IllegalStateException If the client connection has not been
initialized
     */
    String pwd() throws IllegalStateException;

    /**
     * Denotes that the client is done using this service; flushes
     * any pending operations and does all appropriate cleanup.  If
     * already disconnected, this is a no-op.
     */
    void disconnect();

    /**
     * Opens the underlying connections to the target FTP Server,
     * performs any other tasks required before commands may be sent
     * (ie. login, etc)
     *
     * @throws IllegalStateException If already initialized/connected
     */
    void connect() throws IllegalStateException;

}
```

FileTransferException.java

```
    package org.jboss.ejb3.examples.ch06.filetransfer;

    /**
     * Exception to indicate that a problem has occurred during
     * a file transfer operation.
     *
     * @author <a href="mailto:andrew.rubinger@jboss.org">ALR</a>
     */
    public class FileTransferException extends RuntimeException
    {

        //-------------------------------------------------------------------------||
        // Class Members ----------------------------------------------------------||
        //-------------------------------------------------------------------------||
```

```
    private static final long serialVersionUID = 1L;

    //-------------------------------------------------------------------------||
    // Constructor ------------------------------------------------------------||
    //-------------------------------------------------------------------------||

    public FileTransferException()
    {
        super();
    }

    public FileTransferException(final String message, final Throwable cause)
    {
        super(message, cause);
    }

    public FileTransferException(final String message)
    {
        super(message);
    }

    public FileTransferException(final Throwable cause)
    {
        super(cause);
    }

}
```

FileTransferRemoteBusiness.java

```
package org.jboss.ejb3.examples.ch06.filetransfer;

import javax.ejb.Remove;

/**
 * Remote Business interface for the FileTransferEJB.
 * Because this will only be used in EJB environments, we define
 * a method to end the current session.
 *
 * @author <a href="mailto:andrew.rubinger@jboss.org">ALR</a>
 */
public interface FileTransferRemoteBusiness extends FileTransferCommonBusiness
{
    // -----------------------------------------------------------------------||
    // Contracts --------------------------------------------------------------||
    // -----------------------------------------------------------------------||

    /**
     * Ends the current session; will result in a SFSB @Remove call
     * as the bean implementation class will annotate this with
     * {@link Remove}
     */
    void endSession();
}
```

Test Resources

FileTransferIntegrationTestCase.java

```java
package org.jboss.ejb3.examples.ch06.filetransfer;

import java.io.File;

import javax.ejb.EJB;
import javax.ejb.NoSuchEJBException;

import junit.framework.TestCase;

import org.jboss.arquillian.api.Deployment;
import org.jboss.arquillian.junit.Arquillian;
import org.jboss.logging.Logger;
import org.jboss.shrinkwrap.api.ShrinkWrap;
import org.jboss.shrinkwrap.api.spec.JavaArchive;
import org.junit.After;
import org.junit.AfterClass;
import org.junit.BeforeClass;
import org.junit.Test;
import org.junit.runner.RunWith;

/**
 * Test cases to ensure that the FileTransferEJB is working as
 * a Stateful Session Bean from the EJB Container.
 *
 * Inherits some test support from {@link FileTransferTestCaseBase},
 * and additionally tests EJB-specific tasks upon the
 * proxy.  Shows that sessions operate in isolation, and that removal
 * of a session means you cannot use it anymore.
 *
 * @author <a href="mailto:andrew.rubinger@jboss.org">ALR</a>
 */
@RunWith(Arquillian.class)
public class FileTransferIntegrationTestCase extends FileTransferTestCaseBase
{

    //-------------------------------------------------------------------------||
    // Class Members ----------------------------------------------------------||
    //-------------------------------------------------------------------------||

    /**
     * Logger
     */
    private static final Logger log = Logger.getLogger(FileTransferIntegrationTest
Case.class);

    /**
     * Name of the configuration file for the FTP server users
     */
    private static final String FTP_SERVER_USERS_CONFIG_FILENAME = "ftpusers.
properties";
```

```java
/**
 * Port to which the FTP server should bind
 */
private static final int FTP_SERVER_BIND_PORT = 12345;

/**
 * The FTP Server
 */
private static FtpServerPojo ftpServer;

/**
 * The Deployment
 * @return
 */
@Deployment
public static JavaArchive createDeployment()
{
    final JavaArchive archive = ShrinkWrap.create("ftpclient.jar", JavaArchive.
class).addPackage(
            FileTransferBean.class.getPackage());
    log.info(archive.toString(true));
    return archive;
}

//-------------------------------------------------------------------------||
// Instance Members -------------------------------------------------------||
//-------------------------------------------------------------------------||

/**
 * Our view of the EJB, remote business interface type of the Proxy
 */
@EJB
private FileTransferRemoteBusiness client1;

/**
 * Another FTP Client Session
 */
@EJB
private FileTransferRemoteBusiness client2;

//-------------------------------------------------------------------------||
// Lifecycle --------------------------------------------------------------||
//-------------------------------------------------------------------------||

/**
 * Creates and starts the FTP Server
 */
@BeforeClass
public static void startFtpServer() throws Exception
{
    // Create
    final FtpServerPojo server = new FtpServerPojo();

    // Configure
    server.setUsersConfigFileName(FTP_SERVER_USERS_CONFIG_FILENAME);
```

```java
    server.setBindPort(FTP_SERVER_BIND_PORT);

    // Start and set
    server.initializeServer();
    server.startServer();
    ftpServer = server;
}

/**
 * Stops the FTP Server
 * @throws Exception
 */
@AfterClass
public static void stopFtpServer() throws Exception
{
    ftpServer.stopServer();
}

/**
 * Ends the session upon the FTP Client SFSB Proxy
 * and resets
 */
@After
public void endClientSessions() throws Exception
{
    // End the session for client 1
    try
    {
        client1.endSession();
    }
    // If we've already been ended
    catch (final NoSuchEJBException nsee)
    {
        // Ignore
    }

    // End the session for client 2
    try
    {
        client2.endSession();
    }
    // If we've already been ended
    catch (final NoSuchEJBException nsee)
    {
        // Ignore
    }
}

//-------------------------------------------------------------------------||
// Tests ------------------------------------------------------------------||
//-------------------------------------------------------------------------||

/**
 * Tests that two separate sessions will act in isolation from each other
 *
```

```java
 * @throws Exception
 */
@Test
public void testSessionIsolation() throws Exception
{
    // Log
    log.info("testSessionIsolation");

    // Get the existing client as made from the test lifecycle
    final FileTransferRemoteBusiness session1 = this.getClient();

    // Use another client
    final FileTransferRemoteBusiness session2 = this.client2;

    // cd into a home directory for each
    final String ftpHome = getFtpHome().getAbsolutePath();
    session1.cd(ftpHome);
    session2.cd(ftpHome);

    // Now make a new directory for each session, and go into it
    final String newDirSession1 = "newDirSession1";
    final String newDirSession2 = "newDirSession2";
    session1.mkdir(newDirSession1);
    session1.cd(newDirSession1);
    session2.mkdir(newDirSession2);
    session2.cd(newDirSession2);

    // Get the current working directory for each session
    final String pwdSession1 = session1.pwd();
    final String pwdSession2 = session2.pwd();

    // Ensure each session is in the proper working directory
    TestCase.assertEquals("Session 1 is in unexpected pwd", ftpHome + File.
separator + newDirSession1, pwdSession1);
    TestCase.assertEquals("Session 2 is in unexpected pwd", ftpHome + File.
separator + newDirSession2, pwdSession2);

    // End the session manually for session2 (session1 will be ended by test
lifecycle)
    session2.endSession();
}

/**
 * Tests that a call to {@link FileTransferRemoteBusiness#endSession()}
 * results in the SFSB's backing instance removal, and that subsequent
 * operations result in a {@link NoSuchEJBException}
 *
 * @throws Exception
 */
@Test
public void testSfsbRemoval() throws Exception
{
    // Log
    log.info("testSfsbRemoval");
```

```java
        // Get the existing client as made from the test lifecycle
        final FileTransferRemoteBusiness sfsb = this.getClient();

        // cd into the home directory
        final String ftpHome = getFtpHome().getAbsolutePath();
        sfsb.cd(ftpHome);

        // Get and test the pwd
        final String pwdBefore = sfsb.pwd();
        TestCase.assertEquals("Session should be in the FTP Home directory",
    ftpHome, pwdBefore);

        // End the session, resulting in an underlying instance
        // removal due to the annotation with @Remove upon
        // the bean implementation class
        sfsb.endSession();

        // Now try some other operation, and ensure that we get a NoSuchEJBException
        boolean gotExpectedException = false;
        try
        {
            // This should not succeed, because we've called a method marked as
@Remove
            sfsb.pwd();
        }
        catch (final NoSuchEJBException nsee)
        {
            gotExpectedException = true;
        }
        TestCase.assertTrue("Call to end the session did not result in underlying
    removal of the SFSB bean instance",
                gotExpectedException);
    }

    //-------------------------------------------------------------------------||
    // Required Implementations ----------------------------------------------||
    //-------------------------------------------------------------------------||

    /* (non-Javadoc)
     * @see org.jboss.ejb3.examples.ch06.filetransfer.FileTransferTestCaseBase#get
Client()
     */
    @Override
    protected FileTransferRemoteBusiness getClient()
    {
        return this.client1;
    }

}
```

FileTransferTestCaseBase.java

```java
package org.jboss.ejb3.examples.ch06.filetransfer;

import java.io.File;
```

```java
import junit.framework.TestCase;

import org.jboss.logging.Logger;
import org.junit.After;
import org.junit.Before;
import org.junit.Test;

/**
 * Base tests for the file transfer test classes, may
 * be extended either from unit or integration tests.
 *
 * @author <a href="mailto:andrew.rubinger@jboss.org">ALR</a>
 */
public abstract class FileTransferTestCaseBase
{

   //-------------------------------------------------------------------------||
   // Class Members ----------------------------------------------------------||
   //-------------------------------------------------------------------------||

   /**
    * Logger
    */
   private static final Logger log = Logger.getLogger(FileTransferTestCaseBase.
class);

   /**
    * The name of the directory under the writable temp filesystem which
    * will act as the home for these tests
    */
   private static final String RELATIVE_LOCATION_HOME = "ejb31_ch06-example-ftp
Home";

   /**
    * The name of the system property denoting the I/O temp directory
    */
   private static final String SYS_PROP_NAME_IO_TMP_DIR = "java.io.tmpdir";

   /**
    * The File we'll use as the writeable home for FTP operations.  Created and
    * destroyed alongside test lifecycle.
    */
   private static File ftpHome;

   //-------------------------------------------------------------------------||
   // Lifecycle --------------------------------------------------------------||
   //-------------------------------------------------------------------------||

   /**
    * Creates the directory which we'll use as the writeable home
    * for FTP operations; called before each test is run.
    *
    * @throws Exception
    */
```

```java
    @Before
    public void createFtpHome() throws Exception
    {
        final File ftpHome = getFtpHome();
        if (ftpHome.exists())
        {
            throw new RuntimeException("Error in test setup; FTP Home should not yet
exist: " + ftpHome.getAbsolutePath());
        }
        final boolean created = ftpHome.mkdir();
        if (!created)
        {
            throw new RuntimeException("Request to create the FTP Home failed: " +
ftpHome.getAbsolutePath());
        }
        log.info("Created FTP Home: " + ftpHome.getAbsolutePath());
    }

    /**
     * Removes the directory used as the writeable home
     * for FTP operations; called after each test is run.
     *
     * @throws Exception
     */
    @After
    public void deleteFtpHome() throws Exception
    {
        final File ftpHome = getFtpHome();
        if (!ftpHome.exists())
        {
            throw new RuntimeException("Error in test setup; FTP Home should exist:
" + ftpHome.getAbsolutePath());
        }
        final boolean removed = this.deleteRecursive(ftpHome);
        if (!removed)
        {
            throw new RuntimeException("Request to remove the FTP Home failed: " +
ftpHome.getAbsolutePath());
        }
        log.info("Removed FTP Home: " + ftpHome.getAbsolutePath());
    }

    //-------------------------------------------------------------------------||
    // Tests ------------------------------------------------------------------||
    //-------------------------------------------------------------------------||

    /**
     * Tests that a new directory can be made, we can switch
     * into it, and we can obtain the present working directory of our newly created
     * directory
     */
    @Test
    public void testMkdirCdAndPwd() throws Exception
    {
        // Log
```

```
        log.info("testMkdirAndPwd");

        // Get the client
        final FileTransferCommonBusiness client = this.getClient();

        // Switch to home
        final String home = getFtpHome().getAbsolutePath();
        client.cd(home);

        // Ensure we're home
        final String pwdBefore = client.pwd();
        TestCase.assertEquals("Present working directory should be our home", home,
    pwdBefore);

        // Make the directory
        final String newDir = "newDirectory";
        client.mkdir(newDir);

        // cd into the new dir
        client.cd(newDir);

        // Ensure we're in the new directory
        final String pwdAfter = client.pwd();
        TestCase.assertEquals("Present working directory should be our new
directory", home + File.separator + newDir,
            pwdAfter);
    }

    //-------------------------------------------------------------------------||
    // Contracts -------------------------------------------------------------||
    //-------------------------------------------------------------------------||

    /**
     * Obtains the client to be used for the tests
     */
    protected abstract FileTransferCommonBusiness getClient();

    //-------------------------------------------------------------------------||
    // Internal Helper Methods -----------------------------------------------||
    //-------------------------------------------------------------------------||

    /**
     * Recursively deletes all contents of the specified root,
     * including the root itself.  If the specified root does not exist,
     * no action is taken.
     *
     * @param root
     * @return true if deleted, false otherwise
     */
    protected boolean deleteRecursive(final File root)
    {
        // Ensure exists
        if (!root.exists())
        {
            return false;
```

```
        }

        // Get all children
        final File[] children = root.listFiles();
        // If it's a directory
        if (children != null)
        {
            // Remove all children
            for (final File child : children)
            {
                this.deleteRecursive(child);
            }
        }

        // Delete me
        final boolean success = root.delete();
        log.info("Deleted: " + root);
        return success;
    }

    /**
     * Obtains the writeable home for these tests, set under the namespace of the
     * IO Temp directory
     */
    protected static File getFtpHome() throws Exception
    {
        // If the home is not defined
        if (ftpHome == null)
        {

            // Get the property
            final String sysPropIoTempDir = SYS_PROP_NAME_IO_TMP_DIR;
            final String ioTempDir = System.getProperty(sysPropIoTempDir);
            if (ioTempDir == null)
            {
                throw new RuntimeException("I/O temp directory was not specified by
system property: " + sysPropIoTempDir);
            }

            // Make the File
            final File ioTempDirFile = new File(ioTempDir);
            if (!ioTempDirFile.exists())
            {
                throw new RuntimeException("I/O Temp directory does not exist: " + io
TempDirFile.getAbsolutePath());
            }

            // Append the suffix for our home
            final File home = new File(ioTempDirFile, RELATIVE_LOCATION_HOME);
            ftpHome = home;
        }
```

```
            // Return
            return ftpHome;
        }
    }
```

FileTransferUnitTestCase.java

```java
package org.jboss.ejb3.examples.ch06.filetransfer;

import java.io.ByteArrayInputStream;
import java.io.ByteArrayOutputStream;
import java.io.InputStream;
import java.1o.ObjectInput;
import java.io.ObjectInputStream;
import java.io.ObjectOutput;
import java.io.ObjectOutputStream;

import javax.ejb.PostActivate;
import javax.ejb.PrePassivate;

import junit.framework.TestCase;

import org.jboss.logging.Logger;
import org.junit.After;
import org.junit.AfterClass;
import org.junit.Before;
import org.junit.BeforeClass;
import org.junit.Test;

/**
 * Test cases to ensure that the FileTransfer business
 * logic is intact, outside of the container.
 *
 * This is not technically part of the SFSB examples, but is
 * in place to ensure that everything with the example itself
 * is working as expected.
 *
 * @author <a href="mailto:andrew.rubinger@jboss.org">ALR</a>
 */
public class FileTransferUnitTestCase extends FileTransferTestCaseBase
{

    //-------------------------------------------------------------------------||
    // Class Members ----------------------------------------------------------||
    //-------------------------------------------------------------------------||

    /**
     * Logger
     */
    private static final Logger log = Logger.getLogger(FileTransferUnitTestCase.
    class);

    /**
     * The FTP Service to which we'll connect
     */
```

```java
private static FtpServerPojo ftpService;

/**
 * Port to which the FTP Service will bind
 */
private static final int FTP_SERVICE_BIND_PORT = 12345;

/**
 * Name of the users configuration file for the server
 */
private static final String FILE_NAME_USERS_CONFIG = "ftpusers.properties";

//--------------------------------------------------------------------------||
// Instance Members --------------------------------------------------------||
//--------------------------------------------------------------------------||

/**
 * The FTP Client
 */
private FileTransferBean ftpClient;

//--------------------------------------------------------------------------||
// Lifecycle ---------------------------------------------------------------||
//--------------------------------------------------------------------------||

/**
 * Creates, initializes, and starts the FTP Service
 * to which our test clients will connect.
 * Called once before any tests run.
 */
@BeforeClass
public static void createFtpService() throws Exception
{
   // Create the FTP Service
   final FtpServerPojo service = new FtpServerPojo();

   // Configure
   service.setBindPort(FTP_SERVICE_BIND_PORT);
   service.setUsersConfigFileName(FILE_NAME_USERS_CONFIG);

   // Initialize
   service.initializeServer();

   // Start
   service.startServer();

   // Set (on success)
   log.info("Started up test FTP Service: " + service);
   ftpService = service;
}

/**
 * Stops and resets the FTP Service.  Called once after
 * all tests are done.
 *
```

```
 * @throws Exception
 */
@AfterClass
public static void destroyFtpService() throws Exception
{
   // Only run if initialization finished
   if (ftpService == null)
   {
      return;
   }

   // Stop the server
   ftpService.stopServer();

   // Reset
   ftpService = null;
   log.info("Brought down test FTP Service");
}

/**
 * Creates and initializes the FTP Client used in testing.
 * Fired before each test is run.
 */
@Before
public void createFtpClient() throws Exception
{
   // Create client
   final FileTransferBean ftpClient = new FileTransferBean();

   // Connect
   ftpClient.connect();

   // Set
   this.ftpClient = ftpClient;
   log.info("Set FTP Client: " + ftpClient);
}

/**
 * Disconnects and resets the FTP Client.  Fired after each
 * test has completed.
 *
 * @throws Exception
 */
@After
public void cleanup() throws Exception
{
   // Get client
   final FileTransferBean ftpClient = this.ftpClient;

   // If set
   if (ftpClient != null)
   {
      // Disconnect and reset
      ftpClient.disconnect();
      this.ftpClient = null;
```

```
        }
    }

    //---------------------------------------------------------------||
    // Tests ---------------------------------------------------------||
    //---------------------------------------------------------------||

    /**
     * Mocks the passivation/activation process by manually invoking
     * upon the {@link PrePassivate} and {@link PostActivate} lifecycle
     * callbacks.  The client should function properly after these calls are made,
     * reconnecting as expected, and resuming into the correct present working
     * directory
     *
     * @throws Exception
     */
    @Test
    public void testPassivationAndActivation() throws Exception
    {
        // Log
        log.info("testPassivationAndActivation");

        // Get the client
        final FileTransferCommonBusiness client = this.getClient();

        // Switch to home
        final String home = getFtpHome().getAbsolutePath();
        client.cd(home);

        // Test the pwd
        final String pwdBefore = client.pwd();
        TestCase.assertEquals("Present working directory should be set to home",
home, pwdBefore);

        // Mock @PrePassivate
        log.info("Mock @" + PrePassivate.class.getName());
        client.disconnect();

        // Mock passivation
        log.info("Mock passivation");
        final ByteArrayOutputStream outStream = new ByteArrayOutputStream();
        final ObjectOutput objectOut = new ObjectOutputStream(outStream);
        objectOut.writeObject(client);
        objectOut.close();

        // Mock activation
        log.info("Mock activation");
        final InputStream inStream = new ByteArrayInputStream(outStream.toByteArray
());
        final ObjectInput objectIn = new ObjectInputStream(inStream);

        // Get a new client from passivation/activation roundtrip
        final FileTransferCommonBusiness serializedClient = (FileTransferCommon
Business) objectIn.readObject();
```

```
        objectIn.close();

        // Mock @PostActivate
        log.info("Mock @" + PostActivate.class.getName());
        serializedClient.connect();

        // Test the pwd
        final String pwdAfter = serializedClient.pwd();
        TestCase.assertEquals("Present working directory should be the same as
before passivation/activation", home,
                pwdAfter);
    }

    //-------------------------------------------------------------------------||
    // Required Implementations -----------------------------------------------||
    //-------------------------------------------------------------------------||

    /* (non-Javadoc)
     * @see org.jboss.ejb3.examples.ch06.filetransfer.FileTransferTestCaseBase
#getClient()
     */
    @Override
    protected FileTransferCommonBusiness getClient()
    {
        return this.ftpClient;
    }

}
```

FtpServerPojo.java

```
package org.jboss.ejb3.examples.ch06.filetransfer;

import java.net.URL;
import java.security.AccessController;
import java.security.PrivilegedAction;

import org.apache.ftpserver.FtpServer;
import org.apache.ftpserver.FtpServerFactory;
import org.apache.ftpserver.ftplet.FtpException;
import org.apache.ftpserver.ftplet.UserManager;
import org.apache.ftpserver.listener.ListenerFactory;
import org.apache.ftpserver.usermanager.ClearTextPasswordEncryptor;
import org.apache.ftpserver.usermanager.PropertiesUserManagerFactory;
import org.jboss.logging.Logger;

/**
 * POJO Responsible for starting/stopping
 * the Embedded FTP Server.
 *
 * This should be considered part of the test execution environment
 * and is not really part of the SFSB examples themselves.
 * The SFSBs for the examples are a client of the FTP server
 * started by this simple bean.
 *
```

```
 * Not thread-safe.  Intended to be used in single-Threaded environments
 * (or perform your own external synchronization).
 *
 * @author <a href="mailto:andrew.rubinger@jboss.org">ALR</a>
 */
public final class FtpServerPojo
{

   //--------------------------------------------------------------------------||
   // Class Members -----------------------------------------------------------||
   //--------------------------------------------------------------------------||

   /**
    * Logger
    */
   private static final Logger log = Logger.getLogger(FtpServerPojo.class);

   /**
    * Name of the Server's default listener
    */
   private static final String LISTENER_NAME_DEFAULT = "default";

   //--------------------------------------------------------------------------||
   // Instance Members --------------------------------------------------------||
   //--------------------------------------------------------------------------||

   /**
    * Port to which the FTP Server will bind.
    */
   private int bindPort;

   /**
    * The underlying server.  Must not be exported.
    */
   private FtpServer server;

   /**
    * The name of the users/password configuration filename.
    */
   private String usersConfigFileName;

   //--------------------------------------------------------------------------||
   // Lifecycle Methods -------------------------------------------------------||
   //--------------------------------------------------------------------------||

   /**
    * Creates and initializes the underlying server.  Should be
    * called along lifecycle when this POJO is created.
    *
    * @throws IllegalStateException If the properties for the server have not
    *         been properly initialized
    */
   public void initializeServer() throws IllegalStateException
   {
      // Extract properties
```

```
        final int bindPort = this.getBindPort();

        /*
         * Precondition checks
         */

        if (bindPort <= 0)
        {
            throw new IllegalStateException("Property for bind port has not been set
    to a valid value above 0.");
        }

        // Initialize
        final FtpServerFactory serverFactory = new FtpServerFactory();
        final ListenerFactory factory = new ListenerFactory();

        // Set properties
        log.debug("Using FTP bind port: " + bindPort);
        factory.setPort(bindPort);

        // Add default listener to the server factory
        serverFactory.addListener(LISTENER_NAME_DEFAULT, factory.createListener());

        // Get the current CL
        final ClassLoader tccl = AccessController.doPrivileged(new PrivilegedAction
    <ClassLoader>()
        {
            @Override
            public ClassLoader run()
            {
                return Thread.currentThread().getContextClassLoader();
            }
        });

        // Load the properties file to get its URI
        final String usersConfigFileName = this.getUsersConfigFileName();
        log.info("Using users configuration file: " + usersConfigFileName);
        final URL usersConfigUrl = tccl.getResource(usersConfigFileName);
        if (usersConfigUrl == null)
        {
            throw new RuntimeException("Could not find specified users configuration
    file upon the classpath: "
                    + usersConfigFileName);
        }

        // Configure the user auth mechanism
        final PropertiesUserManagerFactory userManagerFactory = new PropertiesUser
    ManagerFactory();
        userManagerFactory.setUrl(usersConfigUrl);
        userManagerFactory.setPasswordEncryptor(new ClearTextPasswordEncryptor());
        final UserManager userManager = userManagerFactory.createUserManager();
        serverFactory.setUserManager(userManager);

        // Create the server
        final FtpServer server = serverFactory.createServer();
```

```java
        this.setServer(server);
        log.info("Created FTP Server: " + server);
    }

    /**
     * Starts the server.
     *
     * @throws IllegalStateException If the server has not been initialized or
     *         if the server has already been started
     * @throws FtpException If there was an error in starting the server
     */
    public void startServer() throws IllegalStateException, FtpException
    {
        // Get the server
        final FtpServer server = this.getServer();

        /*
         * Precondition checks
         */

        // Ensure initialized
        if (server == null)
        {
            throw new IllegalStateException("The server has not yet been initialized
");
        }

        // Ensure not already running or in some other state
        if (!server.isStopped())
        {
            throw new IllegalStateException("Server cannot be started if it is not
currently stopped");
        }

        // Start
        log.debug("Starting the FTP Server: " + server);
        server.start();
        log.info("FTP Server Started: " + server);
    }

    /**
     * Stops the server.
     *
     * @throws IllegalStateException If the server is already stopped or the
server is
     *         not initialized
     * @throws FtpException
     */
    public void stopServer() throws IllegalStateException
    {
        // Get the server
        final FtpServer server = this.getServer();

        /*
         * Precondition checks
```

```
         */

        // Ensure initialized
        if (server == null)
        {
            throw new IllegalStateException("The server has not yet been
initialized");
        }

        // Ensure not already running or in some other state
        if (server.isStopped())
        {
            throw new IllegalStateException("Server cannot be stopped if it's
already stopped");
        }

        // Stop
        log.debug("Stopping the FTP Server: " + server);
        server.stop();
        log.info("FTP Server stopped: " + server);
    }

    //-------------------------------------------------------------------------||
    // Accessors / Mutators ---------------------------------------------------||
    //-------------------------------------------------------------------------||

    /**
     * Obtains the port to which we'll bind
     */
    public int getBindPort()
    {
        return bindPort;
    }

    /**
     * Sets the port to which we'll bind.
     *
     * @param bindPort
     */
    public void setBindPort(final int bindPort)
    {
        this.bindPort = bindPort;
    }

    /**
     * Obtains the underlying FTP Server
     *
     * @return
     */
    protected FtpServer getServer()
    {
        return server;
    }

    /**
```

```
 * Sets the underlying FTP Server.
 *
 * @param server
 */
private void setServer(final FtpServer server)
{
   this.server = server;
}

/**
 * Obtains the name of the users configuration file
 *
 * @return the usersConfigFileName
 */
public String getUsersConfigFileName()
{
   return usersConfigFileName;
}

/**
 * Sets the name of the users configuration file.
 *
 * @param usersConfigFileName the usersConfigFileName to set
 */
public void setUsersConfigFileName(final String usersConfigFileName)
{
   this.usersConfigFileName = usersConfigFileName;
}
}
```

ftpusers.properties

```
# Users / Passwords file
ftpserver.user.user.idletime=0
ftpserver.user.user.userpassword=password
ftpserver.user.user.homedirectory=/
ftpserver.user.user.writepermission=true
ftpserver.user.user.enableflag=true
```

Singleton Session EJB: RSS Cache Example

Description

Often we have a business process best modeled by a single instance instead of a backing pool (like SLSB) or cache (SFSB). New to EJB 3.1, the `@Singleton` EJB creates a sole backing instance to service all incoming requests.

This has two important consequences. First, if this instance is eagerly brought into service (via the `@Startup`) annotation, we may now have application lifecycle events (`@PreConstruct` / `@PostConstruct`).

Second, because all requests are sharing a single instance, for the first time EJB developers must address concurrency of writable, shared state. No SLSB or SFSB bean instance will ever be accessed by more than one thread at a time (thread safety via confinement). This is not the case with `@Singleton`, so the specification introduces container-managed concurrency annotations based on a read/write-lock model to provide declarative thread safety for developers.

Our example models a simple cache which hangs onto an RSS feed. Read operations will not block, but refreshing the cache will block all readers until complete. Assuming a much higher percentage of reads to refreshes, this cache will remain efficient.

Online Companion Information

Wiki article: *http://community.jboss.org/docs/DOC-15569*

Source location: *http://github.com/jbossejb3/oreilly-ejb-6thedition-book-examples/tree/master/ch07-rsscache/*

Source Listing

Following is a full listing of all source code used in this runnable example.

Implementation Resources

ProtectExportUtil.java

```java
package org.jboss.ejb3.examples.ch07.rsscache.impl.rome;

import java.net.MalformedURLException;
import java.net.URL;

/**
 * Package-private utilities to protect against mutable
 * state getting exported
 *
 * @author <a href="mailto:andrew.rubinger@jboss.org">ALR</a>
 */
class ProtectExportUtil
{
    //-------------------------------------------------------------------------||
    // Constructor ------------------------------------------------------------||
    //-------------------------------------------------------------------------||

    /**
     * Internal constructor; protects against instantiation
     */
    private ProtectExportUtil()
    {
    }

    //-------------------------------------------------------------------------||
    // Functional Methods -----------------------------------------------------||
    //-------------------------------------------------------------------------||

    /**
     * Returns a copy of the specified URL; used to ensure that mutable
     * internal state is not leaked out to clients
     * @param url
     * @return
     */
    static URL copyUrl(final URL url)
    {
        // If null, return
        if (url == null)
        {
            return url;
        }

        try
        {
```

```
                // Copy
                return new URL(url.toExternalForm());
            }
            catch (final MalformedURLException e)
            {
                throw new RuntimeException("Error in copying URL", e);
            }
        }
    }
```

RomeRssEntry.java

```java
package org.jboss.ejb3.examples.ch07.rsscache.impl.rome;

import java.net.MalformedURLException;
import java.net.URL;

import org.jboss.ejb3.examples.ch07.rsscache.spi.RssEntry;

import com.sun.syndication.feed.synd.SyndContent;
import com.sun.syndication.feed.synd.SyndEntry;

/**
 * The java.net Rome implementation of an RSS Entry
 *
 * @author <a href="mailto:andrew.rubinger@jboss.org">ALR</a>
 */
public class RomeRssEntry implements RssEntry
{

    //-------------------------------------------------------------------------||
    // Instance Members -------------------------------------------------------||
    //-------------------------------------------------------------------------||

    /**
     * The author of the entry
     */
    private String author;

    /**
     * The short description of the entry
     */
    private String description;

    /**
     * The title of the entry
     */
    private String title;

    /**
     * The link to the entry
     */
    private URL url;
```

```
//-------------------------------------------------------------------------||
// Constructor ------------------------------------------------------------||
//-------------------------------------------------------------------------||

/**
 * Constructor
 *
 * @param entry The Rome API's RSS Entry representation
 * @throws IllegalArgumentException If the entry is not specified
 */
RomeRssEntry(final SyndEntry entry) throws IllegalArgumentException
{
    // Set properties
    this.author = entry.getAuthor();
    final SyndContent content = entry.getDescription();
    this.description = content.getValue();
    this.title = entry.getTitle();
    final String urlString = entry.getLink();
    URL url = null;
    try
    {
        url = new URL(urlString);
    }
    catch (final MalformedURLException murle)
    {
        throw new RuntimeException("Obtained invalid URL from Rome RSS entry: "
+ entry, murle);
    }
    this.url = url;
}

//-------------------------------------------------------------------------||
// Required Implementations -----------------------------------------------||
//-------------------------------------------------------------------------||

/* (non-Javadoc)
 * @see org.jboss.ejb3.examples.ch07.rsscache.spi.RssEntry#getAuthor()
 */
@Override
public String getAuthor()
{
    return this.author;
}

/* (non-Javadoc)
 * @see org.jboss.ejb3.examples.ch07.rsscache.spi.RssEntry#getDescription()
 */
@Override
public String getDescription()
{
    return this.description;
}
```

```
/* (non-Javadoc)
 * @see org.jboss.ejb3.examples.ch07.rsscache.spi.RssEntry#getTitle()
 */
@Override
public String getTitle()
{
   return this.title;
}

/* (non-Javadoc)
 * @see org.jboss.ejb3.examples.ch07.rsscache.spi.RssEntry#getUrl()
 */
@Override
public URL getUrl()
{
   return ProtectExportUtil.copyUrl(this.url);
}

//-------------------------------------------------------------------------||
// Overridden Implementations ---------------------------------------------||
//-------------------------------------------------------------------------||

/* (non-Javadoc)
 * @see java.lang.Object#toString()
 */
@Override
public String toString()
{
   final StringBuilder sb = new StringBuilder();
   sb.append(this.getTitle());
   sb.append(" - ");
   sb.append(this.url.toExternalForm());
   return sb.toString();
}
}
```

RssCacheBean.java

```
package org.jboss.ejb3.examples.ch07.rsscache.impl.rome;

import java.io.IOException;
import java.net.URL;
import java.util.ArrayList;
import java.util.Collections;
import java.util.List;

import javax.annotation.PostConstruct;
import javax.ejb.ConcurrencyManagement;
import javax.ejb.ConcurrencyManagementType;
import javax.ejb.Lock;
import javax.ejb.LockType;
import javax.ejb.Remote;
```

```java
import javax.ejb.Singleton;
import javax.ejb.Startup;

import org.jboss.ejb3.examples.ch07.rsscache.spi.RssCacheCommonBusiness;
import org.jboss.ejb3.examples.ch07.rsscache.spi.RssEntry;
import org.jboss.logging.Logger;

import com.sun.syndication.feed.synd.SyndEntry;
import com.sun.syndication.feed.synd.SyndFeed;
import com.sun.syndication.fetcher.FeedFetcher;
import com.sun.syndication.fetcher.FetcherException;
import com.sun.syndication.fetcher.impl.HttpClientFeedFetcher;
import com.sun.syndication.io.FeedException;

/**
 * Singleton EJB, to be eagerly instantiated upon application deployment,
 * exposing a cached view of an RSS Feed
 *
 * @author <a href="mailto:andrew.rubinger@jboss.org">ALR</a>
 */
@Singleton
@Startup
@Remote(RssCacheCommonBusiness.class)
// Explicitly declare Container Managed Concurrency, which is unnecessary; it's
the default
@ConcurrencyManagement(ConcurrencyManagementType.CONTAINER)
public class RssCacheBean implements RssCacheCommonBusiness
{

   //-------------------------------------------------------------------------||
   // Class Members ----------------------------------------------------------||
   //-------------------------------------------------------------------------||

   /**
    * Logger
    */
   private static final Logger log = Logger.getLogger(RssCacheBean.class);

   //-------------------------------------------------------------------------||
   // Instance Members -------------------------------------------------------||
   //-------------------------------------------------------------------------||

   /**
    * URL pointing to the RSS Feed
    */
   private URL url;

   /**
    * Cached RSS Entries for the feed
    */
   private List<RssEntry> entries;
```

```
    //-------------------------------------------------------------------------||
    // Required Implementations ----------------------------------------------||
    //-------------------------------------------------------------------------||

    /* (non-Javadoc)
     * @see org.jboss.ejb3.examples.ch07.rsscache.spi.RssCacheCommonBusiness#get
Entries()
     */
    @Override
    @Lock(LockType.READ)
    public List<RssEntry> getEntries()
    {
        return entries;
    }

    /* (non-Javadoc)
     * @see org.jboss.ejb3.examples.ch07.rsscache.spi.RssCacheCommonBusiness#get
Url()
     */
    @Lock(LockType.READ)
    @Override
    public URL getUrl()
    {
        // Return a copy so we don't export mutable state to the client
        return ProtectExportUtil.copyUrl(this.url);
    }

    /**
     * @see org.jboss.ejb3.examples.ch07.rsscache.spi.RssCacheCommonBusiness
#refresh()
     * @throws IllegalStateException If the URL has not been set
     */
    @PostConstruct
    @Override
    // Block all readers and writers until we're done here; Optional metadata,
WRITE is the default
    @Lock(LockType.WRITE)
    public void refresh() throws IllegalStateException
    {

        // Obtain the URL
        final URL url = this.url;
        if (url == null)
        {
            throw new IllegalStateException("The Feed URL has not been set");
        }
        log.info("Requested: " + url);

        // Obtain the feed
        final FeedFetcher feedFetcher = new HttpClientFeedFetcher();
        SyndFeed feed = null;
```

```java
        try
        {
            feed = feedFetcher.retrieveFeed(url);
        }
        catch (final FeedException fe)
        {
            throw new RuntimeException(fe);
        }
        catch (final FetcherException fe)
        {
            throw new RuntimeException(fe);
        }
        catch (final IOException ioe)
        {
            throw new RuntimeException(ioe);
        }

        // Make a new list for the entries
        final List<RssEntry> rssEntries = new ArrayList<RssEntry>();

        // For each entry
        @SuppressWarnings("unchecked")
        // The Rome API doesn't provide for generics, so suppress the warning
        final List<SyndEntry> list = (List<SyndEntry>) feed.getEntries();
        for (final SyndEntry entry : list)
        {
            // Make a new entry
            final RssEntry rssEntry = new RomeRssEntry(entry);

            // Place in the list
            rssEntries.add(rssEntry);
            log.debug("Found new RSS Entry: " + rssEntry);
        }

        // Protect the entries from mutation from exporting the client view
        final List<RssEntry> protectedEntries = Collections.unmodifiableList
    (rssEntries);

        // Set the entries in the cache
        this.entries = protectedEntries;
    }

    //-------------------------------------------------------------------------||
    // Internal Helper Methods -------------------------------------------------||
    //-------------------------------------------------------------------------||

    /**
     * Sets the URL pointing to the feed
     *
     * @param url
     * @throws IllegalArgumentException If the URL is null
     */
    void setUrl(final URL url) throws IllegalArgumentException
    {
        // Set the URL
```

```
            this.url = url;

            // Refresh
            this.refresh();
        }
    }
```

RssCacheCommonBusiness.java

```java
package org.jboss.ejb3.examples.ch07.rsscache.spi;

import java.net.URL;
import java.util.List;

/**
 * Common business interface for beans exposing a cached view of an RSS
 * Feed (ie. the EJB Container)
 *
 * @author <a href="mailto:andrew.rubinger@jboss.org">ALR</a>
 */
public interface RssCacheCommonBusiness
{
    // ------------------------------------------------------------------------||
    // Contracts --------------------------------------------------------------||
    // ------------------------------------------------------------------------||

    /**
     * Returns all entries in the RSS Feed represented by {@link RssCacheCommon
Business#getUrl()}.
     * This list will not support mutation and is read-only.
     */
    List<RssEntry> getEntries();

    /**
     * Returns the URL of the RSS Feed
     *
     * @return
     */
    URL getUrl();

    /**
     * Flushes the cache and refreshes the entries from the feed
     */
    void refresh();

}
```

RssEntry.java

```java
package org.jboss.ejb3.examples.ch07.rsscache.spi;

import java.net.URL;

/**
 * Defines the contract for a single RSS Entry
 *
 * @author <a href="mailto:andrew.rubinger@jboss.org">ALR</a>
 */
public interface RssEntry
{
   // -------------------------------------------------------------------------||
   // Contracts ---------------------------------------------------------------||
   // -------------------------------------------------------------------------||

   /**
    * Obtains the author of the entry
    *
    * @return
    */
   String getAuthor();

   /**
    * Obtains the title of the entry
    *
    * @return
    */
   String getTitle();

   /**
    * Obtains the URL linking to the entry
    *
    * @return
    */
   URL getUrl();

   /**
    * Obtains the short description of the entry
    *
    * @return
    */
   String getDescription();
}
```

Test Resources

RssCacheTestCaseBase.java

```java
package org.jboss.ejb3.examples.ch07.rsscache;

import java.io.BufferedReader;
import java.io.BufferedWriter;
import java.io.File;
import java.io.FileReader;
import java.io.FileWriter;
import java.io.IOException;
import java.io.PrintWriter;
import java.net.URI;
import java.net.URISyntaxException;
import java.net.URL;
import java.util.List;

import javax.servlet.ServletException;
import javax.servlet.http.HttpServletRequest;
import javax.servlet.http.HttpServletResponse;

import junit.framework.Assert;

import org.jboss.ejb3.examples.ch07.rsscache.spi.RssCacheCommonBusiness;
import org.jboss.ejb3.examples.ch07.rsscache.spi.RssEntry;
import org.jboss.logging.Logger;
import org.junit.AfterClass;
import org.junit.BeforeClass;
import org.junit.Test;
import org.mortbay.jetty.Handler;
import org.mortbay.jetty.Server;
import org.mortbay.jetty.handler.AbstractHandler;

/**
 * Base tests for the RssCache @Singleton
 * test classes, may be extended either from unit or
 * integration tests.
 *
 * @author <a href="mailto:andrew.rubinger@jboss.org">ALR</a>
 */
public abstract class RssCacheTestCaseBase
{

    //-------------------------------------------------------------------------||
    // Class Members ----------------------------------------------------------||
    //-------------------------------------------------------------------------||

    private static final Logger log = Logger.getLogger(RssCacheTestCaseBase.class);

    /**
     * The number of expected RSS entries from the default RSS Feed
     */
    private static final int EXPECTED_15_RSS_ENTRIES = 15;
```

```java
/**
 * The number of expected RSS entries from the RSS Feed with 5 entries
 */
private static final int EXPECTED_5_RSS_ENTRIES = 5;

/**
 * Filename containing a mock RSS feed for use in testing
 */
static final String FILENAME_RSS_MOCK_FEED_15_ENTRIES = "15_entries.rss";

/**
 * Filename containing a mock RSS feed for use in testing
 */
static final String FILENAME_RSS_MOCK_FEED_5_ENTRIES = "5_entries.rss";

/**
 * Filename of the target RSS feed to be requested of the HTTP server
 */
static final String FILENAME_RSS_FEED = "feed.rss";

/**
 * Port to which the test HTTP Server should bind
 */
static final int HTTP_TEST_BIND_PORT = 12345;

/**
 * Content type of an RSS feed
 */
private static final String CONTENT_TYPE_RSS = "text/rss";

/**
 * The HTTP Server used to serve out the mock RSS file
 */
static Server httpServer;

/**
 * Newline character
 */
private static final char NEWLINE = '\n';

//-------------------------------------------------------------------------||
// Lifecycle --------------------------------------------------------------||
//-------------------------------------------------------------------------||

/**
 * Starts up an embedded HTTP Server to serve out the Mock
 * RSS file (Rome FeedFetcher doesn't support obtaining from
 * file:/ URLs)
 */
@BeforeClass
public static void startHttpServer()
{
    // Start an Embedded HTTP Server
    final Handler handler = new StaticFileHandler();
    final Server httpServer = new Server(HTTP_TEST_BIND_PORT);
```

```
        httpServer.setHandler(handler);
        try
        {
            httpServer.start();
        }
        catch (final Exception e)
        {
            throw new RuntimeException("Could not start server");
        }
        log.info("HTTP Server Started: " + httpServer);
        RssCacheUnitTestCase.httpServer = httpServer;
    }

    /**
     * Creates the RSS feed file from the default mock template
     */
    @BeforeClass
    public static void createRssFeedFile() throws Exception
    {
        writeToRssFeedFile(getMock15EntriesRssFile());
    }

    /**
     * Shuts down and clears the Embedded HTTP Server
     */
    @AfterClass
    public static void shutdownHttpServer()
    {
        if (httpServer != null)
        {
            try
            {
                httpServer.stop();
            }
            catch (final Exception e)
            {
                // Swallow
                log.error("Could not stop HTTP Server cleanly", e);
            }
            log.info("HTTP Server Stopped: " + httpServer);
            httpServer = null;
        }
    }

    /**
     * Removes the RSS feed file
     */
    @AfterClass
    public static void deleteRssFeedFile() throws Exception
    {
        final File rssFile = getRssFeedFile();
        boolean deleted = rssFile.delete();
        if (!deleted)
        {
            log.warn("RSS Feed File was not cleaned up properly: " + rssFile);
```

```
        }
    }

    //-------------------------------------------------------------------------||
    // Tests -----------------------------------------------------------------||
    //-------------------------------------------------------------------------||

    /**
     * Ensures the RSS Entries have been initialized and parsed
     * out as expected.  Additionally tests that {@link RssCacheCommonBusiness
#refresh()}
     * clears the cache and works as expected
     */
    @Test
    public void testRssEntries() throws Exception
    {
        // Log
        log.info("testRssEntries");

        // Get the RSS Cache Bean
        final RssCacheCommonBusiness rssCache = this.getRssCacheBean();

        // Get all entries
        final List<RssEntry> rssEntries = rssCache.getEntries();
        log.info("Got entries: " + rssEntries);

        // Ensure they've been specified/initialized, and parsed out in proper size
        this.ensureExpectedEntries(rssEntries, EXPECTED_15_RSS_ENTRIES);

        // Swap out the contents of the RSS Feed File, so a refresh will pull in
the new contents
        writeToRssFeedFile(getMock5EntriesRssFile());

        // Refresh
        rssCache.refresh();

        // Get all entries
        final List<RssEntry> rssEntriesAfterRefresh = rssCache.getEntries();
        log.info("Got entries after refresh: " + rssEntriesAfterRefresh);

        // Ensure they've been specified/initialized, and parsed out in proper size
        this.ensureExpectedEntries(rssEntriesAfterRefresh, EXPECTED_5_RSS_ENTRIES);

        // Now put back the original 15 mock entries
        writeToRssFeedFile(getMock15EntriesRssFile());
        rssCache.refresh();

        // And ensure we're back to normal
        final List<RssEntry> rssEntriesAfterRestored = rssCache.getEntries();
        log.info("Got entries: " + rssEntriesAfterRestored);
        this.ensureExpectedEntries(rssEntriesAfterRestored, EXPECTED_15_RSS_ENTRIES);

    }
```

```
//---------------------------------------------------------------------||
// Contracts ----------------------------------------------------------||
//---------------------------------------------------------------------||

/**
 * Obtains the RssCache bean to be used for this test
 */
protected abstract RssCacheCommonBusiness getRssCacheBean();

//---------------------------------------------------------------------||
// Internal Helper Methods --------------------------------------------||
//---------------------------------------------------------------------||

/**
 * Ensures that the RSS entries are parsed out and have the specified number
of elements
 * @param entries
 * @param expectedSize
 */
private void ensureExpectedEntries(final List<RssEntry> entries, final int
expectedSize)
{
    // Ensure they've been specified/initialized, and parsed out in proper size
    Assert.assertNotNull("RSS Entries was either not initialized or is
returning null", entries);
    final int actualSize = entries.size();
    Assert.assertEquals("Wrong number of RSS entries parsed out from feed",
expectedSize, actualSize);
    log.info("Got expected " + expectedSize + " RSS entries");
}

/**
 * Obtains the base of the code source
 */
private static URL getCodebaseLocation()
{
    return RssCacheUnitTestCase.class.getProtectionDomain().getCodeSource().get
Location();
}

/**
 * Writes the contents of the template file to the RSS Feed File
 *
 * @param templateFile
 * @throws Exception
 */
private static void writeToRssFeedFile(final File templateFile) throws Exception
{
    // Get a writer to the target file
    final File rssFile = getRssFeedFile();
    final PrintWriter writer = new PrintWriter(new BufferedWriter(new File
Writer(rssFile)));
```

```java
        // Get a reader to the default mock template file
        final BufferedReader reader = new BufferedReader(new FileReader(template
File));

        // Read 'n Write
        String line = null;
        while ((line = reader.readLine()) != null)
        {
            writer.write(line);
            writer.write(NEWLINE);
        }

        // Flush and close
        writer.flush();
        writer.close();
        reader.close();
    }

    /**
     * Obtains the RSS Feed file served by the server
     * @return
     * @throws Exception
     */
    private static File getRssFeedFile() throws Exception
    {
        final File baseFile = getBaseDirectory();
        final File rssFile = new File(baseFile, FILENAME_RSS_FEED);
        return rssFile;
    }

    /**
     * Obtains the Mock RSS Template file with 15 entries
     * @return
     * @throws Exception
     */
    private static File getMock15EntriesRssFile() throws Exception
    {
        return getFileFromBase(FILENAME_RSS_MOCK_FEED_15_ENTRIES);
    }

    /**
     * Obtains the Mock RSS Template file with 5 entries
     * @return
     * @throws Exception
     */
    private static File getMock5EntriesRssFile() throws Exception
    {
        return getFileFromBase(FILENAME_RSS_MOCK_FEED_5_ENTRIES);
    }

    /**
     * Obtains the file with the specified name from the base directory
     *
     * @param filename
     * @return
```

```
 * @throws Exception
 */
private static File getFileFromBase(final String filename) throws Exception
{
    final File baseFile = getBaseDirectory();
    final File mockTemplateFile = new File(baseFile, filename);
    return mockTemplateFile;
}

/**
 * Obtains the base directory in which test files are located
 * @return
 */
private static File getBaseDirectory() throws Exception
{
    final URL baseLocation = getCodebaseLocation();
    final URI baseUri = baseLocation.toURI();
    final File baseFile = new File(baseUri);
    return baseFile;
}

//--------------------------------------------------------------------------||
// Inner Classes -----------------------------------------------------------||
//--------------------------------------------------------------------------||

/**
 * Jetty Handler to serve a static character file from the web root
 */
private static class StaticFileHandler extends AbstractHandler implements
Handler
{
    /*
     * (non-Javadoc)
     * @see org.mortbay.jetty.Handler#handle(java.lang.String, javax.servlet.
http.HttpServletRequest, javax.servlet.http.HttpServletResponse, int)
     */
    public void handle(final String target, final HttpServletRequest request,
final HttpServletResponse response,
            final int dispatch) throws IOException, ServletException
    {
        // Set content type and status before we write anything to the stream
        response.setContentType(CONTENT_TYPE_RSS);
        response.setStatus(HttpServletResponse.SC_OK);

        // Obtain the requested file relative to the webroot
        final URL root = getCodebaseLocation();
        final URL fileUrl = new URL(root.toExternalForm() + target);
        URI uri = null;
        try
        {
            uri = fileUrl.toURI();
        }
        catch (final URISyntaxException urise)
        {
            throw new RuntimeException(urise);
```

```
            }
            final File file = new File(uri);

            // File not found, so 404
            if (!file.exists())
            {
                response.setStatus(HttpServletResponse.SC_NOT_FOUND);
                log.warn("Requested file is not found: " + file);
                return;
            }

            // Write out each line
            final BufferedReader reader = new BufferedReader(new FileReader(file));
            final PrintWriter writer = response.getWriter();
            String line = null;
            while ((line = reader.readLine()) != null)
            {
                writer.println(line);
            }

            // Close 'er up
            writer.flush();
            reader.close();
            writer.close();
        }
    }

}
```

RssCacheUnitTestCase.java

```
    package org.jboss.ejb3.examples.ch07.rsscache;

    import java.net.MalformedURLException;
    import java.net.URL;

    import org.jboss.ejb3.examples.ch07.rsscache.impl.rome.TestRssCacheBean;
    import org.jboss.ejb3.examples.ch07.rsscache.spi.RssCacheCommonBusiness;
    import org.jboss.logging.Logger;
    import org.junit.AfterClass;
    import org.junit.BeforeClass;

    /**
     * Unit Tests for the RssCache classes,
     * used as a POJO outside the context of the EJB container
     *
     * @author <a href="mailto:andrew.rubinger@jboss.org">ALR</a>
     */
    public class RssCacheUnitTestCase extends RssCacheTestCaseBase
    {
```

```
//-----------------------------------------------------------------------||
// Class Members -------------------------------------------------------||
//-----------------------------------------------------------------------||

/**
 * Logger
 */
private static final Logger log = Logger.getLogger(RssCacheUnitTestCase.class);

/**
 * The bean (POJO) instance to test, mocking a @Singleton EJB
 */
private static RssCacheCommonBusiness bean;

//-----------------------------------------------------------------------||
// Lifecycle -----------------------------------------------------------||
//-----------------------------------------------------------------------||

/**
 * Creates a POJO instance to mock the real Container EJB @Singleton
 * before any tests are run
 */
@BeforeClass
public static void createPojo()
{
    // Instantiate and set
    final TestRssCacheBean bean = new TestRssCacheBean();
    RssCacheUnitTestCase.bean = bean;
    log.info("Created POJO instance: " + bean);

    // Set the URL of the Mock RSS File
    URL url = null;
    try
    {
        url = new URL(getBaseConnectUrl(), FILENAME_RSS_FEED);
    }
    catch (final MalformedURLException murle)
    {
        throw new RuntimeException("Error in test setup while constructing the
mock RSS feed URL", murle);
    }
    bean.setUrl(url);

    // Mock container initialization upon the bean
    bean.refresh();
}

/**
 * Resets the POJO instance to null after all tests are run
 */
@AfterClass
public static void clearPojo()
```

```
      {
        // Set to null so we don't ever leak instances between test runs
        bean = null;
      }

      //--------------------------------------------------------------------||
      // Required Implementations -------------------------------------------||
      //--------------------------------------------------------------------||

      /**
       * {@inheritDoc}
       * @see org.jboss.ejb3.examples.ch07.envinfo.EnvironmentInformationTestCase
   Base#getEnvInfoBean()
       */
      @Override
      protected RssCacheCommonBusiness getRssCacheBean()
      {
         return bean;
      }

      //--------------------------------------------------------------------||
      // Internal Helper Methods --------------------------------------------||
      //--------------------------------------------------------------------||

      /**
       * Obtains the base of the code source
       */
      private static URL getBaseConnectUrl()
      {
         try
         {
            return new URL("http://localhost:" + HTTP_TEST_BIND_PORT);
         }
         catch (final MalformedURLException e)
         {
            throw new RuntimeException("Error in creating the base URL during set
   setup", e);
         }
      }

   }
```

TestRssCacheBean.java

```
   package org.jboss.ejb3.examples.ch07.rsscache.impl.rome;

   import java.net.URL;

   /**
    * Extension of the RSS Cache Bean which exposes support to
    * set the Feed URL for testing
    *
    * @author <a href="mailto:andrew.rubinger@jboss.org">ALR</a>
    */
```

```
public class TestRssCacheBean extends RssCacheBean
{

    //----------------------------------------------------------------------||
    // Overridden Implementations --------------------------------------------||
    //----------------------------------------------------------------------||

    /* (non-Javadoc)
     * @see org.jboss.ejb3.examples.ch07.rsscache.impl.rome.RssCacheBean#setUrl
(java.net.URL)
     */
    @Override
    public void setUrl(final URL url) throws IllegalArgumentException
    {
        super.setUrl(url);
    }
}
```

jndi.properties

```
# JNDI Properties for Remote interaction with JBoss Application Server Naming
Service
java.naming.factory.initial=org.jnp.interfaces.NamingContextFactory
java.naming.factory.url.pkgs=org.jboss.naming:org.jnp.interfaces
java.naming.provider.url=jnp://localhost:1099
```

Message-Driven EJB: Status Update Listeners Example

Description

Session beans, as we've seen up to this point, are best suited for servicing client requests. Many enterprise systems, however, use a messaging layer to asynchronously pass requests from application to application. In Java, we use the Java Message Service abstraction to push/pull messages via Queues and Topics, and the integration of JMS with EJB is the message-driven bean.

In this example, we implement social networking status updates via a consumer/publisher Topic. Anyone listening on the Topic will receive incoming status updates, and we create 2 listeners: 1 simple one to log out to the command-line or logfile, and another to push the updates to Twitter.

Note: Set the environment variables below before running to take advantage of the Twitter updates while running the tests.

```
OREILLY_EJB_BOOK_CH08_TWITTER_USERNAME
OREILLY_EJB_BOOK_CH08_TWITTER_PASSWORD
```

Additionally, in this example we show how the use of a single JVM for the test and the server can be used to enable shared memory locking (i.e., `java.util.concurrent`) to reliably test that asynchronous components have completed as expected.

Online Companion Information

Wiki article: *http://community.jboss.org/docs/DOC-15570*

Source location: *http://github.com/jbossejb3/oreilly-ejb-6thedition-book-examples/tree/master/ch08-statusupdate/*

Source Listing

Following is a full listing of all source code used in this runnable example.

Implementation Resources

StatusUpdate.java

```java
package org.jboss.ejb3.examples.ch08.statusupdate.api;

import java.io.Serializable;

/**
 * Encapsulates a single generic status update.
 *
 * As this implementation is only used to show an example of
 * JMS and EJB MDB processing, we don't follow
 * strict contracts for {@link Serializable} and accept
 * the default serialized form.
 *
 * @author <a href="mailto:andrew.rubinger@jboss.org">ALR</a>
 */
public class StatusUpdate implements Serializable
{
   //-------------------------------------------------------------------------||
   // Class Members ----------------------------------------------------------||
   //-------------------------------------------------------------------------||

   /**
    * serialVersionUID
    */
   private static final long serialVersionUID = 1L;

   //-------------------------------------------------------------------------||
   // Instance Members -------------------------------------------------------||
   //-------------------------------------------------------------------------||

   /**
    * Internal status
    */
   private final String status;

   //-------------------------------------------------------------------------||
   // Constructor ------------------------------------------------------------||
   //-------------------------------------------------------------------------||

   /**
    * Creates a new status update with the specified new status
    *
    * @throws IllegalArgumentException If either the status or username is not
    specified
    */
   public StatusUpdate(final String status) throws IllegalArgumentException
```

```java
{
    // Precondition checks
    if (status == null || status.length() == 0)
    {
        throw new IllegalArgumentException("Status must be specified");
    }

    // Set
    this.status = status;
}

//-------------------------------------------------------------------------||
// Functional Methods -----------------------------------------------------||
//-------------------------------------------------------------------------||

/**
 * Returns the new status
 * @return the status
 */
public String getText()
{
    return status;
}

//-------------------------------------------------------------------------||
// Overridden Implementations ---------------------------------------------||
//-------------------------------------------------------------------------||

/**
 * {@inheritDoc}
 * @see java.lang.Object#toString()
 */
@Override
public String toString()
{
    return this.getClass().getSimpleName() + " [status=" + status + "]";
}

/**
 * {@inheritDoc}
 * @see java.lang.Object#hashCode()
 */
@Override
public int hashCode()
{
    final int prime = 31;
    int result = 1;
    result = prime * result + ((status == null) ? 0 : status.hashCode());
    return result;
}

/**
 * {@inheritDoc}
 * @see java.lang.Object#equals(java.lang.Object)
 */
```

```
      @Override
      public boolean equals(Object obj)
      {
         if (this == obj)
            return true;
         if (obj == null)
            return false;
         if (getClass() != obj.getClass())
            return false;
         StatusUpdate other = (StatusUpdate) obj;
         if (status == null)
         {
            if (other.status != null)
               return false;
         }
         else if (!status.equals(other.status))
            return false;
         return true;
      }
   }
```

StatusUpdateConstants.java

```
package org.jboss.ejb3.examples.ch08.statusupdate.api;

import javax.management.ObjectName;

/**
 * Contains constants used in referring to resources shared
 * by clients of the StatusUpdate MDBs.
 *
 * @author <a href="mailto:andrew.rubinger@jboss.org">ALR</a>
 */
public interface StatusUpdateConstants
{
   //-------------------------------------------------------------------------||
   // Contracts --------------------------------------------------------------||
   //-------------------------------------------------------------------------||

   /**
    * JNDI Name of the pub/sub Topic for status updates
    */
   String JNDI_NAME_TOPIC_STATUSUPDATE = "topic/StatusUpdate";

   /**
    * The type of destination used by StatusUpdate MDB implementations
    */
   String TYPE_DESTINATION_STATUSUPDATE = "javax.jms.Topic";

   /**
    * The JMX {@link ObjectName} which will be used as a dependency name for the
Topic
    */
```

```
        String OBJECT_NAME_TOPIC_STATUSUPDATE = "jboss.messaging.destination:service=
    Topic,name=StatusUpdate";

    }
```

EnvironmentSpecificTwitterUtil.java

```java
    package org.jboss.ejb3.examples.ch08.statusupdate.mdb;

    import twitter4j.Twitter;

    /**
     * A stateless class used in creating new instances of the {@link Twitter}
     * client.  In practice we'd never take this approach, where creation is
     * dependent upon a username/password credential set obtained from the
     * environment.  In these examples we must both externalize these properties
     * such that the EJBs using them may be configured, but also hide
     * default values for the sake of security.
     *
     * It is not advised to take this approach in real systems.
     *
     * @author <a href="mailto:andrew.rubinger@jboss.org">ALR</a>
     */
    public class EnvironmentSpecificTwitterClientUtil
    {

       //-------------------------------------------------------------------------||
       // Class Members ----------------------------------------------------------||
       //-------------------------------------------------------------------------||

       /**
        * Environment variable of the Twitter username
        */
       private static final String ENV_VAR_NAME_TWITTER_USERNAME = "OREILLY_EJB_BOOK_
    CH08_TWITTER_USERNAME";

       /**
        * Environment variable of the Twitter password
        */
       private static final String ENV_VAR_NAME_TWITTER_PASSWORD = "OREILLY_EJB_BOOK_
    CH08_TWITTER_PASSWORD";

       /**
        * Message dictating that the environment does not support Twitter integration
        */
       static final String MSG_UNSUPPORTED_ENVIRONMENT = "Both environment variables
    \"" + ENV_VAR_NAME_TWITTER_USERNAME
             + "\" and \"" + ENV_VAR_NAME_TWITTER_PASSWORD + "\" must be specified
    for this test to run";

       //-------------------------------------------------------------------------||
       // Instance Members -------------------------------------------------------||
       //-------------------------------------------------------------------------||
```

```
//------------------------------------------------------------------------||
// Constructor ------------------------------------------------------------||
//------------------------------------------------------------------------||

private EnvironmentSpecificTwitterClientUtil()
{
    throw new UnsupportedOperationException("No instantiation allowed");
}

//------------------------------------------------------------------------||
// Utility Methods --------------------------------------------------------||
//------------------------------------------------------------------------||

static boolean isSupportedEnvironment()
{
    // Obtain the username and password
    final UsernamePasswordCredentials creds = getCredentials();
    final String username = creds.username;
    final String password = creds.password;

    /*
     * Only continue if these are specified, otherwise log out a warning and
skip this
     * test.  Ordinarily you should NOT test based upon the environment, but in
this
     * case we cannot put username/password combinations in SVN due to security
constraints,
     * and this test interacts with an outside service which we do not control
and cannot mock
     * locally (which would default the purpose of showing how MDBs can be used
to asynchronously
     * integrate with other systems).
     *
     * Typically we'd first enforce the executing environment, but we can't
assume that
     * all users of this example have a Twitter account.
     */
    if (username == null || password == null)
    {
        return false;
    }

    // All good
    return true;
}

/**
 * Obtains a Twitter client for the username and password as specified from
 * the environment.  If the environment is not fully set up, an {@link Illegal
StateException}
 * will be raised noting the environment variables expected to be in place.
To avoid the ISE
 * first check for the integrity of the environment by using
 * {@link EnvironmentSpecificTwitterClientUtil#isSupportedEnvironment()}
 *
```

```
    * @throws IllegalStateException If the environment does not support creation
of a Twitter client
    */
   static Twitter getTwitterClient() throws IllegalStateException
   {
      // Obtain the username and password
      final String username = SecurityActions.getEnvironmentVariable(ENV_VAR_NAME
_TWITTER_USERNAME);
      final String password = SecurityActions.getEnvironmentVariable(ENV_VAR_NAME
_TWITTER_PASSWORD);

      /*
       * We're only supported if both the username and password have been set
       */
      if (!isSupportedEnvironment())
      {
         throw new IllegalStateException(MSG_UNSUPPORTED_ENVIRONMENT);
      }

      // Get a Twitter client
      final Twitter twitterClient = new Twitter(username, password);

      // Return
      return twitterClient;
   }

   //-------------------------------------------------------------------------||
   // Internal Helper Methods ------------------------------------------------||
   //-------------------------------------------------------------------------||

   /**
    * Obtains the username/password credentials from the environment
    * @return
    */
   private static UsernamePasswordCredentials getCredentials()
   {
      // Obtain the username and password
      final String username = SecurityActions.getEnvironmentVariable(ENV_VAR_NAME
_TWITTER_USERNAME);
      final String password = SecurityActions.getEnvironmentVariable(ENV_VAR_NAME
_TWITTER_PASSWORD);

      // Return as unified view
      final UsernamePasswordCredentials creds = new UsernamePasswordCredentials();
      creds.username = username;
      creds.password = password;
      return creds;
   }

   //-------------------------------------------------------------------------||
   // Inner Classes ----------------------------------------------------------||
   //-------------------------------------------------------------------------||

   /**
    * Simple value object to encapsulate a username/password pair
```

```
 *
 * @author <a href="mailto:andrew.rubinger@jboss.org">ALR</a>
 * @version $Revision: $
 */
private static class UsernamePasswordCredentials
{
   private String username;

   private String password;
}
}
```

LoggingStatusUpdateMdb.java

```java
package org.jboss.ejb3.examples.ch08.statusupdate.mdb;

import java.util.logging.Logger;

import javax.ejb.ActivationConfigProperty;
import javax.ejb.MessageDriven;
import javax.jms.MessageListener;

import org.jboss.ejb3.examples.ch08.statusupdate.api.StatusUpdate;
import org.jboss.ejb3.examples.ch08.statusupdate.api.StatusUpdateConstants;

/**
 * An MDB which, {@link MessageListener#onMessage(javax.jms.Message)}, will
 * log out the status update at INFO-level.
 *
 * Not explicitly tested by the examples (because we can't test for logging),
 * but its usage should be illustrative.
 *
 * @author <a href="mailto:andrew.rubinger@jboss.org">ALR</a>
 */
@MessageDriven(activationConfig =
{
      @ActivationConfigProperty(propertyName = "destinationType", propertyValue =
   StatusUpdateConstants.TYPE_DESTINATION_STATUSUPDATE),
      @ActivationConfigProperty(propertyName = "destination", propertyValue =
   StatusUpdateConstants.JNDI_NAME_TOPIC_STATUSUPDATE)})
public class LoggingStatusUpdateMdb extends StatusUpdateBeanBase implements
MessageListener
{

   //-------------------------------------------------------------------------||
   // Class Members ----------------------------------------------------------||
   //-------------------------------------------------------------------------||

   /**
    * Logger
    */
   private static final Logger log = Logger.getLogger(LoggingStatusUpdateMdb.
class.getName());
```

```
    //-------------------------------------------------------------------||
    // Required Implementations -----------------------------------------||
    //-------------------------------------------------------------------||

    /**
     * Logs status out at INFO-level
     * @see org.jboss.ejb3.examples.ch08.statusupdate.mdb.StatusUpdateBeanBase
#updateStatus(org.jboss.ejb3.examples.ch08.statusupdate.api.StatusUpdate)
     */
    @Override
    public void updateStatus(final StatusUpdate newStatus) throws IllegalArgument
Exception, Exception
    {
        // Precondition checks
        if (newStatus == null)
        {
            throw new IllegalArgumentException("status must be specified");
        }

        // Get info
        final String status = newStatus.getText();

        // Log
        log.info("New status received: \"" + status + "\"");
    }

}
```

SecurityActions.java

```
    package org.jboss.ejb3.examples.ch08.statusupdate.mdb;

    import java.security.AccessController;
    import java.security.PrivilegedAction;

    /**
     * Protected security actions not to leak outside this package
     *
     * @author <a href="mailto:andrew.rubinger@jboss.org">ALR</a>
     */
    class SecurityActions
    {

        //-------------------------------------------------------------------||
        // Constructor ------------------------------------------------------||
        //-------------------------------------------------------------------||

        /**
         * No external instantiation
         */
        private SecurityActions()
        {

        }
```

```
//--------------------------------------------------------------------------||
// Utility Methods --------------------------------------------------------||
//--------------------------------------------------------------------------||

/**
 * Obtains the Thread Context ClassLoader
 */
static ClassLoader getThreadContextClassLoader()
{
    return AccessController.doPrivileged(GetTcclAction.INSTANCE);
}

/**
 * Sets the specified CL upon the current Thread's Context
 *
 * @param cl
 * @throws IllegalArgumentException If the CL was null
 */
static void setThreadContextClassLoader(final ClassLoader cl) throws Illegal
ArgumentException
{
    if (cl == null)
    {
        throw new IllegalArgumentException("ClassLoader was null");
    }

    AccessController.doPrivileged(new PrivilegedAction<Void>()
    {
        public Void run()
        {
            Thread.currentThread().setContextClassLoader(cl);
            return null;
        };
    });
}

/**
 * Obtains the environment variable with the specified name, or null
 * if not present
 * @param envVarName
 * @return
 * @throws IllegalArgumentException If the environment variable name was not
 * specified
 */
static String getEnvironmentVariable(final String envVarName) throws Illegal
ArgumentException
{
    // Precondition checks
    if (envVarName == null || envVarName.length() == 0)
    {
        throw new IllegalArgumentException("Environment variable name was not
        specified");
    }
```

```
      // Return
      return AccessController.doPrivileged(new GetEnvironmentVariableAction(env
VarName));
   }

   /**
    * Obtains the system property with the specified key
    *
    * @param key
    * @return
    * @throws IllegalArgumentException If the key is null
    */
   static String getSystemProperty(final String key) throws IllegalArgument
Exception
   {
      // Precondition check
      if (key == null)
      {
         throw new IllegalArgumentException("key was null");
      }

      // Get sysprop
      return AccessController.doPrivileged(new GetSystemPropertyAction(key));
   }

   //-------------------------------------------------------------------------||
   // Inner Classes ----------------------------------------------------------||
   //-------------------------------------------------------------------------||

   /**
    * {@link PrivilegedAction} action to obtain the TCCL
    */
   private enum GetTcclAction implements PrivilegedAction<ClassLoader> {
      INSTANCE;

      @Override
      public ClassLoader run()
      {
         return Thread.currentThread().getContextClassLoader();
      }
   }

   /**
    * {@link PrivilegedAction} to access an environment variable
    *
    *
    * @author <a href="mailto:andrew.rubinger@jboss.org">ALR</a>
    * @version $Revision: $
    */
   private static class GetEnvironmentVariableAction implements PrivilegedAction
<String>
   {

      /**
       * Name of the environment variable to get
```

```java
     */
    private String envVarName;

    /**
     * Creates a new instance capable of obtaining the specified environment
variable name
     * @param envVarName
     */
    public GetEnvironmentVariableAction(final String envVarName)
    {
        this.envVarName = envVarName;
    }

    /**
     * {@inheritDoc}
     * @see java.security.PrivilegedAction#run()
     */
    @Override
    public String run()
    {
        return System.getenv(envVarName);
    }
}

/**
 * {@link PrivilegedAction} to access a system property
 *
 *
 * @author <a href="mailto:andrew.rubinger@jboss.org">ALR</a>
 * @version $Revision: $
 */
private static class GetSystemPropertyAction implements PrivilegedAction<String>
{

    /**
     * Name of the sysprop to get
     */
    private String sysPropName;

    /**
     * Creates a new instance capable of obtaining the specified system
property by name
     * @param sysPropName
     */
    public GetSystemPropertyAction(final String sysPropName)
    {
        this.sysPropName = sysPropName;
    }

    /**
     * {@inheritDoc}
     * @see java.security.PrivilegedAction#run()
     */
    @Override
    public String run()
```

```
        {
            return System.getProperty(sysPropName);
        }
    }

}
```

StatusUpdateBeanBase.java

```java
package org.jboss.ejb3.examples.ch08.statusupdate.mdb;

import java.io.Serializable;
import java.util.logging.Logger;

import javax.jms.JMSException;
import javax.jms.Message;
import javax.jms.MessageListener;
import javax.jms.ObjectMessage;

import org.jboss.ejb3.examples.ch08.statusupdate.api.StatusUpdate;

/**
 * Base support for the StatusUpdateEJB.  Responsible for
 * consuming an incoming JMS Message and dispatching to
 * {@link StatusUpdateBeanBase#updateStatus(StatusUpdate)}.  Children
 * are required to supply specialization of this method.
 *
 * @author <a href="mailto:andrew.rubinger@jboss.org">ALR</a>
 */
public abstract class StatusUpdateBeanBase implements MessageListener
{
    //-------------------------------------------------------------------------||
    // Class Members -----------------------------------------------------------||
    //-------------------------------------------------------------------------||

    /**
     * Logger
     */
    private static final Logger log = Logger.getLogger(StatusUpdateBeanBase.class.
getName());

    //-------------------------------------------------------------------------||
    // Contracts ---------------------------------------------------------------||
    //-------------------------------------------------------------------------||

    /**
     * Updates status to the specified value.
     *
     * @throws IllegalArgumentException If the new status is not specified
     * @throws Exception If an error occured in processing
     */
    public abstract void updateStatus(StatusUpdate newStatus) throws Illegal
ArgumentException, Exception;
```

```
//-----------------------------------------------------------------------||
// Required Implementations --------------------------------------------||
//-----------------------------------------------------------------------||

/**
 * {@inheritDoc}
 * @see javax.jms.MessageListener#onMessage(javax.jms.Message)
 */
@Override
public void onMessage(final Message message)
{
    /*
     * Precondition checks
     *
     */
    // Ensure the message is specified
    if (message == null)
    {
        throw new IllegalArgumentException("Message must be specified");
    }

    // Ensure the message is in expected form
    final ObjectMessage objMessage;
    if (message instanceof ObjectMessage)
    {
        objMessage = (ObjectMessage) message;
    }
    else
    {
        throw new IllegalArgumentException("Specified message must be of type "
+ ObjectMessage.class.getName());
    }

    // Extract out the embedded status update
    final Serializable obj;
    try
    {
        obj = objMessage.getObject();
    }
    catch (final JMSException jmse)
    {
        throw new IllegalArgumentException("Could not obtain contents of message
" + objMessage);
    }

    // Ensure expected type
    final StatusUpdate status;
    if (obj instanceof StatusUpdate)
    {
        status = (StatusUpdate) obj;
    }
    else
    {
        throw new IllegalArgumentException("Contents of message should be of
type " + StatusUpdate.class.getName()
```

```
                            + "; was instead " + obj);
        }

        // Process the update
        try
        {
            this.updateStatus(status);
        }
        catch (final Exception e)
        {
            throw new RuntimeException("Encountered problem with processing status
update " + status, e);
        }
    }
}
```

TwitterUpdateMdb.java

```java
package org.jboss.ejb3.examples.ch08.statusupdate.mdb;

import java.util.logging.Logger;

import javax.annotation.PostConstruct;
import javax.jms.MessageListener;

import org.jboss.ejb3.examples.ch08.statusupdate.api.StatusUpdate;

import twitter4j.Twitter;

/**
 * EJB 3.x MDB which will act as an adaptor to the Twitter API, updating
 * Twitter status on incoming messages.
 *
 * The environment must first support Twitter integration by way of a username/
password
 * pair available from environment properties. {@link EnvironmentSpecificTwitter
ClientUtil}
 * has more details.
 *
 * @author <a href="mailto:andrew.rubinger@jboss.org">ALR</a>
 * @see http://twitter.com
 * @see http://yusuke.homeip.net/twitter4j/en/index.html
 */
public class TwitterUpdateMdb extends StatusUpdateBeanBase implements Message
Listener
{

    //-------------------------------------------------------------------------||
    // Class Members ----------------------------------------------------------||
    //-------------------------------------------------------------------------||

    /**
     * Logger
     */
    private static final Logger log = Logger.getLogger(TwitterUpdateMdb.class.get
```

```
Name());

    /**
     * EJB Name
     */
    static final String NAME = "TwitterUpdateMdb";

    //--------------------------------------------------------------------------||
    // Constructors ------------------------------------------------------------||
    //--------------------------------------------------------------------------||

    /**
     * Creates a new instance, required as no-arg ctor by specification
     */
    public TwitterUpdateMdb()
    {

    }

    //--------------------------------------------------------------------------||
    // Instance Members --------------------------------------------------------||
    //--------------------------------------------------------------------------||

    /**
     * Underlying client used in updating Twitter by calling upon its API
     */
    private Twitter client;

    //--------------------------------------------------------------------------||
    // Lifecycle ---------------------------------------------------------------||
    //--------------------------------------------------------------------------||

    /**
     * Lifecycle start to create the Twitter client from supplied environment
properties,
     * if the environment has been configured to do so
     */
    @PostConstruct
    void createTwitterClient()
    {
        if (!EnvironmentSpecificTwitterClientUtil.isSupportedEnvironment())
        {
            log.warning(EnvironmentSpecificTwitterClientUtil.MSG_UNSUPPORTED_
ENVIRONMENT);
            return;
        }

        // Create the client
        client = EnvironmentSpecificTwitterClientUtil.getTwitterClient();
        log.info("Created Twitter client " + client);
    }

    //--------------------------------------------------------------------------||
    // Required Implementations ------------------------------------------------||
    //--------------------------------------------------------------------------||
```

```
    /**
     * Sends incoming status updates to the Twitter account configured in the
     * context properties.
     *
     * @see org.jboss.ejb3.examples.ch08.statusupdate.mdb.StatusUpdateBeanBase
#updateStatus(org.jboss.ejb3.examples.ch08.statusupdate.api.StatusUpdate)
     */
    @Override
    public void updateStatus(final StatusUpdate newStatus) throws IllegalArgument
Exception, Exception
    {
        // Ensure the client's been initialized (if the environment permits)
        if (!EnvironmentSpecificTwitterClientUtil.isSupportedEnvironment())
        {
            // Do nothing and get out
            return;
        }
        if (client == null)
        {
            throw new IllegalStateException("Twitter client has not been initialized
");
        }

        // Extract status
        final String status = newStatus.getText();

        // Update status
        client.updateStatus(status);
    }
}
```

hornetq-jms.xml

```xml
<?xml version="1.0" encoding="UTF-8"?>
<configuration xmlns="urn:hornetq"
  xmlns:xsi="http://www.w3.org/2001/XMLSchema-instance"
  xsi:schemaLocation="urn:hornetq /schema/hornetq-jms.xsd">

  <topic name="StatusUpdate">
    <entry name="/topic/StatusUpdate" />
  </topic>

</configuration>
```

Test Resources

MockObjectMessage.java

```java
package org.jboss.ejb3.examples.ch08.statusupdate.mdb;

import java.io.Serializable;
import java.util.Enumeration;
```

```java
import javax.jms.Destination;
import javax.jms.JMSException;
import javax.jms.ObjectMessage;

/**
 * A Mock {@link ObjectMessage} which supports only the
 * {@link ObjectMessage#getObject()} method; used in testing
 *
 * @author <a href="mailto:andrew.rubinger@jboss.org">ALR</a>
 */
public class MockObjectMessage implements ObjectMessage
{

   //-------------------------------------------------------------------------||
   // Class Members ----------------------------------------------------------||
   //-------------------------------------------------------------------------||

   private static final String MESSAGE_UNSUPPORTED = "This mock implementation
does not support this operation";

   //-------------------------------------------------------------------------||
   // Instance Members -------------------------------------------------------||
   //-------------------------------------------------------------------------||

   /**
    * Object contained in this message
    */
   private final Serializable object;

   //-------------------------------------------------------------------------||
   // Constructor ------------------------------------------------------------||
   //-------------------------------------------------------------------------||

   /**
    * Creates a new instance with the specified backing object
    * to be returned by {@link ObjectMessage#getObject()}
    */
   MockObjectMessage(final Serializable object)
   {
      this.object = object;
   }

   //-------------------------------------------------------------------------||
   // Required Implementations -----------------------------------------------||
   //-------------------------------------------------------------------------||

   /* (non-Javadoc)
    * @see javax.jms.ObjectMessage#getObject()
    */
   @Override
   public Serializable getObject() throws JMSException
   {
      return this.object;
   }
```

```
//-------------------------------------------------------------------||
// Unsupported -----------------------------------------------------||
//-------------------------------------------------------------------||

/*
 * Everything below this line will throw an exception when invoked
 */

/* (non-Javadoc)
 * @see javax.jms.ObjectMessage#setObject(java.io.Serializable)
 */
@Override
public void setObject(Serializable object) throws JMSException
{
    throw new UnsupportedOperationException(MESSAGE_UNSUPPORTED);
}

// ... Omitted for brevity
}
```

StatusUpdateIntegrationTest.java

```
package org.jboss.ejb3.examples.ch08.statusupdate.mdb;

import java.util.concurrent.TimeUnit;
import java.util.logging.Logger;

import javax.jms.Message;
import javax.jms.ObjectMessage;
import javax.jms.Topic;
import javax.jms.TopicConnection;
import javax.jms.TopicConnectionFactory;
import javax.jms.TopicPublisher;
import javax.jms.TopicSession;
import javax.naming.Context;
import javax.naming.InitialContext;

import org.jboss.arquillian.api.Deployment;
import org.jboss.arquillian.api.Run;
import org.jboss.arquillian.api.RunModeType;
import org.jboss.arquillian.junit.Arquillian;
import org.jboss.ejb3.examples.ch08.statusupdate.api.StatusUpdate;
import org.jboss.ejb3.examples.ch08.statusupdate.api.StatusUpdateConstants;
import org.jboss.shrinkwrap.api.ShrinkWrap;
import org.jboss.shrinkwrap.api.spec.JavaArchive;
import org.junit.BeforeClass;
import org.junit.Test;
import org.junit.runner.RunWith;

import twitter4j.Twitter;

/**
 * Integration tests for the StatusUpdateEJBs.  Ensures that
 * the MDBs are working as expected when running inside
 * an EJB Container.
```

```
 *
 * @author <a href="mailto:andrew.rubinger@jboss.org">ALR</a>
 */
@RunWith(Arquillian.class)
@Run(RunModeType.AS_CLIENT)
public class StatusUpdateIntegrationTest extends StatusUpdateTestBase
{

   //-------------------------------------------------------------------------||
   // Class Members ----------------------------------------------------------||
   //-------------------------------------------------------------------------||

   /**
    * Logger
    */
   private static final Logger log = Logger.getLogger(StatusUpdateIntegrationTest
.class.getName());

   /**
    * Name of the archive we'll deploy into the server for testing
    */
   private static final String NAME_MDB_ARCHIVE = "statusUpdateEjb.jar";

   /**
    * Name of the ClassLoader resource for the deployment descriptor making a new
StatusUpdate JMS Topic
    */
   private static final String NAME_RESOURCE_TOPIC_DEPLOYMENT = "hornetq-jms.xml";

   /**
    * The JNDI Context
    */
   private static Context NAMING_CONTEXT;

   /**
    * Name of the Queue Connection Factory in JNDI
    */
   private static final String JNDI_NAME_CONNECTION_FACTORY = "ConnectionFactory";

   /**
    * Creates the EJB JAR to be deployed into the server via Arquillian
    * @return
    */
   @Deployment
   public static JavaArchive getDeployment()
   {
      final JavaArchive archive = ShrinkWrap.create(NAME_MDB_ARCHIVE, JavaArchive
.class).addClasses(StatusUpdate.class,
            StatusUpdateConstants.class, LoggingStatusUpdateMdb.class, Status
UpdateBeanBase.class,
            TwitterUpdateBlockingTestMdb.class, SecurityActions.class, Twitter
UpdateMdb.class,
            EnvironmentSpecificTwitterClientUtil.class).addResource(NAME_RESOURCE
_TOPIC_DEPLOYMENT);
      log.info(archive.toString(true));
```

```java
        return archive;
    }

    //---------------------------------------------------------------------------||
    // Lifecycle ----------------------------------------------------------------||
    //---------------------------------------------------------------------------||

    /**
     * Creates and starts a new JBossAS Server Embedded within this JVM
     */
    @BeforeClass
    public static void setNamingContext() throws Exception
    {
        // Set Naming Context
        NAMING_CONTEXT = new InitialContext();
    }

    //---------------------------------------------------------------------------||
    // Tests --------------------------------------------------------------------||
    //---------------------------------------------------------------------------||

    /**
     * Tests that the {@link TwitterUpdateMdb} updates Twitter when
     * it receives a new status from the JMS Topic upon which it's listening
     */
    @Test
    public void testTwitterUpdateMdb() throws Exception
    {
        // Get a Twitter Client and enforce the environment
        final Twitter twitterClient;
        try
        {
            twitterClient = EnvironmentSpecificTwitterClientUtil.getTwitterClient();
        }
        catch (final IllegalStateException ise)
        {
            log.warning(ise.getMessage() + "; skipping...");
            return;
        }

        // Create a new status
        final StatusUpdate newStatus = this.getUniqueStatusUpdate();

        // Publish the update to a JMS Topic (where it should be consumed by the
        MDB subscriber)
        this.publishStatusUpdateToTopic(newStatus);

        // Wait for the MDB to process, as it's doing so in another Thread.
        // This is *only* possible when we test MDBs in the same JVM as the test.
        try
        {
            log.info("Waiting on the MDB...");
            TwitterUpdateBlockingTestMdb.LATCH.await(10, TimeUnit.SECONDS);
        }
        catch (final InterruptedException e)
```

```
    {
        // Clear the flag and rethrow; some error in setup is in play
        Thread.interrupted();
        throw new RuntimeException(
                "Thread was interrupted while waiting for MDB processing; should
not happen in this test");
    }

    log.info("MDB signaled it's done processing, so we can resume");

    // Test
    this.assertLastUpdateSentToTwitter(twitterClient, newStatus);
}

//-------------------------------------------------------------------------||
// Internal Helper Methods -------------------------------------------------||
//-------------------------------------------------------------------------||

/**
 * Sends a JMS {@link ObjectMessage} containing the specified status to the
 * queue of the specified name
 *
 * @param status
 * @param topicName
 * @throws Exception
 * @throws IllegalArgumentException If either argument is not provided
 */
private void publishStatusUpdateToTopic(final StatusUpdate status) throws
Exception, IllegalArgumentException
{
    // Precondition check
    if (status == null)
    {
        throw new IllegalArgumentException("status must be provided");
    }

    // Get the queue from JNDI
    final Topic topic = (Topic) NAMING_CONTEXT.lookup(StatusUpdateConstants.
JNDI_NAME_TOPIC_STATUSUPDATE);

    // Get the ConnectionFactory from JNDI
    final TopicConnectionFactory factory = (TopicConnectionFactory) NAMING_
CONTEXT
            .lookup(JNDI_NAME_CONNECTION_FACTORY);

    // Make a Connection
    final TopicConnection connection = factory.createTopicConnection();
    final TopicSession sendSession = connection.createTopicSession(false, Topic
Session.AUTO_ACKNOWLEDGE);
    final TopicPublisher publisher = sendSession.createPublisher(topic);

    // Make the message
    final Message message = sendSession.createObjectMessage(status);
```

```
        // Publish the message
        publisher.publish(message);
        log.info("Published message " + message + " with contents: " + status);

        // Clean up
        sendSession.close();
        connection.close();
    }

}
```

StatusUpdateTestBase.java

```java
package org.jboss.ejb3.examples.ch08.statusupdate.mdb;

import java.util.List;
import java.util.UUID;
import java.util.logging.Logger;

import junit.framework.TestCase;

import org.jboss.ejb3.examples.ch08.statusupdate.api.StatusUpdate;

import twitter4j.Paging;
import twitter4j.Status;
import twitter4j.Twitter;
import twitter4j.TwitterException;

/**
 * Base support for tests of the StatusUpdate EJBs in both
 * POJO and JavaEE Environments
 *
 * @author <a href="mailto:andrew.rubinger@jboss.org">ALR</a>
 */
public class StatusUpdateTestBase
{

    //-------------------------------------------------------------------------||
    // Class Members ----------------------------------------------------------||
    //-------------------------------------------------------------------------||

    /**
     * Logger
     */
    private static final Logger log = Logger.getLogger(StatusUpdateBeanBase.class.
getName());

    /**
     * Status update to send
     */
    private static final String STATUS_UPDATE_PREFIX_TWITTER = "I'm testing
Message-Driven EJBs using JBoss EJB 3.x by @ALRubinger/@OReillyMedia!: ";

    //-------------------------------------------------------------------------||
    // Internal Helper Methods ------------------------------------------------||
```

```java
    //-----------------------------------------------------------------------||

    /**
     * Ensures that the last update for the Twitter account represented by the
specified
     * client matches the specified last sent status update
     *
     * @throws TwitterException If an error occurred in obtaining the last update
from the Twitter account
     */
    void assertLastUpdateSentToTwitter(final Twitter twitterClient, final Status
Update sent) throws TwitterException,
        IllegalArgumentException
    {
        // Precondition checks
        if (twitterClient == null)
        {
            throw new IllegalArgumentException("Twitter client must be specified");
        }
        if (sent == null)
        {
            throw new IllegalArgumentException("Last sent status must be specified");
        }

        // Get new status
        final List<Status> statuses = twitterClient.getUserTimeline(new Paging(1,
1));

        // Ensure we've sent one status, and it's as expected
        TestCase.assertEquals("Should have obtained one status (the most recent)
back from request", 1, statuses.size());
        final String roundtrip = statuses.get(0).getText();
        final String expected = sent.getText();
        log.info("Sent status update to Twitter: " + expected);
        log.info("Got last status update from Twitter: " + roundtrip);
        TestCase.assertEquals("Twitter API did not update with last sent status",
expected, roundtrip);
    }

    /**
     * Obtains a unique status update by using {@link StatusUpdateTestBase#STATUS_
UPDATE_PREFIX_TWITTER}
     * prefixed to a UUID.
     */
    StatusUpdate getUniqueStatusUpdate()
    {
        return new StatusUpdate(STATUS_UPDATE_PREFIX_TWITTER + UUID.randomUUID().to
String());
    }

}
```

StatusUpdateUnitTestCase.java

```java
package org.jboss.ejb3.examples.ch08.statusupdate.mdb;

import java.util.logging.Logger;

import javax.jms.MessageListener;
import javax.jms.ObjectMessage;

import junit.framework.TestCase;

import org.jboss.ejb3.examples.ch08.statusupdate.api.StatusUpdate;
import org.junit.Test;

import twitter4j.Twitter;
import twitter4j.TwitterException;

/**
 * Unit tests for the StatusUpdate EJBs.  Ensures that the business
 * logic is intact when running outside the context of an EJB Container.
 *
 * @author <a href="mailto:andrew.rubinger@jboss.org">ALR</a>
 */
public class StatusUpdateUnitTestCase extends StatusUpdateTestBase
{

   //-------------------------------------------------------------------------||
   // Class Members ----------------------------------------------------------||
   //-------------------------------------------------------------------------||

   /**
    * Logger
    */
   private static final Logger log = Logger.getLogger(StatusUpdateUnitTestCase.
class.getName());

   //-------------------------------------------------------------------------||
   // Tests ------------------------------------------------------------------||
   //-------------------------------------------------------------------------||

   /**
    * Ensures that the {@link StatusUpdateBeanBase#updateStatus(StatusUpdate)}
method is
    * invoked for incoming messages
    */
   @Test
   public void testUpdateStatusBase()
   {

      // Make a listener
      final StatusCachingMessageListener listener = new StatusCachingMessage
Listener();

      // Make a status update
      final StatusUpdate newStatus = this.getUniqueStatusUpdate();
```

```java
        // Send to it
        this.sendMessage(newStatus, listener);

        // Extract out the status sent
        final StatusUpdate roundtrip = listener.getLastStatus();

        // Ensure it's what we sent
        TestCase.assertEquals("Status sent was not dispatched and received as
expected", newStatus, roundtrip);
    }

    /**
     * Ensures that the {@link TwitterUpdateMdb} is updating Twitter
     * when {@link MessageListener#onMessage(javax.jms.Message)} is invoked
     */
    @Test
    public void testTwitterUpdateMdb() throws TwitterException
    {
        // Determine if the environment is not set up
        if (!EnvironmentSpecificTwitterClientUtil.isSupportedEnvironment())
        {
            log.warning(EnvironmentSpecificTwitterClientUtil.MSG_UNSUPPORTED_
ENVIRONMENT);
            return;
        }

        // Make a listener (the MDB bean impl class as a POJO)
        final TwitterUpdateMdb listener = new TwitterUpdateMdb();

        // Manually invoke @PostConstruct
        listener.createTwitterClient();

        // Make a status update
        final StatusUpdate newStatus = this.getUniqueStatusUpdate();

        // Send to it
        this.sendMessage(newStatus, listener);

        /*
         * NOTE: This test is flawed, as we do not update then check in one atomic
operation.
         * Someone else could sneak in here and send another status update by the
         * time we check the last one received.  This is for illustrative uses only.
         */

        // Test
        final Twitter twitterClient = EnvironmentSpecificTwitterClientUtil.get
TwitterClient();
        this.assertLastUpdateSentToTwitter(twitterClient, newStatus);
    }

    //-------------------------------------------------------------------------||
    // Internal Helper Methods -----------------------------------------------||
    //-------------------------------------------------------------------------||
```

```java
    /**
     * Sends the specified status update to the specified listener
     */
    private void sendMessage(final StatusUpdate newStatus, final MessageListener
listener)
    {
        // This implementation will send directly (POJO-based)
        final ObjectMessage message = new MockObjectMessage(newStatus);

        // Send manually
        listener.onMessage(message);
    }

    //-------------------------------------------------------------------------||
    // Inner Classes ----------------------------------------------------------||
    //-------------------------------------------------------------------------||

    /**
     * {@link MessageListener} to be invoked in a POJO environment, where the last
     * incoming status update via {@link MessageListener#onMessage(javax.jms.
Message)}
     * is cached and available for retrieval.  Not thread-safe as this is intended
to be used
     * in a single-threaded environment.
     */
    private static class StatusCachingMessageListener extends StatusUpdateBeanBase
    {
        private StatusUpdate lastStatus = null;

        /**
         * Caches the specified status
         * @see org.jboss.ejb3.examples.ch08.statusupdate.mdb.StatusUpdateBeanBase#
updateStatus(org.jboss.ejb3.examples.ch08.statusupdate.api.StatusUpdate)
         */
        public void updateStatus(final StatusUpdate newStatus) throws Illegal
ArgumentException
        {
            this.lastStatus = newStatus;
        }

        /**
         * Obtains the last {@link StatusUpdate} received
         * @return
         */
        StatusUpdate getLastStatus()
        {
            return lastStatus;
        }
    }
}
```

TwitterUpdateBlockingTestMdb.java

```java
package org.jboss.ejb3.examples.ch08.statusupdate.mdb;

import java.util.concurrent.CountDownLatch;
import java.util.logging.Logger;

import javax.ejb.ActivationConfigProperty;
import javax.ejb.MessageDriven;
import javax.jms.MessageListener;

import org.jboss.ejb3.examples.ch08.statusupdate.api.StatusUpdate;
import org.jboss.ejb3.examples.ch08.statusupdate.api.StatusUpdateConstants;

/**
 * Extends the {@link TwitterUpdateMdb} example to add a latch to
 * be shared in testing only, such that tests can be sure we're done
 * processing before they proceed
 *
 * @author <a href="mailto:andrew.rubinger@jboss.org">ALR</a>
 */
@MessageDriven(name = TwitterUpdateMdb.NAME, activationConfig =
{
      @ActivationConfigProperty(propertyName = "destinationType", propertyValue =
StatusUpdateConstants.TYPE_DESTINATION_STATUSUPDATE),
      @ActivationConfigProperty(propertyName = "destination", propertyValue =
StatusUpdateConstants.JNDI_NAME_TOPIC_STATUSUPDATE)})
public class TwitterUpdateBlockingTestMdb extends TwitterUpdateMdb implements
MessageListener
{

   //-------------------------------------------------------------------------||
   // Class Members ----------------------------------------------------------||
   //-------------------------------------------------------------------------||

   /**
    * Logger
    */
   private static final Logger log = Logger.getLogger(TwitterUpdateBlockingTest
Mdb.class.getName());

   /**
    * Shared latch, so tests can wait until the MDB is processed.  In POJO
    * testing this is wholly unnecessary as we've got a single-threaded
environment, but
    * when testing in an EJB Container running in the *same* JVM as the test, the
test
    * can use this to wait until the MDB has been invoked, strengthening the
integrity
    * of the test.  It's not recommended to put this piece into a production EJB;
instead
    * test an extension of your EJB which adds this (and only this) support.
    */
   public static CountDownLatch LATCH = new CountDownLatch(1);
```

```
//------------------------------------------------------------------------||
// Overridden Implementations ---------------------------------------------||
//------------------------------------------------------------------------||

/**
 * {@inheritDoc}
 * Additionally waits upon a shared barrier so that the test can ensure we're
done before
 * it proceeds
 * @see org.jboss.ejb3.examples.ch08.statusupdate.mdb.TwitterUpdateMdb#update
Status(org.jboss.ejb3.examples.ch08.statusupdate.api.StatusUpdate)
 */
@Override
public void updateStatus(final StatusUpdate newStatus) throws IllegalArgument
Exception, Exception
{
    // Call the super implementation
    try
    {
        super.updateStatus(newStatus);
    }
    finally
    {
        // Count down the latch
        log.info("Counting down the latch...");
        LATCH.countDown();
    }
}
}
```

Java Persistence APIs: Employee Registry Example

Description

Enterprise applications frequently need to deal with state which survives application restarts. We call this "persistent state," and it's typically modeled by a program called a *relational database management system* (RDBMS). Handling the transformation/ mapping between the row-based RDBMS and Java objects is a rote process for application developers, so we offload this responsibility to the Java Persistence API (JPA). In this fashion we're free to interact with regular getters/setters on Java objects while the mechanics of getting data into and out of the backing database is handled for us.

EJB integrates with JPA via the entity bean, and Chapters 9 through 14 detail the APIs needed to properly model, map, persist, and retrieve data with a real database. Our example is an employee registry, where we apply a variety of techniques to draw relationships between mapped types and query the DB efficiently.

Online Companion Information

Wiki article: *http://community.jboss.org/docs/DOC-15572*

Source location: *http://github.com/jbossejb3/oreilly-ejb-6thedition-book-examples/tree/ master/ch09-14-employeeregistry/*

Source Listing

Following is a full listing of all source code used in this runnable example.

Implementation Resources

See Chapter 9.

SimpleEmployee.java

```java
package org.jboss.ejb3.examples.employeeregistry.ch09.entitymanager;

import javax.persistence.Entity;
import javax.persistence.Id;

/**
 * Represents an Employee in the system.  Modeled as a simple
 * value object with some additional EJB and JPA annotations.
 *
 * @author <a href="mailto:andrew.rubinger@jboss.org">ALR</a>
 * @version $Revision: $
 */
@Entity
// Mark that we're an Entity Bean, EJB's integration point
// with Java Persistence
public class SimpleEmployee
{

   //-------------------------------------------------------------------------||
   // Instance Members -------------------------------------------------------||
   //-------------------------------------------------------------------------||

   /**
    * Primary key of this entity
    */
   @Id
   // Mark that this field is the primary key
   private Long id;

   /**
    * Name of the employee
    */
   private String name;

   //-------------------------------------------------------------------------||
   // Constructor ------------------------------------------------------------||
   //-------------------------------------------------------------------------||

   /**
    * Default constructor, required by JPA
    */
   public SimpleEmployee()
   {

   }

   /**
    * Convenience constructor
    */
```

```java
public SimpleEmployee(final long id, final String name)
{
    // Set
    this.id = id;
    this.name = name;
}

//-------------------------------------------------------------------------||
// Accessors / Mutators --------------------------------------------------||
//-------------------------------------------------------------------------||

/**
 * @return the id
 */
public Long getId()
{
    return id;
}

/**
 * @param id the id to set
 */
public void setId(final Long id)
{
    this.id = id;
}

/**
 * @return the name
 */
public String getName()
{
    return name;
}

/**
 * @param name the name to set
 */
public void setName(final String name)
{
    this.name = name;
}

/**
 * {@inheritDoc}
 * @see java.lang.Object#toString()
 */
@Override
public String toString()
{
    return SimpleEmployee.class.getSimpleName() + " [id=" + id + ", name=" +
name + "]";
}

/**
```

```
 * {@inheritDoc}
 * @see java.lang.Object#hashCode()
 */
@Override
public int hashCode()
{
   final int prime = 31;
   int result = 1;
   result = prime * result + ((id == null) ? 0 : id.hashCode());
   return result;
}

/**
 * {@inheritDoc}
 * @see java.lang.Object#equals(java.lang.Object)
 */
@Override
public boolean equals(Object obj)
{
   if (this == obj)
      return true;
   if (obj == null)
      return false;
   if (getClass() != obj.getClass())
      return false;
   SimpleEmployee other = (SimpleEmployee) obj;
   if (id == null)
   {
      if (other.id != null)
         return false;
   }
   else if (!id.equals(other.id))
      return false;
   return true;
}
}
```

See Chapter 10.

EmbeddedEmployeePK.java

```
package org.jboss.ejb3.examples.employeeregistry.ch10.mapping;

import java.io.Serializable;

import javax.persistence.Column;
import javax.persistence.Embeddable;
import javax.persistence.EmbeddedId;

/**
 * Composite primary key class to be used as
 * {@link EmbeddedId} on {@link EmployeeWithExternalCompositePK}.
 * The instance members here will together compose
 * an identity in the database (primary key).
 *
```

```
 * @author <a href="mailto:andrew.rubinger@jboss.org">ALR</a>
 * @version $Revision: $
 */
@Embeddable
// Note to JPA that we're intended to be embedded into an Entity
// class as a PK
public class EmbeddedEmployeePK implements Serializable
{

   //-------------------------------------------------------------------------||
   // Class Members ----------------------------------------------------------||
   //-------------------------------------------------------------------------||

   /**
    * serialVersionUID
    */
   private static final long serialVersionUID = 1L;

   //-------------------------------------------------------------------------||
   // Instance Members -------------------------------------------------------||
   //-------------------------------------------------------------------------||

   /**
    * Last Name
    */
   @Column
   private String lastName;

   /**
    * Social Security Number (United States Federal ID)
    */
   @Column
   private Long ssn;

   //-------------------------------------------------------------------------||
   // Functional Methods -----------------------------------------------------||
   //-------------------------------------------------------------------------||

   /**
    * @return the lastName
    */
   public String getLastName()
   {
      return lastName;
   }

   /**
    * @param lastName the lastName to set
    */
   public void setLastName(String lastName)
   {
      this.lastName = lastName;
   }

   /**
```

```java
 * @return the ssn
 */
public Long getSsn()
{
   return ssn;
}

/**
 * @param ssn the ssn to set
 */
public void setSsn(Long ssn)
{
   this.ssn = ssn;
}

//---------------------------------------------------------------------------||
// Overridden Implementations -----------------------------------------------||
//---------------------------------------------------------------------------||

/**
 * {@inheritDoc}
 * @see java.lang.Object#hashCode()
 */
@Override
public int hashCode()
{
   final int prime = 31;
   int result = 1;
   result = prime * result + ((lastName == null) ? 0 : lastName.hashCode());
   result = prime * result + ((ssn == null) ? 0 : ssn.hashCode());
   return result;
}

/**
 * {@inheritDoc}
 * @see java.lang.Object#equals(java.lang.Object)
 */
@Override
public boolean equals(Object obj)
{
   if (this == obj)
      return true;
   if (obj == null)
      return false;
   if (getClass() != obj.getClass())
      return false;
   EmbeddedEmployeePK other = (EmbeddedEmployeePK) obj;
   if (lastName == null)
   {
      if (other.lastName != null)
         return false;
   }
   else if (!lastName.equals(other.lastName))
      return false;
   if (ssn == null)
```

```
        {
            if (other.ssn != null)
                return false;
        }
        else if (!ssn.equals(other.ssn))
            return false;
        return true;
    }

}
```

EmployeeType.java

```java
package org.jboss.ejb3.examples.employeeregistry.ch10.mapping;

import javax.persistence.Enumerated;

/**
 * Types of employees in the system.  Used to show {@link Enumerated}
 * in the entity {@link EmployeeWithProperties}.
 *
 * @author <a href="mailto:andrew.rubinger@jboss.org">ALR</a>
 * @version $Revision: $
 */
public enum EmployeeType {
    MANAGER, PEON;
}
```

EmployeeWithEmbeddedPK.java

```java
package org.jboss.ejb3.examples.employeeregistry.ch10.mapping;

import javax.persistence.EmbeddedId;
import javax.persistence.Entity;

/**
 * Represents an Employee in the system.  The identity
 * (primary key) is determined by embedded properties
 * via the {@link EmbeddedEmployeePK}.
 *
 * @author <a href="mailto:andrew.rubinger@jboss.org">ALR</a>
 * @version $Revision: $
 */
@Entity
// Mark that we're an Entity Bean, EJB's integration point
// with Java Persistence
public class EmployeeWithEmbeddedPK
{

    //-------------------------------------------------------------------------||
    // Instance Members -------------------------------------------------------||
    //-------------------------------------------------------------------------||

    /**
     * Primary key, composite and embedded
```

```java
 */
@EmbeddedId
private EmbeddedEmployeePK id;

//---------------------------------------------------------------------------||
// Constructor -------------------------------------------------------------||
//---------------------------------------------------------------------------||

/**
 * Default constructor, required by JPA
 */
public EmployeeWithEmbeddedPK()
{

}

//---------------------------------------------------------------------------||
// Accessors / Mutators ----------------------------------------------------||
//---------------------------------------------------------------------------||

/**
 * @return the id
 */
public EmbeddedEmployeePK getId()
{
   return id;
}

/**
 * @param id the id to set
 */
public void setId(final EmbeddedEmployeePK id)
{
   this.id = id;
}

//---------------------------------------------------------------------------||
// Overridden Implementations ----------------------------------------------||
//---------------------------------------------------------------------------||

/**
 * {@inheritDoc}
 * @see java.lang.Object#toString()
 */
@Override
public String toString()
{
   return EmployeeWithEmbeddedPK.class.getSimpleName() + " [id=" + id + "]";
}

}
```

EmployeeWithExternalCompositePK.java

```java
package org.jboss.ejb3.examples.employeeregistry.ch10.mapping;

import javax.persistence.Entity;
import javax.persistence.Id;
import javax.persistence.IdClass;

/**
 * Represents an Employee in the system.  The identity
 * (primary key) is determined by composite properties
 * defined by {@link ExternalEmployeePK}.
 *
 * @author <a href="mailto:andrew.rubinger@jboss.org">ALR</a>
 * @version $Revision: $
 */
@Entity
// Mark that we're an Entity Bean, EJB's integration point
// with Java Persistence
@IdClass(ExternalEmployeePK.class)
// Use a composite primary key using a custom PK class
public class EmployeeWithExternalCompositePK
{

   //-------------------------------------------------------------------------||
   // Instance Members -------------------------------------------------------||
   //-------------------------------------------------------------------------||

   /**
    * Last Name
    */
   @Id
   private String lastName;

   /**
    * Social Security Number (United States Federal ID)
    */
   @Id
   private Long ssn;

   //-------------------------------------------------------------------------||
   // Constructor ------------------------------------------------------------||
   //-------------------------------------------------------------------------||

   /**
    * Default constructor, required by JPA
    */
   public EmployeeWithExternalCompositePK()
   {

   }

   //-------------------------------------------------------------------------||
   // Accessors / Mutators ---------------------------------------------------||
   //-------------------------------------------------------------------------||
```

```java
/**
 * @return the lastName
 */
public String getLastName()
{
    return lastName;
}

/**
 * @param lastName the lastName to set
 */
public void setLastName(final String lastName)
{
    this.lastName = lastName;
}

/**
 * @return the ssn
 */
public Long getSsn()
{
    return ssn;
}

/**
 * @param ssn the ssn to set
 */
public void setSsn(final Long ssn)
{
    this.ssn = ssn;
}

//-------------------------------------------------------------------------||
// Overridden Implementations ---------------------------------------------||
//-------------------------------------------------------------------------||

/**
 * {@inheritDoc}
 * @see java.lang.Object#toString()
 */
@Override
public String toString()
{
    return EmployeeWithExternalCompositePK.class.getSimpleName() + " [lastName=
" + lastName + ", ssn=" + ssn + "]";
}

}
```

EmployeeWithMappedSuperClassId.java

```java
package org.jboss.ejb3.examples.employeeregistry.ch10.mapping;

import javax.persistence.Column;
import javax.persistence.Entity;
```

```java
import javax.persistence.Table;

import org.jboss.ejb3.examples.testsupport.entity.AutogenIdentityBase;
import org.jboss.ejb3.examples.testsupport.entity.IdentityBase;

/**
 * Represents an Employee in the system.  Inherits the
 * primary key support from {@link IdentityBase#getId()}.
 *
 * @author <a href="mailto:andrew.rubinger@jboss.org">ALR</a>
 * @version $Revision: $
 */
@Entity
// Mark that we're an Entity Bean, EJB's integration point
// with Java Persistence
@Table(name = "employees_with_autogen_pk")
// Explicitly denote the name of the table in the DB
public class EmployeeWithMappedSuperClassId extends AutogenIdentityBase
{

   //-------------------------------------------------------------------------||
   // Instance Members -------------------------------------------------------||
   //-------------------------------------------------------------------------||

   /**
    * Name of the employee
    */
   // We can use @Column.name to denote the name of the column in the DB
   @Column(name = "employee_name")
   private String name;

   //-------------------------------------------------------------------------||
   // Constructor ------------------------------------------------------------||
   //-------------------------------------------------------------------------||

   /**
    * Default constructor, required by JPA
    */
   public EmployeeWithMappedSuperClassId()
   {

   }

   /**
    * Convenience constructor
    */
   public EmployeeWithMappedSuperClassId(final String name)
   {
      // Set
      this.name = name;
   }

   //-------------------------------------------------------------------------||
   // Accessors / Mutators ---------------------------------------------------||
   //-------------------------------------------------------------------------||
```

```java
/**
 * @return the name
 */
public String getName()
{
    return name;
}

/**
 * @param name the name to set
 */
public void setName(final String name)
{
    this.name = name;
}

/**
 * {@inheritDoc}
 * @see java.lang.Object#toString()
 */
@Override
public String toString()
{
    return EmployeeWithMappedSuperClassId.class.getSimpleName() + " [id=" +
this.getId() + ", name=" + name + "]";
}
}
```

EmployeeWithProperties.java

```java
package org.jboss.ejb3.examples.employeeregistry.ch10.mapping;

import java.util.Arrays;
import java.util.Date;

import javax.persistence.Basic;
import javax.persistence.Entity;
import javax.persistence.EnumType;
import javax.persistence.Enumerated;
import javax.persistence.FetchType;
import javax.persistence.GeneratedValue;
import javax.persistence.Id;
import javax.persistence.Lob;
import javax.persistence.Temporal;
import javax.persistence.TemporalType;
import javax.persistence.Transient;

/**
 * Represents an Employee with a series of properties to
 * show JPA Mapping metadata.
 *
 * @author <a href="mailto:andrew.rubinger@jboss.org">ALR</a>
 * @version $Revision: $
 */
```

```java
@Entity
public class EmployeeWithProperties
{

    //--------------------------------------------------------------------------||
    // Instance Members -------------------------------------------------------||
    //--------------------------------------------------------------------------||

    /**
     * Primary key
     */
    @Id
    @GeneratedValue
    // Automatically manage PK creation for us
    private Long id;

    /**
     * Description of what the Employee's currently
     * working on.  We don't need to store this in the DB.
     */
    @Transient
    // Don't persist this
    private String currentAssignment;

    /**
     * Picture of the employee used in ID cards.
     */
    @Lob
    // Note that this is a binary large object
    @Basic(fetch = FetchType.LAZY, optional = true)
    // Don't load this by default; it's an expensive operation.
    // Only load when requested.
    private byte[] image;

    /**
     * Type of employee
     */
    @Enumerated(EnumType.STRING)
    // Show that this is an enumerated value, and the value to
    // be put in the DB is the value of the enumeration toString().
    private EmployeeType type;

    /**
     * Date the employee joined the company
     */
    @Temporal(TemporalType.DATE)
    // Note that we should map this as an SQL Date field;
    // could also be SQL Time or Timestamp
    private Date since;

    //--------------------------------------------------------------------------||
    // Accessors / Mutators ---------------------------------------------------||
    //--------------------------------------------------------------------------||

    /**
```

```java
 * @return the id
 */
public Long getId()
{
    return id;
}

/**
 * @param id the id to set
 */
public void setId(final Long id)
{
    this.id = id;
}

/**
 * @return the currentAssignment
 */
public String getCurrentAssignment()
{
    return currentAssignment;
}

/**
 * @param currentAssignment the currentAssignment to set
 */
public void setCurrentAssignment(final String currentAssignment)
{
    this.currentAssignment = currentAssignment;
}

/**
 * @return the image
 */
public byte[] getImage()
{
    return image;
}

/**
 * @param image the image to set
 */
public void setImage(final byte[] image)
{
    this.image = image;
}

/**
 * @return the type
 */
public EmployeeType getType()
{
    return type;
}
```

```
    /**
     * @param type the type to set
     */
    public void setType(final EmployeeType type)
    {
        this.type = type;
    }

    /**
     * @return the since
     */
    public Date getSince()
    {
        return since;
    }

    /**
     * @param since the since to set
     */
    public void setSince(final Date since)
    {
        this.since = since;
    }

    //-------------------------------------------------------------------------||
    // Overridden Implementations ---------------------------------------------||
    //-------------------------------------------------------------------------||

    /**
     * {@inheritDoc}
     * @see java.lang.Object#toString()
     */
    @Override
    public String toString()
    {
        return "EmployeeWithProperties [currentAssignment=" + currentAssignment + "
, id=" + id + ", image="
                + Arrays.toString(image) + ", since=" + since + ", type=" + type + "]";
    }

}
```

ExternalEmployeePK.java

```
package org.jboss.ejb3.examples.employeeregistry.ch10.mapping;

import java.io.Serializable;

import javax.persistence.IdClass;

/**
 * Composite primary key class to be used as
 * {@link IdClass} on {@link EmployeeWithExternalCompositePK}.
 * The instance members here will together compose
 * an identity in the database (primary key).
```

```java
 *
 * @author <a href="mailto:andrew.rubinger@jboss.org">ALR</a>
 * @version $Revision: $
 */
public class ExternalEmployeePK implements Serializable
{

   //-------------------------------------------------------------------------||
   // Class Members ----------------------------------------------------------||
   //-------------------------------------------------------------------------||

   /**
    * serialVersionUID
    */
   private static final long serialVersionUID = 1L;

   //-------------------------------------------------------------------------||
   // Instance Members -------------------------------------------------------||
   //-------------------------------------------------------------------------||

   /**
    * Last Name
    */
   private String lastName;

   /**
    * Social Security Number (United States Federal ID)
    */
   private Long ssn;

   //-------------------------------------------------------------------------||
   // Functional Methods -----------------------------------------------------||
   //-------------------------------------------------------------------------||

   /**
    * @return the lastName
    */
   public String getLastName()
   {
      return lastName;
   }

   /**
    * @param lastName the lastName to set
    */
   public void setLastName(String lastName)
   {
      this.lastName = lastName;
   }

   /**
    * @return the ssn
    */
   public Long getSsn()
   {
```

```java
      return ssn;
   }

   /**
    * @param ssn the ssn to set
    */
   public void setSsn(Long ssn)
   {
      this.ssn = ssn;
   }

   //-------------------------------------------------------------------------||
   // Overridden Implementations ----------------------------------------------||
   //-------------------------------------------------------------------------||

   /**
    * {@inheritDoc}
    * @see java.lang.Object#hashCode()
    */
   @Override
   public int hashCode()
   {
      final int prime = 31;
      int result = 1;
      result = prime * result + ((lastName == null) ? 0 : lastName.hashCode());
      result = prime * result + ((ssn == null) ? 0 : ssn.hashCode());
      return result;
   }

   /**
    * {@inheritDoc}
    * @see java.lang.Object#equals(java.lang.Object)
    */
   @Override
   public boolean equals(Object obj)
   {
      if (this == obj)
         return true;
      if (obj == null)
         return false;
      if (getClass() != obj.getClass())
         return false;
      ExternalEmployeePK other = (ExternalEmployeePK) obj;
      if (lastName == null)
      {
         if (other.lastName != null)
            return false;
      }
      else if (!lastName.equals(other.lastName))
         return false;
      if (ssn == null)
      {
         if (other.ssn != null)
            return false;
      }
```

```
            else if (!ssn.equals(other.ssn))
                return false;
            return true;
        }

    }
```

See Chapter 11.

Address.java

```java
package org.jboss.ejb3.examples.employeeregistry.ch11.relationships;

import javax.persistence.Column;
import javax.persistence.Entity;

import org.jboss.ejb3.examples.testsupport.entity.AutogenIdentityBase;

/**
 * Represents a simple Address.  Each {@link Employee} will
 * have one, though the relationship is not bidirectional.
 *
 * @author <a href="mailto:andrew.rubinger@jboss.org">ALR</a>
 * @version $Revision: $
 */
@Entity
// Mark that we're an Entity Bean, EJB's integration point
// with Java Persistence
public class Address extends AutogenIdentityBase
{

    //-------------------------------------------------------------------------||
    // Instance Members -------------------------------------------------------||
    //-------------------------------------------------------------------------||

    /**
     * Street Address
     */
    @Column(length = 100)
    // Length of VARCHAR
    private String street;

    /**
     * City
     */
    @Column(length = 100)
    // Length of VARCHAR
    private String city;

    /**
     * Postal code of the state
     */
    @Column(length = 2)
    // Length of VARCHAR
    private String state;
```

```
//-------------------------------------------------------------------||
// Constructor -----------------------------------------------------||
//-------------------------------------------------------------------||

/**
 * Default constructor, required by JPA
 */
public Address()
{

}

/**
 * Convenience constructor
 */
public Address(final String street, final String city, final String state)
{
    // Set
    this.setStreet(street);
    this.setCity(city);
    this.setState(state);
}

//-------------------------------------------------------------------||
// Accessors / Mutators --------------------------------------------||
//-------------------------------------------------------------------||

/**
 * @return the street
 */
public String getStreet()
{
    return street;
}

/**
 * @param street the street to set
 */
public void setStreet(String street)
{
    this.street = street;
}

/**
 * @return the city
 */
public String getCity()
{
    return city;
}

/**
 * @param city the city to set
 */
```

```
    public void setCity(String city)
    {
        this.city = city;
    }

    /**
     * @return the state
     */
    public String getState()
    {
        return state;
    }

    /**
     * @param state the state to set
     */
    public void setState(String state)
    {
        this.state = state;
    }

    //-------------------------------------------------------------------------||
    // Required Implementations -----------------------------------------------||
    //-------------------------------------------------------------------------||

    /**
     * {@inheritDoc}
     * @see java.lang.Object#toString()
     */
    @Override
    public String toString()
    {
        return Address.class.getSimpleName() + " [city=" + city + ", state=" +
state + ", street=" + street
            + ", getId()=" + getId() + "]";
    }
}
```

Computer.java

```
package org.jboss.ejb3.examples.employeeregistry.ch11.relationships;

import javax.persistence.Column;
import javax.persistence.Entity;
import javax.persistence.OneToOne;

import org.jboss.ejb3.examples.testsupport.entity.AutogenIdentityBase;

/**
 * Represents an {@link Employee}'s computer.  The
 * relationship is bidirectional in the case the computer
 * is lost or in for servicing and needs to be returned.
 *
 * @author <a href="mailto:andrew.rubinger@jboss.org">ALR</a>
 * @version $Revision: $
```

```java
 */
@Entity
public class Computer extends AutogenIdentityBase
{

   //---------------------------------------------------------------------||
   // Instance Members ---------------------------------------------------||
   //---------------------------------------------------------------------||

   /**
    * Manufacturer of the computer
    */
   @Column(length = 100)
   // Length of VARCHAR
   private String make;

   /**
    * Model of the computer
    */
   @Column(length = 100)
   // Length of VARCHAR
   private String model;

   @OneToOne
   // Bidirectional relationship, mappedBy
   // is declared on the non-owning side
   private Employee owner;

   //---------------------------------------------------------------------||
   // Constructor --------------------------------------------------------||
   //---------------------------------------------------------------------||

   //---------------------------------------------------------------------||
   // Accessors / Mutators -----------------------------------------------||
   //---------------------------------------------------------------------||

   /**
    * @return the make
    */
   public String getMake()
   {
      return make;
   }

   /**
    * @param make the make to set
    */
   public void setMake(String make)
   {
      this.make = make;
   }

   /**
    * @return the model
    */
```

```
        public String getModel()
        {
            return model;
        }

        /**
         * @param model the model to set
         */
        public void setModel(String model)
        {
            this.model = model;
        }

        /**
         * @return the owner
         */
        public Employee getOwner()
        {
            return owner;
        }

        /**
         * @param owner the owner to set
         */
        public void setOwner(final Employee owner)
        {
            this.owner = owner;
        }

        //-------------------------------------------------------------------||
        // Required Implementations ------------------------------------------||
        //-------------------------------------------------------------------||

        /**
         * {@inheritDoc}
         * @see java.lang.Object#toString()
         */
        @Override
        public String toString()
        {
            return Computer.class.getSimpleName() + " [make=" + make + ", model=" +
    model + ", owner=" + owner + ", getId()="
                + getId() + "]";
        }

    }
```

Customer.java

```
package org.jboss.ejb3.examples.employeeregistry.ch11.relationships;

import javax.persistence.Entity;
import javax.persistence.ManyToOne;

import org.jboss.ejb3.examples.testsupport.entity.AutogenIdentityBase;
```

```
/**
 * Represents a Customer.  Each customer may have an {@link Employee}
 * which is the primary contact for the account, but the relationship
 * is unidirectional
 *
 * @author <a href="mailto:andrew.rubinger@jboss.org">ALR</a>
 * @version $Revision: $
 */
@Entity
public class Customer extends AutogenIdentityBase
{

   //-------------------------------------------------------------------------------||
   // Instance Members -------------------------------------------------------------||
   //-------------------------------------------------------------------------------||

   /**
    * Name
    */
   private String name;

   /**
    * The primary {@link Employee} contact for this {@link Customer}
    */
   @ManyToOne
   // Unidirectional
   private Employee primaryContact;

   //-------------------------------------------------------------------------------||
   // Constructor ------------------------------------------------------------------||
   //-------------------------------------------------------------------------------||

   /**
    * Default constructor, required by JPA
    */
   public Customer()
   {

   }

   /**
    * Convenience constructor
    */
   public Customer(final String name)
   {
      // Set
      this.name = name;
   }

   //-------------------------------------------------------------------------------||
   // Accessors / Mutators ---------------------------------------------------------||
   //-------------------------------------------------------------------------------||

   /**
```

```
 * @return the name
 */
public String getName()
{
    return name;
}

/**
 * @param name the name to set
 */
public void setName(final String name)
{
    this.name = name;
}

/**
 * @return the primaryContact
 */
public Employee getPrimaryContact()
{
    return primaryContact;
}

/**
 * @param primaryContact the primaryContact to set
 */
public void setPrimaryContact(final Employee primaryContact)
{
    this.primaryContact = primaryContact;
}

//-------------------------------------------------------------------------||
// Overridden Implementations ---------------------------------------------||
//-------------------------------------------------------------------------||

/* (non-Javadoc)
 * @see java.lang.Object#toString()
 */
@Override
public String toString()
{
    return Customer.class.getSimpleName() + " [name=" + name + ", getId()=" +
getId() + "]";
}

}
```

Employee.java

```
package org.jboss.ejb3.examples.employeeregistry.ch11.relationships;

import java.util.ArrayList;
import java.util.Collection;

import javax.persistence.Column;
```

```java
import javax.persistence.Entity;
import javax.persistence.JoinColumn;
import javax.persistence.ManyToMany;
import javax.persistence.ManyToOne;
import javax.persistence.OneToMany;
import javax.persistence.OneToOne;

import org.jboss.ejb3.examples.testsupport.entity.AutogenIdentityBase;

/**
 * Represents an Employee in the system.  Modeled as a simple
 * value object with some additional EJB and JPA annotations.
 *
 * @author <a href="mailto:andrew.rubinger@jboss.org">ALR</a>
 * @version $Revision: $
 */
@Entity
// Mark that we're an Entity Bean, EJB's integration point
// with Java Persistence
public class Employee extends AutogenIdentityBase
{

   //-------------------------------------------------------------------------------||
   // Instance Members -------------------------------------------------------------||
   //-------------------------------------------------------------------------------||

   /**
    * Name
    */
   @Column(unique = true)
   // No two employees are to have the same name; not exactly
   // a real-world restriction, but shows usage. :)
   private String name;

   /**
    * The employee's address
    */
   @OneToOne
   @JoinColumn(name="ADDRESS_ID")
   // Unidirectional relationship
   private Address address;

   /**
    * The employee's computer
    */
   @OneToOne(mappedBy = "owner")
   // Bidirectional relationship
   private Computer computer;

   /**
    * Manager of the {@link Employee}
    */
   @ManyToOne
   private Employee manager;
```

```
/**
 * {@link Employee}s reporting to this {@link Employee}
 */
@OneToMany(mappedBy = "manager")
private Collection<Employee> peons;

/**
 * All {@link Phone}s for this {@link Employee}
 */
@OneToMany
// Unidirectional relationship
private Collection<Phone> phones;

/**
 * The {@link Team}s to which this {@link Employee} belongs
 */
@ManyToMany(mappedBy = "members")
private Collection<Team> teams;

//-------------------------------------------------------------------------||
// Constructor ------------------------------------------------------------||
//-------------------------------------------------------------------------||

/**
 * Default constructor, required by JPA
 */
public Employee()
{
    peons = new ArrayList<Employee>();
    phones = new ArrayList<Phone>();
    teams = new ArrayList<Team>();
}

/**
 * Convenience constructor
 */
public Employee(final String name)
{
    this();
    // Set
    this.name = name;
}

//-------------------------------------------------------------------------||
// Accessors / Mutators ---------------------------------------------------||
//-------------------------------------------------------------------------||

/**
 * @return the name
 */
public String getName()
{
    return name;
}
```

```java
/**
 * @param name the name to set
 */
public void setName(final String name)
{
    this.name = name;
}

/**
 * @return the address
 */
public Address getAddress()
{
    return address;
}

/**
 * @param address the address to set
 */
public void setAddress(final Address address)
{
    this.address = address;
}

/**
 * @return the computer
 */
public Computer getComputer()
{
    return computer;
}

/**
 * @param computer the computer to set
 */
public void setComputer(final Computer computer)
{
    this.computer = computer;
}

/**
 * @return the manager
 */
public Employee getManager()
{
    return manager;
}

/**
 * @param manager the manager to set
 */
public void setManager(final Employee manager)
{
    this.manager = manager;
}
```

```java
/**
 * @return the peons
 */
public Collection<Employee> getPeons()
{
    return peons;
}

/**
 * @param peons the peons to set
 */
public void setPeons(final Collection<Employee> peons)
{
    this.peons = peons;
}

/**
 * @return the teams
 */
public Collection<Team> getTeams()
{
    return teams;
}

/**
 * @param teams the teams to set
 */
public void setTeams(final Collection<Team> teams)
{
    this.teams = teams;
}

/**
 * @return the phones
 */
public Collection<Phone> getPhones()
{
    return phones;
}

/**
 * @param phones the phones to set
 */
public void setPhones(final Collection<Phone> phones)
{
    this.phones = phones;
}

//--------------------------------------------------------------------------||
// Overridden Implementations ----------------------------------------------||
//--------------------------------------------------------------------------||

/* (non-Javadoc)
 * @see java.lang.Object#toString()
```

```
    */
    @Override
    public String toString()
    {
        return Employee.class.getSimpleName() + " [name=" + name + ", getId()=" +
getId() + "]";
    }

}
```

Phone.java

```java
package org.jboss.ejb3.examples.employeeregistry.ch11.relationships;

import javax.persistence.Entity;
import javax.persistence.EnumType;
import javax.persistence.Enumerated;

import org.jboss.ejb3.examples.testsupport.entity.AutogenIdentityBase;

/**
 * Represents a Phone number.  An {@link Employee}
 * may have many, but the relationship is unidirectional.
 *
 * @author <a href="mailto:andrew.rubinger@jboss.org">ALR</a>
 * @version $Revision: $
 */
@Entity
// Mark that we're an Entity Bean, EJB's integration point
// with Java Persistence
public class Phone extends AutogenIdentityBase
{

    //-------------------------------------------------------------------------||
    // Instance Members -------------------------------------------------------||
    //-------------------------------------------------------------------------||

    /**
     * Phone number
     */
    private String number;

    /**
     * Type
     */
    @Enumerated(EnumType.STRING)
    private PhoneType type;

    //-------------------------------------------------------------------------||
    // Accessors / Mutators ---------------------------------------------------||
    //-------------------------------------------------------------------------||

    /**
     * @return the number
     */
```

```
        public String getNumber()
        {
            return number;
        }

        /**
         * @param number the number to set
         */
        public void setNumber(String number)
        {
            this.number = number;
        }

        /**
         * @return the type
         */
        public PhoneType getType()
        {
            return type;
        }

        /**
         * @param type the type to set
         */
        public void setType(PhoneType type)
        {
            this.type = type;
        }

        //-------------------------------------------------------------------------||
        // Required Implementations ------------------------------------------------||
        //-------------------------------------------------------------------------||

        /**
         * {@inheritDoc}
         * @see java.lang.Object#toString()
         */
        @Override
        public String toString()
        {
            return Phone.class.getSimpleName() + " [number=" + number + ", type=" +
    type + ", getId()=" + getId() + "]";
        }

    }
```

PhoneType.java

```
    package org.jboss.ejb3.examples.employeeregistry.ch11.relationships;

    /**
     * Type of number associated with a {@link Phone}
     *
     * @author <a href="mailto:andrew.rubinger@jboss.org">ALR</a>
     * @version $Revision: $
```

```
    */
public enum PhoneType {
    MOBILE, HOME, WORK
}
```

Task.java

```java
package org.jboss.ejb3.examples.employeeregistry.ch11.relationships;

import java.util.ArrayList;
import java.util.Collection;

import javax.persistence.Entity;
import javax.persistence.ManyToMany;

import org.jboss.ejb3.examples.testsupport.entity.AutogenIdentityBase;

/**
 * Represents a task to be completed or tracked as an issue.
 * These may be assigned to any number of {@link Employee}s,
 * and {@link Employee}s may have any number of issues.  However
 * the relationship is unidirectional from task to employee.
 *
 * @author <a href="mailto:andrew.rubinger@jboss.org">ALR</a>
 * @version $Revision: $
 */
@Entity
public class Task extends AutogenIdentityBase
{

    //-------------------------------------------------------------------------||
    // Instance Members -------------------------------------------------------||
    //-------------------------------------------------------------------------||

    /**
     * Name
     */
    private String description;

    /**
     * {@link Employee} in charge of this {@link Task}
     */
    @ManyToMany
    private Collection<Employee> owners;

    //-------------------------------------------------------------------------||
    // Constructor ------------------------------------------------------------||
    //-------------------------------------------------------------------------||

    /**
     * Default constructor, required by JPA
     */
    public Task()
    {
        owners = new ArrayList<Employee>();
```

```
    }

    /**
     * Convenience constructor
     */
    public Task(final String description)
    {
        this();
        // Set
        this.description = description;
    }

    //---------------------------------------------------------------------||
    // Accessors / Mutators -----------------------------------------------||
    //---------------------------------------------------------------------||

    /**
     * @return the description
     */
    public String getDescription()
    {
        return description;
    }

    /**
     * @param description the description to set
     */
    public void setDescription(final String description)
    {
        this.description = description;
    }

    /**
     * @return the owners
     */
    public Collection<Employee> getOwners()
    {
        return owners;
    }

    /**
     * @param owners the owners to set
     */
    public void setOwners(final Collection<Employee> owners)
    {
        this.owners = owners;
    }

    //---------------------------------------------------------------------||
    // Required Implementations -------------------------------------------||
    //---------------------------------------------------------------------||

    /**
     * {@inheritDoc}
     * @see java.lang.Object#toString()
```

```
     */
    @Override
    public String toString()
    {
        return Task.class.getSimpleName() + " [description=" + description + ",
owners=" + owners + ", getId()="
                + getId() + "]";
    }
}
```

Team.java

```java
package org.jboss.ejb3.examples.employeeregistry.ch11.relationships;

import java.util.ArrayList;
import java.util.Collection;

import javax.persistence.Entity;
import javax.persistence.ManyToMany;

import org.jboss.ejb3.examples.testsupport.entity.AutogenIdentityBase;

/**
 * Represents a team of {@link Employee}s who typically
 * work in the same area.  Employees may be a part of many teams.
 *
 * @author <a href="mailto:andrew.rubinger@jboss.org">ALR</a>
 * @version $Revision: $
 */
@Entity
public class Team extends AutogenIdentityBase
{

    //-------------------------------------------------------------------------||
    // Instance Members -------------------------------------------------------||
    //-------------------------------------------------------------------------||

    /**
     * Name of the Team
     */
    private String name;

    /**
     * {@link Employee}s on this {@link Task}.
     */
    @ManyToMany
    private Collection<Employee> members;

    //-------------------------------------------------------------------------||
    // Constructor ------------------------------------------------------------||
    //-------------------------------------------------------------------------||

    /**
     * Default constructor, required by JPA
     */
```

```java
public Team()
{
    members = new ArrayList<Employee>();
}

/**
 * Convenience constructor
 * @param name
 */
public Team(final String name)
{
    this();
    this.name = name;
}

//-------------------------------------------------------------------------||
// Accessors / Mutators ---------------------------------------------------||
//-------------------------------------------------------------------------||

/**
 * @return the members
 */
public Collection<Employee> getMembers()
{
    return members;
}

/**
 * @param members the members to set
 */
public void setMembers(final Collection<Employee> members)
{
    this.members = members;
}

/**
 * @return the name
 */
public String getName()
{
    return name;
}

/**
 * @param name the name to set
 */
public void setName(String name)
{
    this.name = name;
}

//-------------------------------------------------------------------------||
// Required Implementations -----------------------------------------------||
//-------------------------------------------------------------------------||
```

```
    /**
     * {@inheritDoc}
     * @see java.lang.Object#toString()
     */
    @Override
    public String toString()
    {
        return Team.class.getSimpleName() + " [members=" + members + ", name=" +
name + ", getId()=" + getId() + "]";
    }
}
```

Customer.java

```
package org.jboss.ejb3.examples.employeeregistry.ch12.inheritance.joined;

import javax.persistence.Entity;

/**
 * Represents a customer, a {@link Person}
 * associated with a company.  Sits in the middle of an inheritance
 * hierarchy and is extended by employee types, who are a special type of
 * {@link Customer}.
 *
 * @author <a href="mailto:andrew.rubinger@jboss.org">ALR</a>
 * @version $Revision: $
 */
@Entity(name = "JOINED_CUSTOMER")
public class Customer extends Person
{

    //-------------------------------------------------------------------------||
    // Instance Members -------------------------------------------------------||
    //-------------------------------------------------------------------------||

    /**
     * Street-level address
     */
    private String street;

    /**
     * City
     */
    private String city;

    /**
     * State
     */
    private String state;

    /**
     * ZIP
     */
    private String zip;
```

```
//-------------------------------------------------------------------------||
// Accessors / Mutators ---------------------------------------------------||
//-------------------------------------------------------------------------||
/**
 * @return the street
 */
public String getStreet()
{
   return street;
}

/**
 * @param street the street to set
 */
public void setStreet(final String street)
{
   this.street = street;
}

/**
 * @return the city
 */
public String getCity()
{
   return city;
}

/**
 * @param city the city to set
 */
public void setCity(final String city)
{
   this.city = city;
}

/**
 * @return the state
 */
public String getState()
{
   return state;
}

/**
 * @param state the state to set
 */
public void setState(final String state)
{
   this.state = state;
}

/**
 * @return the zip
 */
public String getZip()
```

```
    {
        return zip;
    }

    /**
     * @param zip the zip to set
     */
    public void setZip(final String zip)
    {
        this.zip = zip;
    }

}
```

Employee.java

```java
package org.jboss.ejb3.examples.employeeregistry.ch12.inheritance.joined;

import javax.persistence.Entity;
import javax.persistence.PrimaryKeyJoinColumn;

/**
 * Employee
 *
 * @author <a href="mailto:andrew.rubinger@jboss.org">ALR</a>
 * @version $Revision: $
 */
@Entity(name = "JOINED_EMPLOYEE")
@PrimaryKeyJoinColumn(name = "EMP_PK")
public class Employee extends Customer
{
    //-------------------------------------------------------------------------------||
    // Instance Members -------------------------------------------------------------||
    //-------------------------------------------------------------------------------||

    /**
     * ID of the Employee
     */
    private Integer employeeId;

    //-------------------------------------------------------------------------------||
    // Accessors / Mutators ---------------------------------------------------------||
    //-------------------------------------------------------------------------------||

    /**
     * @return the employeeId
     */
    public Integer getEmployeeId()
    {
        return employeeId;
    }

    /**
     * @param employeeId the employeeId to set
     */
```

```java
    public void setEmployeeId(final Integer employeeId)
    {
        this.employeeId = employeeId;
    }

}
```

Person.java

```java
package org.jboss.ejb3.examples.employeeregistry.ch12.inheritance.joined;

import javax.persistence.Entity;
import javax.persistence.GeneratedValue;
import javax.persistence.Id;
import javax.persistence.Inheritance;
import javax.persistence.InheritanceType;

/**
 * Base class for entities representing a person
 *
 * @author <a href="mailto:andrew.rubinger@jboss.org">ALR</a>
 * @version $Revision: $
 */
@Entity(name = "JOINED_PERSON")
@Inheritance(strategy = InheritanceType.JOINED)
public class Person
{

    //-------------------------------------------------------------------------||
    // Instance Members -------------------------------------------------------||
    //-------------------------------------------------------------------------||

    /**
     * Primary key
     */
    @Id
    @GeneratedValue
    private Long id;

    /**
     * First name of the person
     */
    private String firstName;

    /**
     * Last name of the person
     */
    private String lastName;

    //-------------------------------------------------------------------------||
    // Accessors / Mutators ---------------------------------------------------||
    //-------------------------------------------------------------------------||

    /**
     * @return the id
     */
```

```java
     */
    public Long getId()
    {
        return id;
    }

    /**
     * @param id the id to set
     */
    public void setId(final Long id)
    {
        this.id = id;
    }

    /**
     * @return the firstName
     */
    public String getFirstName()
    {
        return firstName;
    }

    /**
     * @param firstName the firstName to set
     */
    public void setFirstName(final String firstName)
    {
        this.firstName = firstName;
    }

    /**
     * @return the lastName
     */
    public String getLastName()
    {
        return lastName;
    }

    /**
     * @param lastName the lastName to set
     */
    public void setLastName(final String lastName)
    {
        this.lastName = lastName;
    }

    //-------------------------------------------------------------------------||
    // Overridden Implementations ---------------------------------------------||
    //-------------------------------------------------------------------------||

    /*
     * Value equality is based by ID and type only
     */

    /**
```

```
 * {@inheritDoc}
 * @see java.lang.Object#hashCode()
 */
@Override
public int hashCode()
{
   final int prime = 31;
   int result = 1;
   result = prime * result + ((id == null) ? 0 : id.hashCode());
   return result;
}

/**
 * {@inheritDoc}
 * @see java.lang.Object#equals(java.lang.Object)
 */
@Override
public boolean equals(final Object obj)
{
   if (this == obj)
      return true;
   if (obj == null)
      return false;
   if (getClass() != obj.getClass())
      return false;
   Person other = (Person) obj;
   if (id == null)
   {
      if (other.id != null)
         return false;
   }
   else if (!id.equals(other.id))
      return false;
   return true;
}

/**
 * {@inheritDoc}
 * @see java.lang.Object#toString()
 */
@Override
public String toString()
{
   return this.getClass().getSimpleName() + " [firstName=" + firstName + ", id
=" + id + ", lastName=" + lastName
         + "]";
}

}
```

Customer.java

```
package org.jboss.ejb3.examples.employeeregistry.ch12.inheritance.singleclass;

import javax.persistence.DiscriminatorValue;
```

```java
import javax.persistence.Entity;

/**
 * Represents a customer, a {@link Person}
 * associated with a company.  Sits in the middle of an inheritance
 * hierarchy and is extended by employee types, who are a special type of
 * {@link Customer}.
 *
 * @author <a href="mailto:andrew.rubinger@jboss.org">ALR</a>
 * @version $Revision: $
 */
@Entity(name = "SINGLECLASS_CUSTOMER")
@DiscriminatorValue("CUSTOMER")
public class Customer extends Person
{

   //-------------------------------------------------------------------------||
   // Instance Members -------------------------------------------------------||
   //-------------------------------------------------------------------------||

   /**
    * Street-level address
    */
   private String street;

   /**
    * City
    */
   private String city;

   /**
    * State
    */
   private String state;

   /**
    * ZIP
    */
   private String zip;

   //-------------------------------------------------------------------------||
   // Accessors / Mutators ---------------------------------------------------||
   //-------------------------------------------------------------------------||
   /**
    * @return the street
    */
   public String getStreet()
   {
      return street;
   }

   /**
    * @param street the street to set
    */
   public void setStreet(final String street)
```

```java
{
    this.street = street;
}

/**
 * @return the city
 */
public String getCity()
{
    return city;
}

/**
 * @param city the city to set
 */
public void setCity(final String city)
{
    this.city = city;
}

/**
 * @return the state
 */
public String getState()
{
    return state;
}

/**
 * @param state the state to set
 */
public void setState(final String state)
{
    this.state = state;
}

/**
 * @return the zip
 */
public String getZip()
{
    return zip;
}

/**
 * @param zip the zip to set
 */
public void setZip(final String zip)
{
    this.zip = zip;
}

}
```

Employee.java

```java
package org.jboss.ejb3.examples.employeeregistry.ch12.inheritance.singleclass;

import javax.persistence.DiscriminatorValue;
import javax.persistence.Entity;

/**
 * Employee
 *
 * @author <a href="mailto:andrew.rubinger@jboss.org">ALR</a>
 * @version $Revision: $
 */
@Entity(name = "SINGLECLASS_EMPLOYEE")
@DiscriminatorValue("EMPLOYEE")
public class Employee extends Customer
{
   //-------------------------------------------------------------------------||
   // Instance Members -------------------------------------------------------||
   //-------------------------------------------------------------------------||

   /**
    * ID of the Employee
    */
   private Integer employeeId;

   //-------------------------------------------------------------------------||
   // Accessors / Mutators ---------------------------------------------------||
   //-------------------------------------------------------------------------||

   /**
    * @return the employeeId
    */
   public Integer getEmployeeId()
   {
      return employeeId;
   }

   /**
    * @param employeeId the employeeId to set
    */
   public void setEmployeeId(final Integer employeeId)
   {
      this.employeeId = employeeId;
   }

}
```

Person.java

```java
package org.jboss.ejb3.examples.employeeregistry.ch12.inheritance.singleclass;

import javax.persistence.DiscriminatorColumn;
import javax.persistence.DiscriminatorType;
import javax.persistence.DiscriminatorValue;
```

```
import javax.persistence.Entity;
import javax.persistence.GeneratedValue;
import javax.persistence.Id;
import javax.persistence.Inheritance;
import javax.persistence.InheritanceType;

/**
 * Base class for entities representing a person
 *
 * @author <a href="mailto:andrew.rubinger@jboss.org">ALR</a>
 * @version $Revision: $
 */
@Entity(name = "SINGLECLASS_PERSON")
@Inheritance(strategy = InheritanceType.SINGLE_TABLE)
@DiscriminatorColumn(name = "DISCRIMINATOR", discriminatorType = Discriminator
Type.STRING)
@DiscriminatorValue("PERSON")
public class Person
{

   //--------------------------------------------------------------------------||
   // Instance Members --------------------------------------------------------||
   //--------------------------------------------------------------------------||

   /**
    * Primary key
    */
   @Id
   @GeneratedValue
   private Long id;

   /**
    * First name of the person
    */
   private String firstName;

   /**
    * Last name of the person
    */
   private String lastName;

   //--------------------------------------------------------------------------||
   // Accessors / Mutators ----------------------------------------------------||
   //--------------------------------------------------------------------------||

   /**
    * @return the id
    */
   public Long getId()
   {
      return id;
   }

   /**
    * @param id the id to set
```

```java
    */
    public void setId(final Long id)
    {
        this.id = id;
    }

    /**
     * @return the firstName
     */
    public String getFirstName()
    {
        return firstName;
    }

    /**
     * @param firstName the firstName to set
     */
    public void setFirstName(final String firstName)
    {
        this.firstName = firstName;
    }

    /**
     * @return the lastName
     */
    public String getLastName()
    {
        return lastName;
    }

    /**
     * @param lastName the lastName to set
     */
    public void setLastName(final String lastName)
    {
        this.lastName = lastName;
    }

    //---------------------------------------------------------------------------||
    // Overridden Implementations -----------------------------------------------||
    //---------------------------------------------------------------------------||

    /*
     * Value equality is based by ID and type only
     */

    /**
     * {@inheritDoc}
     * @see java.lang.Object#hashCode()
     */
    @Override
    public int hashCode()
    {
        final int prime = 31;
        int result = 1;
```

```java
        result = prime * result + ((id == null) ? 0 : id.hashCode());
        return result;
    }

    /**
     * {@inheritDoc}
     * @see java.lang.Object#equals(java.lang.Object)
     */
    @Override
    public boolean equals(final Object obj)
    {
        if (this == obj)
            return true;
        if (obj == null)
            return false;
        if (getClass() != obj.getClass())
            return false;
        Person other = (Person) obj;
        if (id == null)
        {
            if (other.id != null)
                return false;
        }
        else if (!id.equals(other.id))
            return false;
        return true;
    }

    /**
     * {@inheritDoc}
     * @see java.lang.Object#toString()
     */
    @Override
    public String toString()
    {
        return this.getClass().getSimpleName() + " [firstName=" + firstName + ", id
=" + id + ", lastName=" + lastName
                + "]";
    }

}
```

Customer.java

```java
package org.jboss.ejb3.examples.employeeregistry.ch12.inheritance.tableperclass;

import javax.persistence.Entity;

/**
 * Represents a customer, a {@link Person}
 * associated with a company.  Sits in the middle of an inheritance
 * hierarchy and is extended by employee types, who are a special type of
 * {@link Customer}.
 *
 * @author <a href="mailto:andrew.rubinger@jboss.org">ALR</a>
```

```java
 * @version $Revision: $
 */
@Entity(name = "TABLEPERCLASS_CUSTOMER")
public class Customer extends Person
{

   //--------------------------------------------------------------------------||
   // Instance Members --------------------------------------------------------||
   //--------------------------------------------------------------------------||

   /**
    * Street-level address
    */
   private String street;

   /**
    * City
    */
   private String city;

   /**
    * State
    */
   private String state;

   /**
    * ZIP
    */
   private String zip;

   //--------------------------------------------------------------------------||
   // Accessors / Mutators ----------------------------------------------------||
   //--------------------------------------------------------------------------||
   /**
    * @return the street
    */
   public String getStreet()
   {
      return street;
   }

   /**
    * @param street the street to set
    */
   public void setStreet(final String street)
   {
      this.street = street;
   }

   /**
    * @return the city
    */
   public String getCity()
   {
      return city;
```

```
        }

        /**
         * @param city the city to set
         */
        public void setCity(final String city)
        {
            this.city = city;
        }

        /**
         * @return the state
         */
        public String getState()
        {
            return state;
        }

        /**
         * @param state the state to set
         */
        public void setState(final String state)
        {
            this.state = state;
        }

        /**
         * @return the zip
         */
        public String getZip()
        {
            return zip;
        }

        /**
         * @param zip the zip to set
         */
        public void setZip(final String zip)
        {
            this.zip = zip;
        }

    }
```

Employee.java

```
    package org.jboss.ejb3.examples.employeeregistry.ch12.inheritance.tableperclass;

    import javax.persistence.Entity;

    /**
     * Employee
     *
     * @author <a href="mailto:andrew.rubinger@jboss.org">ALR</a>
     * @version $Revision: $
```

```
 */
@Entity(name = "TABLEPERCLASS_EMPLOYEE")
public class Employee extends Customer
{
   //--------------------------------------------------------------------------||
   // Instance Members --------------------------------------------------------||
   //--------------------------------------------------------------------------||

   /**
    * ID of the Employee
    */
   private Integer employeeId;

   //--------------------------------------------------------------------------||
   // Accessors / Mutators ----------------------------------------------------||
   //--------------------------------------------------------------------------||

   /**
    * @return the employeeId
    */
   public Integer getEmployeeId()
   {
      return employeeId;
   }

   /**
    * @param employeeId the employeeId to set
    */
   public void setEmployeeId(final Integer employeeId)
   {
      this.employeeId = employeeId;
   }

}
```

Person.java

```
package org.jboss.ejb3.examples.employeeregistry.ch12.inheritance.tableperclass;

import javax.persistence.Entity;
import javax.persistence.GeneratedValue;
import javax.persistence.GenerationType;
import javax.persistence.Id;
import javax.persistence.Inheritance;
import javax.persistence.InheritanceType;

/**
 * Base class for entities representing a person
 *
 * @author <a href="mailto:andrew.rubinger@jboss.org">ALR</a>
 * @version $Revision: $
 */
@Entity(name = "TABLEPERCLASS_PERSON")
@Inheritance(strategy = InheritanceType.TABLE_PER_CLASS)
public class Person
```

```
{

    //-------------------------------------------------------------------------||
    // Instance Members -------------------------------------------------------||
    //-------------------------------------------------------------------------||

    /**
     * Primary key
     */
    @Id
    @GeneratedValue(strategy = GenerationType.TABLE)
    // Cannot accept default generation strategy for table-per-class
    private Long id;

    /**
     * First name of the person
     */
    private String firstName;

    /**
     * Last name of the person
     */
    private String lastName;

    //-------------------------------------------------------------------------||
    // Accessors / Mutators ---------------------------------------------------||
    //-------------------------------------------------------------------------||

    /**
     * @return the id
     */
    public Long getId()
    {
        return id;
    }

    /**
     * @param id the id to set
     */
    public void setId(final Long id)
    {
        this.id = id;
    }

    /**
     * @return the firstName
     */
    public String getFirstName()
    {
        return firstName;
    }

    /**
     * @param firstName the firstName to set
     */
```

```java
public void setFirstName(final String firstName)
{
    this.firstName = firstName;
}

/**
 * @return the lastName
 */
public String getLastName()
{
    return lastName;
}

/**
 * @param lastName the lastName to set
 */
public void setLastName(final String lastName)
{
    this.lastName = lastName;
}

//----------------------------------------------------------------------||
// Overridden Implementations ------------------------------------------||
//----------------------------------------------------------------------||

/*
 * Value equality is based by ID and type only
 */

/**
 * {@inheritDoc}
 * @see java.lang.Object#hashCode()
 */
@Override
public int hashCode()
{
    final int prime = 31;
    int result = 1;
    result = prime * result + ((id == null) ? 0 : id.hashCode());
    return result;
}

/**
 * {@inheritDoc}
 * @see java.lang.Object#equals(java.lang.Object)
 */
@Override
public boolean equals(final Object obj)
{
    if (this == obj)
        return true;
    if (obj == null)
        return false;
    if (getClass() != obj.getClass())
        return false;
```

```
        Person other = (Person) obj;
        if (id == null)
        {
            if (other.id != null)
                return false;
        }
        else if (!id.equals(other.id))
            return false;
        return true;
    }

    /**
     * {@inheritDoc}
     * @see java.lang.Object#toString()
     */
    @Override
    public String toString()
    {
        return this.getClass().getSimpleName() + " [firstName=" + firstName + ", id
=" + id + ", lastName=" + lastName
            + "]";
    }

}
```

See Chapter 14.

EntityListenerEmployee.java

```
package org.jboss.ejb3.examples.employeeregistry.ch14.listener;

import java.util.logging.Logger;

import javax.persistence.Entity;
import javax.persistence.PostLoad;
import javax.persistence.PostPersist;
import javax.persistence.PostRemove;
import javax.persistence.PostUpdate;
import javax.persistence.PrePersist;
import javax.persistence.PreRemove;
import javax.persistence.PreUpdate;

import org.jboss.ejb3.examples.testsupport.entity.AutogenIdentityBase;

/**
 * Represents an Employee which is able to receive JPA
 * events.
 *
 * @author <a href="mailto:andrew.rubinger@jboss.org">ALR</a>
 * @version $Revision: $
 */
@Entity
public class EntityListenerEmployee extends AutogenIdentityBase
{
```

```
//--------------------------------------------------------------------||
// Class Members -------------------------------------------------------||
//--------------------------------------------------------------------||

/**
 * Logger
 */
private static final Logger log = Logger.getLogger(EntityListenerEmployee.
class.getName());

//--------------------------------------------------------------------||
// Instance Members ---------------------------------------------------||
//--------------------------------------------------------------------||

/**
 * Name of the employee
 */
private String name;

//--------------------------------------------------------------------||
// Constructor --------------------------------------------------------||
//--------------------------------------------------------------------||

/**
 * No-arg constructor, required by JPA
 */
public EntityListenerEmployee()
{

}

//--------------------------------------------------------------------||
// Accessors / Mutators -----------------------------------------------||
//--------------------------------------------------------------------||

/**
 * @return the name
 */
public String getName()
{
    return name;
}

/**
 * @param name the name to set
 */
public void setName(final String name)
{
    this.name = name;
}

//--------------------------------------------------------------------||
// Overridden Implementations -----------------------------------------||
//--------------------------------------------------------------------||
```

```
/**
 * {@inheritDoc}
 * @see java.lang.Object#toString()
 */
@Override
public String toString()
{
    return EntityListenerEmployee.class.getSimpleName() + " [name=" + name + ",
getId()=" + getId() + "]";
}

//------------------------------------------------------------------------||
// Event Listeners ------------------------------------------------------||
//------------------------------------------------------------------------||

/*
 * Event Listeners; fired by JPA and track state in the EventTracker
 */

@PrePersist
@SuppressWarnings("unused")
private void prePersist()
{
    EventTracker.prePersist = true;
    log.info("prePersist: " + this);
}

@PostPersist
@SuppressWarnings("unused")
private void postPersist()
{
    EventTracker.postPersist = true;
    log.info("postPersist: " + this);
}

@PostLoad
@SuppressWarnings("unused")
private void postLoad()
{
    EventTracker.postLoad = true;
    log.info("postLoad: " + this);
}

@PreUpdate
@SuppressWarnings("unused")
private void preUpdate()
{
    EventTracker.preUpdate = true;
    log.info("preUpdate: " + this);
}

@PostUpdate
@SuppressWarnings("unused")
private void postUpdate()
{
```

```
        EventTracker.postUpdate = true;
        log.info("postUpdate: " + this);
    }

    @PreRemove
    @SuppressWarnings("unused")
    private void preRemove()
    {
        EventTracker.preRemove = true;
        log.info("preRemove: " + this);
    }

    @PostRemove
    @SuppressWarnings("unused")
    private void postRemove()
    {
        EventTracker.postRemove = true;
        log.info("postRemove: " + this);
    }

}
```

EventTracker.java

```
package org.jboss.ejb3.examples.employeeregistry.ch14.listener;

/**
 * Tracks events fired by the {@link EntityListenerEmployee}
 *
 * @author <a href="mailto:andrew.rubinger@jboss.org">ALR</a>
 * @version $Revision: $
 */
public class EventTracker
{

    //-------------------------------------------------------------------------||
    // Class Members ----------------------------------------------------------||
    //-------------------------------------------------------------------------||

    /*
     * Flags denoting whether an event was fired
     */

    public static boolean prePersist;

    public static boolean postPersist;

    public static boolean postLoad;

    public static boolean preUpdate;

    public static boolean postUpdate;

    public static boolean preRemove;
```

```
    public static boolean postRemove;

    //--------------------------------------------------------------------------||
    // Functional Methods ------------------------------------------------------||
    //--------------------------------------------------------------------------||

    /**
     * Resets all events to false
     */
    public static void reset()
    {
        prePersist = false;
        postPersist = false;
        postLoad = false;
        preUpdate = false;
        postUpdate = false;
        preRemove = false;
        postRemove = false;
    }
}
```

persistence.xml

```
<?xml version="1.0" encoding="UTF-8"?>
<persistence xmlns="http://java.sun.com/xml/ns/persistence"
  xmlns:xsi="http://www.w3.org/2001/XMLSchema-instance"
  xsi:schemaLocation="http://java.sun.com/xml/ns/persistence
    http://java.sun.com/xml/ns/persistence/persistence_2_0.xsd"
  version="2.0">
  <persistence-unit name="tempdb">
    <jta-data-source>java:/DefaultDS</jta-data-source>
    <properties>
        <property name="hibernate.hbm2ddl.auto" value="create"/>
        <!--

        You can enable this for Hibernate to dump SQL output to STDOUT
        <property name="hibernate.show_sql" value="true"/>

        -->
    </properties>
  </persistence-unit>
</persistence>
```

Test Resources

EmployeeIntegrationTest.java

```
package org.jboss.ejb3.examples.employeeregistry;

import java.util.Calendar;
import java.util.Collection;
import java.util.Date;
import java.util.concurrent.Callable;
import java.util.logging.Logger;
```

```
import javax.naming.Context;
import javax.naming.InitialContext;
import javax.persistence.EmbeddedId;
import javax.persistence.EntityManager;
import javax.persistence.GeneratedValue;
import javax.persistence.IdClass;
import javax.persistence.criteria.CriteriaBuilder;
import javax.persistence.criteria.CriteriaQuery;
import javax.persistence.criteria.Root;

import org.jboss.arquillian.api.Deployment;
import org.jboss.arquillian.api.Run;
import org.jboss.arquillian.api.RunModeType;
import org.jboss.arquillian.junit.Arquillian;
import org.jboss.ejb3.examples.employeeregistry.ch09.entitymanager.SimpleEmployee;
import org.jboss.ejb3.examples.employeeregistry.ch10.mapping.EmbeddedEmployeePK;
import org.jboss.ejb3.examples.employeeregistry.ch10.mapping.EmployeeType;
import org.jboss.ejb3.examples.employeeregistry.ch10.mapping.EmployeeWithEmbedded
PK;
import org.jboss.ejb3.examples.employeeregistry.ch10.mapping.EmployeeWithExternal
CompositePK;
import org.jboss.ejb3.examples.employeeregistry.ch10.mapping.EmployeeWithMapped
SuperClassId;
import org.jboss.ejb3.examples.employeeregistry.ch10.mapping.EmployeeWith
Properties;
import org.jboss.ejb3.examples.employeeregistry.ch10.mapping.ExternalEmployeePK;
import org.jboss.ejb3.examples.employeeregistry.ch11.relationships.Address;
import org.jboss.ejb3.examples.employeeregistry.ch11.relationships.Computer;
import org.jboss.ejb3.examples.employeeregistry.ch11.relationships.Customer;
import org.jboss.ejb3.examples.employeeregistry.ch11.relationships.Employee;
import org.jboss.ejb3.examples.employeeregistry.ch11.relationships.Phone;
import org.jboss.ejb3.examples.employeeregistry.ch11.relationships.PhoneType;
import org.jboss.ejb3.examples.employeeregistry.ch11.relationships.Task;
import org.jboss.ejb3.examples.employeeregistry.ch11.relationships.Team;
import org.jboss.ejb3.examples.employeeregistry.ch14.listener.EntityListener
Employee;
import org.jboss.ejb3.examples.employeeregistry.ch14.listener.EventTracker;
import org.jboss.ejb3.examples.testsupport.dbquery.EntityManagerExposingBean;
import org.jboss.ejb3.examples.testsupport.dbquery.EntityManagerExposingLocal
Business;
import org.jboss.ejb3.examples.testsupport.entity.IdentityBase;
import org.jboss.ejb3.examples.testsupport.txwrap.TaskExecutionException;
import org.jboss.ejb3.examples.testsupport.txwrap.TxWrappingBean;
import org.jboss.ejb3.examples.testsupport.txwrap.TxWrappingLocalBusiness;
import org.jboss.shrinkwrap.api.ShrinkWrap;
import org.jboss.shrinkwrap.api.spec.JavaArchive;
import org.junit.After;
import org.junit.Assert;
import org.junit.Before;
import org.junit.BeforeClass;
import org.junit.Test;
import org.junit.runner.RunWith;

/**
```

```
 * Tests to ensure that we can do simple CRUD operations
 * upon an object view (Entity beans), and see our changes persisted
 * across transactions.
 *
 * @author <a href="mailto:andrew.rubinger@jboss.org">ALR</a>
 * @version $Revision: $
 */
@RunWith(Arquillian.class)
@Run(RunModeType.AS_CLIENT)
public class EmployeeIntegrationTest
{
   //-------------------------------------------------------------------------||
   // Class Members ----------------------------------------------------------||
   //-------------------------------------------------------------------------||

   /**
    * Logger
    */
   private static final Logger log = Logger.getLogger(EmployeeIntegrationTest.
class.getName());

   /**
    * Naming Context
    * @deprecated Remove when Arquillian will inject the EJB proxies
    */
   @Deprecated
   private static Context jndiContext;

   /**
    * The Deployment into the EJB Container
    */
   @Deployment
   public static JavaArchive getDeployment()
   {
      final JavaArchive archive = ShrinkWrap.create("entities.jar", JavaArchive.
class).addPackages(false,
            SimpleEmployee.class.getPackage(), EmployeeWithMappedSuperClassId.
class.getPackage(),
            Employee.class.getPackage(), TxWrappingLocalBusiness.class.getPackage
(),
            EntityListenerEmployee.class.getPackage(), EntityManagerExposingBean.
class.getPackage(),
            org.jboss.ejb3.examples.employeeregistry.ch12.inheritance.singleclass
.Employee.class.getPackage(),
            org.jboss.ejb3.examples.employeeregistry.ch12.inheritance.tableper
class.Employee.class.getPackage(),
            org.jboss.ejb3.examples.employeeregistry.ch12.inheritance.joined.
Employee.class.getPackage())
            .addManifestResource("persistence.xml");
      log.info(archive.toString(true));
      return archive;
   }

   /*
    * Data for our tests
```

```
    */

    private static final long ID_DAVE = 1L;

    private static final long ID_JOSH = 2L;

    private static final long ID_RICK = 3L;

    private static final String NAME_DAVE = "Dave";

    private static final String NAME_DAVE_NEW = "Dave - The Good Doctor";

    private static final String NAME_JOSH = "Josh";

    private static final String NAME_RICK = "Rick, Jr.";

    //-------------------------------------------------------------------------||
    // Instance Members -------------------------------------------------------||
    //-------------------------------------------------------------------------||

    /**
     * EJB which wraps supplied {@link Callable} instances inside of a new Tx
     */
    // TODO: Support Injection of @EJB here when Arquillian for Embedded JBossAS
will support it
    private TxWrappingLocalBusiness txWrapper;

    /**
     * EJB which provides direct access to an {@link EntityManager}'s method for
use in testing.
     * Must be called inside an existing Tx so that returned entities are not
detached.
     */
    // TODO: Support Injection of @EJB here when Arquillian for Embedded JBossAS
will support it
    private EntityManagerExposingLocalBusiness emHook;

    //-------------------------------------------------------------------------||
    // Lifecycle --------------------------------------------------------------||
    //-------------------------------------------------------------------------||

    /**
     * Performs suite-wide initialization
     */
    @BeforeClass
    public static void init() throws Exception
    {
        // After the server is up, we don't need to pass any explicit properties
        jndiContext = new InitialContext();
    }

    /**
     * Manually looks up EJBs in JNDI and assigns them
     */
    @Before
```

```java
    public void injectEjbsAndClearDB() throws Throwable
    {
        // Fake injection by doing manual lookups for the time being
        //TODO Deprecated portion
        txWrapper = (TxWrappingLocalBusiness) jndiContext.lookup(TxWrappingBean.
class.getSimpleName() + "/local");
        emHook = (EntityManagerExposingLocalBusiness) jndiContext.lookup(Entity
ManagerExposingBean.class.getSimpleName()
            + "/local");

        // Clear all employees before running, just in case
        this.clearAllEmployees();
    }

    /**
     * Resets all entity callbacks
     */
    @Before
    public void clearEntityCallbacks()
    {
        EventTracker.reset();
    }

    /**
     * Issues a deletion to remove all employees from persistent storage
     * @throws Throwable
     */
    @After
    public void clearAllEmployees() throws Throwable
    {
        // Clear the DB of all Employees
        try
        {
            txWrapper.wrapInTx(new Callable<Void>()
            {

                @Override
                public Void call() throws Exception
                {

                    final EntityManager em = emHook.getEntityManager();
                    EmployeeIntegrationTest.this.deleteAllEntitiesOfType(Simple
Employee.class, em);
                    EmployeeIntegrationTest.this.deleteAllEntitiesOfType(EmployeeWith
MappedSuperClassId.class, em);
                    EmployeeIntegrationTest.this.deleteAllEntitiesOfType(EmployeeWith
ExternalCompositePK.class, em);
                    EmployeeIntegrationTest.this.deleteAllEntitiesOfType(EmployeeWith
Properties.class, em);
                    EmployeeIntegrationTest.this.deleteAllEntitiesOfType(Computer.
class, em);
                    EmployeeIntegrationTest.this.deleteAllEntitiesOfType(Phone.class,
em);
                    EmployeeIntegrationTest.this.deleteAllEntitiesOfType(Customer.
class, em);
```

```
                EmployeeIntegrationTest.this.deleteAllEntitiesOfType(Task.class,
em);
                EmployeeIntegrationTest.this.deleteAllEntitiesOfType(Team.class,
em);
                EmployeeIntegrationTest.this.deleteAllEntitiesOfType(Employee.
class, em);

                return null;
            }

        });
        }
        catch (final TaskExecutionException tee)
        {
            // Unwrap
            throw tee.getCause();
        }
    }


    //-------------------------------------------------------------------------||
    // Tests -----------------------------------------------------------------||
    //-------------------------------------------------------------------------||

    /**
     * Tests that we can use the {@link EntityManager} to perform simple
     * CRUD (Create, remove, update, delete) operations on an object view,
     * and these changes will be persisted as expected.
     */
    @Test
    public void persistAndModifyEmployees() throws Throwable
    {

        try
        {

            // Execute the addition of the employees, and conditional checks, in the
    context of a Transaction
            txWrapper.wrapInTx(new Callable<Void>()
            {

                @Override
                public Void call() throws Exception
                {
                    // Create a few plain instances
                    final SimpleEmployee josh = new SimpleEmployee(ID_DAVE, NAME_DAVE);
                    final SimpleEmployee dave = new SimpleEmployee(ID_JOSH, NAME_JOSH);
                    final SimpleEmployee rick = new SimpleEmployee(ID_RICK, NAME_RICK);

                    // Get the EntityManager from our test hook
                    final EntityManager em = emHook.getEntityManager();

                    // Now first check if any employees are found in the underlying
    persistent
                    // storage (shouldn't be)
                    Assert.assertNull("Employees should not have been added to the EM
```

```
yet", em.find(SimpleEmployee.class,
                ID_DAVE));

        // Check if the object is managed (shouldn't be)
        Assert.assertFalse("Employee should not be managed yet", em.
contains(josh));

        // Now persist the employees
        em.persist(dave);
        em.persist(josh);
        em.persist(rick);
        log.info("Added: " + rick + dave + josh);

        // The employees should be managed now
        Assert.assertTrue("Employee should be managed now, after call to
persist", em.contains(josh));

        // Return
        return null;
    }
});

// Now change Employee Dave's name in a Tx; we'll verify the changes
were flushed to the DB later
txWrapper.wrapInTx(new Callable<Void>()
{

    @Override
    public Void call() throws Exception
    {
        // Get an EM
        final EntityManager em = emHook.getEntityManager();

        // Look up "Dave" by ID from the EM
        final SimpleEmployee dave = em.find(SimpleEmployee.class, ID_DAVE);

        // Change Dave's name
        dave.setName(NAME_DAVE_NEW);
        log.info("Changing Dave's name: " + dave);

        // That's it - the new name should be flushed to the DB when the
Tx completes
        return null;
    }
});

// Since we've changed Dave's name in the last transaction, ensure that
we see the changes
// have been flushed and we can see them from a new Tx.
txWrapper.wrapInTx(new Callable<Void>()
{

    @Override
    public Void call() throws Exception
    {
```

```
                // Get an EM
                final EntityManager em = emHook.getEntityManager();

                // Make a new "Dave" as a detached object with same primary key,
but a different name
                final SimpleEmployee dave = new SimpleEmployee(ID_DAVE, NAME_DAVE_
NEW);

                // Merge these changes on the detached instance with the DB
                em.merge(dave);

                // Ensure we see the name change
                Assert.assertEquals("Employee Dave's name should have been changed
", NAME_DAVE_NEW, dave.getName());

                // Now we'll detach Dave from the EM, this makes the object no
longer managed
                em.detach(dave);

                // Change Dave's name again to some dummy value.  Because the
object is
                // detached and no longer managed, we should not see this new value
                // synchronized with the DB
                dave.setName("A name we shouldn't see flushed to persistence");
                log.info("Changing Dave's name after detached: " + dave);

                // Return
                return null;
            }
        });

        // Another check.  We changed Dave's name when the entity was no longer
        // managed and attached to an EM, so ensure that any changes we made
        // were not flushed out
        txWrapper.wrapInTx(new Callable<Void>()
        {

            @Override
            public Void call() throws Exception
            {
                // Get an EM
                final EntityManager em = emHook.getEntityManager();

                // Make a new "Dave" instance
                final SimpleEmployee dave = em.find(SimpleEmployee.class, ID_DAVE);
                log.info("Lookup of Dave after we changed his name on a detached
instance: " + dave);

                // Ensure that the last name change we gave to Dave did not take
effect
                Assert
                    .assertEquals("Detached object values should not have been
flushed", NAME_DAVE_NEW, dave.getName());

                // Return
```

```java
                return null;

            }
        });

        // Uh oh, Rick has decided to leave the company.  Let's delete his record.
        txWrapper.wrapInTx(new Callable<Void>()
        {

            @Override
            public Void call() throws Exception
            {
                // Get an EM
                final EntityManager em = emHook.getEntityManager();

                // Look up Rick
                final SimpleEmployee rick = em.find(SimpleEmployee.class, ID_RICK);

                // Remove
                em.remove(rick);
                log.info("Deleted: " + rick);

                // Return
                return null;

            }
        });

        // Ensure we can no longer find Rick in the DB
        txWrapper.wrapInTx(new Callable<Void>()
        {

            @Override
            public Void call() throws Exception
            {
                // Get an EM
                final EntityManager em = emHook.getEntityManager();

                // Look up Rick
                final SimpleEmployee rick = em.find(SimpleEmployee.class, ID_RICK);

                // Assert
                Assert.assertNull("Rick should have been removed from the DB",
rick);

                // Return
                return null;

            }
        });

    }
    catch (final TaskExecutionException tee)
    {
        // Unwrap
```

```
                throw tee.getCause();
            }

        }

        /**
         * Shows usage of JPA autogeneration of primary keys, using
         * {@link EmployeeWithMappedSuperClassId} which inherits PK support from
         * {@link IdentityBase#getId()}.
         * @throws Throwable
         */
        @Test
        public void autogenPrimaryKeyFromMappedSuperClass() throws Throwable
        {
            try
            {
                // Create a new Employee, and let JPA give us the PK value
                final Long id = txWrapper.wrapInTx(new Callable<Long>()
                {

                    @Override
                    public Long call() throws Exception
                    {
                        // Make a new Employee
                        final EmployeeWithMappedSuperClassId alrubinger = new EmployeeWith
MappedSuperClassId(
                                "Andrew Lee Rubinger");

                        // Ensure we have no ID now
                        Assert.assertNull("Primary key should not be set yet", alrubinger.
getId());

                        // Persist
                        emHook.getEntityManager().persist(alrubinger);

                        // Now show that JPA gave us a primary key as generated
                        final Long id = alrubinger.getId();
                        Assert.assertNotNull("Persisting an entity with PK " + Generated
Value.class.getName()
                                + " should be created", id);
                        log.info("Persisted: " + alrubinger);

                        // Return
                        return id;
                    }

                });

                // Ensure we can look up this new entity by the PK we've been given
                txWrapper.wrapInTx(new Callable<Void>()
                {

                    @Override
                    public Void call() throws Exception
                    {
```

```java
                // Look up the Employee by the ID we just gave
                final EmployeeWithMappedSuperClassId employee = emHook.getEntity
Manager().find(
                    EmployeeWithMappedSuperClassId.class, id);

                // Ensure found
                Assert.assertNotNull("Employee should be able to be looked up by
PK", employee);

                // Return
                return null;
            }

        });
    }
    catch (final TaskExecutionException tee)
    {
        // Unwrap
        throw tee.getCause();
    }
}

/**
 * Shows usage of an entity which gets its identity via an
 * {@link IdClass} - {@link ExternalEmployeePK}.
 * @throws Throwable
 */
@Test
public void externalCompositePrimaryKey() throws Throwable
{
    try
    {
        txWrapper.wrapInTx(new Callable<Void>()
        {

            @Override
            public Void call() throws Exception
            {
                // Define the values to compose a primary key identity
                final String lastName = "Rubinger";
                final Long ssn = 100L; // Not real ;)

                // Create a new Employee which uses a custom @IdClass
                final EmployeeWithExternalCompositePK employee = new EmployeeWith
ExternalCompositePK();
                employee.setLastName(lastName);
                employee.setSsn(ssn);

                // Persist
                final EntityManager em = emHook.getEntityManager();
                em.persist(employee);
                log.info("Persisted: " + employee);

                // Now look up using our custom composite PK value class
                final ExternalEmployeePK pk = new ExternalEmployeePK();
```

```
                    pk.setLastName(lastName);
                    pk.setSsn(ssn);
                    final EmployeeWithExternalCompositePK roundtrip = em.find(Employee
WithExternalCompositePK.class, pk);

                    // Ensure found
                    Assert.assertNotNull("Should have been able to look up record via
a custom PK composite class",
                            roundtrip);

                    // Return
                    return null;
                }

            });
        }
        catch (final TaskExecutionException tee)
        {
            // Unwrap
            throw tee.getCause();
        }
    }

    /**
     * Shows usage of an entity which gets its identity via an
     * {@link EmbeddedId} - {@link EmployeeWithEmbeddedPK}
     * @throws Throwable
     */
    @Test
    public void embeddedCompositePrimaryKey() throws Throwable
    {
        try
        {
            txWrapper.wrapInTx(new Callable<Void>()
            {

                @Override
                public Void call() throws Exception
                {
                    // Define the values to compose a primary key identity
                    final String lastName = "Rubinger";
                    final Long ssn = 100L; // Not real ;)

                    // Create a new Employee which uses an Embedded PK Class
                    final EmployeeWithEmbeddedPK employee = new EmployeeWithEmbeddedPK
();

                    final EmbeddedEmployeePK pk = new EmbeddedEmployeePK();
                    pk.setLastName(lastName);
                    pk.setSsn(ssn);
                    employee.setId(pk);

                    // Persist
                    final EntityManager em = emHook.getEntityManager();
                    em.persist(employee);
                    log.info("Persisted: " + employee);
```

```
                    // Now look up using our custom composite PK value class
                    final EmployeeWithEmbeddedPK roundtrip = em.find(EmployeeWith
EmbeddedPK.class, pk);

                    // Ensure found
                    Assert
                        .assertNotNull("Should have been able to look up record via
a custom embedded PK class", roundtrip);

                    // Return
                    return null;
                }

            });
        }
        catch (final TaskExecutionException tee)
        {
            // Unwrap
            throw tee.getCause();
        }
    }

    /**
     * Shows usage of an entity with a series of nonstandard
     * mappings which require additional JPA metadata to show
     * the ORM layer how things should be represented in the DB.
     */
    @Test
    public void propertyMappings() throws Throwable
    {
        // Define the values for our employee
        final byte[] image = new byte[]
        {0x00};
        final Date since = new Date(0L); // Employed since the epoch
        final EmployeeType type = EmployeeType.PEON;
        final String currentAssignment = "Learn JPA and EJB!";

        try
        {
            final Long id = txWrapper.wrapInTx(new Callable<Long>()
            {

                @Override
                public Long call() throws Exception
                {

                    // Create a new Employee
                    final EmployeeWithProperties employee = new EmployeeWithProperties
();
                    employee.setImage(image);
                    employee.setSince(since);
                    employee.setType(type);
                    employee.setCurrentAssignment(currentAssignment);
```

```java
            // Persist
            final EntityManager em = emHook.getEntityManager();
            em.persist(employee);
            log.info("Persisted: " + employee);

            // Get the ID, now that one's been assigned
            final Long id = employee.getId();

            // Return
            return id;
        }

    });

    // Now execute in another Tx, to ensure we get a real DB load from the EM,
    // and not just a direct reference back to the object we persisted.
    txWrapper.wrapInTx(new Callable<Void>()
    {

        @Override
        public Void call() throws Exception
        {
            // Roundtrip lookup
            final EmployeeWithProperties roundtrip = emHook.getEntityManager()
                    .find(EmployeeWithProperties.class, id);
            log.info("Roundtrip: " + roundtrip);

            final Calendar suppliedSince = Calendar.getInstance();
            suppliedSince.setTime(since);
            final Calendar obtainedSince = Calendar.getInstance();
            obtainedSince.setTime(roundtrip.getSince());

            // Assert all values are as expected
            Assert.assertEquals("Binary object was not mapped properly", image
[0], roundtrip.getImage()[0]);
            Assert.assertEquals("Temporal value was not mapped properly",
suppliedSince.get(Calendar.YEAR),
                    obtainedSince.get(Calendar.YEAR));
            Assert.assertEquals("Temporal value was not mapped properly",
suppliedSince.get(Calendar.MONTH),
                    obtainedSince.get(Calendar.MONTH));
            Assert.assertEquals("Temporal value was not mapped properly",
suppliedSince.get(Calendar.DATE),
                    obtainedSince.get(Calendar.DATE));
            Assert.assertEquals("Enumerated value was not as expected", type,
roundtrip.getType());
            Assert.assertNull("Transient property should not have been
persisted", roundtrip.getCurrentAssignment());

            // Return
            return null;
        }
    });
}
catch (final TaskExecutionException tee)
```

```
        {
            // Unwrap
            throw tee.getCause();
        }
    }

    /**
     * Shows usage of the 1:1 Unidirectional Mapping Between
     * {@link Employee} and {@link Address}
     * @throws Throwable
     */
    @Test
    public void oneToOneUnidirectionalMapping() throws Throwable
    {
        // Create a new Employee
        final Employee alrubinger = new Employee("Andrew Lee Rubinger");

        // Create a new Address
        final Address address = new Address("1 JBoss Way", "Boston", "MA");

        try
        {
            // Persist and associate an Employee and Address
            final Long employeeId = txWrapper.wrapInTx(new Callable<Long>()
            {

                @Override
                public Long call() throws Exception
                {
                    // Get the EM
                    final EntityManager em = emHook.getEntityManager();

                    // Persist
                    em.persist(alrubinger);
                    em.persist(address);

                    // Associate
                    alrubinger.setAddress(address);

                    // Return
                    return alrubinger.getId();
                }

            });

            // Now ensure when we look up the Address again by Employee after Tx has
completed,
            // all's as expected
            txWrapper.wrapInTx(new Callable<Void>()
            {

                @Override
                public Void call() throws Exception
                {
                    // Get the EM
```

```java
            final EntityManager em = emHook.getEntityManager();

            // Look up the employee
            final Employee roundtripEmployee = em.find(Employee.class,
employeeId);

            // Get the address
            final Address persistedAddress = roundtripEmployee.getAddress();

            // Ensure equal
            Assert.assertEquals("Persisted address association was not as
expected", address, persistedAddress);

            // Clean up the association so we can remove
            roundtripEmployee.setAddress(null);

            // Return
            return null;
         }

      });
   }
   catch (final TaskExecutionException tee)
   {
      // Unwrap
      throw tee.getCause();
   }

}

/**
 * Shows usage of the 1:1 Bidirectional Mapping Between
 * {@link Employee} and {@link Computer}
 * @throws Throwable
 */
@Test
public void oneToOneBidirectionalMapping() throws Throwable
{

   // Create a new Computer
   final Computer computer = new Computer();
   computer.setMake("Computicorp");
   computer.setModel("ZoomFast 100");

   // Create a new Employee
   final Employee carloDeWolf = new Employee("Carlo de Wolf");

   try
   {

      /*
       * We don't associate yet; our cascade policy will prohibit
       * persisting entities with relationships that are not themselves
       * yet persisted
       */
```

```java
// Persist and associate
final Long employeeId = txWrapper.wrapInTx(new Callable<Long>()
{

    @Override
    public Long call() throws Exception
    {
        // Get EM
        final EntityManager em = emHook.getEntityManager();

        // Persist
        em.persist(carloDeWolf);
        em.persist(computer);

        // Associate *both* sides of a bidirectional relationship
        carloDeWolf.setComputer(computer);
        computer.setOwner(carloDeWolf);

        // Return
        return carloDeWolf.getId();
    }
});

// Now check all was associated correctly
txWrapper.wrapInTx(new Callable<Void>()
{

    @Override
    public Void call() throws Exception
    {
        // Get the EM
        final EntityManager em = emHook.getEntityManager();

        // Get the Employee
        final Employee carloRoundtrip = em.find(Employee.class, employeeId);

        // Get the Computer via the Employee
        final Computer computerRoundtrip = carloRoundtrip.getComputer();

        // Get the Employee via the Computer
        final Employee ownerOfComputer = computer.getOwner();
        log.info("Employee " + carloRoundtrip + " has computer " +
computerRoundtrip);
        log.info("Computer " + computerRoundtrip + " has owner " + ownerOf
Computer);

        // Assert all's as expected
        Assert.assertEquals("Computer of employee was not as expected ",
computer, computerRoundtrip);
        Assert.assertEquals("Owner of computer was not as expected ",
carloDeWolf, ownerOfComputer);

        // Clean up the associations so we can remove
        ownerOfComputer.setComputer(null);
```

```java
            computerRoundtrip.setOwner(null);

            // Return
            return null;
         }

      });
   }
   catch (final TaskExecutionException tee)
   {
      // Unwrap
      throw tee.getCause();
   }

}

/**
 * Shows usage of the 1:N Unidirectional Mapping Between
 * {@link Employee} and {@link Phone}
 * @throws Throwable
 */
@Test
public void oneToManyUnidirectionalMapping() throws Throwable
{
   // Create an Employee
   final Employee jaikiranPai = new Employee("Jaikiran Pai");

   // Create a couple Phones
   final Phone phone1 = new Phone();
   phone1.setNumber("800-USE-JBOSS");
   phone1.setType(PhoneType.WORK);
   final Phone phone2 = new Phone();
   phone2.setNumber("800-EJB-TIME");
   phone2.setType(PhoneType.MOBILE);

   try
   {
      // Persist and associate
      final Long employeeId = txWrapper.wrapInTx(new Callable<Long>()
      {

         @Override
         public Long call() throws Exception
         {
            // Get EM
            final EntityManager em = emHook.getEntityManager();

            // Persist
            em.persist(jaikiranPai);
            em.persist(phone1);
            em.persist(phone2);

            // Associate
            jaikiranPai.getPhones().add(phone1);
            jaikiranPai.getPhones().add(phone2);
```

```java
                // Return
                return jaikiranPai.getId();
            }
        });

        // Now check all was associated correctly
        txWrapper.wrapInTx(new Callable<Void>()
        {

            @Override
            public Void call() throws Exception
            {
                // Get the EM
                final EntityManager em = emHook.getEntityManager();

                // Get the Employee
                final Employee jaikiranRoundtrip = em.find(Employee.class,
employeeId);

                // Get Phones via the Employee
                final Collection<Phone> phones = jaikiranRoundtrip.getPhones();
                log.info("Phones for " + jaikiranRoundtrip + ": " + phones);

                // Assert all's as expected
                final String assertionError = "Phones were not associated with the
employee as expected";
                Assert.assertEquals(assertionError, 2, phones.size());
                Assert.assertTrue(assertionError, phones.contains(phone1));
                Assert.assertTrue(assertionError, phones.contains(phone2));

                // Clean up the associations so we can remove things
                jaikiranRoundtrip.getPhones().clear();

                // Return
                return null;
            }

        });
    }
    catch (final TaskExecutionException tee)
    {
        // Unwrap
        throw tee.getCause();
    }

}

/**
 * Shows usage of the 1:N Bidirectional Mapping Between
 * {@link Employee} and his/her reports {@link Employee}.  Also
 * shows the Manager of an {@link Employee}.
 * @throws Throwable
 */
@Test
```

```java
public void oneToManyBidirectionalMapping() throws Throwable
{
    // Create a few Employees
    final Employee alrubinger = new Employee("Andrew Lee Rubinger");
    final Employee carloDeWolf = new Employee("Carlo de Wolf");
    final Employee jaikiranPai = new Employee("Jaikiran Pai");
    final Employee bigD = new Employee("Big D");

    try
    {
        // Persist and associate
        final Long managerId = txWrapper.wrapInTx(new Callable<Long>()
        {

            @Override
            public Long call() throws Exception
            {
                // Get EM
                final EntityManager em = emHook.getEntityManager();

                // Persist
                em.persist(jaikiranPai);
                em.persist(alrubinger);
                em.persist(carloDeWolf);
                em.persist(bigD);

                // Associate *both* sides of the bidirectional relationship
                final Collection<Employee> peonsOfD = bigD.getPeons();
                peonsOfD.add(alrubinger);
                peonsOfD.add(carloDeWolf);
                peonsOfD.add(jaikiranPai);
                alrubinger.setManager(bigD);
                carloDeWolf.setManager(bigD);
                jaikiranPai.setManager(bigD);

                // Return
                return bigD.getId();
            }
        });

        // Let the last Tx flush everything out, so lookup again
        // and perform assertions
        txWrapper.wrapInTx(new Callable<Void>()
        {

            @Override
            public Void call() throws Exception
            {
                // Get the EM
                final EntityManager em = emHook.getEntityManager();

                // Get the Employee/Manager
                final Employee managerRoundtrip = em.find(Employee.class, manager
Id);
```

```
                // Get the reports to the manager
                final Collection<Employee> peonsForManager = managerRoundtrip.get
Peons();
                log.info("Reports of " + managerRoundtrip + ": " + peonsForManager);

                // Assert all's as expected
                final String assertionMessage = "The Employee Manager/Reports
relationship was not as expected";
                Assert.assertEquals(assertionMessage, 3, peonsForManager.size());
                Assert.assertTrue(assertionMessage, peonsForManager.contains
(alrubinger));
                Assert.assertTrue(assertionMessage, peonsForManager.contains
(carloDeWolf));
                Assert.assertTrue(assertionMessage, peonsForManager.contains
(jaikiranPai));
                Assert.assertEquals(assertionMessage, bigD, alrubinger.getManager
());
                Assert.assertEquals(assertionMessage, bigD, carloDeWolf.getManager
());
                Assert.assertEquals(assertionMessage, bigD, jaikiranPai.getManager
());

                // Clean up the associations so we can remove things
                for (final Employee peon : peonsForManager)
                {
                    peon.setManager(null);
                }
                peonsForManager.clear();

                // Return
                return null;
            }

        });

    }
    catch (final TaskExecutionException tee)
    {
        // Unwrap
        throw tee.getCause();
    }
}

/**
 * Shows usage of the N:1 Unidirectional Mapping Between
 * {@link Customer} and his/her primary {@link Employee} contact.
 * @throws Throwable
 */
@Test
public void manyToOneUnidirectionalMapping() throws Throwable
{
    // Create an Employee
    final Employee bstansberry = new Employee("Brian Stansberry");

    // Create a couple of Customers
```

```java
        final Customer jgreene = new Customer("Jason T. Greene");
        final Customer bobmcw = new Customer("Bob McWhirter");

        try
        {
            // Persist and associate
            txWrapper.wrapInTx(new Callable<Void>()
            {

                @Override
                public Void call() throws Exception
                {
                    // Get EM
                    final EntityManager em = emHook.getEntityManager();

                    // Persist
                    em.persist(bstansberry);
                    em.persist(jgreene);
                    em.persist(bobmcw);

                    // Associate
                    jgreene.setPrimaryContact(bstansberry);
                    bobmcw.setPrimaryContact(bstansberry);

                    // Return
                    return null;
                }
            });

            // Lookup and perform assertions
            txWrapper.wrapInTx(new Callable<Void>()
            {

                @Override
                public Void call() throws Exception
                {
                    // Get EM
                    final EntityManager em = emHook.getEntityManager();

                    // Get the customers
                    final Customer jgreeneRoundtrip = em.find(Customer.class, jgreene.
getId());
                    final Customer bobmcwRoundtrip = em.find(Customer.class, bobmcw.
getId());

                    // Ensure all's as expected
                    final String assertionMessage = "Primary contact was not assigned
as expected";
                    Assert.assertEquals(assertionMessage, bstansberry, jgreeneRound
trip.getPrimaryContact());
                    Assert.assertEquals(assertionMessage, bstansberry, bobmcwRoundtrip
.getPrimaryContact());

                    // Clean up the associations so we can remove things
                    jgreeneRoundtrip.setPrimaryContact(null);
```

```java
            bobmcwRoundtrip.setPrimaryContact(null);

            // Return
            return null;
        }
    });

    }
    catch (final TaskExecutionException tee)
    {
        // Unwrap
        throw tee.getCause();
    }
}

/**
 * Shows usage of the N:N Unidirectional Mapping Between
 * {@link Customer} and his/her assigned {@link Task}s
 * @throws Throwable
 */
@Test
public void manyToManyUnidirectionalMapping() throws Throwable
{
    // Create a couple of employees
    final Employee smarlow = new Employee("Scott Marlow");
    final Employee jpederse = new Employee("Jesper Pedersen");

    // Create a couple of tasks
    final Task task1 = new Task("Go to the JBoss User's Group - Boston");
    final Task task2 = new Task("Pick up flowers for Shelly McGowan");

    try
    {
        // Persist and associate
        txWrapper.wrapInTx(new Callable<Void>()
        {

            @Override
            public Void call() throws Exception
            {
                // Get EM
                final EntityManager em = emHook.getEntityManager();

                // Persist
                em.persist(smarlow);
                em.persist(jpederse);
                em.persist(task1);
                em.persist(task2);

                // Associate
                task1.getOwners().add(smarlow);
                task1.getOwners().add(jpederse);
                task2.getOwners().add(smarlow);
                task2.getOwners().add(jpederse);
```

```
                // Return
                return null;
            }
        });

        // Lookup and perform assertions
        txWrapper.wrapInTx(new Callable<Void>()
        {

            @Override
            public Void call() throws Exception
            {
                // Get EM
                final EntityManager em = emHook.getEntityManager();

                // Get the tasks
                final Task task1Roundtrip = em.find(Task.class, task1.getId());
                final Task task2Roundtrip = em.find(Task.class, task2.getId());

                // Ensure all's as expected
                final String assertionMessage = "Task owners were not assigned as
expected";
                Assert.assertTrue(assertionMessage, task1Roundtrip.getOwners().
contains(smarlow));
                Assert.assertTrue(assertionMessage, task1Roundtrip.getOwners().
contains(jpederse));
                Assert.assertTrue(assertionMessage, task2Roundtrip.getOwners().
contains(smarlow));
                Assert.assertTrue(assertionMessage, task2Roundtrip.getOwners().
contains(jpederse));

                // Clean up the associations so we can remove things
                task1Roundtrip.getOwners().clear();
                task2Roundtrip.getOwners().clear();

                // Return
                return null;
            }
        });

    }
    catch (final TaskExecutionException tee)
    {
        // Unwrap
        throw tee.getCause();
    }
}

/**
 * Shows usage of the N:N Unidirectional Mapping Between
 * {@link Employee} and his/her team members.
 * @throws Throwable
 */
@Test
public void manyToManyBidirectionalMapping() throws Throwable
```

```
{
    // Create a few employees
    final Employee pmuir = new Employee("Pete Muir");
    final Employee dallen = new Employee("Dan Allen");
    final Employee aslak = new Employee("Aslak Knutsen");

    // Create some teams
    final Team seam = new Team("Seam");
    final Team arquillian = new Team("Arquillian");

    try
    {
        // Persist and associate
        txWrapper.wrapInTx(new Callable<Void>()
        {

            @Override
            public Void call() throws Exception
            {
                // Get EM
                final EntityManager em = emHook.getEntityManager();

                // Persist
                em.persist(pmuir);
                em.persist(dallen);
                em.persist(aslak);
                em.persist(seam);
                em.persist(arquillian);

                // Associate *both* directions
                seam.getMembers().add(dallen);
                seam.getMembers().add(pmuir);
                seam.getMembers().add(aslak);
                arquillian.getMembers().add(dallen);
                arquillian.getMembers().add(pmuir);
                arquillian.getMembers().add(aslak);
                aslak.getTeams().add(seam);
                aslak.getTeams().add(arquillian);
                dallen.getTeams().add(seam);
                dallen.getTeams().add(arquillian);
                pmuir.getTeams().add(seam);
                pmuir.getTeams().add(arquillian);

                // Return
                return null;
            }
        });

        // Lookup and perform assertions
        txWrapper.wrapInTx(new Callable<Void>()
        {

            @Override
            public Void call() throws Exception
            {
```

```java
            // Get EM
            final EntityManager em = emHook.getEntityManager();

            // Get the teams and employees back out as managed objects
            final Team seamRoundtrip = em.find(Team.class, seam.getId());
            final Team arquillianRoundtrip = em.find(Team.class, arquillian.
getId());
            final Employee dallenRoundtrip = em.find(Employee.class, dallen.
getId());
            final Employee pmuirRoundtrip = em.find(Employee.class, pmuir.
getId());
            final Employee aslakRoundtrip = em.find(Employee.class, aslak.
getId());

            // Ensure all's as expected
            final String assertionMessage = "Team members were not assigned as
expected";
            Assert.assertTrue(assertionMessage, seamRoundtrip.getMembers().
contains(pmuir));
            Assert.assertTrue(assertionMessage, seamRoundtrip.getMembers().
contains(aslak));
            Assert.assertTrue(assertionMessage, seamRoundtrip.getMembers().
contains(dallen));
            Assert.assertTrue(assertionMessage, arquillianRoundtrip.getMembers
().contains(pmuir));
            Assert.assertTrue(assertionMessage, arquillianRoundtrip.getMembers
().contains(aslak));
            Assert.assertTrue(assertionMessage, arquillianRoundtrip.getMembers
().contains(dallen));
            Assert.assertTrue(assertionMessage, dallenRoundtrip.getTeams().
contains(seamRoundtrip));
            Assert.assertTrue(assertionMessage, dallenRoundtrip.getTeams().
contains(arquillianRoundtrip));
            Assert.assertTrue(assertionMessage, pmuirRoundtrip.getTeams().
contains(seamRoundtrip));
            Assert.assertTrue(assertionMessage, pmuirRoundtrip.getTeams().
contains(arquillianRoundtrip));
            Assert.assertTrue(assertionMessage, aslakRoundtrip.getTeams().
contains(seamRoundtrip));
            Assert.assertTrue(assertionMessage, aslakRoundtrip.getTeams().
contains(arquillianRoundtrip));

            // Clean up the associations so we can remove things
            aslakRoundtrip.getTeams().clear();
            dallenRoundtrip.getTeams().clear();
            pmuirRoundtrip.getTeams().clear();
            seamRoundtrip.getMembers().clear();
            arquillianRoundtrip.getMembers().clear();

            // Return
            return null;
        }
    });

}
```

```java
        catch (final TaskExecutionException tee)
        {
            // Unwrap
            throw tee.getCause();
        }
    }

    /**
     * Ensures that JPA Entity Callbacks are received
     * @throws Exception
     */
    @Test
    public void entityCallbacks() throws Exception
    {
        // Precondition checks
        final String preconditionMessage = "Test setup is in error";
        Assert.assertFalse(preconditionMessage, EventTracker.postLoad);
        Assert.assertFalse(preconditionMessage, EventTracker.postPersist);
        Assert.assertFalse(preconditionMessage, EventTracker.postRemove);
        Assert.assertFalse(preconditionMessage, EventTracker.postUpdate);
        Assert.assertFalse(preconditionMessage, EventTracker.prePersist);
        Assert.assertFalse(preconditionMessage, EventTracker.preRemove);
        Assert.assertFalse(preconditionMessage, EventTracker.preUpdate);

        // Create a new employee
        final EntityListenerEmployee employee = new EntityListenerEmployee();

        // Put through the full lifecycle
        txWrapper.wrapInTx(new Callable<Void>()
        {

            @Override
            public Void call() throws Exception
            {
                // Get EM
                final EntityManager em = emHook.getEntityManager();

                // Persist
                em.persist(employee);

                // Refresh
                em.refresh(employee);

                // Update
                employee.setName("New Name");
                em.flush();

                // Lookup
                em.find(EntityListenerEmployee.class, employee.getId());

                // Remove
                em.remove(employee);

                // Return
                return null;
```

```
        }
    });

    // Assert events fired
    final String postconditionMessage = "Missing event fired";
    Assert.assertTrue(postconditionMessage, EventTracker.postLoad);
    Assert.assertTrue(postconditionMessage, EventTracker.postPersist);
    Assert.assertTrue(postconditionMessage, EventTracker.postRemove);
    Assert.assertTrue(postconditionMessage, EventTracker.postUpdate);
    Assert.assertTrue(postconditionMessage, EventTracker.prePersist);
    Assert.assertTrue(postconditionMessage, EventTracker.preRemove);
    Assert.assertTrue(postconditionMessage, EventTracker.preUpdate);
}

/**
 * Ensures we may look up an entity by a JPA QL Query
 * @throws Exception
 */
@Test
public void jpaQlFind() throws Exception
{
    // Create an employee
    final SimpleEmployee employee = new SimpleEmployee(ID_DAVE, NAME_DAVE);

    // Persist, then lookup
    txWrapper.wrapInTx(new Callable<Void>()
    {

        @Override
        public Void call() throws Exception
        {
            // Get EM
            final EntityManager em = emHook.getEntityManager();

            // Persist
            em.persist(employee);

            // Lookup
            final String jpaQlQuery = "FROM " + SimpleEmployee.class.getSimple
Name() + " e WHERE e.name=?1";
            final SimpleEmployee roundtrip = (SimpleEmployee) em.createQuery
(jpaQlQuery).setParameter(1, NAME_DAVE)
                    .getSingleResult();

            // Test obtained as expected
            Assert.assertEquals("Employee from JPA QL Query should equal the
record added", employee, roundtrip);

            // Return
            return null;
        }
    });
}

/**
```

```
     * Ensures we may look up an entity by a Criteria API Query
     * @throws Exception
     */
    @Test
    public void criertiaAPIFind() throws Exception
    {
        // Create an employee
        final SimpleEmployee employee = new SimpleEmployee(ID_DAVE, NAME_DAVE);

        // Persist, then lookup
        txWrapper.wrapInTx(new Callable<Void>()
        {

            @Override
            public Void call() throws Exception
            {
                // Get EM
                final EntityManager em = emHook.getEntityManager();

                // Persist
                em.persist(employee);

                // Lookup
                final CriteriaBuilder builder = em.getCriteriaBuilder();
                final CriteriaQuery<SimpleEmployee> query = builder.createQuery
(SimpleEmployee.class);
                Root<SimpleEmployee> root = query.from(SimpleEmployee.class);
                query.select(root).where(builder.equal(root.get("name"), NAME_DAVE));
                final SimpleEmployee roundtrip = (SimpleEmployee) em.createQuery
(query).getSingleResult();

                // Test obtained as expected
                Assert.assertEquals("Employee from Criteria API Query should equal
the record added", employee, roundtrip);

                // Return
                return null;
            }
        });
    }

    //-------------------------------------------------------------------------||
    // Internal Helper Methods ------------------------------------------------||
    //-------------------------------------------------------------------------||

    /**
     * Issues a JPA QL Update to remove all entities of the specified type
     * @param type
     * @param em
     */
    private void deleteAllEntitiesOfType(final Class<?> type, final EntityManager
em)
    {
        assert em != null : EntityManager.class.getSimpleName() + " must be
specified";
```

```
        assert type != null : "type to be removed must be specified";
        // JPA QL String to remove all of the specified type
        log.info("Removed: " + em.createQuery("DELETE FROM " + type.getSimpleName()
    + " o").executeUpdate()
            + " entities of type " + type);
    }
}
```

Security: Secured School Example

Description

Multiuser applications, in order to be secure, must respect that there are differences in user types. For instance, perhaps a system administrator should be given access to alter records hidden to typical users. Coding security logic inside our applications, however, mixes concerns and makes code less maintainable. EJB therefore provides as a service a role-based security model which is both declarative (via metadata) and programmatic (via an API).

In this example we model a school with strict policies about who can open the doors when. Here we showcase the use of `@RolesAllowed`, `@DeclareRoles`, `@RunAs` and `@PermitAll`.

Online Companion Information

Wiki article: *http://community.jboss.org/docs/DOC-15571*

Source location: *http://github.com/jbossejb3/oreilly-ejb-6thedition-book-examples/tree/master/ch15-secureschool/*

Source Listing

Following is a full listing of all source code used in this runnable example.

Implementation Resources

FireDepartmentLocalBusiness.java

```
package org.jboss.ejb3.examples.ch15.secureschool.api;

/**
 * Represents a fire department capable of declaring
```

```
 * a state of emergency.  Anyone may invoke this support,
 * and when an alert is raised we'll close the local school.
 *
 * @author <a href="mailto:andrew.rubinger@jboss.org">ALR</a>
 * @version $Revision: $
 */
public interface FireDepartmentLocalBusiness
{
   // ------------------------------------------------------------------------||
   // Contracts --------------------------------------------------------------||
   // ------------------------------------------------------------------------||

   /**
    * Declares a state of emergency, so we must close the local school
    */
   void declareEmergency();

}
```

SchoolClosedException.java

```
package org.jboss.ejb3.examples.ch15.secureschool.api;

import javax.ejb.ApplicationException;
import javax.ejb.EJBAccessException;

import org.jboss.ejb3.examples.ch15.secureschool.impl.Roles;

/**
 * Thrown when a user in role other than {@link Roles#ADMIN}
 * attempts to open the front door to school while it's closed
 *
 * @author <a href="mailto:andrew.rubinger@jboss.org">ALR</a>
 * @version $Revision: $
 */
@ApplicationException(rollback = true)
// So this isn't wrapped in EJBException
public class SchoolClosedException extends EJBAccessException
{
   //-------------------------------------------------------------------------||
   // Class Members ----------------------------------------------------------||
   //-------------------------------------------------------------------------||

   /**
    * serialVersionUID
    */
   private static final long serialVersionUID = 1L;

   //-------------------------------------------------------------------------||
   // Constructor ------------------------------------------------------------||
   //-------------------------------------------------------------------------||

   /**
    * Constructs a new exception
    */
```

```
    private SchoolClosedException(final String message)
    {
        super(message);
    }

    //-------------------------------------------------------------------------||
    // Factory ----------------------------------------------------------------||
    //-------------------------------------------------------------------------||

    /**
     * Constructs a new exception with the specified, required message
     * @param message
     * @throws IllegalArgumentException If the message is not specified
     */
    public static SchoolClosedException newInstance(final String message) throws
IllegalArgumentException
    {
        // Precondition checks
        if (message == null)
        {
            throw new IllegalArgumentException("message must be specified");
        }

        // Return
        return new SchoolClosedException(message);
    }

}
```

SecureSchoolLocalBusiness.java

```
package org.jboss.ejb3.examples.ch15.secureschool.api;

import org.jboss.ejb3.examples.ch15.secureschool.impl.Roles;

/**
 * Represents a school holding doors which may be
 * opened by various users.  Using the EJB Security model,
 * access to open a particular door may be blocked
 * to certain users.
 *
 * @author <a href="mailto:andrew.rubinger@jboss.org">ALR</a>
 * @version $Revision: $
 */
public interface SecureSchoolLocalBusiness
{
    // -----------------------------------------------------------------------||
    // Contracts -------------------------------------------------------------||
    // -----------------------------------------------------------------------||

    /**
     * Closes the school for business.  At this point the
     * front door will be unlocked for all.
     * This method may only be called by users in role
     * {@link Roles#ADMIN}.
```

```
    */
    void open();

    /**
     * Closes the school for business.  At this point the
     * front door will be locked for all but users
     * in role {@link Roles#ADMIN}
     * This method may only be called by admins.
     */
    void close();

    /**
     * Opens the front door.  While school is open,
     * any authenticated user may open the door, else
     * only the {@link Roles#ADMIN} may open.
     *
     * @throws SchoolClosedException If the current user
     * is not in {@link Roles#ADMIN} and is attempting to open
     * the door while {@link SecureSchoolLocalBusiness#isOpen()}
     * is false.
     */
    void openFrontDoor() throws SchoolClosedException;

    /**
     * Opens the service door. Users in {@link Roles#STUDENT}
     * role may not open this door, but {@link Roles#ADMIN}
     * and {@link Roles#JANITOR} may.
     */
    void openServiceDoor();

    /**
     * Returns whether or not the school is open.  When closed, only
     * the {@link Roles#ADMIN} is allowed access to all doors.  Anyone,
     * even unauthenticated users, may check if school is open.
     * @return
     */
    boolean isOpen();

}
```

FileDepartmentBean.java

```
package org.jboss.ejb3.examples.ch15.secureschool.impl;

import java.util.logging.Logger;

import javax.annotation.security.PermitAll;
import javax.annotation.security.RunAs;
import javax.ejb.EJB;
import javax.ejb.Singleton;

import org.jboss.ejb3.examples.ch15.secureschool.api.FireDepartmentLocalBusiness;
import org.jboss.ejb3.examples.ch15.secureschool.api.SecureSchoolLocalBusiness;

/**
```

```java
 * Bean implementation class of the fire department.
 * Closes the local school in case of emergency.
 *
 * @author <a href="mailto:andrew.rubinger@jboss.org">ALR</a>
 * @version $Revision: $
 */
@Singleton
@RunAs(Roles.ADMIN)
@PermitAll
// Implicit, but included here to show access policy
public class FireDepartmentBean implements FireDepartmentLocalBusiness
{

   //-------------------------------------------------------------------||
   // Class Members ----------------------------------------------------||
   //-------------------------------------------------------------------||

   /**
    * Logger
    */
   private static final Logger log = Logger.getLogger(FireDepartmentBean.class.
getName());

   //-------------------------------------------------------------------||
   // Instance Members -------------------------------------------------||
   //-------------------------------------------------------------------||

   /**
    * School to close in case of emergency
    */
   @EJB
   private SecureSchoolLocalBusiness school;

   //-------------------------------------------------------------------||
   // Required Implementations -----------------------------------------||
   //-------------------------------------------------------------------||

   /**
    * {@inheritDoc}
    * @see org.jboss.ejb3.examples.ch15.secureschool.api.FireDepartmentLocal
Business#declareEmergency()
    */
   @Override
   public void declareEmergency()
   {
      log.info("Dispatching emergency support from the Fire Department, closing
local school");
      school.close();
   }

}
```

Roles.java

```java
package org.jboss.ejb3.examples.ch15.secureschool.impl;

/**
 * Holds the list of roles with which users of the school
 * may be affiliated.  EJB Security is role-based, so this
 * is how we'll determine access.
 *
 * @author <a href="mailto:andrew.rubinger@jboss.org">ALR</a>
 * @version $Revision: $
 */
public interface Roles
{
   // -------------------------------------------------------------------------||
   // Constants ---------------------------------------------------------------||
   // -------------------------------------------------------------------------||

   /*
    * Roles of callers to the system
    */

   /**
    * Role denoting the user is a school administrator
    */
   String ADMIN = "Administrator";

   /**
    * Role denoting the user is a student
    */
   String STUDENT = "Student";

   /**
    * Role denoting the user is a janitor
    */
   String JANITOR = "Janitor";

}
```

SecureSchoolBean.java

```java
package org.jboss.ejb3.examples.ch15.secureschool.impl;

import java.util.logging.Logger;

import javax.annotation.PostConstruct;
import javax.annotation.Resource;
import javax.annotation.security.DeclareRoles;
import javax.annotation.security.PermitAll;
import javax.annotation.security.RolesAllowed;
import javax.ejb.Local;
import javax.ejb.SessionContext;
import javax.ejb.Singleton;
import javax.ejb.Startup;
```

```
import org.jboss.ejb3.examples.ch15.secureschool.api.SchoolClosedException;
import org.jboss.ejb3.examples.ch15.secureschool.api.SecureSchoolLocalBusiness;

/**
 * A secure school which may block requests to
 * open doors depending upon the EJB Security
 * model's configuration
 *
 * @author <a href="mailto:andrew.rubinger@jboss.org">ALR</a>
 * @version $Revision: $
 */
@Singleton
@Local(SecureSchoolLocalBusiness.class)
// Declare the roles in the system
@DeclareRoles(
{Roles.ADMIN, Roles.STUDENT, Roles.JANITOR})
// By default allow no one access, we'll enable access at a finer-grained level
@RolesAllowed(
{})
@Startup
public class SecureSchoolBean implements SecureSchoolLocalBusiness
{

    //-------------------------------------------------------------------------||
    // Class Members ----------------------------------------------------------||
    //-------------------------------------------------------------------------||

    /**
     * Logger
     */
    private static final Logger log = Logger.getLogger(SecureSchoolBean.class.get
Name());

    //-------------------------------------------------------------------------||
    // Instance Members -------------------------------------------------------||
    //-------------------------------------------------------------------------||

    /**
     * Whether or not the school is open
     */
    private boolean open;

    /**
     * Hook to the container to get security information
     */
    @Resource
    private SessionContext context;

    //-------------------------------------------------------------------------||
    // Required Implementations -----------------------------------------------||
    //-------------------------------------------------------------------------||

    /**
     * {@inheritDoc}
     * @see org.jboss.ejb3.examples.ch15.secureschool.api.SecureSchoolLocal
```

```
Business#openFrontDoor()
     */
    // Give everyone access to this method, we may restrict them later
    @RolesAllowed(
    {Roles.ADMIN, Roles.STUDENT, Roles.JANITOR})
    @Override
    public void openFrontDoor()
    {
        // If we've reached this point, EJB security has let us through.  However,
        // we may want to apply some contextual rules.  Because EJB security is
        // declarative at the method level, we use the API to enforce specific logic.

        // Get the caller
        final String callerName = context.getCallerPrincipal().getName();

        // Ensure the school is open
        if (!open)
        {
            // School's closed, so only let admins open the door
            if (!context.isCallerInRole(Roles.ADMIN))
            {
                // Kick 'em out
                throw SchoolClosedException
                        .newInstance("Attempt to open the front door after hours is
prohibited to all but admins, denied to: "
                                + callerName);
            }
        }

        // Log
        log.info("Opening front door for: " + callerName);
    }

    /**
     * {@inheritDoc}
     * @see org.jboss.ejb3.examples.ch15.secureschool.api.SecureSchoolLocal
Business#openServiceDoor()
     */
    @RolesAllowed(
    {Roles.ADMIN, Roles.JANITOR})
    // Students cannot open this door
    @Override
    public void openServiceDoor()
    {
        log.info("Opening service door for: " + context.getCallerPrincipal().get
Name());
    }

    /**
     * {@inheritDoc}
     * @see org.jboss.ejb3.examples.ch15.secureschool.api.SecureSchoolLocal
Business#close()
     */
    @RolesAllowed(Roles.ADMIN)
    // Only let admins open and close the school
```

```
    @Override
    public void close()
    {
        this.open = false;
    }

    /**
     * {@inheritDoc}
     * @see org.jboss.ejb3.examples.ch15.secureschool.api.SecureSchoolLocal
Business#open()
     */
    @Override
    @PostConstruct
    // School is open when created
    @RolesAllowed(Roles.ADMIN)
    // Only let admins open and close the school
    public void open()
    {
        this.open = true;
    }

    /**
     * {@inheritDoc}
     * @see org.jboss.ejb3.examples.ch15.secureschool.api.SecureSchoolLocal
Business#isOpen()
     */
    @Override
    @PermitAll
    // Anyone can check if school is open
    public boolean isOpen()
    {
        return open;
    }
}
```

Test Resources

SecureSchoolIntegrationTest.java

```
package org.jboss.ejb3.examples.ch15.secureschool;

import java.util.HashMap;
import java.util.Map;
import java.util.concurrent.Callable;
import java.util.concurrent.ExecutionException;
import java.util.concurrent.ExecutorService;
import java.util.concurrent.Executors;
import java.util.concurrent.Future;
import java.util.logging.Logger;

import javax.ejb.EJB;
import javax.ejb.EJBAccessException;
import javax.ejb.SessionContext;
import javax.inject.Inject;
```

```
import javax.naming.Context;
import javax.naming.NamingException;

import org.jboss.arquillian.api.Deployment;
import org.jboss.arquillian.junit.Arquillian;
import org.jboss.arquillian.prototyping.context.api.ArquillianContext;
import org.jboss.ejb3.examples.ch15.secureschool.api.FireDepartmentLocalBusiness;
import org.jboss.ejb3.examples.ch15.secureschool.api.SchoolClosedException;
import org.jboss.ejb3.examples.ch15.secureschool.api.SecureSchoolLocalBusiness;
import org.jboss.ejb3.examples.ch15.secureschool.impl.SecureSchoolBean;
import org.jboss.shrinkwrap.api.ShrinkWrap;
import org.jboss.shrinkwrap.api.spec.JavaArchive;
import org.junit.Assert;
import org.junit.Test;
import org.junit.runner.RunWith;

/**
 * Test Cases to ensure the SecureSchoolEJB
 * is working as contracted with regards to
 * its security model.
 *
 * @author <a href="mailto:andrew.rubinger@jboss.org">ALR</a>
 * @version $Revision: $
 */
@RunWith(Arquillian.class)
public class SecureSchoolIntegrationTest
{

   //-------------------------------------------------------------------------||
   // Class Members ----------------------------------------------------------||
   //-------------------------------------------------------------------------||

   /**
    * Logger
    */
   private static final Logger log = Logger.getLogger(SecureSchoolIntegrationTest
.class.getName());

   /**
    * The EJB JAR to be deployed into the server
    * @return
    */
   @Deployment
   public static JavaArchive getDeployment()
   {
      final JavaArchive archive = ShrinkWrap.create("secureSchool.jar", Java
Archive.class).addPackages(false,
            SecureSchoolLocalBusiness.class.getPackage(), SecureSchoolBean.class.
getPackage());
      log.info(archive.toString(true));
      return archive;
   }

   /**
    * Name of a role with "Administrator" role
```

```java
     */
    private static String USER_NAME_ADMIN = "admin";

    /**
     * Password for the "admin" user
     */
    private static String PASSWORD_ADMIN = "adminPassword";

    /**
     * Name of a role with "Student" role
     */
    private static String USER_NAME_STUDENT = "student";

    /**
     * Password for the "student" user
     */
    private static String PASSWORD_STUDENT = "studentPassword";

    /**
     * Name of a role with "Janitor" role
     */
    private static String USER_NAME_JANITOR = "janitor";

    /**
     * Password for the "admin" user
     */
    private static String PASSWORD_JANITOR = "janitorPassword";

    /**
     * JNDI Name at which we'll look up the EJB
     */
    //TODO Would be great to wire up Arquillian to use a supplied JNDI Context
(with login properties) to inject the EJB
    private static final String JNDI_NAME_EJB = "SecureSchoolBeanLocal";

    //-------------------------------------------------------------------------||
    // Instance Members -------------------------------------------------------||
    //-------------------------------------------------------------------------||

    /**
     * Hook to Arquillian so we can create new JNDI Contexts using supplied
properties
     */
    @Inject
    private ArquillianContext arquillianContext;

    /**
     * EJB proxy injected without any explicit login or authentication/authorization.
     * Behind the scenes, Arquillian is using a default JNDI Context without any
     * login properties to inject the proxy into this target.
     */
    @EJB
    private SecureSchoolLocalBusiness unauthenticatedSchool;

    /**
```

```
 * Reference to the fire department from an unauthenticated user.
 * If we use this EJB to declare an emergency, anyone may close
 * the school.
 */
@EJB
private FireDepartmentLocalBusiness fireDepartment;

//--------------------------------------------------------------------------||
// Tests --------------------------------------------------------------------||
//--------------------------------------------------------------------------||

/**
 * Ensures that an unauthenticated user cannot open the front door
 */
@Test(expected = EJBAccessException.class)
public void unauthenticatedUserCannotOpenFrontDoor() throws NamingException
{

    // Try to open the front door before we've authenticated; should fail
    unauthenticatedSchool.openFrontDoor();
}

/**
 * Ensures that the "student" user can open the front door
 */
@Test
public void studentCanOpenFrontDoor() throws NamingException
{

    /*
     * This login and lookup code is specific to OpenEJB container
     */

    // Log in via JNDI as "student" user
    final Context context = this.login(USER_NAME_STUDENT, PASSWORD_STUDENT);

    try
    {
        // Get
        final SecureSchoolLocalBusiness school = this.getEjb(context);

        // Invoke (should succeed, not fail with unauthorized errors)
        school.openFrontDoor();
    }
    finally
    {
        // Clean up, closing the context to log out
        context.close();
    }
}

/**
 * Ensures that the "janitor" user can open the service door
 */
@Test
```

```java
public void janitorCanOpenServiceDoor() throws NamingException
{

    /*
     * This login and lookup code is specific to OpenEJB container
     */

    // Log in via JNDI as "janitor" user
    final Context context = this.login(USER_NAME_JANITOR, PASSWORD_JANITOR);

    try
    {
        // Get
        final SecureSchoolLocalBusiness school = this.getEjb(context);

        // Invoke (should succeed, not fail with unauthorized errors)
        school.openServiceDoor();
    }
    finally
    {
        // Clean up, closing the context to log out
        context.close();
    }
}

/**
 * Ensures that the "student" user cannot open the service door
 */
@Test(expected = EJBAccessException.class)
public void studentCannotOpenServiceDoor() throws NamingException
{

    /*
     * This login and lookup code is specific to OpenEJB container
     */

    // Log in via JNDI as "student" user
    final Context context = this.login(USER_NAME_STUDENT, PASSWORD_STUDENT);

    try
    {
        // Get
        final SecureSchoolLocalBusiness school = this.getEjb(context);

        // Invoke (should fail)
        school.openServiceDoor();
    }
    finally
    {
        // Clean up, closing the context to log out
        context.close();
    }
}

/**
```

```
    * Ensures that the "student" user cannot close the school (and go home early
;) )
    */
    @Test(expected = EJBAccessException.class)
    public void studentCannotCloseSchool() throws NamingException
    {

        /*
         * This login and lookup code is specific to OpenEJB container
         */

        // Log in via JNDI as "student" user
        final Context context = this.login(USER_NAME_STUDENT, PASSWORD_STUDENT);

        try
        {
            // Get
            final SecureSchoolLocalBusiness school = this.getEjb(context);

            // Invoke (should fail)
            school.close();
        }
        finally
        {
            // Clean up, closing the context to log out
            context.close();
        }
    }

    /**
     * Ensures that the "admin" user can close the school
     */
    @Test
    public void adminCanCloseSchool() throws NamingException
    {

        /*
         * This login and lookup code is specific to OpenEJB container
         */

        // Log in via JNDI as "admin" user
        final Context context = this.login(USER_NAME_ADMIN, PASSWORD_ADMIN);

        try
        {
            // Get
            final SecureSchoolLocalBusiness school = this.getEjb(context);

            // Invoke (should succeed)
            school.close();

            // Test
            Assert.assertFalse("School should now be closed", school.isOpen());

            // Reset the school to open for subsequent tests
```

```java
        school.open();

        // Test
        Assert.assertTrue("School should now be open", school.isOpen());
    }
    finally
    {
        // Clean up, closing the context to log out
        context.close();
    }
}

/**
 * Ensures that an unauthenticated user can check if a school is open
 */
@Test
public void unauthenticatedUserCanCheckIfSchoolIsOpen()
{

    // See if school is open
    Assert.assertTrue("Unauthenticated user should see that school is open",
unauthenticatedSchool.isOpen());
}

/**
 * Ensures that a student cannot open the front door
 * when school is closed; tests programmatic security via
 * {@link SessionContext} in the implementation class
 */
@Test(expected = SchoolClosedException.class)
public void studentCannotOpenFrontDoorsWhenSchoolIsClosed() throws Throwable
{
    /*
     * This login and lookup code is specific to OpenEJB container
     */

    try
    {
        // Log in via JNDI as "admin" user
        final Context context = this.login(USER_NAME_ADMIN, PASSWORD_ADMIN);

        // Get
        final SecureSchoolLocalBusiness school = this.getEjb(context);

        // Close the school
        school.close();

        // Log out
        context.close();

        // Test that we're closed
        Assert.assertFalse("School should now be closed", school.isOpen());

        // Now try to open the front doors as a student.  We do this in another
Thread
```

```java
            // because OpenEJB will associate the security context with this
            // Thread to "admin" (from above)
            final Callable<Void> studentOpenDoorTask = new Callable<Void>()
            {

                @Override
                public Void call() throws Exception
                {
                    // Log in via JNDI as "student" user
                    final Context context = SecureSchoolIntegrationTest.this.login
(USER_NAME_STUDENT, PASSWORD_STUDENT);

                    try
                    {
                        // Get
                        final SecureSchoolLocalBusiness school = SecureSchool
IntegrationTest.this.getEjb(context);

                        // Try to open the door (should fail)
                        school.openFrontDoor();

                        // Return
                        return null;
                    }
                    finally
                    {
                        context.close();
                    }
                }
            };
            final ExecutorService service = Executors.newSingleThreadExecutor();
            final Future<Void> future = service.submit(studentOpenDoorTask);
            try
            {
                future.get();// Should fail here
            }
            catch (final ExecutionException ee)
            {

                // Unwrap, should throw SchoolClosedException
                throw ee.getCause();
            }

        }
        finally
        {
            // Cleanup and open the school for other tests
            final Context context = this.login(USER_NAME_ADMIN, PASSWORD_ADMIN);
            final SecureSchoolLocalBusiness school = this.getEjb(context);

            // Reset the school to open for subsequent tests
            school.open();

            // Test
            Assert.assertTrue("School should now be open", school.isOpen());
```

```
        // Clean up, closing the context to log out
        context.close();

    }
}

/**
 * Ensures that any unauthenticated user can declare an emergency, hence
closing the school
 */
@Test
public void anyoneCanDeclareEmergencyAndCloseSchool() throws NamingException
{

    // First check that school's open
    Assert.assertTrue("School should be open to start the test",
unauthenticatedSchool.isOpen());

    // Ensure we can't close the school directly (we don't have access)
    boolean gotAccessException = false;
    try
    {
        unauthenticatedSchool.close();
    }
    catch (final EJBAccessException e)
    {
        // Expected
        log.info("We can't close the school on our own, make an emergency");
        gotAccessException = true;
    }
    Assert.assertTrue("We shouldn't be able to close school directly", got
AccessException);

    // Now declare an emergency via the fire department
    fireDepartment.declareEmergency();

    // The school should now be closed, even though we don't have rights to do
that directly on our own.
    Assert.assertFalse("School should be closed after emergency was declared",
unauthenticatedSchool.isOpen());

    // Reset the school to open
    // Cleanup and open the school for other tests
    final Context context = this.login(USER_NAME_ADMIN, PASSWORD_ADMIN);
    try
    {
        final SecureSchoolLocalBusiness school = this.getEjb(context);

        // Reset the school to open for subsequent tests
        school.open();

        // Test
        Assert.assertTrue("School should now be open", school.isOpen());
    }
```

```
      finally
      {
         // Clean up, closing the context to log out
         context.close();
      }

   }

   //---------------------------------------------------------------------||
   // Internal Helper Methods --------------------------------------------||
   //---------------------------------------------------------------------||

   /**
    * Logs in to JNDI (and by extension, the EJB security system)
    * with the specified username and password.  This mechanism is
    * specific to the OpenEJB container.
    */
   private Context login(final String username, final String password)
   {
      // Precondition checks
      assert username != null : "username must be supplied";
      assert password != null : "password must be supplied";

      // Log in and create a context
      final Map<String, Object> namingContextProps = new HashMap<String, Object>();
      namingContextProps.put(Context.SECURITY_PRINCIPAL, username);
      namingContextProps.put(Context.SECURITY_CREDENTIALS, password);
      final Context context = arquillianContext.get(Context.class, namingContext
Props);

      // Return
      return context;
   }

   /**
    * Obtains a proxy to the EJB via the specified JNDI Context (through
    * which the user may have authenticated)
    * @param context
    * @return
    * @throws NamingException
    */
   private SecureSchoolLocalBusiness getEjb(final Context context) throws Naming
Exception
   {
      // Look up in JNDI specific to OpenEJB
      //TODO Use Global JNDI
      return (SecureSchoolLocalBusiness) context.lookup(JNDI_NAME_EJB);
   }
}
```

groups.properties

```
# OpenEJB Roles Configuration
# Format: Role=Username
Administrator=admin
Janitor=janitor
Student=student
```

users.properties

```
# OpenEJB Users Configuration
# Format: Username=Password
admin=adminPassword
student=studentPassword
janitor=janitorPassword
```

Transactions: Blackjack Game Example

Description

All but the most simple of applications will have the requirement that a composite action, say, "Register a User," succeeds or fails completely. In these cases, the single request is in fact a collection of many smaller pieces of work. If any of these smaller pieces fail halfway through the request, our application can be left in some inconsistent or error state. The use of transactions verifies that all compound actions comply with the ACID properties (atomicity, consistency, isolation, and durability). In other words, compound actions will either complete or fail as a single unit.

EJB offers declarative and programmatic support for transactions via the Java EE `TransactionManager`, and it comes complete with annotations/XML to manage transactional boundaries.

Our example is a transactionally aware poker service, showing the use of `@TransactionAttribute` and the various `TransactionAttributeTypes`.

Online Companion Information

Wiki article: *http://community.jboss.org/docs/DOC-15573*

Source location: *http://github.com/jbossejb3/oreilly-ejb-6thedition-book-examples/tree/master/ch17-transactions/*

Source Listing

Following is a full listing of all source code used in this runnable example.

Implementation Resources

BankLocalBusiness.java

```java
package org.jboss.ejb3.examples.ch17.transactions.api;

import java.math.BigDecimal;

import org.jboss.ejb3.examples.ch17.transactions.entity.Account;

/**
 * Defines the contract for a bank
 *
 * @author <a href="mailto:andrew.rubinger@jboss.org">ALR</a>
 * @version $Revision: $
 */
public interface BankLocalBusiness
{

   //-------------------------------------------------------------------------||
   // Constants --------------------------------------------------------------||
   //-------------------------------------------------------------------------||

   /**
    * JNDI Name to which we'll bind
    */
   String JNDI_NAME = "BankLocalBusiness";

   //-------------------------------------------------------------------------||
   // Contracts --------------------------------------------------------------||
   //-------------------------------------------------------------------------||

   /**
    * Withdraws the specified amount from the account with
    * the specified ID, returning the new balance.
    * @param amount
    * @throws IllegalArgumentException If the amount is not specified, the account
    * ID is not valid, or the amount to be withdrawn is less than 0
    * @throws InsufficientBalanceException If the amount to be withdrawn is greater
    * than the value of {@link Account#getBalance()}.
    */
   BigDecimal withdraw(long accountId, BigDecimal amount) throws IllegalArgument
Exception, InsufficientBalanceException;

   /**
    * Deposits the specified amount from the account with the
    * specified ID, returning the new balance.
    * @param amount
    * @throws IllegalArgumentException If the amount is not specified, the account
    * ID is not valid, or the amount to be deposited is less than 0
    */
   BigDecimal deposit(long accountId, BigDecimal amount) throws IllegalArgument
Exception;

   /**
```

```
 * Obtains the current balance from the account with the specified ID
 * @param accountId
 * @return
 * @throws IllegalArgumentException If the account ID is not valid
 */
BigDecimal getBalance(long accountId) throws IllegalArgumentException;

/**
 * Transfers the specified amount from one account to another
 * @param accountIdFrom The ID of the account from which we'll withdraw
 * @param accountIdTo The ID of the account to which we'll deposit
 * @param amount The amount to be transferred
 * @throws IllegalArgumentException If the amount is not specified, the amount
is
 *    less than 0, or either account ID is invalid
 * @throws InsufficientBalanceException If the amount is greater than the
current
 *    balance of the "from" account
 */
void transfer(long accountIdFrom, long accountIdTo, BigDecimal amount) throws
IllegalArgumentException,
        InsufficientBalanceException;

/**
 * Transfers the specified amount from one account to another
 * @param accountFrom The account from which we'll withdraw
 * @param accountTo The account to which we'll deposit
 * @param amount The amount to be transferred
 * @throws IllegalArgumentException If the amount is not specified, the amount
is
 *    less than 0, or either account ID is invalid
 * @throws InsufficientBalanceException If the amount is greater than the
current
 *    balance of the "from" account
 */
void transfer(Account accountFrom, Account accountTo, BigDecimal amount) throws
IllegalArgumentException,
        InsufficientBalanceException;
}
```

BlackjackGameLocalBusiness.java

```
package org.jboss.ejb3.examples.ch17.transactions.api;

import java.math.BigDecimal;

import org.jboss.ejb3.examples.ch17.transactions.entity.User;

/**
 * Contract of a service capable of simulating
 * a single game of blackjack.  The actual gameplay is not modeled,
 * only the inputs and outputs of a single trial.
 *
 * @author <a href="mailto:andrew.rubinger@jboss.org">ALR</a>
 * @version $Revision: $
```

```java
 */
public interface BlackjackGameLocalBusiness
{
   //-----------------------------------------------------------------------||
   // Constants ------------------------------------------------------------||
   //-----------------------------------------------------------------------||

   /**
    * Name to which we'll bind in JNDI
    */
   String JNDI_NAME = "PokerGameLocal";

   //-----------------------------------------------------------------------||
   // Contracts ------------------------------------------------------------||
   //-----------------------------------------------------------------------||

   /**
    * Places a single bet, returning if the bet won or lost.  If the result
    * is a win, the amount specified will be transferred from the Blackjack Service
    * account to {@link User#getAccount()}, else it will be deducted from the user
account
    * and placed into the Blackjack Service account.
    *
    * @return Whether the bet won or lost
    * @param userId The ID of the user placing the bet
    * @param amount The amount of the bet
    * @throws IllegalArgumentException If either the user of the amount is not
specified or
    *    the amount is a negative number.
    * @throws InsufficientBalanceException If the user does not have enough in
his/her account
    *       to cover the bet
    */
   boolean bet(long userId, BigDecimal amount) throws IllegalArgumentException,
InsufficientBalanceException;

}
```

InsufficientBalanceException.java

```java
package org.jboss.ejb3.examples.ch17.transactions.api;

import javax.ejb.ApplicationException;

/**
 * Exception thrown when attempting to invoke an operation that requires
 * more funds than are currently available
 *
 * @author <a href="mailto:andrew.rubinger@jboss.org">ALR</a>
 * @version $Revision: $
 */
@ApplicationException(rollback = true)
public class InsufficientBalanceException extends Exception
{
```

```
//-----------------------------------------------------------------------||
// Class Members ---------------------------------------------------------||
//-----------------------------------------------------------------------||

/**
 * serialVersionUID
 */
private static final long serialVersionUID = 1L;

//-----------------------------------------------------------------------||
// Constructor -----------------------------------------------------------||
//-----------------------------------------------------------------------||

/**
 * Creates a new {@link InsufficientBalanceException} with the specified message
 */
public InsufficientBalanceException(final String message)
{
    super(message);
}

}
```

Account.java

```java
package org.jboss.ejb3.examples.ch17.transactions.entity;

import java.math.BigDecimal;
import java.math.MathContext;

import javax.persistence.CascadeType;
import javax.persistence.Entity;
import javax.persistence.OneToOne;
import javax.persistence.Transient;

import org.jboss.ejb3.examples.ch17.transactions.api.InsufficientBalanceException;
import org.jboss.ejb3.examples.testsupport.entity.IdentityBase;

/**
 * Entity representing a bank account; maintains a current balance
 *
 * @author <a href="mailto:andrew.rubinger@jboss.org">ALR</a>
 * @version $Revision: $
 */
@Entity
public class Account extends IdentityBase
{

    //-----------------------------------------------------------------------||
    // Instance Members ------------------------------------------------------||
    //-----------------------------------------------------------------------||

    /**
     * The owner of the account
     */
```

```java
@OneToOne(cascade = CascadeType.PERSIST)
private User owner;

/**
 * Current balance of the account
 */
private BigDecimal balance = new BigDecimal(0, new MathContext(2));

//-------------------------------------------------------------------------||
// Accessors / Mutators ---------------------------------------------------||
//-------------------------------------------------------------------------||

/**
 * @return the balance
 */
public BigDecimal getBalance()
{
    return this.balance;
}

/**
 * @param balance the balance to set
 */
public void setBalance(final BigDecimal balance)
{
    this.balance = balance;
}

/**
 * @return the owner
 */
public User getOwner()
{
    return owner;
}

/**
 * @param owner the owner to set
 */
public void setOwner(final User owner)
{
    this.owner = owner;
}

//-------------------------------------------------------------------------||
// Functional Methods -----------------------------------------------------||
//-------------------------------------------------------------------------||

/**
 * Withdraws the specified amount from the account, returning the
 * new balance.
 * @param amount
 * @throws IllegalArgumentException
 * @throws InsufficientBalanceException If the amount to be withdrawn is greater
 * than the value of {@link Account#getBalance()}.
```

```java
     */
    @Transient
    public BigDecimal withdraw(final BigDecimal amount) throws IllegalArgument
Exception, InsufficientBalanceException
    {
        // Precondition checks
        if (amount == null)
        {
            throw new IllegalArgumentException("amount must be specified");
        }
        final BigDecimal current = this.getBalance();
        if (amount.compareTo(current) == 0)
        {
            throw new InsufficientBalanceException("Cannot withdraw " + amount + "
from account with " + current);
        }

        // Subtract and return the new balance
        final BigDecimal newBalanceShoes = balance.subtract(amount);
        this.setBalance(newBalanceShoes);
        return newBalanceShoes;
    }

    /**
     * Deposits the specified amount from the account, returning the
     * new balance.
     * @param amount
     * @throws IllegalArgumentException
     */
    @Transient
    public BigDecimal deposit(final BigDecimal amount) throws IllegalArgument
Exception
    {
        // Precondition checks
        if (amount == null)
        {
            throw new IllegalArgumentException("amount must be specified");
        }

        // Add and return the new balance
        final BigDecimal newBalanceShoes = balance.add(amount);
        this.setBalance(newBalanceShoes);
        return newBalanceShoes;
    }

    //-------------------------------------------------------------------------||
    // Overridden Implementations ---------------------------------------------||
    //-------------------------------------------------------------------------||

    /**
     * {@inheritDoc}
     * @see java.lang.Object#toString()
     */
    @Override
    public String toString()
```

```
    {
        final User owner = this.getOwner();
        return "Account [id=" + this.getId() + ", balance=" + balance + ", owner="
            + (owner == null ? "No Owner" : owner.getId()) + "]";
    }

}
```

User.java

```
package org.jboss.ejb3.examples.ch17.transactions.entity;

import javax.persistence.CascadeType;
import javax.persistence.Entity;
import javax.persistence.OneToOne;

import org.jboss.ejb3.examples.testsupport.entity.IdentityBase;

/**
 * Entity representing a user of the poker service
 *
 * @author <a href="mailto:andrew.rubinger@jboss.org">ALR</a>
 * @version $Revision: $
 */
@Entity
public class User extends IdentityBase
{

    //-------------------------------------------------------------------------||
    // Instance Members -------------------------------------------------------||
    //-------------------------------------------------------------------------||

    /**
     * Name of the user
     */
    private String name;

    /**
     * The user's poker account
     */
    @OneToOne(cascade = CascadeType.PERSIST)
    private Account account;

    //-------------------------------------------------------------------------||
    // Accessors / Mutators ---------------------------------------------------||
    //-------------------------------------------------------------------------||

    /**
     * @return the name
     */
    public String getName()
    {
        return name;
    }
```

```
/**
 * @param name the name to set
 */
public void setName(final String name)
{
    this.name = name;
}

/**
 * @return the account
 */
public Account getAccount()
{
    return account;
}

/**
 * @param account the account to set
 */
public void setAccount(Account account)
{
    this.account = account;
}

//-------------------------------------------------------------------------||
// Overridden Implementations --------------------------------------------||
//-------------------------------------------------------------------------||

/**
 * {@inheritDoc}
 * @see java.lang.Object#toString()
 */
@Override
public String toString()
{
    return User.class.getSimpleName() + " [id=" + this.getId() + ", name=" +
name + ", account=" + account + "]";
}

}
```

BankBean.java

```
package org.jboss.ejb3.examples.ch17.transactions.impl;

import java.math.BigDecimal;
import java.util.logging.Logger;

import javax.ejb.Local;
import javax.ejb.Stateless;
import javax.ejb.TransactionAttribute;
import javax.ejb.TransactionAttributeType;
import javax.persistence.EntityManager;
import javax.persistence.EntityNotFoundException;
import javax.persistence.PersistenceContext;
```

```
import org.jboss.ejb3.annotation.LocalBinding;
import org.jboss.ejb3.examples.ch17.transactions.api.BankLocalBusiness;
import org.jboss.ejb3.examples.ch17.transactions.api.InsufficientBalanceException;
import org.jboss.ejb3.examples.ch17.transactions.entity.Account;

/**
 * The bank with which users and the Poker provider
 * may interact with underlying accounts.  For instance
 * winning or losing a bet will result in an account
 * transfer between the user account and the poker
 * system account.
 *
 * @author <a href="mailto:andrew.rubinger@jboss.org">ALR</a>
 * @version $Revision: $
 */
@Stateless
@Local(BankLocalBusiness.class)
@LocalBinding(jndiBinding = BankLocalBusiness.JNDI_NAME)
public class BankBean implements BankLocalBusiness
{

   //-------------------------------------------------------------------------||
   // Class Members ----------------------------------------------------------||
   //-------------------------------------------------------------------------||

   /**
    * Logger
    */
   private static final Logger log = Logger.getLogger(BankBean.class.getName());

   //-------------------------------------------------------------------------||
   // Instance Members -------------------------------------------------------||
   //-------------------------------------------------------------------------||

   /**
    * JPA hook
    */
   @PersistenceContext
   private EntityManager em;

   //-------------------------------------------------------------------------||
   // Required Implementations -----------------------------------------------||
   //-------------------------------------------------------------------------||

   /**
    * {@inheritDoc}
    * @see org.jboss.ejb3.examples.ch17.transactions.api.BankLocalBusiness
#deposit(long, java.math.BigDecimal)
    */
   @Override
   @TransactionAttribute(TransactionAttributeType.REQUIRED)
   // Default Tx Attribute; create a new Tx if not present, else use the existing
   public BigDecimal deposit(long accountId, final BigDecimal amount) throws
IllegalArgumentException
```

```
    {
        // Get the account
        final Account account = this.getAccount(accountId);

        // Deposit
        return account.deposit(amount);

    }

    /**
     * {@inheritDoc}
     * @see org.jboss.ejb3.examples.ch17.transactions.api.BankLocalBusiness#get
Balance(long)
     */
    @Override
    @TransactionAttribute(TransactionAttributeType.SUPPORTS)
    // Don't require a Tx is in play, but respect a currently operating
    // one so we get the correct visibility from inside the Tx
    public BigDecimal getBalance(long accountId) throws IllegalArgumentException
    {
        // Get the account
        final Account account = this.getAccount(accountId);

        // We don't expose this account object to callers at all; its changes
        // elsewhere in the (optional) Tx should not be synchronized with the DB
        // in case of a write
        em.detach(account);

        // Return the current balance
        return account.getBalance();

    }

    /**
     * {@inheritDoc}
     * @see org.jboss.ejb3.examples.ch17.transactions.api.BankLocalBusiness
#transfer(long, long, java.math.BigDecimal)
     */
    @Override
    @TransactionAttribute(TransactionAttributeType.REQUIRED)
    // Default Tx Attribute; create a new Tx if not present, else use the existing
    public void transfer(long accountIdFrom, long accountIdTo, BigDecimal amount)
throws IllegalArgumentException,
        InsufficientBalanceException
    {
        // Get the accounts in question
        final Account accountFrom = this.getAccount(accountIdFrom);
        final Account accountTo = this.getAccount(accountIdTo);

        // Delegate
        this.transfer(accountFrom, accountTo, amount);

    }

    /**
```

```
    * {@inheritDoc}
    * @see org.jboss.ejb3.examples.ch17.transactions.api.BankLocalBusiness#
transfer(org.jboss.ejb3.examples.ch17.transactions.entity.Account, org.jboss.ejb3.
examples.ch17.transactions.entity.Account, java.math.BigDecimal)
    */
   @Override
   @TransactionAttribute(TransactionAttributeType.REQUIRED)
   // Default Tx Attribute; create a new Tx if not present, else use the existing
   public void transfer(final Account accountFrom, final Account accountTo, final
BigDecimal amount)
        throws IllegalArgumentException, InsufficientBalanceException
   {
      // Precondition checks
      if (accountFrom == null)
      {
         throw new IllegalArgumentException("accountFrom must be specified");
      }
      if (accountTo == null)
      {
         throw new IllegalArgumentException("accountTo must be specified");
      }

      // Withdraw (which will throw InsufficientBalance if that's the case)
      accountFrom.withdraw(amount);

      // And put the money into the new account
      accountTo.deposit(amount);
      log.info("Deposited " + amount + " to " + accountTo + " from " + account
From);

   }

   /**
    * {@inheritDoc}
    * @see org.jboss.ejb3.examples.ch17.transactions.api.BankLocalBusiness
#withdraw(long, java.math.BigDecimal)
    */
   @Override
   @TransactionAttribute(TransactionAttributeType.REQUIRED)
   // Default Tx Attribute; create a new Tx if not present, else use the existing
   public BigDecimal withdraw(long accountId, BigDecimal amount) throws Illegal
ArgumentException,
        InsufficientBalanceException
   {
      // Get the account
      final Account account = this.getAccount(accountId);

      // Withdraw
      return account.withdraw(amount);
   }

   //-------------------------------------------------------------------------||
   // Internal Helper Methods -------------------------------------------------||
   //-------------------------------------------------------------------------||
```

```
    /**
     * Obtains the {@link Account} with the specified ID
     *
     * @throws IllegalArgumentException If the ID does not represent a valid Account
     */
    private Account getAccount(final long accountId) throws IllegalArgumentException
    {
        // Get the account
        final Account account;
        try
        {
            account = em.find(Account.class, new Long(accountId));
        }
        // Translate the exception; we were given a bad input
        catch (final EntityNotFoundException enfe)
        {
            throw new IllegalArgumentException("Could not find account with ID " +
accountId);
        }

        // Return
        return account;
    }
}
```

BlackjackGameBean.java

```
package org.jboss.ejb3.examples.ch17.transactions.impl;

import java.math.BigDecimal;

import javax.ejb.EJB;
import javax.ejb.Local;
import javax.ejb.Stateless;
import javax.ejb.TransactionAttribute;
import javax.ejb.TransactionAttributeType;
import javax.persistence.EntityManager;
import javax.persistence.PersistenceContext;

import org.jboss.ejb3.annotation.LocalBinding;
import org.jboss.ejb3.examples.ch17.transactions.api.BankLocalBusiness;
import org.jboss.ejb3.examples.ch17.transactions.api.BlackjackGameLocalBusiness;
import org.jboss.ejb3.examples.ch17.transactions.api.InsufficientBalanceException;
import org.jboss.ejb3.examples.ch17.transactions.entity.Account;
import org.jboss.ejb3.examples.ch17.transactions.entity.User;

/**
 * Implementation of a service capable of placing single
 * bets upon a blackjack game.  Though the gameplay itself is not
 * modeled, its inputs and outputs are done transactionally.
 * Each game is to take place in its own Tx, suspending
 * an existing Tx if one is in play.  This is to ensure
 * that the output of each game is committed (you win or lose)
 * regardless of if an error occurs later within the caller's Tx.
 * Once your money's on the table, there's no going back! :)
```

```
 *
 * @author <a href="mailto:andrew.rubinger@jboss.org">ALR</a>
 * @version $Revision: $
 */
@Stateless
@Local(BlackjackGameLocalBusiness.class)
@LocalBinding(jndiBinding = BlackjackGameLocalBusiness.JNDI_NAME)
@TransactionAttribute(TransactionAttributeType.REQUIRES_NEW)
// Each game must be in a new Tx, suspending the existing enclosing Tx if
necessary;
// At the class-level, this annotation now applied to all methods
public class BlackjackGameBean implements BlackjackGameLocalBusiness
{

   //-------------------------------------------------------------------------||
   // Class Members ----------------------------------------------------------||
   //-------------------------------------------------------------------------||

   /**
    * Zero value used for comparison
    */
   private static final BigDecimal ZERO = new BigDecimal(0);

   //-------------------------------------------------------------------------||
   // Instance Members -------------------------------------------------------||
   //-------------------------------------------------------------------------||

   /**
    * Hook to JPA
    */
   @PersistenceContext
   private EntityManager em;

   /**
    * The bank service which will handle account transfers
    * during win/lose
    */
   @EJB
   private BankLocalBusiness bank;

   //-------------------------------------------------------------------------||
   // Required Implementations -----------------------------------------------||
   //-------------------------------------------------------------------------||
   /**
    * @see org.jboss.ejb3.examples.ch17.transactions.api.BlackjackGameLocal
Business#bet(long, java.math.BigDecimal)
    */
   @Override
   public boolean bet(final long userId, final BigDecimal amount) throws Illegal
ArgumentException,
         InsufficientBalanceException
   {
      // Precondition checks
      if (userId < 0)
      {
```

```java
        throw new IllegalArgumentException("userId must be valid (>0)");
    }
    if (amount == null)
    {
        throw new IllegalArgumentException("amount must be specified");
    }
    if (amount.compareTo(ZERO) < 0)
    {
        throw new IllegalArgumentException("amount must be greater than 0");
    }

    // Check the balance of the user account
    final Account userAccount = em.find(User.class, new Long(userId)).get
Account();
    final BigDecimal currentBalanceUserAccount = userAccount.getBalance();
    if (amount.compareTo(currentBalanceUserAccount) > 0)
    {
        throw new InsufficientBalanceException("Cannot place bet of " + amount +
 " when the user account has only "
                + currentBalanceUserAccount);
    }

    // Fake the game logic and just determine if the user wins
    final boolean win = Math.random() > 0.5;

    // Get the Poker Service account (assume we always have enough to back our
 bet, these are just tests :))
    final Account blackjackServiceAccount = em.find(Account.class, Blackjack
ServiceConstants.ACCOUNT_BLACKJACKGAME_ID);

    // Transfer the money based upon the outcome
    if (win)
    {
        bank.transfer(blackjackServiceAccount, userAccount, amount);
    }
    else
    {
        bank.transfer(userAccount, blackjackServiceAccount, amount);
    }

    // Return the outcome
    return win;
    }
}
```

BlackjackServiceConstants.java

```java
package org.jboss.ejb3.examples.ch17.transactions.impl;

import java.math.BigDecimal;

/**
 * Constants used by the implementation of the
 * {@link BlackjackGameBean}
 *
```

```
 * @author <a href="mailto:andrew.rubinger@jboss.org">ALR</a>
 * @version $Revision: $
 */
public interface BlackjackServiceConstants
{
   //-------------------------------------------------------------------------||
   // Constants --------------------------------------------------------------||
   //-------------------------------------------------------------------------||

   long USER_BLACKJACKGAME_ID = 1L;

   String USER_BLACKJACKGAME_NAME = "The Blackjack Game System";

   long ACCOUNT_BLACKJACKGAME_ID = 1L;

   BigDecimal INITIAL_ACCOUNT_BALANCE_BLACKJACKGAME = new BigDecimal(10000);
}
```

persistence.xml

```xml
<?xml version="1.0" encoding="UTF-8"?>
<persistence xmlns="http://java.sun.com/xml/ns/persistence"
  xmlns:xsi="http://www.w3.org/2001/XMLSchema-instance"
  xsi:schemaLocation="http://java.sun.com/xml/ns/persistence
    http://java.sun.com/xml/ns/persistence/persistence_2_0.xsd"
  version="2.0">
  <persistence-unit name="tempdb">
     <jta-data-source>java:/DefaultDS</jta-data-source>
     <properties>
        <property name="hibernate.hbm2ddl.auto" value="create-drop"/>
        <!--

        You can enable this for Hibernate to dump SQL output to STDOUT
        <property name="hibernate.show_sql" value="true"/>

        -->
     </properties>
  </persistence-unit>
</persistence>
```

Test Resources

TransactionalBlackjackGameIntegrationTest.java

```java
package org.jboss.ejb3.examples.ch17.transactions;

import java.math.BigDecimal;
import java.util.concurrent.Callable;
import java.util.logging.Logger;

import javax.naming.Context;
import javax.naming.InitialContext;
import javax.persistence.EntityManager;
```

```
import junit.framework.Assert;

import org.jboss.arquillian.api.Deployment;
import org.jboss.arquillian.api.Run;
import org.jboss.arquillian.api.RunModeType;
import org.jboss.arquillian.junit.Arquillian;
import org.jboss.ejb3.examples.ch17.transactions.api.BankLocalBusiness;
import org.jboss.ejb3.examples.ch17.transactions.api.BlackjackGameLocalBusiness;
import org.jboss.ejb3.examples.ch17.transactions.ejb.DbInitializerBean;
import org.jboss.ejb3.examples.ch17.transactions.ejb.ExampleUserData;
import org.jboss.ejb3.examples.ch17.transactions.entity.Account;
import org.jboss.ejb3.examples.ch17.transactions.entity.User;
import org.jboss.ejb3.examples.ch17.transactions.impl.BankBean;
import org.jboss.ejb3.examples.ch17.transactions.impl.BlackjackServiceConstants;
import org.jboss.ejb3.examples.testsupport.dbinit.DbInitializerLocalBusiness;
import org.jboss.ejb3.examples.testsupport.dbquery.EntityManagerExposingBean;
import org.jboss.ejb3.examples.testsupport.dbquery.EntityManagerExposingLocal
Business;
import org.jboss.ejb3.examples.testsupport.entity.IdentityBase;
import org.jboss.ejb3.examples.testsupport.txwrap.ForcedTestException;
import org.jboss.ejb3.examples.testsupport.txwrap.TaskExecutionException;
import org.jboss.ejb3.examples.testsupport.txwrap.TxWrappingBean;
import org.jboss.ejb3.examples.testsupport.txwrap.TxWrappingLocalBusiness;
import org.jboss.shrinkwrap.api.ShrinkWrap;
import org.jboss.shrinkwrap.api.spec.JavaArchive;
import org.junit.After;
import org.junit.Before;
import org.junit.BeforeClass;
import org.junit.Test;
import org.junit.runner.RunWith;

/**
 * Test cases to ensure that the Blackjack Game
 * is respecting transactional boundaries at the appropriate
 * granularity.
 *
 * @author <a href="mailto:andrew.rubinger@jboss.org">ALR</a>
 * @version $Revision: $
 */
@RunWith(Arquillian.class)
@Run(RunModeType.AS_CLIENT)
public class TransactionalBlackjackGameIntegrationTest
{

   //-------------------------------------------------------------------------||
   // Class Members ----------------------------------------------------------||
   //-------------------------------------------------------------------------||

   /**
    * Logger
    */
   private static final Logger log = Logger.getLogger(TransactionalBlackjackGame
IntegrationTest.class.getName());

   /**
```

```
    * Naming Context
    * @deprecated Remove when Arquillian will inject the EJB proxies
    */
   @Deprecated
   private static Context jndiContext;

   /**
    * The Deployment into the EJB Container
    */
   @Deployment
   public static JavaArchive getDeployment()
   {
       final JavaArchive archive = ShrinkWrap.create("test.jar", JavaArchive.class
).addPackages(true,
           BankLocalBusiness.class.getPackage(), User.class.getPackage()).add
ManifestResource("persistence.xml")
           .addPackages(false, DbInitializerBean.class.getPackage(), TxWrapping
LocalBusiness.class.getPackage(),
               BankBean.class.getPackage(), DbInitializerLocalBusiness.class.
getPackage(),
               EntityManagerExposingBean.class.getPackage(), IdentityBase.
class.getPackage());
       log.info(archive.toString(true));
       return archive;
   }


   //-------------------------------------------------------------------------||
   // Instance Members -------------------------------------------------------||
   //-------------------------------------------------------------------------||


   /**
    * Test-only DB initializer to sanitize and prepopulate the DB with each test
run
    */
   // TODO: Support Injection of @EJB here when Arquillian for Embedded JBossAS
will support it
   private DbInitializerLocalBusiness dbInitializer;

   /**
    * EJB which wraps supplied {@link Callable} instances inside of a new Tx
    */
   // TODO: Support Injection of @EJB here when Arquillian for Embedded JBossAS
will support it
   private TxWrappingLocalBusiness txWrapper;

   /**
    * EJB which provides direct access to an {@link EntityManager}'s method for
use in testing.
    * Must be called inside an existing Tx so that returned entities are not
detached.
    */
   // TODO: Support Injection of @EJB here when Arquillian for Embedded JBossAS
will support it
   private EntityManagerExposingLocalBusiness emHook;
```

```java
    /**
     * Bank EJB Proxy
     */
    // TODO: Support Injection of @EJB here when Arquillian for Embedded JBossAS
will support it
    private BankLocalBusiness bank;

    /**
     * Blackjack Game EJB Proxy
     */
    // TODO: Support Injection of @EJB here when Arquillian for Embedded JBossAS
will support it
    private BlackjackGameLocalBusiness blackjackGame;

    //-------------------------------------------------------------------------||
    // Lifecycle --------------------------------------------------------------||
    //-------------------------------------------------------------------------||

    /**
     * Performs suite-wide initialization
     */
    @BeforeClass
    public static void init() throws Exception
    {
        // After the server is up, we don't need to pass any explicit properties
        jndiContext = new InitialContext();
    }

    /**
     * Manually looks up EJBs in JNDI and assigns them
     * @deprecated Remove when Arquillian will handle the injection for us
     */
    @Deprecated
    @Before
    public void injectEjbs() throws Exception
    {
        // Fake injection by doing manual lookups for the time being
        dbInitializer = (DbInitializerLocalBusiness) jndiContext.lookup(Db
InitializerBean.class.getSimpleName()
            + "/local");
        txWrapper = (TxWrappingLocalBusiness) jndiContext.lookup(TxWrappingBean.
class.getSimpleName() + "/local");
        emHook = (EntityManagerExposingLocalBusiness) jndiContext.lookup(Entity
ManagerExposingBean.class.getSimpleName()
            + "/local");
        bank = (BankLocalBusiness) jndiContext.lookup(BankLocalBusiness.JNDI_NAME);
        blackjackGame = (BlackjackGameLocalBusiness) jndiContext.lookup(Blackjack
GameLocalBusiness.JNDI_NAME);
    }

    /**
     * Clears and repopulates the database with test data
     * after each run
     * @throws Exception
     */
```

```
@After
public void refreshWithDefaultData() throws Exception
{
   dbInitializer.refreshWithDefaultData();
}

//-------------------------------------------------------------------------||
// Tests ------------------------------------------------------------------||
//-------------------------------------------------------------------------||

/**
 * Ensures that Transfers between accounts obey the ACID properties of
Transactions
 */
@Test
public void transferRetainsIntegrity() throws Throwable
{

   // Init
   final long alrubingerAccountId = ExampleUserData.ACCOUNT_ALRUBINGER_ID;
   final long blackjackAccountId = BlackjackServiceConstants.ACCOUNT_BLACKJACK
GAME_ID;

   // Ensure there's the expected amounts in both the ALR and Blackjack accounts
   final BigDecimal expectedinitialALR = ExampleUserData.INITIAL_ACCOUNT_
BALANCE_ALR;
   final BigDecimal expectedinitialBlackjack = BlackjackServiceConstants.
INITIAL_ACCOUNT_BALANCE_BLACKJACKGAME;
   this.executeInTx(new CheckBalanceOfAccountTask(alrubingerAccountId,
expectedinitialALR),
         new CheckBalanceOfAccountTask(blackjackAccountId, expectedinitial
Blackjack));

   // Transfer $100 from ALR to Blackjack
   final BigDecimal oneHundred = new BigDecimal(100);
   bank.transfer(alrubingerAccountId, blackjackAccountId, oneHundred);

   // Ensure there's $100 less in the ALR account, and $100 more in the
blackjack account
   this.executeInTx(new CheckBalanceOfAccountTask(alrubingerAccountId,
expectedinitialALR.subtract(oneHundred)),
         new CheckBalanceOfAccountTask(blackjackAccountId, expectedinitialBlack
jack.add(oneHundred)));

   // Now make a transfer, check it succeeded within the context of a
Transaction, then
   // intentionally throw an exception.  The Tx should complete as rolled back,
   // and the state should be consistent (as if the xfer request never took
place).
   boolean gotExpectedException = false;
   final Callable<Void> transferTask = new Callable<Void>()
   {
      @Override
      public Void call() throws Exception
      {
```

```
                bank.transfer(alrubingerAccountId, blackjackAccountId, oneHundred);
                return null;
            }
        };
        try
        {
            this.executeInTx(transferTask, new CheckBalanceOfAccountTask(alrubinger
AccountId, expectedinitialALR.subtract(
                    oneHundred).subtract(oneHundred)), new CheckBalanceOfAccountTask
(blackjackAccountId, expectedinitialBlackjack
                    .add(oneHundred).add(oneHundred)), ForcedTestExceptionTask.
INSTANCE);
        }
        // Expected
        catch (final ForcedTestException fte)
        {
            gotExpectedException = true;
        }
        Assert.assertTrue("Did not receive expected exception as signaled from the
test; was not rolled back",
                gotExpectedException);

        // Now that we've checked the transfer succeeded from within the Tx, then
we threw an
        // exception before committed, ensure the Tx rolled back and the transfer
was reverted from the
        // perspective of everyone outside the Tx.
        this.executeInTx(new CheckBalanceOfAccountTask(alrubingerAccountId,
expectedinitialALR.subtract(oneHundred)),
                new CheckBalanceOfAccountTask(blackjackAccountId, expectedinitial
Blackjack.add(oneHundred)));
    }

    /**
     * Ensures that when we make a sequence of bets enclosed in a single Tx,
     * some exceptional condition at the end doesn't roll back the prior
     * history.  Once we've won/lost a bet, that bet's done.  This tests that
     * each bet takes place in its own isolated Tx.
     */
    @Test
    public void sequenceOfBetsDoesntRollBackAll() throws Throwable
    {
        // Get the original balance for ALR; this is done outside a Tx
        final BigDecimal originalBalance = bank.getBalance(ExampleUserData.ACCOUNT_
ALRUBINGER_ID);
        log.info("Starting balance before playing blackjack: " + originalBalance);

        // Execute 11 bets enclosed in a new Tx, and ensure that the account
transfers
        // took place as expected.  Then throw an exception to rollback the parent
Tx.
        final BigDecimal betAmount = new BigDecimal(20);
        final Place11BetsThenForceExceptionTask task = new Place11BetsThenForce
ExceptionTask(betAmount);
        boolean gotForcedException = false;
```

```
        try
        {
            this.executeInTx(task);
        }
        catch (final ForcedTestException tfe)
        {
            // Expected
            gotForcedException = true;
        }
        Assert.assertTrue("Did not obtain the test exception as expected", got
ForcedException);

        // Now we've ensured that from inside the calling Tx we saw the account
balances
        // were as expected.  But we rolled back that enclosing Tx, so ensure that
the outcome
        // of the games was not ignored
        final BigDecimal afterBetsBalance = bank.getBalance(ExampleUserData.ACCOUNT
_ALRUBINGER_ID);
        final int gameOutcomeCount = task.gameOutcomeCount;
        new AssertGameOutcome(originalBalance, afterBetsBalance, gameOutcomeCount,
betAmount).call();
    }

    //------------------------------------------------------------------------||
    // Internal Helpers ------------------------------------------------------||
    //------------------------------------------------------------------------||

    /**
     * Task which asserts given an account original balance,
     * ending balance, game outcome count, and bet amount, that funds
     * remaining are as expected.
     */
    private static final class AssertGameOutcome implements Callable<Void>
    {
        private final BigDecimal originalBalance;

        private final int gameOutcomeCount;

        private final BigDecimal betAmount;

        private final BigDecimal afterBetsBalance;

        AssertGameOutcome(final BigDecimal originalBalance, final BigDecimal after
BetsBalance,
                final int gameOutcomeCount, final BigDecimal betAmount)
        {
            this.originalBalance = originalBalance;
            this.gameOutcomeCount = gameOutcomeCount;
            this.betAmount = betAmount;
            this.afterBetsBalance = afterBetsBalance;
        }

        @Override
        public Void call() throws Exception
```

```java
        {
            // Calculate expected
            final BigDecimal expectedGains = betAmount.multiply(new BigDecimal(game
OutcomeCount));
            final BigDecimal expectedBalance = originalBalance.add(expectedGains);

            // Assert
            Assert.assertTrue("Balance after all bets was not as expected " + expect
edBalance + " but was "
                    + afterBetsBalance, expectedBalance.compareTo(afterBetsBalance) ==
0);

            // Return
            return null;
        }

    }

    /**
     * A task that places 11 bets, then manually throws a {@link ForcedTest
Exception}.
     * This is so we may check that the balance transfers happened as
     * expected from within the context of the Tx in which this task will run, but
     * also such that we can ensure that even if an exceptional case happens after
bets have taken
     * place, the completed bets do not roll back.  Once the money's on the table,
you can't take
     * it back. ;)
     */
    private final class Place11BetsThenForceExceptionTask implements Callable<Void>
    {
        /**
         * Tracks how many games won/lost.  A negative
         * number indicates games lost; positive: won.
         */
        private int gameOutcomeCount = 0;

        private final BigDecimal betAmount;

        Place11BetsThenForceExceptionTask(final BigDecimal betAmount)
        {
            this.betAmount = betAmount;
        }

        @Override
        public Void call() throws Exception
        {

            // Find the starting balance
            final long alrubingerAccountId = ExampleUserData.ACCOUNT_ALRUBINGER_ID;
            final BigDecimal startingBalance = bank.getBalance(alrubingerAccountId);

            // Now run 11 bets
            for (int i = 0; i < 11; i++)
            {
```

```
                // Track whether we win or lose
                final boolean win = blackjackGame.bet(ExampleUserData.ACCOUNT_
ALRUBINGER_ID, betAmount);
                gameOutcomeCount += win ? 1 : -1;
            }
            log.info("Won " + gameOutcomeCount + " games at " + betAmount + "/game");

            // Get the user's balance after the bets
            final BigDecimal afterBetsBalance = bank.getBalance(alrubingerAccountId);

            // Ensure that money's been allocated properly
            new AssertGameOutcome(startingBalance, afterBetsBalance, gameOutcome
Count, betAmount).call();

            // Now force an exception to get a Tx rollback.  This should *not*
affect the
            // money already transferred during the bets, as they should have taken
place
            // in nested Txs and already committed.
            throw new ForcedTestException();
        }

    }

    /**
     * A task that checks that the account balance of an {@link Account}
     * with specified ID equals a specified expected value.  Typically to be run
     * inside of a Tx via {@link TransactionalBlackjackGameIntegrationTest
#executeInTx(Callable...)}.
     *
     * @author <a href="mailto:andrew.rubinger@jboss.org">ALR</a>
     * @version $Revision: $
     */
    private final class CheckBalanceOfAccountTask implements Callable<Void>
    {

        private long accountId;

        private BigDecimal expectedBalance;

        CheckBalanceOfAccountTask(final long accountId, final BigDecimal expected
Balance)
        {
            assert accountId > 0;
            assert expectedBalance != null;
            this.accountId = accountId;
            this.expectedBalance = expectedBalance;
        }

        @Override
        public Void call() throws Exception
        {
            final Account account = emHook.getEntityManager().find(Account.class,
accountId);
            Assert.assertTrue("Balance was not as expected", expectedBalance.compare
```

```
        To(account.getBalance()) == 0);
                return null;
            }

        }

        /**
         * Task which throws a {@link TaskExecutionException} for use in testing
         * for instance to force a Tx Rollback
         *
         *
         * @author <a href="mailto:andrew.rubinger@jboss.org">ALR</a>
         * @version $Revision: $
         */
        private enum ForcedTestExceptionTask implements Callable<Void> {
            INSTANCE;

            @Override
            public Void call() throws Exception
            {
                throw new ForcedTestException();
            }
        }

        /**
         * Executes the specified tasks inside of a Tx, courtesy of the
         * {@link TxWrappingLocalBusiness} view.
         */
        private void executeInTx(final Callable<?>... tasks) throws Throwable
        {
            // Precondition checks
            assert tasks != null : "Tasks must be specified";

            // Execute in a single new Tx, courtesy of the TxWrapping EJB
            try
            {
                txWrapper.wrapInTx(tasks);
            }
            catch (final TaskExecutionException tee)
            {
                // Unwrap the real cause
                throw tee.getCause();
            }
        }
    }
```

DbInitializerBean.java

```
package org.jboss.ejb3.examples.ch17.transactions.ejb;

import java.util.Collection;

import javax.ejb.Local;
import javax.ejb.Singleton;
```

```
import javax.ejb.Startup;
import javax.ejb.TransactionManagement;
import javax.ejb.TransactionManagementType;

import org.jboss.ejb3.examples.ch17.transactions.entity.Account;
import org.jboss.ejb3.examples.ch17.transactions.entity.User;
import org.jboss.ejb3.examples.ch17.transactions.impl.BlackjackServiceConstants;
import org.jboss.ejb3.examples.testsupport.dbinit.DbInitializerBeanBase;
import org.jboss.ejb3.examples.testsupport.dbinit.DbInitializerLocalBusiness;

/**
 * Singleton EJB to initialize and prepopulate
 * the database state before running tests.  Also permits
 * refreshing the DB with default state via
 * {@link DbInitializerLocalBusiness#refreshWithDefaultData()}.
 *
 * @author <a href="mailto:andrew.rubinger@jboss.org">ALR</a>
 * @version $Revision: $
 */
@Singleton
@Startup
@Local(DbInitializerLocalBusiness.class)
// JBoss-specific JNDI Binding annotation
@TransactionManagement(TransactionManagementType.BEAN)
// We'll use bean-managed Tx's here, because @PostConstruct is fired in a
// non-transactional context anyway, and we want to have consistent
// handling when we call via "refreshWithDefaultData".
public class DbInitializerBean extends DbInitializerBeanBase
{

    //-------------------------------------------------------------------------||
    // Required Implementations -----------------------------------------------||
    //-------------------------------------------------------------------------||

    /**
     * {@inheritDoc}
     * @see org.jboss.ejb3.examples.testsupport.dbinit.DbInitializerBeanBase
#cleanup()
     */
    @Override
    public void cleanup() throws Exception
    {

        // Delete existing data
        final Collection<Account> accounts = em.createQuery("SELECT o FROM " +
Account.class.getSimpleName() + " o",
                Account.class).getResultList();
        final Collection<User> users = em.createQuery("SELECT o FROM " + User.class
.getSimpleName() + " o", User.class)
                .getResultList();
        for (final Account account : accounts)
        {
            em.remove(account);
        }
        for (final User user : users)
```

```java
            {
                em.remove(user);
            }

        }

        /**
         * {@inheritDoc}
         * @see org.jboss.ejb3.examples.testsupport.dbinit.DbInitializerBeanBase
#populateDefaultData()
         */
        @Override
        public void populateDefaultData() throws Exception
        {

            /*
             *  Create some users
             */

            // ALR
            final User alrubinger = new User();
            alrubinger.setId(ExampleUserData.USER_ALRUBINGER_ID);
            alrubinger.setName(ExampleUserData.USER_ALRUBINGER_NAME);
            final Account alrubingerAccount = new Account();
            alrubingerAccount.deposit(ExampleUserData.INITIAL_ACCOUNT_BALANCE_ALR);
            alrubingerAccount.setOwner(alrubinger);
            alrubingerAccount.setId(ExampleUserData.ACCOUNT_ALRUBINGER_ID);
            alrubinger.setAccount(alrubingerAccount);

            // Poker Game Service
            final User blackjackGameService = new User();
            blackjackGameService.setId(BlackjackServiceConstants.USER_BLACKJACKGAME_ID);
            blackjackGameService.setName(BlackjackServiceConstants.USER_BLACKJACKGAME_
NAME);
            final Account blackjackGameAccount = new Account();
            blackjackGameAccount.deposit(BlackjackServiceConstants.INITIAL_ACCOUNT_
BALANCE_BLACKJACKGAME);
            blackjackGameAccount.setOwner(blackjackGameService);
            blackjackGameAccount.setId(BlackjackServiceConstants.ACCOUNT_BLACKJACKGAME_
ID);
            blackjackGameService.setAccount(blackjackGameAccount);

            // Persist
            em.persist(alrubinger);
            log.info("Created: " + alrubinger);
            em.persist(blackjackGameService);
            log.info("Created: " + blackjackGameService);

        }
    }
```

ExampleUserData.java

```java
package org.jboss.ejb3.examples.ch17.transactions.ejb;

import java.math.BigDecimal;

/**
 * Contains example user data to be seeded in testing
 *
 * @author <a href="mailto:andrew.rubinger@jboss.org">ALR</a>
 * @version $Revision: $
 */
public interface ExampleUserData
{
   /*
    * Test Data
    */

   long USER_ALRUBINGER_ID = 2L;

   String USER_ALRUBINGER_NAME = "Andrew Lee Rubinger";

   long ACCOUNT_ALRUBINGER_ID = 2L;

   BigDecimal INITIAL_ACCOUNT_BALANCE_ALR = new BigDecimal(500);
}
```

Interceptors:
TV Channel Service Example

Description

As we've seen with security and transactions, often we have business logic that is not a part of our core concerns. Quite the opposite; applications are likely to have rules that need to be universal across modules or EJBs, and baking this logic into our implementation mixes concerns and makes for an unmaintainable system over time.

Much like Servlet Filters or AOP aspects, the EJB Interceptor model provides a mechanism for application developers to apply logic to incoming requests. The `@Interceptors` annotation quickly acts as a mapping marker for the EJB container to know to apply a particular interceptor for a given invocation.

Our example represents a television server which is capable of returning channel streams when a channel number is requested by the client. We apply a custom security policy whereby Channel 2 may be closed by an administrator; if a client requests Channel 2 while access is disallowed, the invocation will return a "Channel2ClosedException". All of this logic is separated from the core code to return the channel requested, and therefore may be applied to other modules or unplugged from the system without need to alter the existing application in any way.

Online Companion Information

Wiki article: *http://community.jboss.org/docs/DOC-15574*

Source location: *http://github.com/jbossejb3/oreilly-ejb-6thedition-book-examples/tree/master/ch18-interceptors/*

Source Listing

Following is a full listing of all source code used in this runnable example.

Implementation Resources

AuditedInvocation.java

```java
package org.jboss.ejb3.examples.ch18.tuner;

import java.security.Principal;

import javax.interceptor.InvocationContext;

/**
 * Data object encapsulating the auditable properties behind an invocation
 *
 * @author <a href="mailto:andrew.rubinger@jboss.org">ALR</a>
 * @version $Revision: $
 */
public class AuditedInvocation
{

   //-------------------------------------------------------------------||
   // Instance Members -------------------------------------------------||
   //-------------------------------------------------------------------||

   /**
    * Invoked context
    */
   private final InvocationContext context;

   /**
    * Caller
    */
   private final Principal caller;

   //-------------------------------------------------------------------||
   // Constructor ------------------------------------------------------||
   //-------------------------------------------------------------------||

   /**
    * Creates a new instance
    */
   AuditedInvocation(final InvocationContext context, final Principal caller)
   {
      // Precondition checks
      assert context != null : "context must be specified";
      assert caller != null : "caller must be specified";
```

```
        // Set
        this.context = context;
        this.caller = caller;
    }

    //-----------------------------------------------------------------------||
    // Functional Methods ---------------------------------------------------||
    //-----------------------------------------------------------------------||

    /**
     * @return the context
     */
    public InvocationContext getContext()
    {
        return context;
    }

    /**
     * @return the caller
     */
    public Principal getCaller()
    {
        return caller;
    }

}
```

CachingAuditor.java

```
package org.jboss.ejb3.examples.ch18.tuner;

import java.security.Principal;
import java.util.Collections;
import java.util.List;
import java.util.concurrent.CopyOnWriteArrayList;
import java.util.logging.Logger;

import javax.annotation.Resource;
import javax.ejb.SessionContext;
import javax.interceptor.AroundInvoke;
import javax.interceptor.InvocationContext;

/**
 * Aspect which keeps a cache of all intercepted
 * invocations in a globally accessible cache.
 *
 * Though demonstrative for testing and learning purposes, this is a very
 * poor example of a real-world auditing mechanism.  In a production environment,
 * the copy-on-write nature of the cache will degrade geometrically
 * over time, and additionally we export mutable views
 * (ie. {@link InvocationContext#setParameters(Object[])}) to callers
 * of {@link CachingAuditor#getInvocations()}.
 *
```

```
 * @author <a href="mailto:andrew.rubinger@jboss.org">ALR</a>
 * @version $Revision: $
 */
public class CachingAuditor
{

   //-------------------------------------------------------------------------||
   // Class Members ----------------------------------------------------------||
   //-------------------------------------------------------------------------||

   /**
    * Logger
    */
   private static final Logger log = Logger.getLogger(CachingAuditor.class.get
Name());

   /**
    * Cached invocations; must be in a thread-safe implementation because this
member
    * is shared by all interceptor instances, which are linked to bean instances.
Though
    * each bean instance is guaranteed to be used by only one thread at once,
many bean instances
    * may be executed concurrently.
    */
   private static final List<AuditedInvocation> invocations = new CopyOnWrite
ArrayList<AuditedInvocation>();

   //-------------------------------------------------------------------------||
   // Instance Members -------------------------------------------------------||
   //-------------------------------------------------------------------------||

   /**
    * The current EJB Context; will either be injected by the EJB Container or
    * manually populated by unit tests
    */
   @Resource
   SessionContext beanContext;

   //-------------------------------------------------------------------------||
   // Required Implementations -----------------------------------------------||
   //-------------------------------------------------------------------------||

   /**
    * Caches the intercepted invocation in an auditable view such that
    * it may later be obtained
    */
   @AroundInvoke
   public Object audit(final InvocationContext invocationContext) throws Exception
   {
      // Precondition checks
      assert invocationContext != null : "Context was not specified";

      // Obtain the caller
      Principal caller;
```

```java
        try
        {
            caller = beanContext.getCallerPrincipal();
        }
        catch (final NullPointerException npe)
        {
            caller = new Principal()
            {

                @Override
                public String getName()
                {
                    return "Unauthenticated Caller";
                }
            };
        }

        // Create a new view
        final AuditedInvocation audit = new AuditedInvocation(invocationContext,
caller);

        // Add the invocation to the cache
        invocations.add(audit);

        // Carry out the invocation, noting where we've intercepted before and after
the call (around it)
        try
        {
            // Log
            log.info("Intercepted: " + invocationContext);

            // Return
            return invocationContext.proceed();
        }
        finally
        {
            // Log
            log.info("Done with: " + invocationContext);
        }

    }

    //-------------------------------------------------------------------------||
    // Functional Methods ------------------------------------------------------||
    //-------------------------------------------------------------------------||

    /**
     * Returns a read-only view of the {@link InvocationContext}
     * cached by this interceptor
     */
    public static List<AuditedInvocation> getInvocations()
    {
```

```
        // Copy on export
        return Collections.unmodifiableList(invocations);
    }

    /**
     * Test-only hook to clear the invocations
     */
    static void clearInTesting()
    {
        invocations.clear();
    }
}
```

Channel2AccessPolicy.java

```java
package org.jboss.ejb3.examples.ch18.tuner;

/**
 * Defines the authoritative policy governing whether or not
 * Channel 2 should be currently accessible
 *
 * @author <a href="mailto:andrew.rubinger@jboss.org">ALR</a>
 * @version $Revision: $
 */
public class Channel2AccessPolicy
{

    //-------------------------------------------------------------------------||
    // Class Members ----------------------------------------------------------||
    //-------------------------------------------------------------------------||

    /**
     * Flag dictating whether or not Channel 2 should be shown
     */
    private static boolean channel2Permitted = false;

    //-------------------------------------------------------------------------||
    // Constructor ------------------------------------------------------------||
    //-------------------------------------------------------------------------||

    /**
     * No instantiation
     */
    private Channel2AccessPolicy()
    {
        throw new UnsupportedOperationException("No instances permitted");
    }
```

```
//----------------------------------------------------------------------||
// Functional Methods -------------------------------------------------||
//----------------------------------------------------------------------||

/**
 * Returns whether or not requests to view Channel 2 will be honored
 */
public static boolean isChannel2Permitted()
{
    return channel2Permitted;
}

/**
 * Returns whether or not requests to view Channel 2 will be honored
 */
public static void setChannel2Permitted(final boolean channel2Permitted)
{
    Channel2AccessPolicy.channel2Permitted = channel2Permitted;
}
}
```

Channel2ClosedException.java

```java
package org.jboss.ejb3.examples.ch18.tuner;

import javax.ejb.ApplicationException;

/**
 * Denotes that Channel 2 is not currently available for viewing
 *
 * @author <a href="mailto:andrew.rubinger@jboss.org">ALR</a>
 * @version $Revision: $
 */
@ApplicationException
// Denotes that this exception type should be returned to the client as-is, not
wrapped
public class Channel2ClosedException extends Exception
{

    //----------------------------------------------------------------------||
    // Class Members -------------------------------------------------------||
    //----------------------------------------------------------------------||

    /**
     * serialVersionUID
     */
    private static final long serialVersionUID = 1L;

    /**
     * The sole instance, this type has no state
     */
```

```
    public static final Channel2ClosedException INSTANCE;
    static
    {
        INSTANCE = new Channel2ClosedException();
    }

    /**
     * Message for all incoming Exceptions
     */
    private static final String MSG = "Channel 2 is not currently available for
viewing";

    //-------------------------------------------------------------------------||
    // Constructor ------------------------------------------------------------||
    //-------------------------------------------------------------------------||

    /**
     * Constructs a new instance
     */
    private Channel2ClosedException()
    {
        super(MSG);
    }
}
```

Channel2Restrictor.java

```
package org.jboss.ejb3.examples.ch18.tuner;

import java.lang.reflect.Method;
import java.util.logging.Logger;

import javax.interceptor.AroundInvoke;
import javax.interceptor.InvocationContext;

/**
 * Aspect which restricts access to Channel 2 unless
 * the network has allowed broadcasting.
 *
 * @author <a href="mailto:andrew.rubinger@jboss.org">ALR</a>
 * @version $Revision: $
 */
public class Channel2Restrictor
{

    //-------------------------------------------------------------------------||
    // Class Members ----------------------------------------------------------||
    //-------------------------------------------------------------------------||

    /**
     * Logger
     */
    private static final Logger log = Logger.getLogger(Channel2Restrictor.class.
getName());
```

```java
/**
 * Name of the method to request channel content
 */
private static final String METHOD_NAME_GET_CHANNEL;
static
{
    METHOD_NAME_GET_CHANNEL = TunerLocalBusiness.class.getMethods()[0].getName();
}

//-------------------------------------------------------------------------||
// Required Implementations -----------------------------------------------||
//-------------------------------------------------------------------------||

/**
 * Examines the specified request to determine if the caller is attempting
 * to obtain content for Channel 2.  If so, and Channel 2 is currently closed,
 * will block the request, instead throwing {@link Channel2ClosedException}
 */
@AroundInvoke
public Object checkAccessibility(final InvocationContext context) throws
Exception
{
    // Precondition checks
    assert context != null : "Context was not specified";

    // See if we're requesting Channel 2
    if (isRequestForChannel2(context))
    {
        // See if Channel 2 is open
        if (!Channel2AccessPolicy.isChannel2Permitted())
        {
            // Block access
            throw Channel2ClosedException.INSTANCE;
        }
    }

    // Otherwise carry on
    return context.proceed();
}

//-------------------------------------------------------------------------||
// Functional Methods -----------------------------------------------------||
//-------------------------------------------------------------------------||

/**
 * Determines whether or not the specified context represents a request for
 * Channel 2
 */
private static boolean isRequestForChannel2(final InvocationContext context)
{
    // Precondition check
    assert context != null : "Context was not specified";
```

```
            // Get the target method
            final Method targetMethod = context.getMethod();

            // If we're requesting a new channel
            final String targetMethodName = targetMethod.getName();
            if (targetMethodName.equals(METHOD_NAME_GET_CHANNEL))
            {
                log.info("This is a request for channel content: " + context);
                // Get the requested channel
                final int channel = ((Integer) context.getParameters()[0]).intValue();
                if (channel == 2)
                {
                    // Yep, they want channel 2
                    return true;
                }
            }

            // Return
            return false;
        }
}
```

TunerBean.java

```
package org.jboss.ejb3.examples.ch18.tuner;

import java.io.IOException;
import java.io.InputStream;
import java.util.logging.Logger;

import javax.ejb.Local;
import javax.ejb.Stateless;
import javax.interceptor.Interceptors;
import javax.interceptor.InvocationContext;

/**
 * Simple EJB which returns references back to the client.  Used to
 * show configuration of interceptors; here we've configured the
 * {@link CachingAuditor} to remember all previous
 * {@link InvocationContext}s made upon the EJB.
 *
 * @author <a href="mailto:andrew.rubinger@jboss.org">ALR</a>
 * @version $Revision: $
 */
@Stateless
// Class-level interceptors will be run upon requests to every method of this EJB
@Interceptors(CachingAuditor.class)
@Local(TunerLocalBusiness.class)
public class TunerBean implements TunerLocalBusiness
{
```

```
        //------------------------------------------------------------------------||
        // Class Members --------------------------------------------------------||
        //------------------------------------------------------------------------||

        /**
         * Logger
         */
        private static final Logger log = Logger.getLogger(TunerBean.class.getName());

        //------------------------------------------------------------------------||
        // Required Implementations ---------------------------------------------||
        //------------------------------------------------------------------------||

        /**
         * {@inheritDoc}
         * @see org.jboss.ejb3.examples.ch18.tuner.TunerLocalBusiness#getChannel(int)
         */
        // Here we declare method-level interceptors, which will only take place on
this method
        @Interceptors(Channel2Restrictor.class)
        @Override
        public InputStream getChannel(final int channel) throws IllegalArgumentException
        {
            // Declare the stream we'll use
            final InputStream stream;
            switch (channel)
            {
                // We want channel 1
                case 1 :
                    stream = new InputStream()
                    {

                        @Override
                        public int read() throws IOException
                        {
                            return 1;
                        }
                    };
                    break;
                // We want channel 2
                case 2 :
                    stream = new InputStream()
                    {

                        @Override
                        public int read() throws IOException
                        {
                            return 2;
                        }
                    };
                    break;
```

```
                    // We've requested an improper channel
                    default :
                        throw new IllegalArgumentException("Not a valid channel: " + channel);
                }

                // Return
                log.info("Returning stream for Channel " + channel + ": " + stream);
                return stream;
            }
        }
```

TunerLocalBusiness.java

```java
package org.jboss.ejb3.examples.ch18.tuner;

import java.io.InputStream;

/**
 * Local business interface of an EJB which
 * provides access to television streams
 *
 * @author <a href="mailto:andrew.rubinger@jboss.org">ALR</a>
 * @version $Revision: $
 */
public interface TunerLocalBusiness
{
    //-------------------------------------------------------------------------||
    // Contracts -------------------------------------------------------------||
    //-------------------------------------------------------------------------||

    /**
     * Obtains the stream containing viewable content
     * for the specified television channel.  Supported channels are 1 and 2.
     *
     * @param channel
     * @return
     * @throws IllegalArgumentException If the channel is not valid
     */
    InputStream getChannel(int channel) throws IllegalArgumentException;

}
```

Test Resources

CachingInterceptorUnitTestCase.java

```java
package org.jboss.ejb3.examples.ch18.tuner;

import java.security.Identity;
import java.security.Principal;
import java.util.Properties;
import java.util.logging.Logger;

import javax.ejb.EJBHome;
```

```java
import javax.ejb.EJBLocalHome;
import javax.ejb.EJBLocalObject;
import javax.ejb.EJBObject;
import javax.ejb.SessionContext;
import javax.ejb.TimerService;
import javax.interceptor.InvocationContext;
import javax.transaction.UserTransaction;
import javax.xml.rpc.handler.MessageContext;

import junit.framework.TestCase;

import org.jboss.ejb3.examples.ch18.tuner.AuditedInvocation;
import org.jboss.ejb3.examples.ch18.tuner.CachingAuditor;
import org.jboss.ejb3.examples.ch18.tuner.TunerLocalBusiness;
import org.junit.Before;
import org.junit.Test;

/**
 * Tests to ensure that the {@link CachingAuditor}
 * interceptor is working as expected outside the context
 * of a full container.
 *
 * @author <a href="mailto:andrew.rubinger@jboss.org">ALR</a>
 * @version $Revision: $
 */
public class CachingInterceptorUnitTestCase
{

   //-------------------------------------------------------------------------||
   // Class Members ----------------------------------------------------------||
   //-------------------------------------------------------------------------||

   /**
    * Logger
    */
   private static final Logger log = Logger.getLogger(CachingInterceptorUnitTest
Case.class.getName());

   /**
    * Name of the mock user
    */
   private static String NAME_PRINCIPAL = "Mock User";

   /**
    * Principal to return
    */
   private Principal PRINCIPAL = new Principal()
   {

      @Override
      public String getName()
      {
         return NAME_PRINCIPAL;
      }
   };
```

```
//-----------------------------------------------------------------------||
// Instance Members ------------------------------------------------------||
//-----------------------------------------------------------------------||

/**
 * The interceptor instance to test
 */
private CachingAuditor interceptor;

//-----------------------------------------------------------------------||
// Lifecycle -------------------------------------------------------------||
//-----------------------------------------------------------------------||

/**
 * Creates the interceptor instance to be used in testing
 */
@Before
public void createInterceptor()
{
    interceptor = new CachingAuditor();
    // Manually set the EJBContext to a mock view which only supports returning
a principal
    interceptor.beanContext = new SessionContext()
    {

        /**
         * Exception to throw if we invoke any method aside from getCaller
Principal
         */
        private UnsupportedOperationException UNSUPPORTED = new Unsupported
OperationException(
                "Not supported in mock implementation");

        @Override
        public void setRollbackOnly() throws IllegalStateException
        {
            throw UNSUPPORTED;

        }

        @Override
        public Object lookup(String arg0) throws IllegalArgumentException
        {
            throw UNSUPPORTED;
        }

        @Override
        public boolean isCallerInRole(String arg0)
        {
            throw UNSUPPORTED;
        }

        @Override
        @SuppressWarnings("deprecation")
```

```java
public boolean isCallerInRole(Identity arg0)
{
    throw UNSUPPORTED;
}

@Override
public UserTransaction getUserTransaction() throws IllegalStateException
{
    throw UNSUPPORTED;
}

@Override
public TimerService getTimerService() throws IllegalStateException
{
    throw UNSUPPORTED;
}

@Override
public boolean getRollbackOnly() throws IllegalStateException
{
    throw UNSUPPORTED;
}

@Override
public Properties getEnvironment()
{
    throw UNSUPPORTED;
}

@Override
public EJBLocalHome getEJBLocalHome()
{
    throw UNSUPPORTED;
}

@Override
public EJBHome getEJBHome()
{
    throw UNSUPPORTED;
}

@Override
public Principal getCallerPrincipal()
{
    return PRINCIPAL;
}

@Override
@SuppressWarnings("deprecation")
public Identity getCallerIdentity()
{
    throw UNSUPPORTED;
}

@Override
```

```java
        public <T> T getBusinessObject(Class<T> businessInterface) throws
IllegalStateException
        {
            throw UNSUPPORTED;
        }

        @Override
        public EJBLocalObject getEJBLocalObject() throws IllegalStateException
        {
            throw UNSUPPORTED;
        }

        @Override
        public EJBObject getEJBObject() throws IllegalStateException
        {
            throw UNSUPPORTED;
        }

        @Override
        public Class<?> getInvokedBusinessInterface() throws IllegalStateException
        {
            throw UNSUPPORTED;
        }

        @Override
        public MessageContext getMessageContext() throws IllegalStateException
        {
            throw UNSUPPORTED;
        }

        @Override
        public boolean isCancelled() throws IllegalStateException
        {
            throw UNSUPPORTED;
        }
    };
}

//-------------------------------------------------------------------------||
// Tests ------------------------------------------------------------------||
//-------------------------------------------------------------------------||

/**
 * Ensures that contexts passed through the interceptor are cached
 */
@Test
public void testCache() throws Exception
{
    // Ensure the cache is empty to start
    TestCase.assertEquals("Cache should start empty", 0, CachingAuditor.get
Invocations().size());

    // Invoke
    final InvocationContext invocation = new MockInvocationContext(TunerLocal
Business.class.getMethods()[0],
```

```
            new Object[]
            {1});
      interceptor.audit(invocation);

      // Test our invocation was cached properly
      TestCase.assertEquals("Cache should have the first invocation", 1, Caching
Auditor.getInvocations().size());
      final AuditedInvocation audit = CachingAuditor.getInvocations().get(0);
      TestCase.assertEquals("Invocation cached was not the one that was invoked",
  invocation, audit.getContext());
      TestCase.assertEquals("Invocation did not store the caller as expected",
PRINCIPAL, audit.getCaller());
   }

}
```

Channel2RestrictorUnitTestCase.java

```java
package org.jboss.ejb3.examples.ch18.tuner;

import java.lang.reflect.Method;
import java.util.logging.Logger;

import javax.interceptor.InvocationContext;

import junit.framework.TestCase;

import org.jboss.ejb3.examples.ch18.tuner.Channel2AccessPolicy;
import org.jboss.ejb3.examples.ch18.tuner.Channel2ClosedException;
import org.jboss.ejb3.examples.ch18.tuner.Channel2Restrictor;
import org.jboss.ejb3.examples.ch18.tuner.TunerLocalBusiness;
import org.junit.Before;
import org.junit.Test;

/**
 * Tests to ensure that the {@link Channel2Restrictor}
 * interceptor is working as expected outside the context
 * of a full container.
 *
 * @author <a href="mailto:andrew.rubinger@jboss.org">ALR</a>
 * @version $Revision: $
 */
public class Channel2RestrictorUnitTestCase
{

   //-------------------------------------------------------------------------||
   // Class Members ----------------------------------------------------------||
   //-------------------------------------------------------------------------||

   /**
    * Logger
    */
   private static final Logger log = Logger.getLogger(Channel2RestrictorUnitTest
Case.class.getName());
```

```
/**
 * Method to get channel content
 */
private static final Method METHOD_GET_CHANNEL = TunerLocalBusiness.class.get
Methods()[0];

//-------------------------------------------------------------------------||
// Instance Members -------------------------------------------------------||
//-------------------------------------------------------------------------||

/**
 * The interceptor instance to test
 */
private Channel2Restrictor interceptor;

//-------------------------------------------------------------------------||
// Lifecycle --------------------------------------------------------------||
//-------------------------------------------------------------------------||

/**
 * Creates the interceptor instance to be used in testing
 */
@Before
public void createInterceptor()
{
    interceptor = new Channel2Restrictor();
}

//-------------------------------------------------------------------------||
// Tests ------------------------------------------------------------------||
//-------------------------------------------------------------------------||

/**
 * Ensures requests for channel 2 are blocked when the channel's access is
closed
 */
@Test(expected = Channel2ClosedException.class)
public void requestsToChannel2Blocked() throws Exception
{
    // Set the access policy to block
    Channel2AccessPolicy.setChannel2Permitted(false);

    // Invoke
    final InvocationContext invocation = new MockInvocationContext(METHOD_GET_
CHANNEL, new Object[]
    {2});
    interceptor.checkAccessibility(invocation);
}

/**
 * Ensures requests for channel 2 are not blocked when the channel's access is
open
 */
@Test
public void requestsToChannel2NotBlocked() throws Exception
```

```
        {
            // Set the access policy to block
            Channel2AccessPolicy.setChannel2Permitted(true);

            // Invoke
            final InvocationContext invocation = new MockInvocationContext(METHOD_GET_
CHANNEL, new Object[]
            {2});
            try
            {
                interceptor.checkAccessibility(invocation);
            }
            catch (final Channel2ClosedException e)
            {
                TestCase.fail("Should not have been blocked with: " + e);
            }
        }

        /**
         * Ensures requests for channel 1 are not blocked channel 2's access is closed
         */
        @Test
        public void requestsToChannel1NeverBlocked() throws Exception
        {
            // Set the access policy to block
            Channel2AccessPolicy.setChannel2Permitted(false);

            // Invoke
            final InvocationContext invocation = new MockInvocationContext(METHOD_GET_
CHANNEL, new Object[]
            {1});
            interceptor.checkAccessibility(invocation);
        }

}
```

InterceptorIntegrationTest.java

```
package org.jboss.ejb3.examples.ch18.tuner;

import java.io.IOException;
import java.io.InputStream;
import java.lang.reflect.UndeclaredThrowableException;
import java.util.logging.Logger;

import javax.ejb.EJB;
import javax.interceptor.Interceptors;
import javax.naming.NamingException;

import junit.framework.TestCase;

import org.jboss.arquillian.api.Deployment;
import org.jboss.arquillian.junit.Arquillian;
import org.jboss.ejb3.examples.ch18.tuner.CachingAuditor;
import org.jboss.ejb3.examples.ch18.tuner.Channel2AccessPolicy;
```

```
import org.jboss.ejb3.examples.ch18.tuner.Channel2ClosedException;
import org.jboss.ejb3.examples.ch18.tuner.Channel2Restrictor;
import org.jboss.ejb3.examples.ch18.tuner.TunerBean;
import org.jboss.ejb3.examples.ch18.tuner.TunerLocalBusiness;
import org.jboss.shrinkwrap.api.ShrinkWrap;
import org.jboss.shrinkwrap.api.spec.JavaArchive;
import org.junit.After;
import org.junit.Test;
import org.junit.runner.RunWith;

/**
 * Integration test ensuring that an EJB with {@link Interceptors}
 * declared are intercepted when invoked
 *
 * @author <a href="mailto:andrew.rubinger@jboss.org">ALR</a>
 * @version $Revision: $
 */
@RunWith(Arquillian.class)
public class InterceptionIntegrationTest
{

   //-------------------------------------------------------------------------||
   // Class Members ----------------------------------------------------------||
   //-------------------------------------------------------------------------||

   /**
    * Logger
    */
   private static final Logger log = Logger.getLogger(InterceptionIntegrationTest
.class.getName());

   //-------------------------------------------------------------------------||
   // Instance Members -------------------------------------------------------||
   //-------------------------------------------------------------------------||

   /**
    * Archive representing the deployment
    */
   @Deployment
   public static JavaArchive createDeployment()
   {
      final JavaArchive deployment = ShrinkWrap.create("echo.jar", JavaArchive.
class).addClasses(
            TunerLocalBusiness.class, TunerBean.class, CachingAuditor.class,
Channel2Restrictor.class);
      log.info(deployment.toString(true));
      return deployment;
   }

   /**
    * The bean to invoke upon
    */
   @EJB
   private TunerLocalBusiness bean;
```

```
//-------------------------------------------------------------------------||
// Lifecycle -------------------------------------------------------------||
//-------------------------------------------------------------------------||

/**
 * Cleanup
 */
@After
public void clearInvocationsAfterTest()
{
   // Clean up
   CachingAuditor.clearInTesting();
}

//-------------------------------------------------------------------------||
// Tests -----------------------------------------------------------------||
//-------------------------------------------------------------------------||

/**
 * Ensures that invocation upon an EJB with {@link CachingAuditor} declared
 * results in the interception of targeted methods
 */
@Test
public void testCachingInterception() throws NamingException, IOException
{
   // Ensure no invocations intercepted yet
   TestCase.assertEquals("No invocations should have yet been intercepted", 0,
CachingAuditor.getInvocations()
         .size());

   // Invoke
   final int channel = 1;
   final InputStream content = bean.getChannel(channel);

   // Test the response is as expected
   TestCase.assertEquals("Did not obtain expected response", channel, content.
read());

   // Test the invocation was intercepted
   TestCase.assertEquals("The invocation should have been intercepted", 1,
CachingAuditor.getInvocations().size());
}

/**
 * Ensures that requests to obtain Channel 2 while restricted are blocked with
 * {@link Channel2ClosedException}
 */
@Test(expected = Channel2ClosedException.class)
public void testChannel2Restricted() throws Throwable
{
   // Set the policy to block channel 2
   Channel2AccessPolicy.setChannel2Permitted(false);

   // Invoke
   try
```

```
        {
            bean.getChannel(2);
        }
        // Expected
        catch (final UndeclaredThrowableException ute)
        {
            throw ute.getCause();
        }

        // Fail if we reach here
        TestCase.fail("Request should have been blocked");
    }

    /**
     * Ensures that requests to obtain Channel 2 while open succeed
     */
    @Test
    public void testChannel2Allowed() throws NamingException, IOException
    {
        // Set the policy to block channel 2
        Channel2AccessPolicy.setChannel2Permitted(true);

        // Invoke
        final int channel = 2;
        final InputStream stream = bean.getChannel(channel);

        // Test
        TestCase.assertEquals("Unexpected content obtained from channel " + channel
, channel, stream.read());
    }
}
```

MockInvocationContext.java

```
package org.jboss.ejb3.examples.ch18.tuner;

import java.lang.reflect.Method;
import java.util.Map;

import javax.interceptor.InvocationContext;

/**
 * {@link InvocationContext} implementation which throws {@link Unsupported
OperationException}
 * for all required methods except {@link InvocationContext#proceed()}, which
will always return null,
 * {@link InvocationContext#getMethod()}, and {@link InvocationContext#get
Parameters()}.
 *
 * @author <a href="mailto:andrew.rubinger@jboss.org">ALR</a>
 * @version $Revision: $
 */
class MockInvocationContext implements InvocationContext
{
```

```
//---------------------------------------------------------------------||
// Class Members -------------------------------------------------------||
//---------------------------------------------------------------------||

/**
 * Message used to denote that the operation is not supported
 */
private static final String MSG_UNSUPPORTED = "Not supported in mock implement
ation";

//---------------------------------------------------------------------||
// Instance Members ----------------------------------------------------||
//---------------------------------------------------------------------||

/**
 * Method invoked
 */
private final Method method;

/**
 * Parameters in the request
 */
private final Object[] params;

//---------------------------------------------------------------------||
// Constructor ---------------------------------------------------------||
//---------------------------------------------------------------------||

/**
 * Constructs a new instance with the specified required arguments
 * @param method
 * @param params
 */
MockInvocationContext(final Method method, final Object[] params)
{

    assert method != null : "method must be specified";
    assert params != null : "params must be specified";
    this.method = method;
    this.params = params;
}

//---------------------------------------------------------------------||
// Required Implementations --------------------------------------------||
//---------------------------------------------------------------------||

@Override
public Map<String, Object> getContextData()
{
    throw new UnsupportedOperationException(MSG_UNSUPPORTED);
}
```

```java
    @Override
    public Method getMethod()
    {
        return method;
    }

    @Override
    public Object[] getParameters()
    {
        return params;
    }

    @Override
    public Object getTarget()
    {
        throw new UnsupportedOperationException(MSG_UNSUPPORTED);
    }

    @Override
    public Object proceed() throws Exception
    {
        return null;
    }

    @Override
    public void setParameters(final Object[] arg0)
    {
        throw new UnsupportedOperationException(MSG_UNSUPPORTED);
    }
}
```

SecurityActions.java

```java
package org.jboss.ejb3.examples.ch18.tuner;

import java.security.AccessController;
import java.security.PrivilegedAction;

/**
 * Protected security actions not to leak outside this package
 *
 * @author <a href="mailto:andrew.rubinger@jboss.org">ALR</a>
 * @version $Revision: $
 */
class SecurityActions
{

    //-------------------------------------------------------------------------||
    // Constructor -----------------------------------------------------------||
    //-------------------------------------------------------------------------||
```

```java
    /**
     * No external instantiation
     */
    private SecurityActions()
    {

    }

    //-----------------------------------------------------------------------||
    // Utility Methods ------------------------------------------------------||
    //-----------------------------------------------------------------------||

    /**
     * Obtains the Thread Context ClassLoader
     */
    static ClassLoader getThreadContextClassLoader()
    {
        return AccessController.doPrivileged(GetTcclAction.INSTANCE);
    }

    /**
     * Sets the specified CL upon the current Thread's Context
     *
     * @param cl
     * @throws IllegalArgumentException If the CL was null
     */
    static void setThreadContextClassLoader(final ClassLoader cl) throws Illegal
ArgumentException
    {
        if (cl == null)
        {
            throw new IllegalArgumentException("ClassLoader was null");
        }

        AccessController.doPrivileged(new PrivilegedAction<Void>()
        {
            public Void run()
            {
                Thread.currentThread().setContextClassLoader(cl);
                return null;
            };
        });
    }

    /**
     * Obtains the system property with the specified key
     *
     * @param key
     * @return
     * @throws IllegalArgumentException If the key is null
     */
    static String getSystemProperty(final String key) throws IllegalArgument
Exception
    {
```

```java
        // Precondition check
        if (key == null)
        {
            throw new IllegalArgumentException("key was null");
        }

        // Get sysprop
        return AccessController.doPrivileged(new GetSystemPropertyAction(key));
    }

    //-------------------------------------------------------------------------||
    // Inner Classes ----------------------------------------------------------||
    //-------------------------------------------------------------------------||

    /**
     * {@link PrivilegedAction} action to obtain the TCCL
     */
    private enum GetTcclAction implements PrivilegedAction<ClassLoader> {
        INSTANCE;

        @Override
        public ClassLoader run()
        {
            return Thread.currentThread().getContextClassLoader();
        }
    }

    /**
     * {@link PrivilegedAction} to access a system property
     *
     *
     * @author <a href="mailto:andrew.rubinger@jboss.org">ALR</a>
     * @version $Revision: $
     */
    private static class GetSystemPropertyAction implements PrivilegedAction<String>
    {

        /**
         * Name of the sysprop to get
         */
        private String sysPropName;

        /**
         * Creates a new instance capable of obtaining the specified system
property by name
         * @param sysPropName
         */
        public GetSystemPropertyAction(final String sysPropName)
        {
            this.sysPropName = sysPropName;
        }
```

```
    /**
     * {@inheritDoc}
     * @see java.security.PrivilegedAction#run()
     */
    @Override
    public String run()
    {
        return System.getProperty(sysPropName);
    }
}

}
```

Timer Service: Credit Card Processor Example

Description

As we've seen with message-driven beans, a client request is not the only way to start a business taskflow. In addition to listening on incoming messages like MDB, events can be fired based on some timed criteria. EJB handles this via the Timer Service.

EJB 3.1 has seen significant advancements to the bean provider's view of the Timer Service with a completely revamped natural-language syntax. This example models a credit card processing operation, which at the beginning of every hour will process all queued transactions. Scheduling the job is done both programmatically via the `javax.ejb.TimerService` API, as well as declaratively via the `@Timeout` and `@Schedule` annotations.

Online Companion Information

Wiki article: *http://community.jboss.org/docs/DOC-15575*

Source location: *http://github.com/jbossejb3/oreilly-ejb-6thedition-book-examples/tree/master/ch19-timer/*

Source Listing

Following is a full listing of all source code used in this runnable example.

Implementation Resources

CreditCardTransaction.java

```java
package org.jboss.ejb3.examples.ch19.timer.api;

import java.math.BigDecimal;

/**
 * Value object representing a single credit card transaction.
 * Immutable.
 *
 * @author <a href="mailto:andrew.rubinger@jboss.org">ALR</a>
 * @version $Revision: $
 */
public class CreditCardTransaction
{
   //-------------------------------------------------------------------||
   // Instance Members -------------------------------------------------||
   //-------------------------------------------------------------------||

   /**
    * The card number
    */
   private final String cardNumber;

   /**
    * The amount to be charged
    */
   private final BigDecimal amount;

   //-------------------------------------------------------------------||
   // Constructor ------------------------------------------------------||
   //-------------------------------------------------------------------||

   /**
    * Creates a new instance with the specified card number and amount
    * @param cardNumber
    * @param amount
    * @throws IllegalArgumentException If either argument is null
    */
   public CreditCardTransaction(final String cardNumber, final BigDecimal amount)
      throws IllegalArgumentException
   {
      // Precondition checks
      if (cardNumber == null || cardNumber.length() == 0)
      {
         throw new IllegalArgumentException("card number must be specified");
      }
      if (amount == null)
      {
         throw new IllegalArgumentException("amount must be specified");
      }

      // Set
```

```
            this.amount = amount;
            this.cardNumber = cardNumber;
        }

        //------------------------------------------------------------------||
        // Required Implementations ---------------------------------------||
        //------------------------------------------------------------------||

        /**
         * {@inheritDoc}
         * @see java.lang.Object#toString()
         */
        @Override
        public String toString()
        {
            return "CreditCardTransaction [amount=" + amount + ", cardNumber=" + card
Number + "]";
        }

        //------------------------------------------------------------------||
        // Functional Methods ---------------------------------------------||
        //------------------------------------------------------------------||

        /**
         * @return the cardNumber
         */
        public String getCardNumber()
        {
            return cardNumber;
        }

        /**
         * @return the amount
         */
        public BigDecimal getAmount()
        {
            return amount;
        }
    }
```

CreditCardTransactionProcessingLocalBusiness.java

```
package org.jboss.ejb3.examples.ch19.timer.api;

import java.util.Date;
import java.util.List;

import javax.ejb.ScheduleExpression;
import javax.ejb.Timer;

/**
 * Contract of a service capable of storing a series
 * of {@link CreditCardTransaction}s to be processed,
 * scheduling processing, and processing payment of
 * all pending transactions.
```

```
 *
 * @author <a href="mailto:andrew.rubinger@jboss.org">ALR</a>
 * @version $Revision: $
 */
public interface CreditCardTransactionProcessingLocalBusiness
{
   //-----------------------------------------------------------------------||
   // Contracts -------------------------------------------------------------||
   //-----------------------------------------------------------------------||

   /**
    * Returns an immutable view of all transactions
    * pending processing
    * @return
    */
   List<CreditCardTransaction> getPendingTransactions();

   /**
    * Proceses all pending {@link CreditCardTransaction}s,
    * clearing them from the pending list when complete
    */
   void process();

   /**
    * Adds the specified {@link CreditCardTransaction} to be processed
    * @param transaction
    * @throws IllegalArgumentException If the transaction is null
    */
   void add(CreditCardTransaction transaction) throws IllegalArgumentException;

   /**
    * Schedules a new {@link Timer} to process pending payments
    * according to the supplied {@link ScheduleExpression}.  Returns
    * the {@link Date} representing when the next job is to fire.
    * @param expression
    * @return
    * @throws IllegalArgumentException If the expression is null
    */
   Date scheduleProcessing(ScheduleExpression expression) throws IllegalArgument
Exception;
}
```

CreditCardTransactionProcessingBean.java

```
package org.jboss.ejb3.examples.ch19.timer.impl;

import java.util.ArrayList;
import java.util.Collections;
import java.util.Date;
import java.util.List;
import java.util.logging.Logger;

import javax.annotation.Resource;
import javax.ejb.ConcurrencyManagement;
import javax.ejb.ConcurrencyManagementType;
```

```
import javax.ejb.Local;
import javax.ejb.Lock;
import javax.ejb.LockType;
import javax.ejb.Schedule;
import javax.ejb.ScheduleExpression;
import javax.ejb.SessionContext;
import javax.ejb.Singleton;
import javax.ejb.Timeout;
import javax.ejb.Timer;
import javax.ejb.TimerService;

import org.jboss.ejb3.examples.ch19.timer.api.CreditCardTransaction;
import org.jboss.ejb3.examples.ch19.timer.api.CreditCardTransactionProcessing
LocalBusiness;

/**
 * Implementation of a Service capable of storing pending
 * {@link CreditCardTransaction}s for later processing.
 * These may either be processed via a business call to
 * {@link CreditCardTransactionProcessingLocalBusiness#process()}
 * or via any number of configured timers using the EJB Timer Service.
 * At deployment, a default timer will be set to run
 * every hour on the hour (as configured by the {@link Schedule}
 * annotation atop {@link CreditCardTransactionProcessingBean#processViaTimeout
(Timer)}.
 * The {@link CreditCardTransactionProcessingBean#scheduleProcessing(Schedule
Expression)}
 * method shows programmatic creation of timers given a supplied
 * {@link ScheduleExpression}.
 *
 * @author <a href="mailto:andrew.rubinger@jboss.org">ALR</a>
 * @version $Revision: $
 */
@Singleton
@Local(CreditCardTransactionProcessingLocalBusiness.class)
@ConcurrencyManagement(ConcurrencyManagementType.CONTAINER)
public class CreditCardTransactionProcessingBean implements CreditCardTransaction
ProcessingLocalBusiness
{

   //-------------------------------------------------------------------------||
   // Class Members ----------------------------------------------------------||
   //-------------------------------------------------------------------------||

   /**
    * Logger
    */
   private static final Logger log = Logger.getLogger(CreditCardTransaction
ProcessingBean.class.getName());

   /**
    * Wildcard denoting "all" in timer expressions
    */
   private static final String EVERY = "*";
```

```java
/**
 * Timer value denoting 0
 */
private static final String ZERO = "0";

//-------------------------------------------------------------------------||
// Instance Members -------------------------------------------------------||
//-------------------------------------------------------------------------||

/**
 * {@link SessionContext} hook to the EJB Container;
 * from here we may obtain a {@link TimerService} via
 * {@link SessionContext#getTimerService()}.
 */
@Resource
private SessionContext context;

/**
 * We can directly inject the {@link TimerService} as well.
 */
@Resource
@SuppressWarnings("unused")
// Just for example
private TimerService timerService;

/**
 * {@link List} of all pending transactions.  Guarded
 * by the concurrency policies of this EJB.
 */
private final List<CreditCardTransaction> pendingTransactions = new ArrayList
<CreditCardTransaction>();

//-------------------------------------------------------------------------||
// Functional Methods -----------------------------------------------------||
//-------------------------------------------------------------------------||

@Timeout
// Mark this method as the EJB timeout method for timers created
programmatically.  If we're
// just creating a timer via @Schedule, @Timer is not required.
@Schedule(dayOfMonth = EVERY, month = EVERY, year = EVERY, second = ZERO,
minute = ZERO, hour = EVERY)
// This timeout will be created on deployment and fire every hour on the hour;
 declarative creation
@Lock(LockType.WRITE)
public void processViaTimeout(final Timer timer)
{
    // Just delegate to the business method
    this.process();
}

//-------------------------------------------------------------------------||
// Required Implementations -----------------------------------------------||
//-------------------------------------------------------------------------||
```

```java
   /**
    * {@inheritDoc}
    * @see org.jboss.ejb3.examples.ch19.timer.api.CreditCardTransactionProcessing
LocalBusiness#add(org.jboss.ejb3.examples.ch19.timer.api.CreditCardTransaction)
    */
   @Override
   @Lock(LockType.WRITE)
   public void add(final CreditCardTransaction transaction) throws Illegal
ArgumentException
   {
      // Precondition check
      if (transaction == null)
      {
         throw new IllegalArgumentException("transaction must be specified");
      }

      // Add
      this.pendingTransactions.add(transaction);
      log.info("Added transaction pending to be processed: " + transaction);
   }

   /**
    * {@inheritDoc}
    * @see org.jboss.ejb3.examples.ch19.timer.api.CreditCardTransactionProcessing
LocalBusiness#getPendingTransactions()
    */
   @Override
   @Lock(LockType.READ)
   public List<CreditCardTransaction> getPendingTransactions()
   {
      // Return immutable so callers can't modify our internal state
      return Collections.unmodifiableList(pendingTransactions);
   }

   /**
    * {@inheritDoc}
    * @see org.jboss.ejb3.examples.ch19.timer.api.CreditCardTransactionProcessing
LocalBusiness#process()
    */
   @Override
   @Lock(LockType.WRITE)
   public void process()
   {
      // Process all pending transactions
      for (final CreditCardTransaction transaction : pendingTransactions)
      {
         // Fake it, we're not really gonna
         // charge you in the EJB Book examples!
         log.info("Processed transaction: " + transaction);
      }

      // Clear the pending payments as we've "charged" all now
      pendingTransactions.clear();
   }
```

```
    /**
     * {@inheritDoc}
     * @see org.jboss.ejb3.examples.ch19.timer.api.CreditCardTransactionProcessing
LocalBusiness#scheduleProcessing(javax.ejb.ScheduleExpression)
     */
    @Override
    public Date scheduleProcessing(final ScheduleExpression expression) throws
IllegalArgumentException
    {
        // Precondition checks
        if (expression == null)
        {
            throw new IllegalArgumentException("Timer expression must be specified");
        }

        // Programmatically create a new Timer from the given expression via the
TimerService from the SessionContext
        final TimerService timerService = context.getTimerService();
        final Timer timer = timerService.createCalendarTimer(expression);
        final Date next = timer.getNextTimeout();
        log.info("Created " + timer + " to process transactions; next fire is at: "
 + timer.getNextTimeout());
        return next;
    }
}
```

Index

Symbols

2-PC (two-phase commit), 297
\<binding\> element, 377
\<complexType\> element, 357
\<definitions\> element, 372
\<entity\> element, 154
\<entity-listeners\> element, 238
\<env-entry\> element, 275
\<id\> element, 154
\<injection-target\> element, 260, 268
\<message\> element, 374
\<message-destination-ref\> element, 277
\<persistence-unit-ref\> element, 268
\<portType\> element, 374
\<service\> element, 377
\<service-ref\> deployment element, 388
\<types\> element, 375
@ActivationConfigProperty annotation, 103
@ApplicationException annotation, 315
@AroundInvoke annotation, 325
@AroundInvoke method, 338
@Asynchronous, 60
@AttributeOverrides annotation, 163
@Basic annotation, 164
@Column annotation, 156
@DeclareRoles annotation, 248
@DiscriminatorColumn annotation, 197
@EJB annotation, 259, 264
@Embedded annotation, 167–169
@EmbeddedId annotation, 162
@Entity annotation, 153
@EntityListeners annotation, 237
@Enumerated annotation, 167
@ExcludeClassInterceptors annotation, 331

@ExcludeDefaultInterceptors annotation, 331
@ExcludeDefaultListeners annotation, 238
@ExcludeSuperclassListeners annotation, 239
@FieldResult annotation, 232
@GeneratedValue annotation, 158
@Id annotation, 153, 157
@IdClass annotation, 160
@Inheritance annotation, 197
@Interceptors annotation, 327
@JoinColumn annotation, 174
@Lob annotation, 166
@Local and @Remote annotations, 56
@ManyToMany annotation, 185
@ManyToOne annotation, 181
@MapKey annotation, 189
@MappedSuperclass annotation, 203
@MessageDriven annotation, 103
@NamedNativeQuery annotation, 233
@NamedQuery annotation, 232
@OneToMany annotation, 180
@OneToOne annotation, 174
@OrderBy annotation, 188
@PermitAll annotation, 249
@PersistenceContext annotation, 131
@PersistenceUnit annotation, 267, 270
@PostActivate method, 67, 70
@PostActivate annotation, 72
@PostConstruct annotation, 57, 70, 72, 110
@PostConstruct method, 50
@PreDestroy annotation, 70
    stateless session beans with timers, 352
@PreDestroy method, 51
@PrePassivate annotation, 67
@PrePassivate method, 70
@PrePersist and @PostPersist events, 235

@PreRemove and @PostRemove events, 236
@PreUpdate event, 236
@PrimaryKeyJoinColumn annotation, 175
@Remove method, 71
@Resource annotation, 57, 259
    shareable resources, 274
@Resource annotation, 272
@RolesAllowed annotation, 248
@RunAs annotation, 251
@Schedule annotation, 344
@SequenceGenerator annotation, 159
@SqlResultSetMapping annotation, 231
@Startup annotation, 87
@Stateful annotation, 71
@Table annotation, 156
@Table.uniqueConstraints( ) attribute, 156
@TableGenerator annotation, 158
@Temporal annotation, 166
@Timeout annotation, 345
@TransactionAttribute annotation, 286, 287
@Transient annotation, 164
@Version annotation, 302
@WebService annotation
    endpointInterface( ) attribute, 401
@WebServiceClient annotation, 402
\ (backslash) character, 224
= (equals) operator, 219
> (greater-than) operator, 219
#jboss-dev Freenode IRC Channel, xx
< (less-than) operator, 219
<> (not equals) operator, 219
% (percent) character, 224
_ (underscore) character, 224

A

ABS (number) function, 226
abstract schema names, 211
ACID, 23
ACID transactions, 279–286
    BlackjackEJB example, 281–286
        testing with helper EJBs, 283
    database locks, 299
    isolation, 298
        dirty, repeatable, and phantom reads, 298
    optimistic locking, 302
    performance versus consistency, 301
        controlling isolation levels, 301
    programmatic locking, 303

transaction isolation levels, 300
acknowledgments, 105
ALL CascadeType, 193
AND operator, 219
Apache Ant, 36
Apache Commons FTP Client, 71
app-name, 255
application development, 3
    core concerns, 4
    cross-cutting concerns, 4
    planning, 6
    plumbing, 5
application exceptions, 54, 315
Application Server team, xx
arithmetic operators in WHERE clauses, 219
AS operator, 212
aspects, 4
asynchronous, 99
asynchronous methods, 60
atomicity, 23
atomicity in transactions, 281
    BlackjackEJB example, 284
auditing, 351
Auditor listener, 238
authentication, 243, 244
authenticationType( ) attribute, 273
authorization, 243, 245
AVG( ) function, 227

B

B2B (business-to-business) taskflow and integration, 107
backslash (\) character, 224
batch jobs, 341
batch processing, 351
BEAN concurrency management type, 86
bean implementation class, 29, 34, 55
bean instances, 29
bean provider, 23
bean setter methods, 260
begin( ) method, 309
BETWEEN clause, 221
bidirectional relationships, peculiarities of, 178
built-in types, 357
Burke, Bill, xv, xx
business interfaces, 31, 54
business logic, 4
business objects, 11

C

call-by-value and call-by-reference semantics, 54

callback events, 235

callback( ) method, 310

callbacks on entity classes, 236

cascade( ) attribute, 191–194

ALL CascadeType, 193

MERGE CascadeType, 192

PERSIST CascadeType, 192

REFRESH CascadeType, 193

REMOVE CascadeType, 193

CascadeType, 192

catalog( ) attribute, 156

.class files, 34

Class.newInstance method, 50

clear( ) method, 148, 210

client view, 30

CMC (container-managed concurrency), 86

code reuse, negative example, 323

coding EJBs, 33–39

bean implementation class, 34

contracts, 33

integration testing, 36

client, 37

deployment, 37

packaging, 36

out-of-container testing, 35

coding standards, 6

Collection type, 180

collection-based relationships, mapping, 188

map-based relationships, 189

ordered list-based relationships, 188

commit( ) method, 309

common business names, 32

comparison operators in WHERE clauses, 219

complex native queries, 231

with multiple entries, 231

component interface, 31

component types, 11

server-side component types, 12–16

composite keys, 160

CONCAT (String1, String2) function, 225

concurrency, 21

singleton session beans, 82–87

CONCURRENCY_NOT_SUPPORTED concurrency management type, 86

ConnectionFactory, 116

Connections, 116

consistency, 23

consistency in transactions, 281

BlackjackEJB example, 285

CONTAINER concurrency management type, 86

Container Services, 19–27

container-managed concurrency (see CMC)

containers, 7

container services, 11

contains( ) method, 148

contracts, 33

conversational state, 43, 63

COUNT( ) function, 226

createEntityManager( ) method, 137

createQuery( ) method, 207

createQuery( ), createNamedQuery( ), and createNativeQuery( ) methods, 146

createSession( ) method, 117

Criteria API, 205

CRUD (Create, Read, Update, Delete), 141

cryptographic hashing, 52

CURRENT_DATE, CURRENT_TIME, and CURRENT_TIMESTAMP functions, 226

D

database locks, 299

de Wolf, Carlo, xx

declarative transaction management, 286

transaction attributes, 287

attributes defined, 289–292

EJB 3.0 persistence, 292

EJB endpoints and, 293

MDBs and, 293

transaction propagation, 293

persistence context propagation, 297

transaction scope, 286

DELETE operator, 229

Dependency Injection (see DI)

detached entities, 132, 190

DI (Dependency Injection), 20

dirty reads, 298

DISTINCT keyword, 217

DISTINCT operator

using with aggregate functions, 227

distributed transactions, 297

division of labor, 19

Document/Literal message, 369

DTD (Document Type Definition), 356

durability, 23
durability in transactions, 281
    BlackjackEJB example, 285
dynamic proxies, 382

E

EARs (Enterprise Archives), 36
EJB deployment descriptor
    transaction management using, 286
EJB endpoints, 391
EJB Proxy, 30
EJB QL, 205
EJB references, JNDI ENC, 264–266
EJB Timer Service (see Timer Service)
EJBContext interface, 47, 259
    obsolete methods, 49
    programmatic security using, 250
EJBs (Enterprise JavaBeans)
    coding, 33–39
    composition, 29
    EJB specification, 8
    version 3.1, xvi
    web services and, 381
EJBs (Enterprise JavaBeans) 3.1
    SOAP messaging RPCEncoded mode
        support, 369
ejbTimeout( ) method, 342
Employee class, 152
ENC (Enterprise Naming Context), 57 (see
        JNDI ENC)
EncryptionCommonBusiness interface, 54
EncryptionEJB, 52–59
    accessing environment properties, 57
    application exceptions, 54
    bean implementation class, 55
    contract, 53
endpoint interface, 31
endSession( ) method, 70, 78
enterprise messaging systems, 98
Enterprise Naming Context (see JNDI ENC)
entities, 151
entities, managed versus unmanaged, 130–
        133
    detached entities, 132
    extended persistence context, 132
    persistence context, 130
    transaction-scoped persistence context,
        131
entity beans, 16, 127, 151

entity callbacks, 235
    (see also callback events; entity listeners)
entity inheritance, 195–204
    mixing strategies, 203
    nonentity base classes, 203
    single table per class hierarchy, 196
        advantages and disadvantages, 198
    table per concrete class strategy, 199
        advantages and disadvantages, 200
    table per subclass strategy, 200
        advantages and disadvantages, 203
entity listeners, 235, 237–239
    default listeners, 238
    inheritance, 238
entity relationships, 171–194
    cascading, 191–194
        ALL, 193
        MERGE, 192
        PERSIST, 192
        REFRESH, 193
        REMOVE, 193
        when to use, 194
    detached entities and FetchType, 190
    many-to-many bidirectional relationships,
        184–186
    many-to-many unidirectional relationships,
        187
    many-to-one unidirectional relationships,
        181–182
    mapping collection-based relationships,
        188–190
    one-to-many bidirectional relationships,
        182–183
    one-to-many unidirectional relationships,
        178–181
    one-to-one bidirectional relationships, 176–
        178
    one-to-one unidirectional relationships,
        173–176
    relationship types, 171
EntityManager, 16, 127–149
    interacting with an EntityManager, 140
    obtaining an EntityManager, 136–140
        EntityManagerFactory, 137
        EntityManagerFactory in Java EE, 137
        obtaining a persistence context, 138
    persistence units, packaging, 133–136
        persistence unit class set, 135

persistent employee registry example, 141–149
    finding and updating entities, 144–147
    locking, 149
    persisting entities, 142
    removing entities, 147
    transactional abstraction, 141
    unwrap( ) and getDelegate( ), 149
EntityManager interface
    lock( ) method, 303
    native query methods, 230
EntityManagerFactory references, 266
    XML-based references, 268
EntityNotFoundException, 148
environment entries, 57, 275–276
equals (=) operator, 219
examples workbook, xvii
exceptions
    application exceptions, 54
    system exceptions, 68
exclusive write locks, 299
explicit transaction demarcation, 286
explicit transaction management, 304–312
    EJBContext rollback methods, 312
    heuristic decisions, 308
    Status interface, 310
    transaction propagation, bean-managed transactions, 307–308
    UserTransaction interface, 309
extended persistence context, 132

F

fault message, 374
fetch( ) attribute, 165
    set to FetchType.LAZY, 190
find( ) method, 144
flush( ) method, 148
FlushMode
    using in the query API, 210
FlushModeType enumeration, 149
foreign keys, 173
FQN, 255
FROM clause, 212

G

get ResultList( ) method, 208
getBalance( ) method, 294
getBusinessObject( ) method, 46

getCallerPrincipal( ) method, 48, 250
getDelegate( ) method, 149
getEJBObject( ) and getEJBLocalObject( ) methods, 46
getEntries( ) method, 92
getInvokedBusinessInterface( ) method, 47
getReference( ) method, 144
getResultList( ) method, 213
getRollbackOnly( ) method, 312
getSingleResult( ) method, 207
getStatus( ) method, 310
getter and setter methods, 152, 154
getTimeRemaining( ) method, 350
getTimers( ) method, 348
getTimerService( ) method, 47
Global JNDI, 255
greater-than (>) operator, 219

H

headers, 117
home interface, 31
HTTP tunneling, 370

I

IllegalArgumentException, 145, 148
IN operator, 216, 221
info objects, 349
injection, 57, 255
INNER JOINs, 216
input message, 374
instance pooling, 22
integration, 6
integration testing, 36
interceptors, 26, 323
    applying, 327
        annotated methods and classes, 327
        default interceptors, 329
        through XML, 328
    bean class @AroundInvoke methods, 338
    disabling, 330
    exception handling, 335–338
        aborting a method invocation, 336
        catch and rethrow exceptions, 336
    injection and, 331
    intercepting lifecycle events, 333–335
        custom injection annotations, 333
    intercepting methods, 323
    interceptor class, 325

lifecycles, 338
Interceptors 1.1 Specification, 323
interoperability, 25
interval timers, 347
IS EMPTY operator, 223
IS NULL comparison operator, 222
isCallerInRole( ) method, 48, 250
isolation, 23
isolation in transactions, 281
    BlackjackEJB example, 285
isolation levels
    performance impacts, 301

J

jar tool, 36
JARs (Java Archives), 36
Java Connector Architecture (see JCA)
Java Message Service (see JMS)
Java Naming and Directory Interface (see JNDI)
Java Persistence programming model, xvi, 152–
        155
    bean class, 152
    Employee entity, 152
    inheritance hierarchy mapping, 195
    primary keys (see primary keys)
    property mappings (see property mappings)
    relational mapping (see relational mapping)
    reserved words, 212
    XML mapping files, 154
Java Transaction Service (see JTS)
javax.ejb.SessionContext interface, 46
javax.naming classes, 37
javax.persistence.EntityManager, 16
JAX-RPC (Java API for XML-based RPC), 381–
        396
    <service-ref> deployment element, 388–
            389
    defining web services, 391–396
        deployment files, 394–396
        service endpoint interface, 393
        stateless bean class, 393
        WSDL documents, 392
    EJBs, calling services from, 387–388
    execution loop, 382
    JAX-RPC mapping files, 394
    mapping files, 389
    service endpoint interfaces, 382
    WSDL web service generation, 382–386

XML Schema built-in types and Java types,
        384
JAX-WS (Java API for XML-based Web
        Services), 371, 381, 396–405
    @OneWay annotation, 401
    @SOAPBinding annotation, 398
    @WebMethod annotation, 397
    @WebParam annotation, 399
    @WebResult annotation, 400
    @WebService annotation, 396
    @WebServiceRef annotation, 403
    separating web services contracts, 401
    Service class, 402
    service endpoint interface, 403
JAXB (Java Architecture for XML Binding),
        405
JCA (Java Connector Architecture), 98
    Service Provider Interface, 112
JMS (Java Message Service), 98–103
    acknowledgment mode, 105
    APIs, 115
    asynchronous messaging, 99
    JMS clients, JMS providers, and JMS
            applications, 98
    message types, 117
    messaging models, 100
    supporting messaging systems, 98
JMS gateways, 111
JNDI (Java Naming and Directory Interface),
        25, 37
    authentication using, 245
    ENC (see JNDI ENC)
    Global JNDI, 255
    InitialContext, 245
JNDI ENC
    annotation population, 257
    reference and injection types, 264–278
        EJB references, 264–266
        EntityManager references, 269–271
        EntityManagerFactory references, 266–
                269
        environment entries, 275–276
        message destination references, 277–
                278
        resource environment and administered
                objects, 275
        resource references, 271–274
    referencing from the ENC, 258–263
        annotation injection, 259

default ENC name, 260
  injection and inheritance, 263
  using EJBContext, 259
  XML injection, 260
  XML overrides, 261
what can be registered, 257
XML population, 257
jndi.properties file, 38
JOIN FETCH, 217
JPA (Java Persistence API) Version 2.0, 17, 127
  QL (query language) (see JPA QL)
JPA QL query language, 205, 211–230
  abstract schema names, 211
  bulk UPDATE and DELETE, 229
  constructor expressions, 215
  DISTINCT keyword, 217
  functional expressions, 224
    aggregate function in SELECT, 226
    AVG( ) and SUM( ) functions, 227
    COUNT( ) function, 226
    date and time functions, 226
    DISTINCT, nulls, and empty arguments, 227
    MAX( ) and MIN( ) functions, 226
  IN operator and INNER JOIN, 215
  JOIN FETCH syntax, 217
  LEFT JOIN, 216
  ORDER BY clause, 228
  selection of entity and relationship properties, 213
  simple queries, 212
  WHERE clause (see WHERE clause)
JSR-181, 396
JTA (Java Transaction API), 304
JTS (Java Transaction Service), 23, 304
JUnit testing framework, 35

L

LEFT JOIN, 216
LENGTH (String) function, 225
less-than (<) operator, 219
lifecycle callbacks, 25
LIKE comparison operator, 224
List type, 188
local and remote, 30
local business interfaces, 54
LOCATE (String1, String2 [, start]) function, 225

lock( ) method, 303
LockModeType.READ and LockModeType.WRITE, 303
logical operators in WHERE clauses, 219
lookup APIs, 25
lookup( ) method, 47
LOWER (String) function, 225

M

managed objects, 16
Mandatory attribute, 291
manual lookup, 57
many-to-many bidirectional relationships, 172, 184–186
  programming model, 185
  relational database schema, 184
many-to-many unidirectional relationships, 172, 187–188
  programming model, 187
  relational database schema, 187
many-to-one unidirectional relationships, 172, 181–182
  programming model, 181
  relational database schema, 181
Map interface, 189
mappedby( ) attribute, 177
mappedName( ) attribute, 273
Maven, 36
MAX( ) function, 226
MDBs (message-driven beans), 15, 97–124
  connector-based beans, 111–113
  Java Message Service and, 98–103
  JMS-based beans, 103–108
    @MessageDriven, 103–108
  lifecycle, 108–111
  message linking, 114–124
    JMS APIs, 115
    prohibition of receipt of messages by session beans, 114
    StatusUpdateEJBs example, 118–124
  RunAs security identifier and, 251
MEMBER OF operator, 223
MERGE CascadeType, 192
merge( ) method, 144, 148
message bodies, 117
message destination references, 277
  @Resource annotation, using for, 278
  XML-based resource references, 277
message interface, 31

Message interface, 104
message selectors, 104
message-driven beans (see MDBs)
message-oriented middleware, 98
MessageDrivenContext, 106
MessageListener interface, 107
MessageProducers, 117
messaging domains, 100
META-INF/persistence.xml file, 133
Method-Ready Pool, 49–52, 109
MIN( ) function, 226
MOD (int, int) function, 226
module-name, 255
modules, 4
Monson-Haefel, Richard, xx
myapp.ear, 256
myejb.jar, 256

N

name( ) attribute, 55
named parameters, 208
named queries, 232–234
    named native queries, 233
naming conventions, 32
    for the examples, 32
naming services, 24
native queries, 230–232
network-protocol agnostic, 370
Never attribute, 291
new operator, 127
nillable types, 385
no-arg constructors, 50
nonentity base classes, 203
nonrepeatable reads, 299
nontransactional EJBs, 303
NonUniqueResultException, 207
not equals (<>) operator, 219
NOT operator, 219
notification messaging, 375
NotSupported attribute, 289
NULL comparison operator, 222
numeric primitives, 221
numeric types, comparisons with WHERE,
    220

O

object binding, 25
OBJECT( ) operator, 212

object-relational mapping, 16
occurrence attributes, 358
one-to-many bidirectional relationships, 172,
    182–183
    programming model, 183
    relational database schema, 182
    usage, 183
one-to-many unidirectional relationships, 172,
    178–181
    programming model, 180
    relational database schema, 179
one-to-one bidirectional relationships, 171,
    176–178
    relational database schema, 177
one-to-one unidirectional relationships, 171,
    173–176
    default relationship mapping, 176
    primary-key join columns, 175
    programming model, 173
    relational database schema, 173
one-way messaging, 374
onMessage( ) method, 107
operator precedence in WHERE clauses, 218
optimistic locking, 302
optional( ) attribute, 165
OR operator, 219
ORDER BY clause, 228
orm.xml file, 154
OTS (Object Transaction Service), 304
output message, 374

P

Pai, Jaikiran, xx
passivation, 14
percent (%) character, 224
PERSIST CascadeType, 192
persist( ) method, 148, 235
persistence, 17, 127
    entities as POJOs, 128
persistence context, 130
persistence units, 133, 269
persistence.xml deployment descriptor, 134,
    154
persistence.xml files, 134
phantom reads, 299
platform integration, 27
point-to-point (p2p) messaging model, 102
POJO (Plain Old Java Object) class, 11
positional parameters, 208

primary keys, 157–164
    @EmbeddedId annotation, 162
    @Id annotation, 157
    @IdClass annotation, 160
    primary-key classes and composite keys,
        160
    sequence generators, 159
    TABLE generators, 158
Project Rome, 90
property mappings, 164–167
    @Basic and FetchType, 164
    @Enumerated annotation, 167
    @Lob annotation, 166
    @Temporal annotation, 166
    @Transient annotation, 164
publish-and-subscribe (pub/sub) messaging
    model, 100
pull- or polling-based messaging models, 102
push-based messaging model, 101

Q

queries, 205
    JPA QL (see JPA QL)
    named queries (see named queries)
    native queries (see native queries)
    query API (see query API)
query API, 206–211
    date parameters, 209
    EntityManager query creating methods,
        207
    FlushMode, 210
    hints, 210
    paging results, 209
    parameters, 208
Query interface, 206
queues, 102

R

Read Committed isolation level, 300
read locks, 86, 299
Read Uncommitted isolation level, 300
REFRESH CascadeType, 193
refresh( ) method, 148
relational mapping, 151, 155–157
    elementary schema mappings, 155
relational mappings
    @Column annotation, 156
    @Table annotation, 156

remote business interfaces, 54
REMOVE CascadeType, 193
remove( ) method, 148, 235
Repeatable Read isolation level, 300
repeatable reads, 298
request-response messaging, 374
Required attribute, 290
RequiresNew attribute, 291
reserved words, Java Persistence programming,
    212
resource references, 271–274
    resource types, 272
    shareable resources, 274
role-based security, 24
    authorization, 245
roles, 243
RPC/Literal style, 369
RuntimeException, 55

S

scalar native queries, 230
ScheduleExpression, 344
scheduling systems, 341
schema( ) attribute, 156
schemalocation attribute, 364
scope, 364
security, 23, 243–252
    authentication, 243, 244
    authorization, 243, 245
    role-based security, 243
    secured school example, 246–252
        business interface, 246
        method permissions, assigning, 247
        programmatic security, 249
        RunAs security identifier, 251
    session beans and, 244
SELECT clause, 212, 213
    aggregate functions in, 226
    JPA QL constructor, specification within,
        215
SEQUENCE generators, 159
Serializable isolation level, 300
server-side component types, 12–16
    session beans, 12
service endpoint interface, 382
Service Provider interface (SPI), 112
session beans, 12
    security (see security)
SessionContext interface, 46

Sessions, 116
SessionSynchronization interface, 65, 318
Set type, 185
setFirstResult( ) method, 209
setFlushMode( ) method, 149, 211
setHint( ) method, 210
setMaxResults( ) method, 209
setParameter( ) method, 208
setRollbackOnly( ) method, 310, 312
setter and getter methods, 152, 154
setTransactionTimeout(int seconds) method,
    310
SFSBs (stateful session beans), 13, 63–79
    Does Not Exist state, 65
    FileTransferEJB example, 68–79
        bean implementation class, 70
        contract, 69
        exceptions, 70
        integration testing, 77
        POJO testing, 74
    lifecycle, 64–68
    Method-Ready state, 65
    Passivated state, 66
    system exceptions, 68
    transactional beans, 318–320
simple entity native queries, 230
Simple Object Access Protocol (see SOAP)
single-action timers, 347
singleton beans, 14
singleton session beans, 81–95
    concurrency, 82–87
        bean-managed concurrency, 87
        container-managed concurrency, 86
        shared mutable access, 84
    lifecycle, 87
    RSSCacheEJB example, 88–95
        bean implementation class, 92
        contract, 92
        value objects, 89
size( ) method, 190
SLSBs (stateless session beans), 12, 43–59
    death of a bean instance, 51
    declaration, 29
    Encryption EJB, 52–59
    lifecycle, 49–52
        Does Not Exist state, 50
        Method-Ready Pool, 50
    SessionContext, 46
        EJBContext, 47

uses, 45
    XML deployment descriptor, 45
snapshots, 299
SOAP (Simple Object Access Protocol) 1.1,
    368–371
    JAX-WS, 371
    reliance on XML, 368
    RPC/Encoded messaging mode, 369
    SOAP message exchange with HTTP, 370
    standard SOAP elements, 368
    web services styles, 369
solicitation messaging, 375
SORT (double) function, 226
SPI (Service Provider interface), 112
standards, 6
stateful session beans (see SFSBs)
stateless session beans (see SLSBs)
Status interface, 310
subscription durability, 106
SUBSTRING (String1, start, length) function,
    225
SUM( ) function, 227
Supports attribute, 289
suspended transactions, 289
synchronized keyword, 87
system exceptions, 68, 313

T

TABLE generators, 158
targetNamespace attribute, 363
TemporalType parameter, 209
TimedObject interface, 345
Timer class, 342
Timer object, 348
    canceling timers, 349
    exceptions, 350
    identifying timers, 349
    retrieving information from timers, 349
    TimerHandle object, 350
Timer Service, 342
    batch credit card processing example, 342–
        350
        bean implementation class, 345
        business interface, 343
        ScheduleExpression and @Schedule,
            344
        Timer object (see Timer object)
        TimerService interface, 347
    message-driven bean timers, 352

stateless session bean timers, 351–352
transactions, 350
timers, 24
topic, 101
Topic and TopicConnectionFactory, 116
transaction-scoped persistence context, 131
TransactionRequiredException, 148
transactions, 23, 279
ACID (atomic, consistent, isolated, and
durable) transactions (see ACID
transactions)
business transaction examples, 279
conversational persistence contexts, 321
declarative transaction management (see
declarative transaction
management)
exception summary for message-driven
beans, 317
exception summary for session and entity
beans, 315
exceptions, 313–317
application exceptions, 315
system exceptions, 313
explicit transaction management (see
explicit transaction management)
SFSBs and, 318–320
Transactional Method-Ready state, 318–
320
transfer( ) method, 294
TRIM (String) function, 225
two-phase commits, 297

U

UBR (Universal Business Registry), 379
UDDI (Universal Description, Discovery, and
Integration), 379
underscore (_) character, 224
UniqueConstraint annotation, 156
unit testing, 35
Unit Tests, 6
unit-of-work, 279
Universal Description, Discovery, and
Integration (see UDDI)
unwrap( ) method, 149
UPDATE operator, 229
UPPER (String) function, 225
URI (Universal Resource Identifier), 362
URL (Universal Resource Locator), 362
UserTransaction interface, 305, 309

V

valid XML, 356
volatile keyword, 87

W

Web Service Description Language 1.1 (see
WSDL)
web services, 355
JAX-RPC, accessing with (see JAX-RPC)
JAX-WS, accessing with (see JAX-WS)
services APIs, purpose, 381
SOAP (see SOAP)
supporting Java APIs in EJB 3.1, 381
UDDI, 379
WSDL (see WSDL)
XML namespaces, 361
XML Schema, 356
webservices.xml files, 395
well-formed XML, 356
WHERE clause, 218
arithmetic operators, 219
BETWEEN clause, used with, 221
comparison operators, 219
equality semantics, 220
functional expressions in, 225
IN operator, use with, 221
IS EMPTY operator, 223
IS NULL comparison operator, 222
LIKE comparison operator, 224
logical operators, 219
MEMBER OF operator, 223
operator precedence, 218
withdraw( ) method, 48
workflow applications, 341
wrapInTx( ) method, 286
write locks, 86, 299
WSDL (Web Service Description Language)
1.1, 371–379
<binding> and <service> elements, 377
<definitions> element, 372
<portType> and <message> elements, 374
<types> element, 375
WSDL files for JAX-RPC web services, 394

X

XML deployment descriptor, 45
overriding injection annotations, 261
XML mapping files, 154

XML markup language, 361
XML Namespaces, 361–368
    default namespaces, 363
    namespace declaration, 365
    namespaces and attributes, 364
    URIs, 362
    usage by XML Schema, 366
    XML Namespace declarations, 362
XML Schema, 356–361
    <element> declarations, 358
    built-in types
        corresponding Java types, 357
        mapping to Java types, 384
    correctness, 356
    example schema, 356
    XSD built-in types, 357
xsd prefix, 373

About the Authors

Andrew Lee Rubinger is Senior Software Engineer at JBoss, a division of Red Hat, and is primarily responsible for development of the company's EJB 3.x implementation. He was an early adopter of JEE technologies and is an active contributor in the tech community.

Bill Burke is Chief Architect at JBoss Inc. Besides co-leading the EJB 3.0 and AOP projects at JBoss, he represents JBoss as an expert on the EJB 3.0 and Java EE 5 specification committees. Bill was coauthor of the JBoss workbook included with *Enterprise JavaBeans*, Fourth Edition, and has published numerous articles in various print and online magazines.

Colophon

The animals on the cover of *Enterprise JavaBeans 3.1*, Sixth Edition, are a wallaby and her joey. Wallabies are medium-sized marsupials belonging to the kangaroo family (*Macropodidae*; the second-largest marsupial family). They are grazers and browsers, native to Australia, and found in a variety of habitats on that continent. Female wallabies have a well-developed anterior pouch in which they hold their young. When they are born, the tiny, still-blind joeys instinctively crawl up into their mothers' pouches and begin to nurse. They stay in the pouch until they are fairly well grown. A female wallaby can support joeys from up to three litters at once: one in her uterus, one in her pouch, and one that has graduated from the pouch but still returns to nurse.

Like all *Macropodidae*, wallabies have long, narrow hind feet and powerful hind limbs. Their long, heavy tails are used primarily for balance and stability and are not prehensile. Wallabies resemble kangaroos but are smaller: they measure from less than two feet to over five feet long, with the tail accounting for nearly half of their total length. Oddly enough, although they can hop along quite quickly (reaching speeds of up to 50 kilometers per hour), it is physically impossible for wallabies to walk backward!

The three main types of wallaby are brush, rock, and nail-tailed. There are eleven species of brush wallaby (genus *Macropus*) and six named species of rock wallaby (*Petrogale*). Brush wallabies usually live in brushland or open woods. Rock wallabies, which are notable for their extreme agility, are usually found among rocks and near water. There are only three species of nail-tailed wallaby (*Onychogalea*), which are so named because of the horny growth that appears on the tip of their tails. The major threats to wallabies today are hunting, habitat destruction, and predation by and competition with introduced species.

The cover image is from *The Illustrated Natural History: Mammalia*, by J. G. Wood. The cover font is Adobe ITC Garamond. The text font is Linotype Birka; the heading font is Adobe Myriad Condensed; and the code font is LucasFont's TheSansMono-Condensed.

Related Titles from O'Reilly

Java

Ajax on Java

Ant: The Definitive Guide, *2nd Edition*

Better, Faster, Lighter Java

Beyond Java

Eclipse

Eclipse Cookbook

Eclipse IDE Pocket Guide

Enterprise JavaBeans 3.0, *5th Edition*

Hardcore Java

Harnessing Hibernate

Head First Design Patterns

Head First Java, *2nd Edition*

Head First Servlets and JSP, *2nd Edition*

Head First EJB

Hibernate: A Developer's Notebook

J2EE Design Patterns

Java 5.0 Tiger: A Developer's Notebook

Java & XML Data Binding

Java & XML, *3rd Edition*

Java Cookbook, *2nd Edition*

Java Data Objects

Java Database Best Practices

Java Enterprise Best Practices

Java Enterprise in a Nutshell, *3rd Edition*

Java Examples in a Nutshell, *3rd Edition*

Java Extreme Programming Cookbook

Java in a Nutshell, *5th Edition*

Java I/O, *2nd Edition*

Java Management Extensions

Java Message Service

Java Network Programming, *3rd Edition*

Java NIO

Java Performance Tuning, *2nd Edition*

Java Pocket Guide

Java Power Tools

Java RMI

Java Security, *2nd Edition*

Java SOA Cookbook

JavaServer Faces

JavaServer Pages Pocket Reference

Java Servlet & JSP Cookbook

Java Servlet Programming, *2nd Edition*

Java Swing, *2nd Edition*

Java Web Services in a Nutshell

Java Web Services: Up and Running

JBoss: A Developer's Notebook

JBoss at Work: A Practical Guide

Learning Java, *3rd Edition*

Mac OS X for Java Geeks

Maven: A Developer's Notebook

Maven: The Definitive Guide

Programming Jakarta Struts, *2nd Edition*

QuickTime for Java: A Developer's Notebook

Spring: A Developer's Notebook

Swing Hacks

Tomcat: The Definitive Guide, *2nd Edition*

WebLogic: The Definitive Guide

Get even more for your money.

Join the O'Reilly Community, and register the O'Reilly books you own. It's free, and you'll get:

- $4.99 ebook upgrade offer
- 40% upgrade offer on O'Reilly print books
- Membership discounts on books and events
- Free lifetime updates to ebooks and videos
- Multiple ebook formats, DRM FREE
- Participation in the O'Reilly community
- Newsletters
- Account management
- 100% Satisfaction Guarantee

Signing up is easy:

1. **Go to: oreilly.com/go/register**
2. **Create an O'Reilly login.**
3. **Provide your address.**
4. **Register your books.**

Note: English-language books only

To order books online:

oreilly.com/store

For questions about products or an order:

orders@oreilly.com

To sign up to get topic-specific email announcements and/or news about upcoming books, conferences, special offers, and new technologies:

elists@oreilly.com

For technical questions about book content:

booktech@oreilly.com

To submit new book proposals to our editors:

proposals@oreilly.com

O'Reilly books are available in multiple DRM-free ebook formats. For more information:

oreilly.com/ebooks

Spreading the knowledge of innovators | oreilly.com